Frommer's®

Cancún & the Yucatán 2011
with Tabasco & Chiapas

by David Baird, Shane Christensen & Christine Delsol
with Maribeth Mellin

Wiley Publishing, Inc.

Published by:
Wiley Publishing, Inc.
111 River St.
Hoboken, NJ 07030-5774

ISBN 978-0-470-61432-7 (paper); ISBN 978-0-470-40623-6 (ebk); ISBN 978-0-470-93296-4 (ebk); ISBN 978-0-470-93297-1 (ebk)

Editor: Jennifer Polland and Melinda Quintero
Production Editor: M. Faunette Johnston
Cartographer: Guy Ruggiero
Photo Editor: Alden Gewirtz
Cover Photo Editor: Richard Fox
Production by Wiley Indianapolis Composition Services

Front cover photo: Hammock on Puerto Morelos Beach © Michael Alberstat / Masterfile

Back cover photos: *Left:* El Castillo Piramide de Kukulcan, Mayan Toltec ruins, Chichen Itza © Witold Skrypczak / Alamy Images. *Middle:* Aktun Chen Cenote cave park, Tulum parakeet in aviary © Shirley Kilpatrick / Alamy Images. *Right:* A light ray streams down onto the water inside Dzitnup, an underground cenote near Valladolid © James May / Stock Connection / Alamy Images.

For information on our other products and services or to obtain technical support, please contact our Customer Care Department within the U.S. at 877/762-2974, outside the U.S. at 317/572-3993 or fax 317/572-4002.

Wiley also publishes its books in a variety of electronic formats. Some content that appears in print may not be available in electronic formats.
Manufactured in the United States of America

5 4 3 2 1

CONTENTS

4 SUGGESTED YUCATÁN ITINERARIES 86

5 CANCÚN 101

6 ISLA MUJERES & COZUMEL 138

7 THE RIVIERA MAYA & THE SOUTHERN CARIBBEAN COAST 176

8 MÉRIDA, THE MAYA INTERIOR & CHICHÉN ITZÁ 246

9 TABASCO & CHIAPAS 321

10 FAST FACTS 363

11 SURVIVAL SPANISH 367

Index 377

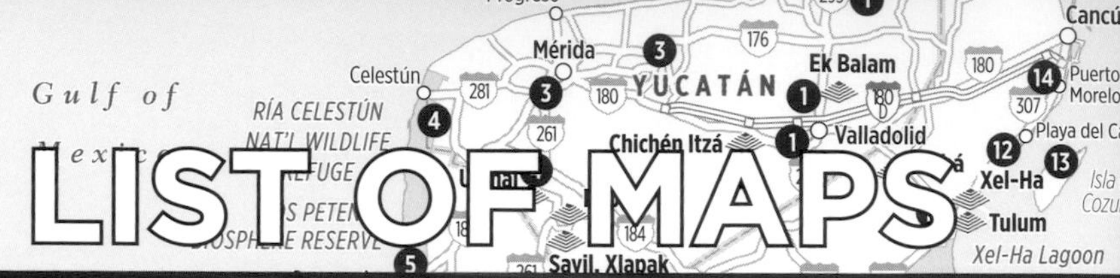
Progreso
Mérida
Celestún
Gulf of
RÍA CELESTÚN
YUCATÁN
Ek Balam
Valladolid
Chichén Itzá
Cancún
Puerto Morelos
Xel-Ha
Tulum
Xel-Ha Lagoon
Savil, Xlapak

LIST OF MAPS

ABOUT THE AUTHORS

A writer, editor, and translator, **David Baird** has lived several years in different parts of Mexico. Now based in Austin, Texas, he spends as much time in Mexico as possible. A former resident of Mexico City, **Shane Christensen** has written extensively for Frommer's throughout Mexico, and is the author of *Frommer's Dubai* and *Frommer's Grand Canyon*. He resides in New York, and goes back to Mexico at every chance he gets. Author of *Pauline Frommer's Cancún & the Yucatán*, **Christine Delsol** has been traveling to Mexico at every opportunity for 30 years. She has spent most of her career in newspapers and is the recipient of an Associated Press award and two Lowell Thomas awards. **Maribeth Mellin** first drove the two-lane road from Cancún to Chetumal when tires hanging on sticks marked sandy roads to secluded campgrounds. She's kept track of the changes ever since, and is constantly amazed to see highway overpasses and gigantic resorts and parks. She's the author of *Traveler's Mexico Companion*, which won the country's prestigious Pluma de Plata award, and has covered Mexico and Latin America for dozens of newspapers, magazines, websites, and guides.

HOW TO CONTACT US

In researching this book, we discovered many wonderful places—hotels, restaurants, shops, and more. We're sure you'll find others. Please tell us about them, so we can share the information with your fellow travelers in upcoming editions. If you were disappointed with a recommendation, we'd love to know that, too. Please write to:

Frommer's Cancún & the Yucatán 2011

Wiley Publishing, Inc. * 111 River St. * Hoboken, NJ 07030-5774

frommersfeedback@wiley.com

AN ADDITIONAL NOTE

Please be advised that travel information is subject to change at any time—and this is especially true of prices. We therefore suggest that you write or call ahead for confirmation when making your travel plans. The authors, editors, and publisher cannot be held responsible for the experiences of readers while traveling. Your safety is important to us, however, so we encourage you to stay alert and be aware of your surroundings. Keep a close eye on cameras, purses, and wallets, all favorite targets of thieves and pickpockets.

FROMMER'S STAR RATINGS, ICONS & ABBREVIATIONS

Every hotel, restaurant, and attraction listing in this guide has been ranked for quality, value, service, amenities, and special features using a star-rating system. In country, state, and regional guides, we also rate towns and regions to help you narrow down your choices and budget your time accordingly. Hotels and restaurants are rated on a scale of zero (recommended) to three stars (exceptional). Attractions, shopping, nightlife, towns, and regions are rated according to the following scale: zero stars (recommended), one star (highly recommended), two stars (very highly recommended), and three stars (must-see).

In addition to the star-rating system, we also use **eight feature icons** that point you to the great deals, in-the-know advice, and unique experiences that separate travelers from tourists. Throughout the book, look for:

Special finds—those places only insiders know about

Fun facts—details that make travelers more informed and their trips more fun

Kids—best bets for kids and advice for the whole family

Special moments—those experiences that memories are made of

Overrated—places or experiences not worth your time or money

Insider tips—great ways to save time and money

Great values—where to get the best deals

Warning—traveler's advisories are usually in effect

The following abbreviations are used for credit cards:

AE American Express
DC Diners Club
DISC Discover
MC MasterCard
V Visa

TRAVEL RESOURCES AT FROMMERS.COM

Frommer's travel resources don't end with this guide. Frommer's website, **www.frommers.com**, has travel information on more than 4,000 destinations. We update features regularly, giving you access to the most current trip-planning information and the best airfare, lodging, and car-rental bargains. You can also listen to podcasts, connect with other Frommers.com members through our active-reader forums, share your travel photos, read blogs from guidebook editors and fellow travelers, and much more.

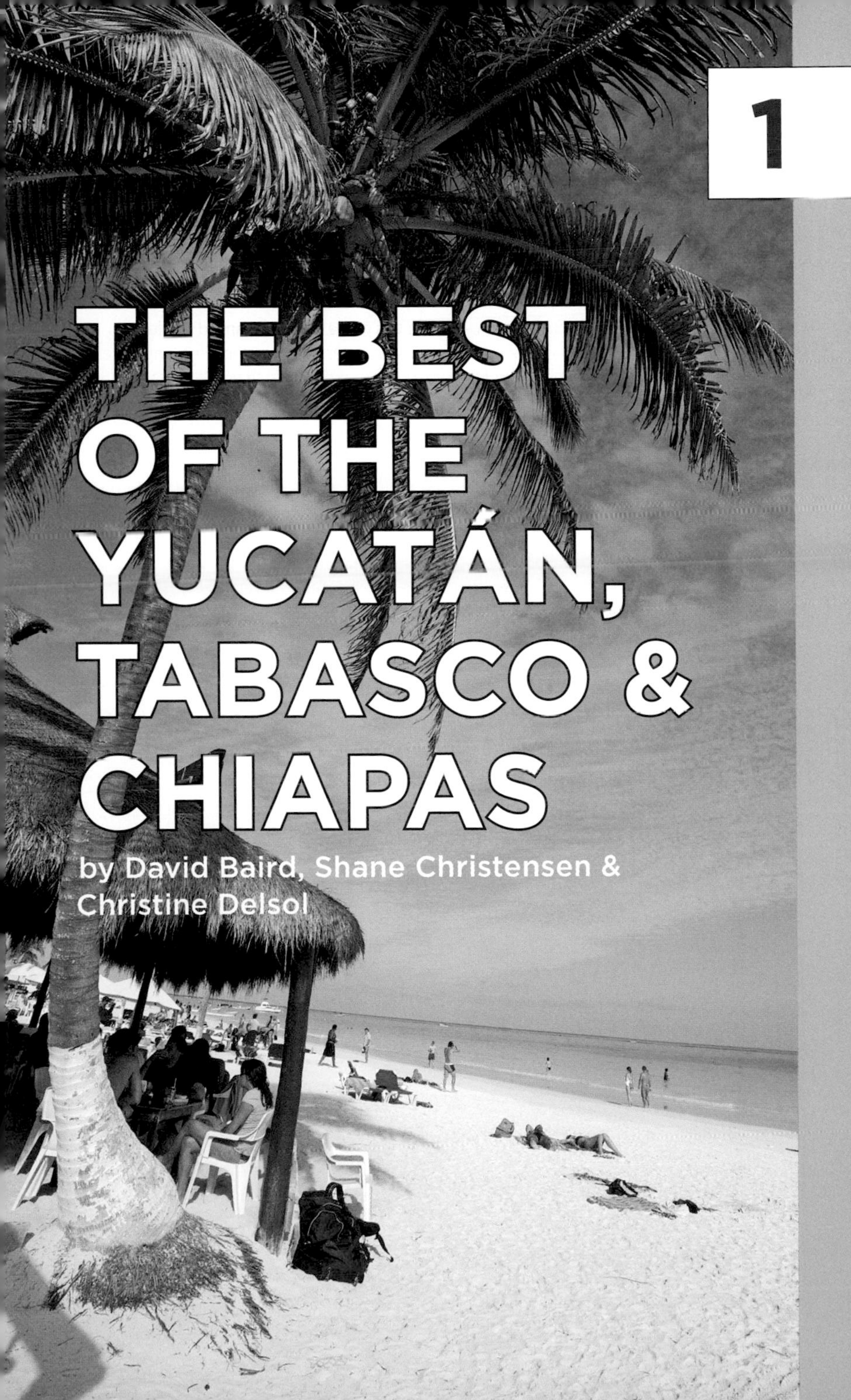

1

THE BEST OF THE YUCATÁN, TABASCO & CHIAPAS

by David Baird, Shane Christensen & Christine Delsol

The Yucatán Peninsula welcomes more visitors than any other part of Mexico. Its tremendous variety attracts every kind of traveler with an unrivaled mix of sophisticated resorts, rustic inns, ancient Maya culture, exquisite beaches, and exhilarating adventures. Between the three of us, we've logged thousands of miles crisscrossing the peninsula, and these are our personal favorites—the best places to visit, the best hotels and restaurants, plus must-see, one-of-a-kind experiences.

THE best BEACH VACATIONS

- **Cancún:** Whether or not you believe Cancún is an unrelenting spring break party in which Americans compete with Mexicans for the city's real identity—and I'd say the truth lies in the timing of your visit—you're likely to agree this man-made resort has some of the most spectacular beaches in the country. The powdery white sand is complemented by warm Caribbean waters the color of a Technicolor dream; it's so clear that you can see through to the coral reefs below. You can come here just to relax, but this is of course also one of the world's most popular entertainment destinations. Cancún offers Mexico's widest selection of beachfront resorts, with more restaurants, nightlife, and activities than any other resort destination in the country. See chapter 5.

PREVIOUS PAGE: **Tulum Beach.** ABOVE: **A luxury resort in Cancún.**

The Tulum ruins, overlooking the Caribbean Sea.

- **Isla Mujeres:** If uninterrupted relaxation is what you're after, Isla Mujeres offers a quintessential laid-back vacation. Most accommodations are small, inexpensive inns, with a few luxury boutique hotels tempting you for at least a night. Bike—or take a golf cart—around the island to explore rocky coves and sandy beaches, or focus your tanning efforts on the wide beachfront of Playa Norte. Here you'll find calm waters perfect for swimming and snorkeling as well as beachfront *palapa* restaurants beckoning you for a fresh fish lunch. If island fever starts to take over, you're only a ferry ride away from the action in Cancún. See chapter 6.
- **Cozumel:** It may not offer lots of big, sandy beaches, but Cozumel promises something the mainland doesn't: the calm, flat waters of the sheltered western shore. It's so calm that it could be mistaken for a giant swimming pool, only this pool has lots of brilliantly colored fish, so take your snorkeling mask even if you don't plan to do any diving. See chapter 6.
- **Playa del Carmen:** Stylish and hip, Playa del Carmen has a beautiful beach and an eclectic assortment of small hotels, inns, and cabañas. The social scene focuses on the beach by day and the pedestrian-only Avenida Quinta (Fifth Avenue) by night, with its assortment of restaurants, clubs, sidewalk cafes, and shops offering all the entertainment you could want. You're also close to the coast's major attractions, including nature parks, ruins, and cenotes (sinkholes or natural wells). Playa is Mexico's fastest-growing city and is becoming homogenized (think Dairy Queen and Starbucks). Enjoy it while it's still a manageable size. See chapter 7.
- **Tulum:** Fronting some of the best beaches on the entire coast, Tulum's small *palapa* hotels offer guests a little slice of paradise far from the crowds and megaresorts. The bustling town lies inland; at the coast, things are quiet, because all these small hotels must generate their own electricity. If you can pull yourself away from the beach, there are ruins to marvel at and a vast nature preserve to explore. See chapter 7.

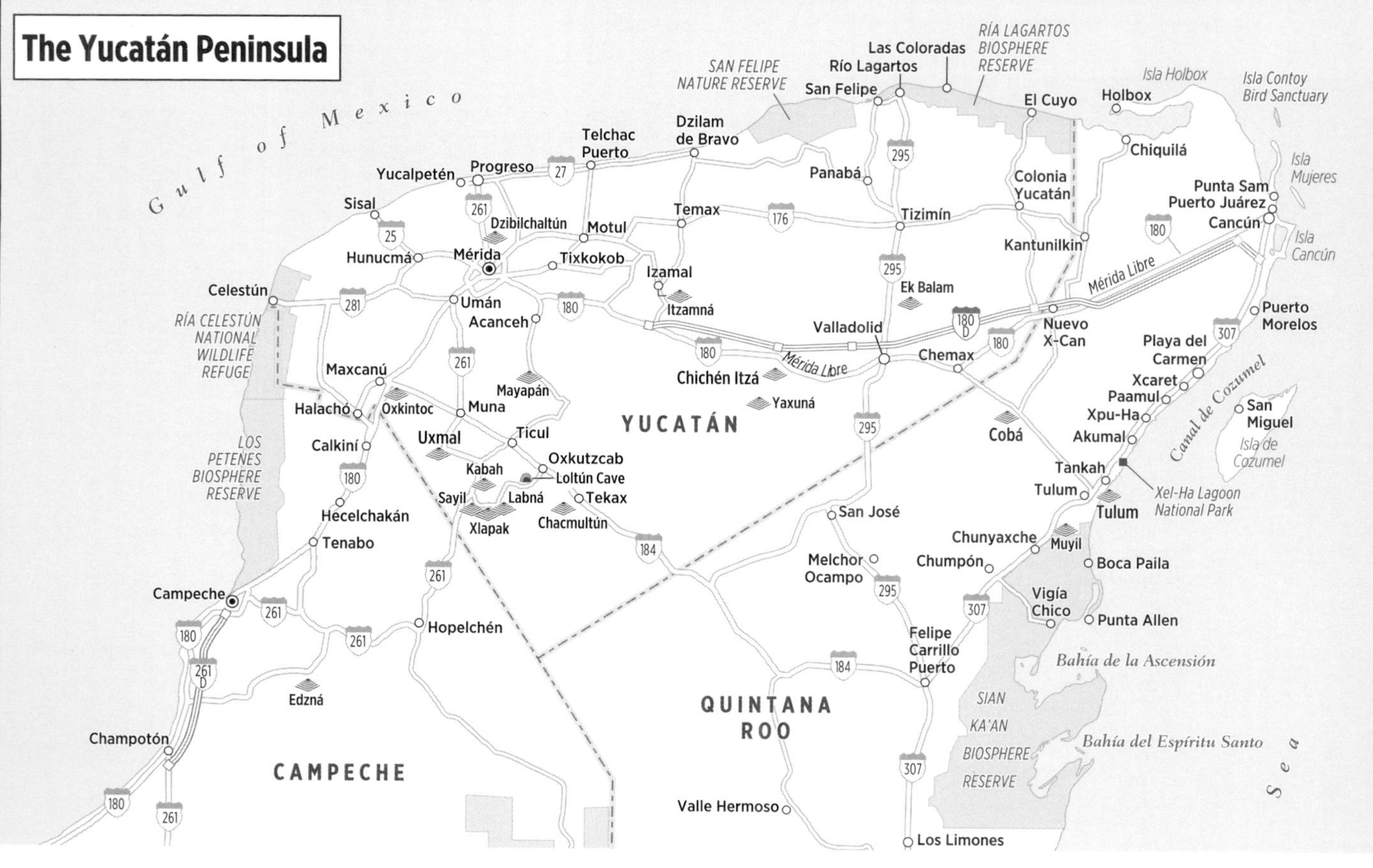

The Yucatán Peninsula
Gulf of Mexico
Sea
RÍA LAGARTOS BIOSPHERE RESERVE
Las Coloradas
Río Lagartos
San Felipe
SAN FELIPE NATURE RESERVE
El Cuyo
Holbox
Isla Holbox
Isla Contoy Bird Sanctuary
Isla Mujeres
Isla Cancún
Chiquilá
Punta Sam
Puerto Juárez
Cancún
Dzilam de Bravo
Telchac Puerto
Progreso
Yucalpetén
Sisal
Panabá
Colonia Yucatán
Kantunilkín
Temax
Tizimín
Motul
Dzibilchaltún
Hunucmá
Mérida
Tixkokob
Izamal
Itzamná
Ek Balam
Mérida Libre
Celestún
RÍA CELESTÚN NATIONAL WILDLIFE REFUGE
Umán
Acanceh
Valladolid
Nuevo X-Can
Puerto Morelos
Playa del Carmen
Xcaret
Paamul
Xpu-Ha
Akumal
San Miguel
Isla de Cozumel
Canal de Cozumel
Chemax
Chichén Itzá
Yaxuná
Maxcanú
Halachó
Oxkintoc
Muna
Mayapán
YUCATÁN
Cobá
Uxmal
Ticul
Calkiní
LOS PETENES BIOSPHERE RESERVE
Oxkutzcab
Loltún Cave
Kabah
Tekax
Sayil
Labná
Xlapak
Chacmultún
Hecelchakán
Tenabo
Tankah
Tulum
Xel-Ha Lagoon National Park
San José
Chunyaxche
Muyil
Boca Paila
Melchor Ocampo
Chumpón
Vigía Chico
Punta Allen
Campeche
Hopelchén
Felipe Carrillo Puerto
Bahía de la Ascensión
Edzná
QUINTANA ROO
SIAN KA'AN BIOSPHERE RESERVE
Bahía del Espíritu Santo
Champotón
CAMPECHE
Valle Hermoso
Los Limones
180
180 D
307
295
176
184
27
261
261 D
25
281

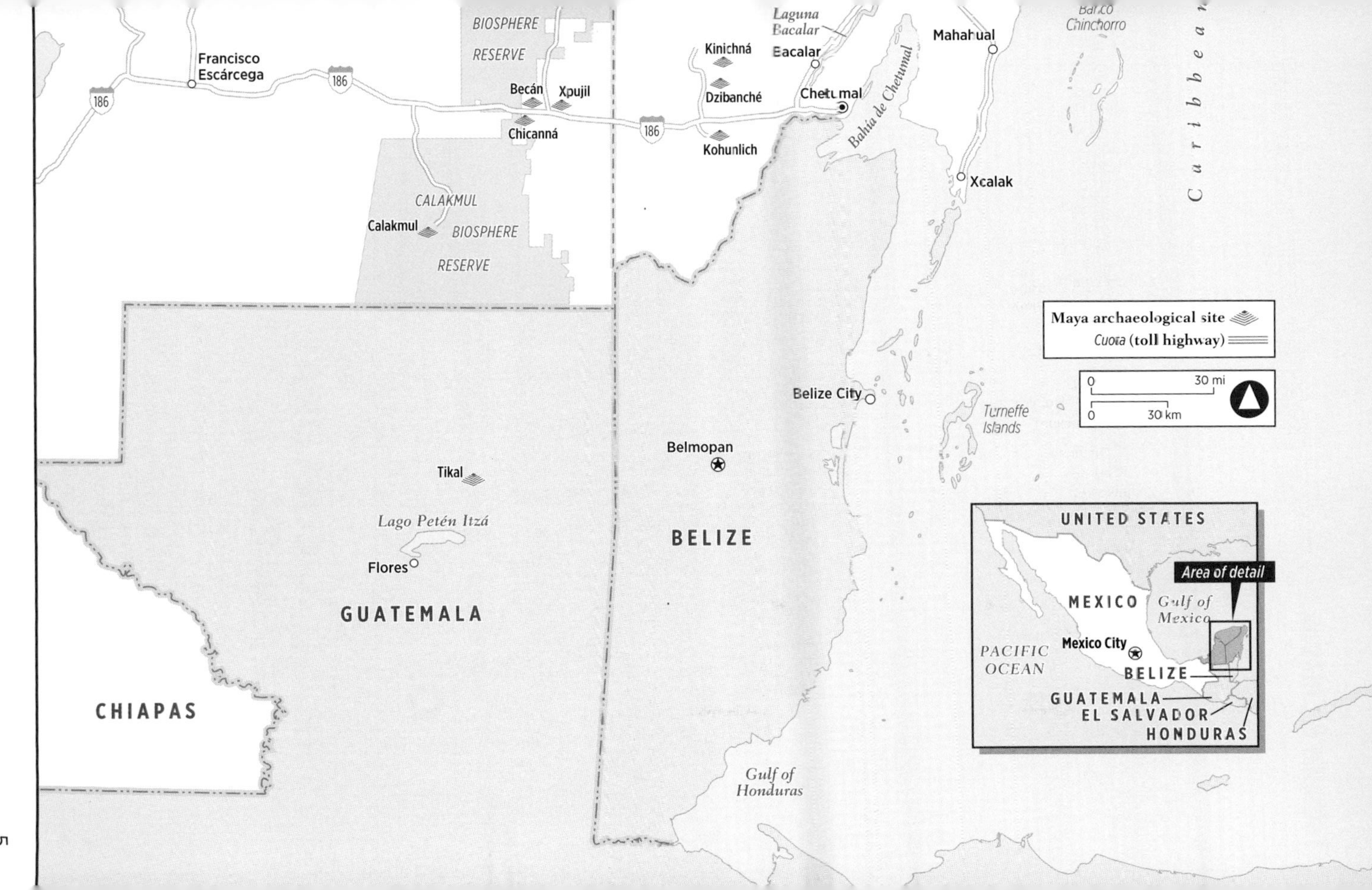

Francisco Escárcega
186
BIOSPHERE
RESERVE
Becán
Xpujil
Chicanná
CALAKMUL
BIOSPHERE
RESERVE
Calakmul
Kinichná
Dzibanché
Kohunlich
Laguna Bacalar
Bacalar
Chetumal
Bahía de Chetumal
Mahahual
Xcalak
Chinchorro
Maya archaeological site
Cuota (toll highway)
0
30 mi
0
30 km
Belize City
Turneffe Islands
Belmopan
BELIZE
Tikal
Lago Petén Itzá
Flores
GUATEMALA
CHIAPAS
Gulf of Honduras
UNITED STATES
Area of detail
MEXICO
Gulf of Mexico
Mexico City
PACIFIC OCEAN
BELIZE
GUATEMALA
EL SALVADOR
HONDURAS

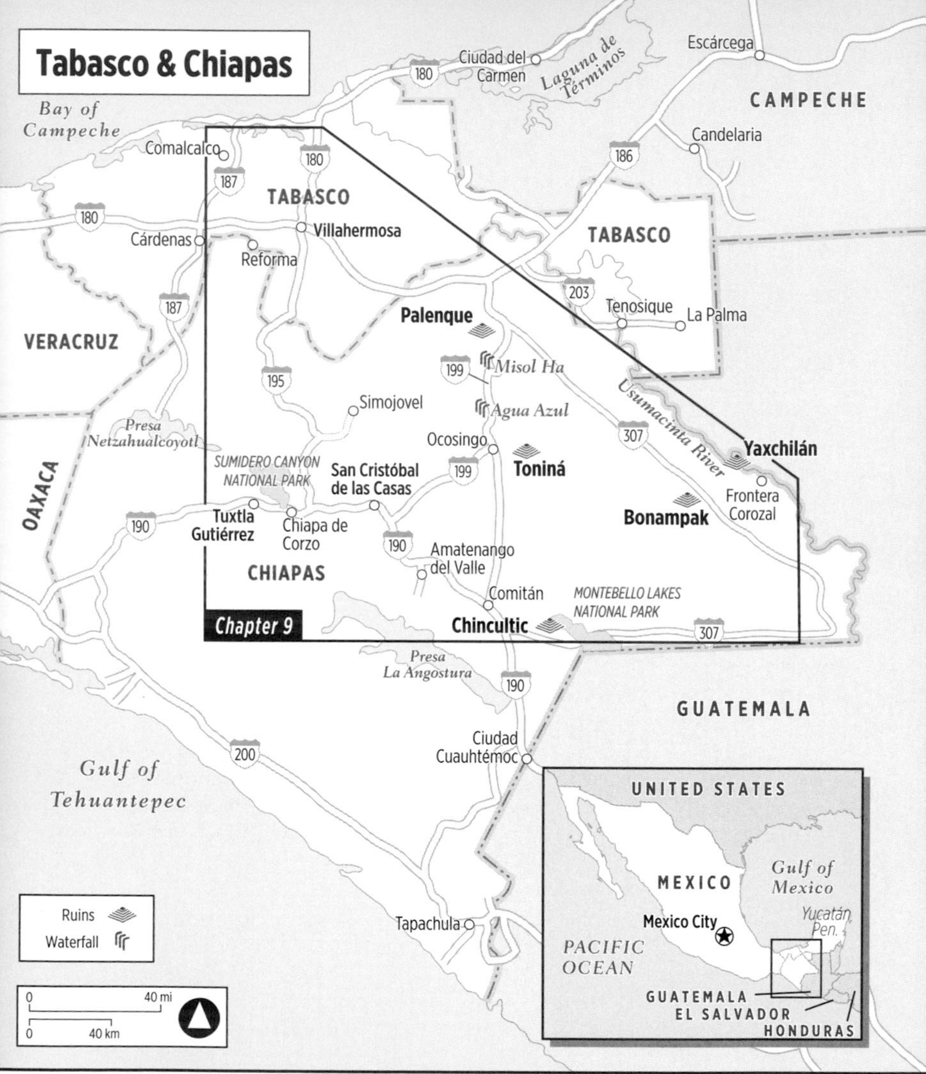

THE best CULTURAL EXPERIENCES

- **Exploring the Inland Yucatán Peninsula:** Travelers who venture only to the Yucatán's resorts and cities miss the rock-walled inland villages, where women wear brightly embroidered dresses and life proceeds almost as if the modern world (with the exception of highways) didn't exist. The adventure of seeing secluded cenotes, unrestored haciendas, and newly uncovered ruins, deep in jungle settings, is not to be missed. See chapter 8.
- **Street & Park Entertainment in Mérida:** Few cities have so vibrant a street scene as Mérida. Every night throughout the week you can catch music and

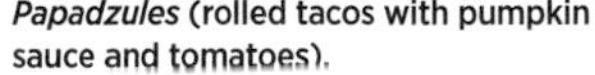

Papadzules (rolled tacos with pumpkin sauce and tomatoes).

Mérida by night.

dance performances in plazas about town. Then, on Sunday, Mérida really gets going—streets are closed off, food stalls spring up everywhere, and you can enjoy a book fair, a flea market, comedy acts, band concerts, and dance groups. At night, the main plaza is the place to be, with people dancing to mambos and rumbas in the street in front of the city hall. See chapter 8.

- **San Cristóbal de las Casas:** The city of San Cristóbal is a living museum, with 16th-century colonial architecture and pre-Hispanic native influences. The highland Maya live in surrounding villages and arrive daily in town wearing colorful handmade clothing. A visit to the villages is a window into another world, giving visitors a glimpse of traditional Indian dress, religious customs, churches, and ceremonies. See chapter 9.
- **Regional Cuisine:** A trip to the Yucatán allows for a culinary tour of some of Mexico's finest foods. Don't miss specialties such as *pollo* or *cochinita pibil* (chicken or pork in savory *achiote* sauce), the uniquely Campechan *pan de cazón,* great seafood dishes, the many styles of *tamal* found throughout Chiapas and the Yucatán, and Caribbean-influenced staples such as fried bananas, black beans, and yucca root. For a glossary of popular regional dishes, see chapter 11.

THE best ARCHAEOLOGICAL SITES

- **Tulum:** Tulum isn't the most important ancient Maya city, either historically or architecturally, but its seaside setting is uniquely beautiful. The stark contrast of its crumbling stone walls against the clear turquoise ocean just beyond is an extraordinary sight. See "Tulum" in chapter 7.
- **Calakmul:** Of the many elegantly built Maya cities of the Río Bec area, in the lower Yucatán, Calakmul is the broadest in scope and design. It's also one of the hardest to reach—about 48km (30 miles) from the Guatemalan border and completely surrounded by the jungle of the Calakmul Biological Reserve.

The Palenque ruins.

Calakmul is a walled city with the tallest pyramid in the Yucatán—a city that continuing research might prove to be the largest in the Maya world, more than equal to Guatemala's Tikal. Go now, while it remains infrequently visited. See "Side Trips to Maya Ruins from Chetumal" in chapter 7.

- **Uxmal:** No matter how many times we see Uxmal, the splendor of its stone carvings remains awe-inspiring. A stone rattlesnake undulates across the facade of the Nunnery complex, and 103 masks of Chaac—the rain god—project from the Governor's Palace. See "The Ruins of Uxmal" in chapter 8.
- **Chichén Itzá:** Stand beside the giant serpent head at the foot of El Castillo and marvel at the architects and astronomers who positioned the building so precisely that shadow and sunlight form a serpent's body slithering from peak to the earth at each equinox (Mar 21 and Sept 21). See "The Ruins of Chichén Itzá" in chapter 8.
- **Ek Balam:** In recent years, this is the site where some of Mexico's most astounding archaeological discoveries have been made. Ek Balam's main pyramid is taller than Chichén Itzá's, and it holds a sacred doorway bordered with elaborate stucco figures of priests and kings and rich iconography. See "Ek Balam: Dark Jaguar" in chapter 8.
- **Palenque:** The ancient builders of these structures carved histories in stone that scholars have only recently deciphered. Imagine the magnificent ceremony in A.D. 683 when King Pacal was buried deep inside his pyramid—his tomb unspoiled until its discovery in 1952. See "Palenque" in chapter 9.

THE best ACTIVE VACATIONS

- **Scuba Diving in Cozumel & along the Yucatán's Caribbean Coast:** The coral reefs off the island, Mexico's premier diving destination, are among the top five dive spots in the world. The Yucatán's coastal reef, part of the planet's second-largest reef system and a national marine park, affords excellent diving all along the coast. Diving from Isla Mujeres is quite spectacular. Especially beautiful is the Chinchorro Reef, lying 32km (20 miles) offshore from Mahahual or Xcalak. See chapters 6 and 7.

Scuba diving in Cozumel.

- **Fly-Fishing off the Punta Allen & Mahahual Peninsulas:** Serious anglers will enjoy the challenge of fly-fishing the saltwater flats and lagoons on the protected sides of these peninsulas. See "Sian Ka'an & the Punta Allen Peninsula" and "Mahahual, Xcalak & the Chinchorro Reef" in chapter 7.
- **Cenote Diving on the Yucatán Mainland:** Dive into the clear depths of the Yucatán's cenotes for a whole new world of underwater exploration. The Maya considered the cenotes sacred—and their vivid colors do indeed seem otherworldly. Most are between Playa del Carmen and Tulum, and dive shops in these areas regularly run trips for experienced divers. For recommended dive shops, see "Cozumel" in chapter 6, and "Playa del Carmen" and "South of Playa del Carmen" in chapter 7.
- **Birding:** The Yucatán Peninsula, Tabasco, and Chiapas are ornithological paradises. Two very special places are Isla Contoy, with more than 70 species of birds as well as a host of marine and animal life (p. 129) and the Huitepec Cloud Forest, with its flocks of migratory species (p. 350) North America's

Herons in Isla Contoy.

Exploring the ruins of Yaxchilán.

largest flamingo breeding and nesting grounds lie at opposite ends of Yucatán state's Gulf Coast, in Celestún (p. 275) and Ría Lagartos (p. 318).

- **An Excursion to Bonampak & Yaxchilán:** Bonampak and Yaxchilán—two remote, jungle-surrounded Maya sites along the Usumacinta River—are accessible by car and motorboat. The experience could well be the highlight of any trip. See "Road Trips from San Cristóbal" in chapter 9.

THE best PLACES TO GET AWAY FROM IT ALL

- **Isla Mujeres:** Isla Mujeres in low season is about as low-key as you can get. You'll find an ample selection of hotels and restaurants, and they're as laid-back as their patrons. Here life moves along in pure *mañana* mode, with little sign of the bustling commercialism that exists just across the bay. Visitors stretch out and doze beneath shady palms or languidly stroll about. In fact, Isla Mujeres feels worlds removed from Cancún, yet remains comfortably close (about 15 minutes by ferry) for those who choose to reconnect. See "Isla Mujeres" in chapter 6.
- **The Yucatán's Riviera Maya:** Away from the busy resort of Cancún, a string of quiet getaways, including Paamul, Punta Bete, and Xpu-ha, offer tranquility on extraordinarily beautiful beaches. See "North of Playa del Carmen" and "South of Playa del Carmen" in chapter 7. For the kind of sleepy fishing village atmosphere— and low prices—that once belonged to Playa del Carmen, pull off the highway at Puerto Morelos. See "Puerto Morelos & Vicinity" in chapter 7.

Relaxing on a beach in Isla Mujeres.

- **Tulum:** Near the Tulum ruins, about two dozen beachside *palapa* inns still offer peaceful getaways despite their burgeoning popularity. This stretch just might offer the best sandy beaches on the entire coast. Life here among the birds and coconut palms is decidedly unhurried. See "Tulum" in chapter 7.
- **Balamkú Inn on the Beach** (Mahahual; www.balamku.com): Beach bungalows just don't get any more comfortable than these large, stylish rooms, all with terraces looking onto groomed white sands and turquoise waves, standing 5.7km (3.5 miles) outside of town; you'd never suspect they are completely self-sustained by wind and solar power and a rainwater collection and recycling system that replenishes the wetlands. Unless you're here to dive the Chinchorro Reef, your main sources of exertion will be snorkeling, kayaking, boat trips to Bird Island, excursions to little-known ruins, and climbing into and out of *palapa*-shaded hammocks. See p. 230.
- **Hacienda San José Cholul** (www.luxurycollection.com): Operated by Starwood Hotels, this hacienda is only an hour east of the bustling city of Mérida, toward Izamal, but it feels like another world. The quiet, unhurried manner of both guests and staff, and the beautiful tropical surroundings make it the perfect place to recoup some of the silence and slow time lost to the modern world. See "Haciendas & Hotels" on p. 260.

Puerto Morelos on the Riviera Maya.

THE best MUSEUMS

- **Museo de la Cultura Maya** (Chetumal; ✆ **983/832-6838**): This modern museum, one of the best in the country, explores Maya archaeology, architecture, history, and mythology. It has interactive exhibits and a glass floor that allows visitors to walk above replicas of Maya sites. See p. 235.
- **Museo Regional de Antropología** (Mérida; ✆ **999/923-0557**): Housed in the Palacio Cantón, one of the most beautiful 19th-century mansions in a city overendowed with beautiful mansions, this museum showcases local archaeology and anthropological studies in handsome exhibits. See p. 269.
- **Parque-Museo La Venta** (Villahermosa; ✆ **993/314-1652**): The Olmec, considered Mexico's mother culture, are the subject of this park/museum, which features the magnificent stone remains that were removed from the La Venta site not far away. Stroll through a jungle setting where tropical birds alight, and examine the giant carved stone heads of the mysterious Olmec. See p. 325.

THE best SHOPPING

Some tips on bargaining: Although haggling over prices in markets is expected and part of the fun, don't try to browbeat the vendor or bad-mouth the goods. Vendors won't bargain with people they consider disrespectful unless they are desperate to make a sale. Be insistent but friendly.

- **Resort Wear in Cancún:** Resort clothing—especially if you can find a sale—can be a good value here. And the selection may be wider than what's available at home. Almost every mall on the island contains trendy boutiques that

Shopping in San Cristóbal.

specialize in locally designed and imported clothing. The best is La Isla Shopping Center. Less expensive local fashions are widely available in the original downtown known as El Centro. See "Shopping" in chapter 5.

- **Duty-Free in Cancún:** If you're looking for European perfume, fine watches, or other imported goods, you'll find the prices in Cancún's duty-free shops (at the major malls on the island and in downtown Cancún) hard to beat.
- **Avenida Quinta, Playa del Carmen:** This pedestrian-only street offers leisurely shopping at its best—no cars, no hassle; even the touts are laid-back. Simply stroll the street and let your eye pick out objects of interest. New Age types will be in their glory, with the abundance of batik clothing and fabric, Guatemalan textiles, and inventive jewelry and artwork. But you'll also find quality Mexican handicrafts, premium tequilas, and (genuine) Cuban cigars. See "Playa del Carmen" in chapter 7.
- **Mérida:** This is *the* marketplace for the Yucatán—count on the best prices and the best quality in hammocks, *guayaberas,* Panama hats, and Yucatecan *huipiles.* See "Exploring Mérida" in chapter 8.
- **San Cristóbal de las Casas:** Deep in the heart of the Maya highlands, San Cristóbal has shops, open plazas, and markets that feature the distinctive waist-loomed wool and cotton textiles of the region, as well as leather shoes, handsome pottery, and Guatemalan textiles. Highland Maya Indians sell direct to tourists from their armloads of textiles, pottery, and wood carvings. See "San Cristóbal de las Casas" in chapter 9.

THE hottest NIGHTLIFE

Although, as expected, Cancún is the source of much of the Yucatán's nightlife, that resort city isn't the only place to have a good time after dark. Along the Caribbean coast, beachside dance floors with live bands and extended happy hours in seaside bars dominate the nightlife. Here are some favorite hot spots, from live music in hotel lobby bars to hip techno dance clubs.

- **Cancún:** Longstanding Cancún favorites **Carlos 'n' Charlie's** and **Señor Frog's** offer potent drinks, hot music, and wild (if sometimes sloppy) dance floors. For a more cosmopolitan setting, **La Madonna** is a fashionable martini bar and restaurant in the La Isla Shopping Village, while **Bling,** with its outdoor terrace overlooking the lagoon, is the city's most chic cocktail venue. See chapter 5.
- **Grupo Dady:** Longstanding favorite Dady'O, as well as its offsprings Terresta, UltraClub, Dady Rock, and Dos Equis Bar, all lie within a block of each other pulsating with music and happy revelers. Grupo Dady offers a package rate that includes open bar and entrance to these popular venues. See p. 135.
- **Forum by the Sea:** This seaside entertainment center in Cancún has it all: a dazzling array of dance clubs, sports bars, fast food, and fine dining, with shops open late as well. You'll find plenty of familiar names here, including the Hard Rock Cafe and Rainforest Cafe. It's also the home of what remains Cancún's hottest club, **CoCo Bongo,** which regularly packs in up to 3,000 revelers. See p. 136.
- **The City:** One of Cancún's hottest nightclubs, the City is a raging day-and-night club, offering a beach club with beach and pool activities and food and bar service, as well as the sizzling nightclub with nine bars at which the

world's top DJs spin their grooves. This is truly a City that never sleeps. See p. 136.

- **Avenida Quinta (Playa del Carmen):** Stroll along lively, pedestrian-only Fifth Avenue to find the bar that's right for you. With live-music venues, tequila bars, sports bars, and cafes, you're sure to find something to fit your mood. The intersection with Calle 12 is becoming the de facto club central. See p. 190.
- **San Cristóbal de las Casas:** This city, small though it may be, has a live-music scene that can't be beat for fun and atmosphere. The bars and clubs are all within walking distance, and they're a real bargain. See "San Cristóbal de las Casas" in chapter 9.

Playa del Carmen's bustling Avenida Quinta.

THE most LUXURIOUS HOTELS

- **Aqua** (Cancún; www.feel-aqua.com): This is the trendiest resort in Cancún, a privileged spa-retreat for the urban jet-set. Completely rebuilt after having been destroyed by Hurricane Wilma, Aqua features spacious oceanview rooms, eight beachfront pools, an invigorating spa, world-class cuisine, and exceptional service. See p. 110.
- **Fiesta Americana Grand Coral Beach** (Cancún; www.fiestamericanagrand.com): This refined resort sits on one of Cancún's most alluring stretches of beach, although you'll be equally tempted by the spectacular multi-tiered

The free-form infinity pools at the JW Marriott in Cancún.

pools surrounded by lush grounds. This all-suite resort, renovated in 2009, attracts an international crowd and offers outstanding service. See p. 113.

- **JW Marriott** (Cancún; www.jwmarriottcancun.com): This gorgeous resort affords elegance without pretense, combining classic and Caribbean styling with warm Mexican service. The inviting free-form infinity pool extends to the white-sand beach, and families feel just as comfortable here as romance-seeking couples. The hotel includes a spectacular 3,250-sq.-m (35,000-square-foot) spa. See p. 114.
- **Ritz-Carlton Cancún** (Cancún; www.ritzcarlton.com): For years, thick carpets, sparkling glass and brass, and rich mahogany have surrounded guests at this hotel, the standard-bearer of luxury in Cancún. The service is impeccable, leaving guests with an overall sense of pampered relaxation. Its restaurants are among the best in the city, and the resort's beach just got bigger as a result of a large sand restoration project. See p. 115.
- **Presidente InterContinental Cozumel** (Cozumel; www.intercontinental cozumel.com): Surrounded by shady palms, this resort sits on the island's best beach, right in front of Paraíso Reef. There's an excellent dive center here, and the Maya-inspired service is warm and personalized. Beachfront "reef" rooms and suites occupy the resort's most exclusive section and include 24-hour butler service and hammocks. See p. 171.
- **The Tides Riviera Maya** (north of Playa del Carmen; www.tidesrivieramaya.com): Small, secluded, and supremely private, the Tides offers extraordinary personal service—some villas come with a mayordomo on call—and spa treatments. Rooms are spread throughout the jungle, and there's a beautiful seaside pool and restaurant. See p. 186.
- **Grand Velas** (south of Puerto Morelos; http://rivieramaya.grandvelas.com): Put away your old notions of all-inclusive resorts as cheap and tacky. This new "one price for everything" wonder pampers guests with elegant, understated decor, award-winning gourmet restaurants, luxe suites with beachfront plunge pools, a spa that outshines most others … in short, just about every luxury accoutrement ever invented. See p. 185.
- **Hacienda Xcanatún** (outskirts of Mérida; www.xcanatun.com): With its large, boldly designed suites built with extravagance in mind, acres of tropical gardens, private spa, excellent restaurant, and ample staff, this hotel masters the difficult trick of being compact in size but expansive in offerings. See "Haciendas & Hotels" on p. 260.
- **Hacienda Puerta Campeche** (Campeche; www.luxurycollection.com): Not a hacienda at all, really, this gorgeous hotel was created out of several adjoining colonial houses. This makes for a large property (especially for having only 15 rooms), with an open area in back featuring a pool and tropical gardens under ancient crumbling walls. From any vantage point the hotel is beautiful—both in overall layout and design details. And the service is impeccable. See p. 298.
- **Parador San Juan de Dios** (San Cristóbal; www.sanjuandios.com): Any luxury hotel in San Cristóbal must capture the atmosphere of this ancient town balanced between European and native worlds. Here it is presented with grace and beauty, a place where one can relax in the oversize colonial rooms or outside amid the extensive grounds. See p. 352.

THE best INEXPENSIVE INNS

- **Rey del Caribe Hotel** (Cancún; www.reycaribe.com): An inexpensive retreat in downtown Cancún, this hotel has considered every detail in its quest for an organic and environmentally friendly atmosphere. Set in a tropical garden, the Rey del Caribe provides sunny rooms, warm service, yoga and other themed classes, and healthful dining—all a welcome respite from party-hearty Cancún. See p. 120.
- **Luz en Yucatán** (Mérida; www.luzenyucatan.com): This inn, just 3 blocks from the main plaza, has a marvelous variety of thoughtfully decorated rooms, suites, studios, and apartments tucked into a sweet garden around a pool. The beds are superior, and guests have use of a large kitchen and dining room. You determine your own price, depending on your perceived level of success—and it's the only place I know of that offers a free bar cart. See p. 259.
- **Hotel López** (Campeche; www.hotellopezcampeche.com): The recently restored López departs from the historic center's colonial restorations with its Art Deco loops and curves. The lobby, courtyard and new waterfall pool are sheer eye candy; rooms are more modest but quite comfy and equipped with gleaming tile bathrooms. In a city that's already kind to the budget, it's the best hotel in its price range.
- **Hotel Posada La Media Luna** (San Cristóbal; www.hotellamedialuna.com): In a city of inexpensive lodgings, this beats all the other bargain hotels for its combination of location, room size, and service. See p. 353.

THE best UNIQUE INNS

- **Hotel Na Balam** (Isla Mujeres; www.nabalam.com): This eco-friendly hotel sits on an idyllic stretch of beach with calm turquoise waters just in front. Bleached white rooms and suites are almost hidden amidst the lush grounds, which torches and candles illuminate at night. The resort offers excellent yoga classes during the week. See p. 151.
- **Hotel Villa Rolandi Gourmet & Beach Club** (Isla Mujeres; www.villarolandi.com): In addition to being steps away from an exquisite private cove, a tranquil infinity pool, and Isla's finest restaurant, this intimate inn also pampers guests with every conceivable in-room amenity. Each unit even has a private Jacuzzi on the balcony and a shower that converts into a steam room. Guests are offered free transportation from Cancún via the hotel's private yacht. See p. 150.
- **Deseo Hotel + Lounge** (Playa del Carmen; www.hoteldeseo.com): Perhaps it should be Hotel = Lounge. That might be an overstatement, but the lounge is at the center of everything, making Deseo the perfect fit for outgoing types who are into an alternative lodging experience. Enjoy a cocktail at the bar or on one of the large daybeds and chill to the modern, er, lounge music. See p. 194.
- **Hacienda Yaxcopoil Casa de Visitas** (south of Mérida; www.yaxcopoil.com): You can truly be lord of the manor at this hacienda, a popular stop on the way to Uxmal. A single large guest house, with a sitting and dining room, opens onto a garden behind the manor house. When the hacienda closes to visitors at night, it's just you and the stars and the utter silence, except for the woman from town who brings you a home-cooked dinner and breakfast. See p. 279.

- **Casa Na-Bolom** (San Cristóbal de las Casas; www.nabolom.org): This unique house-museum is terrific for anthropology buffs. Built as a seminary in 1891, it was transformed into the headquarters of two anthropologists. The 12 guest rooms, named for surrounding villages, are decorated with local objects and textiles; all rooms have fireplaces and private bathrooms, and the room rate includes breakfast. See p. 344.

THE best RESTAURANTS

Best doesn't necessarily mean most luxurious. Although some of the restaurants listed here are fancy affairs, others are simple places to get fine, authentic Yucatecan cuisine.

- **Gustino** (Cancún; ✆ **998/848-9600**): The JW Marriott's signature restaurant is a gourmand's paradise, with fresh seafood, steaks, and homemade pastas prepared in the open kitchen using classic Italian ingredients. The beautiful dining room makes this one of the city's most romantic places to dine. See p. 122.
- **The Club Grill** (Cancún; ✆ **998/881-0808**): Two of the only AAA five-diamond restaurants in Mexico lie in the Ritz Carlton Cancún. Under the expert direction of Executive Chef Rainer Zinngrebe, The Club Grill serves exquisite international food. The resort has an outstanding culinary center offering cooking classes, as well. See p. 116.
- **Labná** (Ciudad Cancún; ✆ **998/892-3056**): Steep yourself in traditional Yucatecan culture at this downtown eatery, which showcases Maya cuisine and music. The Labná Special samples four of the region's best dishes, including baked suckling pig with guacamole. See p. 125.
- **Thai** (Cancún; ✆ **998/144-0364**): This enchanting Thai restaurant offers a handful of secluded tables in individual *palapas* over the lagoon. The waterfront setting provides a romantic backdrop to the classic and contemporary Thai cuisine. Plus, the restaurant's chill-out lounge makes for a perfect before- or after-dinner drink. See p. 124.
- **100% Natural for *Licuados:*** This casual eatery serves terrific breakfasts and healthy snacks throughout the day. Come for one of the *licuados,* drinks made from fresh fruit mixed with water or milk. The chain offers a wide selection, including innovative mixtures such as the Cozumel (spinach, pineapple, and orange) and the Caligula (orange, pineapple, beet, celery, parsley, carrot, and lime juices)—a healthy indulgence. Cancún has several branches; others are in Playa del Carmen and Mérida. See p. 126.

Dine on fresh seafood.

- **Casa Rolandi** (Isla Mujeres; ✆ **998/877-0700**): This exquisite restaurant attached to the Casa Rolandi boutique hotel serves the island's finest cuisine. The open-air establishment sits adjacent to the Caribbean and offers wonderful fresh fish, seafood, and pastas. See p. 134.
- **Cabaña del Pescador** (Cozumel; no phone): If you want an ideally seasoned, succulent lobster dinner, Cabaña del Pescador (Lobster House) is the place. If you want anything else, you're out of luck—lobster dinner, expertly prepared, is all it serves. When you've achieved perfection, why bother with anything else? See p. 172.
- **La Cocay** (Cozumel; ✆ **987/872-5533**): The most original cooking on the island is served in an enchanted dining room and outdoor courtyard. The emphasis is Mediterranean-prepared seafood with Spanish accents. Don't miss the excellent *tapas* and mixed grilled seafood served with Spanish rice. See p. 173.
- **Yaxché** (Playa del Carmen; ✆ **984/873-2502**): Few restaurants in the Riviera Maya explore the region's culinary traditions and use of local ingredients to the degree that this one does. Its menu presents several pleasant surprises and is a welcome relief from the standard offerings of most tourist restaurants. See p. 196.
- **La Pigua** (Campeche; ✆ **981/811-3365**): Campeche's regional specialty is seafood, and nowhere else will you find seafood like this. Mexican caviar, coconut-battered shrimp, and chiles stuffed with shark are just a few of the unique specialties. Thinking about La Pigua's pompano in a fine green herb sauce makes me want to start checking flight schedules. See p. 300.
- **Jangada** (Villahermosa; ✆ **993/317-6050**): Here you can dine on fresh fish and seafood prepared in a variety of ways, both classic and original. Try the freshwater *pejelagarto,* found only here, in the state of Tabasco. *Pigua,* the freshwater lobster, a rare delicacy elsewhere, can be had daily here. But the dish that keeps drawing me back is the shrimp and yuca soup. All the Mexican classics are represented, too, from ceviche to the fish tacos and *empanadas*. Here you can have it all. See p. 328.

Panucho **(tortilla filled with beans, chicken, lettuce, and red onion).**

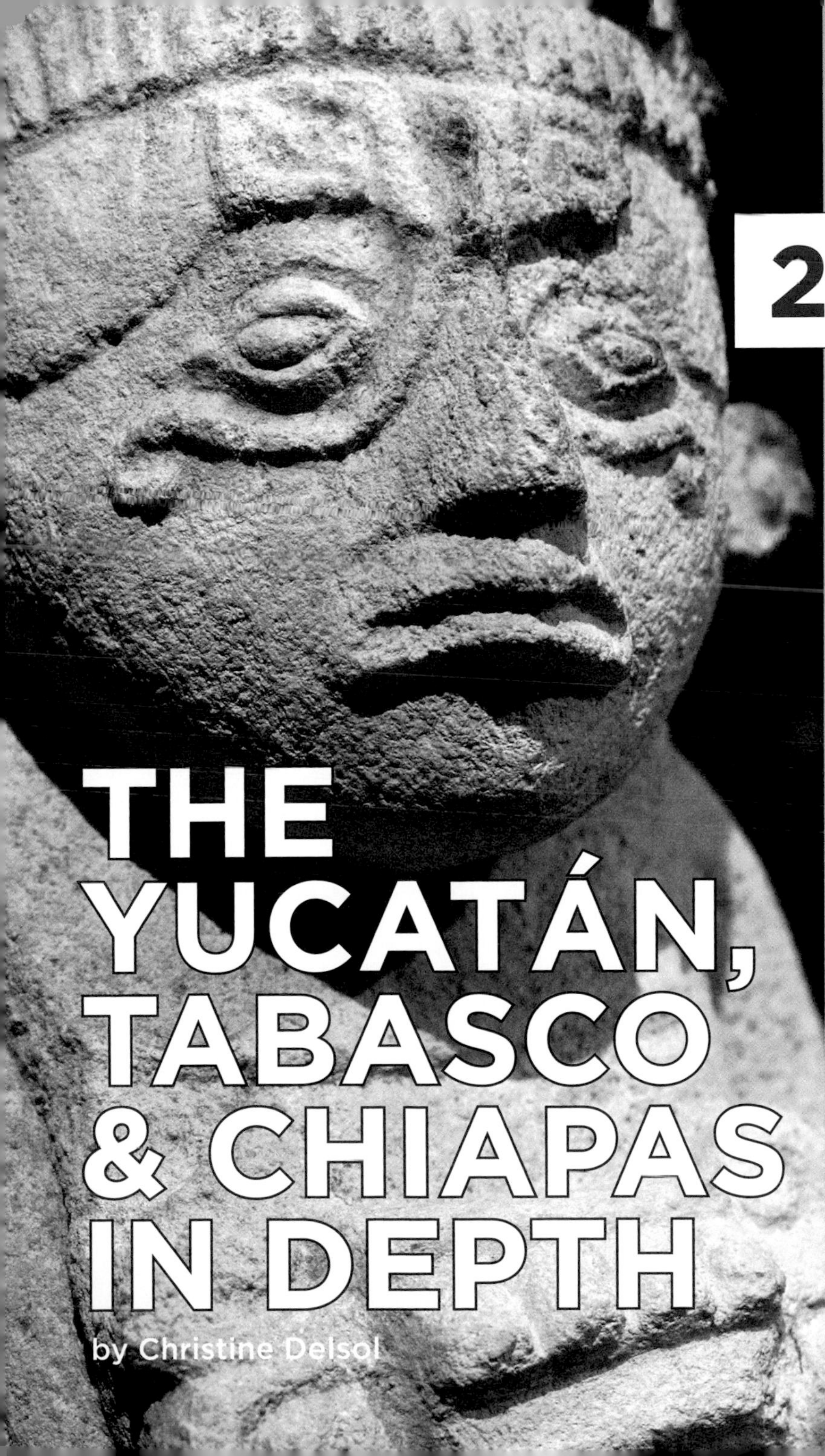

2

THE YUCATÁN, TABASCO & CHIAPAS IN DEPTH

by Christine Delsol

Barely 35 years ago, the Yucatán's only visitors were archaeologists headed to the ruins and scuba divers bound for Cozumel. Mile upon mile of Caribbean coast sat ignored, except for the occasional fisherman. Within the span of a single generation, the changes wrought on the Yucatán Peninsula and even distant Chiapas by Cancún's creation and growth have transformed the region from a forgotten backwater to a major international destination and one of Mexico's biggest cash cows.

Tourism, once an afterthought, is now the big enchilada. The change is most visible on the coast, where fishing villages and coconut plantations have given way to modern developments marching in lock step south to Tulum and inching beyond. For the young Maya of the interior villages, growth has brought new work opportunities, an end to isolation, and their first close contact with the modern world—specifically the modern world in vacation mode. The shift from village society to vacation paradise is the very definition of culture shock, which the implacable Maya meet with equanimity.

Less dramatically, tourism also made its way inland to the splendid Yucatán capital of Mérida and the major ruins—Chichén Itzá, Uxmal, and Palenque—and eventually to the barely uncovered ancient cities and time-warp villages of the deep interior. The ruins are wonders to behold, and every year seems to bring new archaeological discoveries.

Curiously, all the excavation and renovation has left small town life little changed. Coastal natives not swept up in the tourism boom were relocated inland, where they continue their ancestors' ways. Families of workers in the tourist palaces remain in the tropical forest, living in round thatch houses with no electricity, indoor plumbing, or paved roads, gathering plants for food and medicine, cooling off in hidden cenotes, and appealing to the gods for successful crops. To explore an older world where the Mayan tongue's distinctive intonations fill the air and traditions carry on as they have for untold centuries, you have only to drive inland from the Caribbean coast, venture to Campeche on the Gulf shore, or cross over into Chiapas.

The turquoise waters and tropical climate may beckon first, but what will ultimately draw you back, again and again, is the unique character of this land and its people.

THE YUCATÁN, TABASCO & CHIAPAS NOW

In the five states that make up the Yucatán and southeastern Mexico, great wealth lives alongside abject poverty. Paradoxically, the indexes of both wealth

PREVIOUS PAGE: **A Maya sculpture.**

and poverty in this region are higher than the national average. A tremendous amount of money flows into the area—from tourism in Yucatán and Quintana Roo, the oil industry in Campeche, Tabasco, and Chiapas. Yet most residents reap little from this prosperity. These five states have a total population of almost 10 million—10% of Mexico's population—but account for only about 6% of the economic activity.

In some cases, development has increased demand for local products and services. For example, fishermen and *palaperos,* the native people who create the thatched roofs *(palapas)* crowning so many restaurants and hotels, are in high demand whenever a hurricane brushes the coast. At the same time, development has destroyed the livelihood of other locals. Coastal coconut growers were wiped out when Cancún developers brought turf from Florida to build a golf course, unwittingly introducing a disease that killed the coconut palms; destruction of mangroves, crucial to the coastal food chain, has diminished fishermen's catches. A similar give-and-take is at play within the oil economies of Tabasco and Chiapas.

While residents' incomes have not improved, tourism and oil money has brought indirect benefits. Lacking a coherent policy to combat social ills, the government still has paved most of the peninsula's roads and fitted out remote villages with electricity. Purified water is widely available. And with the increasing emphasis on ecotourism, some remote villages have formed partnerships with tour companies that allow them to profit from tourism while controlling the number and type of visitors.

Today's Maya Culture & People

The Yucatán peninsula, Tabasco, and Chiapas often feel like a country apart from Mexico. Their *jarana* music, sweetened by clarinets, and a cuisine redolent with capers, achiote, and saffron, exude Caribbean sensuality. And the region's proud, gentle people display little of the machismo or the relentless salesmanship that tries visitors' patience in northern and central Mexico.

The sense of "otherness" grows partly from geographical isolation but even more from the Maya's fierce, centuries-long resistance to being absorbed into the

The old and new combine as people surf the Internet in a centuries-old plaza.

A Maya family in Yokdzonot, a small town near Chichén Itzá.

Spanish spoils; some Maya refuse to recognize Mexican sovereignty even today. All of which makes their warm, generous natures as much a wonder as their famous pyramid at Chichén Itzá.

In the Yucatán, especially, your simplest transaction with a local easily evolves into spirited conversation. In the Peninsula's interior, where some Maya Indians are uneasy speaking Spanish, you are more likely to encounter some initial reticence. Usually, it's quickly overcome with smiles and inventive gestures.

You don't need to leave Cancún to meet the Maya; thousands travel from the interior to jobs at hotels and restaurants. More than 350,000 Maya living in the peninsula's three states speak Yucatec, the local Mayan language. Most, especially men, also speak Spanish, and workers in Cancún usually know at least basic English.

The estimated 1 million Tabascan and Chiapan Maya, who speak four Mayan languages with dozens of dialects, are more reserved. Highland Maya around San Cristóbal de las Casas tend to remain aloof from outside cultures, preferring to live in mountain hamlets and meeting only for ceremonies and market days. In their chilly cloud-forest homeland they, too, live much as their ancestors did, but with beliefs distinct from their peninsular relatives.

Though they held fast to their language through the Spanish conquest, the Maya lost much of their living memory of pre-Hispanic life; what they retained is cloaked in myth and worked into elements of Catholicism. That process of syncretism, as anthropologists call it, continues today in the many Maya communities that have native churches.

The question of their ancestors' rightful place among the world's ancient civilizations might be as much a mystery to today's Maya people as it is to scholars. But nearly every year, archaeological discoveries of the art and architecture of the ancients add to the growing picture of a complex urban culture that thrived where only sparsely populated jungle exists today.

The Well-Lived Life

Despite economic inequities, Mexican society remains tremendously resilient and cohesive—due in no small part to the way Mexicans live. They place paramount value on family and friends, social gatherings, and living in the present; worrying about the future takes a back seat. Mexicans always have time to meet with friends for a drink or a cup of coffee or attend a family get-together. The many spirited public celebrations Mexico is known for are simply another manifestation of this attitude.

You won't find more amiable people anywhere on earth, and you can invite the full force of their natural gregariousness by being mindful of some social norms. Here's a start:

SLOW DOWN The stereotype of "*mañana* time" is mostly true. Life obeys slower rhythms, and "on time" is a flexible concept. Arriving 30 minutes to two hours late to a party in someone's home is acceptable—in fact, coming at the specified hour would be rude, for your hosts almost certainly will not be ready. Here's the "mostly" part: Dinner invitations are less flexible; arrive within 30 minutes of the appointed hour. And be on time for business appointments, public performances, weddings, and funerals.

MEET & GREET Don't short-circuit the hellos and goodbyes; social values are valued over time efficiency. A Mexican must at least say "*¡Buenos días!*" even to strangers. When meeting a group of people, an individual will greet each one separately, no matter how long it takes. Handshakes, *abrazos* (embraces), and, among women, kisses abound. Stick to handshakes until your host decides you rate a more intimate greeting. But don't back away from an embrace—that would amount to a rejection of friendship.

HAVE A LITTLE RESPECT Mexicans are lavish with titles of respect, so dispense *señor, señora,* and *señorita* (Mr., Mrs., Miss) freely. Teachers, lawyers, architects, and other professionals have earned the right to a title: *licenciado* for lawyers (and some other professions requiring a college degree), *maestro* or *maestra* for elementary school teachers, *profesor* or *profesora* for secondary or college teachers, and so forth. Mexicans have two surnames, father's first and mother's second. Both appear on business cards (the mother's name might be abbreviated to an initial), but when addressing people, use just the first (paternal) surname.

DON'T GET HUFFY Mexicans are genuinely interested in foreigners. If they stare, it's friendly curiosity. They like to practice their English, and will ask about family, friends, money, and other intimate matters. If you are over 30 and have no children, they may express deep concern. Don't take it personally.

SHOW SOME CULTURE Mexicans tend to divide the world into the well-raised and cultured *(bien educado)* and the poorly raised *(mal educado)*. Don't be shy about trying out your rudimentary Spanish; even the most elementary attempt is appreciated because it shows your interest in the culture. To be categorized as a foreigner is no big deal. What's important in Mexico is to be categorized as a cultured foreigner and not one of the barbarians.

In the Beginning

The animals showed them the road. And then grinding the yellow corn and the white corn, Xmucané made nine drinks...and with it they created the muscles and the strength of man... After that they began to talk about the creation and the making of our first mother and father; of yellow corn and of white corn they made their flesh; of corn meal dough they made the arms and the legs of man. —Popol Vuh

MAYAN TERMS & PHRASES

Hundreds of thousands of Maya living on the Yucatán Peninsula today speak at least some of their mother tongue. Most speak Yucatec Maya (commonly called simply "Maya"), one of more than 30 Mayan languages used today that can be traced back about 4,000 years to a single language believed to have originated in northwestern Guatemala. You will see numerous spelling variations around the peninsula. ***Note:*** The term "Mayan" is reserved for Mayan languages. The noun or the adjective for the people is "Maya."

Mayan vowels are pronounced very much as they are in Spanish. Double vowels are pronounced like their single counterparts but are held longer. The "x" is pronounced "sh," as in "ship"; the "j" sounds like "h," as in "home." Consonants that come before an accent (') are glottalized. Though the difference is hard for a newcomer to discern, glottalized consonants have a harder, more emphatic sound. Accents in Mayan words usually fall on the last syllable (unlike Spanish, which emphasizes the second-to-last syllable unless an accent mark indicates otherwise). Plurals in Mayan are formed by adding the suffix –ob.

ENGLISH	MAYAN	PRONUNCIATION
Hello	**Ola**	*oh*-lah
How are you?	**Biix a beel?**	Beesh a bell
What is your name?	**Bix a k'aaba**	Beesh ah k-ah-*bah*
My name is . . .	. . . in k'aaba	. . . een k-ah-*bah*
So long	**Tu heel k'iin**	Too heel k-*een*
Goodbye/Take care/Good luck	**Xi'ik tech utsil**	Shee-*eek* tech oot-*seel*
See you tomorrow	**Asta sa'amal**	Ahs-*ta* sah-ah-*mahl*
Okay (fine, well)	**Ma'aloob**	Mah-ah-*lohby*
Yes (That's the way it will be)	**He'le'**	Hey-*leh*
No	**Ma'**	Mah
I don't understand	**Min na'atik**	Meen na-ah-*teek*
Thank you	**Dyos bo'otik**	Dee-*yos* boh-oh-*teek*
You're welcome	**Mixba'al**	Meesh-bah-*ahl*
Stop	**Wa'alen**	Wah-ah-*lehn*
I'm hungry	**Wi'hen**	Wee-*hehn*
I'm going home	**Kin bin tin nah**	Keen been teen nah
Bon appetit	**Hach ki' a wi'ih**	Hach kee ah wee-*ee*
Let's (go)	**Ko'ox (tun)**	Koh-*osh* (toon)
Where is the beach?	**Tuxan há?**	Too-*shan* hah

A BASIC MAYAN GLOSSARY

Ah kin A high priest.

Aktun Cave.

Atl-atl Spear-throwing device.

Bacab A class of important gods.

Balam Jaguar spirit that keeps evil away.

Cán Serpent.

Cenote A natural waterhole created by the collapse of limestone caves; corruption by the Spanish of the Maya word dzonot.

Ch'en Pool.

Chilan A soothsayer or medium.

Chultun A bottle-shaped, underground cistern

Corte Indian woman's traditional full-length skirt.

Há Cacao seed.

Huipil A traditional Maya wraparound, woven cotton dress, worn leaving the shoulders bare.

Ka'a'anab, háal ha Beach.

Kayab A turtle-shell drum.

Kayem Ground maize.

Kin The sun, the day, unity of time.

Ku'um Pumpkin.

Manta A square of cloth, used as a cloak or blanket; still worn by the Maya today.

Milpa A cornfield.

Muxubbak Tamale.

Nohoch Important, big.

P'ac Tomatoes.

Palapa Traditional thatched-roof Maya structure built without nails.

Pok-a-tok A Maya ball game.

Pom Resin of the copal tree, used for rubber, chewing gum, and incense.

Quetzal A rare Central American bird, now almost extinct, prized by Maya kings for its long, brilliant blue-green tail feathers.

Sacbé Literally "white road," a raised limestone causeway linking Maya buildings and settlements.

Xibalbá The Maya underworld.

A LOOK AT THE PAST

Pre-Hispanic Civilizations

The earliest "Mexicans" might have been Stone Age hunter-gatherers from the north, descendants of a race that crossed the Bering Strait and reached North America around 12,000 B.C. A more recent theory points to an earlier crossing of peoples from Asia to the New World. What we do know is that Mexico was populated by 10,000 B.C. Sometime between 5200 and 1500 B.C., these early people began practicing agriculture and domesticating animals.

THE OLMECS & MAYA: THE PRECLASSIC PERIOD (1500 B.C.–A.D. 300)

Agriculture eventually yielded enough food to support large communities, with enough surplus to free some people from agricultural work. A civilization emerged that we call the **Olmec**—an enigmatic people who settled the coast of today's Tabasco and Veracruz states. Anthropologists regard them as Mesoamerica's mother culture because they established a pattern for later civilizations from northern Mexico to Central America. The Olmec developed a basic calendar, established principles of urban layout and architecture, and originated the cult of the jaguar and the sacredness of jade. They probably also bequeathed the sacred ball game common to all Mesoamerican culture.

A defining feature of the Olmec was its colossal carved stone heads, several of which reside today in the Parque Museo La Venta in Villahermosa, Tabasco. Their significance remains a mystery, but they were immense projects, sculpted from basalt mined miles inland and transported to the coast, probably by river rafts. Their rounded, baby-faced look, marked by a peculiar, high-arched lip—a "jaguar mouth"—is an identifying mark of Olmec sculpture.

A colossal Olmec head in Villahermosa.

IT'S ALL in the game

The ancient Maya played a game with a solid rubber ball of such importance that ball courts (pictured below) appear in virtually every Maya city (Bonampak is a rare exception). They were laid out in a capital I shape with sloping walls in the center. Similar ball courts have been found as far south as Nicaragua and as far north as Arizona.

Though we know little about this sacred game, ancient depictions of the game, early accounts by the Spanish, and the Popol Vuh (the Maya "bible"), show that the ball was heavy and could inflict injury. Wearing thick padding and protective gear, players formed teams of 2 to 10 members, the object being to propel the ball through a stone ring or other goal using mainly the hips.

We also know the ball game was part sport and part religious ritual based on the Maya's cosmological belief system. It sometimes involved sacrifice, though we're not sure whether the winners, the losers, or perhaps prisoners of war were sacrificed. In the Popol Vuh, the hero twins, Hunahpu and Xbalanque, challenge the lords of the underworld to a ball game, played in part with the head of one brother. Eventually the twins win and are allowed to return to the world of the living. Playing the ball game, then, might have been one way to cheat the underworld.

The **Maya** civilization began developing in the pre-Classic period, around 500 B.C. Understanding of this period is sketchy, but Olmec influences show up everywhere. The Maya perfected the Olmec calendar and developed both their ornate system of hieroglyphic writing and their early architecture. The people of **Teotihuacán,** north of present-day Mexico City, and the **Zapotec** of Monte Albán, in the valley of Oaxaca, also emerged around this time.

TEOTIHUACÁN, MONTE ALBÁN & PALENQUE: THE CLASSIC PERIOD (A.D. 300–900)

The rise and fall of these three city-states are bookends to the Classic Period, the height of pre-Columbian Mesoamerican art and culture. Achievements include the pyramids and palaces of Teotihuacán; the ceremonial center of Monte Albán; and the stelae and temples of Palenque, Bonampak, and Calakmul. The Maya also made significant scientific discoveries, including the concept of zero in mathematics and a complex calendar with which priests predicted eclipses and the movements of the stars.

Teotihuacán (100 B.C.–A.D. 700—near present-day Mexico City), a well-organized city built on a grid, is thought to have had 100,000 or more inhabitants at its zenith, led by an industrious, literate, and cosmopolitan ruling class. The city exerted tremendous influence as far away as Guatemala and the Yucatán. Its feathered serpent god, Quetzalcóatl, joined the pantheon of many succeeding cultures, including the Toltecs, who brought the cult to the Yucatán. Teotihuacán's refined aesthetics, evident in its beautiful, highly stylized sculpture and ceramics, show up in Maya and Zapotec objects. Around the 7th century, the city was abandoned. Who these people were and where they went remains a mystery.

TOLTECS & AZTEC INVASIONS: THE POST-CLASSIC PERIOD (A.D. 900–1521)

Warfare became more pervasive during this period, and these later civilizations were less sophisticated than those of the Classic period. The **Toltec** of central Mexico established their capital at Tula in the 10th century. Originally one of the barbarous hordes that periodically migrated from the north, they were influenced by remnants of Teotihuacán culture at some point and adopted the feathered-serpent god Quetzalcóatl. The Toltec maintained a large military class, and Tula spread its influence across Mesoamerica. But their might was played out by the 13th century, probably because of civil war and battles with invaders from the north.

The Maya of the Yucatán, especially the **Xiu** and **Itzáes,** might have departed from the norm with their broad trading networks and multiple influences from the outside world. They built beautiful cities in and around the Yucatán's Puuc hills, south of Mérida, their architecture characterized by elaborate exterior stonework above door frames and extending to the roofline. Impressive examples include the Codz Poop at Kabah and the palaces at Uxmal, Sayil, and Labná. Chichén Itzá, also ruled by Itzáes, was associated with the Puuc cities but shows strong Toltec influence in its architectural style and its cult of Quetzalcóatl, renamed Kukulkán.

Elaborate stonework from a Maya construction.

The exact nature of the Toltec influence on the Maya is a subject of debate, but an intriguing myth in central Mexico tells how Quetzalcóatl quarrels with Tezcatlipoca and is tricked into leaving Tula. Quetzalcóatl heads east toward the morning star, vowing someday to return. In the language of myth, this could be a metaphor for a civil war between two factions in Tula, each led by the priesthood of a particular god. Could the losing faction have migrated to the Yucatán and later ruled Chichén Itzá? Perhaps. What we do know is that this myth of Quetzalcóatl's eventual return became, in the hands of the Spanish, a powerful weapon of conquest.

Cortez, Moctezuma & the Spanish Conquest

In 1517, the first Spaniards arrived in Mexico and skirmished with Maya Indians off the coast of Campeche. A shipwreck left several Spaniards stranded as prisoners of the Maya. Another Spanish expedition, under **Hernán Cortez,** landed on Cozumel in February 1519. The coastal Maya were happy to tell Cortez about the gold and riches of the Aztec empire in central Mexico. Disobeying all orders from his superior, the governor of Cuba, Cortez promptly sailed to the mainland and embarked on one of history's most bizarre culture clashes.

He sailed with his army to Tabasco, established a settlement in Veracruz, and worked his way up the Gulf Coast during the height of the Aztec empire's wealth and power. **Moctezuma II** ruled the central and southern highlands and extracted tribute from lowland peoples; his greatest temples were literally plated with gold and encrusted with the blood of sacrificial captives. A fool, a mystic, and something of a coward, Moctezuma dithered in Tenochtitlán while Cortez blustered and negotiated his way into the highlands. Moctezuma, terrified, was convinced that Cortez was the returning Quetzalcóatl. By the time he arrived in the Aztec capital, Cortez had accumulated 6,000 indigenous allies who resented paying tribute to the Aztec. In November 1519, he took Moctezuma hostage in an effort to leverage control of the empire.

In the middle of Cortez's manipulations, another Spanish expedition arrived with orders to end Cortez's unauthorized mission. Cortez hastened to the coast, routed the rival force, and persuaded the vanquished to join him on his return to Tenochtitlán. The capital had erupted in his absence, and the Aztec chased his garrison out of the city. Moctezuma was killed during the attack—whether by the Aztec or the Spaniards is not clear. For a year and a half, Cortez laid siege to Tenochtitlán, aided by rival Indians and a devastating smallpox epidemic. When the Aztec capital fell, all of central Mexico lay at the conquerors' feet, vastly expanding the Spanish empire. The king legitimized Cortez after his victory and ordered the forced conversion to Christianity of the new colony, to be called New Spain. By 1540, New Spain included possessions from Vancouver to Panama. In the 2 centuries that followed, Franciscan and Augustinian friars converted millions of Indians to Christianity, and Spanish lords built huge feudal estates with Indian farmers serving as serfs. The silver and gold that Cortez looted made Spain the richest country in Europe.

The Rise of Mexico City & Spanish Colonialism

Cortez set about building a new city upon the ruins of the Aztec capital, collecting the tributes that the Indians once paid to Moctezuma. Many paid in labor. This became the model for building the new colony.

Benito Juárez.

Over the 3 centuries of the colonial period, Spain grew rich from New World gold and silver chiseled out by Indian labor. The Spanish elite built lavish homes filled with ornate furniture and draped themselves in imported velvets, satins, and jewels. Under the new class system, those born in Spain considered themselves superior to the *criollos,* or Spaniards born in Mexico. People of other races and the *castas* (Spanish-Indian, Spanish-African, or Indian-African mixes) formed society's bottom rungs. Wealthy colonists lived extravagantly despite the Crown's insatiable demand for taxes and contributions.

Criollo discontent with Spanish rule following the 1767 expulsion of the Jesuits simmered for years. In 1808, **Napoleon** invaded Spain, deposed Charles IV and crowned his brother **Joseph Bonaparte.** To many in Mexico, allegiance to France was unthinkable. The next logical step was revolt.

Hidalgo, Juarez & Mexico's Independence

In 1810, **Father Miguel Hidalgo** set off the rebellion with his *grito,* the fabled cry for independence, in the town of Dolores, Guanajuato. With **Ignacio Allende** and a citizen army, Hidalgo marched toward Mexico City. Although he ultimately failed and was executed, Hidalgo is honored as "the Father of Mexican Independence." Another priest, José María Morelos, kept the revolt alive with several successful campaigns until he, too, was captured and executed in 1815.

When the Spanish king who replaced Joseph Bonaparte decided to institute social reforms in the colonies, Mexico's conservative powers concluded they didn't need Spain after all. Royalist **Agustín de Iturbide** defected in 1821 and conspired with the rebels to declare independence from Spain, with himself as emperor. However, internal dissension soon deposed Iturbide, and Mexico was instead proclaimed a republic.

The young, politically unstable republic ran through 36 presidents in 22 years, in the midst of which it lost half its territory in the disastrous **Mexican-American War (1846-48).** The central figure, **Antonio López de Santa Anna,** assumed the presidency no fewer than 11 times and just might hold the record for frequency of exile. He was ousted for good in 1855 and finished his days in Venezuela.

Amid continuing political turmoil after ragtag Mexican troops defeated the well-equipped French force in a battle near Puebla in 1862 (now celebrated as Cinco de Mayo), conservatives hit upon the idea of bringing in a Habsburg to regain control. With French backing, **Archduke Maximilian** of Austria stepped in as emperor in 1864. After 3 years of civil war, the French finally abandoned the emperor's cause, leaving Maximilian to be captured and executed in 1867. His adversary and successor as president was **Benito Juárez,** a Zapotec Indian lawyer and one of Mexico's greatest heroes. Juárez did his best to unify and strengthen

A mural depicting the subjugation of the people of the Yucatán.

his country before dying of a heart attack in 1872, and his plans and visions bore fruit for decades.

Yucatecan Independence & the Caste War

In 1845, with a stable form of government still eluding the country, the Yucatán's landed oligarchy decided to declare independence from Mexico. They armed the populace—including Indians who had slaved their entire lives on the haciendas—to defend the territory from invasion. The Indians, resentful of their serfdom, realized it didn't much matter whether their oppressors lived in Mexico City or Mérida, and raised their arms against the landowners in what became the War of the Castes. The slaughter would continue, off and on, for 60 years.

The peasants soon controlled most of the countryside, capturing several towns and the city of Valladolid. Mérida, too, was on the verge of surrender just as planting season arrived. Rather than press their advantage and take the capital, the Maya inexplicably laid down their weapons to return to their corn fields. Yucatecan troops quickly regrouped, swore fealty to Mexico and called for a government army. Eventually the Maya rebels were driven back into what is now Quintana Roo, where they were largely left on their own, virtually a nation within a nation, until a Mexican army with modern weaponry finally penetrated the region at the turn of the 20th century.

Diaz, Zapata, Pancho Villa & the Mexican Revolution

A few years after Juárez's death, one of his generals, **Porfirio Díaz,** seized power in a coup. He ruled Mexico from 1877 to 1911, a period now called the "Porfiriato," maintaining power through repression and by courting favor with powerful nations. With foreign investment came the concentration of great wealth in few hands, and discontent deepened.

In 1910, **Francisco Madero** led an armed rebellion that became the Mexican revolution ("La Revolución" in Mexico; the revolution against Spain is the "Guerra de Independencia"). Díaz was exiled and is buried in Paris. Madero became president, but **Victoriano Huerta,** in collusion with U.S. ambassador Henry Lane Wilson, betrayed and executed him in 1913. Those who had answered Madero's call rose up again—the great peasant hero **Emiliano Zapata** in the south, and the seemingly invincible **Pancho Villa** in the central north,

OF henequén & haciendas

Commercial production of *henequén*, the thorny agave that yields the rope fiber we know as sisal (pictured), began in 1830. Demand reached fever pitch during World War I; with a virtual monopoly on the *oro verde* ("green gold"), Yucatán blossomed from one of Mexico's poorest states to one of its richest. In addition to their baronial homes along Mérida's Paseo de Montejo, landowners built plantations to meet their every comfort when they traveled to the countryside. Their haciendas were small, self-contained cities supporting hundreds of workers, and each had its own school, infirmary, store, church, cemetery, and even a jail.

Invention of synthetic fibers during World War II devastated the henequén industry; abandoned haciendas became grand derelicts until a new generation of wealthy Mexicans began turning them into hotels in the early 1990s.

flanked by **Alvaro Obregón** and **Venustiano Carranza.** They eventually routed Huerta and began hashing out a new constitution.

For the next few years, Carranza, Obregón, and Villa fought among themselves; Zapata did not seek national power, though he fought tenaciously for land for the peasants. Carranza, who was president at the time, betrayed and assassinated Zapata. Obregón finally consolidated power and probably had Carranza assassinated. He, in turn, was assassinated when he tried to break one of the tenets of the revolution—no re-election. Not until **Lázaro Cárdenas** was elected in 1934 did the Revolution appear to have a chance. He implemented massive land redistribution, nationalized the oil industry, instituted many reforms, and gave shape to the ruling political party (precursor to today's Partido Revolucionario Institucional, or **PRI**). Cárdenas is practically canonized by most Mexicans.

Modern Mexico

The presidents who followed were noted more for graft than leadership, and the party's reform principles were abandoned. In 1968, the government quashed a democratic student demonstration in Mexico City, killing hundreds of people. Though the PRI maintained its grip on power, it lost its image as a progressive party.

Economic progress, particularly in the form of large development projects, became the PRI's sole basis for legitimacy. In 1974 the government decided to build a new coastal megaresort. To determine the ideal location, data crunchers loaded all the variables into a computer. Out popped Cancún, and Mexico's economy changed forever.

The government weathered several bouts of social unrest caused by periodic devaluations of the peso. But in 1985, the devastating Mexico City earthquake brought down many new, supposedly earthquake-proof buildings, exposing the widespread corruption that had fostered the shoddy construction, and triggering criticism of the government's relief efforts.

Meanwhile, opposition parties were gaining strength. The two largest were the **PRD** (Partido de la Revolución Democrática) on the left and the **PAN** (Partido Acción National) on the right. To ensure its candidate, Carlos Salinas de Gortari, would win the 1988 presidential election over the PRD's Cuauhtémoc Cárdenas (formerly of the PRI and son of former President Lázaro Cárdenas), the government simply unplugged election computers and declared a system failure.

Under pressure at home and abroad, the government moved to demonstrate a new commitment to democracy and even began to concede electoral defeats for state governorships and legislative seats. Power struggles between reformist factions and hardliners within the party led to several political assassinations, most notably of the PRI's next candidate, Luis Colosio. After that assassination and the crippling economic crisis of 1994, Gortari's successor, Ernesto Zedillo, spent his 6 years in office trying to stabilize the economy and bring transparency to government.

In 2000 he shepherded the first true elections in 70 years of one-party rule. The winner was PAN candidate **Vicente Fox,** a former businessman who ran on a platform of economic liberalization and anti-corruption. Many Mexicans voted for him to see if the PRI would relinquish power more than for any other reason. It did, but Fox didn't prove to be the master politician that the situation required.

A TALE OF two hurricanes

By 1988, when Hurricane Gilbert swept through, Cancún had more than 200,000 residents, with more than 12,000 hotel rooms and another 11,000 on the drawing boards. The storm's destruction barely slowed the explosive growth; existing resorts were promptly remodeled and reopened, followed by dozens of new ones. But the decision to slash hotel rates to lure tourists back, combined with the drinking age of 18, had the unintended effect of making Cancún the spring-break capital of North America. Images of binge-drinking college hordes replaced idyllic scenes of couples and families playing tag with turquoise waves.

Ironically, an even more devastating hurricane was the occasion for turning this image around. On Oct. 18, 2005, Hurricane Wilma parked on top of the region, battering it with 240kmph (150 mph) winds. Bridges linking the Hotel Zone with the city collapsed, electricity and water were out for 10 days, and the world's most celebrated beaches were scoured down to rock. Tens of thousands of tourists were stranded in shelters for as much as a week by the most destructive natural disaster in Mexican history, surpassing even the 1985 Mexico City earthquake.

The government, insurance companies, and major resort hotel chains mobilized a massive recovery effort. Restoration of more than 11km (7 miles) of white-powder beach with sand pumped 35km (22 miles) from the ocean bottom grabbed the headlines, but a more important transformation was in the works. Within 3 months, 18,000 of the 22,000 hotel rooms were ready for guests. Crews built new roads, installed better street lamps, planted thousands of palms, and installed modern sculptures. In rebuilding, in some cases from the ground up, resorts took pains to distance themselves from the spring-break crowd, going bigger, better, and more luxurious than ever, with price hikes to match.

A sticky HABIT

Cigar smoking and gum chewing are two pleasures we have the Maya to thank for. Gum, the more innocuous of the two, comes from the sap of a species of zapote tree that grows in the Yucatán and Guatemala. Chewing releases its natural sugars and a mild, agreeable taste. The chewing-gum habit spread from the Maya to other cultures and eventually to the non-Indian population. In the second half of the 19th century, a Mexican (said to have been General Santa Anna) introduced gum to the American Thomas Adams, who realized that it could be sweetened further and given other flavors. He marketed chewing gum in the U.S. with great success. Chemists have since figured out how to synthesize the gum, but the sap is still collected in parts of the Yucatán and Guatemala for making natural chewing gum. *Chicle* is the Spanish word originally from the Nahuatl (Aztec) *tzictli,* and those who live in the forest and collect the sap are called *chicleros.* Because the tree takes so long to produce more sap, there is no way to cultivate it commercially, so it is still collected in the wild.

His efforts to build a coalition with segments of the PRI failed, and he accomplished little during his last 3 years in office.

The whisker-close and bitterly disputed presidential election of 2006 tested Mexico's nascent pluralism. The elections tribunal's ruling, declaring PAN's **Felipe Calderón** the winner while denying the PRD's request for a recount, was profoundly unpopular. Losing candidate **Andrés Manuel López Obrador** did not take defeat gracefully and provoked a constitutional crisis that only time managed to heal. President Calderón, recognizing the PRD campaign's resonance with the poor, announced programs to boost employment, alleviate poverty, and stabilize the skyrocketing price of tortillas.

His biggest challenge, however, has proved to be the alarming escalation of drug-related violence—a conflagration widely attributed to his crackdown on traffickers who ferry contraband through Mexico on its way to the United States. The violence, directed at journalists and government officials as well as rival drug cartels, is concentrated in five counties along the U.S.-Mexico border and parts of northern and central Mexico.

Several high-profile captures and killings of key drug lords have disrupted the cartels but have not quelled the violence: Each loss of a leader spurs infighting within the beheaded cartel, while other gangs make a grab for new territory. Calderón, who has held fast to his strategy, is facing increasing criticism; meanwhile, the PRI has gained new strength since the July 2009 legislative elections ended the majority rule of Calderón s PAN. He has until 2012 to turn things around, perhaps with law-enforcement reforms, but high levels of violence could well continue at least until then.

Southern Mexico especially Yucatán and Campeche has some of the lowest casualty counts in the country and remains among the safest places to travel. Yet blaring headlines about the drug wars, combined with reports of the H1N1 flu virus surfacing first in Mexico City, have scared travelers away in droves. Mexico has taken the brunt of the worldwide tourism slump, and even though the unprecedented deals that surfaced in the wake of the flu scare are gone, travel costs generally remain equal to or even lower than they were a year ago.

ART & ARCHITECTURE

Mexico's art, architecture, politics, and religion were inextricable for more than 3,000 years. The Maya were perhaps the most gifted artists in the Americas, producing fantastically lifelike stone sculptures, soaring temples clad in colors we can only guess at today, and delicately painted pottery. The Spanish conquest in A.D. 1521 influenced the style and subject of Mexican art, yet failed to stamp out its roots.

Pre-Hispanic Forms

Nowhere is the interplay of religion and art more striking than in Mexico's renowned pyramids, which were temples crowning a truncated platform. Maya structures also served as navigation aids, administrative and ceremonial centers, tombs, astronomical observatories, and artistic canvases.

Circular buildings such as Chichén Itzá's El Caracol and Palenque's observatory tower aided Maya priests' remarkably accurate astral calculations, used primarily for astrological divination but surprisingly accurate by modern astronomical standards. Chichén Itzá's El Castillo itself is a massive and stunningly accurate calendar, with four staircases of 91 steps, equaling the 365 days of the solar year when the central platform is added. The 18 terraces on each face of the pyramid symbolize the number of months in the Maya calendar, and the 52 panels on the terraces symbolize the 52-year cycle, when the solar and religious calendars converge. Architects aligned the temple to create the equinox phenomenon of the stairway's shadow slithering down a corner of the pyramid to the giant serpent's head at the bottom.

Chichén Itzá's El Castillo.

The ancient architecture shows a variety of influences, though the practice of building one pyramid on top of another was widespread. Chichén Itzá's strong Toltec influence, with its angular, stepped profiles, emphasizes war and human sacrifice; Uxmal's refined and more purely Maya geometry, including the beautifully sloped and rounded Temple of the Magician, incorporates the varied elevations of the Puuc hills.

The unjustly overlooked Edzná in Campeche state displays roof combs and corbeled arches resembling those of Palenque and giant stone masks similar to Guatemala's Petén style. The alternating vertical and sloping panels of Toltec and Aztec architecture surfaces in Dzibanché, too, a recently excavated site near Laguna de Bacalar in southern Quintana Roo.

The true arch was unknown in Mesoamerica, but the Maya devised the corbeled arch (or Maya arch) by stacking each successive stone to cantilever beyond the one below, until the two sides met at the top in an inverted V.

The Olmecs, who reigned over the Gulf coastal plains, are considered Mesoamerica's parent culture. Little survives of their pyramids, which were built of clay. We still have their enormous sculptural legacy, from small, intricately carved pieces of jade to the 40-ton carved basalt rock heads still found at La Venta, Tabasco (some of which are on view in the museum in Villahermosa).

More intact later cities, built of stone, give us a better glimpse of ancient Maya art, but their exuberant color is all but lost to us. The stones originally were covered with a layer of painted stucco that gleamed red, blue, and yellow through the jungle foliage. Most of the fantastic murals that adorned their buildings are also lost to time, though surprisingly well-preserved fragments have been found at Bonampak and Ek Balam. Vestiges also remain at Mayapán, and Cobá.

Artisans also crafted marvelous stone murals and mosaics from thousands of pieces of fitted stone, adorning facades with geometric designs or figures of warriors or snakes. Uxmal, in fact, evidently had not a single mural; all its artistry is in the intricate stonework.

A corbeled arch in Uxmal.

Murals and stone carvings were more religious or historical than ornamental in purpose. Deciphering the hieroglyphs—rich, elegant symbols etched in stone or painted on pottery—allows scholars to identify rulers and untangle dynastic history. Michael Coe's *Breaking the Maya Code* traces centuries-long efforts to decode Maya script and outlines recent breakthroughs that make it possible to decipher 90% of the glyphs. "Cracking the Maya Code," a "Nova" program based on Coe's book, is available for viewing on www.pbs.org or on DVD.

Good hieroglyphic examples appear in Palenque's site museum. Several stelae, the large, free-standing

A mural from Bonampak.

Detailed stonework from Uxmal.

stone slabs where the Maya etched their history, are in place at Cobá. Calakmul is known for its many stelae, and good examples are displayed in Mexico City's Museum of Anthropology and the archaeology museum in Villahermosa.

Spanish Influence

The Spaniards brought new forms of architecture to Mexico; in many cases they built Catholic churches, public buildings, and palaces with limestone from razed Maya cities. In the Yucatán, churches at Izamal, Tecoh, Santa Elena, and Muna rest atop former pyramids. Indian artisans recruited to build the new structures frequently implanted traditional symbolism, such as a plaster angel swaddled in feathers, reminiscent of the god Quetzalcóatl; they determined how many florets to carve around church doorways based on the ancient cosmos' 13 steps of heaven and nine levels of the underworld.

Spanish priests and architects altered their teaching and building methods in order to convert native populations. Church adornment became more explicit to combat the language barrier; frescoes of Biblical tales were splashed across church walls, and Christian symbols in stone supplanted pre-Hispanic figures.

Remnants of 16th-century missions, convents, monasteries, and parish churches dot almost every Yucatán village. Examples worth visiting include the Mission of San Bernardino de Sisal in Valladolid; the cathedral of Mérida; the vast atrium and church at Izamal; and the *retablos* (altarpieces), altars, and crucifixes in churches along the Convent Route, between the Puuc Hills and Mérida.

Porfirio Díaz's 35-year rule (1876–1911) brought a new infusion of European sensibility. Díaz commissioned imposing European-style public buildings and provided European scholarships to artists who returned to paint Mexican subjects using techniques from abroad. Mérida is a veritable museum of opulent, European-style buildings built during the Díaz years; the most striking are the Palacio Cantón, now housing the Regional Anthropology Museum, and the Teatro Peón Contreras.

The Advent of Mexican Muralism

The Mexican revolution that ripped the country apart from 1910 to 1920 gave rise to a new social and cultural era. In 1923, as one way to reach the illiterate masses, Diego Rivera and other budding artists were invited to paint Mexican history on the walls of the Ministry of Education building and the National Preparatory School in Mexico City. Thus was born Mexico's tradition of public murals.

The courtyard and History Room of the Governor's Palace in Mérida display 31 works of Castro Pacheco, the Yucatán's most prominent muralist. Though he painted on large panels rather than directly on the walls, he aligned with other great muralists in his affinity for strong colors and the belief that art is meant for public enjoyment, not just private collectors. Pacheco's murals are a chilling depiction of the bloody subjugation of the Yucatán, including the Popol Vuh legend, a jaguar with fierce warriors in headdresses, a Maya *henequén* worker's hands, and portraits of such heroes as Felipe Carrillo Puerto, the martyred Yucatecan governor who instituted agrarian and other reforms.

RELIGION, MYTH & FOLKLORE

Nearly 90% of Mexicans subscribe to Roman Catholicism, but Catholicism in much of Mexico is laced with pre-Hispanic spiritual tradition. You need only to visit the *curandero* section of a Mexican market (where you can buy such talismans as copal, an incense agreeable to the gods; rustic beeswax candles, a traditional offering; the native species of tobacco used to ward off evil) or watch pre-Hispanic dances performed at a village festival to sense the supernatural beliefs running parallel with Christian ones.

Spanish Catholicism was disseminated by pragmatic Jesuit missionaries who grafted Christian tradition onto indigenous ritual to make it palatable to their flock. Nearly 500 years after the conquest, a large minority of Mexicans—faithful Catholics every one—adhere to this hybrid religion, nowhere more so than in Chiapas and the Yucatán.

The padres' cause enjoyed a huge boost when a dark-skinned image of the Virgin Mary appeared to an Aztec potter near Mexico City in 1531. The Virgin of Guadalupe, fluent in the local language and acquainted with indigenous gods, provided a crucial link between Catholic and native spiritual traditions. She remains Mexico's most beloved religious figure, smiling from countless shrines, saloons, and kitchen walls. Millions of pilgrims walk and crawl to her Mexico City shrine on her December 12 feast day.

The equally pragmatic native people chose the path of least resistance, dressing their ancestral beliefs in Catholic garb. They gave their familiar gods the names of Christian saints and celebrated their old festivals on the nearest saint's day. Thus we find the Catholic feasts of All Saints' Day and All Souls' Day superimposed on the ancient Day of the Dead celebration, and the cult of

Santa Elena Church is located atop a former pyramid.

the "Black Christ"—an amalgam of Jesus Christ and the cave-dwelling Maya god Ik'al—entrenched in the Yucatán, Chiapas, and Tabasco. In one of the most dramatic examples of this spiritual hybridization, the Tzotzil Maya of San Juan Chamula in highland Chiapas carpet their church with pine needles, kneeling among candles and Coke bottles to pray in an archaic dialect under the painted eyes of helpful saints. They bring offerings of flower petals, eggs, feathers, or live chickens prescribed by local *curanderos* (medicine men) in an effort to dispel the demons of disease.

Common themes in the Catholic and Maya belief systems also made the Jesuits' task easier. The Catholics had the Bible, the Maya had the Popol Vuh. Both had long oral and written traditions (although Bishop Diego de Landa burned the Maya codices of Maní in the infamous *auto-da-fè* of 1562). Ceremonial processions with elaborate robes and incense were common to both religions, as were baptism by water and the symbol of the cross.

But the differences intrigue us most. The Maya's multitude of deities, 166 by some counts, is just the beginning. The Popol Vuh's creation myth, similar to Genesis in making man on the last day and striking down imperfect creations with an apocalyptic flood, departs from the Genesis plot in striking ways, not the least of which is fashioning man from corn after failed tries with mud and wood. Maya mythology is a collection of convoluted tales, full of images placing nature on a level equal to man, that attempt to make sense of the universe, geography, and seasons.

The tall, straight *ceiba* tree was revered as a symbol of the cosmos. Its leaves and branches represented the 13 levels of heaven, the tree trunk the world of humans, and its roots the nine-level underworld—not hell but a cold, damp, dark place called Xibalba. The manner of death determined one's resting place: Men who died in battle or women who died in childbirth, for example, went straight to the sun. Everyone else had to journey first through the underworld.

Foremost among the Maya pantheon were those who influenced the growth of corn. The Maya worked hard to please their gods through prayer, offerings, and

THE maya PANTHEON

Every ancient culture had its gods and goddesses, and their characteristics or purposes, if not their names, often crossed cultures. Chaac, the hook-nosed rain god of the Maya, was Tlaloc, the squat rain god of the Aztecs; Quetzalcóatl, the plumed-serpent man/god of the Toltecs, became the Maya's Kukulkán. Sorting out the ancient deities and beliefs can become a life's work, but here are some of the most important gods of the Maya world.

Itzamná Often called the Supreme Diety; creator of mankind and inventor of corn, cacao, writing, and reading; patron of the arts and sciences.

Chaac God of rain, striking the clouds with a lightning ax; sometimes depicted as four separate gods based in the four cardinal directions.

Kinich Ahau Sun god, sometimes regarded as another manifestation of Itzamná; appeared in the shape of a firebird.

Kukulkán Mortal who took on godly virtues, sometimes symbolized as Venus, the morning star.

Ixchel Wife of Kinich Ahau; multitasking goddess of the moon, fertility and childbirth, water, medicine, and weaving.

Bacab Generic name for four brothers who guarded the four points of the compass; closely associated with the four Chaacs.

Yumil Kaxob God of maize, or corn, shown with a crown or headdress of corn and distinguished by his youth.

Balam One of numerous jaguar spirits; symbol of power and protector of fields and crops.

Ixtab Goddess of suicide; suicide was an honorable way to die, and Ixtab received those souls into heaven.

sacrifices, which could be anything from a priest giving his own blood to human sacrifice. They were obsessed with time, maintaining both a 260-day religious calendar and a 365-day solar calendar that guided crop planting and other practicalities. In fact, religion, art, and science were so entwined that the Maya might not even have perceived them as separate pursuits. So from a kernel of corn grew some of civilization's earliest and greatest accomplishments.

THE LAY OF THE LAND

The Yucatán Peninsula is truly a freak of nature—a flat, nearly 134,400 sq. km (51,892 sq. mile) slab of limestone with almost 1,600km (1,000 miles) of shoreline that is virtually devoid of surface water. The peninsula's geology, found nowhere else on Earth, was shaped by the same meteor thought to have extinguished the dinosaurs 65 million years ago. The impact wracked the brittle limestone, fracturing it into an immense network of fissures that drain all rainwater away from the surface. You'll see no bridges, no rivers, lakes, or streams in the northern and central Yucatán, but fresh rainwater courses through a vast underground river system stretching for hundreds of miles.

Cenote X`keken in Valladolid.

Breaches in the ceiling of this subterranean basin have created an estimated 3,000 cenotes—sinkholes that reveal the underground to the world above. The Maya called them *dzonots,* or sacred wells, and regarded them as gateways to the underworld. Precious stones, ceramics, and bones unearthed in cenotes suggest that they were ancient ceremonial sites.

Quiet, dark, and cool, cenotes offer respite from the bright, often steamy glare above. Some are underground, with only a small breach in a roof perforated by ropy, water-seeking tree roots. Others open to the surface like a lake. Most tourists get their introduction to this subterranean world at Chichén Itzá, with its Grand Cenote, and Hidden Worlds Cenotes Park, with underground caverns and waterways north of Tulum. But thousands more lie at the ends of narrow dirt roads throughout the peninsula, the greatest concentration being inland from the Playa del Carmen–Tulum corridor. The largest is the sea-like Cenote Azul, at the end of Laguna de Bacalar in southern Quintana Roo.

The thin layer of soil coating the Yucatán's limestone shelf supports a surprisingly uniform terrain of dense, scrubby jungle full of wild ginger and orchids, jaguars, monkeys, and tropical birds. The only elevation is in the Puuc Hills. Rising south of Chichén Itzá and extending into northwestern Campeche, they peak at less than 300m (984 ft.).

The geography changes abruptly at the peninsula's isthmus. Hot, marshy Tabasco is a low-lying state bordering the Gulf of Mexico. With about 30% of Mexico's surface freshwater, Tabasco is said

The Endemic Birds of the Yucatán

The following 14 bird species are endemic to the Yucatán. See them while you're here, because you won't find them anywhere else on the planet: the black catbird, Cozumel emerald, Cozumel vireo, Cozumel thrasher, ocellated turkey, orange oriole, red-vented woodpecker, rose-throated tanager, yellow-lored (Yucatán) parrot, Yucatán poorwill, Yucatán nightjar, Yucatán flycatcher, Yucatán jay, and the Yucatán wren.

The Lay of the Sea

Cozumel has been one of the world's top dive sites since Jacques Cousteau unveiled its wonders in a 1961 documentary film. The island is fringed by a coral reef system that grows into towering walls, peaks, valleys, arches, and tunnels inhabited by more than 4,000 species of fish and thousands of other plants and animals. Its colors and textures rival New England's fall foliage displays. This underwater mountain range, running for 32km (20 miles) along Cozumel's southwest coast, is part of the massive Great Mesoamerican Reef (also called the Great Mayan Reef) stretching from the Gulf of Mexico to Honduras—second in size only to Australia's Great Barrier Reef.

to be more water than land. Parts of the state are cloaked in thick rainforest, which extends through Chiapas. The capital, Villahermosa, lies in a shallow basin about an hour from the coast at the confluence of two rivers. Small lakes break up the landscape, especially in the modern parts of the city.

Chiapas, a much larger state of wildly varying elevations, extends from Tabasco all the way to the Pacific on one side and Guatemala on the other. It is washed by abundant lagoons, waterfalls, and rivers, including the Usumancinta, which forms the border with Guatemala. The high central plateau of a dramatic, pine-covered mountain range is the uncommonly chilly domain of San Cristóbal de las Casas, a small and ancient colonial city surrounded by Maya villages. Nearby Sumidero Canyon is a winding river gorge with some walls reaching 1,000m (3,281 ft.) into the sky. Palenque, one of Mexico's most exquisite ruins, sits where the northern highlands slide down to the Gulf coastal plain.

Southern Mexico is blessed with an astounding diversity of wildlife. North America's only two flamingo breeding grounds flank the northern Yucatán's Gulf

Marshland in Tabasco.

Coast, and whale sharks convene off the peninsula's northeastern tip. Jaguars, howler monkeys, crocodiles, sea turtles, and hundreds of bird species populate the Sian Ka'an Biosphere Reserve south of the Riviera Maya.

A coati.

Odd critters such as the paca (kind of a spotted guinea pig on steroids), the coati, and the kinkajou (tree-dwelling raccoon kin), might pop up as you roam ancient Maya cities or hike through mangrove thickets. Though less often seen, Jaguars, ocelots, margays, and other smaller cats roam the region's tropical forests.

Most of Mexico's 1,000 species of colorful tropical birds inhabit southern Mexico. The resplendent quetzal, which inspired the "plumed serpent" god of Maya legend, is among the world's most spectacular feathered creatures, with its shimmering, 2-foot-long tail. Its numbers have dwindled, but it can still be found in Chiapas' highlands.

Tabasco's wetlands are a paradise for bird-watchers. Crocodiles are also common, and you might spot howler monkeys, big cats, and manatees. Coastal waters throughout the region teem with dolphins, rays, and sea turtles.

And those are just the animals you might have heard of. Others in this region include the Mexican caecilian, a primitive amphibian resembling a half-meter (2-ft.) long earthworm; the striped basilisk, called the "Jesus Christ lizard" for its ability to skip across the water's surface; the roseate spoonbill, a flamingo burdened with an elongated duck's bill; and other strange and wondrous creatures.

EATING & DRINKING

The tacos and burritos familiar north of the border are mere appetizers on Mexico's vast and varied menu. Some staples grace plates throughout the country, but long distances and two formidable mountain ranges gave rise to distinct regional cuisines that evolved independently. It is not only possible but also one of life's greatest pleasures to eat your way through Mexico without downing a single taco or burrito.

When the Spanish arrived, they found Mexico's natives cooking with corn, beans, chiles, tomatoes, and squash, combined with turkey and other wild game. Local women promptly incorporated beef, pork, lamb, nuts, fruits, cheese, spices, and sugar cane (by way of the Caribbean) contributed by the conquistadors. To the dismay of the Spaniards—and the delight of travelers today—the result was not a simulation of European cuisine but new versions of native dishes.

Mexican cooking remains simple at its core; most of the *picante* flavor is added afterward with the chile and salsa found on every table. Regional variations range from the basic but nutritious dishes of the north to seafood specialties of the coastal regions to the complex variety of Mexico City and the central states to the earthy, piquant creations of the Maya in the south.

Tequila and lime.

The Staples

TORTILLAS The tortilla is Mexico's bread, and sometimes its fork and spoon, used to scoop up food. Corn is cooked in water and lime, ground into grainy *masa* dough, patted and pressed into thin cakes, and cooked on a *comal* (hot griddle). Even restaurants that serve bread always have tortillas available. The flour tortilla was developed in northern Mexico and is less common in the south.

ENCHILADAS The most famous of numerous Mexican dishes based on the tortilla was originally called *tortilla enchilada,* meaning a tortilla dipped in a chile sauce; variations include *entomatada* (dipped in tomato sauce) and *enfrijolada* (in a bean sauce). The basic enchilada, still sold in food stands, is a tortilla dipped first in hot oil and then chile (usually ancho) sauce, folded or rolled on a plate, and sprinkled with chopped onions and *queso cotija* (crumbly white cheese). It's often served with fried potatoes and carrots. Restaurants serve more elaborate enchiladas filled with cheese, chicken, pork, or seafood. In Southern Mexico, they are enchiladas often bathed in a rich *mole* sauce.

TACOS Anything folded or rolled into a tortilla—sometimes two, either soft or fried—is a taco. *Flautas* and quesadillas (except in Mexico City, where they are a different animal) are species of tacos. This is the quintessential Mexican fast food, sold in *taquerías* everywhere.

FRIJOLES Most Mexican households eat beans daily. Pinto beans are predominant in northern Mexico, but black beans are the Yucatán's legumes of choice. Mexicans add only a little onion and garlic and a pinch of herbs, as beans are meant to be a counterpoint to spicy foods. They also may appear at the end of a meal with a spoonful of sour cream. Fried leftover beans often appear as *frijoles refritos,* a side dish commonly translated as "refried beans." In fact, they are fried just once; the prefix *re* means "well" (as in "thoroughly"), so a better translation would be "well-fried beans."

TAMALES The ultimate takeout meal, tamales (singular: *tamal*) developed in pre-Hispanic Mexico and became more elaborate after the Spanish introduced pork and other ingredients. To make a *tamal,* you mix corn *masa* with

Local Wisdom

"The chile runs in our veins."

—Laura Esquivel, author of ***Like Water for Chocolate*** (1989) in introduction to ***La Cocina del Chile*** (2003)

lard, beat the batter, add a filling, wrap it, and cook it. Every region has its own specialty. The most popular *rellenos* (fillings) are pork and cheese, but they might be anything from fish to iguana, augmented by pumpkin, pineapple, rice, or peanuts, and tucked into a blanket of yellow, black, or purple masa. Tamales are usually steamed but may be baked or grilled; the jackets are most often dried corn husks or fresh corn or banana leaves but are sometimes fashioned from palm, avocado, or *chaya* (a spinach-like vegetable) leaves.

A DEBT OF gratitude

Lost among the laurels heaped upon the ancient Maya for their contributions to science, mathematics, architecture, astronomy, and writing is the wide array of foods they introduced. It's no exaggeration to say the Maya changed the world's eating habits in the 1500s. Just try to imagine life without:

Avocado From its origins in southern Mexico, where it was used as an aphrodisiac, the avocado spread to the Rio Grande and central Peru before the Europeans learned about it.

Black Beans Archaeological digs indicate the black bean originated in southern Mexico and Central America more than 7,000 years ago. Still the favorite in and around the Yucatán, it has spread widely throughout Latin America, the Caribbean, and the U.S.

Chiles Chiles have been cultivated in the Americas for more than 6,000 years. Blame Christopher Columbus for calling them "peppers," but credit him for their worldwide reach. Southern Mexico's Capsicum annuum species, with its many cultivars, is crucial to nearly every fiery cuisine in the world.

Chocolate The Maya's "food of the gods," made from the toasted, fermented seeds of the cacao tree, is arguably the New World's greatest gift to civilization. Though Cortez learned of chocolate from the Aztecs, the Maya ate it many centuries earlier and used cacao beans as currency.

Corn The creation myth in *Pópul Vuh,* the Maya "bible," attributes humankind's very existence to this domesticated strain of wild grass, easily the most important food in the Americas. Thousands of years after corn became a dietary staple, the Maya started cultivating it around 2500 B.C. and abandoned their nomadic ways to settle in villages surrounded by cornfields.

Papaya The large, woody, fast-growing herb—commonly referred to as a tree—was used to treat stomach ailments. After spreading from southern Mexico, it now grows in every tropical country.

Tomatoes Even the Italians had to make do without tomato sauce before discovery of the New World. Precursors originated in Peru, but the tomato as we know it came from the Yucatán, where the Maya cultivated it long before the conquest.

Vanilla The elixir from a special species of orchid originally flavored Maya chocolate drinks. Southern Mexico's jungle is still the only place the orchid grows wild, pollinated by native stingless bees that produce Maya honey. The prized Tahitian vanilla, must be hand-pollinated.

Yucatecan tamales have a distinctly Maya flavor, filled with pork or chicken marinated in *achiote* (an earthy, mildly tangy paste made from the annatto seed) and cooked in an underground pit or oven that chars the banana leaf black. Tabasco makes liberal use of freshwater fish and seafood, rice, and an array of exotic produce. Chiapas' marvelous variety of tamales might be filled with *mole, chicharrón* (crispy, fried pork rind), or even flower buds; the best known are *tamales de bola,* with pork rib, a prune, and a small dried chili, all wrapped up in a corn husk tied on top to form a ball *(bola).*

CHILES Hardly a traditional dish in all of Mexico lacks chiles. Appearing in wondrous variety throughout Mexico, they are bestowed different names depending on whether they are fresh or dried. Chiles range from blazing hot with little discernible taste to mild with a rich, complex flavor, and they can be pickled, smoked, stuffed, or stewed. Among the best-known are the *pimiento,* the large, harmless bell pepper familiar in the U.S.; the fist-sized poblano, ranging from mild to very hot; the short, torpedo-shaped *serrano;* the skinny and seriously fiery *chile de árbol;* the stubby, hot *jalapeño;* the *chipotle,* a dried and smoked jalapeño usually served in *adobo* (vinegar and garlic paste); and the tiny, five-alarm *pequín.*

If you suffer from misadventure by chile, a drink of milk, a bite of banana or cucumber, a spoonful of yogurt, or—if all else fails—a bottle of beer will help extinguish the fire.

Regional Specialties

The Yucatán evolved in isolation from the rest of the country until recent decades, and its cuisine is an amalgam of native, European, Caribbean, and Middle Eastern flavors and techniques. Some of the most recognizable tastes are *achiote,* sour oranges, lime juice, pumpkin seeds, and pickled onions. Turkey *(pavo),* still the most common meat in Yucatecan homes, is prominent on most menus, though beef, pork, and chicken have also become staples. Fish and seafood reign along the coast.

Achiote and sour orange came to the Yucatán by way of the Caribbean; Edam cheese through historical trade with the Dutch; and peas likely from the English. A wave of Lebanese immigration around the turn of the 20th century also made its mark; the spit-broiled *tacos al pastor* is basically Mexican gyros, and you might come across *kibbeh* made of beef or potatoes instead of lamb or *dolmas* wrapped in chaya instead of grape leaves.

The Yucatán's trademark dishes are *pollo* or *cochinita* (chicken or pork) *pibil,* meat marinated in achiote, bitter orange and spices, wrapped in banana leaves and barbecued or baked in a pit; *poc chuc,* pork slices marinated in sour orange and garnished with

Food Hygiene

The days when you had to carry water purification tablets to return from a trip to Mexico with your intestines intact are long gone. Nearly all restaurants that serve middle-class Mexicans use filtered water, disinfect their vegetables, and buy ice made from purified water. If in doubt, look for ice with a rough cylindrical shape and a hollow center, produced by the same kind of machinery across the country. Street vendors and market stalls are less consistent. I love street food, so I find clean, busy places and stick with cooked foods and unpeeled fruit.

pickled onions; and *sopa de lima* (lime soup), made of shredded, lime-marinated turkey or chicken and topped with sizzling tortilla strips.

Try starting your day with *huevos motuleños*—fried eggs over sliced plantains, beans, and fried tortillas, topped with a dusting of salty cheese, tomato sauce, and peas—but only if you're ravenous. *Cochinita pibil* is also served in the morning. The best place to have the former is in any reputable restaurant; the best place for the latter would be a market such as El Mercado de Santa Ana in Mérida.

Customary dishes for the afternoon meal include *relleno negro,* turkey cooked with a paste of charred chiles and vegetables with bits of hard-boiled eggs; *escabeche blanco,* chicken or turkey cooked in a vinegar-based sauce; or *queso relleno,* mild Edam cheese stuffed with seasoned ground beef. The unique *Tikinxic* (or some variant of this name) is grilled fish that has been lightly marinated in an achiote paste. All are served in restaurants for the afternoon meal; in Cancún and on the coast, they also appear on the evening menu. Traditional evening foods are based on turkey and include such finger foods as *salbutes* and *panuchos,* two dishes of tortillas or masa cakes layered with shredded turkey or chicken; panuchos add a layer of *frijoles*.

Campeche has its own culinary traditions, a marriage of Spanish cuisine, recipes brought by pirates from all over the world, and local fruits and vegetables. The signature dish, *pan de cazón* (baby shark casserole)—layers of tortillas, black beans, and shredded baby shark meat, smothered in tomato sauce—reaches its greatest heights at La Pigua. Lying on the Gulf Coast, Tabasco has more in common with the Caribbean flavors of Veracruz, which developed close ties to Cuba

A Lebanese restaurant.

A food stall in a Mérida market.

Fresh produce at a local market.

during colonial times. *Veracruzana,* a lightly spiced blend of tomato and onion, bathes fresh fish, meat, and seafood. The specialty is the fish *pejelagarto,* whose mild, nutty taste is enhanced by chile and lemon; La Jangada in Villahermosa is a favorite place to indulge. *Camarón* (shrimp), *ostión* (oyster), and *pulpo* (octopus) are ubiquitous, delicious, and cheap.

The Maya of Chiapas were great mathematicians and astronomers, like their kin throughout the Yucatán, but they also were particularly accomplished farmers. Though they depended above all on corn, native herbs such as chipilin, a fragrant, thin-leaved plant, and hoja santa, the large anise-scented leaves that characterize much of southern Mexico's cooking, flavor the many varieties of Chiapas' famous tamales, which are heavier and larger than central Mexican tamales. With the introduction of European cattle, Chiapans also became expert ranchers and, as a corollary, cheese makers. Similar to neighboring Guatemala, Chiapas' cooking uses a lot of beef, either grilled or in a stew.

Be sure to read the food glossary in "Chapter 11: Survival Spanish," to learn more about regional dishes.

Drinks

Coca-Cola is nearly as entrenched in Mexico's drinking habits as tequila, having been a fixture since 1926. Pepsi is also sold in every city and town. These and other American *refrescos* outsell Mexican brands such as Manzana, a carbonated apple juice. If you like your soft drinks cold, specify *frío,* or you may get them *clima* (room temperature).

Better yet, treat yourself to ***licuados***—refreshing smoothies of fresh fruit (or juice), milk, and ice, sold all over Mexico. ***Aguas frescas*** ("fresh waters") are lighter drinks made by adding a small amount of fresh fruit juice and sugar to water. Hibiscus, melon, tamarind, and lime are common, but rice, flowers, cactus fruit (*tuna* in Spanish), and other exotic ingredients find their way into these refreshments. And inexpensive, fresh-squeezed juices from every fruit you can name—and a few you can't—are one of Mexico's greatest pleasures.

Coffee is one of Mexico's most important exports, and Chiapas grows some of the best. Tarted-up coffee isn't Mexico's style. Your basic choices are *café Americano,* the familiar gringo-style brew; espresso and sometimes cappuccino, served in cafes; and the widely popular *café con leche,* translated as "coffee with milk" but more accurately described as milk with coffee. Potent, delicious *café de olla,* traditionally brewed in a clay pot with raw sugar and cinnamon, is harder to find.

Hot chocolate is a traditional drink, usually made with cinnamon and often some crushed almonds. Another traditional hot drink is *atole,* made from cornmeal, milk, cinnamon, and pureed fresh fruit, often served for breakfast.

Mexican **beer** generally is light and well-carbonated, all the better to tame the chile burn. Brands such as Bohemia, Corona, Dos Equis, Pacifica, Tecate, and Modelo are favorites around the world. Mérida's Cerveceria Yucateca, alas, was bought by Modelo in 1979 and closed in 2002, but its Leon Negra and Montejo beers are still produced in central Mexico.

Tequila's poorer cousins, **pulque** and **mescal,** originated with *octli,* an Aztec agave drink produced strictly for feasts. Mexicans drank *pulque,* made from juice straight from the plant, for more than 5,000 years, but it has recently given way to more refined—and more palatable—spirits. The Spanish learned to create serious fire power by roasting the agave hearts, then extracting, fermenting, and distilling the liquids. Thus were born tequila and *mescal. Mescal,* famous for the traditional worm at the bottom of the bottle, is more potent than *pulque* but easier to swallow. It's also available commercially; *pulque* is found mostly in central Mexico's *pulquerías.*

Tequila, once consigned to a stereotype in bad Westerns, has lately acquired a sophisticated aura. A growing coterie of connoisseurs has spotlighted high-quality varieties and is making inroads on the knock-back-a-shot mentality in favor of sipping and swirling as you would with fine Scotch or French cognac.

Don't overlook southern Mexico's **local spirits.** Kahlúa, the Arabica coffee-flavored liquor ubiquitous in U.S. bars, is the Yucatán's best-known product. Xtabentún, a honey-anisette liqueur based on the Maya's ceremonial drink produced from the morning glory whose nectar fueled local honey production,

Tequila 101

Tequila is a variety of mescal produced from the *A. tequilana* agave species, or blue agave, in the Tequila area of Jalisco state. Its quality and the popularity have soared in the past 15 years. Distillers—all but one still based in Jalisco—have formed an association to establish standards for labeling and denomination. The best tequilas are 100% agave, made with a set minimum of sugar to prime the fermentation process. These tequilas come in three categories based on how they were stored: *Blanco* is white tequila aged very little, usually in steel vats. *Reposado* (reposed) is aged in wooden casks for between 2 months and a year. The coveted *añejo* (aged) tequila is stored in oak barrels for a year or more.

dining service TIPS

- The afternoon meal is the main meal of the day, and many restaurants offer a multicourse daily special called *comida corrida* or *menú del día.* This is the least expensive way to get a full dinner.
- In Mexico you need to ask for your check; it is considered rude to present the bill to someone who hasn't requested it. If you're in a hurry, ask for the check when your food arrives.
- Tips are about the same as in the U.S. Restaurants sometimes include a 15% value-added tax, which shows up on the bill as "IVA." This is effectively the tip, which you may augment if you like, but make sure you're not tipping twice.
- To summon the waiter, wave or raise your hand, but don't motion with your index finger, which is a demeaning gesture. If you need your check, it's OK to summon any waiter and ask, "La Cuenta, por favor"—or simply catch someone's eye and pantomime a scribbling motion against the palm of your hand.

is a popular after-dinner cordial. Its best-known maker, D'Aristi of Mérida, also makes Caribe rum and the lesser-known Kalani, a coconut liqueur. Other after-dinner liqueurs are flavored with native flowers such as hibiscus *(jamaica)* or fruit such as bananas *(plátano)* and pomegranate *(granada)*.

BOOKS, FILM & MUSIC

HISTORY & CULTURE For an overview of pre-Hispanic cultures, pick up Michael D. Coe's *Mexico: From the Olmecs to the Aztecs* or Nigel Davies's *Ancient Kingdoms of Mexico.* Coe's *The Maya* is probably the best general account of the Maya. For a survey of Mexico's history through modern times, *A Short History of Mexico* by J. Patrick McHenry is both thorough and concise.

John L. Stephens's two-volume *Incidents of Travel in the Yucatán* is not only one of the great books of archaeological discovery but a travel classic. Before his expeditions, beginning in 1841, the world knew little about the region and nothing about the Maya. Stephens' account of 44 Maya sites is still the most authoritative.

Marimba.

Graham Greene's *The Lawless Roads,* covering the brutal religious oppression of the late 1930s, is a dyspeptic travelogue of Chiapas and Tabasco. This compelling look at what was then a remote region—flawed though it is by the author's distaste for Mexico—also was the basis for his masterpiece, *The Power and the Glory.*

For contemporary culture, start with Octavio Paz's classic, *The Labyrinth of Solitude*, still controversial because of some of Paz' cultural generalizations. *Our Word Is Our Weapon,* a collection of articulate, often poetic writings by Zapatista leader Subcomandante Marcos, provides insight into Chiapas' armed revolt in the 1990s.

Lesley Byrd Simpson's *Many Mexicos* is a comprehensive cultural history; *Distant Neighbor* by Alan Riding is a classic of cultural insight.

ART & ARCHITECTURE *Art and Time in Mexico: From the Conquest to the Revolution* by Elizabeth Wilder Weismann covers religious, public, and private architecture. *Maya Art and Architecture* by Mary Ellen Miller showcases the best of Maya artistic expression.

NATURE *A Naturalist's Mexico* by Roland H. Wauer, is getting hard to find, but *A Hiker's Guide to Mexico's Natural History* by Jim Conrad is a good alternative. *Peterson Field Guides: Mexican Birds* by Roger Tory Peterson and Edward L. Chalif is predictably excellent. Les Beletsky's *Southern Mexico* is a richly illustrated, engagingly written field guide and ecotourism manual.

LITERATURE Jorge Ibargüengoitia, one of Mexico's most famous modern writers, died in 1983 but remains popular in Mexico and is available in translation. His novels *Estas Ruinas Que Ves (These Ruins You See)* and *The Dead Girls* (a fictional account of a famous 1970s crime) display deft characterization and a sardonic view of Mexican life.

The earlier novels of Carlos Fuentes, Mexico's pre-eminent living writer, are easier to read than more recent works; try *The Death of Artemio Cruz.* Angeles Mastretta's delightful *Arráncame la vida (Tear Up My Life)* is a well-written novel about a young woman's life in postrevolutionary Puebla. Laura Esquivel's *Like Water for Chocolate* (and the subsequent movie) covers roughly the same period through a lens of magical realism and helped to popularize Mexican food abroad.

Hasta No Verte Jesús Mío by Elena Poniatowska, and anything by Pulitzer winner Luis Alberto Urrea, offer hard looks at third-world realities.

Guillermo Arriaga, screenwriter for *Amores Perros,* is a brilliant novelist, too. *El Bufalo de la Noche,* about a young man reeling from his best friend's suicide, is available in English. *Retorno 201,* a collection of stories set on the Mexico City street where Arriaga grew up, is rumored to be coming out in English soon.

Mexican Cinema

GOLDEN AGE & CLASSICS

During Mexico's "Golden Age of Cinema" in the 1940s, studios stopped trying to mimic Hollywood and started producing unabashedly Mexican black- and-white films whose stars are still cultural icons in Mexico. **Mario Moreno,** a.k.a. Cantinflas, was a comedic genius who personalized the *el pelado* archetype—a poor, picaresque, slightly naughty character trading on his wits alone and getting nowhere. Mexican beauty **Dolores del Río** played the steamy Latin babe in Hollywood. **Pedro Infante,** the singing cowboy, embodied the ideal of Mexican manhood.

Luis Buñuel's dark *Los Olvidados* (1950) was the Spanish surrealist's third Mexican film, exploring the life of young hoodlums in Mexico City's slums.

THE NEW CINEMA

After a long fallow period, a new generation of filmmakers came along in the 1990s. The first big *El Nuevo Cine Mexicano* (The New Cinema) hit outside of Mexico was *Like Water for Chocolate* (1992), directed by **Alfonso Arau,** then author Laura Esquivel's husband. He continues to make films, mainly in Mexico. *Sexo, Pudor y Lágrimas* (1999), by director **Antonio Serrano,** is an unflinching look at the battle of the sexes in Mexico City.

After **Alfonso Cuarón**'s debut film, the mordant social satire *Sólo con tu Pareja* (1991), scored critical and commercial success in Mexico, he garnered international acclaim with his ironic *Y Tu Mamá También* (2001), which touches on class hypocrisy while following a pair of teenage boys on an impromptu road trip with a sexy older woman. Cuarón has since directed *Harry Potter and the Prisoner of Azkaban,* the science fiction thriller *Children of Men,* and other international productions.

In *Amores Perros* (2000), **Alejandro González Iñárritu** (director of *21 Grams*) presents a keen glimpse of contemporary Mexican society through three stories about different ways of life in Mexico City that converge at the scene of a horrific car accident. His Academy Award–nominated *Babel* (2006), another tour de force, features a Mexican border scene that is realistic, exhilarating, and frightening all at once.

Guillermo del Toro's debut, the dark, atmospheric *Cronos* (1993), won critical acclaim in Mexico. Moving into the international arena, he has directed similarly moody films such as *Hellboy* (2004) and Oscar winner *Pan's Labyrinth* (2006).

Julie Taymor's *Frida* (2002), with Mexican actress Salma Hayek producing and starring, is an enchanting biopic about Frida Kahlo's life and work, from her devastating accident to relationships with Diego Rivera and Leon Trotsky. The exquisite cinematography captures the magic realism evinced in Kahlo's work.

Views from the Outside: Films Starring Mexico

Elia Kazan's 1952 classic, *Viva Zapata!,* written by John Steinbeck, stars Marlon Brando as revolutionary Emiliano Zapata. Orson Welles' 1958 film-noir *Touch of Evil* (preposterously billing Charlton Heston as a Mexican narcotics agent) looks at drugs and corruption in Tijuana—still compelling, even though it feels sanitized compared with today's screaming headlines.

HBO's 2003 flick, *And Starring Pancho Villa as Himself* with Antonio Banderas, is the true story of how revolutionaries allowed Hollywood to film Pancho Villa in battle. *Man on Fire* (2004), with Denzel Washington as a bodyguard hired to protect a little girl, is full of great Mexico City scenes, though the plot is depressing and all too real. Dylan Verrechia's *Tijuana Makes Me Happy* (2005), focusing on Tijuana's humanity rather than its perceived sins, has won awards in Latin America and at U.S. film festivals. Stephen Soderbergh's Academy Award–winning *Traffic* (2000), with Benicio del Toro, has powerful scenes focusing on Tijuana's drug war, while the documentary *Tijuana Remix* (2002) unveils the city's unique and idiosyncratic culture. Mel Gibson's controversial *Apocalypto* (2006) cast indigenous Maya to depict the Maya empire's waning days; the rain forests of Veracruz state stand in for the lush jungles that must have covered the Yucatán centuries ago.

Dancing in Tuxtla Gutiérrez's Parque de la Marimba.

Director **Robert Rodriguez**'s breakout film, *El Mariachi* (1992), is set in a small central Mexican town. Made on a shoestring budget, the somewhat cheesy action flick is at least highly entertaining. His *Once Upon a Time in Mexico* (2003) isn't as great, but it's fun to see scenes of San Miguel Allende. Ditto for San Luis Potosí in *The Mexican* (2001) with Brad Pitt and Julia Roberts.

Music

MARIMBA & SON

Marimba music flourishes in much of southern and central Mexico but is considered traditional only in Chiapas and the port city of Veracruz, whose bands travel to play in places like Oaxaca and Mexico City. You can hear marimba any night for free in Tuxtla Gutiérrez's Parque de la Marimba.

Son, a native art form from many parts of Mexico, employs a variety of stringed instruments. Ritchie Valens' "La Bamba" popularized one of the most famous forms, *son jarocho,* in the '50s. Often fast-paced, with lots of strumming and fancy string picking, it originated in southern Veracruz. *Jarana,* the Yucatán's principal dance music, is a form of *son jarocho* that adds woodwinds and a sensuous Caribbean beat. The dance was born as part of the haciendas' annual *Vaquerías,* or country fiestas, and are still performed every week in Mérida's Plaza Grande and many smaller parks.

DANZÓN & BOLERO

These musical forms came from Cuba in the late 19th century and gained great popularity, especially in Veracruz and Mexico City. *Danzón* is orchestra music that combines Latin flavor with a stateliness uncommon in later Latin music.

The Yucatán had strong ties to Cuba, and its *son yucateca* probably influenced *bolero* and the related *trova,* or classical guitar trios. This soft, romantic, and often slightly melancholy music is a lynchpin of Yucatecan tradition, and singers sometimes use Mayan lyrics. Mérida's free nightly cultural events include *trova yucateca,* and the city stages an annual trova festival.

MARIACHI & RANCHERA

Mariachis, with their big sombreros, waist-length jackets and tight pants, embody Mexican spirit. The music originated from Jalisco state's *son,* arranged for guitars, violins, string bass, and trumpets. Now heard across Mexico and much of the American southwest, it is at its traditional best in Jalisco and its capital, Guadalajara. Mariachi is also common in the Yucatán, especially in cantinas and during national celebrations. Yucatecan *trova* music even has mariachi adaptations.

Trova, a classical guitar trio.

The national pride, individualism, and sentimentality expressed in mariachi's kin, *ranchera,* earns it favored status as drinking music. Many Mexicans know the songs of famous composer **José Alfredo Jiménez** by heart.

ROCK EN ESPAÑOL

Mexican rock forged its identity in the 1980s and exploded during the 1990s with bands such as **Los Jaguares** and **Molotov** out of Mexico City and **Maná,** based in Guadalajara. Named for the 1920s cafe in the capital's Centro Histórico, **Café Tacvba** has been at it since 1989. Their music is influenced by indigenous Mexican music as much as folk, punk, bolero, and hip-hop. The fast-rising **Yucatán a Go Go**—hailing, despite the name, from central Mexico—fuses a bouncy pop beat to lyrics firmly rooted in cultural tradition.

A Vaquería, or country fiesta.

3

PLANNING YOUR TRIP TO THE YUCATÁN, TABASCO & CHIAPAS

By Shane Christensen

Unless you intend to stick to the well-serviced beaches of the Caribbean, a trip to Mexico's Yucatán Peninsula or the southern states of Tabasco and Chiapas will require planning, patience, and flexibility. Quintana Roo is by far the most advanced tourist state in this region, playing host to about half of all tourism to Mexico. It's easy to travel between Cancún and the beaches of the Riviera Maya, where tourist infrastructure is well developed. You can either plan on resort hopping along the Caribbean coast in a rental car, or taking buses to visit the Maya ruins in the Yucatán peninsula. Getting to and around Chiapas and Tabasco requires a little more ingenuity, although infrastructure (particularly roads) has improved here in recent years.

Travelers to Mexico should be aware of security concerns in certain parts of the country and take precautions to maximize their safety. For the most part, Mexico is safe for travelers who steer clear of drugs and those who sell them, but visitors should still exercise caution in unfamiliar areas and remain aware of their surroundings at all times. See "Safety," below, for more details; and visit the U.S. State Department's website, www.state.gov, for up-to-date information on travel to Mexico.

For additional help in planning your trip and for more on-the-ground resources in the Yucatán peninsula, Tabasco, and Chiapas, please turn to "Fast Facts," on p. 363.

WHEN TO GO

High season in the Yucatán begins around December 20 and continues to Easter week. This is the best time for calm, warm weather; snorkeling, diving, and fishing (the calmer weather means clearer and more predictable seas); and for visiting the ruins that dot the interior of the peninsula. Book well in advance if you plan to be in Cancún around the holidays.

Low season begins the day after Easter and continues to mid-December; during low season, prices may drop 20% to 50%. However, in Cancún and along the Riviera Maya, demand by Mexican and European visitors is creating a summer middle season.

Generally speaking, Mexico's **dry season** runs from November to April, with the **rainy season** stretching from May to October. It isn't a problem if you're staying close to the beaches, but for those bent on road-tripping to Chichén Itzá, Uxmal, or other sites, temperatures and humidity in the interior can be downright stifling from May to July. Later in the rainy season, the frequency of **tropical storms** and **hurricanes** increases; such storms, of course, can put a crimp in your vacation. But they can lower temperatures, making climbing ruins more

PREVIOUS PAGE: **A Carnaval performer in Cozumel.**

fun, accompanied by cool air and a slight wind. November is especially ideal for Yucatán travels. Cancún, Cozumel, and Isla Mujeres also have a rainy season from November to January, when northern storms hit. This usually means diving visibility is diminished—and conditions may prevent boats from even going out.

Villahermosa is sultry and humid all the time. San Cristóbal de las Casas, at an elevation of 2,152m (7,059 ft.), is much cooler than the lowlands and is downright cold in winter.

Cancún's Average Temperatures

	JAN	FEB	MAR	APR	MAY	JUNE	JULY	AUG	SEPT	OCT	NOV	DEC
AVG. HIGH (°C)	27	27	28	29	31	31	32	32	31	30	28	27
AVG. HIGH (°F)	81	82	84	85	88	89	90	90	89	87	84	82
AVG. LOW (°C)	19	20	21	22	25	25	25	25	24	23	22	20
AVG. LOW (°F)	67	68	71	73	77	78	78	77	76	74	72	69

Calendar of Events

Religious and secular festivals are a part of life in Mexico. Every town, city, and state holds its own specific festivals throughout the year commemorating religious and historic figures. Indeed, in certain parts of the country it sometimes feels like the festivities never die down, and the Yucatán, Tabasco, and Chiapas are no exception.

For an exhaustive list of events beyond those listed here, check **http://events.frommers.com**, where you'll find a searchable, up-to-the-minute roster of what's happening in cities all over the world.

JANUARY

Año Nuevo (New Year's Day), nationwide. This national holiday is perhaps the quietest day in all of Mexico. Most people stay home or attend church. All businesses are closed. In traditional indigenous communities, new tribal leaders are inaugurated with colorful ceremonies rooted in the pre-Hispanic past. January 1.

Día de los Reyes (Three Kings' Day), nationwide. This day commemorates the Three Kings' presenting gifts to the Christ Child. On this day, children receive presents, much like they do at Christmas in the United States. Friends and families gather to share the *Rosca de Reyes,* a special cake. Inside the cake is a small doll representing the Christ Child; whoever receives the doll must host a tamales-and-*atole* (a warm drink made of masa) party on February 2. January 6.

FEBRUARY

Día de la Candelaria (Candlemas), nationwide. Music, dances, processions, food, and other festivities lead up to a blessing of seed and candles in a ceremony that mixes pre-Hispanic and European traditions marking the end of winter. Those who attended the Three Kings celebration reunite to share *atole* and tamales at a party hosted by the recipient of the doll found in the Rosca. February 2.

Día de la Constitución (Constitution Day), nationwide. This national holiday is in honor of the current Mexican constitution, signed in 1917 as a result of the revolutionary war of 1910. It's celebrated through small parades. February 5.

Carnaval, nationwide. Carnaval takes place the 3 days preceding Ash Wednesday and the beginning of Lent. In Cozumel, the celebration resembles New Orleans's Mardi Gras, with a festive atmosphere and parades. In Chamula, the event harks back to pre-Hispanic times, with ritualistic running on flaming branches. Cancún also celebrates with parade floats and street parties.

Ash Wednesday, nationwide. The start of Lent and time of abstinence, this is a day of reverence nationwide; some towns honor it with folk dancing and fairs.

MARCH

Benito Juárez's Birthday, nationwide. This national holiday celebrating one of Mexico's most beloved leaders is observed through small hometown celebrations, especially in Juárez's birthplace, Guelatao, Oaxaca. March 21.

Spring Equinox, Chichén Itzá. On the first day of spring, the Temple of Kukulkán—Chichén Itzá's main pyramid—aligns with the sun, and the shadow of the plumed serpent moves slowly from the top of the building down. When the shadow reaches the bottom, the body joins the carved stone snake's head at the base of the pyramid. According to ancient legend, at the moment that the serpent is whole, the earth is fertilized. Visitors come from around the world to marvel at this sight, so advance arrangements are advisable. Elsewhere, equinox festivals and celebrations welcome spring, in the custom of the ancient Mexicans, with dances and prayers to the elements and the four cardinal points. It's customary to wear white with a red ribbon. March 21 (the shadow appears Mar 19–23).

APRIL

Semana Santa (Holy Week), nationwide. Mexico celebrates the last week in the life of Christ, from Palm Sunday to Easter Sunday, with somber religious processions, spoofing of Judas, and reenactments of biblical events, plus food and craft fairs. Some businesses close during this traditional week of Mexican national vacations, and almost all close on Maundy Thursday, Good Friday, Saturday, and Easter Sunday.

If you plan to travel to Mexico during Holy Week, make your reservations early. Airline seats into Cancún in particular will be reserved months in advance. Planes and buses to towns across the Yucatán and to almost anywhere else in Mexico will be full, so try arriving on the Wednesday or Thursday before Good Friday. Easter Sunday is quiet, and the week following is a traditional vacation period. Early April.

MAY

Labor Day, nationwide. Workers' parades countrywide; everything closes. May 1.

Cinco de Mayo, nationwide. This holiday celebrates the defeat of the French at the Battle of Puebla, although it (ironically) tends to be a bigger celebration in the United States than in Mexico. May 5.

Feast of San Isidro. The patron saint of farmers is honored with a blessing of seeds and work animals. May 15.

Cancún Jazz Festival. Over Memorial Day weekend, the Parque de las Palapas, as well as the area around the Convention Center, has live performances from jazz musicians from around the world. To confirm dates and schedule information, check www.cancun.travel.

International Gay Festival. This 5-day event in Cancún kicks off with a welcome fiesta of food, drinks, and mariachi music. Additional festivities include a tequila party, tour of Cancún, sunset Caribbean cruise, bar and beach parties, and a final champagne breakfast. For schedule information, check www.cancun.eventguide.com.

JUNE

Navy Day (Día de la Marina). All coastal towns celebrate with naval parades and fireworks. June 1.

Corpus Christi, nationwide. The day honors the Body of Christ (the Eucharist) with religious processions, Masses, and food. Dates vary.

Día de San Pedro (St. Peter and St. Paul's Day), nationwide. Celebrated wherever St. Peter is the patron saint, this holiday honors anyone named Pedro or Peter. June 26.

AUGUST

Assumption of the Virgin Mary, nationwide. This is celebrated throughout the country with special Masses and in some places with processions. August 15 to August 17.

SEPTEMBER

Independence Day, nationwide. This day of parades, picnics, and family reunions throughout the country celebrates Mexico's independence from Spain. At 11pm on September 15, the president of Mexico gives the famous independence *grito* (shout) from the National Palace in Mexico City, and local mayors do the same in every town and municipality all over Mexico. On September 16, every city and town conducts a parade in which both government and civilians display their pride in being Mexican. For these celebrations, all important government buildings are draped in the national colors—red, green, and white—and the towns blaze with decorative lights. September 15 and 16; September 16 is a national holiday.

Fall Equinox, Chichén Itzá. The same shadow play that occurs during the spring equinox repeats at the fall equinox. September 21 to September 22.

OCTOBER

'Ethnicity Day' or Columbus Day (Día de la Raza), nationwide. This commemorates the fusion of the Spanish and Mexican peoples. October 12.

NOVEMBER

Day of the Dead (Día de los Muertos), nationwide. What's commonly called the Day of the Dead is actually 2 days: All Saints' Day, honoring saints and deceased children, and All Souls' Day, honoring deceased adults. Relatives gather at cemeteries countrywide, carrying candles and food to create an altar, and sometimes spend the night beside the graves of loved ones. Weeks before, bakers begin producing bread (called *pan de muerto*) formed in the shape of mummies or round loaves decorated with bread "bones." Decorated sugar skulls emblazoned with glittery names are sold everywhere. Many days ahead, homes and churches erect special altars laden with Day of the Dead bread, fruit, flowers, candles, favorite foods, and photographs of saints and of the deceased. On the 2 nights, children dress in costumes and masks, often carrying through the streets mock coffins and pumpkin lanterns, into which they expect money to be dropped. November 1 and 2; November 1 is a national holiday.

Annual Yucatán Bird Festival (Festival de las Aves de Yucatán), Mérida, Yucatán. Bird-watching sessions, workshops, and exhibits are the highlights of this festival, designed to illustrate the special role birds play in our environment and in the Yucatán territory. Check out www.yucatanbirds.org.mx for details. Mid-November.

Revolution Day, nationwide. This commemorates the start of the Mexican Revolution in 1910 with parades, speeches, rodeos, and patriotic events. November 20.

DECEMBER

Feast of the Virgin of Guadalupe, nationwide. Throughout the country, religious processions, street fairs, dancing, fireworks, and Masses honor the patroness of Mexico. This is one of Mexico's most moving and beautiful displays of traditional culture. The Virgin of Guadalupe appeared to a young man, Juan Diego, in December 1531, on a hill near Mexico City. He convinced the bishop that he had seen the apparition by revealing his cloak, upon which the Virgin was emblazoned. It's customary for children to dress up as Juan Diego, wearing mustaches and red bandannas. One of the most famous and elaborate celebrations takes place at the Basílica of Guadalupe, north of Mexico City, where the Virgin appeared. Every village celebrates this day, though, often with processions of children carrying banners of the Virgin and with *charreadas* (rodeos), bicycle races, dancing, and fireworks. December 12.

Festival of San Cristóbal de las Casas, San Cristóbal de las Casas, Chiapas. This 10-day festival in Chiapas includes a procession by the Tzotzil and Tzetzal Indians, *marimba* music, and a parade of horses. December 12 to December 21.

Christmas Posadas, nationwide. On each of the 9 nights before Christmas, it's customary to reenact the Holy Family's search for an inn, with door-to-door candlelit processions in cities and villages nationwide. These are also hosted by most businesses and community organizations, taking the place of the northern tradition of a Christmas party. December 15 to December 24.

Christmas. Mexicans extend this celebration and often leave their jobs beginning 2 weeks before Christmas all the way through New Year's Day. Many businesses close, and resorts and hotels fill up. Significant celebrations take place on December 24.

New Year's Eve. As in the rest of the world, New Year's Eve in Mexico is celebrated with parties, fireworks, and plenty of noise. December 31.

what's biting WHEN?

It's fishing season year-round along the Caribbean coast. Here's a general breakdown of what to look for during your trip, and a handy guide for more information can be found at: www.deepseafishingcancun.com/season.htm.

- **Blue Marlin:** March through August
- **White Marlin:** March through August
- **Sailfish:** January through August
- **Grouper:** Most of the year, except July and August
- **Wahoo:** November through August
- **Amberjack:** August through March
- **Dolphin Fish:** March through September
- **Blackfin Tuna:** December through August
- **Bonita:** February through October
- **Barracuda:** June through March
- **Kingfish:** October through February
- **Red Snapper**: August through June

ENTRY REQUIREMENTS

Passports

Citizens from most countries are required to present a valid passport for entry to Mexico. Citizens from some countries will need a Mexican visa. U.S. citizens can enter Mexico with any U.S. official ID; passports are not required. Nonetheless, U.S. Citizens need to be mindful of re-entry requirements, outlined below.

Virtually every air traveler **entering the U.S.** is required to show a passport. All U.S. and Canadian citizens traveling by **air or sea** to Mexico are required to present a valid passport or other valid travel document to enter or reenter the United States. In addition, all travelers, including U.S. and Canadian citizens, attempting to enter the United States by **land** or **sea** must have a valid passport or other WHTI compliant document.

Other valid travel documents (known as WHTI-compliant documents) include the new **Passport Card** and SENTRI, NEXUS, FAST, and the U.S. Coast Guard Mariner Document. Members of the U.S. Armed Forces on active duty traveling on orders are exempt from the passport requirement. U.S. citizens may apply for the limited-use, wallet-size **Passport Card.** The card is valid only for land and sea travel between the U.S. and Canada, Mexico, the Caribbean region, and Bermuda. For more details on application restrictions, see www.dhs.gov/files/programs/gc_1200693579776.shtm.

From our perspective, it's easiest just to travel with a valid passport. Safeguard your passport in an inconspicuous, inaccessible place, like a money belt, and keep a copy of the critical pages with your passport number in a separate place. If you lose your passport, visit the nearest consulate of your native country as soon as possible for a replacement.

Visas

For detailed information regarding visas to Mexico, visit the **National Immigration Institute** at www.inm.gob.mx/EN/index.php.

American and Canadian tourists are not required to have a visa or a tourist card for stays of 72 hours or less within the border zone (20–30km/12–19 miles from the U.S. border). For travel to Mexico beyond the border zone, all travelers from Australia, Canada, New Zealand, the U.K., and the U.S., among others, can get their visas upon arrival. Many other countries require a pre-approved visa. For the latest requirements, please check www.inm.gob.mx/EN/index.php. Once in Mexico, all travelers must be in possession of a tourist card, also called **Tourist Migration Form.** This document is provided by airlines or by immigration authorities at the country's points of entry. Be careful not to lose this card, as you will be required to surrender it upon departure and you will be fined if you lose it.

Your tourist card is stamped on arrival. If traveling by bus or car, ensure you obtain such a card at the immigration module located at the border and have it stamped by immigration authorities at the border. If you do not receive a stamped tourist card at the border, ensure that, when you arrive at your destination within Mexico, you immediately go to the closest National Institute of Immigration office, present your bus ticket, and request a tourist card. Travelers who fail to have their tourist card stamped may be fined, detained, or expelled from the country.

An immigration official will determine the number of days you can remain in Mexico. Do not assume that you will be granted the full 180 days. An extension of your stay can be requested for a fee at the National Institute of Immigration of the Ministry of the Interior or its local offices.

If you plan to enter Mexico by car, please read the vehicle's importation requirements (p. 64).

Note on travel of minors: Mexican law requires that any non-Mexican citizen under the age of 18 departing Mexico without both parents must carry notarized written permission from the parent or guardian who is not traveling with the child to or from Mexico. This permission must include the name of the parent, the name of the child, the name of anyone traveling with the child, and the notarized signature(s) of the absent parent(s). The U.S. Department of State recommends that permission include travel dates, destinations, airlines, and a summary of the circumstances surrounding the travel. The child must be carrying the original letter (not a facsimile or scanned copy), and proof of the parent/child relationship (usually a birth certificate or court document) and an original custody decree, if applicable. Travelers should contact the Mexican Embassy or closest Mexican Consulate for current information.

Customs

Mexican Customs inspection has been streamlined. At most points of entry, tourists are requested to press a button in front of what looks like a traffic signal, which alternates on touch between red and green. Green light and you go through without inspection; red light and your luggage or car may be inspected. If you have an unusual amount of luggage or an oversized piece, you may be subject to inspection anyway. Passengers that arrive by air will be required to put their bags through an x-ray machine, and then move to the kiosk and push a button to determine whether their luggage will be selected for any further inspection.

WHAT YOU CAN BRING INTO MEXICO

When you enter Mexico, Customs officials will be tolerant if you are not carrying illegal drugs or firearms. Tourists are allowed to bring in their personal effects duty-free. A laptop computer, camera equipment, and sports equipment that could feasibly be used during your stay are also allowed. The underlying guideline is: Don't bring anything that looks as if it's meant to be resold in Mexico. Those entering Mexico by air or sea can bring in gifts worth a value of up to $300 duty-free, except alcohol or tobacco products. The website for Mexican Customs (*Aduanas*) is **www.aduanas.gob.mx/aduana_mexico/2008/home.asp**.

WHAT YOU CAN TAKE HOME FROM MEXICO

For information on what you're allowed to bring home, contact one of the following agencies:

Australian Citizens: Australian Customs Service, Customs House, 5 Constitution Avenue, Canberra City, ACT 2601 (✆ **1300/363-263;** from outside Australia, 612/6275-6666; www.customs.gov.au).

Canadian Citizens: Canada Border Services Agency, Ottawa, Ontario, K1A 0L8 (✆ **800/461-9999** in Canada, or 204/983-3500; www.cbsa-asfc.gc.ca).

New Zealand Citizens: New Zealand Customs, The Customhouse, 17–21 Whitmore St., Box 2218, Wellington, 6140 (✆ **04/473-6099** or 0800/428-786; www.customs.govt.nz).

U.K. Citizens: HM Customs & Excise, Crownhill Court, Tailyour Road, Plymouth, PL6 5BZ (✆ **0845/010-9000;** from outside the U.K., 020/8929-0152; www.hmce.gov.uk).

U.S. Citizens: **U.S. Customs & Border Protection (CBP),** 1300 Pennsylvania Ave., NW, Washington, DC 20229 (✆ **877/287-8667;** www.cbp.gov).

Medical Requirements

No special vaccinations are required for entry into Mexico. For other medical requirements and health-related recommendations, see "Health," p. 71.

GETTING THERE & GETTING AROUND

Getting There

BY PLANE

Mexico has dozens of international and domestic airports. Among the airports in the Yucatán region are Cancún (CUN), Cozumel (CZM), and Mérida (MID). The major airport in Chiapas is in Tuxtla Gutierrez (NTR) and in Tabasco, Villahermosa (VSA). We list which airlines fly to the local airports in the relevant "Getting There: By Air" sections throughout this book. For a list of the major international airlines with service to Mexico, turn to "Fast Facts," p. 363.

Arriving at the Airport

Immigration and Customs clearance at Mexican airports is generally efficient. Expect longer lines during peak seasons, but you can usually clear immigration and customs within an hour. For more on what to expect when passing through Mexican Customs, see "Customs," above.

BY CAR

Driving is not the cheapest way to get to Mexico, and it is definitely not the easiest way to get to the Yucatán peninsula. While driving is a convenient way to see the country, you may think twice about taking your own car south of the U.S. border, once you've pondered the bureaucracy involved. One option is to rent a car once you arrive and tour around a specific region. The Yucatán peninsula is a great place to do this. Rental cars in Mexico generally are clean and well maintained, although they are often smaller than rentals in the U.S., may have manual rather than automatic transmission, and are comparatively expensive due to pricey mandatory insurance. Discounts are often available for rentals of a week or longer, especially when you make arrangements in advance online or from the United States. Be careful about estimated online rates, which often fail to include the price of the mandatory insurance. (See "Car Rentals," below, for more details.)

If, after reading the section that follows, you have additional questions or you want to confirm the current rules, call your nearest Mexican consulate or the Mexican Government Tourist Office. Although travel insurance companies

Carrying Car Documents

You must carry your temporary car-importation permit, tourist permit (see "Car Documents," below), and, if you purchased it, your proof of Mexican car insurance in the car at all times. The temporary car-importation permit papers are valid for 6 months to a year, while the tourist permit is usually issued for 30 days. It's a good idea to overestimate the time you'll spend in Mexico so if you have to (or want to) stay longer, you'll avoid the hassle of getting your papers extended. Whatever you do, don't overstay either permit. Doing so invites heavy fines, confiscation of your vehicle (which will not be returned), or both. Also remember that 6 months does not necessarily equal 180 days—be sure that you return before the earlier expiration date.

generally are helpful, they may not have the most accurate information. To check on road conditions or to get help with any travel emergency while in Mexico, call ✆ **800/482-9832,** or 55/5089-7500 in Mexico City. English-speaking operators staff both numbers.

In addition, check with the **U.S. Department of State** (www.state.gov) for warnings about dangerous driving areas.

Car Documents

To drive your car into Mexico, you'll need a **temporary car-importation permit,** which is granted after you provide a required list of documents (see below). The permit can be obtained after you cross the border into Mexico through Banco del Ejército (Banjercito) officials with Mexican Customs (*aduanas*), or at Mexican consulates in Austin, San Francisco, Phoenix, Albuquerque, Chicago, Houston, Dallas, Los Angeles, Sacramento, and San Bernardino. For more information, call ✆ **877-210-9469** in the U.S. or visit www.banjercito.com.mx.

The following requirements for border crossing were accurate at press time:

- **Passport.**
- **A valid driver's license,** issued outside of Mexico.
- **Current, original car registration and a copy of the original car title.** If the registration or title is in more than one name and not all the named people are traveling with you, a notarized letter from the absent person(s) authorizing use of the vehicle for the trip is required; have it ready. The registration and your credit card (see below) must be in the same name.
- **Original immigration documentation.** Likely your tourist card (see above).
- **Processing fee and posting of a bond.** You have three options for covering the car-importation fee: pay $29 at the border, pay $39 in advance at a Mexican Consulate, or pre-pay $49 online at www.banjercito.com.mx. You will generally need a credit card to make this payment. Mexican law also requires the posting of a bond at a Banjercito office to guarantee the export of the car from Mexico within a time period determined at the time of the application. For this purpose, American Express, Visa, or MasterCard credit card holders will be asked to provide credit card information; others will need to make a cash deposit of $200 to $400, depending on the make/model/year of the vehicle. In order to recover this bond or avoid credit card charges, travelers must go to any Mexican Customs office immediately before leaving Mexico.

If you receive your documentation at the border, Mexican officials will make two copies of everything and charge you for the copies. For up-to-the-minute information, a great source is the Customs office in Nuevo Laredo, or *Módulo de Importación Temporal de Automóviles, Aduana Nuevo Laredo* (✆ **867/712-2071**).

Important reminder: Someone else may drive, but the person (or relative of the person) whose name appears on the car-importation permit must *always* be in the car. (If stopped by police, a nonregistered family member driving without the registered driver must be prepared to prove familial relationship to the registered driver—no joke.) Violation of this rule subjects the car to impoundment and the driver to imprisonment, a fine, or both. You can drive a car with foreign license plates only if you have a foreign (non-Mexican) driver's license.

Point-to-Point Driving Directions Online

You can get point-to-point driving directions in English for anywhere in Mexico from the website of the Secretary of Communication and Transport. The site will also calculate tolls, distance, and travel time. Go to http://aplicaciones4.sct.gob.mx/sibuac_internet and click on "Rutas punto a punto" in the left-hand column. Then select the English version.

Mexican Auto Insurance *(Seguros de Auto)*

Liability auto insurance is legally required in Mexico. U.S. insurance is invalid; to be insured in Mexico, you must purchase Mexican insurance. Any party involved in an accident who has no insurance may be sent to jail and have his or her car impounded until all claims are settled. This is true even if you just drive across the border to spend the day. U.S. companies that broker Mexican insurance are commonly found at the border crossing, and several quote daily rates.

You can also buy car insurance through **Sanborn's Mexico Insurance,** P.O. Box 52840, 2009 S. 10th, McAllen, TX (✆ **800/222-0158;** fax 800/222-0158 or 956/686-0732; www.sanbornsinsurance.com). The company has offices at all U.S. border crossings. Its policies cost the same as the competition's do, but you get legal coverage (attorney and bail bonds if needed) and a detailed guide for your proposed route. Most of the Sanborn's border offices are open Monday through Friday; a few are staffed on Saturday and Sunday. **AAA** auto club (www.aaa.com) also sells insurance.

Returning to the U.S. with Your Car

You *must* return the car documents you obtained when you entered Mexico when you cross back with your car, or within 180 days of your return. (You can cross as many times as you wish within the 180 days.) If the documents aren't returned, serious fines are imposed (50 pesos for each day you're late), your car may be impounded and confiscated, or you may be jailed if you return to Mexico. You can only return the car documents to a Banjercito official on duty at the Mexican *aduana* building *before* you cross back into the United States. Some border cities have Banjercito officials on duty 24 hours a day, but others do not; some do not have Sunday hours.

BY SHIP

Numerous cruise lines serve Mexico. Some (such as Carnival and Royal Caribbean) cruise from Houston or Miami to the Caribbean (which often includes stops in Cancún, Playa del Carmen, and Cozumel). Several cruise-tour specialists sometimes offer last-minute discounts on unsold cabins. One such company is **CruisesOnly** (✆ **800/278-4737;** www.cruisesonly.com).

BY BUS

Greyhound (✆ **800/231-2222;** www.greyhound.com), or its affiliates, offers service from around the United States to the Mexican border, where passengers disembark, cross the border, and buy a ticket for travel into Mexico. Many border crossings have scheduled buses from the U.S. bus station to the Mexican bus station.

More than likely, if you travel to the Yucatán by bus from the northern border you will pass through Mexico City, the country's capitol and main transportation hub. Expect a trip from the border to last several grueling days of all day (and/or all night) travel on roads of varying quality.

We've listed bus arrival information in each applicable section of this book.

Getting Around

BY PLANE

Mexico has two large private national carriers: **Mexicana** (✆ **800/531-7921** in the U.S., or 01-800/801-2010 in Mexico; www.mexicana.com) and **Aeroméxico** (✆ **800/237-6399** in the U.S., or 01-800/021-4000 in Mexico; www.aeromexico.com), in addition to several low-cost carriers. Mexicana and Aeroméxico offer extensive connections to the United States as well as within Mexico.

Low-cost carriers include **Aviacsa** (www.aviacsa.com), **Click Mexicana** (www.mexicana.com), **InterJet** (www.interjet.com.mx), and **Volaris** (www.volaris.com.mx). In each applicable section of this book, we've mentioned regional carriers with all pertinent telephone numbers.

Because major airlines may book some regional carriers, check your ticket to see if your connecting flight is on a smaller carrier—they may use a different airport or a different counter.

AIRPORT TAXES Mexico charges an airport tax on all departures. Passengers leaving the country on international flights pay about $24 or the peso equivalent. It has become a common practice to include this departure tax in your ticket price. Taxes on each domestic departure within Mexico are around $17, unless you're on a connecting flight and have already paid at the start of the flight.

BY CAR

Many Mexican roads are not up to U.S., Canadian, and European standards of smoothness, hardness, width of curve, grade of hill, or safety markings. Driving at night is dangerous—the roads are rarely lit; trucks, carts, pedestrians, and bicycles usually have no lights; and you can hit potholes, animals, rocks, dead ends, or uncrossable bridges without warning.

The spirited style of Mexican driving sometimes requires keen vision and reflexes. Be prepared for new customs, as when a truck driver flips on his left turn signal when there's not a crossroad for many kilometers. He's probably telling you the road's clear ahead for you to pass. Another custom that's very important to respect is turning left. Never turn left by stopping in the middle of a highway with your left-turn signal on. Instead, pull onto the right shoulder, wait for traffic to clear, and then proceed across the road.

GASOLINE There's one government-owned brand of gas and one gasoline station name throughout the country—**Pemex** (Petroleras Mexicanas). There are two types of gas in Mexico: *magna,* 87-octane unleaded gas, and *premio* 93 octane. In Mexico, fuel and oil are sold by the liter, which is slightly more than a quart (1 gal. equals about 3.8L). Many franchise Pemex stations have bathroom facilities and convenience stores—a great improvement over the old ones. Gas stations accept both credit and debit cards for gas purchases.

TOLL ROADS Mexico charges some of the highest tolls in the world for its network of new toll roads, so they are rarely used. Generally, though, using toll roads cuts travel time. Older toll-free roads are generally in good condition, but travel times tend to be longer.

BREAKDOWNS If your car breaks down on the road, help might already be on the way. Radio-equipped green repair trucks, run by uniformed English-speaking officers, patrol major highways during daylight hours (approximately 8am to 6pm). These **"Green Angels/Angeles Verdes"** perform minor repairs and adjustments free, but you pay for parts and materials. To contact them in Mexico, dial ✆ **078.** For more information, see www.sectur.gob.mx

Your best guide to repair shops is the Yellow Pages. For repairs, look under *Automóviles y Camiones: Talleres de Reparación y Servicio;* auto-parts stores are under *Refacciones y Accesorios para Automóviles.* To find a mechanic on the road, look for the sign TALLER MECÁNICO.

Places called *vulcanizadora* or *llantera* repair flat tires, and it is common to find them open 24 hours a day on the most traveled highways.

MINOR ACCIDENTS When possible, many Mexicans drive away from minor accidents, or try to make an immediate settlement, to avoid involving the police. If the police arrive while the involved persons are still at the scene, the cars will likely be confiscated and both parties will likely have to appear in court. Both parties may also be taken into custody until liability is determined. Foreigners who don't speak fluent Spanish are at a distinct disadvantage when trying to explain their version of the event. Three steps may help the foreigner who doesn't wish to do as the Mexicans do: If you were in your own car, notify your Mexican insurance company, whose job it is to intervene on your behalf. If you were in a rental car, notify the rental company immediately and ask how to contact the nearest adjuster. (You did buy insurance with the rental, right?) Finally, if all else fails, ask to contact the nearest Green Angel, who may be able to explain to officials that you are covered by insurance. See also "Mexican Auto Insurance," in "Getting There," earlier in this chapter.

CAR RENTALS You'll get the best price if you reserve a car at least a week in advance. For a list of car-rental firms operating in this region, turn to "Fast Facts: Airline, Hotel & Car Rental Websites," p. 366.

Cars are easy to rent if you are 25 or older and have a major credit card, valid driver's license, and passport with you. Without a credit card, you must leave a cash deposit, usually a big one. One-way rentals are usually simple to arrange, but they are more costly.

Car-rental costs are high in Mexico because cars are more expensive. The condition of rental cars has improved greatly over the years, and clean new cars are the norm. You will pay the least for a manual car without air-conditioning. Prices may be considerably higher if you rent around a major holiday. Also double-check charges for insurance—some companies will increase the insurance rate after several days. Always ask for detailed information about all charges you will be responsible for.

Car-rental companies often charge on a credit card in U.S. dollars.

DEDUCTIBLES Be careful—these vary greatly; some are as high as $2,500 which comes out of your pocket immediately in case of damage.

INSURANCE Insurance is offered in two parts: **Collision and damage** insurance covers your car and others if the accident is your fault, and **personal accident** insurance covers you and anyone in your car. Note that insurance may be invalid if you have an accident while driving on an unpaved road.

Bus Hijackings

The U.S. Department of State notes that bandits target long-distance buses. First-class buses on toll *(cuota)* roads sustain a markedly lower crime rate than second-class and third-class buses that travel the less secure "free" *(libre)* highways.

DAMAGE Inspect your car carefully and note every damaged or missing item, no matter how minute, on your rental agreement, or you may be charged.

BY TAXI

Taxis are the preferred way to get around almost all of Mexico's resort areas. Fares for short trips within towns are generally preset by zone, and are quite reasonable compared with U.S. rates. For longer trips or excursions to nearby cities, taxis can generally be hired for around $15 to $20 per hour, or for a negotiated daily rate. A negotiated one-way price is usually much less than the cost of a rental car for a day, and a taxi travels much faster than a bus. For anyone who is uncomfortable driving in Mexico, this is a convenient, comfortable alternative. A bonus is that you have a Spanish-speaking person with you in case you run into trouble. Many taxi drivers speak at least some English. Your hotel can assist you with the arrangements.

BY BUS

Mexican buses run frequently, are readily accessible, and can transport you almost anywhere you want to go. Taking the bus is common in Mexico, and the executive and first-class coaches can be as comfortable as business class on an airplane. Buses are often the only way to get from large cities to other nearby cities and small villages. Don't hesitate to ask questions if you're confused about anything, but note that little English is spoken in bus stations.

Dozens of Mexican companies operate large, air-conditioned, Greyhound-type buses between most cities. Classes are *segunda* (second), *primera* (first), and *ejecutiva* (deluxe), which goes by a variety of names. Deluxe buses often have fewer seats than regular buses, show movies, are air-conditioned, and make few stops. Many run express from point to point. They are well worth the few dollars more. In rural areas, buses are often of the school-bus variety, with lots of local color.

Whenever possible, it's best to buy your reserved-seat ticket, often using a computerized system, a day in advance on long-distance routes and especially before holidays.

For each relevant destination, we list bus arrival and contact information. The following website provides reservations and bookings for numerous providers throughout Mexico: www.ticketbus.com.mx/wtbkd/autobus.jsp.

MONEY & COSTS

Frommer's lists exact prices in the local currency. The currency conversions quoted below were correct at press time. However, rates fluctuate, so before departing consult a currency exchange website such as **www.oanda.com/convert/classic** to check up-to-the-minute rates.

In general, the southern region of Mexico is considerably cheaper not just than most U.S. and European destinations, but also than many other parts of Mexico, although prices vary significantly depending on the specific location. The most expensive destinations are those with the largest number of foreign visitors, such as Cancún and Playa del Carmen. The least expensive are those off the beaten path and in small rural villages, particularly in the poorer states of Tabasco and Chiapas. In the major cities, prices vary greatly depending on the neighborhood. As you might imagine, tourist zones tend to be much more expensive than local areas.

The currency in Mexico is the **peso.** Paper currency comes in denominations of 20, 50, 100, 200, and 500 pesos. Coins come in denominations of 1, 2, 5, 10, and 20 pesos, and 20 and 50 **centavos** (100 centavos = 1 peso). The current exchange rate for the U.S. dollar, and the one used in this book, is 12 pesos; at that rate, an item that costs 12 pesos would be equivalent to $1.

THE VALUE OF THE MEXICAN PESO VS. OTHER POPULAR CURRENCIES

Pesos	US$	Can$	UK£	Euro (€)	Aus$	NZ$
100	US$8.20	C$50.24	£5.34	€6.09	A$8.79	NZ$11.46

Many establishments that deal with tourists, especially in coastal resort areas, quote prices in U.S. dollars. To avoid confusion, they use the abbreviations "Dlls." for dollars and "M.N." (*moneda nacional*, or national currency) or "M.X.P." for Mexican Pesos. ***Note:*** Establishments that quote their prices primarily in U.S. dollars are listed in this guide with U.S. dollars.

Getting **change** is a problem. Small-denomination bills and coins are hard to come by, so start collecting them early in your trip. Shopkeepers and taxi drivers everywhere always seem to be out of change and small bills; that's doubly true in markets. There seems to be an expectation that the customer should provide appropriate change, rather than the other way around.

Don't forget to have enough pesos to carry you over a weekend or Mexican holiday, when banks are closed. In general, avoid carrying the U.S. $100 bill, the bill most commonly counterfeited in Mexico and therefore the most difficult to exchange, especially in smaller towns. Because small bills and coins in pesos are hard to come by in Mexico, the $1 bill is very useful for tipping. ***Note:*** A tip of U.S. coins, which cannot be exchanged into Mexican currency, is of no value to the service provider.

Casas de cambio (exchange houses) are generally more convenient than banks for money exchange because they have more locations and longer hours; the rate of exchange may be the same as at a bank or slightly lower. Before leaving a bank or exchange-house window, count your change in front of the teller before the next client steps up.

Large airports have currency-exchange counters that often stay open whenever flights are operating. Though convenient, they generally do not offer the most favorable rates.

A hotel's exchange desk com-monly pays less favorable rates than banks; however, when the currency is in a state of flux, higher-priced hotels are known to pay higher rates than banks, in an effort to attract dollars. ***Note:*** In

Money Matters

The universal currency sign ($) is sometimes used to indicate pesos in Mexico. The use of this symbol in this book, however, denotes U.S. currency.

almost all cases, you receive a better rate by changing money first, then paying.

The bottom line on exchanging money: Ask first, and shop around. Banks generally pay the top rates.

Banks in Mexico have expanded and improved services. Except in the smallest towns, they tend to be open weekdays from 9am until 5pm, and often for at least a half day on Saturday. In larger resorts and cities, they can generally accommodate the exchange of dollars (which used to stop at noon) anytime during business hours. Some, but not all, banks charge a 1% fee to exchange traveler's checks. But you can pay for most purchases directly with traveler's checks at the establishment's stated exchange rate. Don't even bother with personal checks drawn on a U.S. bank—the bank will wait for your check to clear, which can take weeks, before giving you your money.

Travelers to Mexico can easily withdraw money from **ATMs** called *"cajeras"* in most major cities and resort areas. The U.S. Department of State recommends caution when you're using ATMs in Mexico, stating that they should only be used during business hours and in large protected facilities, but this pertains primarily to Mexico City, where crime remains a significant problem. In most resorts in Mexico, the use of ATMs is perfectly safe—just use the same precautions you would at any ATM. However, beware of using ATMs in dubious locations as there have been reports of people having their card numbers "skimmed" (where information is copied and monies stolen or cards fraudulently charged). The ATM exchange rate is generally more favorable than at *casas de cambio*. Most machines offer Spanish/English menus and dispense pesos, but some offer the option of withdrawing dollars.

In Mexico, Visa, MasterCard, and American Express are the most accepted cards. You'll be able to charge most hotel, restaurant, and store purchases, as well as almost all airline tickets, on your credit card. Most Pemex gas stations now accept credit card purchases for gasoline, though this option may not be available everywhere and often not at night—check before you pump. Generally you receive the favorable bank rate when paying by credit card. However, be aware that some establishments in Mexico add a 5% to 7% surcharge when you pay with a credit card. This is especially true when using American Express. Many times, advertised discounts will not apply if you pay with a credit card.

A Few Words about Prices

Many hotels in Mexico—except places that receive little foreign tourism—quote prices in U.S. dollars or in both dollars and pesos. Thus, currency fluctuations are unlikely to affect the prices most hotels charge.

Mexico has a value-added tax of 15% (*Impuesto de Valor Agregado,* or IVA; pronounced "*ee*-bah") on most everything, including restaurant meals, bus tickets, and souvenirs. (Exceptions are Cancún, Cozumel, and Los Cabos, where the IVA is 10%; as ports of entry, they receive a break on taxes.) Hotels charge the usual 15% IVA, plus a locally administered bed tax of 2% (in most areas), for a total of 17%. In Cancún, Los Cabos, and Cozumel, hotels charge the 10% IVA plus 2% room tax. The prices quoted by hotels and restaurants do not necessarily include IVA. You may find that upper-end properties (three or more stars) often quote prices without IVA included, while lower-priced hotels include IVA. Ask to see a printed price sheet and ask if the tax is included.

WHAT THINGS COST IN THE YUCATÁN	PESOS (US$ WHERE INDICATED)
Shuttle from airport to Cancún Hotel Zone	US$15.00
Cancún beachfront double room, moderate	US$120.00
Akumal beachfront double room, moderate	US$100.00–$140.00
Tulum beachfront double room, moderate	US$150.00–$200.00
Cancún 3-course dinner for one without wine, moderate	400.00–500.00
Tacos in San Cristóbal de las Casas	30.00
Admission to most archaeological sites	31.00–51.00
Night out in Cancún	US$40.00

HEALTH

The 2009 world outbreak of H1N1 ("swine flu") began in central Mexico and quickly spread to over 74 countries. Though the World Health Organization (WHO) issued a pandemic alert at the time, that alert is no longer in effect. For the latest information on health risks when traveling to Mexico, and what to do if you get sick, consult the **U.S. State Department**'s website at www.travel.state.gov, the **CDC website** at www.cdc.gov, or the website of the **World Health Organization** at www.who.int.

General Availability of Health Care

In most of Mexico's resort destinations, you can usually find health care that meets U.S. standards. Care in more remote areas is limited. Standards of medical training, patient care, and business practices vary greatly among medical facilities in beach resorts throughout Mexico. Cancún has first-rate hospitals, for example, but other cities along the Caribbean coast do not. In recent years, some U.S. citizens have complained that certain health-care facilities in beach resorts have taken advantage of them by overcharging or providing unnecessary medical care. On the other hand, Mexican doctors often spend more time with patients than doctors do north of the border, and may be just as good for less cost. Only rudimentary health care is generally available in much of Chiapas, Tabasco, and the Yucatán.

Prescription medicine is broadly available at Mexico pharmacies; however, be aware that you may need a copy of your prescription or to obtain a prescription from a local doctor.

Common Ailments

SUN/ELEMENTS/EXTREME WEATHER EXPOSURE Mexico is synonymous with sunshine; much of the country is bathed in intense sunshine for much of the year. Avoid excessive exposure, especially in the tropics where UV rays are more dangerous. The hottest months in Mexico's south are April and May, but the sun is intense most of the year.

DIETARY RED FLAGS Travelers' diarrhea (locally known as *turista,* the Spanish word for "tourist")—persistent diarrhea, often accompanied by fever, nausea, and vomiting—used to attack many travelers to Mexico. (Some in the U.S. call this "Montezuma's revenge," but you won't hear it called that in Mexico.) Widespread improvements in infrastructure, sanitation, and education have greatly diminished this ailment, especially in well-developed resort areas. Most travelers make a habit of drinking only bottled water, which also helps to protect against unfamiliar bacteria. In resort areas, and generally throughout Mexico, only purified ice is used. If you do come down with this ailment, nothing beats Pepto Bismol, readily available in Mexico. Imodium is also available in Mexico and is used by many travelers for a quick fix. A good high-potency (or "therapeutic") vitamin supplement and even extra vitamin C can help; yogurt is good for healthy digestion.

Over-the-Counter Drugs in Mexico

Antibiotics and other drugs that you'd need a prescription to buy in the States are often available over the counter in Mexican pharmacies. Mexican pharmacies also carry a limited selection of common over-the-counter cold, sinus, and allergy remedies. Contact lenses can be purchased without an exam or prescription, should you run out.

Since dehydration can quickly become life-threatening, be careful to replace fluids and electrolytes (potassium, sodium, and the like) during a bout of diarrhea. Drink Pedialyte, a rehydration solution available at most Mexican pharmacies, or natural fruit juice, such as guava or apple (stay away from orange juice, which has laxative properties), with a pinch of salt added.

The U.S. Public Health Service recommends the following measures for preventing travelers' diarrhea: **Drink only purified water** (boiled water, canned or bottled beverages, beer, or wine). **Choose food carefully.** In general, avoid salads (except in first-class restaurants), uncooked vegetables, undercooked protein, and unpasteurized milk or milk products, including cheese. Choose food that is freshly cooked and still hot. Avoid eating food prepared by street vendors. In addition, something as simple as **clean hands** can go a long way toward preventing *turista.*

HIGH-ALTITUDE HAZARDS Travelers to certain regions of Mexico occasionally experience **elevation sickness,** which results from the relative lack of oxygen and the decrease in barometric pressure that characterizes high elevations (more than 1,500m/5,000 ft.). Symptoms include shortness of breath, fatigue, headache, insomnia, and even nausea. Mexico City is at 2,240m (7,349 ft.) above sea level, as are a number of other central and southern cities, such as San Cristóbal de las Casas (even higher than Mexico City). At high elevations, it takes about 10 days to acquire the extra red blood corpuscles you need to adjust to the scarcity of oxygen. To help your body acclimate, drink plenty of fluids, avoid alcohol, and don't overexert yourself during the first few days. If you have heart or lung trouble, consult your doctor before flying above 2,400m (7,872 ft.).

BUGS, BITES & OTHER WILDLIFE CONCERNS **Mosquitoes** and **gnats** are prevalent along the coast and in the Yucatán lowlands. *Repelente contra insectos* (insect repellent) is a must, and you can buy it in most pharmacies. If you'll be in these areas and are prone to bites, bring along a repellent that contains the active ingredient DEET. Avon's Skin So Soft also works extremely well. Another good remedy to keep the mosquitoes away is to mix citronella essential oil with basil, clove, and lavender essential oils. If you're sensitive to bites, pick up some antihistamine cream from a drugstore at home.

Most readers won't ever see an *alacrán* (scorpion). But if one stings you, go immediately to a doctor. The one lethal scorpion found in some parts of Mexico is the *Centruroides*, part of the Buthidae family, characterized by a thin body, thick tail, and triangular-shaped sternum. Most deaths from these scorpions result within 24 hours of the sting as a result of respiratory or cardiovascular failure, with children and elderly people most at risk. Scorpions are not aggressive (they don't hunt for prey), but they may sting if touched, especially in their hiding places. In Mexico, you can buy scorpion-toxin antidote at any drugstore. It is an injection, and it costs around $25. This is a good idea if you plan to camp in a remote area, where medical assistance can be several hours away. Note that not all scorpion bites are lethal, but a doctor's visit is recommended regardless.

TROPICAL ILLNESSES You shouldn't be overly concerned about tropical diseases if you stay on the normal tourist routes and don't eat street food. However, both dengue fever and cholera have appeared in Mexico in recent years. Talk to your doctor or to a medical specialist in tropical diseases about precautions you should take. You can protect yourself by taking some simple precautions: Watch what you eat and drink; don't swim in stagnant water (ponds, slow-moving rivers, or wells); and avoid mosquito bites by covering up, using repellent, and sleeping under netting. The most dangerous areas seem to be on Mexico's west coast, away from the big resorts.

On occasion, coastal waters from the Gulf of Mexico can become contaminated with rapid growth in algae (phytoplankton), leading to a phenomenon known as harmful algal bloom or a "red tide." The algal release of neurotoxins threatens marine life and can cause rashes and even flu-like symptoms in exposed humans. Although red tides happen infrequently, you should not enter the water if you notice a reddish-brown color or are told there is a red tide.

Smoke-Free Mexico?

In early 2008, the Mexican president signed into law a nationwide smoking ban in workplaces and public buildings, and on public transportation. Under this groundbreaking law, private businesses are only permitted to allow public smoking in enclosed ventilated areas. Hotels may maintain up to 25% of guest rooms for smokers. Violators face stiff fines, and smokers refusing to comply could receive up to 36-hour jail sentences. The law places Mexico—where a significant percentage of the population smokes—at the forefront of efforts to curb smoking and improve public health in Latin America. So before you light up, be sure to ask about the application of local laws in Mexican public places and businesses you visit.

If You Get Sick

Any English-speaking embassy or consulate staff in Mexico can provide a list of area doctors who speak English. If you get sick in Mexico, consider asking your hotel concierge to recommend a local doctor—even his or her own. You can also try the emergency room at a local hospital or urgent care facility. Many hospitals also have walk-in clinics for emergency cases that are not life-threatening; you may not get immediate attention, but you won't pay emergency room prices.

For travel to Mexico, you may have to pay all medical costs upfront and be reimbursed later. Before leaving home, find out what medical services your health insurance covers. To protect yourself, consider buying medical travel insurance.

We list **emergency numbers** and **embassies** in "Fast Facts," p. 364 and p. 363 respectively.

CRIME & SAFETY

Mexico is one of the world's great travel destinations and millions of visitors travel safely here each year. In most places, it's uncommon for foreign visitors to face anything worse than petty crime. Always use common sense and exercise caution when in unfamiliar areas. Leave valuables and irreplaceable items in a safe place, or don't bring them at all. Use hotel safes when available. Avoid driving alone, especially at night. You can generally trust a person whom you approach for help or directions, but be wary of anyone who approaches you offering the same. The more insistent a person is, the more cautious you should be. Stay away from areas where drug dealing and prostitution occur. These tips should help make your trip even more enjoyable.

Mexico has experienced a serious escalation in drug-related and border violence in the past couple years, including cities that previously received significant tourism, such as Mexico City, Tijuana, Ciudad Juarez, Nuevo Laredo and Acapulco.

The U.S. and Mexico share a border more than 3,000km (nearly 2,000 miles) long and Americans comprise the vast majority of tourists to Mexico. Due to this close and historically intertwined relationship, we recommend that all travelers read the **U.S. Department of State travel advisories** for Mexico (**www.state.gov**). The U.S. State Department encourages its citizens to use main roads during daylight hours, stay in well-known tourist destinations and tourist areas with better security, and provide an itinerary to a friend or family member not traveling with them. Kidnapping continues to happen at an alarming rate. It can be useful to travel with a working cellphone, as well. This is good advice for all travelers to Mexico.

For emergency numbers, turn to p. 364.

Crime in Resort Towns

There have been a significant number of rapes reported in Cancún and other resort areas, usually at night or in the early morning. Women should not walk alone late at night. Armed street crime is a serious problem in all the major cities. Some bars and nightclubs, especially in resort cities such as Cancún, can be havens for drug dealers and petty criminals.

The U.S. State Department offers specific safety and security information for travelers on spring break in Mexico: http://travel.state.gov/travel/cis_pa_tw/spring_break_mexico/spring_break_mexico_2812.html.

ONE MORE AUTHOR GIVES HIS TWO CENTS: safety in mexico

Stories of murder and mayhem are making all the headlines about Mexico these days. Stories of assassinations, kidnappings, and shootouts sell newspapers but are of no help evaluating the risk in traveling through the country. They are newsworthy in that they document the gravity of the problem Mexico faces in gaining control of its borders and ensuring public safety. The best way to understand the risk of traveling in Mexico is to read the U.S. State Department Travel Alert (www.state.gov).

The current situation has changed the way I travel in two ways beyond the usual precautions—such as not flashing a lot of money, not wearing an expensive watch, keeping aware of my surroundings, and not driving on the highway at night (for reasons that have more to do with practicalities than issues of crime). The changes I've made can be boiled down to two objectives: Avoid being in the wrong place at the wrong time, and avoid the possibility of mistaken identity. The **first** is largely met by not lingering in Mexico's northern border states (including Durango and the interior of Sinaloa). This is where the immense majority of the violence is occurring. The **second** is meant to minimize any risk of being held up or nabbed by kidnappers, and it is achieved by looking as much like a tourist as possible. Kidnappers in Mexico don't target tourists. They have targeted resident foreigners who have family in the country or business people who have associates. They do this because they need someone to demand the ransom from. The risk here is from small-time gangs who act opportunistically. (Serious kidnappers aren't a threat because they won't do anything without planning and surveillance.) In the last few years, small-time gangs have increased. The best way I know of to avoid this risk is not to carry a briefcase or satchel, which is a business symbol. What's more, by hauling around a backpack, you will automatically escape scrutiny because businesspersons in Mexico never use them. The backpack (*mochila*) in Mexico is a strong cultural identifier. It's associated with students and counterculture types, so much so that the word *mochilero* has come to describe hippies. For this very reason, I used to lug my computer around in a briefcase and now I always use a backpack.

–David Baird

It is also advised that you should not hike alone in backcountry areas nor walk alone on less-frequented beaches, ruins, or trails.

Highway Safety

Travelers should exercise caution while traveling Mexican highways, avoiding travel at night, and using toll (*cuota*) roads rather than the less secure free (*libre*) roads whenever possible. Cooperate with official checkpoints when traveling on Mexican highways.

Bus travel should take place during daylight hours on first-class conveyances. Although bus hijackings and robberies have occurred on toll roads, buses on toll roads have a markedly lower rate of incidents than second-class and third-class buses that travel the less secure "free" highways.

Bribes & Scams

As is the case around the world, there are the occasional bribes and scams in Mexico, targeted at people believed to be naive, such as telltale tourists. For years, Mexico was known as a place where bribes—called *mordidas* (bites)—were expected; however, the country is rapidly changing. Frequently, offering a bribe today, especially to a police officer, is considered an insult, and it can land you in deeper trouble.

Many tourists have the impression that everything works better in Mexico if you "tip"; however, in reality, this only perpetuates the *mordida* tradition. If you are pleased with a service, feel free to tip. But you shouldn't tip simply to attempt to get away with something illegal or inappropriate—whether it is evading a ticket that's deserved or a car inspection as you're crossing the border.

Whatever you do, **avoid impoliteness;** you won't do yourself any favors if you insult a Mexican official. Extreme politeness, even in the face of adversity, rules Mexico. In Mexico, *gringos* have a reputation for being loud and demanding. By adopting the local custom of excessive courtesy, you'll have greater success in negotiations of any kind. Stand your ground, but do it politely.

As you travel in Mexico, you may encounter several types of **scams,** which are typical throughout the world. One involves some kind of a **distraction** or feigned commotion. While your attention is diverted, for example, a pickpocket makes a grab for your wallet. In another common scam, an **unaccompanied child** pretends to be lost and frightened and takes your hand for safety. Meanwhile the child or an accomplice plunders your pockets. A third involves **confusing currency.** A shoeshine boy, street musician, guide, or other individual might offer you a service for a price that seems reasonable—in pesos. When it comes time to pay, he or she tells you the price is in dollars, not pesos. Be very clear on the price and currency when services are involved. An **ATM scam** involves ATMs in questionable locations where card numbers are "skimmed" and information is copied, money stolen, or cards fraudulently charged.

SPECIALIZED TRAVEL RESOURCES

In addition to the destination-specific resources listed below, please visit Frommers.com for additional specialized travel resources.

LGBT Travelers

Mexico is a conservative country, with deeply rooted Catholic religious traditions. Public displays of same-sex affection are rare and still considered surprising for men, especially outside of urban or resort areas. Women in Mexico frequently walk hand in hand, but anything more would cross the boundary of acceptability. However, gay and lesbian travelers are generally treated with respect and should not experience harassment, assuming they give the appropriate regard to local customs.

Things are changing here. On December 21, 2009, Mexico City became the first Latin American jurisdiction to legalize same-sex marriage, and 14th overall after the Netherlands, Belgium, Spain, Canada, South Africa, Norway, Sweden, and six U.S. jurisdictions.

While much of Mexico is socially conservative, Cancún and Playa del Carmen are not. Popular with many gay travelers, both coastal resorts offer gay-friendly accommodations, bars, and activities. For more information, visit **MexGay Vacations** at www.mexgay.com. Information about gay-friendly accommodations in Mérida, Yucatán is available at www.gayplaces2stay.com.

Travelers with Disabilities

Mexico may seem like one giant obstacle course to travelers in wheelchairs or on crutches. At airports, you may encounter steep stairs before finding a well-hidden elevator or escalator—if one exists. Airlines will often arrange wheelchair assistance to the baggage area. Porters are generally available to help with luggage at airports and large bus stations, once you've cleared baggage claim.

Mexican airports are upgrading their services, but it is not uncommon to board from a remote position, meaning you either descend stairs to a bus that ferries you to the plane, which you board by climbing stairs, or you walk across the tarmac to your plane and ascend the stairs. Deplaning presents the same problem in reverse.

Escalators (and there aren't many in the country) are often out of order. Stairs without handrails abound. Few restrooms are equipped for travelers with disabilities; when one is available, access to it may be through a narrow passage that won't accommodate a wheelchair or a person on crutches. Many deluxe hotels (the most expensive) now have rooms with bathrooms designed for people with disabilities. Those traveling on a budget should stick with one-story hotels or hotels with elevators. Even so, there will probably still be obstacles somewhere. Generally speaking, no matter where you are, someone will lend a hand, although you may have to ask for it.

For a bit of underwater sight-seeing, **Yucatek Divers** (**✆ 984/803-2836;** www.yucatek-divers.com), in Playa del Carmen, specializes in dives for people with disabilities.

Family Travel

If you have trouble getting your kids out of the house in the morning, dragging them to a faraway foreign country may seem like an insurmountable challenge. But family travel can be immensely rewarding, giving you new ways of seeing the world through the eyes of children.

Children are considered the national treasure of Mexico, and Mexicans will warmly welcome and cater to your children. Many parents were reluctant to bring young children into Mexico in the past, primarily due to health concerns, but I can't think of a better place to introduce children to the exciting adventure of exploring a different culture. One of the best destinations for kids is Cancún. Hotels can often arrange for a babysitter.

Before leaving, ask your doctor which medications to take along. Disposable diapers cost about the same in Mexico but are of poorer quality. You can get Huggies Supreme and Pampers identical to the ones sold in the United States, but at a higher price. Many stores sell Gerber's baby foods. Dry cereals, powdered formulas, baby bottles, and purified water are easily available in midsize and large cities or resorts.

Cribs may present a problem; only the largest and most luxurious hotels provide them. However, rollaway beds are often available. Child seats or high chairs at restaurants are common.

Consider bringing your own car seat; they are not readily available for rent in Mexico.

Every country's regulations differ, but in general children traveling abroad should have plenty of documentation on hand, particularly if they're traveling with someone other than their own parents (in which case a notarized form letter from a parent is often required). For details on entry requirements for children traveling abroad, turn to p. 61.

To locate accommodations, restaurants, and attractions that are particularly kid-friendly, refer to the "Kids" icon throughout this guide.

Women Travelers

Women do not frequently travel alone in Mexico, including driving alone on the highways. Walking on the street could net you a catcall, and walking alone at night is not advisable except in well-protected tourist areas. I've known people who have had uncomfortable experiences in crowded places such as subways. In general, however, Mexicans are extremely gracious, and will help a woman carry heavy items, open doors, and provide information.

Senior Travel

Mexico is a popular country for retirees. For decades, North Americans have been living indefinitely in Mexico by returning to the border and recrossing with a new tourist permit every 6 months. Mexican immigration officials have caught on, and now limit the maximum time in the country to 6 months within any year. This is to encourage even partial residents to acquire proper documentation.

AIM-Adventures in Mexico, Apartado Postal 31–70, 45050 Guadalajara, Jalisco, is a well-written, informative newsletter for prospective retirees. Subscriptions are $29 to the United States.

Sanborn Tours, 2015 S. 10th St., P.O. Box 936, McAllen, TX 78505-0519 (✆ **800/395-8482;** www.sanborns.com), offers a "Retire in Mexico" orientation tour.

Student Travel

Because Mexicans consider higher education a luxury rather than a birthright, there is no formal network of student discounts and programs. Most Mexican students travel with their families rather than with other students, so student discount cards are not commonly recognized.

The U.S. State Department offers information designated specifically for students traveling abroad: www.studentsabroad.state.gov.

More hostels have entered the student travel scene. **Hostels.com.mx** offers a list of hostels in Cancún, Mérida, Playa del Carmen, and San Cristóbal Las Casas.

RESPONSIBLE TOURISM

Mexico's ecological diversity is among the broadest of any country in the world, with an abundance of ecosystems that ranges from the northern deserts to the central conifer forests, and the southern tropical rainforests. Mexico also supports a population of 111 million people and welcomes more than 20 million visitors each year. Tourism is one of the country's biggest and most lucrative industries, and while tourism has brought jobs and growth to much of Mexico,

Biodegradable Sunscreen

Recent scientific studies have shown that the chemicals in commercial sunscreen can do long-term damage to coral reefs, collect in freshwater, and even build up in your own body system. The Riviera Maya receives more than 2.5 million visitors every year, many of them drawn to its rare marine environment—a unique combination of freshwater cenotes and the world's second-largest coral reef. A few ounces of sunscreen multiplied by 2.5 million is equal to a substantial amount of harmful chemicals suspended in the ocean and freshwater. That's why tours to the Sian Ka'an Biosphere Reserve and water parks Xcaret and Xel-Ha ask that you use only biodegradable sunscreen or wear none at all when swimming in their ocean or cenotes. You might just be inspired to use a biodegradable formula wherever you swim.

The label of a biodegradable sunscreen should state that it is 100% biodegradable (and only 100% will do). Xcaret gives out packets of biodegradable formula, but Xel-Ha charges $16 for theirs. If you're curious, you can obtain a list of banned chemicals by contacting the parks directly. Buy a supply of biodegradable formula before you go from www.mexitan.com or www.caribbean-sol.com.

it has also created and even accelerated many of Mexico's ecological problems. **Cancún** may be the most high-profile example: Rapidly developed from a rural outpost to an international resort destination, Cancún imported turf from Florida for its golf courses, inadvertently introducing a disease that wiped out the local coconut palms. The region's mangroves, a key habitat for native species and vital to protecting the land from hurricanes and erosion, have also suffered.

However, tourism has also encouraged the development of ecological conservation. Mexico is home to seven of the world's eight species of sea turtle, and the entire sea turtle population was decimated on both coasts as a result of tourism growth and local overfishing. A recent success story comes from the **Riviera Maya,** where marine biologists are working with hotels to guard nesting turtles and their eggs.

Mexico's people are proud of their land and culture, and through your travels, especially in rural areas, you will likely encounter ***ejidos,*** and ***cooperativos,*** or local cooperatives, that offer small-scale tourism services—this may be as simple as taking visitors on a boat ride through a lake or as visible as controlling access to archeological ruins. *Ejidos* will also run tours to popular eco-tourism destinations similar to those offered by large travel agencies. When you deal with *ejidos,* everyone you encounter will be from the community and you know that your money goes directly back to them. States with a strong network of cooperatives include Chiapas, Quintana Roo, and Yucatán. Playa del Carmen's **Alltournative** (www.alltournative.com) is one example of a private company that has created tour options that include local input and grow by sustainable development.

The Mexican Caribbean supports the Great Mesoamerican Barrier Reef, the second largest reef in the world, which extends down to Honduras. This reef and other marine ecosystems face increasing pressure from sedimentation, pollution, overfishing, and exploitative recreational activities, all newly associated with growing regional tourism. The **Coral Reef Alliance** (CORAL; www.coral.org) is an example of an organization that, by teaming up with the **World**

Wildlife Fund (WWF; www.wwf.org) and **United Nations Environmental Program** (UNEP; www.unep.org), has been working to address threats to the Mesoamerican Barrier Reef and improve environmental sustainability throughout the region. CORAL partners with Mexican Amigos de Sian Ka'an, Conservation International, and the Cozumel Reefs National Park in an effort to build sustainability into mass tourism (such as cruise ships and hotels). CORAL assists marine tourism operators in implementing a voluntary code of conduct for best environmental practices. CORAL is soon to spread its influence to the Yum Balam region of the Yucatán Peninsula, where guidelines for whale shark interactions are greatly needed.

One of the best contributions a diver can make to support a healthy reef while diving is to avoid physical contact with the reef. Talk to your scuba outfitter about proper buoyancy control and body position to avoid damaging these fragile ecosystems.

Tabasco suffered severe flooding in 2007 that devastated much of the land and brought widespread suffering to the population, which is among Mexico's poorest. The floods also affected Chiapas, though to a lesser extent. Tabasco's sinking land, and the extraction of oil and gas, land erosion, and deforestation all contributed to the state's vulnerability to flooding.

Ecotourism and sustainable tourism opportunities abound in **Chiapas,** where a growing number of small, local tourism cooperatives have organized to take tourists on guided hikes, treks, and even kayak expeditions into the state's isolated jungles and nature reserves. The **Chiapas Tourism Secretariat** has information in Spanish about ecotourism at locations across the state (www.turismo chiapas.gob.mx). Two private companies that run ecotours throughout Chiapas are **Ecochiapas** (Primero de Marzo 30, San Cristóbal de las Casas; ✆ **967/674-6660;** www.ecochiapas.com) and **Latitud 16** (Calle Real de Guadalupe 23, San Cristóbal de las Casas; ✆ **967/678-3909;** www.latitud16.com).

The **Mesoamerican Ecotourism Alliance** (✆ **800/682-0584** in the U.S.; www.travelwithmea.org) offers award- winning ecotours recognized by *National Geographic* to the Yucatán and Chiapas.

Animal-Rights Issues

The Yucatán presents many opportunities to **swim with dolphins.** The capture of wild dolphins was outlawed in Mexico in 2002. The only dolphins added to the country's dolphin swim programs since then were born in captivity. This law may have eased concerns about the death and implications of capturing wild dolphins, but the controversy is not over. Local organizations have been known to staple notes to Dolphin Discovery ads in magazines distributed in Cancún hotels. Marine biologists who run the dolphin swim programs say the mammals are thriving and that the programs provide a forum for research, conservation, education, and rescue operations. Animal rights advocates maintain that keeping these intelligent mammals in captivity is nothing more than exploitation. Their argument is that these private dolphin programs don't qualify as "public display" under the Marine Mammal Protection Act because the entry fees bar most of the public from participating.

Visit the website of the **Whale and Dolphin Conservation Society** at www.wdcs.org or the **American Cetacean Society,** www.acsonline.org, for further discussion on the topic.

ONLINE TRAVELER'S toolbox

- **Regional Travel** (www.travelyucatan.com; www.yucatantoday.com; www.sac-be.com; www.cozumelmycozumel.com)
- **Regional Airports** (www.asur.com.mx)
- **Cancún Convention & Visitor's Bureau** (http://cancun.travel/en/)
- **Riviera Maya Tourism Board** (www.rivieramaya.com)
- **Yucatán Tourism Board** (www.mayayucatan.com.mx)
- **Campeche Tourism Board** (www.campeche.travel)
- **Expat Life on the Peninsula** (www.locogringo.com; www.yucatanliving.com)
- **Local Government** (www.yucatan.gob.mx; www.qroo.gob.mx; www.campeche.travel/en; www.chiapas.gob.mx; www.tabasco.gob.mx)
- **Travel Warnings** (www.state.gov; www.fco.gov.uk/travel; www.voyage.gc.ca; www.smartraveller.gov.au)

Bullfighting is considered an important part of Latin culture, but you should know, before you attend a *correo,* that the bulls (at least four) will ultimately be killed in a gory spectacle. This is not the case in some countries, such as France and Portugal, but the Mexicans follow the Spanish model. That said, a bullfight is a portal into understanding Mexico's Spanish colonial past, although nowadays bullfights are more of a tourist attraction, especially in tourist laden Cancún. To read more about the implications of attending a bullfight, visit **www.peta.org**, the website of People for the Ethical Treatment of Animals (PETA) (or see specifically: www.peta.org/mc/factsheet_display.asp?ID=64).

SPECIAL INTEREST & ESCORTED TRIPS

Academic Trips & Language Classes

For Spanish-language instruction, **IMAC** (✆ **866/306-5040;** www.spanish-school.com.mx) offers programs in Guadalajara, Puerto Vallarta, and Playa del Carmen. The **Spanish Institute** (✆ **800/539-9710;** www.spanishtoday.com) is affiliated with intensive Spanish language schools in Puebla and Mérida.

To explore your inner Frida or Diego while in Mexico, look into **Mexico Art Tours,** 9323 E. Lupine Ave, Scotsdale, AZ 85260 (✆ **888/783-1331** or 480/730-1764; www.mexicanarttours.com). Typically led by Jean Grimm, a specialist in the arts and cultures of Mexico, these unique tours feature compelling speakers who are themselves respected scholars and artists. Itineraries include visits to Chiapas, Guadalajara, Guanajuato, Puebla, Puerto Vallarta, Mexico City, San Miguel de Allende, and Veracruz—and other cities. Special tours involve archaeology, architecture, interior design, and culture—such as a Day of the Dead tour.

The **Archaeological Conservancy,** 5301 Central Ave. NE, Suite 402, Albuquerque, NM 87108 (✆ **505/266-1540;** www.americanarchaeology.com), presents various trips each year, led by an expert, usually an archaeologist. The trips change from year to year and space is limited; make reservations early.

ATC Tours and Travel, Av. 16 de Septiembre 16, 29200 San Cristóbal de las Casas, Chis. (✆ **967/678-2550,** -2557; fax 967/678-3145; www.atctours.com), a Mexico-based tour operator with an excellent reputation, offers specialist-led trips, primarily in southern Mexico. In addition to trips to the ruins of Palenque and Yaxchilán (extending into Belize and Guatemala by river, plane, and bus if desired), ATC runs horseback tours to Chamula or Zinacantán, and day trips to the ruins of Toniná around San Cristóbal de las Casas; birding in the rainforests of Chiapas and Guatemala (including in the El Triunfo Reserve of Chiapas); hikes to the shops and homes of textile artists of the Chiapas highlands; and walks from the Lagos de Montebello in the Montes Azules Biosphere Reserve, with camping and canoeing. The company can also prepare custom itineraries.

Adventure Trips

Mexico Sagaz (Asociación Mexicana de Turismo de Aventura y Ecoturismo) is an active association of ecotourism and adventure tour operators. It publishes an annual catalog of participating firms and their offerings, all of which must meet certain criteria for security, quality, and training of the guides, as well as for sustainability of natural and cultural environments. For more information, contact (✆ **800/654-4452** toll-free in Mexico or 55/5544-7567; www.mexicosagaz.org).

The California Native, 6701 W. 87th Place, Los Angeles, CA 90045 (✆ **800/926-1140** or 310/642-1140; www.calnative.com), offers small-group deluxe 7-, 8-, 11-, and 14-day escorted tours through the Riviera Maya, the Yucatán, and Chiapas.

MexicoTravel.net, 300-3665 Kingsway, Vancouver, BC V5R 5W2 Canada (✆ **604/454-9044;** fax 604/454-9088; www.mexicotravel.net), runs adventure, cultural, and sports tours to Mexico City and surrounding areas, Baja, Veracruz, the Copper Canyon, the Mayan Route, and other destinations.

Trek America, 16/17 Grange Mills Weir Road, LONDON, SW12ONE, UK (✆ **800/873-5872** in the U.S.; 0845/313-2614 in the UK; www.trekamerica.com); organizes lengthy, active trips that combine trekking, hiking, van transportation, and camping along the Mayan Route and across the Yucatán.

Food & Wine Trips

If you're looking to eat your way through Mexico, sign up with **Culinary Adventures,** 6023 Reid Dr. NW, Gig Harbor, WA 98335 (✆ **253/851-7676;** fax 253/851-9532; www.marilyntausend.com). It runs a short but select list of cooking tours in Mexico. Culinary Adventures features well-known cooks, with travel to regions known for excellent cuisine. Destinations vary each year, though often include the Yucatán. The owner, Marilyn Tausend, is the author of *Cocinas de la Familia* (Family Kitchens), *Savoring Mexico,* and *Mexican,* and co-author of *Mexico the Beautiful Cookbook.*

STAYING CONNECTED

Mobile Phones

Telcel is Mexico's expensive, primary cellphone provider. It has upgraded its systems to GSM and offers good coverage in much of the country, including the major cities and resorts. Most Mexicans buy their cellphones without a specific coverage plan and then pay as they go or purchase prepaid cards with set amounts of air-time credit. These cellphone cards with scratch-off pin numbers can be purchased in Telcel stores as well as many newspaper stands and convenience stores.

Many North American and European cellphone companies offer networks with roaming coverage in Mexico. Rates can be very high, so check with your provider before committing to making calls this way. An increasing number of Mexicans, particularly among the younger generation, prefer the less expensive rates of **Nextel** (www.nextel.com.mx), which features push-to-talk service. **Cellular Abroad** (www.cellularabroad.com) offers cellphone rentals and purchases as well as SIM cards for travel abroad. Whether you rent or purchase the cellphone, you need to purchase a SIM card that is specific for Mexico.

Internet & E-mail

Wi-Fi is increasingly common in Mexico's major cities and resorts. Mexico's largest airports offer Wi-Fi access provided for a fee by Telcel's Prodigy Internet service. Most five-star hotels now offer Wi-Fi in the guest rooms, although you will need to check in advance whether this service is free or for a fee. Hotel lobbies often have Wi-Fi as well. To find public Wi-Fi hotspots in Mexico, go to **www.jiwire.com**; its Hotspot Finder holds the world's largest directory of public wireless hotspots.

Many large Mexican airports have **Internet kiosks,** and quality Mexican hotels usually have business centers with Internet access. You can also check out such copy stores as **FedEx Office** or **OfficeMax,** which offer computer stations with fully loaded software (as well as Wi-Fi).

Telephones

Mexico's telephone system is slowly but surely catching up with modern times. Most telephone numbers have 10 digits. Every city and town that has telephone access has a two-digit (Mexico City, Monterrey, and Guadalajara) or three-digit (everywhere else) area code. In Mexico City, Monterrey, and Guadalajara, local numbers have eight digits; elsewhere, local numbers have seven digits. To place a local call, you do not need to dial the area code. Many fax numbers are also regular phone numbers; ask whoever answers for the fax tone (*"me da tono de fax, por favor"*).

The **country code** for Mexico is **52.**

To call Mexico:

1. Dial the international access code: 011 from the U.S. and Canada; 00 from the U.K., Ireland, or New Zealand; or 0011 from Australia.
2. Dial the country code: 52.
3. Dial the two- or three-digit area code, then the eight- or seven-digit number. For example, if you wanted to call the U.S. consulate in Acapulco, the entire number would be 011-52-744-469-0556. If you wanted to dial the U.S. embassy in Mexico City, the entire number would be 011-52-55-5209-9100.

To make international calls: To make international calls from Mexico, dial 00, then the country code (U.S. or Canada 1, U.K. 44, Ireland 353, Australia 61, New Zealand 64). Next, dial the area code and number. For example, to call the British Embassy in Washington, you would dial 00-1-202-588-7800.

To call a Mexican cellular number: From the same area code, dial 044 and then the number. To dial the cellular phone from anywhere else in Mexico, first dial 01, and then the three-digit area code and the seven-digit number. To place an international call to a cellphone (e.g., from the U.S.), you now must add a 1 after the country code: for example, 011-52-1 + 10-digit number.

For directory assistance: Dial ✆ **040** if you're looking for a number inside Mexico. ***Note:*** Listings usually appear under the owner's name, not the name of the business, and your chances to find an English-speaking operator are slim.

For operator assistance: If you need operator assistance in making a call, dial ✆ **090** to make an international call, and ✆ **020** to call a number in Mexico.

Toll-free numbers: Numbers beginning with 800 within Mexico are toll-free, but calling a U.S. toll-free number from Mexico costs the same as an overseas call. To call an 800 number in the U.S., dial 001-880 and the last seven digits of the toll-free number. To call an 888 number in the U.S., dial 001-881 and the last seven digits of the toll-free number. For a number with an 887 prefix, dial 882; for 866, dial 883.

TIPS ON ACCOMMODATIONS

Mexico's Hotel Rating System

The hotel rating system in Mexico is called "Stars and Diamonds." Hotels may qualify to earn one to five stars or diamonds. Many hotels that have excellent standards are not certified, but all rated hotels adhere to strict standards. The guidelines relate to service, facilities, and hygiene more than to prices.

Five-diamond hotels meet the highest requirements for rating: The beds are comfortable, bathrooms are in excellent working order, all facilities are renovated regularly, infrastructure is top-tier, and services and hygiene meet the highest international standards.

Five-star hotels usually offer similar quality, but with lower levels of service and detail in the rooms. For example, a five-star hotel may have less luxurious linens or, perhaps, room service during limited hours rather than 24 hours.

Four-star hotels are less expensive and more basic, but they still guarantee cleanliness and basic services such as hot water and purified drinking water.

Boutique Lodgings

Mexico lends itself beautifully to the concept of small, private hotels in idyllic settings. They vary in style from grandiose estate to palm-thatched bungalow. Mexico Boutique Hotels (www.mexicoboutiquehotels.com) specializes in smaller places to stay with a high level of personal attention and service. Most options have less than 50 rooms, and the accommodations consist of entire villas, *casitas,* bungalows, or a combination. The Yucatán is especially noted for the luxury haciendas (p. 260) throughout the peninsula.

Three- two-, and one-star hotels are at least working to adhere to certain standards: Bathrooms are cleaned and linens are washed daily, and you can expect a minimum standard of service. Two- and one-star hotels generally provide bottled water rather than purified water.

The nonprofit organization Calidad Mexicana Certificada, A.C., known as **Calmecac** (www.calmecac.com.mx), is responsible for hotel ratings; visit their website for additional details about the rating system.

Hotel Chains

In addition to the major international chains, you'll run across a number of less-familiar brands as you plan your trip to Mexico. They include:

- **Brisas Hotels & Resorts** (www.brisas.com.mx). These were the hotels that originally attracted jet-set travelers to Mexico. Spectacular in a retro way, these properties offer the laid-back luxury that makes a Mexican vacation so unique.
- **Fiesta Americana** and **Fiesta Inn** (www.posadas.com). Part of the Mexican-owned Grupo Posadas company, these hotels set the country's midrange standard for facilities and services. They generally offer comfortable, spacious rooms and traditional Mexican hospitality. Fiesta Americana hotels offer excellent beach-resort packages. Fiesta Inn hotels are usually more business-oriented. Grupo Posadas also owns the more luxurious Caesar Park hotels and the eco-oriented Explorean hotels.
- **Hoteles Camino Real** (www.caminoreal.com). Hoteles Camino Real remains Mexico's premier hotel chain with beach resorts, city hotels, and colonial inns scattered throughout the country. Its beach hotels are traditionally located on the best beaches in the area. This chain also focuses on the business market. The hotels are famous for their vivid and contrasting colors.
- **NH Hoteles** (www.nh-hotels.com). The NH hotels are noted for their family-friendly facilities and quality standards. The beach properties' signature feature is a pool, framed by columns, overlooking the sea.
- **Quinta Real Grand Class Hotels and Resorts** (www.quintareal.com). These hotels, owned by Summit Hotels and Resorts, are noted for architectural and cultural details that reflect their individual regions. At these luxury properties, attention to detail and excellent service are the rule. Quinta Real is the top-line Mexican hotel brand.

House Rentals & Swaps

House and villa rentals and swaps are becoming more common in Mexico, but no single recognized agency or business provides this service exclusively for Mexico. In the chapters that follow, we have provided information on independent services that we have found to be reputable.

You'll find the most extensive inventory of homes at **Vacation Rentals by Owner** (**VRBO;** www.vrbo.com). They have more than 33,000 homes and condominiums worldwide, including a large selection in Mexico. Another good option is **VacationSpot** (✆ **888/903-7768;** www.vacationspot.com), owned by Expedia and a part of its sister company Hotels.com. It has fewer choices, but the company's criteria for adding inventory is much more selective and often includes on-site inspections. They also offer toll-free phone support.

4 SUGGESTED YUCATÁN ITINERARIES

by Shane Christensen

The following itineraries assume you're flying in and out of Cancún, by far the most common port of entry for the Yucatán. The airport is south of town in the direction of the Riviera Maya, so if you rent a car to drive down the coast, you won't have to deal with city traffic. Those preferring to skip the coast and stick to the peninsula's interior could fly directly to Mérida, capital of the state of Yucatán, and adjust their itineraries accordingly.

For traveling around the Yucatán, rental cars work well. The roads are generally easy to figure out, and there's not much traffic when you move inland. Finding your way around Mérida is a little tricky, but Cancún and the other cities of the peninsula are easy. You can take inexpensive, comfortable buses for long distances during your entire trip, but keep in mind that buses in the Riviera Maya do not run along the small roads that connect the highway to the beach. Your bus may drop you on the side of the highway right at the junction with the road to your paradise, and you'll have to flag a taxi to take you the rest of the way. This is a fine method, but can be time-consuming.

These itineraries are merely suggestions; you should tweak them to your specific tastes and interests. The 14-day itinerary is very busy and will keep you moving quickly; it's an attempt to be comprehensive in hitting the top sites, but you may well want to skip a few of these and spend more time at others. Though I've included an itinerary that takes you south into Tabasco and Chiapas, interested travelers should consider taking a fully dedicated trip to these states on their own. I recommend against being too ambitious with your vacation time. The heat and humidity bring about a lethargy that can be enjoyable if you're not preoccupied with a timetable. Keep in mind as well that it gets dark early here, and it's not a good idea to do much night driving.

THE REGIONS IN BRIEF

Travelers to the peninsula have an opportunity to see pre-Hispanic ruins—such as **Chichén Itzá, Uxmal,** and **Tulum**—and the living descendants of the cultures that built them, as well as the ultimate in resort Mexico: **Cancún.** The Yucatán peninsula borders the aquamarine Gulf of Mexico on the west and north, and the clear blue Caribbean Sea on the east. It covers almost 134,400 sq. km (51,892 sq. miles), with nearly 1,600km (1,000 miles) of shoreline. Underground rivers and natural wells, called cenotes, are a peculiar feature of this region.

Of course, the primary allure of the Yucatán peninsula for tourists is its long Caribbean coast, stretching the entire coast of the state of **Quintana Roo.** The swath of coast from Cancún south to **Tulum** has been dubbed the **Riviera Maya;** south from there to the Belize border is the **Costa Maya.** This coastline has an enormous array of wildlife, including hundreds of species of birds. The Gulf Coast beaches, while good enough, don't compare to those on the

FACING PAGE: **Snorkelers at Xel-Ha.**

The Caribbean Coast

Caribbean. National parks near **Celestún** and **Río Lagartos** on the Gulf Coast are home to amazing flocks of flamingos.

Things change, however, when you move inland, into the states of **Yucatán,** the northern portion of the peninsula, and **Campeche,** the western portion. The landscape is dotted by crumbling haciendas and the stark ruins of ancient cities. This is the world of the present-day Maya, where life moves slowly in simple villages bordered by rock walls and small cornfields. And in the cities and towns, such as **Mérida** and **Izamal** in Yucatán state, and **Campeche** in Campeche state, you'll find the traditional Yucatán, with its highly pronounced regional flavor, and a way of life informed by centuries-old traditions.

To present the Maya world in its entirety, this book also covers the states of **Tabasco** and **Chiapas.** The Gulf Coast state of Tabasco was once home to the Olmec, the mother culture of Mesoamerica. At Villahermosa's Parque–Museo La Venta, you can see the impressive 40-ton carved rock heads that the Olmec left behind.

San Cristóbal de las Casas, in Chiapas, inhabits cooler, greener mountains, and is more in the mold of a provincial colonial town. Approaching San Cristóbal from any direction, you see small plots of corn tended by colorfully clad Maya. The surrounding villages are home to many craftspeople, from woodcarvers to potters to weavers. In the eastern lowland jungles of Chiapas lie the classic Maya ruins of **Palenque.** Deeper into the interior, for those willing to make the trek, are the ruins of **Yaxchilán** and **Bonampak.**

NATURAL LIFE & PROTECTED AREAS The Yucatán state's nature preserves include the 47,200-hectare (116,584-acre) **Ría Lagartos Biosphere Reserve** north of Valladolid—where you'll find North America's largest flock of nesting flamingos—and the 5,600-plus-hectare (13,832-acre) **Celestún Wildlife Refuge,** which harbors most of the flamingos during non-nesting season. The state also has incorporated nature trails into the archaeological site of **Dzibilchaltún,** north of Mérida.

In 1989, Campeche state set aside 71,480 hectares (176,556 acres) in the **Calakmul Biosphere Reserve** that it shares with Guatemala. The area includes the ruins of Calakmul, as well as acres of thick jungle.

Quintana Roo's protected areas are some of the region's most wild and beautiful lands. In 1986, the state set aside the 520,000-hectare (1.3-million-acre) **Sian Ka'an Biosphere Reserve,** conserving a significant part of the coast in the face of development south of Tulum. **Isla Contoy,** also in Quintana Roo, off the coast of Isla Mujeres and Cancún, is a beautiful island refuge for hundreds of birds, turtles, plants, and other wildlife. Cozumel's **Chankanaab National Park** gives visitors an idea of the biological importance of Yucatán's lengthy shoreline: Four of Mexico's eight marine turtle species—loggerhead, green, hawksbill, and leatherback—nest on Quintana Roo's shores, and more than 600 species of birds, reptiles, and mammals have been counted.

Tabasco, though a small state, has set aside a vast preserve of wetlands called **Pantanos de Centla,** just northeast of Villahermosa. Three reserves in Chiapas encompass jungles and lakes, and some of Mexico's most bio diverse lands. The largest by far is the nature preserve called **Montes Azules,** the old homeland of the Lacandón Indians in the extreme eastern lowlands bordering Guatemala. Not far from San Cristóbal de las Casas is also a small preserve of high cloud forest habitat called **Huitepec.** A good distance west of Tuxtla Gutiérrez, the state capital, is an extensive nature preserve containing upland forests called **Selva del Ocote.**

FROM TOP: **Flamingos in Celestún Wildlife Refuge; Lush Montes Azules.**

A crowded beach in Playa del Carmen.

NORTHERN YUCATÁN IN A WEEK

You could extend this itinerary to 10 days, even 2 weeks—it all depends on how much time you want to spend on the beach. Once you've spent a little time in that clear blue water, it's hard to pull yourself away to move inland.

DAYS 1 & 2: Playa del Carmen ★ & Tulum ★★★

I recommend starting your trip in fashionable **Playa del Carmen** (p. 188), which offers gorgeous beaches and an artsy main strip called Avenida Quinta with bustling shops, cafes, and restaurants. "Playa," as it is known locally, is the gateway to **Cozumel** (p. 155), which makes for an easy day trip by ferry. **Xcaret** and **Xel-Ha** (p. 209 and 201 respectively), two outstanding eco-parks, also lie within easy driving distance. Spend your second day in any of these tempting spots or in the ancient Mayan city of **Tulum** (p. 211) visiting its beaches, ruins, and the Sian Ka'an Biosphere Reserve (p. 223).

DAY 3: Ek Balam ★★★ & Chichén Itzá ★★★

Head for the ruins of **Ek Balam** (p. 317), which lie north of the colonial city of **Valladolid** (p. 311). From Tulum, take the highway to **Cobá** (p. 219) and consider stopping first at the ruins here. When you get to Valladolid, continue north on Highway 295 to the turnoff for Ek Balam. After climbing the main pyramid and inspecting the beautifully worked sacred doorway, head back to Valladolid for a late lunch. You can then drive to Chichén Itzá via the old highway. If there's time, stop at **Cenote Dzitnup** (p. 317), just outside Valladolid. Continue on to the ancient Mayan city of **Chichén Itzá** (p. 302) and check into a hotel in the area. In the evening, see the sound-and-light show, and then visit the ruins the next morning.

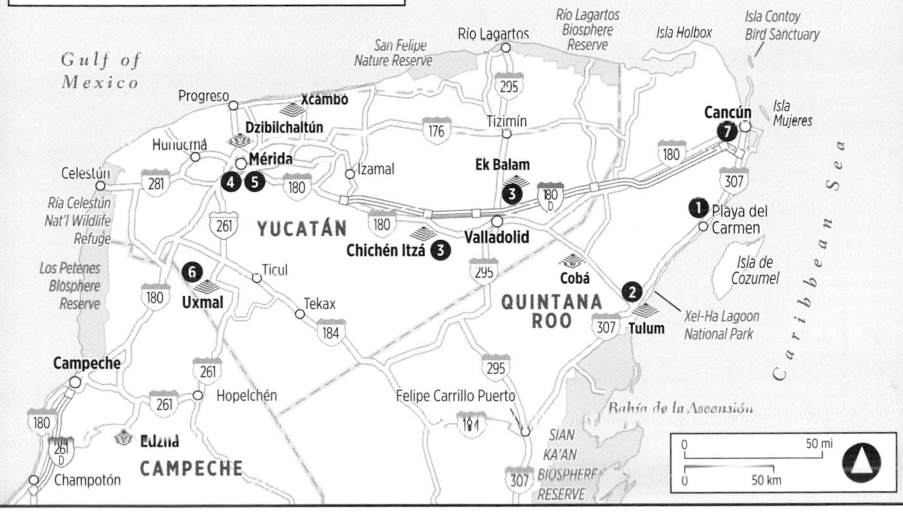

DAYS 4 & 5: Mérida ★★

After you've taken in Chichén Itzá, head west to **Mérida** (p. 248) and enjoy an evening in this bustling capital city. The next day, you can further explore the tropical town, or may wish to take a side trip during the day and enjoy Mérida in the evening. Choices include the **Celestún National Wildlife Refuge** (p. 275), where you can take a boat ride and see some pink flamingos, or the ruins of **Dzibilchaltún** (p. 276). You might also consider visiting **Progreso** and **Xcambó** (p. 277), for another good chance of seeing flamingos.

DAY 6: Uxmal ★★★

No matter whether you take the short way or the long way, try to get to **Uxmal** by late afternoon, so that you can rest and cool off before seeing the sound-and-light show at night. Uxmal's **Pyramid of the Magician** is one of the most dramatic structures in the Maya world and it becomes even more intriguing when lit at night. The next morning, you can explore the ruins in more detail. See p. 283.

DAY 7: Cancún or Puerto Morelos

This last day will necessarily include a good bit of driving. Take the short route back via Umán, then use the loop or *periférico* to avoid entering Mérida. After about 45 minutes, you'll see signs for the highway to Cancún. If you prefer to stay in a quiet beach location near Cancún, try **Puerto Morelos** (p. 177).

The ruins of Uxmal.

IF YOU HAVE even less time . . .

Given Cancún and the Riviera Maya's proximity to the United States, the vast majority of visitors to this region are weekenders and snowbirds from the East Coast looking for a quick beach fix. Of course, that's what Cancún was made for and even if you have a mere 3 days, you can still experience a taste of what this fascinating region has to offer.

Here are a few suggestions if you're prepared to leave the beach cabaña of your resort and explore a bit of the area. Ease yourself into a state of relaxation by spending a day and perhaps a night in sleepy **Isla Mujeres** (p. 139), just 15 minutes by ferry from Cancún; or check in to a seriously luxurious **spa resort** just 20 minutes south of Cancún (p. 114). A more ambitious beach vacation would have you head a couple hours south to stylish **Playa del Carmen** (p. 188) and then to either **Tulum** (p. 211) or **Cozumel** (p. 155). For a bit of culture off the beach, you can easily do a half-day trip to the unforgettable Mayan ruins of **Chichén Itzá** (p. 302), stopping for lunch and a stroll in colonial **Valladolid** (p. 311). Since Cancún's **nightlife** is legendary (p. 135), you may want to spend at least one evening in this world-famous resort partying the night away.

THE YUCATÁN IN 2 WEEKS

The Yucatán's quality roads and fairly contained shape allow for a complete circuit of the peninsula within a 2-week time frame. By moving counterclockwise, you'll save the best beach time for the end of your trip. This is a packed itinerary, and can be done at a more relaxed pace if you leave out Palenque and San Cristóbal de las Casas in Chiapas. Plan on arriving in and departing from Cancún.

DAY 1: Ría Lagartos Biosphere Reserve ★, Ek Balam ★★★ & Valladolid ★

Begin with a trip from Cancún to **Ría Lagartos** (p. 318), at the peninsula's northern tip, where you can take a boat tour of the wildlife sanctuary, explore the mangrove and saltwater estuaries as well as lakes filled with pink flamingos, pelicans, eagles, and other species. After taking a swim, head south on Highway 295 toward the ruins of **Ek Balam** (p. 317), noted for a beautifully sculpted sacred doorway on the tallest pyramid in northern Yucatán. Spend the night in **Valladolid** (p. 311).

DAY 2: Cenote Dzitnup ★ & Chichén Itzá ★★★

Shortly after leaving Valladolid on the old highway, stop to enjoy **Cenote Dzitnup** (p. 317). Continue on to the fascinating ruins of **Chichén Itzá** (p. 302). If you wish to stay near Chichén Itzá, you can watch a surreal sound-and-light show in the evening.

DAY 3: Izamal & Mérida ★★

The next day, go west to **Izamal** (p. 273), to visit the few remaining Mayan buildings, main square, and local market before continuing on to

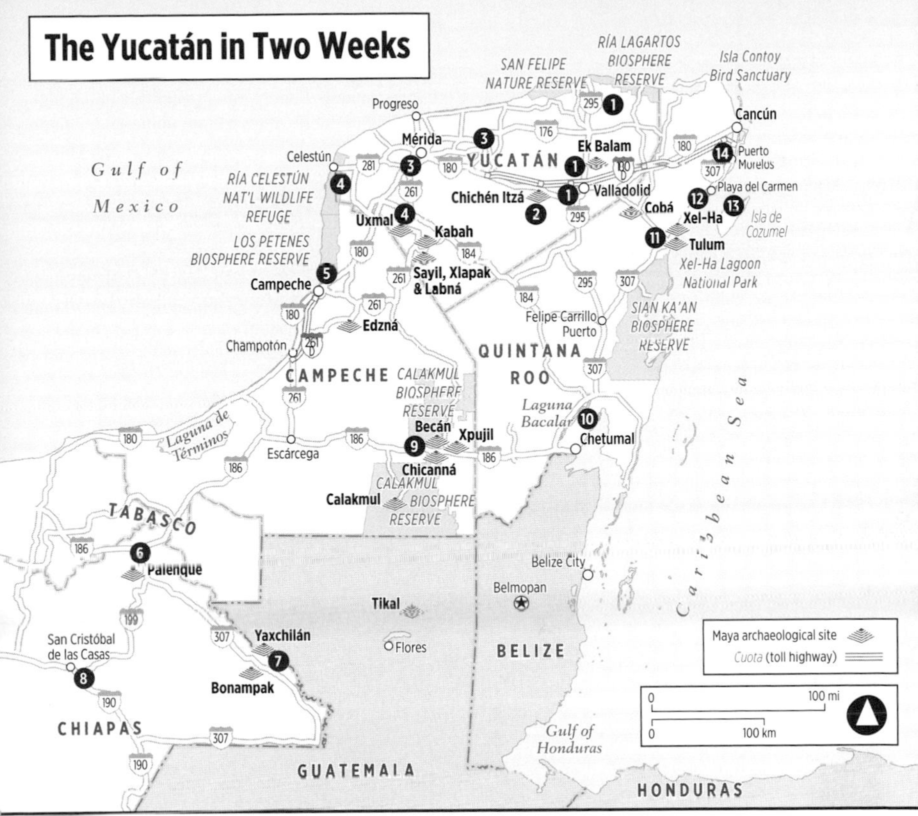

Mérida (p. 248), the region's cultural center. Get an overview of Mérida on a bus/trolley tour and stroll the main plaza surrounded by 500-year-old buildings, built from the stone of Mayan pyramids torn down by the Spanish Conquistadors. Each evening, free cultural events take place in the historic district. Sunday is a big day for festivities that last all day.

DAY 4: Celestún & Uxmal ★★★

From Mérida, **Celestún** (p. 275) is an easy day trip where travelers can combine a half-day on the beach with a boat trip to see flocks of flamingos in the ecological biosphere. From there, head south to the Mayan ruins of **Uxmal** (p. 283). If you're driving, choose from two different routes (p. 279) that take you past tiny Maya villages, crumbling Spanish haciendas, and more archaeological finds. Check into a hotel near Uxmal and tour the ruins; return in the evening for the light show. Explore the ruins further the next morning, when the temperature is much cooler.

DAY 5: Campeche ★

Campeche (p. 292) is the best-preserved walled city in the Americas. The United Nations declared it a World Heritage Site in 2000, which secures protection for its narrow cobblestone streets and colonial-era buildings, painted in pastel colors. Check in and rest up: The next 3 days involve lots of road time.

DAYS 6, 7 & 8: Palenque & San Cristóbal de las Casas

Head south on Highways 180, 186, and finally 199 to **Palenque** (p. 328). You can explore the magnificent pyramids here and, if you like, also see the ruins of **Bonampak** and **Yaxchilán** (p. 336), the next day. Spend one night in Palenque and the second night in **San Cristóbal de las Casas** (p. 339), the most interesting city in Chiapas. From San Cristóbal, go with one of the local guides to see the fascinating Mayan communities of **San Juan Chamula** and **Zinacantán** (p. 347).

DAY 9: Calakmul, Xpujil & the Río Bec Ruins

Leave San Cristóbal early to head back up Highway 186 to the Calakmul Biosphere Reserve. It's a long drive through Escárcega to **Xpujil** (p. 240) and the ruins of the **Río Bec** area (p. 236). Easy-to-access local ruins are Xpujil, Chicanná, and Becán. The ruins of **Calakmul** (p. 242) are perhaps the Yucatán's most mysterious and difficult to reach—a 90-minute drive off the highway. The best way to see these ruins is to overnight in Xpujil or the eco-village of Chicanná and set out at dawn. If you decide to go to Calakmul, devote an extra day.

DAY 10: Lago Bacalar ★

Xpujil marks the geographic halfway point; from here you're on your way back to Cancún. Head west to **Lago Bacalar** (p. 232), and stop on the way to see the stone masks in the **Kohunlich** ruins (p. 239), and then have a late lunch in **Chetumal** (p. 234). Spend the night 37km (23 miles) north of the city at **Rancho Encantado** (p. 233), a lovely eco-lodge on the edge of Lago Bacalar.

Campeche's main square.

Lago Bacalar at sunset.

The Tulum ruins.

DAY 11: Tulum ★★

After an hour-and-a-half drive's north to **Tulum** (p. 211), you'll reach one of Mexico's most alluring Caribbean towns. Plan to spend a night at a beach hotel, allowing time to visit the **Tulum ruins** (p. 283) and check out the incredible beach in front of them. Also consider a nature tour of the **Sian Ka'an Biosphere** (p. 223), just south of town, with one of the local collectives of guides.

DAYS 12 & 13: Playa del Carmen ★ & Cozumel

Take the drive up to **Playa del Carmen** (p. 188), which can serve as a base to explore cenotes or even the ruins of **Cobá** (p. 219). Playa is a chic town with a somewhat European flavor; be sure to allow yourself time to take in the cobblestone Avenida Quinta.

The next morning, you can take the ferry to **Cozumel** (p. 155) for a day trip of diving, snorkeling, swimming with dolphins, or simply enjoying the beach. Stay for an early dinner and return to Playa for the night.

DAY 14: Puerto Morelos

Spend your last day in **Puerto Morelos** (p. 177), a slow-paced beach town just 31km (20 miles) south of Cancún.

AN ECO-ADVENTURE FOR THE WHOLE FAMILY

If you've got your own mask and snorkel (and fins, too) bring them for this trip; you can always get rentals, but you're better off with gear that fits well.

DAY 1: The Lower Riviera Maya

For this itinerary, I recommend staying in the lower Riviera Maya in or near **Playa del Carmen** (p. 188) or **Tulum** (p. 211). That puts you close to most of the places you'll be visiting. The drive from the airport to this part of the coast is at most 2 hours.

DAY 2: Xel-Ha & the Ruins of Tulum ★★★

Spend a day snorkeling, swimming, and frolicking in **Xel-Ha**'s natural lagoons and open-sea aquarium (p. 209). You can stay here the entire day or combine this with a trip to see the mystical ruins in **Tulum** (which you should do in the morning, when the air is cooler). See p. 283.

DAY 3: Hidden Worlds ★★★ & Aktun Chen ★

Between Akumal and Tulum are two attractions, each interesting in its own way. At **Hidden Worlds** (p. 211), you can snorkel in cenotes and subterranean rivers. Wet suits and snorkel gear are provided if you don't bring your own. **Aktun Chen** (p. 209) is a cavern that you can hike through and see lots of rock formations. The small zoo houses local species such as spider monkeys and tropical birds.

DAY 4: Alltournative

Consider spending today with **Alltournative,** an adventure tour agency based in Playa del Carmen. Its day trips combine adventure with nature

Xel-Ha Lagoon.

An Eco-Adventure for the Whole Family

and interactions with contemporary Maya in one of their own villages. The tour company will pick you up at almost any hotel in the Riviera Maya. See p. 79.

DAY 5: Sian Ka'an Biosphere Reserve ★

Explore the largest wildlife preserve in the Yucatán; snorkel down canals built by the Maya, visit the large, pristine lagoon at the center of the park, and observe various forms of wildlife as you get an up-close-and-personal view of the peninsula's natural habitat. See p. 223.

DAY 6: Chichén Itzá ★★★

Go for a morning snorkel trip with one of the local dive shops, and then drive to **Chichén Itzá** in the afternoon. Check into a hotel, and in the evening you can enjoy the sound-and-light show at the ruins. Return the next morning to get a closer look in daylight. See p. 302.

DAY 7: Cenote Dzitnup ★, Ek Balam ★★★ & Ría Lagartos Nature Reserve ★

After seeing the ruins, head east on the old federal highway until you get to **Cenote Dzitnup** (p. 317), shortly before the town of Valladolid. You'll find a dark cenote with a beautiful pool of water illuminated by a column of sunlight that penetrates the roof. Nearby is a second cenote. After a quick dip, continue into **Valladolid** (p. 311) for lunch. After you're nourished, head north on Highway 295 to the turnoff for the ruins of **Ek Balam** (p. 317), a remarkable pre-Columbian archaeological site. Then continue north, past the town of Tizimín, until you get to the coastal village of **Río Lagartos.** Check-in to one of the economical hotels fronting the water and arrange for an early-morning boat tour of the wildlife sanctuary. See p. 318.

DAY 8: Cancún

After your visit with pink flamingos, it's time to get back to Cancún and civilization. See chapter 5.

LA RUTA MAYA

This route, which connects the major Maya sites in Mexico, could be done moving quickly over 2 weeks, or more slowly in a month or perhaps broken up into two trips. I've condensed the trip by leaving out Mérida, but you may want to visit the beautiful Yucatán capital. There's a risk of overdosing on ruins by seeing too many in too short a time, so feel free to pick and choose at your own pace. The best mode of travel is by rental car: The highways have little traffic and are, for the most part, in good shape.

DAY 1: Cancún

After you arrive, enjoy the rest of the day with a swim in the Caribbean or an afternoon by the pool. See chapter 5.

DAY 2: Ek Balam ★★★ & Chichén Itzá ★★★

Get on the modern toll highway that heads toward Mérida and take the exit for Valladolid. Head north, away from town, to visit the ruins of **Ek Balam** (p. 317). Then head back to **Valladolid** (p. 311) for lunch before driving the short distance to **Chichén Itzá** (p. 302). Just outside of Valladolid, stop to see the cenotes of **Dzitnup** and **Sammulá** (for both, see p. 317). Further on is the **Balankanché Cave** (p. 311). When you get to Chichén Itzá, check into your hotel, and then go to the **ruins** later in the evening for the sound-and-light show. See p. 302.

DAY 3: Uxmal ★★★

Spend more time at the ruins of **Chichén Itzá** in the morning, then continue west on the toll highway toward Mérida, and turn off at Ticopó. Head south toward the town of **Acanceh** (p. 280) and Highway 18. Stop to see the small but interesting ruins in the middle of town, and then proceed down

Chichén Itzá ruins.

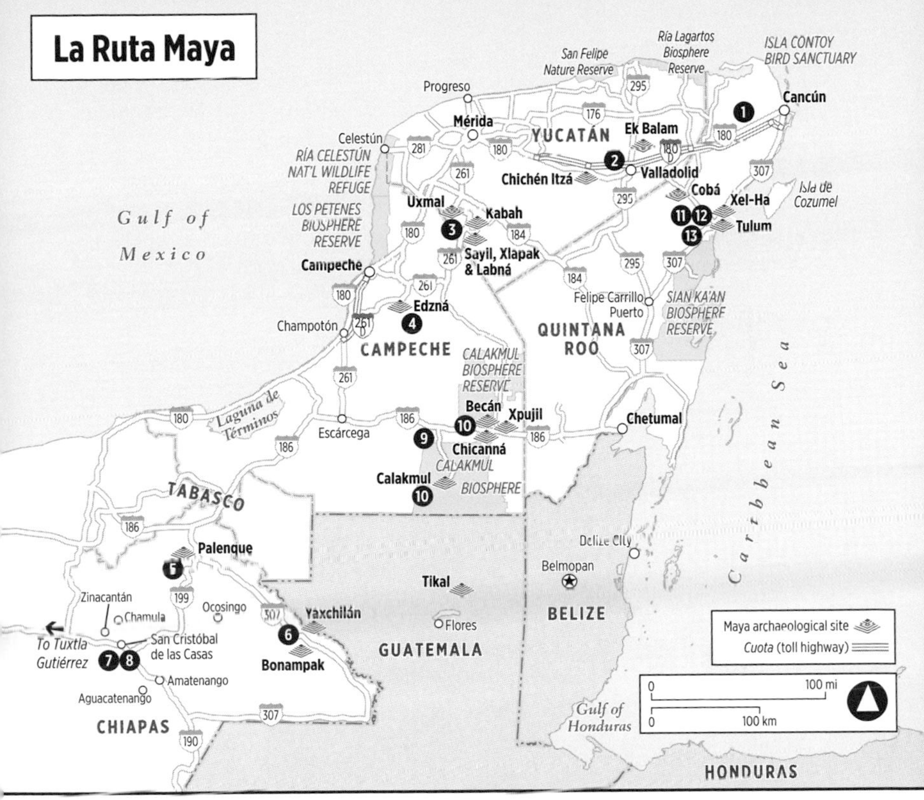

Highway 18 to the ruins of **Mayapán** (p. 281). Afterward, continue through Ticul to Santa Elena and **Uxmal** (p. 283) for the sound-and-light show.

DAY 4: Edzná

Visit **Uxmal** (p. 283) in the morning, then drive back toward Santa Elena and take Highway 261 south to Hopelchén and on to the impressive ruins of **Edzná** (p. 301). Nearby is a fancy hacienda-turned-hotel, called **Uayamón** (p. 261). Better still, stay at the sister property in old-town Campeche, **Hacienda Puerta Campeche** (p. 298). Or choose from several more modest digs.

DAYS 5 & 6: Palenque ★★, Bonampak & Yaxchilán

Stay on Highway 261 to Escárcega, then head west on Highway 186 toward Villahermosa, then south on Highway 199 to the town of **Palenque** (p. 328) with its magnificent pyramids. The next day go to the ruins of **Bonampak** and **Yaxchilán** (p. 336).

DAYS 7 & 8: San Cristóbal de las Casas ★★

Keep south on Highway 199 toward **San Cristóbal de las Casas** (p. 339). On the way, take a swim at **Misol Ha** (p. 337), and visit the ruins of

Toniná (p. 338) outside of Ocosingo. From San Cristóbal, go with one of the local guides to see the Maya communities of **San Juan Chamula** and **Zinacantán** (p. 347).

DAY 9: Calakmul ★★★

Retrace your steps to Escárcega and continue east on Highway 186. If you have time, visit the fascinating sculptures of **Balamkú** (p. 245). Spend the night at one of the hotels in the vicinity of the turnoff for **Calakmul,** one of the prime city-states of the Classic age of the Maya, and not often visited.

DAY 10: Calakmul & Becán ★★★

Get to **Calakmul** (p. 242) early. Keep your eyes open for wildlife as you drive along a narrow jungle road. All the area surrounding the city is a wildlife preserve. Afterward, continue east on Highway 186 to see the ruins of **Becán** (p. 241), a large ceremonial center with tall temples. Also in the vicinity are **Xpujil** (p. 240) and **Chicanná** (p. 242). Spend the night on the shores of **Lake Bacalar** (p. 232), where you can cool off in its blue waters.

DAYS 11, 12 & 13: Tulum

Drive north on Highway 307 to **Tulum** and settle into one of the small beach hotels there. In the morning, walk through the ruins and enjoy the lovely view of the coast. On your last day, depending on your schedule, you can enjoy some more beach time, or head straight to the airport (25 min. south of Cancún) and depart.

The San Cristóbal de las Casas cathedral.

The Calakmul ruins, located in a dense jungle.

CANCÚN

by Shane Christensen

5

It may be commercialized and more American than Mexican in design, but Cancún remains one of the finest resort destinations in the world—with breathtaking beaches and enough pleasure-pursuits to make even the most unrelenting hedonists blush. And while Cancún may be a top travel destination for Americans and other Western travelers who flock here like sun-seeking swallows in winter and spring, it's also a favorite for Mexicans who come to holiday year-round.

Due to Cancún's ideal mix of elements—its transparent turquoise sea, powdery white sand, and immense potential for growth—a group of Mexican government computer analysts targeted the town for tourism development in 1974, transforming it from a deserted beach area to a five-star resort. Since then, Cancún has sustained the devastations of hurricanes and other powerful tropical storms, only to emerge stronger and more irresistible. In the wake of Hurricane Wilma, which tore through the Yucatán peninsula in 2005, wreckage rapidly gave way to exacting renovations, luxurious upgrades, and brand-new destinations. Today Cancún is better than ever.

The double whammy of the worldwide economic crisis and worries caused by swine flu has not made for an easy time in Cancún in the past couple years. Hotels, restaurants, and tourist services across the board have suffered here, just as they have elsewhere in the region. But what's amazing to me is the resilience of Cancún's tourist industry, and the high hopes for all those involved of a hefty rebound. And as of press time that rebound seems to be gathering steam.

The allure hasn't changed much over the years—it's still the spectacular Caribbean beach. Cancún (which means "golden snake" in Mayan) stretches from the downtown area known as Cancún City east to the Hotel Zone, also known as Isla Cancún, which is a narrow 24-km (15-mile) island that runs southwest and is framed on one side by the beautiful Caribbean Sea and on the other by the picturesque Nichupté lagoon.

Cancún is home to breathtaking resorts; an unrivaled range of shopping, dining, and nightlife; and endless outdoor activities. Air travel is easy, with major airlines flying here from destinations across Mexico, the United States, Canada, and Europe. And it's a gateway to the nearby ruins of Tulum, Chichén Itzá, and Cobá.

Cancún embodies Caribbean splendor and the exotic joys of Mexico, but even a Western traveler feeling apprehensive about visiting foreign soil will feel completely at ease here. English is spoken and dollars accepted; roads are well paved and lawns manicured. Some travelers are surprised to find that Cancún is more like a U.S. beach resort than a part of Mexico. Indeed, signs of Americanism are rampant. U.S. college students continue to descend in droves during spring break—which, depending on your perspective, may be reason to rush headlong into the party or stay far, far away during this season. One astonishing statistic suggests that more Americans travel to Cancún than to any other foreign

PREVIOUS PAGE: **An infinity pool overlooking the Caribbean Sea.**

Sunbathers on a Cancún beach.

destination in the world. Indeed, almost three million people visit annually—most of them on their first trip to Mexico.

You won't find much in the way of authentic Mexican charm in the Hotel Zone, although you can get a glimpse of this in Cancún City, where most of the local population lives. You'll find good value hotels, a number of outstanding traditional restaurants, and some excellent shopping here. Cancún is also a convenient distance from the more traditional Mexican resorts of Isla Mujeres and the coastal stretch known as the Riviera Maya making for easy day trips.

You will likely run out of vacation days before you run out of things to do in Cancún. Snorkeling, dolphin swims, jungle tours, and visits to ancient Maya ruins and modern ecological theme parks are among the most popular diversions. A dozen malls sell name-brand and duty-free goods (with European imports for less than in the U.S.). With tens of thousands of hotel rooms and more than 350 restaurants and nightclubs, there's something for every taste and budget.

A day here could easily combine time at the pool or beach with a nearby excursion. After soaking up the sun, you might want to browse some of the shops or head for a sunset cocktail. Choose a restaurant for fresh Caribbean seafood or creative Mexican cuisine before heading to a tequila bar or chill lounge to get the night started. Then end up at a rocking bar or dance club filled with nighttime revelers who can't bear going to sleep until the dawn.

Cancún's luxury hotels have swimming pools so spectacular that you may find it tempting to turn into what I'd like to call a pool potato—but don't. Set aside some time to get yourself to the beach and wriggle your toes in the fine, brilliant white sand. It is, after all, what put Cancún on the map—and no tempest of nature has been able to sweep it away.

ORIENTATION

Getting There

BY PLANE If this is not your first trip to Cancún, you'll notice that the **airport**'s (✆ **998/848-7200**) facilities and services continue to expand. Most international flights, including those to and from the U.S. (except for JetBlue, which uses Terminal 2), now go through the new Terminal 3, which has money-exchange services, duty-free shops, restaurants, medical services, an express spa, and even a welcome bar serving beer and margaritas just outside the terminal. **Aeroméxico** (✆ **800/237-6639** in the U.S., or 01-800/021-4000 in Mexico; www.aeromexico.com) operates connecting service to Cancún through Mexico City. **Mexicana** (✆ **800/531-7921** in the U.S., 01-800/801-2010 in Mexico, or 998/881-9090; www.mexicana.com) runs connecting flights to Cancún through Miami or Mexico City. In addition to these carriers, many **charter** companies—such as Apple Vacations (www.applevacations.com) and Funjet (www.funjet.com)—travel to Cancún; these package tours make up as much as half of arrivals by U.S. visitors.

Regional carrier **Click Mexicana,** a Mexicana affiliate (✆ **01-800/112-5425** in Mexico; www.mexicana.com), flies from Havana, Cuba, and Chetumal, Cozumel, Mexico City, Mérida, and other points within Mexico. You'll want to confirm departure times for flights to the U.S. **Interjet** (✆ **01-800/01-12345** in Mexico; www.interjet.com.mx) and **Volaris** (✆ **01-800/122-8000** in Mexico; www.volaris.com.mx) are two other regional carriers that fly to Cancún from Mexico City. Domestic flights generally use Terminal 1, and flights to and from other destinations in Latin America use Terminal 2.

An aerial view of the Cancún Hotel Zone.

The following major international carriers serve Cancún: **Alaska** (✆ 800/426-0333 in the U.S.; www.alaskaair.com), **American** (✆ 800/433-7300 in the U.S.; www.aa.com), **Continental** (✆ 800/231-0856 in the U.S.; www.continental.com), **Delta** (✆ 800/221-1212 in the U.S.; www.delta.com), **Frontier** (✆ 800/432-1359 in the U.S.; www.frontierairlines.com), **JetBlue** (✆ 800/538-2583 in the U.S.; www.jetblue.com), **Spirit** (✆ 800/225-2525 in the U.S.; www.spiritair.com), **United** (✆ 800/772-7117 in the U.S.; www.united.com), and **US Airways** (✆ 800/428-4322 in the U.S.; www.usairways.com).

Most major car-rental firms have outlets at the airport, so if you're renting a car, consider picking it up and dropping it off at the airport, to save on airport-transportation costs. Another way to save money is to arrange for the rental before you leave home. If you wait until you arrive, the daily cost will be around $50 to $75 for a compact vehicle. Major agencies include **Alamo** (✆ 800/462-5266 in the U.S., or 998/886-0448; www.alamo.com), **Avis** (✆ 800/331-1212 in the U.S., or 998/886-0221; www.avis.com), **Budget** (✆ 800/527-0700 in the U.S., or 998/886-0417; fax 998/884-4812; www.budget.com), **Hertz** (✆ 800/654-3131 in the U.S. and Canada, or 998/884-1326; www.hertz.com), **National** (✆ 800/227-7368 in the U.S., or 998/886-0153; www.nationalcar.com), and **Thrifty** (✆ 800/847-4389 in the U.S., or 998/886-0333; www.thrifty.com). The Zona Hotelera (Hotel Zone) lies 10km (6¼ miles)—a 20-minute drive—from the airport along wide, well-paved roads.

The rate for a **private taxi** from the airport is $60 to Ciudad Cancún (downtown) or the Hotel Zone. The return trip with an airport taxi is discounted by 50%. Green Line and Gray Line **van shuttles** (✆ **01-800/021-9097;** www.graylinecancun.com) run from the airport into town approximately every 20 minutes. Buy tickets, which cost about $15, from the booth to the far right as you exit the airport. These services accept U.S. dollars, though you'll get a more favorable rate if you pay in pesos. **Local bus** transportation on ADO (40 pesos) goes from the airport to Ciudad Cancún. From there, you can take another bus for less than a dollar to Puerto Juárez, where passenger ferries leave to Isla Mujeres regularly. There is no shuttle service returning to the airport from Ciudad Cancún or the Hotel Zone, so you'll have to take a taxi, but the rate will be much less than for the trip from the airport. (Only federally chartered taxis may take fares *from* the airport, but any taxi may bring passengers *to* the airport.) Ask at your hotel what the fare should be, but expect to pay about half what you paid from the airport to your hotel.

BY CAR From Mérida or Campeche, take **Highway 180** east to Cancún. This is mostly a winding, two-lane road that branches off into the express **toll road 180D** between Izamal and Nuevo Xcan. Nuevo Xcan is approximately 40km (25 miles) from Cancún. Mérida is about 320km (198 miles) away.

BY BUS Cancún's **ADO bus terminal** (✆ **01-800/702-8000** or 998/884-4352; www.ado.com.mx) is in downtown Ciudad Cancún at the intersection of avenidas Tulum and Uxmal. All out-of-town buses arrive here. Buses run to Playa del Carmen, Tulum, Chichén Itzá, other nearby beach and archaeological zones, and other points within Mexico. ADO buses also operate between the airport and downtown.

Visitor Information

The **Cancún Municipal Tourism Office** is downtown at Avenida Nader at the corner of Avenida Cobá (✆ **998/887-3379**). It's open Monday through Friday from 8am to 6pm, Saturday from 9am to 2pm. The office lists hotels and their rates, as well as ferry schedules. For information prior to your arrival in Cancún, visit the Convention Bureau's website, **www.cancun.travel**. The state tourism website is in Spanish, at www.qroo.gob.mx.

Pick up copies of the free booklet ***Cancún Tips*** (www.cancuntips.com.mx), and a seasonal tabloid of the same name.

City Layout

There are really two Cancúns: **Ciudad Cancún (Cancún City)** and **Isla Cancún (Cancún Island).** Ciudad Cancún, on the mainland, is the original downtown area, where most of the local population lives. It's home to traditional restaurants, shops, and less expensive hotels, as well as pharmacies, dentists, automotive shops, banks, travel and airline agencies, and car-rental firms—all within an area about 9 square blocks. The city's main thoroughfare is **Avenida Tulum.** Heading south, Avenida Tulum becomes the highway to the airport and to Tulum and Chetumal; heading north, it intersects the highway to Mérida and the road to Puerto Juárez and the Isla Mujeres ferries.

Isla Cancún is a sandy strip 22km (14 miles) long, shaped like a 7. It's home to the famed **Zona Hotelera,** or Hotel Zone (also called the Zona Turística, or Tourist Zone), connected to the mainland by the Playa Linda Bridge at the north end and the Punta Nizuc Bridge at the southern end. Between the two areas lies Laguna Nichupté. Avenida Cobá from Cancún City becomes Bulevar Kukulkán, the island's main traffic artery. Cancún's international airport is just inland from the south end of the island.

the best websites FOR CANCÚN

- **All About Cancún: www.cancunmx.com** This site is a good place to start planning. Their database, called "The Online Experts," answers many of the most common questions. It's slow but current, with input from lots of recent travelers to the region.
- **Cancún Convention & Visitors Bureau: www.cancun.travel** The official site of the Cancún Convention & Visitors Bureau lists excellent information on events and attractions. Its hotel guide is one of the most complete available and includes events and news related to Cancún.
- **Cancún Online: www.cancun.com** This comprehensive guide has lots of information about things to do and see in Cancún, though most details come from paying advertisers. The site lets you reserve package trips, accommodations, activities, and tee times.
- **Cancún Travel Guide: www.go2cancun.com** These online information specialists are also an excellent resource for Cancún rentals, hotels, and attractions. Note that this site lists only paying advertisers, which means you'll find most of the major players here.

FINDING AN ADDRESS Cancún City's street-numbering system is a holdover. Addresses are still given by the number of the building lot and by the *manzana* (block) or *supermanzana* (group of blocks). The city is relatively compact, and the downtown commercial section is easy to cover on foot.

On the island, addresses are given by kilometer number on Bulevar Kukulkán or by reference to some well-known location. In Cancún, streets are named after famous Maya cities. Boulevards are named for nearby archaeological sites, Chichén Itzá, Tulum, and Uxmal.

Getting Around

BY TAXI Taxi prices in Cancún are clearly set by zone, although keeping track of what's in which zone can take some doing. The minimum fare within the Hotel Zone is 70 pesos per ride, making it one of the most expensive taxi areas in Mexico. In addition, taxis operating in the Hotel Zone feel perfectly justified in having a discriminatory pricing structure: Local residents pay about half of what tourists pay, and prices for guests at higher-priced hotels are about double those for budget hotel guests—these are all established by the taxi union. Rates should be posted outside your hotel; if you have a question, all drivers are required to have an official rate card in their taxis, though it's generally in Spanish. Taxi drivers will accept dollars, though at a less favorable rate than pesos.

Within the downtown area, the cost is about 20 pesos per cab ride (not per person); within any other zone, it's 70 to 110 pesos. It'll cost about 180 pesos to travel between the Hotel Zone and downtown. Settle on a price in advance, or check at your hotel. Trips to the airport from most zones cost about 280 pesos (up to 4 people). Taxis can also be rented for 250 pesos per hour for travel around the city and Hotel Zone. To hire a taxi to take you to Chichén Itzá or along the Riviera Maya, you'll pay about 350 pesos per hour—many taxi drivers feel that they are also providing guide services.

BY BUS Bus travel within Cancún continues to improve and is increasingly popular. In town, almost everything lies within walking distance. **Ruta 1** and **Ruta 2** (HOTELES) city buses travel frequently from Puerto Juárez on the mainland to the beaches along Avenida Tulum (the main street) and all the way to Punta Nizuc at the far end of the Hotel Zone on Isla Cancún. **Ruta 8** buses go to Puerto Juárez/Punta Sam for ferries to Isla Mujeres. They stop on the east side of Avenida Tulum. All these city buses run between 6am and 10pm daily. Buses also go up and down the main strip of the Hotel Zone day and night. Public buses have the fare painted on the front; at press time, the fare was 7.50 pesos.

A Ruta 2 bus heading to the Hotel Zone.

BY SCOOTER Scooters are a convenient but dangerous way to cruise through the very congested traffic. Rentals start at about $30 for a day, not including insurance, and a credit card voucher is required as security. You should receive a crash helmet (it's the law) and instructions on how to lock the wheels when you park. Read the fine print on the back of the rental agreement regarding liability for repairs or replacement in case of accident, theft, or vandalism.

Area Code The telephone area code is **998.**

[Fast FACTS] CANCÚN

ATMs & Banks Most banks sit downtown along Avenida Tulum and are usually open Monday through Friday from 9am to 3pm, although some are open later and even half the day on Saturday. Many have ATMs for after-hours cash withdrawals. In the Hotel Zone, you'll find an HSBC bank in Kukulcán Plaza that's open Monday through Saturday from 9am to 7pm.

Consulates The **U.S. Consular Agent** is in the Plaza Caracol Dos, Bl. Kukulkán Km 8.5, 3rd level, 320–323 (✆ **998/883-0272;** cancunagency@gmail.com); open Monday through Friday from 9am to 2pm. The **Canadian Consulate** is in the Plaza Caracol Dos, 3rd level, Loc. 330 (✆ **998/883-3360;** cancun@canada.org.mx); open Monday through Friday from 9am to 3:30pm. The **United Kingdom** has a consular office at the Royal Sands Hotel (✆ **998/881-0100;** information@britishconsulatecancun.com); open Monday through Friday from 9am to 5pm. Irish, Australian, and New Zealand citizens should contact their embassies in Mexico City.

Crime Car break-ins are just about the only frequent crime here. They happen repeatedly, especially around the shopping centers in the Hotel Zone. Rapes have also been reported in Cancún. Most have taken place at night or in the early morning.

Currency Exchange Cancún has many *casas de cambio* (exchange houses). Downtown merchants are eager to change cash dollars, but island stores don't offer very good exchange rates. Avoid changing money at the airport as you arrive, especially at the first exchange booth you see—its rates are less favorable than those of any in town or others farther inside the airport. Dollars are widely accepted throughout Cancún.

Drugstores Across the street from Señor Frog's in the Hotel Zone, at Bulevar Kukulkán Km 9.5, **Farmacías del Ahorro** (✆ **998/892-7291**) is open from 7am to 11pm. Plenty of drugstores are in the major shopping malls in the Hotel Zone and are open until 10pm. In downtown Cancún, **Farmacía Cancún** is located at Av. Tulum 17 (✆ **998/884-1283**). It's open Monday to Saturday from 9am to 10pm, and Sunday from 10am to 10pm. You can stock up on over-the-counter and many prescription drugs without a prescription.

Emergencies The local **Red Cross** (✆ **998/884-1616**), is open 24 hours on Av. Yaxchilán between avenidas Xcaret and Labná, next to the Telmex building.

Hospital **Galenia Hospital** is one of the city's most modern, offering full emergency and other services with excellent care, at Av. Tulum, SM 12, at Nizuc (✆ **998/891-5200;** www.hospitalgalenia.com). **AMAT,** Av. Nader 13, SM 2, at Avenida Uxmal (✆ **998/887-4422**), is a small emergency hospital with some English-speaking doctors open 24 hours. Desk staff may have limited command of English. **U.S. Air Ambulance** (Global Ambulance) service is available by calling ✆ **800/948-1214** in the U.S., or 01-800/305-9400 in Mexico (www.usair ambulance.net).

Internet Access All of **Kukulcán Plaza,** Bl. Kukulkán Km 13, offers free Wi-Fi. You'll need to pick up a password at Customer Services, near the main entrance. Also in Kukulcán Plaza, **Cyber Terrace** offers computers with Internet access for 60 pesos per hour. There's a cafe here, and it's open daily from 10am to 10pm. Most hotels now have Internet access, and five-star hotels have business centers.

Luggage Storage & Lockers Hotels will generally tag and store luggage while you travel elsewhere.

Newspapers & Magazines Most hotel gift shops and newsstands carry English-language magazines and English-language, Mexican-edition newspapers, such as *USA Today. Cancún Tips* (www.cancuntips.com.mx) is an entertainment magazine that offers descriptions of local activities, maps, and tourist information.

Police Dial ✆ **066** for the police in an emergency. Cancún also has a fleet of English-speaking tourist police to help travelers. Dial ✆ **998/885-2277.** The **Procuraduría Federal del Consumidor ("Profeco," the consumer protection agency),** Av. Cobá 9–11 (✆ **998/884-2634**), is opposite the Social Security Hospital and upstairs from the Fenix drugstore. It's open Monday through Friday from 9am to 3pm.

Post Office The main *correo* lies at the intersection of avenidas Sunyaxchen and Xel-Ha (✆ **998/884-1418**). It's open Monday through Friday from 9am to 4pm, and Saturday from 9am to noon for the purchase of stamps only.

Seasons Technically, high season runs from December 15 to April; low season extends from May to December 15, when prices drop 10% to 30%. Some hotels are starting to charge high-season rates during June and July, when Mexican, European, and school-holiday visitors often travel, although rates may still be lower than in winter months.

Weather It's hot but not overwhelmingly humid. The rainy season is May through October. August to November is hurricane season, which brings erratic weather. November through February is generally sunny but can also be cloudy, windy, somewhat rainy, and even cool.

WHERE TO STAY

Island hotels—almost all of them offering modern facilities and English-speaking staffs—line the beach like concrete dominoes. Extravagance is the byword in the newer hotels. Some hotels, while exclusive, affect a more relaxed attitude. The water on the upper end of the island facing Bahía de Mujeres is placid, while beaches lining the long side of the island facing the Caribbean are subject to choppier water and crashing waves on windy days. (For more information on swimming safety, see "Beaches, Watersports & Boat Tours," later in this chapter.) Be aware that the farther south you go on the island, the longer it takes (20–30 min. in traffic) to get back to the "action spots," which are primarily between the Plaza Flamingo and Punta Cancún on the island and along Avenida Tulum on the mainland.

The "concrete dominoes" of Cancún's Hotel Zone.

Following Hurricane Wilma's devastation, the news item that received the most coverage was the destruction of Cancún's famed white-sand beaches. Immediately following the storm, literally all of the sand was washed away from the northern border of Isla Cancún, and from Punta Cancún. The Mexican government has since made a series of efforts to pump the dislocated sand back to the beach, most recently in late 2009. The southern beaches of Isla Cancún actually benefited from the storm, and now they have especially wide beachfronts.

Almost all major hotel chains have real estate on Cancún Island (the "Hotel Zone"). The reality is that Cancún is so popular as a **package destination** from the U.S. that prices and special deals are often the deciding factor for consumers rather than loyalty to any one hotel brand. Ciudad Cancún offers independently owned, smaller, less-expensive lodging. For condo, home, and villa rentals, check with **Cancún Hideaways** (**✆ 817/522-4466;** www.cancun-hideaways.com), an American company specializing in luxury properties, downtown apartments, and condos—many at prices much lower than comparable hotel stays. Owner Maggie Rodriguez, a former resident of Cancún, has made this niche market her specialty.

The hotel listings in this chapter begin on Cancún Island and finish in Cancún City (the real downtown), where bargain lodgings are available. Unless otherwise indicated, parking is free at Cancún's hotels.

Isla Cancún

VERY EXPENSIVE

Aqua ★★ Resurrected after being destroyed by Hurricane Wilma in 2005, Aqua once again stands at the pinnacle of Cancún's hotel scene. The ultramodern resort— New Age music seems to be piped in from each corner, behind every palm tree, and around the eight tempting pools—attracts a chic clientele pampered by an exceptionally gracious staff. The spa is outstanding, with indoor and outdoor treatments that incorporate the best techniques from around the globe.

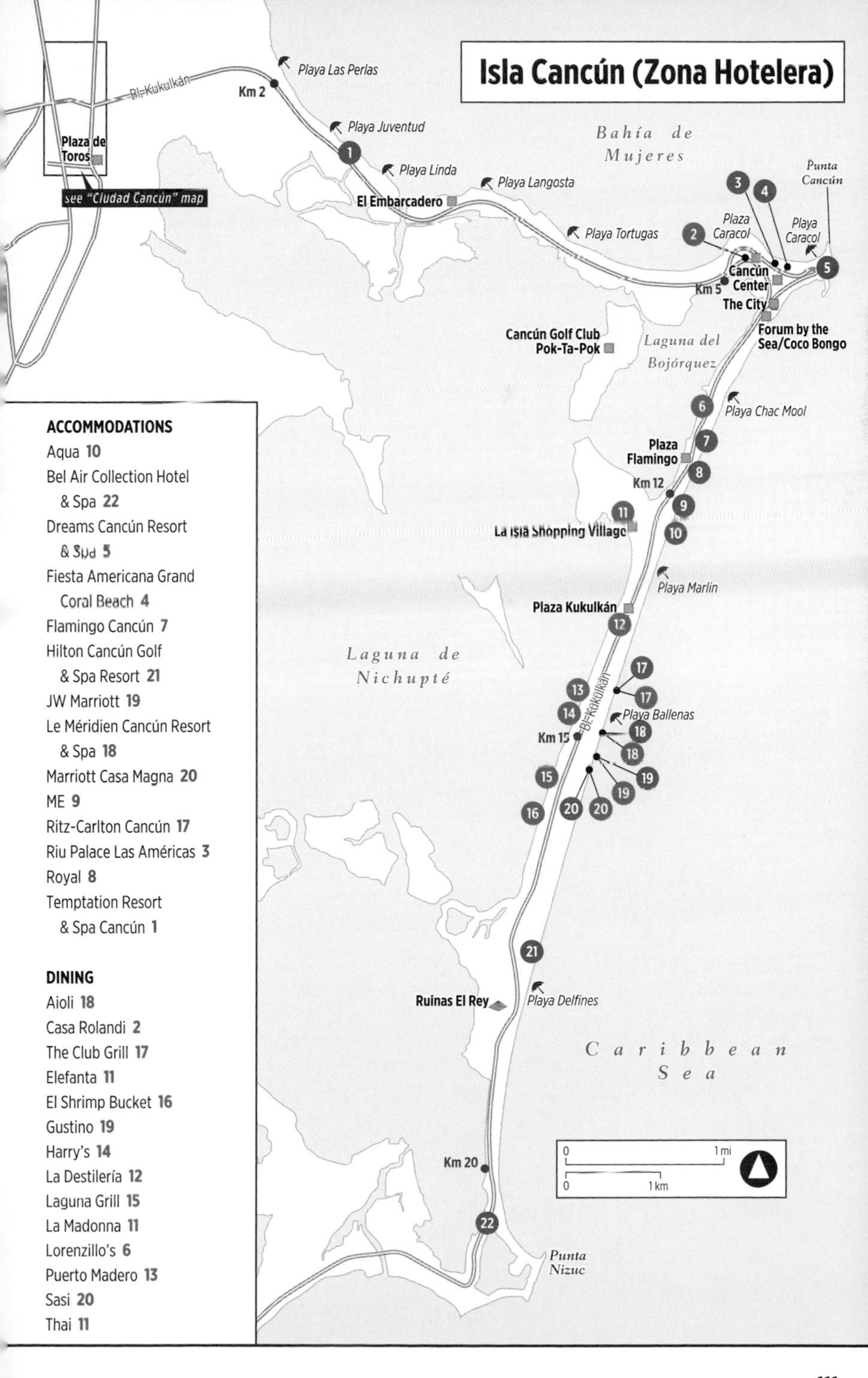

Isla Cancún (Zona Hotelera)
Bl. Kukulkán
Km 2
Playa Las Perlas
Playa Juventud
Plaza de Toros
see "Ciudad Cancún" map
Playa Linda
Playa Langosta
El Embarcadero
Bahía de Mujeres
Punta Cancún
Plaza Caracol
Playa Caracol
Playa Tortugas
Cancún Center
Km 5
The City
Forum by the Sea/Coco Bongo
Cancún Golf Club Pok-Ta-Pok
Laguna del Bojórquez
Playa Chac Mool
Plaza Flamingo
Km 12
La Isla Shopping Village
Playa Marlin
Plaza Kukulkán
Laguna de Nichupté
Bl. Kukulkán
Playa Ballenas
Km 15
Ruinas El Rey
Playa Delfines
Caribbean Sea
0
1 mi
0
1 km
Km 20
Punta Nizuc
ACCOMMODATIONS
Aqua 10
Bel Air Collection Hotel & Spa 22
Dreams Cancún Resort & Spa 5
Fiesta Americana Grand Coral Beach 4
Flamingo Cancún 7
Hilton Cancún Golf & Spa Resort 21
JW Marriott 19
Le Méridien Cancún Resort & Spa 18
Marriott Casa Magna 20
ME 9
Ritz-Carlton Cancún 17
Riu Palace Las Américas 3
Royal 8
Temptation Resort & Spa Cancún 1
DINING
Aioli 18
Casa Rolandi 2
The Club Grill 17
Elefanta 11
El Shrimp Bucket 16
Gustino 19
Harry's 14
La Destilería 12
Laguna Grill 15
La Madonna 11
Lorenzillo's 6
Puerto Madero 13
Sasi 20
Thai 11

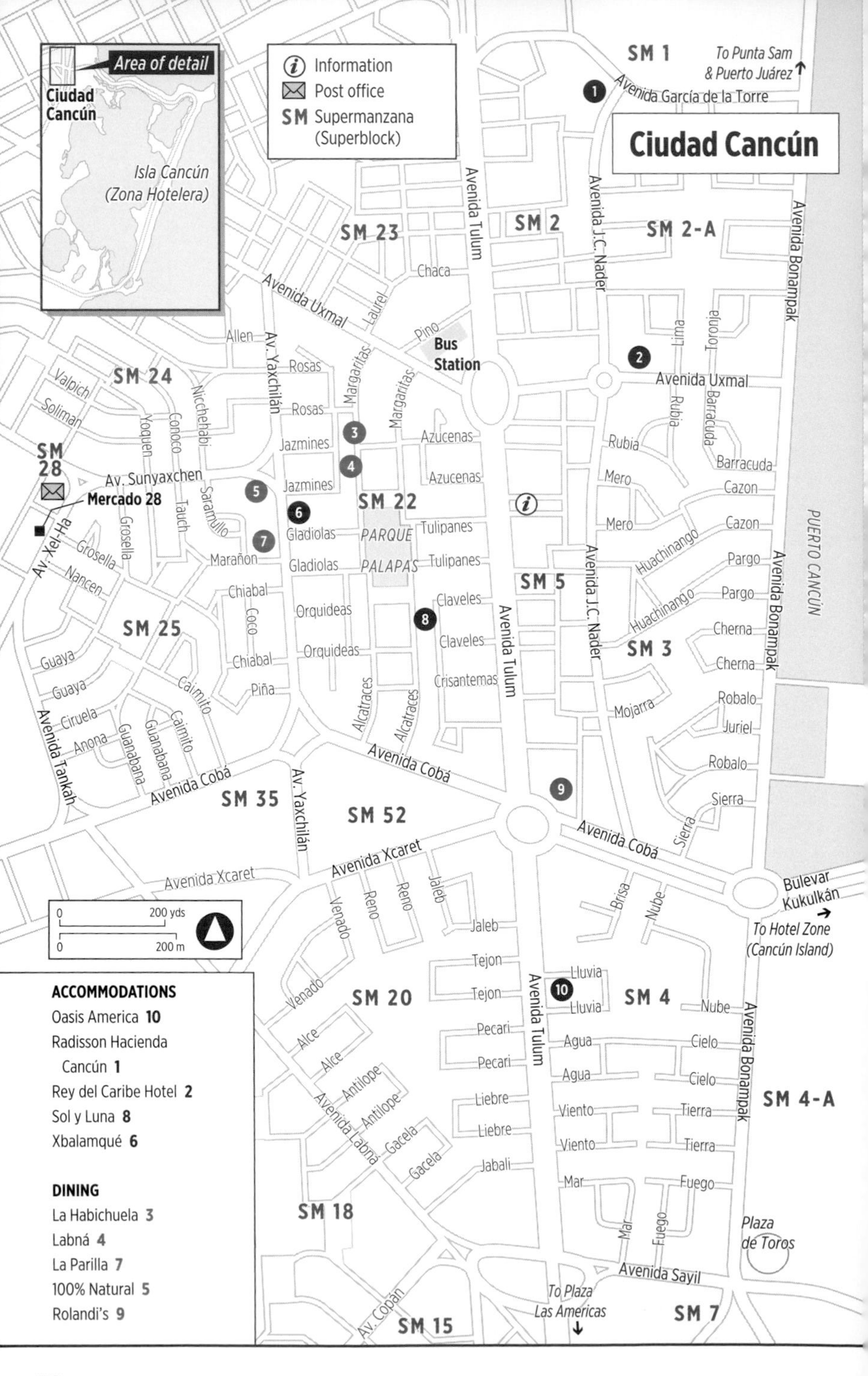

Ciudad Cancún
Area of detail
Ciudad Cancún
Isla Cancún (Zona Hotelera)
Information
Post office
SM Supermanzana (Superblock)
To Punta Sam & Puerto Juárez
Avenida García de la Torre
SM 1
SM 2
SM 2-A
SM 23
SM 24
SM 28
SM 22
SM 5
SM 3
SM 25
SM 35
SM 52
SM 20
SM 4
SM 4-A
SM 18
SM 15
SM 7
Avenida Tulum
Avenida J.C. Nader
Avenida Bonampak
Avenida Uxmal
Av. Yaxchilán
Avenida Cobá
Avenida Xcaret
Avenida Tankah
Avenida Labná
Avenida Sayil
Av. Copán
Av. Sunyaxchen
Av. Xel-Ha
Bus Station
Mercado 28
PARQUE PALAPAS
PUERTO CANCÚN
Bulevar Kukulkán
To Hotel Zone (Cancún Island)
Plaza de Toros
To Plaza Las Americas
0 200 yds
0 200 m
ACCOMMODATIONS
Oasis America 10
Radisson Hacienda Cancún 1
Rey del Caribe Hotel 2
Sol y Luna 8
Xbalamqué 6
DINING
La Habichuela 3
Labná 4
La Parilla 7
100% Natural 5
Rolandi's 9

Ruins near a modern Cancún hotel.

All of the soothing guest rooms face the ocean and have i-Home sound systems, aromatherapy menus, and Molton Brown bath amenities and artisan soaps. I don't remember the last time I slept in such a comfortable bed; Egyptian cotton sheets share company with a plush collection of form-fitting pillows. The only thing calling you out of bed is likely to be the clear blue skies, deep turquoise waters, and brilliant white sand outside your window. Some of Mexico's top chefs oversee the gourmet restaurants, including acclaimed chef Martha Ortiz, who created **Siete,** featuring floor-to-ceiling windows overlooking the Caribbean and the resort pools.

Bulevar Kukulkán Km 12.5, 77500 Cancún, Q. Roo. ✆ **800/343-7821** in the U.S., or 998/881-7600. Fax 998/881-7635. www.feel-aqua.com. 371 units. High season $370 and up double, $630 and up suite; low season $150–$311 double, $442 and up suite. AE, MC, V. **Amenities:** 3 gourmet restaurants; 3 bars; concierge w/multilingual staff; fitness center; 8 outdoor pools w/luxury cabañas for rent; room service; sauna; boutique spa; 2 tennis courts. *In room:* A/C, flatscreen TV w/DVD, i-Home, aromatherapy and pillow menu, hair dryer, minibar, Wi-Fi (for a fee).

Fiesta Americana Grand Coral Beach ★★★ ☺ This grand coral-colored resort sits on Punta Cancún, offering relative seclusion despite lying within easy walking distance of the Hotel Zone's key entertainment. Most of the hotel was renovated in 2009, and looks as magnificent as ever. In front, the whitest sand beach glides into emerald waters, where the surf is calm and perfect for swimming. Yet you may feel tempted not to leave the beautiful multitiered pools with waterfalls, fountains, swim-up bars, and lush surroundings. The all-suites hotel includes junior suites with sunken sitting areas, whitewashed furniture, marble bathrooms, and soothing California colors. Guests staying in Grand Club suites enjoy access to a private rooftop lounge, exclusive check-in, continental breakfast, hors d'oeuvres, and beverages. Service throughout this luxury property is gracious and attentive, and the magnificent lobby is embellished with elegant dark-green granite and fresh flowers. The Fiesta Kids Activities include nonstop games, contests, and shows for the little ones, and there are daylong sports and social activities planned for adults as well. The resort's international clientele includes many European, Japanese, Mexican, and American visitors. An American Express travel agency is located here.

Bulevar Kukulkán Km 9.5, 77500 Cancún, Q. Roo. ✆ **800/343-7821** in the U.S., or 998/881-3200. Fax 998/881-3288. www.fiestamericanagrand.com. 602 units. High season $403 and up double, $571 and up club-floor double; low season $200 and up double, $350 and up club-floor double. AE, MC, V. **Amenities:** 5 restaurants; 4 bars; babysitting; kids' club; concierge w/ multilingual staff; fitness center; concierge floor; outdoor pool w/swim-up bars; room service; sauna; boutique spa; watersports. *In room:* A/C, flatscreen TV, i-Home, hair dryer, minibar, Wi-Fi (for a fee).

Hilton Cancún Golf & Spa Resort ★★ ☺ Full of energy, this is a grand resort in every sense of the word. The Hilton Cancún sits on 100 hectares (247 acres) of prime beachside property, which means every room has a sea view (some have both sea and lagoon views). And there's an 18-hole par-72 golf course across the street. Like the sprawling resort, guest rooms are spacious and decorated in minimalist style. The Beach Club villas are the largest and best-located rooms, and come with continental breakfast and an evening cocktail hour. This Hilton is a kid-friendly hotel, with one of the island's best children's activity programs, children's pool, and babysitting. The spectacular multisection swimming pool stretches out to the gorgeous beach. The Hilton is especially appealing to golfers because it's one of only two in Cancún with an on-site course (the other is the Meliá). Greens fees for guests during high season are $79 for 9 holes, $159 for 18 holes (low season and twilight discounts offered), and come with use of a cart. The Wellness Spa includes oceanfront massage cabañas, yoga, and aromatherapy. This Hilton has a friendly vibe and excellent service.

Bulevar Kukulkán Km 17, Retorno Lacandones, 77500 Cancún, Q. Roo. ✆ **800/548-8690** in the U.S., or 998/881-8000. Fax 998/881-8080. www.hiltoncancun.com. 426 units. High season $249 and up double, $309 and up villa room, $409 and up suite; low season $159 and up double, $199 and up villa room, $279 and up suite. AE, DC, MC, V. **Amenities:** 4 restaurants; 2 bars; babysitting; kids' club; concierge; golf course across the street; golf clinic; 10 interconnected outdoor pools w/swim-up bar; 2 whirlpools; room service; wellness spa and fully equipped gym; 2 lighted tennis courts; watersports. *In room:* A/C, flatscreen TV, CD/MP3 player, hair dryer, minibar, Wi-Fi (for a fee).

JW Marriott ★★★ This remains my favorite resort in Cancún, a refined oasis that offers exceptional service without pretense. Despite its many touches of elegance, the JW is friendly and even family friendly—although more families stay at the neighboring and less expensive Marriott CasaMagna (p. 117). From the beautifully decorated marble and flower-filled lobby to the luxurious

Deciphering Hotel Prices

In all price categories, Cancún's hotels generally set their rates in dollars, so they are immune to variations in the peso. Travel agents and wholesalers always have air/hotel packages available. Cancún also has numerous all-inclusive properties, which allow you to take a fixed-cost vacation. Note that the price quoted when you call a hotel's reservation number may not include Cancún's 12% tax (a 10% federal tax and 2% state lodging tax). Prices can vary considerably throughout the year and have dropped considerably during the global financial crisis, so it pays to consult a travel agent or shop around.

oceanview guest rooms, the resort combines classic and Caribbean styling with warm Mexican service. Guest rooms feature exquisite marble bathrooms with separate tub and shower, private balconies, flatscreen TVs, bathrobes and slippers, and twice-daily maid service. The wonderful free-form infinity pool meanders through the property and overlooks the sea. A spectacular 3,252 sq.-m (35,004-sq.-ft.) spa includes an indoor pool and Jacuzzi, high-tech fitness center, and full range of massages, body scrubs and polishes, facials, and healing water treatments. **Gustino** (p. 122) is the hotel's outstanding Italian restaurant seated off the lobby.

Bulevar Kukulkán Km 14.5, 77500 Cancún, Q. Roo. ✆ **800/223-6388** in the U.S., or 998/848-9600. Fax 998/848-9601. www.jwmarriottcancun.com. 448 units. High season $449 and up double; low season $300 and up double. AE, DC, MC, V. **Amenities:** 3 restaurants; deli; lobby bar and pool bar; access to kids' club at Marriott CasaMagna; concierge; club floor w/special amenities and complimentary cocktails; expansive outdoor pool; dive pool w/waterfalls; indoor pool; 3 whirlpools; room service; sauna; full-service spa; steam room. *In room:* A/C, flatscreen TV, hair dryer, minibar, Wi-Fi (for a fee).

Le Méridien Cancún Resort & Spa ★★ Frequented by Europeans familiar with this fine chain of hotels, Le Méridien is among Cancún's most inviting luxury options. The elegant lobby, featuring original artwork, fresh flowers, and subtle lighting, creates a sense of intimacy that extends throughout the hotel. Guest rooms are generous in size, with small balconies overlooking the pool; due to the hotel's design, they do not have full ocean views. Each has a large marble bathroom with a separate tub and glassed-in shower. The resort's **Spa del Mar** is one of Mexico's most complete European spa facilities, with more than 4,570 sq. m (49,191 sq. ft.) of services dedicated to your body and soul. It consists of an extensive fitness center, full-service salon, selection of treatment rooms, men's and women's steam rooms, saunas, whirlpools, and cold plunge pools. **Aioli** (p. 121) is the splendid fine-dining restaurant connected to the lobby. The hotel staff offers calm, personalized service.

Retorno del Rey Km 14, Zona Hotelera, 77500, Cancún, Q. Roo. ✆ **800/543-4300** in the U.S., or 998/881-2200. Fax 998/881-2201. www.meridiencancun.com.mx. 213 units. $300 and up double, $400 and up suite. Ask about special spa packages. AE, DC, MC, V. Small dogs accepted with prior reservation. **Amenities:** 2 restaurants; bar; babysitting; supervised children's program w/ clubhouse, play equipment, wading pool; concierge; 3 cascading outdoor pools; whirlpool; room service; spa; 2 lighted championship tennis courts; watersports. *In room:* A/C, flatscreen TV, CD player, hair dryer, minibar, Wi-Fi (for a fee).

Ritz-Carlton Cancún ★★★ ☺ The exclusive Ritz-Carlton fronts a gorgeous white-sand beach, having recently added a significant stretch of sand as part of Cancún's $71 million beach recovery project. Rooms and public areas overlook the pools and beach and offer the low-key elegance that's a hallmark of the Ritz chain—think plush carpets; chandeliers; fresh flowers; and rooms with marble baths, fluffy featherbeds, and 400-count bed linens. Several features will enhance your stay, including a fabulous culinary center under the direction of acclaimed Executive Chef Rainer Zinngrebe offering gourmet cooking classes, as well as wine and tequila tastings. A group of specially designed "Itzy Bitzy Ritz Kids" guest rooms offer baby-friendly amenities and conveniences. In addition to the daytime Kids Camp, the Ritz offers a "Kids' Night Out" program that allows parents to steal away for the evening. The beachfront Kayantá Spa bases many of its treatments on traditional Maya rituals and therapies. The resort's oceanfront restaurant, **Casitas,** is the only beachside dining spot in Cancún, where you can dine on steakhouse fare in candlelit cabañas. The hotel's primary restaurant, **The Club Grill,** is reviewed in the "Where to Dine" section, below; **Fantino,** is similarly outstanding and focuses on Mediterranean cuisine; and the **Lobby Lounge** (p. 137) is a refined space for an evening out. The resort itself, as well as The Club Grill and Fantino, another Ritz-Carlton restaurant, have received AAA five diamonds.

Retorno del Rey 36, off Bulevar Kukulkán Km 13.5, 77500 Cancún, Q. Roo. ✆ **800/241-3333** in the U.S. and Canada, or 998/881-0808. Fax 998/881-0815. www.ritzcarlton.com. 365 units. May 1–Dec 21 $309–$409 double, $489 and up club floor and suites; Dec 21–Jan 3 $799–$1,099 double, $1,679 and up club floor and suites; Jan 4–Apr 30 $549–$629 double, $769 and up club floor and suites. Ask about golf, spa, and weekend packages. AE, MC, V. **Amenities:** 6 restaurants; lounge w/sushi bar; babysitting; Kids Camp; concierge; fully equipped fitness center; club floors; 2 outdoor pools (heated in winter); room service; spa; a Cliff Drysdale tennis center w/3 lighted tennis courts. *In room:* A/C, flatscreen TV, CD player, hair dryer, minibar, Wi-Fi (for a fee).

Riu Palace Las Américas ★ ☺ The all-inclusive Riu Palace is part of a family of Riu resorts in Cancún known for their grand, opulent style. This one is the smallest of the three and the most over-the-top, steeped in pearl-white Greco architecture. It looks more like it belongs on the Las Vegas strip than next to the Caribbean Sea, but then again, no one ever said Cancún had a consistent style. The location is prime—near the central shopping, dining, and nightlife centers, and just a 5-minute walk to the Convention Center. All rooms are spacious junior suites with an ocean or lagoon view, separate seating area with sofa or sofa bed, and a balcony or terrace. Eight have Jacuzzis. The beautiful central pools overlook the ocean and a small stretch of beach. Riu Palace offers guests virtually 24 hours of all-inclusive snacks, meals, and beverages. Activities include watersports, daytime entertainment for adults and kids, live music and shows at night, and access to other Riu hotels in Cancún. The hotel's European opulence stands in contrast to the mostly informal North American guests.

Bulevar Kukulkán Km 8.5, Lote 4, 77500 Cancún, Q. Roo. ✆ **888/666-8816** in the U.S., or 998/891-4300. Fax 998/891-4301. www.riu.com. 372 units. High season $412 and up double; low season $322 and up double. Rates are all-inclusive, and a 2-night stay may be required. AE, MC, V. **Amenities:** 6 restaurants; 2 bars; access to golf and tennis; fitness center; 2 outdoor pools; room service; spa; nonmotorized watersports, including introductory scuba lessons; free Wi-Fi in lobby. *In room:* A/C, TV, minibar, hair dryer.

Royal ★★ Opened in early 2007, this adults-only all-suites hotel is my favorite of Cancún's all-inclusive establishments, offering a level of services and amenities unmatched almost anywhere. From the stunning infinity pools and gorgeous beach to the gourmet restaurants and sophisticated spa, the owners have spared no expense. The elegant marble lobby looks out one side to the Caribbean and the other to the lagoon, with sitdown check-in and a champagne welcome. All of the innovative suites feature flatscreen TVs with CD/DVD players, marble bathrooms with rain showers, two-person Jacuzzis, and oceanview balconies with hammocks. Swim-up master suites have semiprivate plunge pools facing the resort's pool and beach; guests in the top-category suites have access to BMW Mini Coopers. The Maya-inspired oceanview spa includes a massage room, Jacuzzi, sauna, traditional *temazcal* steam bath, massage waterfall, and state-of-the-art fitness center. Actually, the range of services is almost hard to believe, except that you will be paying top dollar for it. The all-inclusive package includes gourmet meals, premium drinks, and evening entertainment.

Bulevar Kukulkán Km 11.5, 77500 Cancún, Q. Roo. ✆ **800/760-0944** in the U.S., or 998/881-7340. www.realresorts.com.mx. 288 units. $400–$800 double. AE, DC, MC, V. No children younger than 16. **Amenities:** 6 restaurants; 8 bars; concierge; well-equipped fitness center; expansive outdoor pool; room service; sauna; full-service spa; steam room. *In room:* A/C, flatscreen TV, CD/DVD player, hair dryer, minibar, Wi-Fi (free).

EXPENSIVE

Dreams Cancún Resort & Spa ☺ Operated by the Apple Vacations charter group, the all-inclusive Dreams Resort enjoys one of the island's most idyllic locations—29 hectares (72 acres) at the tip of Punta Cancún. The setting is casual, and the hotel welcomes children. Bright colors and strategic angles define the design, which now looks somewhat dated relative to Cancún's newer establishments. Choose from two sets of rooms: those in the 17-story club section with ocean views and extra services and amenities, and those in the pyramid overlooking the dolphin-filled lagoon. The all-inclusive concept here includes meals, 24-hour room service, and premium-brand drinks, as well as the use of all resort amenities, nonmotorized watersports, theme-night entertainment, and tips. The spa costs extra. One of the resort's restaurants is **Paloma Bonita,** for Mexican cuisine. Unfortunately, service at the resort is inconsistent.

Bulevar Kukulkán, 77500 Punta Cancún (Apdo. Postal 14), Cancún, Q. Roo. ✆ **866/237-3267** in the U.S., or 998/848-7000. Fax 998/848-7001. www.dreamsresorts.com. 376 units. High season $400 and up double; low season $285 and up double. AE, DC, MC, V. **Amenities:** 5 restaurants; 5 bars; babysitting; bikes; kids' club; fitness center w/steam bath; 2 outdoor pools; private saltwater lagoon w/dolphins and tropical fish; lighted tennis court; watersports including kayaks, Catamarans, paddleboats, snorkeling equipment, and scuba lessons; cooking classes; beach volleyball; dance lessons; yoga. *In room:* A/C, TV w/DVD/CD player, hair dryer, minibar.

Marriott CasaMagna ★★ ☺ This picture-perfect Marriott resort is one of the most enticing family destinations in Cancún. Entering through a half-circle of Roman columns, you'll pass through a domed foyer to a wide, lavishly marbled lobby filled with plants and shallow pools. It looks out to the sparkling pool and enormous whirlpool at the edge of the beach. Guest rooms are decorated with Mexican-Caribbean furnishings and have balconies facing the sea or lagoon. The Marriott caters to family travelers (up to two children stay free with parent), and the supervised children's program is one of the best of any resort here. That said, the resort never feels overrun by kids, and young couples will also have a wonderful time. Among the many places to dine, my favorite is the *teppanyaki*-style (cook-at-your-table) Mikado Japanese restaurant. Service throughout the resort is excellent.

Bulevar Kukulkán Km 14.5, 77500 Cancún, Q. Roo ✆ **800/228-9290** in the U.S., or 998/881-2000. Fax 998/881-2085. www.casamagnamarriott.com. 450 units. $249–$309 double; $454 and up suite. Ask about packages. AE, MC, V. **Amenities:** 5 restaurants (including Sasi, p. 124); lobby bar w/live music; babysitting; concierge; health club w/sauna and aerobics; outdoor pool and whirlpool; room service; spa; 2 lighted tennis courts. *In room:* A/C, flatscreen TV, hair dryer, minibar.

ME ★ The Spanish ME hotel by Meliá brings to Cancún a new level of minimalist chic with an atmosphere befitting a trendy nightclub more than a beach resort. Bathed in hues of beige and mauve, with polished marble, onyx lamps, and modern artwork, the hotel creates its own fashion statement—and the hip clientele reflects it. The modern lobby feels a bit like an urban cocktail lounge, with designer bars and chill-out music filling the space. Guest rooms have distinctive contemporary furnishings, plasma TVs, MP3 players, and marble bathrooms with rain showers and Aveda bath products; half look to the Caribbean Sea and the other half to the lagoon. The super-stylish Yhi Spa overlooks the ocean and offers body glows and exfoliations, aromatherapy massages, body masks, and wraps. The Beach House restaurant appears sunken into the main pool and joins the beach in front. One drawback: Service is not as consistent as you might expect from such an upscale resort.

Bulevar Kukulkán Km 12, 77500 Cancún, Q. Roo. ✆ **877/954-8363** in the U.S., or 998/881-2500. Fax 998/881-2501. www.mecancun.travel. 448 units. $239 and up double. AE, MC, V. **Amenities:** 3 restaurants; Internet cafe; 2 bars; beach club; concierge; fitness center; concierge floor; 3 outdoor pools; whirlpool; full-service luxury spa. *In room:* A/C, flatscreen TV, MP3 player, hair dryer, minibar, Wi-Fi (for a fee).

MODERATE

Bel Air Collection Hotel & Spa ★ This trendy boutique hotel attracts the young, hip, and hot—making this beachfront hotel into something you'd expect to find in Miami, standing in direct contrast to the nearby all-inclusive mega-resorts. Of the hotel's 156 rooms, nearly half face the ocean; the rest face the lagoon, which offers splendid sunset views. Guest rooms are modern and spacious, with minimalist white and red decor. There's an asymmetrical infinity pool that seems to spill over onto the turquoise Caribbean Sea, with guests lazing around it on comfortable mattresses while lounge music plays in the background. The Collection Spa offers a variety of moderately priced services, including a chocolate facial. ***Note:*** This hotel is a 15-minute ride from the center of the Hotel Zone, and children under 12 are not allowed, so if you're looking for privacy and peace, this is the place for you.

Bulevar Kukulkán Km 20.5, 77500 Cancún, Q. Roo. ✆ **998/193-1770.** www.belaircollection.com. 156 units. High season $150 and up double; low season $100 and up double. Meal plans available. AE, MC, V. No children 11 and under. **Amenities:** 2 restaurants; sushi bar; 2 bars; concierge; exercise room; Jacuzzi; infinity outdoor pool; room service; spa; free Wi-Fi in lobby. *In room:* A/C, satellite TV/DVD, hair dryer, minibar.

Flamingo Cancún ☺ The all-inclusive Flamingo seems to have been inspired by the dramatic, slope-sided architecture of the Dreams Cancún, but the Flamingo is considerably smaller and less expensive (guests can opt out of the all-inclusive package, which includes three meals and domestic drinks). With two pools and a casual vibe, it's also a friendly, accommodating choice for families. The bright guest rooms—all with balconies—border a courtyard facing the interior swimming pool and *palapa* pool bar. Some, but not all, of the rooms have been remodeled in recent years. The Flamingo lies in the heart of the island hotel district, opposite the Flamingo Shopping Center and close to other hotels, shopping centers, and restaurants.

Bulevar Kukulkán Km 11, 77500 Cancún, Q. Roo. ✆ **998/848-8870.** Fax 998/883-1029. www.flamingocancun.com. 260 units. High season $199 double, low season $112 double, all-inclusive plan high season $400 double; low season $200 double. AE, MC, V. **Amenities:** 2 restaurants; 2 bars; kids' club; fitness center; 2 outdoor pools; room service; free Wi-Fi in lobby. *In room:* A/C, TV, hair dryer, minibar.

Temptation Resort & Spa Cancún This adults-only (21 and over) getaway is a spirited all-inclusive resort favored by those looking for significant social interaction. Although it's not advertised as such, the hotel is widely known for its popularity with "swingers." By day, pool time is all about flirting, seducing, and getting a little wacky with adult games such as teasing time and a dirty jokes contest. The main pools are top-optional. Note that tops are also optional on the beach in front, which has calm waters for swimming. Come night, theme dinners, shows, and other live entertainment keep the party going. The small, somewhat dated rooms are housed in two sections, with quiet rooms in one and "sexy" rooms, complete with red lighting, in another. Surrounded by acres of tropical gardens, this moderate hotel lies at the northern end of the Hotel Zone, close to the major shopping plazas, restaurants, and nightlife. It reminds me of a Carnival Cruise, but on land.

Bulevar Kukulkán Km 3.5, 77500 Cancún, Q. Roo. ✆ **877/485-8367** in the U.S., or 998/848-7900. Fax 998/848-7994. www.temptationresort.com. 384 units. High season $179 per person per night double occupancy; low season $139 per person per night double occupancy. Rates include food, beverages, and activities. AE, MC, V. Guests must be at least 21 years old. **Amenities:** 6 restaurants; 5 bars; exercise room w/daily classes; 3 outdoor pools; 7 whirlpools; limited room service; spa; nonmotorized watersports; marina; snorkeling and scuba lessons. *In room:* A/C, TV, hair dryer, Wi-Fi (for a fee).

Ciudad Cancún

MODERATE

Oasis America One of downtown's better hotels, Oasis America sits off the main business street and is a 20-minute ride from the Hotel Zone. Of the hotel's two sections, the "Sens" side is superior, offering handsomely appointed rooms decorated in muted tones with king beds, flatscreen TVs, plenty of work space, and bathrooms with showers only. The "standard" rooms have smaller beds and more basic furnishings. The swimming pool is the highlight of the hotel, surrounded by palm trees, waterways, and lounge chairs and beds. There's also a small spa offering among the best massage rates of any spa you'll find in Cancún. Service throughout the hotel is polite but unexceptional.

Av. Tulum (corner of Brisa), Centro, 77500 Cancún, Q. Roo. ✆ **998/848-9144** or 848-8600. Fax 998/884-1953. www.oasishoteles.com. 177 units. 1,500 pesos and up double. AE, MC, V. **Amenities:** 2 restaurants; bar; small gym; outdoor pool with separate wading area for children; limited room service; spa; free Wi-Fi in lobby. *In room:* A/C, TV, minibar.

Radisson Hacienda Cancún ★ This is the top hotel in downtown Cancún, and one of the best values in the area. The business-friendly Radisson offers all the expected comforts of the chain, yet resembles a hacienda with the distinct manner of Mexican hospitality. Guest rooms surround a warm, rotunda-style lobby with a cool onyx bar, as well as lush gardens and an inviting pool area. All have brightly colored fabric accents; views of the garden, the pool, or the street; and a small sitting area and balcony. The hotel lies within walking distance of downtown Cancún.

Av. Nader 1, SM2, Centro, 77500 Cancún, Q. Roo. ✆ **800/333-3333** in the U.S., or 998/881-6500. Fax 998/884-7954. www.radissoncancun.com. 248 units. $100 and up double; $120 and up junior suite. AE, MC, V. **Amenities:** Restaurant; lobby bar; small gym; free Wi-Fi in lobby; outdoor pool w/adjoining bar and separate wading area for children; limited room service; sauna; lighted tennis courts. *In room:* A/C, TV, hair dryer.

Rey del Caribe Hotel ★★ 🎁 This ecological hotel is a unique oasis where every detail works toward establishing harmony with the environment. You might easily forget you're in the midst of downtown Cancún in the tropical garden setting, with blooming orchids and other flowering plants. The lovely grounds include statues of Maya deities, hammocks, and a tiled swimming pool. There's a regularly changing schedule of hatha and flow yoga, as well as special classes on astrology, tarot, and other subjects. The on-site spa offers facial and body treatments. Guest rooms, many of which were renovated in 2009, are large and sunny, with a kitchenette and your choice of one king-size or two full-size beds; some have a terrace. The extent of ecological sensitivity is impressive—ranging from the use of collected rainwater to waste composting. Recycling is encouraged, and solar power is used wherever possible.

Av. Uxmal SM 2A (corner of Nader), 77500 Cancún, Q. Roo. ✆ **998/884-2028.** Fax 988/884-9857. www.elreydelcaribe.com. 31 units. High season $85 double; low season $65 double. Rates include breakfast. MC, V. **Amenities:** Outdoor pool; Jacuzzi; spa. *In room:* A/C, TV, kitchenette, free Wi-Fi.

INEXPENSIVE

Sol y Luna This simple but cheerful hotel next to the Parque Las Palapas has 11 individually decorated rooms with small balconies, and mosaic-trimmed baths with showers only. A tiny bridge crosses the small pool at the entrance. Come here if you want to explore the downtown and experience Cancún's more local flavor, but don't expect much in the way of service or amenities. The hotel sits up one flight of stairs, just above a tapas and wine bar.

Calle Alcatraces 33, 77500 Cancún, Q. Roo. ✆ **998/887-5579.** www.hotelsolylunacancun.com. 11 units. $50–$70 double. AE, MC, V. Street parking. **Amenities:** Restaurant/bar; outdoor pool; free Wi-Fi. *In room:* A/C, TV, fridge.

Xbalamqué ★ Creatively designed to resemble a Maya temple, this downtown hotel features a lovely pool and waterfall, full-service spa, and authentic Mexican cantina. Live music plays evenings in the bookstore/cafe adjacent to the lobby. Guest rooms and 10 junior suites have rustic furnishings with regional touches, colorful tilework, and small bathrooms with showers. Ask for a room overlooking the ivy-filled courtyard. A tour desk is available to help you plan your vacation activities, and the spa offers some of the best rates of any hotel in Cancún.

Av. Yaxchilán 31, Sm. 22, Mza. 18, 77500 Cancún, Q. Roo. ✆ **998/884-9690.** Fax 998/884-9690. www.xbalamque.com. 99 units. $75 double, $85 suite. AE, MC, V. **Amenities:** Restaurant; cafe; cantina; lobby bar; outdoor pool; spa. *In room:* A/C, TV.

WHERE TO DINE

More than 300 restaurants spanning North American, European, and Asian cuisines have opened across Cancún. They have come to supplement the many U.S.-based franchise chains that have long dominated the Cancún restaurant scene. These include Hard Rock Cafe, Rainforest Cafe, Tony Roma's, Ruth's Chris Steak House, and the gamut of fast-food burger places. One inexpensive, reliable Mexican chain that serves tasty meals, including breakfasts, is **Vips,** across from the Convention Center. The establishments listed below are typically locally owned, one-of-a-kind restaurants or exceptional selections at area hotels. Many schedule live music. Unless otherwise indicated, parking is free.

One unique way to combine dinner with sightseeing is aboard the **Lobster Dinner Cruise** (✆**998/849-4748;** www.thelobsterdinner.com). Cruising around the tranquil, turquoise waters of the lagoon, passengers feast on steak and lobster dinners accompanied by wine. Cost is $79 per person for the surf-and-turf menu. The two daily departures are from the Aquatours Marina (Bulevar Kukulkán 6.5). A sunset cruise leaves at 5pm during the winter and 5:30pm during the summer; a moonlight cruise leaves at 8pm winter, 8:30pm summer. Another—albeit livelier—lobster dinner option is the **Captain Hook Lobster Dinner Cruise** (✆**998/849-4451;** www.pirateshipcancun.com), which is similar, but with the added attraction of a pirate show involving two 28m (93-ft.) replicas of 18th-century Spanish galleons, making this a fun choice for families. The steak option costs 1,026 pesos per person, and the lobster option is 1,130 pesos per person. It departs at 7pm from El Embarcadero at Playa Linda, and returns at 10:30pm.

Isla Cancún

VERY EXPENSIVE

Aioli ★★ FRENCH The Provençal—but definitely not provincial—Aioli offers exquisite French and Mediterranean gourmet specialties in a warm and cozy country French setting. Though it serves perhaps the best breakfast buffet in Cancún (for 312 pesos), most diners from outside the hotel come here in the evening, when low lighting and superb service promise a romantic experience. To start, the *foie gras* medallions and caramelized figs with a cherry Brandy sauce are the obvious choice. Among my favorite main courses are roasted sea bass with an artichoke fricassee and basil cream sauce, rack of lamb with polenta sauce, and seared breast of duck. Desserts are decadent, especially the signature "Fifth Element" with chocolate and a rich berry sauce.

In Le Méridien Cancún Resort & Spa (p. 115), Retorno del Rey Km 14. ✆ **998/881-2200.** Reservations recommended. No sandals or tennis shoes; men must wear long pants. Main courses 324–540 pesos. AE, MC, V. Daily 6:30am–11pm.

The Club Grill ★★★ INTERNATIONAL Under the direction of Executive Chef Rainer Zinngrebe, the five-diamond Club Grill is one of Mexico's top restaurants. Even rival restaurateurs give it an envious thumbs-up. The gracious service starts as you enter the anteroom, with its elegant seating and superb selection of cocktails and wines. It continues in the candlelit dining room, with shimmering silver and crystal. Sophisticated plates of prime cuts, escargot, seared scallops, foie gras, truffles, and roasted duck arrive at a leisurely pace. Don't miss the soufflé station before concluding your meal. There's a martini bar next door, and a jazz band plays from 7:30pm on. Guests seeking an even more gastronomically rich experience can sign up for the chef's table or take a gourmet cooking class at the hotel's fabulous culinary school.

In the Ritz-Carlton Cancún (p. 115), Retorno del Rey, 36 Bulevar Kukulkán Km 13.5. ✆ **998/881-0808.** Reservations required. No sandals or tennis shoes; men must wear long pants and collared shirts. Main courses $30–$46. AE, DC, MC, V. Tues–Sun 7–11pm.

Lorenzillo's ★★ ☺ SEAFOOD This longtime Cancún favorite hasn't changed much over the years. Lobster remains the star, and part of the appeal is selecting your dinner out of the giant lobster tank set in the lagoon (Lorenzillo's sits right on the lagoon under a giant *palapa* roof). A dock leads down to the main dining area, and when that's packed, a wharf-side bar handles the overflow. You'll find a large captain's wheel at the entrance to this nautical-themed restaurant. To start, I recommend *El Botin,* which consists of two soft-shell crabs breaded and fried to perfection. Good bets for the entree include lobster (which comes prepared in any of 20 different ways), shrimp stuffed with cheese and wrapped in bacon, the *Pescador* (Caribbean grouper prepared to taste), and steak and seafood combinations. Desserts include the tempting crêpes suzette, prepared tableside. Lorenzillo's is as popular with families as it is with couples looking for lagoon-side romance. It's connected by a walkway to Limoncello, the waterfront Italian restaurant next door.

Bulevar Kukulkán Km 10.5. ✆ **998/883-1254.** www.lorenzillos.com.mx. Reservations recommended. Main courses $22–$49. AE, MC, V. Daily 1pm–midnight.

EXPENSIVE

Casa Rolandi ★★★ INTERNATIONAL Trained in Lyon, France, chef-owner Danielle Muller has taken the reigns and redesigned both the dining space and the menu of Casa Rolandi. Famous personalities, from international actors to Mexican presidents, have dined here over the years, and Casa Rolandi remains one of Cancún's best tables. Among the artfully presented selections are homemade ravioli stuffed with wild mushrooms over a creamy Alba truffle sauce, fresh seafood tagliolini draped in black ink, red snapper or sea bass baked in salt, and grilled 18-ounce rib-eye served sizzling. Finish with the sublime tiramisu accompanied by Kalhua and coffee. Special international menus are offered each month. Service remains personalized and friendly, and a sophisticated cigar and wine lounge called **Very Wine** has been added upstairs (p. 137).

Bulevar Kukulkán Km 8.5, in Plaza Caracol. ✆ **998/883-2557.** www.rolandi.com. Reservations recommended. Main courses 182–385 pesos. AE, MC, V. Daily 1–11:30pm.

Elefanta ★★ INDIAN Opened in April 2009 as a partner restaurant to Thai (p. 124), Elefanta is the trendiest new table to hit Cancún's dining scene. The exotic waterfront space has two open kitchens overseen by an Indian chef—one for tandoori cooking and the other for curries. The kitchens focus on fish, shrimp, and chicken dishes, and there are plentiful vegetarian options. Dishes can be ordered on regular or half-size plates and are perfect for sharing with friends or family. Elefanta's chill-out music is coordinated with Thai, next door, and a DJ here spins hot mixes Thursday through Saturday nights. If you're in the mood for a cocktail, try one of the 30 exotic martinis.

La Isla Shopping Center, Bulevar Kukulcán 12.5. ✆ **998/176-8070.** Reservations recommended during high season. Main courses 200–400 pesos. AE, MC, V. Daily 4–11:30pm.

Gustino ★★★ ITALIAN JW Marriott's signature restaurant Gustino offers romantic Italian dining unsurpassed in Cancún. The exquisite dining room includes a gorgeous centerpiece candle display, floor-to-ceiling windows looking out to a lazy man-made lagoon and the beach beyond, and live saxophone. For an *antipasto,* I recommend the unusual pear carpaccio with parmesan nuggets and caramelized grapes, or the sautéed shrimp in a white wine sauce with capers and roasted celery crouton. The warm tossed spinach salad is one of the best I've ever tasted, topped with pancetta, mushrooms, sun-dried tomatoes, and walnuts. Expertly prepared main dishes include open lasagna with lobster and black olives, and roasted loin of venison with a stuffed potato croquette. The menu, which changes seasonally, features other homemade pastas and succulent steak and seafood selections. Gustino has a wine cellar with an excellent variety of international grapes. Service is outstanding.

In the JW Marriott (p. 114), Bulevar Kukulkán Km 14.5. ✆ **998/848-9600.** www.jwmarriott restaurants.com. Reservations required. Main courses 195–585 pesos. AE, DC, MC, V. Daily 6–11pm.

Harry's ★★ STEAK Situated adjacent to the Nichupté Lagoon, this prime steakhouse and raw bar is a hot addition to Cancún's dining scene. The dining room and waterfront terrace combine local stone and wood with burned orange marble and large expanses of glass to create a sense of California chic. The attentive waitstaff brings to your table a tempting selection of different cuts of beef, as well as a presentation from the raw bar. The New York strips, rib-eyes, and other cuts of beef are broiled in a 1,700°F (1,000°C) oven, while the fish and seafood are grilled on a *parilla*. Dishes are served a la carte, and the food is prepared with careful attention to detail. Don't expect a kids' menu here: Even the Kobe beef burger is so big it could feed a family. An excellent selection of international and Mexican boutique wines accompanies the menu.

Bulevar Kukulkán Km 14.2. ✆ **998/840-6550.** www.harrys.com.mx. Reservations recommended. Main courses 300–1,250 pesos. AE, MC, V. Daily 1pm–1am.

Laguna Grill ★★ FUSION Laguna Grill offers diners a contemporary culinary experience in a picturesque setting overlooking the lagoon. A tropical garden welcomes you at the entrance, while a small creek traverses the *palapa*-covered dining room set with tables made from the trunks of tropical trees. As magical as the decor is, the real star here is the kitchen, with its selection of contemporary international cuisine fused with regional flavors. Starters include a light lobster bisque or martini *gyoza* (steamed dumplings) filled with shrimp and vegetables. Fish and seafood dominate the menu. Grilled shrimp come marinated in rum, mint, and lime; surf-and-turf fusion dishes may include grilled lobster, beef, and shrimp skewers. For beef-lovers, the rib-eye served with mashed potatoes and black olives is excellent. For dessert, I recommend the crème brûlée served with a touch of Bailey's. If you're an early diner, request a table on the outside deck for a spectacular sunset view. An impressive selection of wines is available.

Bulevar Kukulkán Km 16.5. ✆ **998/885-0320.** www.lagunagrill.com.mx. Reservations recommended. Main courses 150–400 pesos. AE, MC, V. Daily 5–11pm.

La Madonna ★ SWISS/ITALIAN This architecturally dazzling restaurant and bar emerges unexpectedly from La Isla shopping center like an Italian Renaissance showroom along the canal. Inside, the dining room resembles one of the mystical international Buddha Bars, with an enormous replica of the Mona Lisa looking over the dazzled clientele. La Madonna offers authentic Italian and Swiss cuisine, including pasta, grilled fish, steak, and fondues. Among the best main dishes is the battered veal chop with fresh mozzarella, tomato sauce, and parmesan cheese over homemade basil pasta. For dessert, request the tableside flambéed strawberries. Many people come just for dessert and drinks, too (p. 137).

La Isla Shopping Center, Bulevar Kukulcán 12.5. ✆ **998/883-2222.** Reservations recommended. Main courses 150–800 pesos. AE, MC, V. Daily noon–1am.

Puerto Madero ★★ ARGENTINE/STEAK/SEAFOOD As a tribute to the famed Puerto Madero of Buenos Aires, this trendy restaurant has quickly earned a reputation for its steak and fish as well as its buzzing atmosphere. Overlooking the Nichupté Lagoon, the decor re-creates a 20th-century dock warehouse similar to what you'd find in the real Puerto Madero, with dark woods, exposed brick, and visible pipes. This steakhouse offers an extensive selection of prime-quality beef cuts, pastas, grilled fish, and shellfish, meticulously prepared with Argentine gusto. In addition to the classic carpaccio, the tuna tartar and halibut steak are favorites, but the real standouts here are the tender grilled steaks (particularly the rib-eye), served in ample portions. Enjoy a cocktail or glass of wine from the extensive selection, while viewing the sunset from the lagoon-side deck. Service is excellent and the restaurant stays open late.

Marina Barracuda, Bulevar Kukulkán Km 14. ✆ **998/885-2829, -2830.** www.puertomadero restaurantes.com. Reservations recommended. Main courses 170–630 pesos. AE, MC, V. Daily 1pm–1am.

Sasi ★★ THAI One of two outstanding Thai restaurants in Cancún—and the more family friendly of the two—Sasi sparkles under a series of *palapas* lit by soft onyx lamps. To start, I recommend ordering the Sasi Sampler which comes with a selection of shrimp, pork, beef, and chicken dumplings presented in a *Domburi* basket. Excellent main courses include stir-fried rice plates with chicken or shrimp, two versions of Phad Thai, and a variety of curries prepared with toasted herbs and Jasmine rice. Those looking for spicy selections will find worthy contenders in the Tom Yang Goong shrimp soup and the chicken and shrimp green curry. Dishes arrive carefully prepared and artfully presented, and the bartender mixes among the best martinis I've found in this city. The wait staff is Mexican, and the service every bit as gracious as you'd find if you were in Thailand.

In the Marriott CasaMagna (p. 117), Bulevar Kukulkán Km 14.5. ✆ **998/881-2092.** Reservations recommended. Main courses 140–240 pesos. AE, MC, V. Daily 5:30–11pm.

Thai ★★★ THAI This sensual restaurant and lounge feels like it should be in Southeast Asia rather than the edge of a Mexican shopping plaza. The stunning outdoor setting includes thick foliage and bamboo, with private *palapas* (open-air huts, each with its own table, sofa, and flickering candles) constructed like tiny islands over the expansive lagoon. Unobtrusive service, soft red and blue lighting, and Asian chill and lounge music contribute to the chic ambience. Classic Thai specialties such as spicy shrimp soup with lemon grass and mushrooms, glass noodle salad, chicken satay, and chicken and shrimp curries and stir-fries are served alongside exotic cocktails to the beautiful crowd. A DJ works the stylish lounge on weekends. Thai opens at sunset.

La Isla Shopping Center, Bulevar Kukulcán Km 12.5. ✆ **998/176-8070.** Reservations recommended during high season. Main courses 220–395 pesos. AE, MC, V. Daily 6pm–1am.

MODERATE

El Shrimp Bucket ☺ SEAFOOD This festive, family-friendly restaurant on the lagoon is all about "meaty, magnificent, and tender" shrimp cooked to your liking—peel-and-eat, breaded, beer-battered, coconut, grilled, and even bacon-barbecued. The kitchen serves only wild-caught shrimp from the Pacific coast of Mexico, which are extremely rich in flavor. The menu offers other fish and seafood selections, including ceviches, fish tacos, seafood pastas, and fish sandwiches. The casual eatery features a fun kids' playground that advises the children to "keep an eye on your parents." The indoor and outdoor seating is decorated with fish nets, shrimp buckets, and other nautical knickknacks. Salsa music plays in the background, and the servers are as cheerful as the atmosphere.

Bulevar Kukulkán Km 15. ✆ **998/840-6466.** www.shrimpbucket.com. Main courses 100–300 pesos. AE, MC, V. Daily noon–midnight.

La Destilería MEXICAN To experience Mexico's favorite export on an enticing terrace overlooking the lagoon, this is your place (keep an eye out for Tequila, the lagoon crocodile who often comes to visit). Renovated in 2009, La Destilería is more than a tequila-inspired restaurant; it's a minimuseum honoring the "spirit" of Mexico. It serves over 150 brands of tequila, including some treasures that never find their way across the country's northern border. A tequila tour is offered daily at 4:30pm, and patrons can always order tequila "samplers" at their tables. No surprise, the margaritas are also among the island's best. When you decide to order food with your tequila, you'll find a creative Mexican menu, with everything from quesadillas with zucchini flower, cheese, and poblano pepper to *arrachera* beef fajitas served in a hot pot with roasted *nopales* (cactus), Mexican sausage, and avocado.

Bulevar Kukulkán Km 12.65, across from Kukulcán Plaza. ✆ **998/885-1086,** -1087. www.ladestileria.com.mx. Main courses 150–470 pesos. AE, MC, V. Daily 1pm–midnight.

Ciudad Cancún

EXPENSIVE

La Habichuela ★★ 📷 SEAFOOD In a musically accented garden setting with flowering white-lit hibiscus trees, this longtime favorite remains downtown's most elegant table. For an unforgettable culinary adventure, order crème of *habichuela* (string bean) soup; giant shrimp in any number of sauces, including Jamaican tamarind, tequila, or ginger and mushroom; and exotic Mayan coffee prepared tableside with Xtabentun (a strong, sweet, anise-based liqueur). Grilled seafood and steaks are excellent, and the menu includes luscious ceviches, Caribbean lobsters, an inventive seafood "parade," and shish kabob flambé with shrimp and lobster or beef. For something divine, try *cocobichuela,* lobster and shrimp in sweet curry served in a coconut shell with rice and topped with fruit. Top it off with one of the boozy butterscotch crepes. La Habichuela now has a second branch in the Hotel Zone called **La Habichuela Sunset,** which features giant windows overlooking the lagoon and is close to La Isla shopping center. It's open daily from noon to midnight.

Margaritas 25. ✆ **998/884-3158.** (La Habichuela Sunset at Bulevar Kukulkán Km 12.6, ✆ 998/840-6280). www.lahabichuela.com. Reservations recommended in high season. Main courses 157–396 pesos. AE, MC, V. Daily noon–midnight.

MODERATE

Labná ★★ YUCATECAN Coming for a meal at Labná is like a very special trip to a Yucatecan home, a place that serves delicious Maya food and treats you like a friend. Specialties include a sublime lime soup, *poc chuc* (marinated, barbecue-style pork), chicken or pork *pibil* (sweet and spicy barbecue sauce served over shredded meat wrapped in banana leaves), and appetizers such as *papadzules* (tortillas stuffed with boiled eggs in a pumpkin-seed sauce). The Labná Special is a sampler of four typically Yucatecan main courses, including *poc chuc,* while another specialty of the house is baked suckling pig, served with guacamole. The refreshing Yucatecan beverage, *agua de chaya*—a blend of sweetened water and the leaf of the *chaya* plant, abundant in the area, to which sweet Xtabentun liquor (a type of anise) can be added for an extra kick—is also served here. The vaulted ceiling dining room is decorated with a mural of a pre-Hispanic Yucatecan scene, as well as with black-and-white photographs of Mérida, the capital of the Yucatán, dating from the 1900s. A local trio plays weekends from 3 to 5pm.

Margaritas 29, next to Cristo Rey church and the Habichuela restaurant. ✆ **998/892-3056.** www.labna.com. Reservations recommended. Main courses 78–198 pesos. AE, MC, V. Daily noon–10pm.

La Parilla ★★ MEXICAN A downtown institution, La Parilla is a celebration of Mexican folklore featuring a colorful open-air dining room, nightly Mariachi music, and a rich menu promising excellent food. You'll find authentic dishes from the garden, the kettle, and the Caribbean, as well as Mexican specialties like *mole* enchiladas or grilled Aztec steak wrapped in cactus leaves and stuffed with onions. There are also tacos of every variety, sumptuous grilled steaks and seafood, and Maya treats such as "poc-chuc" pork tenderloin. This is a place to eat, drink, and be merry, and tequila samplers are available for those willing to risk a hangover tomorrow morning. One drawback: there are fans but no air-conditioning, so take a cold shower before you come here on a hot, humid night.

Av. Yaxchilán 51. ✆ **998/287-8118.** www.laparilla.com.mx. Reservations not accepted. Main courses 150–350 pesos. AE, MC, V. Daily noon–2am.

INEXPENSIVE

100% Natural ★ BREAKFAST/HEALTH FOOD If you want a healthy reprieve from an overindulgent night—or just like your meals as fresh and natural as possible—this is your oasis. No matter what your dining preference, you owe it to yourself to try a Mexican tradition, the fresh-fruit *licuado.* These tropical smoothies combine fresh fruit, ice, and water or milk. More creative combinations may mix in yogurt, granola, or other goodies. 100% Natural serves more than just quality drinks—there's a bountiful selection of healthy Mexican plates and terrific sandwiches served on whole-grain bread, with options for vegetarians. Breakfast is delightful and the attached bakery features all-natural baked goods such as chocolate croissants and apple-cinnamon muffins. There are several 100% Natural locations in town, including branches at Playa Chac-Mool, in front of Señor Frog's, and downtown.

Av. Sunyaxchen 63. ✆ **998/884-0102.** www.100natural.com.mx. Reservations not accepted. Main courses 50–184 pesos. AE, MC, V. Daily 7am–11pm.

Rolandi's ☺ ITALIAN At this shaded patio bar, restaurant, and pizzeria known for dependably tasty Italian delights, you can choose from an enticing selection of spaghetti, calzones, and Italian-style chicken and beef, as well as from almost two dozen delicious, if greasy, wood-oven pizzas (individual size). Why not try the deliciously spicy "Fiesta Mexicana" pizza with tomato, cheese, Mexican pepperoni, and jalapeños or the "Pizza del Patrone" with prosciutto and arugula? A Cancún institution here since 1979, Rolandi's has additional branches in Cozumel and Isla Mujeres (see chapter 6). It's as popular with locals as with tourists.

Av. Cobá 12. ✆ **998/884-4047.** Fax 998/884-4047. www.rolandi.com. Reservations recommended. Pasta 90–120 pesos; pizza and main courses 70–140 pesos. AE, MC, V. Daily 12:30pm–12:30am.

BEACHES, WATERSPORTS & BOAT TOURS

THE BEACHES Cancún recently added significant stretches of sand to its beaches as part of a $71 million beach recovery project to counter the amount of sand eroded by various storms in recent years. Big hotels dominate the best stretches of beach. All of Mexico's beaches are public property, so you can use the beach of any hotel by walking through the lobby or directly onto the sand. Be especially careful on the east-facing beaches fronting the open Caribbean, where the undertow can be quite strong. By contrast, the waters of **Bahía de Mujeres** (Mujeres Bay), at the north end of the island, are usually calm and ideal for swimming. Get to know Cancún's water-safety pennant system, and make sure to check the flag at any beach or hotel before entering the water. Here's how it goes:

Sailing off of the Cancún coast.

White Excellent

Green Normal conditions (safe)

Yellow Changeable, uncertain (use caution)

Black or **red** Unsafe—use the swimming pool instead!

In the Caribbean, storms can arrive and conditions can change from safe to unsafe in a matter of minutes, so be alert: If you see dark clouds heading your way, make for the shore and wait until the storm passes.

Playa Tortuga (Turtle Beach), Playa Langosta (Lobster Beach), Playa Linda (Pretty Beach), and Playa Las Perlas (Beach of the Pearls) are some of the public beaches. At most beaches, you can rent a sailboard and take lessons, ride a parasail, or partake in a variety of watersports. There's a

Learn to scuba dive in Cancún's clear, vibrant waters.

Snorkelers look for sealife off the Cancún coast.

small but beautiful portion of public beach on Playa Caracol, by the Xcaret Terminal. It faces the calm waters of Bahía de Mujeres and, for that reason, is preferable to those facing the Caribbean.

WATERSPORTS Many beachside hotels offer watersports concessions that rent rubber rafts, kayaks, and snorkeling equipment. On the calm Nichupté lagoon are outlets for renting **sailboats, jet skis, sailboards,** and **water skis.** Prices vary and are often negotiable, so check around.

DEEP-SEA FISHING You can arrange a shared or private deep-sea fishing charter at one of the numerous piers or travel agencies. Prices fluctuate widely depending on the length of the excursion (there's usually a 4-hr. minimum), number of people, and quality of the boat. Marinas will sometimes assist in putting together a group. Charters include a captain, a first mate, bait, gear, and beverages. Rates are lower if you depart from Isla Mujeres or from Cozumel—and, frankly, the fishing is better closer to those departure points. **Lagoonview Marina & Fishing Club** (✆ **998/845-0749**), located at Bulevar Kukulkán Km 13.5, rents 9.6m (32-ft.) Welcraft boats (maximum 6 people) for $450 for 4 hours, $675 for 6 hours, and $795 for 8 hours.

SCUBA & SNORKELING Known for its shallow reefs, dazzling color, and diversity of life, Cancún is one of the best places in the world for beginning scuba diving. Punta Nizuc is the northern tip of the **Gran Arrecife Maya (Great Mesoamerican Reef),** the largest reef in the Western Hemisphere and one of the largest in the world. In addition to the sea life along this reef system, several sunken boats add a variety of dive options. Inland, a series of caverns and cenotes (wellsprings) are fascinating venues for the more experienced diver. Drift diving is the norm here, with popular dives going to the reefs at **El Garrafón** and the **Cave of the Sleeping Sharks**—although be aware that the famed "sleeping sharks" have departed, driven off by too many people watching them snooze.

A variety of hotels offer resort courses that teach the basics of diving—enough to make shallow dives and slowly ease your way into this underwater world of unimaginable beauty. One preferred dive operator is **Scuba Cancún,** Bulevar Kukulkán Km 5 (✆ **998/849-4736;** www.scubacancun.com.mx), on the lagoon side. Full open-water PADI certification takes 3 days and costs $410. A half-day resort course for beginners with theory, pool practice, and a one-tank dive at a reef costs $88. Scuba Cancún is open daily from 7am to 8pm. For certified divers, Scuba Cancún also offers PADI specialty courses and diving trips in good weather to 18 nearby reefs, as well as to cenotes (9m/30 ft.) and Cozumel. The average dive is around 11m (36 ft.), while advanced divers descend farther (up to 18m/59 ft.). Two-tank dives to reefs around Cancún cost $68, and one-tank dives cost $54; those to farther destinations cost $140. Discounts apply if you bring your own gear. Dives usually start around 9:30am and return by 1:30pm. Snorkeling trips cost $29 and leave daily at 1:30pm and 4pm for shallow reefs about a 20-minute boat ride away.

The largest dive operator is **Aquaworld,** across from the Meliá Cancún at Bulevar Kukulkán Km 15.2 (✆ **998/848-8300;** www.aquaworld.com.mx). It offers resort courses and diving at a reef barrier, as well as snorkeling, parasailing, jet-ski "jungle tours," fishing, day trips to Isla Mujeres and Cozumel, and other watersports activities. Single-tank dives cost $65; two-tank dives $75. Aquaworld has the **Sub See Explorer,** a boat with picture windows beneath the surface. The vessel doesn't submerge—it's an updated version of a glass-bottom boat—but it does provide nondivers with a worthwhile peek at life beneath the sea. It costs $40 per person.

Another interesting option is **BOB Submarines** (✆ **998/849-7284**), located at El Embarcadero next to Playa Linda, which rents propelled breathing observation bubbles (BOBs). These personal minisubs let you discover the Caribbean with a big air bubble over your head and operate much like a scooter would. The tours include instruction, soft drinks, and a 30-minute assisted dive. The cost is $80 per person and the minimum age is 12, with departures at 9am, 11:30am, and 2pm.

Besides snorkeling at **El Garrafón Natural Park** (see "Boating Excursions," below), travel agencies offer an all-day excursion to the natural wildlife habitat of **Isla Contoy,** which usually includes time for snorkeling. The island, 90 minutes past Isla Mujeres, is a major nesting area for birds and a treat for nature lovers. You can call any travel agent or see any hotel tour desk to get a selection of boat tours to Isla Contoy. Prices range from $50 to $80, depending on the length of the trip, and generally include drinks and snorkeling equipment.

A frigate bird at Isla Contoy.

The Great Mesoamerican Reef also offers exceptional snorkeling opportunities. In Puerto Morelos, 37km (23 miles; p. 128) south of Cancún, the reef hugs the coastline for 15km (9¼ miles). The reef is so close to the shore (about 460m/1,509 ft.) that it forms a natural barrier for the village and keeps the waters calm on the inside of the reef. The water here is shallow, from 1.5 to 9m (5–30 ft.), resulting in ideal conditions for snorkeling. Stringent environmental regulations implemented by the local community have kept the reef here unspoiled. Only a select few companies are allowed to offer snorkel trips, and they must adhere to guidelines that will ensure the reef's preservation.

Cancún Mermaid (✆ **998/843-6517;** www.cancunmermaid.com), in Puerto Morelos, is considered the best—it's a family-run ecotour company that has operated in the area since the 1970s. It's known for highly personalized service. The tour typically takes snorkelers to two sections of the reef, spending about an hour in each area. When conditions allow, the boat drops off snorkelers and then follows them along with the current—an activity known as "drift snorkeling," which enables snorkelers to see as much of the reef as possible. The trip costs $50 for adults, $35 for children, and includes boat, snorkeling gear, life jackets, a light lunch, bottled water, sodas, and beer, plus round-trip transportation to and from Puerto Morelos from Cancún hotels. Departures are Monday through Saturday at 9am. For snorkelers who just can't get enough, a combo tour for $30 more adds a bicycle tour to additional snorkeling destinations. Reservations are required at least 1 day in advance; MasterCard and Visa are accepted.

JET-SKI/FAST BOAT TOURS Several companies offer the thrilling **Jungle Cruise,** in which you drive your own small speed boat (called a *lancha*) or WaveRunner rapidly through Cancún's lagoon and mangrove estuaries out into the Caribbean Sea and a shallow reef. The excursion lasts about 2½ hours and costs $60 to $70, including snorkeling equipment. Many people prefer the companies offering two-person boats rather than WaveRunners, since they can sit side by side rather than one behind the other.

Jungle cruise operators and names offering excursions change often. To find out what's available, check with a local travel agent or hotel tour desk. The popular **Aquaworld,** Bulevar Kukulkán Km 15.2 (✆ **998/848-8300**), calls its trip the Jungle Tour and charges $66 for the 2½-hour excursion, which includes 30 minutes of snorkeling time. It even gives you a free snorkel and has the WaveRunner-style one-behind-the-other seating configuration. Departures are daily at 9am, noon, and 2:30pm. If you'd prefer a side-by-side boat so that you and your partner can talk or at least look at each other, try **Blue Ray,** Bulevar Kukulkán Km 13.5, next to Mambo Café (✆ **998/885-1108**), which charges $55, with departures every hour between 9am and 3pm. Expect to get wet, and wear plenty of sunscreen. If you just want to rent a Wave Runner, Aquaworld offers them for $45 per half hour.

Boating Excursions

ISLA MUJERES The island of **Isla Mujeres,** just 13km (8 miles) offshore, is one of the most pleasant day trips from Cancún. At one end is **El Garrafón Natural Park,** which is good for snorkeling. At the other end is a captivating village with small shops, restaurants, and hotels, and **Playa Norte,** the island's best beach. If you're looking for relaxation and can spare the time, it's worth several days. For complete information about the island, see chapter 6.

There are four ways to get there: **public ferry** from Puerto Juárez, which takes between 15 and 20 minutes; **shuttle boat** from Playa Linda or Playa Tortuga, an hour-long ride, with irregular service; **water taxi** (more expensive, but faster), next to the Xcaret Terminal; and daylong **pleasure-boat cruises,** most of which leave from the Playa Linda pier.

The inexpensive but fast Puerto Juárez **public ferries** ★ lie just a few kilometers from downtown Cancún. From Cancún City, take the Ruta 8 bus on Avenida Tulum to Puerto Juárez. The air-conditioned ***Ultramar*** (**✆ 998/843-2011;** www.granpuerto.com.mx) boats cost 70 pesos per person each way and take 15 to 20 minutes. Departures are every half-hour from 5am to 8:30pm and then at 9:30pm, 10:30pm, and 11:30pm. Upon arrival, the ferry docks in downtown Isla Mujeres near all the shops, restaurants, hotels, and Norte beach. You'll need a taxi to get to El Garrafón park at the other end of the island. You can stay as long as you like on the island and return by ferry, but be sure to confirm the time of the last returning ferry.

An All-Terrain Tour

Cancún Mermaid (✆ 998/843-6517; www.cancunmermaid.com), about 30 minutes south of Cancún, offers all-terrain-vehicle (ATV) jungle tours for $49 per person if riding double or $66 if riding single. The ATV tours travel through the jungles of Cancún and emerge on the beaches of the Riviera Maya. The 5-hour tour (including transportation time from your hotel to the destination) includes gear, instruction, the services of a tour guide, lunch, and bottled water; it departs Monday through Saturday at 8am and 1:30pm. Reservations are required.

Pleasure-boat cruises to Isla Mujeres are a favorite pastime. Modern motor yachts, sailboats (including the "Sea Passion" catamaran), and even old-time sloops—more than 25 boats a day—take swimmers, sun lovers, snorkelers, and shoppers out on the translucent waters. Some tours include a snorkeling stop at El Garrafón, lunch on the beach, and a short time for shopping in downtown Isla Mujeres. Most leave at 9:30 or 10am, last about 5 or 6 hours, and include continental breakfast, lunch, and rental of snorkel gear. Others, particularly sunset and night cruises, go to beaches away from town for pseudo-pirate shows and include a lobster dinner or Mexican buffet (p. 121). If you want to actually see Isla Mujeres, go on a morning cruise, or travel on your own using the public ferry from Puerto Juárez. Prices for the day cruises run around $80 per person. Reservations aren't necessary.

An all-inclusive entrance fee of $69, $50 for children to **Garrafón Natural Reef Park ★★** (**✆ 998/849-4748;** www.garrafon.com), includes transportation from Playa Langosta in Cancún; meals; open bar with domestic drinks; access to the reef; and use of snorkel gear, kayaks, inner tubes, life vests, the pool, hammocks, and public facilities and showers (but not towels, so bring your own). There are also nature trails and several on-site restaurants.

Other excursions go to the **reefs** in glass-bottom boats, so you can have a near-scuba-diving experience and see many colorful fish. However, the reefs are some distance from the shore and are impossible to reach on windy days with choppy seas. They've also suffered from overvisitation, and their condition is far from pristine. Nautibus's **Atlantis Sub-marine** (**✆ 987/872-5671;** www.atlantisadventures.com) takes you close to the aquatic action. Departures vary, depending on weather conditions. Prices are $79 for adults, $45 for children ages 4 to 12. The submarine descends to a depth of 30m (98 ft.). Atlantis Submarine departs daily at 9am, 11am, and noon; the tour lasts about 40 minutes. The submarine departs from Cozumel, so you need to either take a ferry to get there or purchase a package that includes round-trip transportation from your hotel in Cancún ($103 adults, $76 children 4–12). Reservations are recommended.

OUTDOOR ACTIVITIES & ATTRACTIONS

DOLPHIN SWIMS On Isla Mujeres, you have the opportunity to swim with dolphins at **Dolphin Discovery** ★★ (✆ **998/877-0207** or 849-4757; www.dolphindiscovery.com). Groups of eight people swim with two dolphins and one trainer. Swimmers view an educational video and spend time in the water with the trainer and the dolphins before enjoying 15 minutes of free swimming time with them. Reservations are recommended (you can book online), and you must arrive an hour before your assigned swimming time, at 10:30am, noon, 2pm, or 3:30pm. The cost is $149 per person for the Dolphin Royal Swim. There are less expensive programs that allow you to learn about, touch, and hold the dolphins (but not swim with them) starting at $69. Ferry transfers from Playa Langosta in Cancún are available.

La Isla Shopping Center, Bulevar Kukulkán Km 12.5, has an impressive **Interactive Aquarium** (✆ **998/883-0411,** -0436, -0413; www.aquariumcancun.com.mx), with dolphin swims and shows and the chance to feed a shark while immersed in the water in an acrylic cage. Guides inside the main tank use underwater microphones to point out the sea life, and even answer your questions. Open exhibition tanks enable visitors to touch a variety of marine life, including sea stars and manta rays. The educational program and dolphin swim costs 1,120 pesos and the shark-feeding experience runs 790 pesos. The entrance fee to the aquarium is 140 pesos for adults, 90 pesos for children under 11, and it's open daily from 9am to 6pm.

GOLF & TENNIS The 18-hole **Cancún Golf Club at Pok-Ta-Pok** (✆ **998/883-0871;** www.cancungolfclub.com), located at Bulevar Kukulkán Km. 7.5, is a Robert Trent Jones II design on the northern leg of the island. Greens

The Hilton Cancún Golf club.

fees run $145 for 18 holes, including breakfast or lunch and golf cart (discounted fees after 2pm), with clubs renting for $45. A caddy costs $20 plus tip. The club is open daily from 6:30am to 5pm and accepts American Express, MasterCard, and Visa.

The **Hilton Cancún Golf & Spa Resort** (✆ **998/881-8016;** www.hiltongolfclub.com/golf) has a championship 18-hole, par-72 course around the Ruinas Del Rey. Greens fees during high season for the public are typically $199 for 18 holes and $125 for 9 holes; Hilton Cancún guests pay discounted rates of $159 for 18 holes, or $79 for 9 holes, which includes a golf cart. Low-season and twilight discounts are available. Golf clubs and shoes are available for rent. The club is open daily from 6am to 6pm and accepts American Express, MasterCard, and Visa. The **Gran Meliá Cancún** (✆ **998/881-1100**) has a 9-hole executive course; the fee is $30. The club is open daily from 7am to 3pm and accepts American Express, MasterCard, and Visa.

The first Jack Nicklaus Signature Golf Course in the Cancún area has opened at the **Moon Palace Spa & Golf Club** (✆ **998/881-6000;** www.palaceresorts.com), along the Riviera Maya. The $260 greens fee includes cart, snacks, and drinks.

HORSEBACK RIDING **Cancún Mermaid** (✆ **998/843-6517;** www.cancunmermaid.com), about 30 minutes south of town at the Rancho Loma Bonita, is a popular option for horseback riding. Five-hour packages include 2 hours of riding through the mangrove swamp to the beach, where you have time to swim and relax. The tour costs $66 for adults and $60 for children under 13. Tours include transportation to the ranch, riding, soft drinks, and lunch, plus a guide and insurance. Only cash or traveler's checks are accepted.

SHOPPING

Aside from the surrounding natural splendor, Cancún is known throughout Mexico for its diverse shops and festive malls catering to international tourists. Visitors from the United States may find apparel more expensive in Cancún, but the selection is much broader than at other Mexican resorts. Numerous duty-free shops offer excellent value on European goods. The largest is **Ultrafemme,** Av. Tulum, SM 25 (✆ **998/884-1402**), specializing in imported cosmetics, perfumes, and fine jewelry and watches. The downtown Cancún location offers slightly lower prices than branches in Plaza Caracol, La Isla, and Kukulcán Plaza. It's open Monday to Saturday from 9:30am to 9pm and Sunday from 2 to 9pm.

Handicrafts are more limited and more expensive in Cancún than in other regions of Mexico because they are not produced here. They are available, though; the best **open-air crafts market** is Mercado 28 in Cancún City. A less enticing open-air market in the Hotel Zone is **Coral Negro,** Bulevar Kukulkán Km 9.5, next to Plaza Dady'O, open daily from 7am to 11pm. **Plaza La Fiesta,** next to the Cancún Center (✆ **998/883-4519**), is a large Mexican outlet store selling handicrafts, jewelry, tequila, leather, and accessories. It's open daily from 7am to midnight.

Cancún's main venues are the **malls**—not quite as grand as their U.S. counterparts, but close. All are air-conditioned, sleek, and sophisticated. Most are on Bulevar Kukulkán between Km 7 and Km 12. They offer everything from fine

La Isla Shopping Village by night.

crystal and silver to designer clothing and decorative objects, along with numerous restaurants and clubs. Stores are generally open daily from 10am to 10pm.

The **Kukulcán Plaza** (✆ **998/885-2200;** www.kukulcanplaza.com) houses more than 300 shops, restaurants, and entertainment. It has a bank, a bowling alley, several crafts stores, a Play City with gambling machines, a liquor and tobacco store, several bathing-suit specialty stores, music stores, a drugstore, a leather-goods shop (including shoes and sandals), and a store specializing in silver from Taxco. U.S. franchise eateries include Häagen-Dazs and Ruth's Chris Steak House. The adjacent Luxury Avenue complex features designer labels such as Cartier, Coach, Fendi, Louis Vuitton, Salvatore Ferragamo, and Ultrafemme. The mall is open daily from 10am to 10pm, until 11pm during high season. Assistance for those with disabilities is available upon request, and wheelchairs, strollers, and lockers are available at the information desk.

The long-standing **Plaza Caracol** (✆ **998/883-1038;** www.caracolplaza.com) is one of Cancún's least glamorous malls but holds, among other things, Casa Rolandi (p. 122) restaurant and its Very Wine lounge. It's just before you reach the Convention Center as you come from downtown Cancún, and is open daily from 10am to 10pm.

Most people come to entertainment-oriented **Forum by the Sea,** Bulevar Kukulkán Km 9 (✆ **998/883-4425;** www.forumbythesea.com.mx), for the food and fun, choosing from Hard Rock Cafe, Carlos 'n' Charlie's, Rainforest Cafe, and CoCo Bongo, plus an extensive food court. Shops include Diesel, Harley-Davidson, Massimo Dutti, Señor Frog's, Sunglass Island, and Zingara Beachwear and Swimwear. The mall is open daily from 10am to midnight (bars remain open later).

One of Mexico's most appealing malls is the **La Isla Shopping Village,** Bulevar Kukulkán Km 12.5 (✆ **998/883-5025;** www.laislacancun.com.mx), a wonderful open-air complex that borders the lagoon. Walkways lined with quality shops and restaurants cross little canals (boat rides are even offered through the canals), and an attractive boardwalk lines the lagoon itself, as well as an interactive aquarium and dolphin swim facility (p. 132). Shops include Bulgari, Guess, Nautica, Nine West, Puma, Tommy Hilfiger, Ultrafemme, and Zara, as well as a large Mexican handicrafts store called Casa Mexicana. Among the dining choices are Johnny Rockets, Chili's, Italianni's, Planet Hollywood, the romantic Thai restaurant (p. 124), and the new Elefanta (p. 122). You will also find a movie theater, video arcade, and several bars, including La Madonna (p. 137).

CANCÚN AFTER DARK

Cancún's party reputation is not confined to spring break—the action here continues year-round. While the revelry often begins by day at the beach, the sun-drenched crowd heads at happy hour to the rocking bars located along the Hotel Zone, which often serve two-for-one drinks at sunset. Hotels play in the happy hour scene, with special drink prices to entice visitors and guests from other resorts. Come night, the hottest centers of action are also along Kukulkán, and include **Plaza Dady'O, Forum by the Sea,** and **La Isla Shopping Village.** These entertainment plazas transform into true spring break madness for most of March and April.

The Club & Music Scene

Clubbing in Cancún is a favorite part of the vacation experience and can go on each night until the sun rises over that incredibly blue sea. Several big hotels have nightclubs or schedule live music in their lobby bars. At the clubs, expect to stand in lines on weekends, pay a cover charge of about $40 with open bar, or $15 to $25 without open bar; and then pay $8 to $10 for a drink. Some of the higher-priced clubs include live entertainment. The places listed in this section are air-conditioned and accept American Express, MasterCard, and Visa.

Numerous restaurants, such as **Carlos 'n' Charlie's, Hard Rock Cafe,** and **Señor Frog's**, double as nighttime party spots, offering wildish fun at a fraction of the price of more costly clubs.

Grupo Dady offers a package deal enticing clubbers to party in all five of its neighboring bars, including Dady'O, Terresta, UltraClub, Dady Rock, and Dos Equis Bar. It costs $45 to $55 per person depending on the night and includes open bar; buy tickets at any of the Grupo Dady bars.

If you have been drinking when you're ready to go back to your accommodations, take public transportation or have someone with you rather than drive or get in a taxi alone.

Bling ★★ This is one of the coolest nightspots in Cancún, featuring a chic outdoor terrace overlooking the lagoon. A fashionable 30-something crowd congregates amid sofas under the stars, a killer sound system, and flowing cocktails. A sushi and sashimi bar and some Mediterranean dishes are also offered. This upscale lounge is considerably more sophisticated than Cancún's typical frat-style bars, and it's open daily from 6pm to 2am. Bl. Kukulkán Km 13.5. ✆ **998/840-6014.** www.blingcancun.com.

The City ★★ One of Cancún's hottest and largest nightclubs, The City features nine bars over three floors with progressive electronic music spun by visiting DJs from New York, L.A., and Mexico City (the DJ station looks like an airport control tower). This is where celebrities come to party when they're in town. You actually need never leave, as The City is a day-and-night club. The Playa Cabana beach club opens at 10am and features beach cabañas, a pool, and food and bar service with frequent activities, pool parties, and bikini contests. The Terrace Bar, overlooking the action on Bulevar Kukulkán, serves food and drinks all day long. For a relaxing evening vibe, the Lounge features comfy couches, chill music, and an extensive menu of martinis, snacks, and desserts. Open from 10:30pm to 4am, the 743-sq.-m (8,000-sq.-ft.) nightclub features a one million watt sound system, stunning light shows, and several VIP areas. Bl. Kukulkán Km 9.5. ✆ **998/848-8380.** www.thecitycancun.com. Cover $25; $45 with open bar.

CoCo Bongo ★★★ Continuing its reputation as the hottest party venue in town, CoCo Bongo combines an enormous dance club with extravagant theme shows. It has no formal dance floor, so you can dance anywhere—and that includes on the tables, on the bar, or even on the stage with the occasional live band. This place regularly packs in as many as 3,000 people—you have to experience it to believe it. Despite its capacity, lines are long on weekends and in high season. The music alternates between Caribbean, salsa, house, hip-hop, techno, and classics from the '70s, '80s, and '90s. Open from 10:30pm to 3:30am, CoCo Bongo draws a hip young crowd. Forum by the Sea, Bl. Kukulkán Km 9.5. ✆ **998/883-5061.** www.cocobongo.com.mx. Weekend cover $60 with open bar, $50 weekdays with open bar.

Dady'O This is a popular rave among the young and brave, with frequent long lines. Grupo Dady offers a package deal that includes open bar and entrance to all five of its neighboring bars (see above), and this is the grand daddy of them. It opens nightly at 10pm and has a giant dance floor and awesome light system. Bl. Kukulkán Km 9.5. ✆ **998/883-3333.** www.dadyo.com. Cover $20–$25.

Dady Rock Bar and Club The offspring of Dady'O, Dady Rock opens at 8pm and goes as long as any other nightspot, offering a combination of live rock bands and DJs spinning grooves, along with an open bar, full meals, a buffet, and dancing. Bl. Kukulkán Km 9.5. ✆ **998/883-1626.** www.dadyo.com. Cover $20–$25.

Club-goers wait to get in to CoCo Bongo.

La Madonna With more than 150 creative martini selections accompanied by ambient music, La Madonna also offers authentic Swiss-Italian cuisine, including fondues, as well as delicious desserts (p. 123). Enjoy your red mandarin, lychee, or green apple martini or glass of wine elbow to elbow with Cancún's beautiful people on the outdoor patio. Bossa nova and lounge music are the norm. It's open daily from noon to 1am. La Isla Shopping Village, Bl. Kukulkán Km 12.5. ✆ **998/883-2222.** www.lamadonna.com.

The Lobby Lounge ★ This is the most refined of Cancún's nightly gathering spots, with a terrace overlooking the lagoon, a special martini collection, and a list of more than 80 premium tequilas for tasting or sipping. There's also a sushi and seafood bar, as well as a humidor collection of Cuban cigars. It's open daily from 5pm to 12am, with live music Wednesday through Saturday. Ritz-Carlton Cancún (p. 115), Retorno del Rey 36, off Bl. Kukulkán Km 13.5. ✆ **998/881-0808.**

Very Wine ★ This elegant wine bar sits on the upper level of Casa Rolandi (p. 122), a relaxed place to come for a predinner drink or a nightcap. The gourmet bar has a fine wine and liquor selection, and also offers tapas, fondues, and desserts, as well as cigars. This is a refined alternative to Cancún's more raucous bars and clubs. It's open from 1pm until the last customer leaves. Plaza Caracol, Bl. Kukulkán Km 8.5. ✆ **998/883-1817.**

The Performing Arts

Several hotels host **Mexican fiesta nights,** including a buffet dinner and a folkloric dance show; admission with dinner and open bar costs about $50, unless you're at an all-inclusive resort that includes this as part of the package. Check out the show at **Hacienda Sisal** (✆ **998/848-8220**), located at Bulevar Kukulkán Km 13.5, which is offered Tuesday and Thursday nights at 8pm.

6

ISLA MUJERES & COZUMEL

by Shane Christensen

These two Caribbean islands are am back beach destinations in Mexico from Cancún and the Riviera Maya. high season, both receive a lot of cruise-ship visitors, but if you stay o the relaxed pace of island life is yours to enjoy. Nei nor Cozumel is particularly large, and they still have that island feel—with small roads that don't go very far, lots of mopeds, few (if any) trucks, and a sense of remoteness from the rest of the world. Both offer a range of lodging options, ample outdoor activities, and a relaxed atmosphere that contrasts with much of the mainland experience.

Isla Mujeres

Fish-shaped **Isla Mujeres** is 13km (8 miles) northeast of Cancún, a quick boat ride away. Hotels range from rustic to regal. Passenger ferries travel to Isla Mujeres from Puerto Juárez, and car ferries leave from Punta Sam, both near Cancún. More expensive passenger ferries, with fewer departures, leave from the Playa Linda pier on Cancún Island.

Larger than Isla Mujeres and farther from the mainland (19km/12 miles off the coast from Playa del Carmen), **Cozumel** has its own international airport. Life here revolves around two major activities: scuba diving and cruise ships making a port of call. Cozumel remains far and away the most popular destination along this coast for both activities, although tourism here declined dramatically in the wake of the global recession and swine flu.

The result is that Cozumel feels as relaxed as ever. There's just one town, San Miguel de Cozumel; to the north and south lie resorts. The rest of the shore is deserted and predominantly rocky, with a scattering of small sandy coves that you can have all to yourself. Unfortunately, there's no way to travel directly between Cozumel and Isla Mujeres, but you can get from one to the other by traveling via Cancún and Playa del Carmen.

ISLA MUJERES ★★★

13km (8 miles) N of Cancún

Isla Mujeres (Island of Women) is a casual, easygoing refuge from the heady tempo of Cancún. It lies not far off the coast and is visible from the resort. As Caribbean islands go, Isla is a bargain and a good fit for anyone who prefers simplicity and ease over variety and action. The island's only town is right next to North Beach, the best beach on the island. With beach towel in hand, you can leisurely stroll to the beach from any hotel in town; there's no need for transportation unless you want to tour the whole island, in which case a golf cart will do. Isla Mujeres is small, the town is small, the hotels (with a couple of exceptions) are small, the restaurants, the bars, the excursion boats—small, small, small.

FACING PAGE: **An isolated beach on Cozumel.**

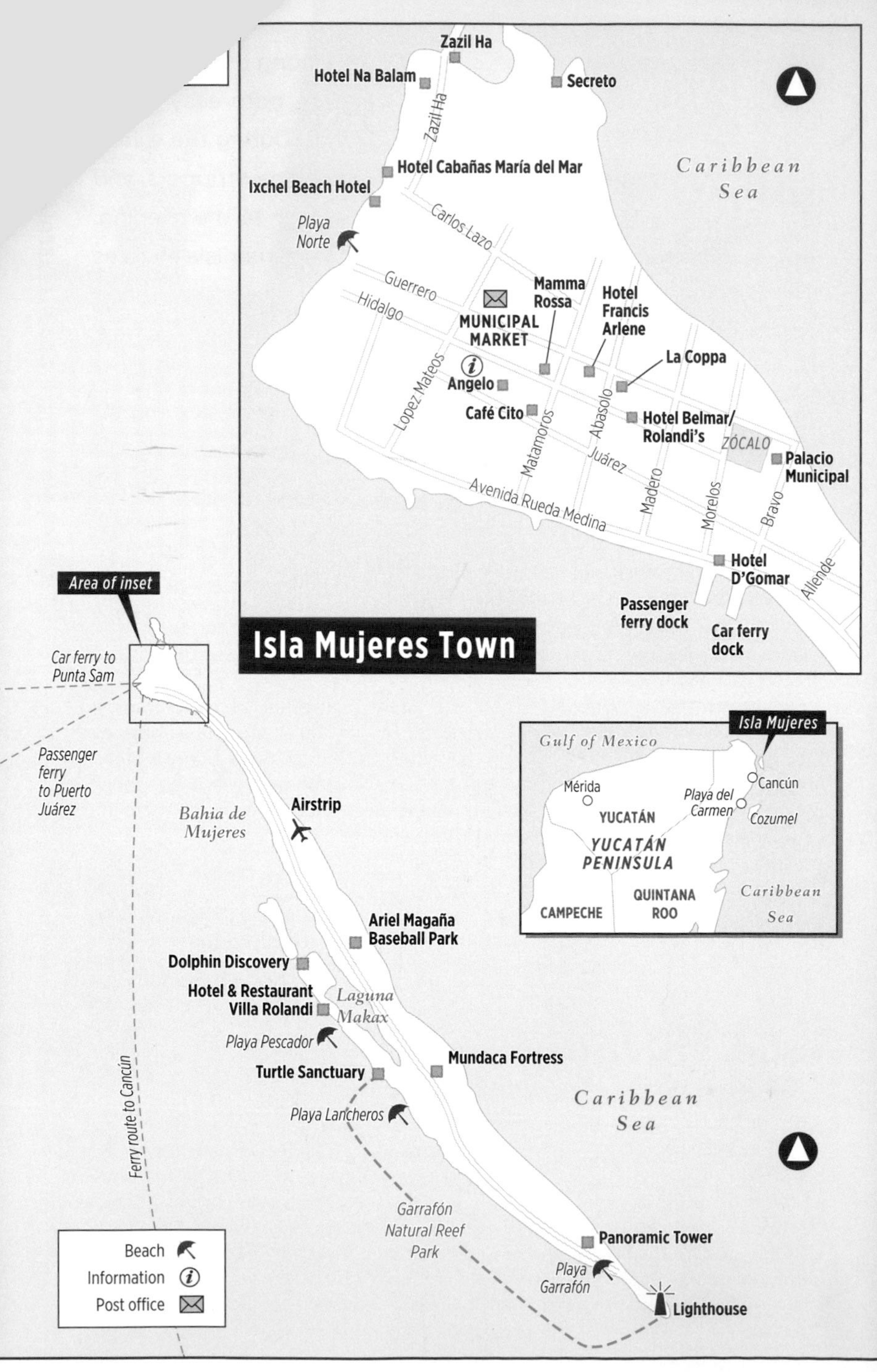
Isla Mujeres Town
Zazil Ha
Hotel Na Balam
Secreto
Zazil Ha
Hotel Cabañas María del Mar
Ixchel Beach Hotel
Caribbean Sea
Playa Norte
Carlos Lazo
Guerrero
Hidalgo
Mamma Rossa
MUNICIPAL MARKET
Hotel Francis Arlene
La Coppa
Angelo
Lopez Mateos
Café Cito
Matamoros
Abasolo
Hotel Belmar/ Rolandi's
ZÓCALO
Palacio Municipal
Juárez
Avenida Rueda Medina
Madero
Morelos
Bravo
Hotel D'Gomar
Allende
Passenger ferry dock
Car ferry dock
Area of inset
Car ferry to Punta Sam
Passenger ferry to Puerto Juárez
Bahia de Mujeres
Airstrip
Gulf of Mexico
Isla Mujeres
Mérida
Cancún
Playa del Carmen
Cozumel
YUCATÁN
YUCATÁN PENINSULA
CAMPECHE
QUINTANA ROO
Caribbean Sea
Ariel Magaña Baseball Park
Dolphin Discovery
Hotel & Restaurant Villa Rolandi
Laguna Makax
Playa Pescador
Mundaca Fortress
Turtle Sanctuary
Caribbean Sea
Playa Lancheros
Ferry route to Cancún
Garrafón Natural Reef Park
Panoramic Tower
Playa Garrafón
Lighthouse
Beach
Information
Post office

Choose from several inexpensive hotels, mostly in town, and a smattering of luxury boutique hotels spread out to other parts of the island.

The scale of the island heightens the contrast between high season and low season, making the crowds and bustle much more noticeable at peak travel times. At midday, suntanned visitors from the Cancún tour boats hang out in open-air cafes and stroll the pedestrian streets lined with zealous souvenir vendors calling attention to their wares. The scene takes on a carnivalesque hue during the hours when the tour-boat traffic is at its peak. Then, later in the afternoon, things settle down.

Trips to the Isla Contoy bird sanctuary are popular, as are the diving, snorkeling, and fishing jaunts. In 1998, the island's coral coast became part of Mexico's Marine National Park system. The reef suffered substantial hurricane damage in 2005, but continues to rebound. The water clarity illuminates the wonderful array of coral and tropical fish living here. The underwater life you are likely to see includes French angelfish, longspine squirrelfish, trumpet fish, four-eye butterfly fish, green angelfish, stoplight parrotfish, southern stingrays, sharp-nose puffer fish, blue tang, and great barracuda.

The island and several of its hotels attract regular gatherings of yoga practitioners. In the evening, most people find the slow, casual pace one of the island's biggest draws. The cool night breeze offers a perfect accompaniment to casual open-air dining and drinking in small street-side restaurants. This is just how island living is meant to be.

Essentials

GETTING THERE & DEPARTING **Puerto Juárez,** just north of Cancún, is the dock (✆ **998/877-0382**) for passenger ferries to Isla Mujeres.

THE BEST WEBSITES FOR isla mujeres & cozumel

- **Isla Mujeres Tourist Information: www.isla-mujeres.net** The official site of the Isla Mujeres Tourism Board provides complete information on Isla, from getting there to where to stay.
- **My Isla Mujeres: www.myislamujeres.com** Get a local's view of the island; the active message boards are especially good.
- **Cozumel.net: www.cozumel.net** This site is a cut above the typical dining/lodging/activities sites. Click on "About Cozumel" to find schedules for ferries and island-hop flights, and to check the latest news. There's also a comprehensive listing of B&Bs and vacation-home rentals.
- **Cozumel Travel Planner: www.go2cozumel.com** This is a well-done guide to area businesses and attractions, by an online Mexico specialist.
- **Cozumel Hotel Association: www.islacozumel.com.mx** Operated by the tourism-promotion arm of the hotel association, this site gives more than just listings of the member hotels. There's info on packages and specials, plus brief descriptions of most of the island's attractions, restaurants, and recreational activities.

Ultramar (✆ **998/843-2011;** www.granpuerto.com.mx) has fast boats leaving every half-hour from "Gran Puerto" in Puerto Juárez, making the trip in 15 minutes. There is storage space for luggage and the fare is 70 pesos each way. These boats operate daily, starting at 6am and usually ending at 10:30pm (check beforehand for latest schedules). They might leave early if they're full, so arrive ahead of schedule. Pay at the ticket office or on board if the ferry is about to leave.

Note: Upon arrival by taxi or bus in Puerto Juárez, be wary of pirate "guides" who tell you either that the ferry is canceled or that it's several hours until the next ferry. They'll offer the services of a private *lancha* (small boat) for about 450 pesos—and it's nothing but a scam. Small boats are available and, on a co-op basis, charge 200 to 350 pesos one-way, based on the number of passengers. They take about 50 minutes and are not recommended on days with rough seas. Check with the ticket office—the only accurate source for information.

On your return to Puerto Juárez, you'll see taxi fares posted by the street where the taxis park, so be sure to check the rate before agreeing to a taxi for the ride back to Cancún. Rates generally run 120 to 150 pesos, depending upon your destination. Moped and bicycle rentals are also readily available as you depart the ferry. This small complex also has public bathrooms, luggage storage, a snack bar, and souvenir shops.

Isla Mujeres is so small that a vehicle isn't necessary, but if you're taking one to the island, you'll use the **Punta Sam** port a little beyond Puerto Juárez. The 40-minute car ferry (✆ **998/877-0065**) runs five or six times daily between 8am and 8pm, year-round except in bad weather. Times are generally as follows: Cancún to Isla 8 and 11am and 2:45, 5:30, and

The Isla Mujeres Ferry Terminal.

Avenida Rueda Medina, or the malecón

8:15pm; Isla to Cancún 6:30 and 9:30am and 12:45, 4:15, and 7:15pm. Always check with the tourist office in Cancún to verify this schedule. Cars should arrive an hour before the ferry departure to register for a place in line and pay the posted fee, which varies depending on the weight and type of vehicle. A gas pump is at Avenida Rueda Medina and Calle Abasolo, northwest of the ferry docks.

Ferries to Isla Mujeres also depart from **Playa Linda,** known as the Embarcadero pier in Cancún, but they're less frequent and more expensive than those from Puerto Juárez. There are four to six scheduled departures per day to Isla Mujeres, depending upon the season. Adult fares are 150 pesos round-trip; kids ages 3 to 12 pay 75 pesos; children younger than 3 ride free. A **Water Taxi** (✆ **998/886-4270**) to Isla Mujeres operates from the Embarcadero (just off Kukulkán Km 4 on the northern tip of the Hotel Zone/Isla Cancun).

To get to Puerto Juárez or Punta Sam from **Cancún,** take any Ruta 8 city bus from Avenida Tulum. From the Cancún airport, take the shuttle bus to the pier (160 pesos).

VISITOR INFORMATION The **City Tourist Office** (✆/fax **998/877-0767,** -0307) is at Av. Rueda Medina 130, just across the street from the pier. It's open Monday through Friday from 9am to 4pm, closed on Saturday and Sunday. *Islander* is a free publication with local information, advertisements, and event listings.

ISLAND LAYOUT Isla Mujeres is about 8km (5 miles) long and 4km (2½ miles) wide, with the town at the northern tip. "Downtown" is a compact 4 blocks by 6 blocks, so it's very easy to get around. The **passenger ferry docks** are at the center of town, within walking distance of most hotels, restaurants, and shops. The street running along the waterfront and in front of the ferry docks is **Avenida Rueda Medina,** commonly called the ***malecón*** **(boardwalk).** The **Mercado Municipal (town market)** is by the post office on **Calle Guerrero,** an inland street at the north edge of town, which, like most streets in the town, is unmarked.

GETTING AROUND A popular form of transportation on Isla Mujeres is the electric **golf cart,** available for rent at many hotels or rental shops for 180 pesos per hour or 600 pesos for 24 hours. Prices are set the same at all rental locations. **El Sol Golf Cart Rental,** Av. Benito Juárez Mza 3 no. 20 (corner of Matamoros; ✆ **998/877-0791**), is one good option in the town center. The golf carts don't go more than 30kmph (19 mph), but they're fun. Anyway, you aren't on Isla Mujeres to hurry. Many people enjoy touring the island by ***moto*** **(motorized bike or scooter).** Fully automatic versions are available for around 450 pesos per day or 100 pesos per hour. They come with helmets and seats for two people. There's only one main road with a couple of offshoots, so you won't get lost. Be aware that the rental price does not include insurance, and any injury to yourself or the vehicle will come out of your pocket. **Bicycles** are also available for rent at some hotels for about 35 pesos an hour or 120 pesos per day, usually including a basket and a lock.

Tricycle taxis are the least expensive and easiest way to get to your hotel if it's in town. From the ferry pier to any of the downtown hotels will cost about 20 to 30 pesos. If you ask the guys, they'll say "Oh, whatever you care to give." I will let them haul my bags and lead the way while I walk.

If you prefer to use a taxi, rates are about 25 pesos for trips within the downtown area, or 50 pesos for a trip to the southern end of Isla. You can also hire them for about 100 pesos per hour. Regular taxis are always lined up in a parking lot to the right of the pier, with their rates posted. The number to call for taxis is ✆ **998/877-0066.**

Playa Norte Beach in Isla Mujeres.

[FastFACTS] ISLA MUJERES

Area Code The telephone area code is **998.**

ATMs & Banks Isla has only one bank, **HSBC Bank** (✆ **998/877-0005**), across from the ferry docks. It's open Monday through Friday from 8:30am to 6pm, and Saturday from 9am to 2pm. It has ATM machines.

Consumer Protection You can reach the local branch of **Profeco** consumer protection agency at ✆ **998/887-3960.**

Currency Exchange Isla Mujeres has numerous *casas de cambio,* or currency exchanges, along the main streets. Most of the hotels listed here change money for their guests, although often at less favorable rates than the commercial enterprises.

Drugstore **Isla Mujeres Farmacía** (✆ **998/877-0178**) has the best selection of prescription and over-the-counter medicines. It's open daily from 9am to 10pm.

Hospital The **Hospital de la Armada** is on Avenida Rueda Medina at Ojón P. Blanco (✆ **998/877-0001**). It's less than a kilometer (a half-mile) south of the town center. It will treat you only in an emergency. Otherwise, you're referred to the **Centro de Salud,** on Avenida Guerrero, a block before the beginning of the *malecón* (✆ **998/877-0117**).

Internet Access **L'Argentina,** at Hidalgo and Matamoros, offers Wi-Fi and computers for 20 pesos per hour. It's open daily from 11am to 2am and serves coffee and grilled foods, too.

Post Office The *correo* is at Calle Guerrero 12 (✆ **998/877-0085**), at the corner of López Mateos, near the market. It's open Monday through Friday from 9am to 4pm.

Seasons Isla Mujeres's tourist season (when hotel rates are higher) is a bit different from that of other places in Mexico. High season runs December through May, a month longer than in Cancún. Some hotels raise their rates in August, and some raise their rates beginning in mid-November. Low season is from June to mid-November.

Beaches & Outdoor Activities

BEACHES & SWIMMING The most popular beach in town, and the best for swimming, is **Playa Norte ★**. It's a long stretch of beach extending around the northern tip of the island. This is perhaps the world's best municipal beach—a wide swath of fine white sand and calm, translucent, turquoise-blue water. The beach is easily reached on foot from the ferry and from all downtown hotels. Watersports equipment, beach umbrellas, and lounge chairs are available for rent. Areas in front of restaurants usually cost nothing if you use the restaurant as your headquarters for drinks and food, and the best of them have hammocks and swings from which to sip your piña coladas.

Garrafón Natural Reef Park ★★ (p. 148) is best known as a snorkeling area, but there is a nice stretch of beach on either side of the park. **Playa Lancheros** is on the Caribbean side of Laguna Makax and is probably the second-best for swimming. Local buses go to Lancheros and then turn inland and return downtown. The beach at Playa Lancheros is nice, with a variety of casual restaurants.

There are no lifeguards on duty on Isla Mujeres, which does not use the system of water-safety flags employed in Cancún and Cozumel. The bay between Cancún and Isla Mujeres is calm, with warm, transparent waters ideal for swimming, snorkeling, and diving. The east side of the island facing the open Caribbean Sea is typically rougher, with much stronger currents.

FISHING To arrange a day of fishing, ask at the **Sociedad Cooperativa Turística** (the boatmen's cooperative), on Avenida Rueda Medina (© **998/877-1363**), next to Mexico Divers and Las Brisas restaurant. Four to six others can share the cost, which includes lunch and drinks. Capt. Tony Martínez (© **998/877-0274**) also arranges fishing trips aboard the ***Marinonis,*** with advanced reservations recommended. Year-round you'll find bonito, mackerel, kingfish, and amberjack. Sailfish and sharks (hammerhead, bull, nurse, lemon, and tiger) are in good supply in April and May. In winter, larger grouper and jewfish are prevalent. Four hours of fishing close to shore costs around $125; 8 hours farther out goes for $250. The cooperative is open Monday through Saturday from 8am to 1pm and 5 to 8pm, and Sunday from 7:30 to 10am and 6 to 8pm.

SCUBA DIVING Most of the dive shops on the island offer the same trips for similar prices, including reef, drift, deep, and night dives: one-tank dives cost about $55 to $75; two-tank dives about $65 to $85. **Bahía Dive Shop,** Rueda Medina 166, across from the car-ferry dock (© **998/877-0340**), is a full-service shop that offers dive equipment for sale or rent. Another respected dive shop is **Carey Dive Center,** at Matamoros 13A and Rueda Medina (© **998/877-0763**). Both offer 2-hour snorkeling trips for about $25.

Cuevas de los Tiburones (Caves of the Sleeping Sharks) is Isla's most renowned dive site—but the name is slightly misleading, as shark sightings are rare these days. Two sites where you could traditionally see the sleeping shark are the Cuevas de Tiburones and **La Punta,** but the sharks have mostly been driven off, and a storm collapsed the arch featured in a Jacques Cousteau film showing them, but the caves survive. Other dive sites include a **wreck** 15km (9¼ miles) offshore; **Banderas** reef, between Isla Mujeres and Cancún, where there's always a strong current; **Tabos** reef on the eastern shore; and **Manchones** reef, 1km (a half-mile) off the southeastern tip of the island, where the water is 4.5 to 11m (15–36 ft.) deep. **The Cross of the Bay** is close to Manchones reef. A bronze cross, weighing 1 ton and standing 12m (39 ft.) high, was placed in the water between Manchones and Isla in 1994, as a memorial to those who have lost their lives at sea.

SNORKELING One of the most popular places to snorkel is **Garrafón Natural Reef Park ★★** (p. 148). **Manchones Reef,** off the southeastern coast, is also good. It's just offshore and accessible by boat. You can snorkel around *el faro* (the lighthouse) in the **Bahía de Mujeres** at the southern tip of the island. The water is about 2m (6½ ft.) deep. Boatmen will take you for around 250 pesos per person if you have your own snorkeling equipment or 300 pesos if you use theirs.

YOGA Increasingly, Isla is becoming popular among yoga enthusiasts. The trend began at **Hotel Na Balam ★★** (p. 151; © **998/877-0279,** -0058; www.nabalam.com), which offers yoga classes on weekdays under its large poolside *palapa,* complete with yoga mats and props. The hotel also offers yoga instruction vacations featuring respected teachers and a more extensive

Snorkeling off of Isla Mujeres.

practice schedule; the current schedule of yoga retreats is posted on their website. Another yoga center that has sprung up and is drawing together a community is **Elements of the Island** (www.elementsoftheisland.com). It's located at Juárez 64, between López Mateos and Matamoros.

Attractions

DOLPHIN DISCOVERY ★★ You can swim with dolphins (✆ **998/849-4748** or 849-4757; fax 998/849-4751; www.dolphindiscovery.com) in an enclosure at Treasure Island, on the side of Isla Mujeres that faces Cancún. Groups of eight people swim with two dolphins and one trainer. Swimmers view an educational video and spend time in the water with the trainer and the dolphins before enjoying 15 minutes of free swimming time with them. Reservations are necessary, and you must arrive an hour before your assigned swimming time, at 10:30am, 12:15pm, 2:15pm, or 3:30pm. The cost is $149 per person for the Dolphin Royal Swim. There are less expensive programs that allow you to learn about, touch, and hold the dolphins (but not swim with them), starting at $79 ($69 for kids).

TURTLE SANCTUARY ★★ Years ago, fishermen converged on the island nightly from May to September to capture turtles when they would come ashore to lay eggs. Then a concerned fisherman, Gonzalo Chale Maldonado, began convincing others to spare the eggs, which he protected. It was a start. Following his lead, the fishing ministry founded the **Centro de Investigaciones Pesqueras** to find ways to protect the species and increase the turtle populations. Although the local government provides some assistance, most of the funding comes from private-sector donations. Since the center opened, tens of thousands of young turtles have been released, and local schoolchildren have participated, helping to educate a new generation of islanders for the cause. Releases are scheduled from May to October, and visitors are invited to take part. Inquire at the center.

Three species of sea turtles nest on Isla Mujeres. An adult green turtle, the most abundant species, is 1 to 1.5m (3¼–5 ft.) long and can weigh 204kg (450 lb.). At the center, visitors walk through the indoor and outdoor turtle pool areas, where the creatures paddle around. Turtles are separated by age, from newly hatched up to 1 year. People who come here usually end up staying at least an hour, especially if they opt for the guided tour, which I recommend. They also have a small gift shop and snack bar. The sanctuary is on a spit of land jutting out from the island's west coast. The address is Carretera Sac Bajo #5; you'll need a taxi to get there. Admission is 30 pesos; the shelter is open daily from 9am to 5pm. For more information, call **✆ 998/877-0595.**

GARRAFÓN NATIONAL PARK & PUNTA SUR ★★ El Garrafón (**✆ 998/849-4748;** www.garrafon.com) is at the southern end of the island. The pricey but well-equipped park has two restaurant/bars, beach chairs, a swimming pool, kayaks, changing rooms, rental lockers, showers, a gift shop, and snack bars. Once a public national underwater park, Garrafón is now operated by Dolphin Discovery. Activities include snorkeling, kayaking, and swimming (for an extra fee, there are swim-with-dolphins packages, too). On land are tanning decks, shaded hammocks, a 12m (39-ft.) climbing tower, and—of course—a souvenir superstore. Admission is $68 ($50 for children under 12); the all-inclusive package includes round-trip transportation between Cancún and Isla Mujeres, continental breakfast, domestic open bar, buffet lunch, and use of snorkeling equipment and kayaks. The park is open daily in high season from 9am to 5pm. In low season, it may close a couple days per week.

Next to the panoramic tower, you'll find **Sculptured Spaces,** an impressive and extensive garden of large sculptures donated to Isla Mujeres by internationally renowned sculptors as part of the 2001 First International Sculpture Exhibition. Among Mexican sculptors represented by works are José Luis Cuevas and Vladimir Cora.

Cliff of the Dawn.

The Cross of the Bay.

Nearby is the **Caribbean Village,** with narrow lanes of colorful clapboard buildings that house cafes and shops displaying folk art. You can have lunch or a snack here at the kiosk and stroll around before heading on to the lighthouse and Maya ruins.

Also at this southern point of the island, and part of the ruins, is **Cliff of the Dawn,** the southeasternmost point of Mexico. Services are available from 9am to 5pm, but you can enter at any time; if you make it there early enough to see the sunrise, you can claim you were the first person in Mexico that day to be touched by the sun!

ISLA CONTOY ★ Try to visit this pristine uninhabited island, 30km (19 miles) by boat from Isla Mujeres. It became a national wildlife reserve in 1981. The 6km- (3¾-miles) long island is covered in lush vegetation and harbors 70 species of birds, as well as a host of marine and animal life. Bird species that nest on the island include pelicans, brown boobies, frigates, egrets, terns, and cormorants. Flocks of flamingos arrive in April. Most excursions troll for fish (which will be your lunch), anchor en route for a snorkeling expedition, skirt the island at a leisurely pace for close viewing of the birds without disturbing the habitat, and then pull ashore. While the captain prepares lunch, visitors can swim, sun, follow the nature trails, and visit the fine nature museum, which has bathroom facilities. The trip from Isla Mujeres takes about 45 minutes each way and can be longer if the waves are choppy. Because of the tight-knit boatmen's cooperative, prices for this excursion are the same everywhere: $55 for adults; half price for children under 9 (cash only). You can buy a ticket at the **Sociedad Cooperativa** (**✆ 998/877-1363**), on Avenida Rueda Medina, next to Mexico Divers and Las Brisas restaurant. Trips leave at 9am and return around 4pm. Boat captains should respect the cooperative's regulations regarding ecological sensitivity and boat safety, including the availability of life jackets for everyone on board. If you're not given a life jacket, ask for one. Snorkeling equipment is usually included in the price, but double-check before heading out.

A MAYA RUIN ★★ Just beyond the lighthouse, at the southern end of the island, are the remains of a small Maya temple. Archaeologists believe it was dedicated to the moon and fertility goddess Ixchel. The location, on a lofty bluff overlooking the sea, is worth seeing and makes a great place for photos. It is believed that Maya women traveled here on annual pilgrimages to seek Ixchel's blessings of fertility.

A PIRATE'S FORTRESS Almost in the middle of the island is a large building purported to have been a pirate fortress. A slave trader who arrived here in the

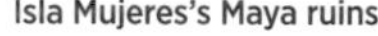

Isla Mujeres's Maya ruins.

Hacienda Mundaca, an old pirate's fortress.

early 19th century claimed to have been the pirate Mundaca Marecheaga. He set up a business selling slaves to Cuba and Belize, and prospered here. According to island lore, a charming local girl captivated him, only to spurn him in favor of a local.

Shopping

Shopping is a casual activity here. Several shops, especially concentrated on Avenida Hidalgo, sell Saltillo rugs, onyx, silver, Guatemalan clothing, blown glassware, masks, folk art, crafts, beach paraphernalia, and T-shirts in abundance. Prices are lower than in Cancún or Cozumel.

Where to Stay

You'll find plenty of hotels in all price ranges on Isla Mujeres. The rates listed below include the 12% room tax. They do not necessarily apply to the brief Christmas/New Year's season, when many hotels charge extra. High season runs from December through May and sometimes includes August. Low season is the rest of the year.

Those interested in private home rentals or longer-term stays can contact **Mundaca Travel and Real Estate** on Isla Mujeres (✆ **866/646-0536** in the U.S., or 998/877-0025; www.mundaca.com.mx), or book online with **Isla Beckons** property rental service (www.islabeckons.com). Another helpful website for booking accommodations is www.travelyucatan.com.

VERY EXPENSIVE

Hotel Villa Rolandi Gourmet & Beach Club ★★★ Villa Rolandi is a romantic escape on a little sheltered cove with a pristine white-sand beach. Each of the luxurious suites holds a separate sitting area and large terrace or balcony with private whirlpool overlooking the sea. All rooms feature in-room sound systems, subtle lighting, and marble surfaces. The bathrooms have Bulgari products and enticing showers with multiple showerheads that convert into steam baths. In-room breakfast is delivered through a small portal. The hotel spa also offers an outdoor Thalasso therapy whirlpool and beachside massages. The owner is a Swiss-born restaurateur who made a name for himself with his restaurants on Isla Mujeres and in Cancún. You can eat well without having to go off property, which is reached directly by boat (provided by the resort) or via a 20-minute drive from the town.

Fracc. Lagunamar, SM 7, Mza. 75, Locs. 15 and 16, 77400 Isla Mujeres, Q. Roo. ✆ **998/999-2000.** Fax 998/877-0100. www.villarolandi.com. 35 units. High season $357 and up double, $438 and up junior suite; low season $254–$323 double, $288–$357 junior suite. Rates include continental breakfast. AE, MC, V. **Amenities:** Restaurant (see "Where to Dine," below); airport transfer via van (for a fee) and catamaran (included); concierge; small fitness room; salt water Jacuzzi; infinity pool w/waterfall; spa; room service. *In room:* TV, hair dryer, minibar, Wi-Fi.

EXPENSIVE

Hotel Na Balam ★★★ 🎁 This ecologically-friendly hotel on Playa Norte promises a piece of Maya heaven on the beach, and I'd say that's just about right. Bleached white rooms lie in three sections separated only by sand, palms, and flowers; some face the beach and others lie in a garden setting with a swimming pool. They're individually decorated with a king-size or two double beds, seating area, folk-art decorations, and terrace or balcony with hammocks. Master suites feature additional amenities, including small pools with hydromassage. The older section is well kept and surrounds a lush inner courtyard and Playa Norte. Yoga practitioners take advantage of the numerous classes offered throughout the week; check with the reception for schedules. The beautiful turquoise cove in front of the hotel makes for perfect swimming and snorkeling. At night, tiki torches illuminate the enchanted grounds. Na Balam's restaurant, **Zazil Ha,** remains one of the island's most popular (see "Where to Dine," below), and the beachside bar is a beautiful spot for sunsets.

Zazil Ha 118, 77400 Isla Mujeres, Q. Roo. ✆ **998/877-0279.** Fax 998/877-0446. www.nabalam.com. 33 units. $127 standard, $142 beach view, $234 and up suite. Ask about weekly and monthly rates. Children under 12 stay free. AE, MC, V. **Amenities:** Restaurant; bar; diving and snorkeling trips available; spa; Wi-Fi; yoga. *In room:* A/C, hair dryer, minibar, no phone.

Secreto ★★ This boutique hotel oozes a chic Mediterranean feel. Twelve suites overlook an infinity pool, Jacuzzi, and the open sea. Located on the northern end of the island, Secreto lies within walking distance of town, yet feels removed enough to make for an idyllic retreat. Tropical gardens surround the exquisite pool, and an outdoor living area offers large couches and small dining areas. Guest rooms are contemporary, featuring lots of space, simple and bold design lines, individual balconies, and rich amenities. Nine suites include king-size beds, while the remaining three have two double beds. Secreto is distinguished by its style and service. A spa and fitness center were under construction at press time.

Sección Rocas, Lote 1, 77400 Isla Mujeres, Q. Roo. ✆ **998/877-1039.** Fax 998/877-1048. www.hotelsecreto.com. 12 units. $252–$336 double. Extra person $25. One child younger than 5 stays free in parent's room. Rates include continental breakfast. AE, MC, V. **Amenities:** Bar; outdoor pool; watersports equipment/rentals (diving and snorkeling). *In room:* A/C, TV/DVD, iHome, fridge, hair dryer, minibar.

MODERATE

Hotel Cabañas María del Mar ★ A good choice for simple beach accommodations, the Cabañas María del Mar sits on the popular Playa Norte. The older two-story section behind the reception area and beyond the garden offers nicely outfitted rooms facing the beach. All have two single or double beds, refrigerators, and oceanview balconies. Twenty-two single-story cabañas closer to the reception area are decorated in a rustic Mexican style. The third section, **El Castillo,** lies across the street, over and beside Buho's restaurant. All rooms are "deluxe," though some are larger than others. The five rooms on the ground floor have large patios and king-size beds. Upstairs rooms offer small balconies, and most have ocean views. The central courtyard contains a small pool.

Av. Arq. Carlos Lazo 1 (on Playa Norte, a half-block from the Hotel Na Balam), 77400 Isla Mujeres, Q. Roo. ✆ **998/877-0179.** Fax 998/877-0213. www.cabanasdelmar.com. 73 units. High season $130–$150 double; low season $66–$90 double. MC, V. **Amenities:** Restaurant; bar; pool. *In room:* A/C, TV, fridge.

Ixchel Beach Hotel ☺ This moderately priced "condohotel" enjoys a privileged location on Playa Norte. Most of the stylish rooms have balconies with ocean and pool views, as well as small kitchens. Especially popular with families, Ixchel sits right on an idyllic stretch of beach with lounge chairs and umbrellas and nearby access to water sports. The swimming pool and bar sit adjacent to the beach, and the hotel is less than a 10-minute walk from the ferry dock and town center.

Calle Guerrero at Playa Norte, 77400 Isla Mujeres, Q. Roo. ✆/fax **998/999-2010.** www.ixchelbeachhotel.com. 117 units. High season $175–$205 double, $265 suite; low season $99–$119 double, $155 suite. MC, V. **Amenities:** Restaurant; snack bar; babysitting; pool; Wi-Fi. *In room:* A/C, TV, kitchenette.

INEXPENSIVE

Hotel Belmar ★★ In the center of Isla's entertainment district, this charming three-story hotel (no elevator) sits above the usually packed Rolandi's restaurant. The simple, attractive rooms come with tile floors, nicely finished bathrooms, and either a king bed or two twins or two doubles. The rooms are well maintained and have quiet air-conditioning. One large suite features a sitting area, large patio, and whirlpool. The rooms have double-glazed windows. Though I had no trouble with noise from the restaurant in my third-floor room, light sleepers might want to look elsewhere.

Av. Hidalgo 110 (btw. Madero and Abasolo, 3½ blocks from the passenger-ferry pier), 77400 Isla Mujeres, Q. Roo. ✆ **998/877-0430.** Fax 998/877-0429. www.rolandi.com. 11 units. High season 985 pesos double, 1,495 pesos suite; low season 695 pesos double, 1,495 pesos suite. Full breakfast included. AE, MC, V. **Amenities:** Restaurant/bar (see "Where to Dine," below); room service. *In room:* A/C, fan, TV.

Hotel D'Gomar This very simple hotel sits at the bottom of the inexpensive range; it's comfortable but don't expect any thrills. Rooms have two double beds and a wall of windows affording gentle breezes. The higher prices are for air-conditioned rooms with refrigerators. The hotel stretches four stories with no elevator, and is conveniently located cater-corner from the ferry pier (look right). The name of the hotel is the most visible sign on the "skyline."

Rueda Medina 150, 77400 Isla Mujeres, Q. Roo. ✆/fax **998/877-0541.** www.hoteldgomar-islamujeres.com. 20 units. High season 550 pesos double; low season 350–450 pesos double. MC, V. *In room:* A/C, fan, TV and fridge (in some), no phone.

Hotel Francis Arlene ★ The Magaña family operates this neat little two-story inn built around a shady courtyard. It's bright, cheerful, and well managed, and features attractive common spaces. For these reasons, it gets a lot of return guests and remains especially popular with families and seniors. Some rooms have ocean views, and many are remodeled or updated each year. They are comfortable, with tile floors, tiled bathrooms, balconies or patios, and a very homey feel. Standard rooms include a coffeemaker and a refrigerator; top-floor rooms come with kitchenettes and offer an ocean view. Ten rooms have only a ceiling fan and are the lowest-priced doubles.

Guerrero 7 (5½ blocks inland from the ferry pier, btw. Abasolo and Matamoros), 77400 Isla Mujeres, Q. Roo. ✆/fax **998/877-0310,** -0861. www.francisarlene.com.mx. 24 units. High season $65–$75 double, $90 top-floor double; low season $45–$60 double, $80 top-floor double. MC, V. *In room:* A/C (in some), fridge, kitchenette (in some), no phone.

Where to Dine

At the **Municipal Market,** next to the post office on Avenida Guerrero, obliging, hardworking women operate several little food stands. When you're in the mood for an ice cream, stop by **La Coppa** (no phone), at Hidalgo and Abasolo, where you can choose from among 18 flavors of Italian *gelato*. It's open daily from 3 to 11pm.

EXPENSIVE

Casa Rolandi ★★ ITALIAN/SEAFOOD This gourmet restaurant in the Villa Rolandi hotel offers a beautiful setting with windows over the island's western shore and an open-air terrace. The menu here is more sophisticated than Rolandi's downtown, with an open kitchen that serves fresh lobster, grilled salmon, shrimp brochettes, homemade pastas, and other creatively prepared dishes. Both restaurants make good use of wood-burning stoves to produce some great baked fish dishes. And take care with the wood-oven-baked bread—it arrives looking like a puffer fish and is so divine you're apt to fill up on it. This is a great place to enjoy the sunset, and there's a selection of fine international wines and more than 80 premium tequilas.

On the pier of Villa Rolandi (p. 150), Lagunamar SM 7. ✆ **998/999-2000.** Reservations necessary. Main courses 182–303 pesos. AE, MC, V. Daily 7am–10:30pm.

MODERATE

Angelo ★ ITALIAN An Italian restaurant in the town center, Angelo offers a selection of antipasti, pasta, grilled seafood, and wood-oven-baked pizzas. The Sardinian-born owner instills his menu with the flavors of his homeland, including a rich tomato sauce. Consider starting with a bowl of seafood soup or black mussels au gratin and continuing with the grilled shrimp kabobs or seafood pasta in an olive oil and white-wine sauce. The open-air restaurant includes an inviting sidewalk terrace and lies across the street from a casual Cuban restaurant also owned by Angelo.

Av. Hidalgo 14 (btw. Lopez Mateos and Matamoros). ✆ **998/877-1273.** Main courses 120–235 pesos. MC, V. Daily 4pm–midnight.

Rolandi's ★ ITALIAN/SEAFOOD This casual Italian eatery is an Isla institution, and usually the most crowded place in town. The thin-crust pizzas and calzones feature wide-ranging ingredients—from traditional tomato, olive, basil, and salami to more exotic seafood selections. A wood-burning oven imparts the signature flavor of the pizzas, as well as fish kabobs, baked chicken, and roast beef. The extensive menu offers a wealth of salads and appetizers, plus an ample

Open-air restaurants line the streets of Isla Mujeres.

array of homemade pasta dishes, steaks, fish, and desserts. The restaurant sits adjacent to the Hotel Belmar (p. 152), with sidewalk tables brushing up against the action on Avenida Hidalgo. Rolandi's serves breakfast, too.

Av. Hidalgo 10 (3½ blocks inland from the pier, btw. Madero and Abasolo). ✆ **998/877-0430.** Reservations recommended. Breakfast 30–50 pesos; main courses 80–160 pesos. AE, MC, V. Daily 7:30am–11pm.

Zazil Ha ★★ CARIBBEAN/INTERNATIONAL Here you can enjoy some of the island's best food while sitting at tables on the sand among palms and gardens. Come night, candlelit tables sparkle underneath the open-air *palapa.* Specialties include the "surf and turf" lobster and rib-eye, and the Maya chicken stuffed with corn mushroom and goat cheese. A selection of fresh juices complements the vegetarian options, and there's even a special menu for those participating in yoga retreats. The delicious breads are baked in-house. Between the set meal times, you can order all sorts of enticing food, such as tacos and sandwiches, ceviche, terrific nachos, and vegetable and fruit drinks.

At the Hotel Na Balam (at the end of Playa Norte, almost at the end of Calle Zazil Ha; p. 151). ✆ **998/877-0279.** www.nabalam.com. Reservations recommended. Breakfast 60–120 pesos; main courses 80–250 pesos. AE, MC, V. Daily 7:30am–10:30pm.

INEXPENSIVE

Café Cito CAFE Brisa and Luis Rivera own this adorable, Caribbean-blue corner restaurant where you can begin the day with flavorful coffee and a croissant and cream cheese (this is the only place in town where you can have breakfast until 2pm). Terrific crepes come with yogurt, ice cream, fresh fruit, or *dulce de leche* (caramel sauce made from goat's milk), as well as ham and cheese. The cafe now serves dinner as well, offering Caribbean dishes such as coconut shrimp and stuffed chicken with a rich mushroom sauce.

Calle Matamoros 42, at Juárez. ✆ **998/877-1470.** Reservations not accepted. Crepes 30–60 pesos; breakfast 40–60 pesos; sandwiches 35–50 pesos; dinner 120–150 pesos. No credit cards. Daily 7:30am–2pm and 5–10pm.

Mamma Rosa ★★ ITALIAN Opened in early 2009 by a northern Italian family, Mamma Rosa serves mouth-watering pizzas and homemade pasta to happy patrons seated at candlelit sidewalk tables. The most extravagant pizza is the Diamante smothered with lobster, mozzarella, and tomatoes. For pasta, I recommend the simple meat lasagna or tortelli with ricotta cheese and spinach. The filet of grouper makes for a perfect main course, unless you're in the mood for an Angus steak with green pepper. Lots of olive oil is used in the light, Mediterranean-inspired cooking. Finish with the rich tiramisu. Waiters here speak Italian and little Spanish or English.

Av. Hidalgo 10 (at Matamoros). ✆ **998/200-1969.** Pizzas and pasta 75–220 pesos; main courses 105–220 pesos. MC, V. Wed–Mon 8am–noon and 5–11pm. Dinner only in low season.

Isla Mujeres after Dark

Those in a party mood by day's end may want to start out at the beach bar of the **Na Balam** hotel on Playa Norte, which usually hosts a crowd until around midnight. On Saturday and Sunday in high season, live music plays between 4 and 7pm. **Jax Bar & Grill,** on Avenida Rueda Medina, close to Hotel Posada del Mar, is a Texas-style sports bar offering live music nightly. **Las Palapas Chimbo's** restaurant on the beach becomes a jammin' dance joint with a live band from 9pm until whenever. Farther along the same stretch of beach, **Buho's,** the restaurant/beach bar of the Cabañas María del Mar, has its moments as a popular, low-key hangout, complete with swinging seats over the sand. If you want to sample one of nearly 100 tequila brands on a relaxing sidewalk terrace, stop by **Fayne's**, located at Av. Hidalgo 12 and open nightly from 7pm to midnight or later. It offers excellent live music that usually gets going after 10pm. Close by at Av. Hidalgo 17, **El Patio** has tables in the sand and live music nightly, including guitar, saxophone, and reggae. It's open nightly from 7pm to midnight or later except for Sundays, when it's closed. **Om Bar and Chill Lounge,** on Calle Matamoros, serves cocktails in an atmosphere that includes jazzy Latino music, open from 6pm to 2am.

COZUMEL ★★★

70km (43 miles) S of Cancún; 19km (12 miles) SE of Playa del Carmen

You might not expect such a sleepy island to be one of the world's top diving spots, but Cozumel's clear turquoise waters are spectacular for snorkeling and scuba diving. Tall reefs line the southwest coast, creating towering walls that offer divers a fairy-tale landscape to explore. The island is far quieter than Cancún, and there are no big highways, high-rises, or construction projects. One of my favorite things about Cozumel is that the water on the protected side (western shore) stays as calm as an aquarium, unless a front is blowing through. The island is 45km (28 miles) long and 18km (11 miles) wide, and lies 19km (12 miles) from the mainland. Most of the terrain is flat and clothed in a low tropical forest.

A strong sense of family and community continues to prevail here. There are about 80,000 people on the island, 2,000 of whom are Americans and the rest of whom are mostly Maya, Yucatecans, and Mexicans from elsewhere in the country. The only town on the island is San Miguel, which, despite the growth of the last 20 years, can't be called anything more than a small town. It's not a stunningly beautiful town, but its inhabitants are welcoming—life moves along at a slow pace, and every Sunday evening, residents congregate around the plaza to enjoy live music and see their friends. Staying in town can be fun and convenient. Avenida Rafael Melgar is the main waterfront road and includes a boardwalk with benches and sculptures along the way. A number of restaurants and nightspots line the avenue.

Because Cozumel is a frequent stop on the cruise ship circuit, the waterfront section of town holds wall-to-wall jewelry stores and duty-free and souvenir shops. This and the area around the town's main square are about as far as most cruise-ship passengers venture into town, and they're usually just here for a few hours in the middle of the day.

During pre-Hispanic times, Maya women would cross over to the island to make offerings to the goddess of fertility, Ixchel. More than 40 sites containing shrines remain around the island, and archaeologists still uncover the small dolls that were customarily part of those offerings. Though the island has its own ruins, they cannot compare with the major sites of the mainland.

Essentials

GETTING THERE & DEPARTING

BY PLANE During high season, several more international commercial flights fly in and out of Cozumel's airport (CZM) than in low season, including a few flights from northern U.S. cities. Airlines include **Aeroméxico, American, Continental, Delta, Frontier,** and **US Airways.** You might also inquire about buying a ticket on one of the charter flights in high season. Some packagers, such as **Fun Jet** (www.funjet.com), will sell you just a ticket. But look into packages, too. Several of the island's independent hotels work with packagers.

BY FERRY Passenger ferries run to and from Playa del Carmen. **México Waterjets** (✆ **987/872-1508**) and ***Ultramar*** (✆ **998/881-5890;** www.granpuerto.com.mx) offer departures almost every hour in the morning and about every 2 hours in the afternoon. The schedules change according to seasons but generally start at 7am and continue until 9 or 10pm. The trip takes 30 to 45 minutes, depending on conditions, and costs 140 pesos one-way. The boats are air-conditioned. In Playa del Carmen, the ferry dock is 1½ blocks from the main square. In Cozumel, the ferries use Muelle Fiscal, the town pier, a block from the main square. Luggage storage at the Cozumel dock costs 20 pesos per day.

The car ferry that used to operate from Puerto Morelos now uses the Calica pier just south of Playa del Carmen. The fare for a standard car is 600 pesos. **TransCaribe** (✆ **987/872-7688;** www.transcaribe.com.mx) has six departures daily; check the website for exact scheduling. The ferry docks in Cozumel at the **Muelle Internacional** (the **International Pier,** which is south of town near La Ceiba Hotel).

BY BUS If you plan to travel on the mainland by bus, purchase tickets in advance from the ticket office for **ADO buses** called **Ticket Bus** on the municipal pier (open while the ferries are running). Another is on Calle 2 Norte and Avenida 10 (✆ **987/872-1706**). Hours are from 8am to 9pm daily. ADO buses make the 1-hour trip from Cancún airport to Playa del Carmen (and back) throughout the day for 100 pesos; you can easily catch the ferry to Cozumel from Playa.

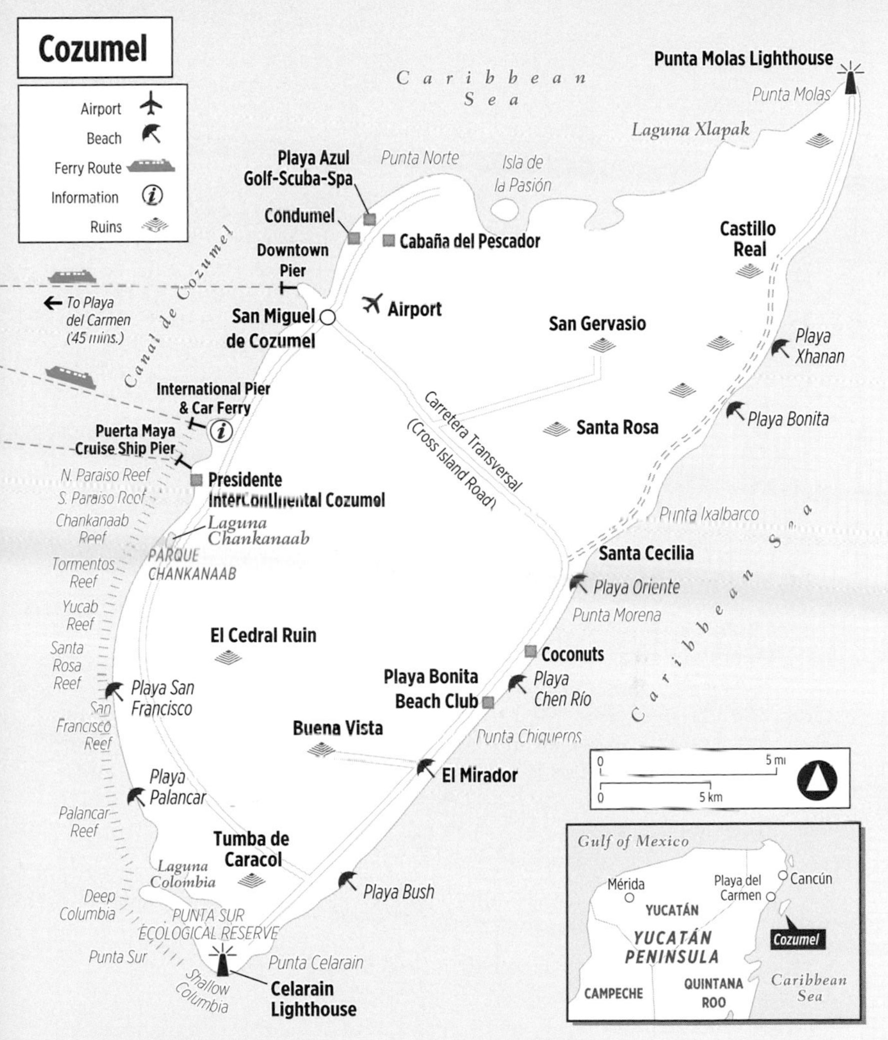

ORIENTATION

ARRIVING Cozumel's **airport** is inland from downtown. **Transportes Terrestres** provides hotel transportation in air-conditioned Suburbans. Buy your ticket as you exit the terminal. To hotels downtown, the fare is 70 pesos per person; to hotels along the north shore, 100 pesos; and to hotels along the south shore, up to 150 pesos. Passenger ferries arrive at the Muelle Fiscal, the municipal pier, by the town's main square. Cruise ships dock at the **Punta Langosta** pier, several blocks south of the Muelle Fiscal, and at the **International Pier,** which is at Km 4 of the southern coastal road. A third cruise-ship pier, the **Puerta Maya** near the International Pier, is also operational.

The ferry runs between Cozumel and Playa del Carmen.

VISITOR INFORMATION The **Municipal Tourism Office** (©/fax **987/869-0212**; www.cozumel.gob.mx) has information booths at the International Pier and Punta Langosta Pier. They're open 8am to 3pm Monday to Friday.

CITY LAYOUT San Miguel's main waterfront street is **Avenida Rafael Melgar.** Running parallel to Rafael Melgar are *avenidas* numbered in multiples of five—5, 10, 15. **Avenida Juárez** runs perpendicular to these, heading inland from the ferry dock. Avenida Juárez divides the town into northern and southern halves. The *calles* (streets) that parallel Juárez to the north have even numbers. The ones to the south have odd numbers, except for Calle Rosado Salas, which runs between calles 1 and 3. Vehicles on the *avenidas* have the right ofway.

ISLAND LAYOUT One road runs along the western coast of the island, which faces the Yucatán mainland. It has different names. North of town, it's **Santa Pilar** or **San Juan;** in the city, it is **Avenida Rafael Melgar;** south of town, it's **Costera Sur.** Hotels stretch along this road north and south of town. The road runs to the southern tip of the island (Punta Sur), passing **Chankanaab National Park. Avenida Juárez** (and its extension, the **Carretera Transversal**) runs east from the town across the island. It passes the airport and the turnoff to the ruins of San Gervasio before reaching the undeveloped ocean side of the island. It then turns south and follows the coast to the southern tip, where it meets the Costera Sur.

Be Streetwise

North-south streets—the *avenidas*—have the right of way, and traffic doesn't slow down or stop.

GETTING AROUND You can walk to most destinations in town, and

AN all-inclusive vacation IN COZUMEL

Booking a room at an all-inclusive resort should be done through a vacation packager. Booking lodging directly through the hotel usually doesn't make sense, even with frequent-flier mileage to burn, because the discounts offered by most packagers are so deep. I include websites for you to find out more info about the properties, but don't expect to find clear info on rates. The game of setting rates with these hotels is complicated and always in flux.

Two all-inclusives are north of town: **El Cozumeleño** (www.elcozumeleno.com) and the **Meliá Cozumel** (www.solmelia.com). Both occupy multistory modern buildings and have attractive rooms. El Cozumeleño is the larger of the two resorts and has the nicest hotel pool on the island. It's best suited for active types. The Meliá is quieter and offers golf discounts for the nearby golf course. The Cozumeleño's small beach has to be replenished with sand periodically. The Meliá's beach is long, narrow, and pretty, but occasionally seaweed washes up, which doesn't happen on the rest of the island's coast. The advantages of staying in these two are the proximity to town, with its restaurants, clubs, movie theaters, and so on, and the fact that most rooms at these hotels come with views of the ocean.

The **Cozumel Palace** (www.palaceresorts.com) is right on the water on the southern fringes of town, occupying the property that used to be Plaza las Glorias. Despite the location, it doesn't have a beach. But that's not so bad. The water is usually so calm on Cozumel's west shore that swimming here is like swimming in a pool, and you can snorkel right out of the hotel.

Of the all-inclusives to the south, my favorites are the **Occidental** resort (**Grand Cozumel;** www.occidentalhotels.com) and the **Iberostar Cozumel** (www.iberostar.com). These are "village" style resorts with two- and three-story buildings, often with thatched roofs, spread over a large area at the center of which is the pool and activities area. Rooms at the Grand Cozumel are larger and more attractive than the all-inclusives in the south. Like the Occidental chain, Iberostar has several properties in the Mexican Caribbean. This one is the smallest. I like its food and service and the beauty of the grounds. The rooms are attractive and well maintained. The advantage to staying in these places is that you're close to a lot of dive sites; the disadvantage is that you're somewhat isolated from town, and you don't have many rooms with ocean views.

Other all-inclusives include the **Wyndham Cozumel Resort and Spa** (www.wyndham.com), which used to be the Reef Club, and the **Holiday Village White Sands**, which used to be the Allegro Cozumel but is now a First Choice property (www.firstchoice.co.uk). It probably has one of the nicest beaches on the island. And finally, there's the **Hotel Cozumel & Resort** (formerly the Costa Club; www.hotelcozumel.com.mx), which is on the inland side of the road in a crowded section of the island.

Although the **Fiesta Americana Cozumel Dive Center** (www.fiestamericana.com) does not call itself an all-inclusive resort, it offers guests the option of a meal plan that includes all meals and domestic drinks. Among other services, the family-friendly resort offers an excellent variety of outdoor activities, including a first-rate dive center next to the oldest and largest coral reef in the hemisphere.

it's very safe. Getting to outlying hotels and beaches requires a taxi, rental car, or moped.

Car rentals are about $45 for a VW bug and $60 for a Jeep Wrangler. **Avis** (✆ **987/872-0099**) and **Executive** (✆ **987/872-1308**) have counters in the airport. Other major rental companies have offices in town, including **Thrifty** (✆ **987/869-2957**) at Juárez 181, between Avenidas 5 and 10 Norte. Rentals are easy to arrange through your hotel or at any of the many local rental offices.

Moped rentals are readily available and cost 250 to 500 pesos for 24 hours, depending upon the season. If you rent a moped, be careful. Riding a moped made a lot more sense when Cozumel had less traffic; now it involves a certain amount of risk as taxi drivers and other motorists have become more numerous and pushier. Moped accidents easily rank as the greatest cause of injury in Cozumel. Before renting one, inspect it carefully to see that all the gizmos—horn, light, starter, seat, mirror—are in good shape. I've been offered mopeds with unbalanced wheels, which made them unsteady at higher speeds, but the renter quickly exchanged them upon my request. You are required to stay on paved roads. It's illegal to ride a moped without a helmet outside of town (subject to a 300 peso fine).

Cozumel has lots of **taxis** and a strong drivers' union. Fares have been standardized—there's no bargaining. Here are a few sample fares for two people (there is an additional charge for extra passengers to most destinations): island tour, 500 pesos; town to southern Hotel Zone, 110 to 180 pesos; town to northern hotels, 50 to 70 pesos; town to Chankanaab, 100 pesos for up to four people; in and around town, 30 to 40 pesos.

[FastFACTS] COZUMEL

Area Code The telephone area code is **987.**

ATMs, Banks & Currency Exchange The island has several banks and *casas de cambio,* as well as ATMs. Most places accept dollars, but you usually get a better deal paying in pesos.

Climate From October to December, there can be strong winds all over the Yucatán, as well as some rain. June through October is the rainy season.

Hospital **Médica San Miguel** (✆ **987/872-0103**) works for most things and includes intensive-care facilities. It's on Calle 6 Norte between avenidas 5 and 10. **Centro Médico Cozumel** (✆ **987/872-3545**) is an alternative. It's at the intersection of Calle 1 Sur and Avenida 50.

Internet Access Several cybercafes are in and about the main square. If you go just a bit off Avenida Rafael Melgar and the main square, prices drop. **Modutel,** Av. Juárez 15 (at Av. 10), offers good rates. Hours are Monday through Saturday from 10am to 8pm.

Post Office The *correo* is on Avenida Rafael Melgar at Calle 7 Sur (✆ **987/872-0106**), at the southern edge of town. It's open Monday through Friday from 9am to 3pm, Saturday from 9am to noon.

Recompression Chamber Cozumel has four *cámaras de recompresión.* The best are **Buceo Médico Mexicano,** staffed 24 hours, at Calle 5 Sur 21-B, between Avenida Rafael Melgar and Avenida 5 Sur (✆ **987/872-2387, -1430**); and the **Hyperbaric Center of Cozumel** (✆ **987/872-3070**), at Calle 6 Norte, between avenidas 5 and 10.

Seasons High season is from Christmas to Easter and August.

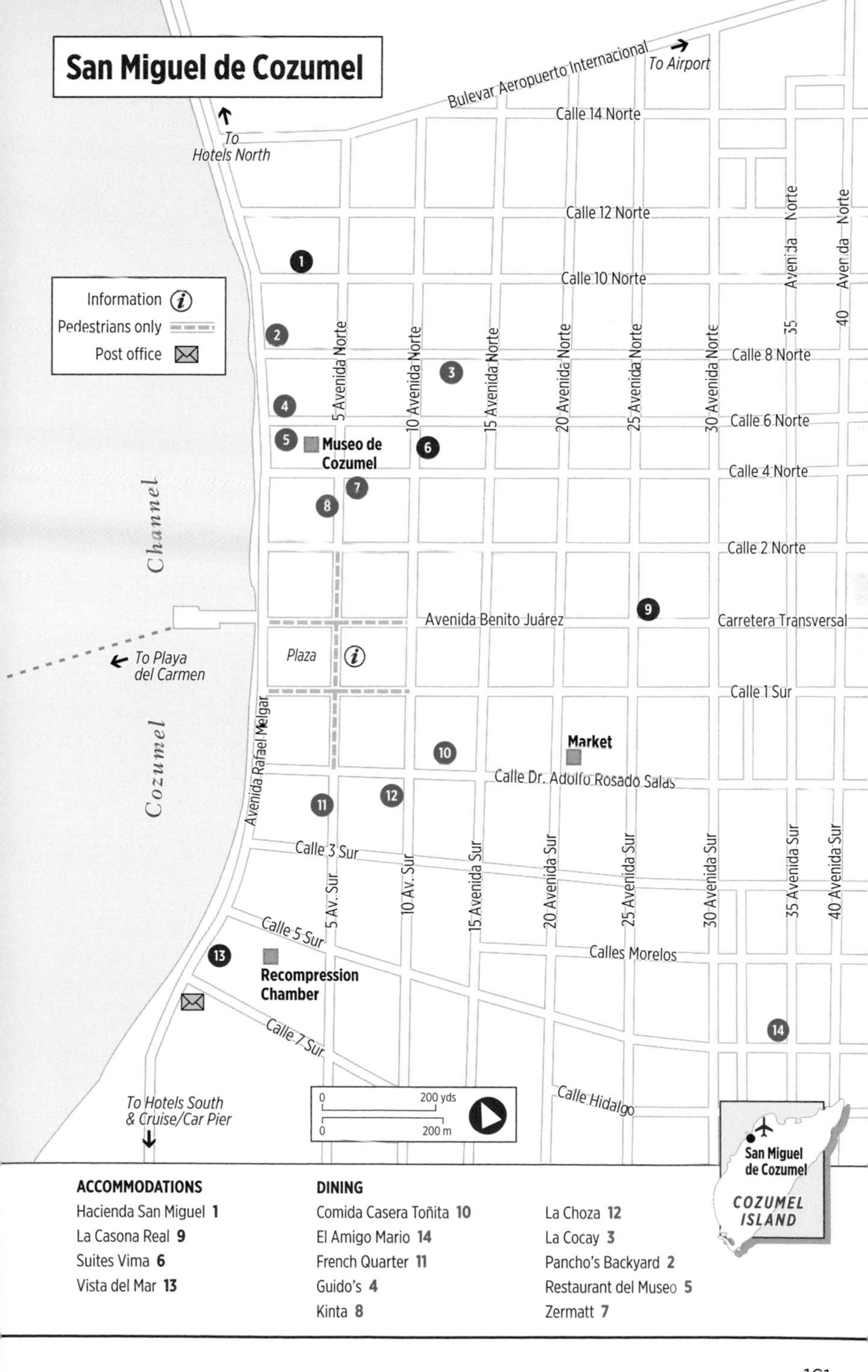

ACCOMMODATIONS
Hacienda San Miguel **1**
La Casona Real **9**
Suites Vima **6**
Vista del Mar **13**

DINING
Comida Casera Toñita **10**
El Amigo Mario **14**
French Quarter **11**
Guido's **4**
Kinta **8**
La Choza **12**
La Cocay **3**
Pancho's Backyard **2**
Restaurant del Museo **5**
Zermatt **7**

Carnaval festivities.

Exploring the Island

For **diving** and **snorkeling,** you have plenty of dive shops to choose from. For **island tours, ruins tours** on and off the island, **evening cruises,** and other activities, go to a travel agency, such as **InterMar Cozumel Viajes,** Calle 2 Norte 101-B, between avenidas 5 and 10 (✆ **987/872-1535;** www.intermar.com.mx). Office hours are Monday through Saturday from 8am to 8pm, Sunday from 9am to 5pm.

WATERSPORTS

SCUBA DIVING Cozumel is the number-one dive destination in the Western Hemisphere. Don't forget your dive card and dive log. Dive shops will rent you scuba gear but won't take you out on a boat until you show some documentation. If you have a medical condition, bring a letter signed by a doctor stating that you've been cleared to dive. A two-tank morning dive costs about $75 to $90; some shops offer an additional one-tank dive for a modest additional fee. A lot of divers save some money by buying a dive package with a hotel. These usually include two dives a day.

Diving in Cozumel is drift diving, which can be a little disconcerting for novices. The current that sweeps along Cozumel's reefs, pulling nutrients into them and making them as large as they are, also dictates how you dive here. The problem is that it pulls at different speeds at different depths and in different places. When it's pulling strong, it can quickly scatter a dive group. The role of the dive master becomes more important, especially with choosing the dive location. Cozumel has a lot of dive locations. To mention but a few: the famous **Palancar Reef,** with its caves and canyons, plentiful fish, and sea coral; the monstrous **Santa Rosa Wall,** famous for its depth, sea life, coral, and

Carnaval

Carnaval **(similar to Mardi Gras) is Cozumel's most colorful fiesta. It begins the Thursday before Ash Wednesday, with daytime street dancing and nighttime parades on Thursday, Saturday, and Monday (the best).**

Cenote Diving on the Mainland

A popular activity in the Yucatán is cave diving. The peninsula's underground **cenotes** (seh-*noh*-tehs)—sinkholes or wellsprings—lead to a vast system of underground caverns. The gently flowing water is so clear that divers seem to float on air through caves complete with stalactites and stalagmites. If you want to try this but didn't plan a trip to the mainland, contact **Yucatech Expeditions,** Avenida 5, on the corner of Calle 3 Sur (✆ /fax **987/872-5659;** www.yucatech.net), which offers a trip five times a week. Cenotes are 30 to 45 minutes from Playa del Carmen, and a dive in each cenote lasts around 45 minutes. Dives are within the daylight zone, about 40m (131 ft.) into the caverns, and no more than 18m (59 ft.) deep. Open water certification and at least five logged dives are required. For those without diving certifications, a cenote snorkeling tour is also offered.

sponges; the **San Francisco Reef,** with a shallower drop-off wall and fascinating sea life; and the **Yucab Reef,** with its beautiful coral.

Finding a dive shop in town is even easier than finding a jewelry store. Cozumel has more than 50 dive operators. I can recommend **Aqua Safari,** which has a location on Avenida Rafael Melgar 429 at Calle 5 (✆ **987/872-0101;** www.aquasafari.com). **Liquid Blue Divers** (✆ **987/869-2812;** www.liquidbluedivers.com), on Avenida 5 between Rosado Salas and Calle 3 Sur, offers quality tours with no more than 12 divers. **Scuba Du** (✆ **987/872-9505;** www.scubadu.com), based at the Intercontinental President resort (p. 171), offers excellent diving excursions, refresher courses, and all levels of diving certification.

SNORKELING Most resorts offer snorkeling equipment, and many dive shops do, as well. When contracting for a snorkel tour, stay away from the companies that cater to the cruise ships. Those tours are crowded and not very fun. For a good snorkeling tour, contact **Victor Casanova** (✆ **987/112-2553;** boshms.angelfire.com/wild_cat_diver/). He speaks English, owns a couple of boats, and does a good 5-hour tour. He takes his time and doesn't rush through the trip. Even though you won't see a lot of the more delicate structures, such as fan coral, you will still see plenty of sea creatures and enjoy the clear, calm water of Cozumel's protected west side.

Cozumel's underwater dive sites.

BOAT TRIPS Travel agencies and hotels can arrange boat trips, a popular pastime on Cozumel. Choose from evening cruises, cocktail cruises, glass-bottom boat cruises, and other options. One novel boat ride is offered by **Atlantis Submarines** (✆ **987/872-5671;** www.atlantisadventures.com). It operates almost 3km (1¾ miles) south of town in front of the

Casa del Mar hotel and costs $89 per adult, $59 for kids ages 4 to 12. The tour duration is 1½ hours with 40 minutes underwater, and the sub can hold 48 people. This is a superior experience to the **Sub See Explorer** offered by **AquaWorld,** which is really just a glorified glass-bottom boat. You can make reservations online and get a bit of a discount.

For Experienced Divers

Bring proof of your diver's certification and your log. Underwater currents can be strong, and many of the reef drops are quite steep, so dive operators want to make sure divers are experienced.

FISHING The best months for fishing are March through June, when the catch includes blue and white marlin, sailfish, tarpon, and swordfish. The least expensive option would be to contact a boat owner directly. Try Victor Casanova, listed above under "Snorkeling." A reliable operator offering deep-sea fishing and bonefishing in Cozumel is **Aquarius Fishing** (✆ **987/872-1092;** www.aquariusflatsfishing.com), located at 20 Avenida Sur between Calle 3 Sur and Calle Rosado Salas.

CHANKANAAB NATIONAL PARK & FARO CELERAIN ECOLOGICAL RESERVE (PUNTA SUR)

Chankanaab National Park ★ is the pride of many islanders. In Mayan, Chankanaab means "little sea," which refers to a beautiful land-locked pool connected to the sea through an underwater tunnel—a sort of miniature ocean. Snorkeling in this natural aquarium is not permitted, but the park itself has a beach for sunbathing and snorkeling. Arrive before 9am to stake out a chair and *palapa* before the cruise-ship crowd arrives. The snorkeling is also best before noon. The park has bathrooms, lockers, a gift shop, several snack huts, a restaurant, and a *palapa* for renting snorkeling gear.

You can also swim with dolphins. **Dolphin Discovery** (✆ **800/293-9698;** www.dolphindiscovery.com) has several programs for experiencing these

ANATOMY OF the coral reef

Corals are polyps, tiny animals with hollow, cylindrical bodies that attach by the thousands to hard surfaces of the sea floor. The polyps extract calcium carbonate from the seawater to create hard, cup-shaped skeletons that assume an endless variety of shapes and sizes. These massive limestone structures shelter nearly one-fourth of all marine life. The soft, delicate polyps retreat into their skeletons during the day, but their protruding tentacles can be seen when they feed at night.

Two distinct types of coral formations dominate Cozumel's waters. Bases of the less developed platform reefs, such as Colombia Shallows, Paradise, and Yucab, are rarely more than 9 to 15m (30–50 ft.) in depth. Edge reefs are more complex structures built up over many millennia, and their layered structures peak high above the edge of the drop-off, extending as much as 55m (180 ft.) below the surface. These are found mostly in the south; examples include Palancar, Colombia Deep, Punta Sur, and Maracaibo.

Chankanaab National Park.

sea creatures. These are popular, so plan ahead—you should make reservations well in advance. The surest way is through the website—make sure to pick the Cozumel location, as there are a couple of others on this coast. There are three different programs for swimming with dolphins. The one of longest duration costs $149 and features close interaction with the beautiful swimmers. There are also swim-and-snorkel programs for about $100 that get you in the water with these creatures.

Admission to the park is $16, and half price for children under 12. It's open daily from 8am to 5pm and lies south of town, just past the Fiesta Americana Hotel. Taxis run constantly between the park, the hotels, and town (100 pesos from town for up to four people).

Faro Celerain Ecological Reserve (admission $10), also called Punta Sur, is an ecological reserve at the southern tip of the island that includes the Columbia Lagoon. A number of crocodiles make the lagoon their home, so

Crocodiles in the Faro Celerain Ecological Reserve.

swimming is not only a bad idea, it's not allowed. The only practical way of going out to the lighthouse, which lies 8km from the entrance, is to rent a car or scooter; there's no taxi stand, and usually few people. At the entrance to Punta Sur, you'll find a reggae beach bar and a sea turtle nesting area. The lovely beaches just in front are kept as natural as possible, but be cautious about swimming or snorkeling here depending on the winds and currents. Regular hours are daily 9am to 4pm. If you have a rental car, getting here is no problem, and this is usually a great place to get away from the crowds and have a lot of beach to yourself. Occasionally, boat tours of the lagoon are offered. Ask at the information office.

BEACHES

Along both the west and east sides of the island you'll see signs advertising beach clubs. A "beach club" in Cozumel can mean just a *palapa* hut that's open to the public and serves soft drinks, beer, and fried fish. It can also mean a recreational beach with the full gamut of offerings, from banana boats to parasailing. They also usually have locker rooms, a pool, and food. The biggest of these is **Mr. Sancho's** (✆ **987/871-9174;** www.mrsanchos.com), south of downtown San Miguel at Km 15 on the main road between the Reef Club and Allegro Resort. It offers a restaurant, bar, massage service, and motorized and non-motorized watersports. Quieter versions of beach clubs are **Playa San Francisco** (no phone), **Paradise Beach** (no phone, next to Playa San Francisco), and **Playa Palancar** (no phone). All of these beaches are south of Chankanaab Park and easily visible from the road. Several have swimming pools with beach furniture, a restaurant, and snorkel rental. Most of these beaches cost around 50 pesos.

Once you get to the end of the island, the beach clubs become simple places where you can eat, drink, and lay out on the beach for free. **Paradise Cafe** is on the southern tip of the island across from Punta Sur Nature Park, and as you go up the eastern side of the island you pass **Playa Bonita, Chen Río,** and **Punta Morena.** Except on Sunday, when the locals head for the beaches, these places are practically deserted. Most of the east coast is unsafe for swimming because of the surf. The beaches tend to be small and occupy gaps in the rocky coast.

ISLAND TOURS

Travel agencies can arrange a variety of tours, including horseback, Jeep, and ATV tours. Taxi drivers charge 700 pesos for a 3-hour tour of the island, which most people would consider only mildly amusing, depending on the driver's personality. The best horseback tours are offered at **Rancho Palmitas** (no phone), on the Costera Sur highway, across from the Occidental Cozumel resort. Rides can be from 1 to 2½ hours long and cost 200 to 300 pesos.

OTHER ATTRACTIONS

MAYA RUINS A popular island excursion is to **San Gervasio** (100 B.C.–A.D. 1600). Follow the paved transversal road, and you'll see the well-marked turnoff about halfway between town and the eastern coast. For what you see, it's a bit overpriced. You have to pay a 70-pesos fee charged by the local institute; camera permits cost an additional 50 pesos. A small tourist center at the entrance sells handicrafts, cold drinks, and snacks. The ruins are open from 7am to 4pm.

When it comes to Cozumel's Maya ruins, getting there is most of the fun—do it for the mystique and for the trip, not for the size or scale of

San Gervasio Maya ruins.

the ruins. The buildings, though preserved, are crudely made and would not be much of a tourist attraction if they were not the island's principal ruins. More significant than beautiful, this site was once an important ceremonial center where the Maya gathered, coming even from the mainland. The important deity was Ixchel, the goddess of weaving, women, childbirth, pilgrims, the moon, and medicine. Although you won't see any representations of Ixchel at San Gervasio today, Bruce Hunter, in his *Guide to Ancient Maya Ruins,* writes that priests hid behind a large pottery statue of her and became the voice of the goddess, speaking to pilgrims and answering their petitions. Ixchel was the wife of Itzamná, the sun god.

Guides charge 200 pesos for a tour for one to six people. A better option is to find a copy of the green booklet *San Gervasio,* sold at local checkout counters and bookstores, and tour the site on your own. Seeing it takes 30 to 60 minutes. Taxi drivers offer transportation for about 600 pesos, which includes the driver waiting for you outside the ruins.

A HISTORY MUSEUM The **Museo de la Isla de Cozumel ★**, Av. Rafael Melgar between calles 4 and 6 Norte (✆ **987/872-1475**), is more than just a nice place to spend a rainy hour. On the first floor, an exhibit illustrates endangered species, the origin of the island, and its present-day topography and plant and animal life, including an explanation of coral formation. The second-floor galleries feature the history of the town, artifacts from the island's pre-Hispanic sites, and Colonial-era cannons, swords, and ship paraphernalia. It's open daily from 9am to 5pm (but closes at 4pm on Sun). Admission is 36 pesos. There's also a gift shop and a picturesque rooftop cafe that serves breakfast and lunch (p. 175; you don't need to pay admission to eat here, unless you plan to visit the museum, too).

GOLF Cozumel has an 18-hole course designed by Jack Nicklaus. It's at the **Cozumel Country Club** (✆ **987/872-9570;** www.cozumelcountryclub.com.mx), north of San Miguel. Greens fees are $169 for a morning tee time, including cart rental and tax. Afternoon tee times cost $105. Tee times can be reserved 3 days in advance. A few hotels have special memberships with discounts for guests and advance tee times; guests at Playa Azul Golf and Beach Club pay no greens fees, but the cart costs $25.

Trips to the Mainland

CHICHÉN ITZÁ, TULUM & COBÁ Travel agencies can arrange day trips to the ruins of **Chichén Itzá** ★★★. The ruins of **Tulum** ★, overlooking the Caribbean, and **Cobá** ★, in a dense jungle setting, are closer and cost less to visit. These latter two cities are quite a contrast to Chichén Itzá. Cobá is a large, mostly unrestored city beside a lake in a remote jungle setting, while Tulum is smaller, more compact, and right on the beach. It's more intact than Cobá. A trip to both Cobá and Tulum begins at 8am and returns around 6pm. A shorter, more relaxing excursion goes to Tulum and the nearby nature park of Xel-Ha.

PLAYA DEL CARMEN & XCARET Going on your own to the nearby seaside town of **Playa del Carmen** and the **Xcaret** nature park is as easy as a quick ferry ride from Cozumel (for ferry information, see "Getting There & Departing," earlier in this chapter). For information on Playa and Xcaret, see chapter 7. Cozumel travel agencies offer an Xcaret tour that includes the ferry ride, transportation to the park, and the admission fee.

Shopping

If you're looking for silver jewelry or other souvenirs, go no farther than the town's coastal avenue, Rafael Melgar. Along this road, you'll find one store after another selling jewelry, Mexican handicrafts, and other souvenirs and duty-free merchandise. There are also some import/export stores in the Punta Langosta Shopping

Souvenir stores line Avenida Rafael Melgar.

Center in the southern part of town in front of the cruise-ship pier. Prices for serapes, T-shirts, and the like are lower on the side streets off Avenida Melgar.

Where to Stay

I've grouped Cozumel's hotels by location—**north** of town, **in town,** and **south** of town. The prices quoted are public rates and include the 12% tax. High season is from December to Easter. Expect rates from Christmas to New Year's to be still higher than the regular high-season rates quoted here. Low season is the rest of the year, though a few hotels raise their rates in August, when Mexican families go on vacation.

All of the beach hotels in Cozumel, even the small ones, have deals with vacation packagers. Keep in mind that some packagers will offer last-minute deals to Cozumel with hefty discounts; if you're the flexible sort, keep an eye open for these.

Most hotels have an arrangement with a dive shop and offer dive packages. These can be good deals, but if you don't buy a dive package, it's quite okay to stay at one hotel and dive with a third-party operator—any dive boat can pull up to any hotel pier to pick up customers. Most dive shops won't pick up from the hotels north of town.

In addition to the hotels listed below, another reliable option is the **Fiesta Americana** (✆ **987/872-9600;** www.fiestamericana.com), located on Carretera Chankanaab Km. 7.5, which is popular with families and has its own dive center. As an alternative to a hotel, you can try **Cozumel Vacation Villas and Condos,** Av. Rafael Melgar 685 (btw. calles 3 and 5 Sur; ✆ **800/224-5551** in the U.S. or 987/872-0729; www.cozumel-villas.com), which offers accommodations by the week.

NORTH OF TOWN

Carretera Santa Pilar, or San Juan, is the name of Avenida Rafael Melgar's northern extension. All the hotels lie close to each other on the beach side of the road a short distance from town and the airport.

Very Expensive

Playa Azul Golf-Scuba-Spa ★★ This quiet hotel is perhaps the most relaxing of the island's properties. It's smaller than the others, and an excellent choice for golfers; guests pay no greens fees, only cart rental. The hotel's small beautiful beach with shade *palapas* has a quiet little beach bar. All three categories of guest rooms have ocean views. The units in the original section are suites—very large, with oversize bathrooms with showers. The new wing has mostly standard rooms that are comfortable and large. The corner rooms are master suites with large balconies and Jacuzzis overlooking the sea. If you prefer lots of space over having a Jacuzzi, opt for a suite in the original building. Rooms contain a king-size or two double beds; some suites offer two convertible single sofas in the separate living room. The hotel also offers deep-sea- and fly-fishing trips.

Carretera San Juan Km 4, 77600 Cozumel, Q. Roo. ✆ **987/869-5160.** Fax 987/869-5173. www.playa-azul.com. 51 units. High season $210–$272 double, $255–$390 suite; low season $185–$255 double, $230–$340 suite. Rates include unlimited golf and full breakfast. Internet specials available. AE, MC, V. Free guarded parking. **Amenities:** 2 restaurants; 3 bars; babysitting; unlimited golf privileges at Cozumel Country Club; medium-size pool; room service; dive shop; snorkeling equipment; spa. ***In room:*** A/C, TV, fridge, hair dryer, Wi-Fi.

Expensive

Condumel Condobeach Apartments If you want some distance from the crowds, consider lodging here. It's not a full-service hotel, but in some ways, it's more convenient. The one-bedroom waterfront apartments are designed and furnished in practical fashion—airy, with sliding glass doors that face the sea and allow for good cross-ventilation (especially in the upper units). They also have ceiling fans, air-conditioning, and two twin beds or one king-size. Each apartment has a separate living room and a full kitchen with a partially stocked fridge, so you don't have to run to the store on the first day. There's a small, well-tended beach area (with shade *palapas* and a grill for guests' use) that leads to a low, rocky fall-off into the sea.

Carretera Hotelera Norte s/n, 77600 Cozumel, Q. Roo. ✆ **987/872-0892.** Fax 987/872-0661. www.condumel.com. 10 units. High season $142 double; low season $120 double. Dive packages available. No credit cards. *In room:* A/C, kitchen, no phone, Wi-Fi.

IN TOWN

Staying in town is not like staying in the town on Isla Mujeres, where you can walk to the beach. The oceanfront in town is too busy for swimming, and there's no beach, only the *malecón*. Prices are considerably lower, but you'll have to drive or take a cab to the beach; it's pretty easy. English is spoken in almost all of the hotels.

Moderate

Hacienda San Miguel ★ This is a peaceful hotel built in Mexican colonial style around a large garden courtyard. The property is well maintained and the service is good. It's located a half-block from the shoreline on the town's north side. The large guest rooms offer rustic Mexican furnishings and fully equipped kitchens. Most of the studios have a queen-size bed or two doubles, while the junior suites have more living area and a queen-size as well as a twin bed. The two-bedroom suite comes with four double beds. For this hotel, high season runs from January to August; low season is from September to December, excluding the holiday season.

Calle 10 Norte 500 (btw. Rafael Melgar and Av. 5), 77600 Cozumel, Q. Roo. ✆ **866/712-6387** in the U.S., or 987/872-1986. Fax 987/872-7043. www.haciendasanmiguel.com. 11 units. High season 1,222 pesos studio, 1,313 pesos junior suite, 2,002 pesos 2-bedroom suite; low season 1,027 pesos studio, 1,222 pesos junior suite, 1,586 pesos 2-bedroom suite. Rates include continental breakfast and free entrance to Mr. Sancho's beach club. MC, V. Guarded parking on street. *In room:* A/C, TV, hair dryer, kitchen, no phone, Wi-Fi.

Vista del Mar ★ This hotel is located on the town's shoreline boulevard. Guest rooms have been renovated and are bright and cheerfully decorated with bamboo furnishings. Bathrooms are medium size or a little smaller and have showers. The rooms in front offer ocean views with wrought-iron balconies. The rooms in back go for 100 pesos less than the oceanview rooms and look out over a small pool and large Jacuzzi. This hotel is operated by the same people who run Hacienda San Miguel, and it has the same high season/low season split, with higher rates for Carnaval and Christmas time.

Av. Rafael Melgar 45 (btw. calles 5 and 7 Sur), 77600 Cozumel, Q. Roo. ✆ **888/309-9988** in the U.S., or 987/872-0545. Fax 987/872-7036. www.hotelvistadelmar.com. 20 units. High season $110 double; low season $78–$90. Discounts sometimes available. AE, MC, V. Limited street parking. **Amenities:** Bar; Jacuzzi; outdoor pool. *In room:* A/C, TV, fridge, hair dryer, free local calls, Wi-Fi.

Inexpensive

La Casona Real Five blocks from the waterfront, this cheerful two-story hotel is a bargain for those wanting a hotel with a pool. The simple rooms are small to medium in size, with a king or two double beds, good air-conditioning, and colorful Mexican decor. A courtyard with an oval pool is on the west side of the building, and some rooms have views of the pool while others look toward the town (and are a bit noisier). Families can make good use out of the one-bedroom suite, which has a futon in the living room, full kitchen, and cable TV with a DVD player.

Av. Juárez 501, 77600 Cozumel, Q. Roo. ✆ **987/872-5471.** www.hotel-la-casona-real-cozumel.com. 15 units. $45–$55 double, $80 suite. No credit cards. Limited street parking. **Amenities:** Medium-size outdoor pool. *In room:* A/C, TV, no phone.

Suites Vima This three-story hotel sits 4 blocks from the main square. It offers large, plainly furnished rooms for a good price. The lighting is okay, the showers are good, and every room comes with its own fridge, which for island visitors can be a handy feature. The rooms are fairly quiet. Choose between two doubles or one king-size bed. There is no restaurant, but there is a pool and lounge area. As is the case with other small hotels on the island, the staff at the front desk doesn't speak English. Reservations through e-mail can be made in English. This is one of the few hotels in town that doesn't use high season/low season rates.

Av. 10 Norte btw. calles 4 and 6, 77600 Cozumel, Q. Roo. ✆ **987/872-5118.** 12 units. 550 pesos double. No credit cards. Limited street parking. **Amenities:** Tiny pool. *In room:* A/C, fridge.

SOUTH OF TOWN

The hotels in this area tend to be more spread out and farther from town than hotels to the north. Some are on the inland side of the road; some are on the beach side, which means a difference in price. Those farthest from town are all-inclusive properties. The beaches tend to be slightly better than those to the north, but all the hotels have swimming pools and piers from which you can snorkel, and all of them accommodate divers. Head south on Avenida Rafael Melgar, which becomes the coastal road **Costera Sur** (also called Carretera a Chankanaab).

Very Expensive

Presidente InterContinental Cozumel ★★★ Widely considered the best resort in Cozumel, the Presidente spreads out across a long stretch of coast with only distant hotels for neighbors. Rooms come in seven categories offering pool, ocean, or beachfront views and are separated by quiet corridors displaying vivid original art. Even if the resort seems a bit architecturally dated, the rooms are not: guests enjoy Egyptian cotton sheets, marble bathrooms, Mexican artwork and onyx lamps, Maya-inspired turndown service, and complementary tea or coffee in the morning. Beachfront "reef" rooms and suites occupy the resort's most exclusive section and include 24-hour butler service and hammocks. There's a full-service spa here, and a pyramid of iguanas out by the pool that is thrilling for children to see. The excellent poolside dive shop (**Scuba Du,** p. 163) offers introductory and one- and two-tank dives as well as certification programs. A long stretch of sandy beach, dotted with *palapas* and palm trees, fronts the entire hotel, and the sunsets are amazing. Service here is first class.

Costera Sur Km 6.5, 77600 Cozumel, Q. Roo. ✆ **800/327-0200** in the U.S., or 987/872-9500.

Fax 987/872-9528. www.intercontinentalcozumel.com. 220 units. High season $330 pool view, $398 ocean view, $582 and up for beach fronts and suites; low season $257–$291 pool view, $302–$358 ocean view, $370–$504 and up for beach fronts and suites. Internet specials sometimes available. AE, MC, V. Free valet parking. **Amenities:** 3 restaurants; 4 bars; babysitting; 24-hr. butler service in reef section; kid's club; concierge; dive shop; access to golf club; putting green; 2 outdoor pools including adults-only pool; deep-sea fishing trips; full-service spa with salon and fully equipped fitness center; room service; 2 lighted tennis courts; tennis lessons; watersports; yoga. ***In room:*** A/C, flatscreen TV w/pay movies, iHome, hair dryer, minibar, Wi-Fi.

Where to Dine

The island offers a number of tasty restaurants. Taxi drivers will often steer you toward restaurants that pay them commissions; don't heed their advice.

Zermatt (© **987/872-1384**), a nice little bakery, is on Avenida 5 at Calle 4 Norte. It's open Monday to Saturday from 7am to 9pm. For inexpensive local fare during the day, I like **Comida Casera Toñita** (© **987/872-0401**), at Calle Rosado Salas 265 between avenidas 10 and 15. It's daily hours are from 8am to 6pm. For morning tacos of *cochinita pibil* (traditionally a breakfast item), go to **El Amigo Mario** (© **987/872-0742**), on Calle 5 Sur, between Francisco Mújica and Avenida 35. The doors close at 12:30pm.

EXPENSIVE

Cabaña del Pescador (Lobster House) ★★ LOBSTER The story's a little strange, but brothers Fernando and Enrique, who no longer speak with each other due to a business dispute, run adjacent restaurants both called the Lobster House. They have slight differences in decor, but both restaurants are excellent. Fresh lobster is weighed, then grilled or boiled with a hint of spices, and served with melted butter or garlic, accompanied by sides of rice, vegetables, and bread. Does lobster require anything more? Lobster is the only thing on the menu at Fernando's restaurant, but Enrique will also cook up steaks, shrimp, or fish. The setting is quite tropical—a pair of thatched bungalows bordering a pond with lily pads and reeds, traversed by a small footbridge. The open-air rooms are softly lit with the glow of candles and furnished with rustic tables and chairs. The restaurants ramble around quite a bit, so explore until you find the spot most to your taste. Finish with the signature key lime pie.

Carretera Santa Pilar Km 4 (across from Playa Azul Hotel). No phone. Reservations not accepted. Lobster (by weight) $13–$40. No credit cards. Daily 6–10:30pm.

French Quarter ★★ SOUTHERN Owner Mike Slaughter brings his Louisiana roots to this downtown favorite where you can order Southern and Creole classics, such as jambalaya and étouffée, or the daily catch blackened, grilled, or stuffed. The restaurant also serves Black Angus beef, and a filet mignon with red-onion marmalade that's delicious. I appreciate the uniqueness of the menu, but the dishes are pricey for this area. The downstairs bar is a popular hangout for many locals, especially for sports events.

Av. 5 Sur 18. © **987/872-6321.** Reservations recommended during Carnaval. Main courses $15–$36. AE, MC, V. Wed–Mon 5–10:30pm.

Guido's ★★ MEDITERRANEAN The inviting terrace, with director's chairs and rustic wood tables, makes this a restful place in daytime and a romantic spot at night. The specialties are oven-baked pizzas and homemade pastas, including

A laid-back outdoor restaurant in Cozumel.

lasagna with a Bolognese and béchamel sauce, ravioli stuffed with spinach and beef, and spaghetti with shrimp, garlic, olive oil, and parmesan. My favorite main courses include sautéed grilled shrimp and the spinach-stuffed chicken breast. The other item people love here is the *pan de ajo*—a house creation of fresh bread prepared with olive oil, garlic, and rosemary. In addition to an impressive wine list, pitchers of sangria are available.

Av. Rafael Melgar, btw. calles 6 and 8 Norte. ✆ **987/872-0946.** Reservations accepted. Main courses 162–312 pesos; pizzas 150–174 pesos. AE, MC, V. Mon–Sat 11am–11pm.

La Cocay ★★★ MEDITERRANEAN/SEAFOOD La Cocay, which means "firefly" in Mayan, serves the most original cooking on the island. The intimate dining room and outdoor courtyard, glittering with white lights wrapped around a sprawling palm tree, create an alluring atmosphere. For an appetizer, the empanadas with goat cheese and caramelized apples make for excellent tapas, as do the figs with prosciutto. For a main course, try the 8-oz. filet mignon, roasted stuffed chicken breast, or mixed grilled seafood served with Spanish rice. Give special consideration to the daily specials and the wonderful chocolate torte. It takes a little extra time to prepare, so order it early. The wine list offers excellent selections from South America.

Calle 8 Norte 208 (btw. avenidas. 10 and 15). ✆ **987/872-5533.** www.lacocay.com. Reservations recommended. Main courses 130–340 pesos. AE, MC, V. Mon–Sat 5:30–11pm.

MODERATE

Coconuts ★★ 🎁 SEAFOOD This fun-filled beach restaurant and bar sits on the highest point in Cozumel, which really isn't saying much but nevertheless offers a magnificent view of the Caribbean. Coconuts is open only during the day and has no electricity—running only a daytime generator using solar power. Grab a plastic table in the sand or a seat under the open-air *palapa* and check out the proverbs around you. One says, "beer, so much more than just a breakfast drink," while another advises, "sex is like air, it's really not that important until you're not getting any." If you do nothing else here, please order the mixed seafood *ceviche*.

It's just too delicious. There are also sumptuous shrimp quesadillas, the freshest guacamole, and all kinds of tacos and fajitas.

Carratera Oriente Km 43.5 ✆ **987/105-7622.** Reservations not accepted. Main courses 100–180 pesos. No credit cards. Daily 10am–6pm.

El Moro ★ REGIONAL El Moro is an out-of-the-way place that has been around for a long time and has always been popular with the locals, who come for the food, the service, and the prices—but not the decor, which is orange, orange, orange, and Formica. Get there by taxi, which will cost a couple of bucks. Portions are generous. Any of the shrimp dishes use the real jumbo variety when available. For something different, try the *pollo Ticuleño,* a specialty from the town of Ticul, a layered dish of tomato sauce, mashed potatoes, crispy baked corn tortillas, and fried chicken breast, topped with shredded cheese and green peas. Other specialties include enchiladas and seafood prepared many ways, plus grilled steaks and sandwiches.

75 bis Norte 124 (btw. calles 2 and 4 Norte). ✆ **987/872-3029.** Reservations not accepted. Main courses 50–150 pesos. MC, V. Fri–Wed 1–11pm.

Kinta ★★ CARIBBEAN An excellent example of Mexican creativity, this chic restaurant blends tropical decor with a cool urban style. Chill-out music fills the air of the lush garden terrace decorated with palms, tiny white lights, stone and wood designs, and a pond. Chef Kris Wallenta, who previously worked at Guido's and trained at New York's French Culinary Institute, has created a menu celebrating contemporary Mexican cuisine. I recommend the "Mexikanissimo" to start—crispy warm *panela* cheese over a green tomato sauce with herbs. Then order a *chile relleno*—a *poblano* pepper with vegetable ratatouille and cheese, baked and cooked over red sauce with a *chipotle* cream. The filet mignon with *huitlacoche* (corn mushroom), mashed potatoes, and *poblano* pepper sauce is terrific, too. Service is a bit slow on busy nights, so come for a leisurely evening.

5 Av. 148B (btw. calles 2 and 4 Norte). ✆ **987/869-0544.** Reservations not accepted. Main courses 120–195 pesos. MC, V. Tues–Sun 5:30–11:30pm, closed Mon.

La Choza ★ YUCATECAN/MEXICAN A favorite among locals, La Choza is an open-air restaurant with well-spaced tables under a tall thatched roof. Platters of poblano chiles stuffed with shrimp, grilled *brochetas* (kabobs), and *pollo en relleno negro* (chicken in a sauce of blackened chiles) are all delicious. Be sure to add some of the zesty table sauces and guacamole to your meal. Breakfasts are tasty here, as well.

Rosado Salas 198 (at Av. 10 Sur). ✆ **987/872-0958.** Reservations accepted for groups of 6 or more. Breakfast 45 pesos; main courses 100–160 pesos. AE, MC, V. Daily 7am–10pm.

Pancho's Backyard ★★★ MEXICAN Despite its popularity with visitors, the number of locals also eating here attests to Pancho's authenticity. Owned by father and son duo Pancho and Panchito, this charming open-air restaurant surrounded by palms, banana trees, and fountains occupies one of the town's original buildings. Cuisine here focuses on traditional Mexican fare—corn, beans, vegetables, and rice—with a healthy selection of chicken and fish plates. My favorite is the mahi-mahi filet topped with an almond, mango, orange, and pineapple *pico de gallo*. Homemade tortilla chips are served with fresh tomato and onion salsa, as well as a bowl of extraordinarily spicy *habanero* sauce. Crisply dressed waiters wearing white *guayaberas* with blue bandanas offer friendly,

Downtown San Miguel de Cozumel.

efficient service. There's also an outstanding artesian store selling quality arts and crafts here.

Av. Melgar 27 at Calle 8 Norte. © **987/872-2141.** www.panchosbackyard.com. Lunch $6–$16; dinner $12–$18. AE, MC, V. Mon–Sat 10am–11pm, Sun 6pm–11pm.

INEXPENSIVE

Restaurant del Museo BREAKFAST/MEXICAN The museum's rooftop restaurant and cafe remains my favorite place in San Miguel for breakfast or lunch (weather permitting). It offers a serene view of the water, removed from the traffic noise below and sheltered from the sun above. Breakfasts include *huevos rancheros* with corn tortillas, fried eggs, and salsa; Mexican and American omelets; fresh fruit platters; and pancakes. The Spanish menu offers even more choices than the English menu (including dishes with *nopales*, or cactus). Simple lunch dishes include sandwiches and enchiladas.

Av. Rafael Melgar (corner of Calle 6 Norte). © **987/872-0838.** Reservations not accepted. Breakfast 55–75 pesos; lunch main courses 64–110 pesos. No credit cards. Daily 7am–2pm.

Cozumel After Dark

Most of the music and dance venues are along Avenida Rafael Melgar. **Carlos 'n' Charlie's** (© **987/869-1648**), which is in the Punta Langosta shopping center, is practically next to **Señor Frog's** (© **987/869-1650**). Punta Langosta lies just south of Calle 7 Sur. The **Hard Rock Cafe** (© **987/872-5271**) is also on Avenida Rafael Melgar, at no. 2, just north of the municipal pier, and remains open until 2am or later with live music on weekends.

In town, there are a few Latin music clubs. These open and close with every high season, prospering when people have cash in their pockets, but closing down when the flow of tourism stops bringing in money. Calle 1 Sur between 5 Av. Sur and 10 Av. Sur is a pedestrian walking street housing a number of local bars, some with live music.

For sports events, the best bar is at the **French Quarter** (p. 172), open Wednesday to Monday from 5pm to midnight. On Sunday evenings, the place to be is the main square, which usually has a free concert and lots of people strolling about and visiting with friends. Various cafes and bars surround the square.

San Miguel's **movie theater** is Cinépolis, the modern multicinema in the Chedraui Plaza Shopping Center at the south end of town. It mainly shows Hollywood movies. Most of these are in English with Spanish subtitles (*película subtitulada*); before buying your tickets, make sure the movie hasn't been dubbed (*doblada*).

7

THE RIVIERA MAYA & THE SOUTHERN CARIBBEAN COAST

by Christine Delsol & Maribeth Mellin

You've heard it more times than you can count: "Caribbean coast," "endless stretch of pristine beach," "soft white sand caressed by turquoise waves ..." So let's skip the prose and move on to what you really need to know.

The Yucatán's Caribbean coast stretches 380km (236 miles) from Cancún to Chetumal, at the Belize border. The northern part of the coast from Cancún to Tulum has been dubbed the Riviera Maya; the southern half, the Costa Maya. In between is the vast Sian Ka'an Biosphere Reserve.

The Great Mesoamerican Reef, the second-longest mountain of coral in the world, protects most of the shoreline. You usually find the best beaches where the reef is far from shore, such as around Playa del Carmen, Xpu-Ha, and Tulum. However, feverish construction along this coastline has harmed many beaches, and currents can carry away all the sand. Some resorts are using unsightly sandbags as artificial reefs to protect their beaches. Others have created sandy terraces above the shore.

But sand is secondary to the Caribbean's gorgeous aquamarine water, and it's easy to find places to snorkel and dive with lots of fish and other sea creatures. Mangroves growing inland are now protected by the federal government, which is slowly helping the coastline return to its more natural state. You'll also find jungle, caverns, underground rivers, and the peninsula's famous cenotes (freshwater sinkholes) inland—and the even more famous Maya archaeological sites. Sights and activities abound.

So do lodging options. On this coast, you can stay in a variety of communities or distance yourself from all of them. You can bunk down in rustic cabins, secluded spa resorts, boutique hotels, all-inclusive megaresorts, bed-and-breakfasts, family-run guesthouses. You've got some decisions to make. I hope this chapter will help.

A single road, Hwy. 307, traces the coastline for 380km from Cancún to Chetumal, a 4½-hour trip by car. The section between Cancún's airport and Tulum is now a four-lane divided highway with speed limits up to 110kmph (68 mph). Overpasses have replaced the traffic lights and reduced-speed zones at Puerto Morelos, Playa del Carmen, and Tulum. It takes about 1½ hours to make the 130km (81 mile) drive from the Cancún airport to Tulum.

From Tulum, the highway turns inland to skirt the edges of Sian Ka'an. The roadway is two lanes, but here, too, the government has been hard at work, bypassing a significant fraction of the *tope*-pocked villages and providing shoulders almost as wide as the lanes, making passing easier and safer. Driving from Tulum to Chetumal takes 3 hours.

PUERTO MORELOS & VICINITY

Between Cancun & Playa del Carmen

The coast directly south of the Cancún airport has several roadside attractions, all-inclusives, small cabaña hotels, and some spa resorts. Much of the latest

FACING PAGE: **Sunbathers at Akumal Bay beach in Akumal.**

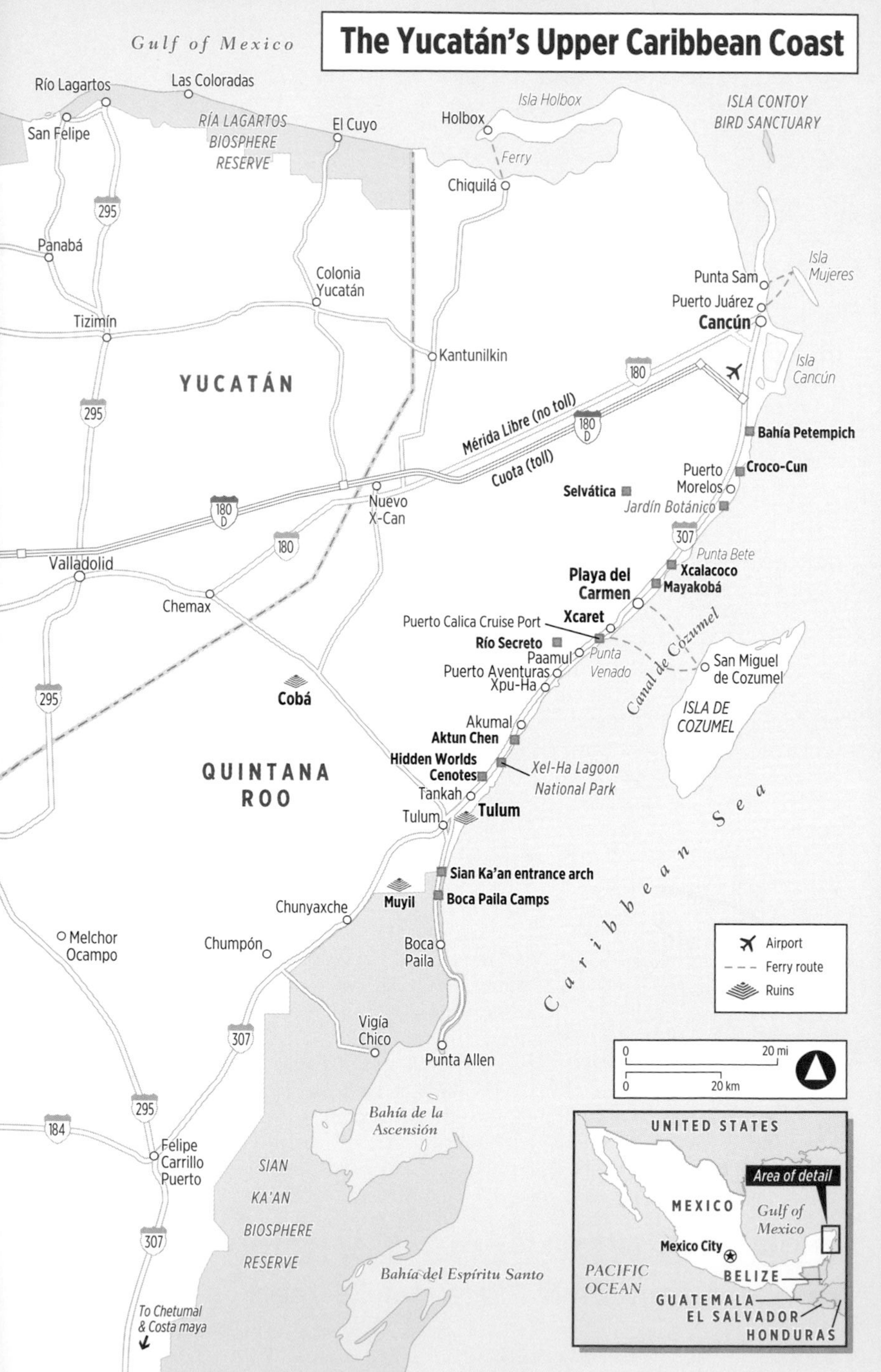
The Yucatán's Upper Caribbean Coast
Gulf of Mexico
Río Lagartos
Las Coloradas
San Felipe
RÍA LAGARTOS BIOSPHERE RESERVE
El Cuyo
Holbox
Isla Holbox
ISLA CONTOY BIRD SANCTUARY
Ferry
Chiquilá
Panabá
Colonia Yucatán
Punta Sam
Isla Mujeres
Puerto Juárez
Cancún
Tizimín
Kantunilkin
Isla Cancún
YUCATÁN
Mérida Libre (no toll)
Cuota (toll)
Bahía Petempich
Croco-Cun
Puerto Morelos
Selvática
Jardín Botánico
Nuevo X-Can
Punta Bete
Xcalacoco
Valladolid
Playa del Carmen
Mayakobá
Chemax
Puerto Calica Cruise Port
Xcaret
Río Secreto
Paamul
Punta Venado
Canal de Cozumel
San Miguel de Cozumel
Puerto Aventuras
Xpu-Ha
Cobá
ISLA DE COZUMEL
Akumal
Aktun Chen
Hidden Worlds Cenotes
Xel-Ha Lagoon National Park
QUINTANA ROO
Tankah
Tulum
Caribbean Sea
Sian Ka'an entrance arch
Muyil
Boca Paila Camps
Chunyaxche
Melchor Ocampo
Chumpón
Boca Paila
Airport
Ferry route
Ruins
Vigía Chico
Punta Allen
0
20 mi
0
20 km
Bahía de la Ascensión
Felipe Carrillo Puerto
SIAN KA'AN BIOSPHERE RESERVE
Bahía del Espíritu Santo
To Chetumal & Costa maya
UNITED STATES
Area of detail
MEXICO
Gulf of Mexico
Mexico City
PACIFIC OCEAN
BELIZE
GUATEMALA
EL SALVADOR
HONDURAS

development targets the well-heeled traveler—small boutique hotels and astonishingly luxurious all-inclusives. The agreeable town of **Puerto Morelos** lies midway along this 51km (32-mile) stretch of coast between the airport and Playa del Carmen.

ROADSIDE ATTRACTIONS

Near the Puerto Morelos turnoff is Rancho Loma Bonita, which offers horseback riding and ATV tours, but I prefer **Rancho Punta Venado** (p. 200), just south of Playa. You'll also find **Jardín Botánico Dr. Alfredo Barrera** (✆ **998/206-9223;** www.ecosur.mx/jb/YaaxChe). Opened in 1990 and named after a biologist who studied tropical forests, this botanical garden is the largest swath of undeveloped land along the coast, save for the Sian Ka'an Biosphere Reserve (p. 224). Ceiba trees, sacred to the Maya, stand tall amid bromeliads, ferns, orchids, and small archaeological sites. Biology students working here are happy to share details (it helps to speak Spanish). Spider monkeys, nearly extinct along the coast, frolic here along with tropical birds. The park is open Monday to Saturday from 9am to 5pm. Admission is 70 pesos. Wear insect repellent!

Kids are more likely to enjoy the interactive zoo, **CrocoCun ★** (✆ **998/850-3719;** www.crococunzoo.com), a mile north of Puerto Morelos. Formerly a crocodile farm, it now runs a captive breeding program that has helped to restore the reptiles' population in Cancún's Nichupté Lagoon. Currently, it protects all animals native to the Yucatán; those in residence include iguanas, spider

driving THE RIVIERA MAYA

Driving along this coast isn't difficult, but it takes eagle-eyed attention, especially for first timers. With only one highway, you can't get too lost unless you miss the signs for your hotel. Turnoffs can be from either the right or left lane; if you miss the one you want, go a bit farther and circle back. You're not allowed to stop on the highway to make a left turn, but there are several short left turn lanes at many points across the road from major resorts. In some places, the exit leads to the right, where you should stop before charging across the road to the other side. I can't stress enough just how dangerous this highway can be, especially during high season when you've got locals speeding to work, tour buses clogging the lanes, truck and bus drivers barreling along, and confused or distracted tourists changing lanes on whim. Speed limits are clearly posted and change constantly. Keep an eye out for speed signs, especially around towns and resorts. Lots of drivers ignore speed limits, often to their chagrin. The police have become ever more sophisticated at ticketing speeders and are eagle-eyed around stoplights and one-way streets.

All that said, I can't imagine traveling around the Riviera Maya without a rental car. So many wonderful places to explore are right beside the highway and along side roads to the beach and jungle. First-class gas station plazas with mini-marts and fast-food spots are becoming a common sight. Attendants pump the gas (be sure they don't overfill the tank) and will check your oil. Make sure you receive the right change, and tip attendants if they provide extra services. As long as you study your maps in advance and keep your wits about you, driving allows freedom for serendipitous discoveries.

Children will love seeing the reptiles at CrocoCun.

monkeys, a boa constrictor, and immense tarantulas. A guided tour with one of the enthusiastic veterinary students who volunteer here lasts 1 hour. Again, wear bug repellent. Open daily from 9am to 5pm. Entrance fees are high, as are most roadside attractions on this coast: $20 adults, $12 children 6 to 12, free for children younger than 6.

SPA RESORTS ★★★

Several resorts with first-rate spas are clustered between Puerto Morelos and the Cancún airport. They're actually more convenient for quick getaways than those along Cancún's Hotel Zone, and all offer airport transfers for the 15- to 20-minute commute. Rates quoted below are for high season, but don't include the often exorbitant holiday periods. These hotels are mostly all-inclusive (there are few other dining choices nearby). Some add a 10% or 15% service charge.

Ceiba del Mar ★★ Closest to the town of Puerto Morelos, this peaceful resort consists of seven three-story buildings along a landscape of gardens, ponds, and pools. Rooms are large, with a terrace or balcony complete with hammocks. The bathrooms have both showers and tubs, some with an ocean view. Service is attentive and unobtrusive—exemplified by the morning coffee and juice delivery quietly slipped into a niche by the door. The spa's excellent therapists quickly assess each client's needs and preferences. I try to spend at least one night here after my travels through the Riviera Maya for a pre-flight massage.

Av. Niños Héroes s/n, 77580 Puerto Morelos, Q. Roo. ✆ **877/545-6221** in the U.S., or 998/872-8060. Fax 998/872-8061. www.ceibadelmar.com. 88 units. High season $316–$445 deluxe and junior suite, from $445 master suite; low season $133–$257 deluxe and junior suite, from $468 master suite. Spa and dining packages available. AE, MC, V. Free parking. **Amenities:** 2 restaurants; 2 bars; babysitting; bikes; concierge; dive shop w/watersports; state-of-the-art gym w/ sauna, steam room, whirlpool, and Swiss showers; 2 outdoor pools (1 heated); room service; smoke-free rooms; spa. ***In room:*** A/C, TV/VCR, CD player, hair dryer, minibar, Wi-Fi.

Zoëtry Paraíso de la Bonita ★★ Both a luxurious all-inclusive hotel and a serious wellness center with an elaborate thalassotherapy spa, this resort offers a bit of everything. Macaws squawk and lovebirds coo in an indoor aviary. Drinks are served in the library amid celeb photos, shared computers, and plush sofas. Guest rooms are decorated around global themes—guests reside in Bali, India, or Africa. The over-the-top design melds sunken marble tubs, beds so puffy short people have to hop to get on, and stone carvings jutting from lintels. Ground-floor rooms have a plunge pool; upstairs rooms have balconies. Artfully placed sculptures of Chinese dragons and Maya deities are spread through hallways and gardens between the two restaurants, pool, and outdoor cocktail lounge. Weddings and incentive trips are popular here.

Carretera Cancún–Chetumal Km 328, Bahía Petempich, 77710 Q. Roo. ✆ **888/496-3879** in the U.S., or 998/872-8300. Fax 998/872-8301. www.zoetryparaisodelabonita.com. 90 units. High season $1,000 and up suite; low season $800 and up suite. Rates include ground transfer and meals, drinks, and some activities. AE, MC, V. Free valet parking. No children 11 and under. **Amenities:** 2 restaurants; 2 bars; concierge; 2 Jacuzzis; 4 outdoor pools; room service; smoke-free rooms; spa; lighted tennis court, watersports. *In room:* A/C, TV/DVD, hair dryer, minibar, Wi-Fi.

Puerto Morelos

Puerto Morelos remains a quiet fishing village, perfect for lying on the white-sand beach and reading, with the occasional foray into snorkeling, diving, windsurfing or kayaking. This was the coast's boomtown 100 years ago, when its port shipped hardwood and *chicle* to the U.S. and Europe. Today, the biggest attraction is its idyllic small-town atmosphere and easy pace.

Puerto Morelos' section of the Great Maya Reef has been protected as a national park. The reef is close to the surface and easy to snorkel, and it protects the coast from storm surges. The government-maintained beaches are great, and the water is shallow, calm, and clear, with sea grass growing on the bottom.

Puerto Morelos brims with foreign tourists at times during the high season, but low season is so low that many businesses close for the season, earning it the affectionate nickname, Muerto Morelos (*muerto* means "dead").

ESSENTIALS

GETTING THERE By Car Puerto Morelos is at Km 31, about a ½ hour from Cancún. You'll need to exit the highway onto the frontage road, then turn left under the new overpass.

BY BUS Buses from Cancún to Tulum and Playa del Carmen usually stop here, but be sure to ask in Cancún if your bus makes the Puerto Morelos stop.

EXPLORING IN & AROUND PUERTO MORELOS

The biggest draw is the **coral reef ★★★** rising directly in front of the village to top out just a couple of feet below the water's surface. Divers have nothing over snorkelers here; everyone gets a close-up of the convoluted passages and large caverns burgeoning with fish and sea flora. Restrictions on fishing and boating make this the coast's most pristine patch of coral. Several dive shops in town offer snorkeling tours and gear rentals, but my choice is the local **fishing cooperative ★** (**✆ 998/121-1524**) at the foot of the pier. Its 22 member fishing families are national park-certified guides who rotate tour gigs to supplement their income. The fixed fee is 300 pesos for a 2-hour trip that visits two snorkeling sites. Tours leave approximately every half-hour, Monday through Saturday from 9am to 3pm. During whale shark season, the manager, Paco González, also runs tours to Isla Holbox (p. 319) on his day off.

Dive shops around town charge $45 to $50 for one-tank dives; PADI certification costs $350 to $400. One of the best is **Almost Heaven Adventures** (©/fax **998/871-0230;** www.almostheavenadventures.com), on Javier Rojo Gómez a block north of the plaza. Enrique Juárez, in business for 15 years, holds groups to five divers and is known for thorough briefings and attentive boat crews. Also recommended: **Dive In Puerto Morelos** (© **998/206/9084;**www.diveinpuertomorelos.com) and **Wet Set Diving Adventure** (©**998 871 0198;** www.wetset.com).

Snorkelers enter the water at Puerto Morelos.

The small, modern **central plaza** is less beguiling than the adjacent sea walk, but it is the fulcrum of local life (and the site of many restaurants). On the south side, **Alma Libre** (© **998/871-0713;** www.almalibrebooks.com) sells more English-language books than any other bookstore in the Yucatán. The owners, Canadians Joanne and Rob Birce, stock everything from beach reads to English classics, cookbooks to volumes on Maya culture, as well as regional maps. The store also serves as a book exchange, tourist information center, and vacation rental agency. This year it expanded its hours to 7 days a week, 10am to 3pm and 6 to 9pm.

About a block south of the plaza on Javier Rojo Gómez, the local artisans' cooperative runs **Hunab Kú market,** a collection of *palapa* stands selling hammocks, hand-embroidered clothes, jewelry, blankets, ceramics, and other handicrafts. The wares are high quality, and there are some bargains. Vendors don't hustle you, so it's worth a stroll just for the parklike setting. The market is open daily from 9am to 8pm.

On Wednesday and Friday, you can get a good massage and other treatments at the **Jungle Spa ★★** (© **998/208-9148;** www.mayaecho.com), a short distance west of Hwy. 307. This is a cooperative endeavor by Maya women who have been trained in spa techniques. Massages cost $40 for 1 hour, $60 for 1½ hours—a fraction of what nearby spa hotels charge—and the money directly supports local Maya families. The same group holds a Sunday Jungle Market to sell unique handicrafts.

Selvática (© **866/552-8825** in the U.S., or 998/847-4581; www.selvatica.com.mx), operating out of offices in Cancún, offers guests a little jungle adventure, with 2.5km (1½ miles) of zip lines strung up in the forest canopy 19km (12 miles) west of Puerto Morelos. The program also includes biking and swimming in cenotes. In high season, you should make reservations a month in advance. The cost ($90–$120) includes transportation, activities, a light lunch, locker, and all equipment.

WHERE TO STAY

For condo rentals, see the website of Alma Libre books (above).

Club Marviya ★ Guest rooms in the original Club Marviya occupy the second floor of a converted mansion on the town's main street, where small terraces offer terrific views and refreshing breezes. Mexican style and color infuse the airy contemporary rooms, which have firm beds and ceramic tile floors. A large communal kitchen and lounge encourage socializing, and the hospitable Canadian and Mexican owners often schmooze with guests in the covered courtyard during the evening. Around the corner, the same owners offer nine newly renovated studios geared toward longer stays (but available by the night). Neither property has air-conditioning, but sea breezes suffice most of the year. They are three blocks from the main square, but only a block from the best beach in town.

Av. Javier Rojo Gómez (at Ejército), SM2, 77580 Puerto Morelos, Q. Roo. ✆ **998/871-0049.** www.marviya.com. 15 units. High season $110; low season $60–$75. High-season rates include breakfast. Studios $80–$110 a night (no breakfast). Weekly/monthly rates available. MC, V. **Amenities:** Communal kitchen/lounge; bikes; on-site massage therapist; sailboard and kayak rentals; Wi-Fi in lobby. *In room:* Ceiling fans, fridge.

Hotel Ojo de Agua ☺ This family-run hotel's perch on the town's best stretch of beach, two long blocks from the main square, would be enough to recommend it, but it also has a good dive shop, watersports, and a popular beach restaurant. Utilitarian rooms are brightened by rattan furniture and bold paint. Studios with kitchenettes and small yards come with one king-size bed or a double and two twins—they have ceiling fans but no air-conditioning—and are well-suited for families. The beach's excellent snorkeling includes the undersea cenote for which the hotel is named.

Puerto Morelos's waterfront.

Av. Javier Rojo Gómez 16, SM2, M 2, 77580 Puerto Morelos, Q. Roo. ✆ **998/840-3942.** www.ojo-de-agua.com. 36 units. High season $70–$80 double, $90 studio; low season $60–$70 double, $80 studio. AE, MC, V. **Amenities:** Restaurant; dive shop; outdoor pool. *In room:* A/C (in some), kitchen (in some).

Posada El Moro ★★★ ☺ One of the town's most appealing hotels also happens to be a great deal. Renting a room is akin to ordering dim sum: Add $5 a night for air-conditioning, $5 more for TV, and another $5 for a kitchenette. French-paned sliding doors and windows flood the rooms with natural light, and the tile bathrooms are new and sparkling clean. Simple, cheery furnishings include queen-size beds with nearly perfect mattresses, plus a futon. Junior suites have a single bed as well; full suites have two double beds, a futon, and a kitchenette. Guests have use of the kitchen off the lobby. The pretty, compact garden has a small pool perfect for kids, and the amiable family that runs the place creates a homey atmosphere. The hotel is about a half-block off the square on the town square.

Av. Rojo Gómez, SM2, M 5, Lote 17 (north of José Morelos), 77580 Puerto Morelos, Q. Roo. ✆/fax **998/871-0159.** www.posadaelmoro.com. 31 units. High season $60–$80 double, $90 suite; low season $50–$70 double, $80 suite. Rates include ample continental breakfast. MC, V. Limited free parking. **Amenities:** Small outdoor pool. *In room:* A/C (in some), TV (in some), Wi-Fi.

WHERE TO DINE

Most of Puerto Morelos' restaurants are on or around the main square. These include **Doña Triny's** for Mexican and Yucatecan standards; **Los Pelícanos** for seafood; **David Lau's** for Asian food; enduring local favorite **Hola Asia** for Chinese, Japanese, and Thai; **El Pirata** if you have kids (for its large menu); and **Le Café d'Amancia** for coffee, pastries, and downright addictive smoothies.

John Gray's Kitchen ★★★ SEAFOOD If I could splurge only once on my entire Riviera Maya stay, this would be the place. After chef John Gray left the Ritz-Carlton Cancún, where he elevated the Club Grill to iconic status, he cooked his way around the world before settling in Puerto Morelos in 2002. He's since opened restaurants in Playa del Carmen and Cancún, but this is where it all began, and where he still captains the kitchen most nights. The menu changes with Gray's mood and what's fresh in the market; the first time I ate there, he burst out of the kitchen to scribble swordfish and fresh clams on menus that diners were already studying. Pick out three of the appetizers, such as crab cakes with a Mexican twist or ambrosial baked red chili cauliflower, and split them among two people for a very *haute* meal at a bargain price. Newcomer **La Suegra,** just north of the square near the lighthouse, is owned by Gray's mother-in-law. The food is good, if a bit expensive, and it has a full bar, but its greatest virtue is the two-level deck overlooking the ocean.

Av. Niños Heroes Lote 6 (north of Av. José Morelos). ✆ **998/871-0665.** Reservations recommended. Main courses $12–$29. MC, V. Mon–Sat 6–10pm.

Posada Amor ★ BREAKFAST/YUCATECAN Puerto Morelos' oldest restaurant, now run by the founder's son, has patrons who have been eating here for nearly 30 years. The *palapa*-roofed dining room, a half-block south of the plaza, is a great place for a complete breakfast or the bargain-priced Sunday breakfast buffet. A few sidewalk tables are perfect for nighttime. The dinner menu focuses on fresh seafood and Yucatecan-influenced dishes.

Avs. Javier Rojo Gómez and Tulum. ✆ **998/871-0033.** Main courses 48–200 pesos, breakfast 45–70 pesos. AE, MC, V. Daily 7am–10pm.

South of Puerto Morelos

The beaches, bays, mangrove lagoons, and jungles between Puerto Morelos and Playa del Carmen are constantly undergoing transformation. Punta Maroma, home to the coast's first exclusive hideaway, is being carved into several resort and residential compounds. Massive all-inclusive resorts rise on beaches where campgrounds once thrived. Mayakobá, a master-planned resort just north of Playa del Carmen, is a fine example of an ecologically responsible development, though many other resorts are just using the land as they wish without much thought to conservation. This area is packed with adventures and attractions, and new playtime projects open frequently.

Grand Velas ★★★ All-inclusive resorts, some with nearly 1,000 rooms, claim much of the Riviera Maya's coastline. I've ignored them, for the most part. But I couldn't resist checking out the Grand Velas just south of Mayakobá. From afar, it looks massive and imposing. But I quickly learned that this small hotel chain has merged all-inclusive with all the luxuries of the area's finest hotels. Suites are clustered in three categories—the adults-only Grand Class, an Ambassador Family Ambience, and Jungle Suite Ambience. The first two all have ocean views; jungle suites are located beside the spa and convention center and have the most amenities for business travelers, including large desks facing canals and jungle. Sleek, dark brown furnishings and cream walls, ceiling, and floors give all suites an open-air feeling. The restaurants are top-notch: the Cocina de Autor has won numerous accolades thanks to its creative Spanish chefs, as has the French restaurant Piaf. I could easily spend hours in the spa's hydrotherapy area ($50 for a full day or free with spa treatment), with its bubbling jets, gushing water spouts, "experience showers," saunas, and cushy lounge chairs. Everything is over the top, in a good way—it's no wonder guests spend multiple nights and hold destination weddings here.

Carretera 307 Km 62, Playa del Carmen, 77710 Q. Roo. ✆ **866/335-4640** in the U.S. and Canada, or 984/877-4414. http://rivieramaya.grandvelas.com. 481 suites. From $450 double. Rates include meals (one at each of the 3 gourmet restaurants, unlimited at others), drinks, and gratuities. AE, MC, V. Free valet parking. **Amenities:** 8 restaurants; 3 bars; children's programs; concierge; butler service; fitness center; 2 outdoor pools; room service; spa; watersports. *In room:* A/C, TV/CD/DVD, fan, hair dryer, Internet (for a fee), MP3 dock.

Maroma ★★ This resort has been around the longest, owns a large inland parcel that somewhat protects from development, and has a gorgeous beach and beautifully manicured grounds. Two- and three-story buildings house the large guest rooms; most have king-size beds. The grounds are lovely, and the beach is fine white sand. The hotel has also spent a lot of effort and money upgrading the rooms. Nine new suites are outrageously extravagant. The beach bar is an enjoyable place to pass the evening. A replica of the pyramid at Uxmal rises above the entrance to the stylish spa.

Carretera 307 Km 51, Riviera Maya (Solidaridad), 77710 Q. Roo. ✆ **866/454-9351** in the U.S., or 998/872-8200. www.maromahotel.com. 65 units. $765 and up double and junior suite, $1,520 master suite. Rates include ground transfer, full breakfast, and snorkeling tour. AE, MC, V. Free valet parking. No children 15 and under. **Amenities:** Restaurant; 3 bars; concierge; fitness center; Jacuzzi; 3 outdoor spring-fed pools; room service; spa; steam bath; watersports. *In room:* A/C, hair dryer, Internet.

Petit Lafitte Hotel ★ One kilometer (a half-mile) south of the original Posada Lafitte, this new property has the same easy-going attitude that characterized the old one. In relative isolation, you still get all the amenities of a relaxing vacation. The three-story building, with 30 rooms, is surrounded by 13 bungalows. Spacious, attractive rooms are larger than those in the original property but have a similar beach-hotel simplicity. The staff came from the old property, so service is still personal and attentive.

Carretera Cancún–Tulum Km 63 (Punta Bete), 77710 Playa del Carmen, Q. Roo. ✆ **800/538-6802** in the U.S. and Canada, or 984/877-4000. www.petitlafitte.com. 43 units. High season $200–$375 double; low season $175–$350 double. Minimum 2 to 4 nights. Rates include breakfast and dinner. MC, V. Free guarded parking. **Amenities:** Restaurant; bar; outdoor pool. *In room:* A/C, TV, minibar, Wi-Fi.

El Camaleón golf course.

The Tides Riviera Maya ★★ The smallest resort in this area once held sway over a seemingly endless white beach. New hotels and neighborhoods are rising all around it these days, but the Tides (formerly Ikal del Mar) is still all about privacy and tranquility. Thirty well-separated bungalows—each with its own piece of jungle, a little pool, and an outdoor shower—are connected by sparsely lit pathways through the vegetation. The bungalows are large and designed to blend with the setting, using louvered shutters, crocheted hammocks, and minimal decorations in a modern, spare style. The bathrooms have two showers (though the private pools are perfect for long soaks). Mayordomos are on call for some villas, and service at all levels is understated and professional. The bar and restaurant, overlooking an inviting pool, make for an attractive common area. And, of course, there's the eco-spa surrounded by jungle.

Playa Xcalacoco, Carretera Cancún–Tulum (Playa Xcalacoco), 77710 Q. Roo. ✆ **800/578-0281** in the U.S. and Canada, or 984/877-3000. Fax 713/528-3697. www.tidesrivieramaya.com. 30 units. High season $700 and up double; low season $585 and up double. Rates include full breakfast. AE, MC, V. Free secure parking. No children 17 and under except during some holidays. **Amenities:** Restaurant; 2 bars; concierge; 2 Jacuzzis; large outdoor pool; room service; courtesy shuttle to Playa; spa; steam bath; watersports. *In room:* A/C, TV/DVD, hair dryer, minibar, Wi-Fi.

Mayakobá Residential Golf & Spa Resort

One of the most impressive ecologically sensitive developments I've seen, **Mayakobá** (www.mayakoba.com) incorporates three upscale hotels, including Banyan Tree's first foray into Mexico, and a championship golf course into more than 607 hectares (1,500 acres) of healthy mangroves, lagoons, cenotes, and beaches. Less than 243 hectares (600 acres) have been developed thus far, all on the ocean side of Hwy. 307. The compound's concept is unusual—it's a beach resort with precious few oceanview rooms. Instead, the hotels line a series of freshwater canals. It takes some getting used to, but the idea works.

Guests travel about in electric boats and golf carts and may use the restaurants, spas, and other facilities in all three hotels. Some guests have trouble with the jungle setting bug repellent is a must, especially at dusk, and swimming is forbidden in the canals. I've spotted small crocodiles in the canals and have been assured they're removed to more suitable homes on Mayakobá's wild side. The **El Camaleón** golf course, designed by Greg Norman, is an Audubon-certified bird reserve—and a challenge for the pros competing in Mexico's only PGA tournament, usually scheduled for late February/early March. The first fairway sits beside a large cenote. The development is extremely private, and you must have a reservation or appointment to get past the gates. Consider booking a meal or spa treatment at one of the superb restaurants or spas and take a look around.

Fairmont Mayakobá ☺ Families, groups, and recluses are all happy with the thoughtful layout and facilities at Mayakobá's first resort. Active types head for the beach, pool island (with a 929-sq.-m/10,000-sq.-ft. freeform pool), 24-hour gym or El Camaleón golf course. Sybarites spend hours at the Willow Stream Spa, alternating between treatments and lazy laps in a peaceful rooftop pool. Dining choices range from a gourmet deli to lagoon-side breakfast buffets to two excellent formal restaurants. Rooms come in 13 categories, including a suite on its own island. All open out to gardens, lagoons, or the Caribbean Sea. Wooden shutter doors close off the bathing and sleeping areas or can be open to nature. In keeping with the eco setting, rooms have trash cans for recyclable materials and the spa uses soaps and lotions made at a local community co-op.

Carretera Cancún–Tulum Km 298, 77710 Playa del Carmen, Q. Roo. ✆ **800/435-2600** in the U.S. and Canada, or 984/206-3000. www.fairmont.com/mayakoba. 401 units. High season $409–$659 casitas, $809 and up signature casitas; low season $219–$469 casitas, $299 and up signature casistas. AE, MC, V. Free guarded parking. **Amenities:** 3 restaurants; 3 bars; fitness center; 5 outdoor pools; spa; watersports. *In room:* A/C, fan, TV/CD, hair dryer, Internet, minibar.

The Mayakobá development is surrounded by healthy mangroves and lagoons.

Rosewood Mayakobá ★★★ Privacy is the hallmark of this pricey resort designed with sail-like roofs on open-air spaces that take full advantage of the natural setting. Classy two-story suites face various mangrove-backed lagoons and have awe-inspiring sea views from rooftop pools and sundecks—starlit nights are pretty perfect as well. Over-water decks and plunge pools are almost totally hidden, though motorized boats sometimes pass by when ferrying new guests around the property. Beachfront suites are a bit less secluded—you can't keep folks from strolling the mile-long stretch of soft sand. Interiors have a fresh, airy look, with sliding shuttered doors connecting bedrooms, spacious closet areas, and outdoor showers and tubs buried in foliage. Private butlers and housekeepers anticipate your needs. Guests linger over newspapers during leisurely breakfasts at Casa del Lago, tequila tastings and ceviches at the Agua Azul bar, and Mexican cuisine at Punta Bonita.

Carretera Cancún–Tulum Km 298, 77710 Playa del Carmen, Q. Roo. ✆ **800/435-2600** in the U.S. and Canada, or 984/875-8000. www.rosewoodmayakoba.com. 128 suites. High season $790 and up lagoon-view suites; $1,350 and up oceanview suites; low season $590–$850 lagoon-view suites, $1,050 and up oceanview suites. AE, MC, V. Free guarded parking. **Amenities:** 3 restaurants; 3 bars; fitness center; 3 outdoor pools; spa; watersports. ***In room:*** A/C, fan, TV/CD/DVD, hair dryer, Internet, minibar.

PLAYA DEL CARMEN ★★★

32km (20 miles) S of Puerto Morelos; 70km (43 miles) S of Cancún; 10km (6½ miles) N of Xcaret; 13km (8 miles) N of Puerto Calica

Though it no longer has the feel of a village, Playa still provides a combination of simplicity (at its core, still primarily a beach town) and variety (unique hotels, restaurants, and stores). The local architecture has adopted such elements of native building as rustic clapboard walls, stucco, thatched roofs, rough-hewn wood, and in many structures, a ramshackle, unplanned look. Cheap-looking commercial architecture has intruded, and chain restaurants and stores detract from the individuality, but Playa retains the feel of a cosmopolitan getaway with a counterculture ethos.

A strong European influence has made topless sunbathing (nominally against the law in Mexico) an accepted practice at beaches north and south of town (away from families). The beach grows and shrinks, from broad and sandy to narrower with rocks, depending on currents and wind. When this happens, head to the beaches in north Playa.

Essentials

GETTING THERE & DEPARTING

BY AIR Fly into Cancún and take a bus directly from the airport (see "By Bus," below), or fly into Cozumel and take the passenger ferry.

BY CAR **Hwy. 307** is the only highway that passes through Playa. The highway divides as you approach from Cancún. The two main arteries into town are Avenida Constituyentes, which works well for destinations in northern Playa, and Avenida Juárez, which leads to the town's main square. Keep to the inside lanes to permit turning left at any of the traffic lights; otherwise you will have to continue past Playa until you get to the turnaround, then double-back, staying to your right.

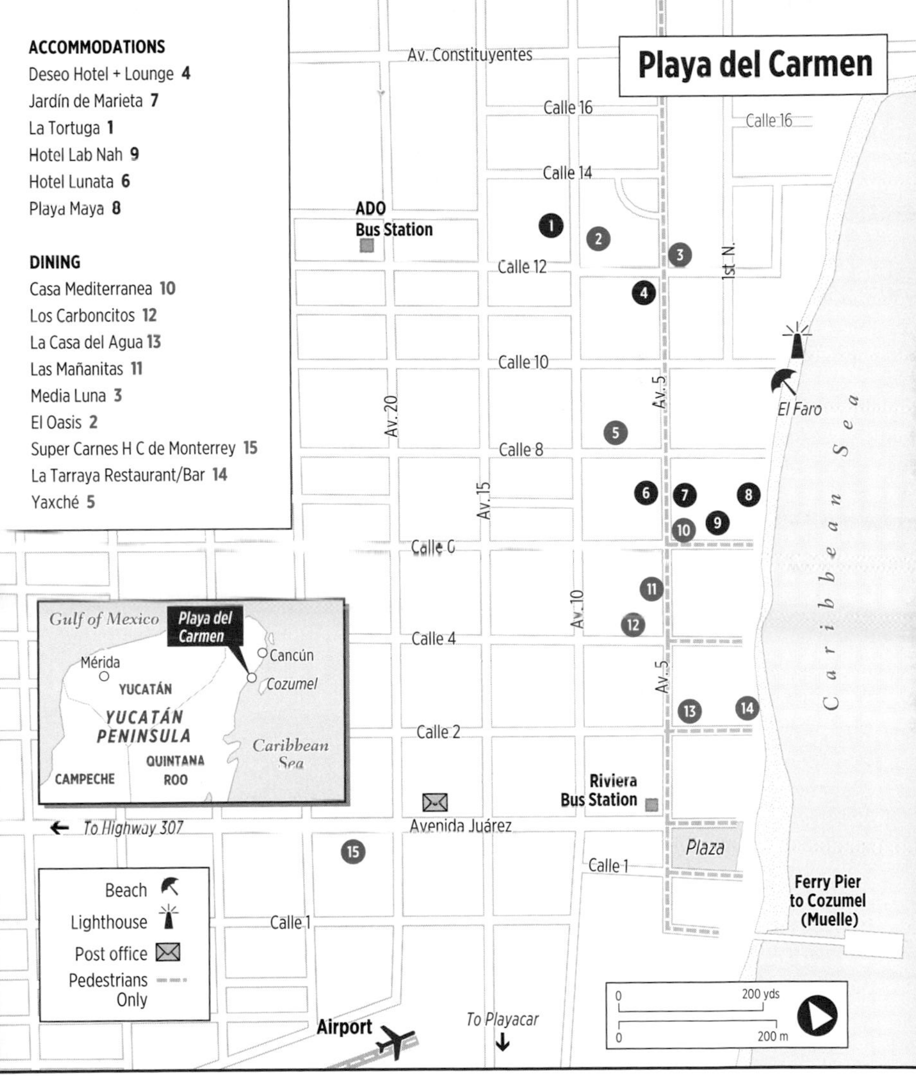

BY FERRY Air-conditioned passenger ferries to Cozumel leave from the pier, 1 block from the main square. There is also a car ferry to Cozumel from the Calica pier just south of Playacar. The schedule for passenger ferries changes with demand. You can usually count on hourly departures in the morning and late afternoon—just like rush hour on land. Ferries typically depart every 2 hours around midday. For more information about both ferries, see "Getting There & Departing" in the Cozumel section of chapter 6.

BY TAXI Taxi fares from the Cancún airport are about 650 to 750 pesos one-way.

BY BUS **Autobuses Riviera** offers service from the Cancún airport about 10 times a day between 8:10am and 8pm. Cost is 106 pesos one-way. If you arrive at Terminal 2, you'll see a ticket counter in the corridor to your right as you approach the doors out of the terminal. The buses leave from the end of the parking lot all the way to the right after you exit. From Terminal 3, go outside after you depart customs/immigrations, and the bus is to the right. At either terminal, you can also pay the driver, in either pesos or U.S. dollars. For a higher fee ($10 to Playa, $4 to Cancún) you can also reserve your seat online at www.cancun-airport.com/public-buses.htm; an airport representative will meet you outside the terminal and escort you to the bus. From the downtown Cancún bus station, buses depart almost every 30 minutes and cost 40 pesos.

ORIENTATION

ARRIVING Playa has two **bus** stations. Buses from Cancún and places along the coast, such as Tulum, arrive at the Riviera bus station, at the corner of Juárez and Avenida Quinta, by the town square. Buses from interior destinations arrive at the new ADO station on Avenida 20 between calles 12 and 14.

A word of caution: Most "information" stands along Avenida Quinta are associated with timeshare and vacation ownership properties. The salespeople are usually generous with information, hoping you'll agree to a sales tour of the properties they represent. Some tourists are wise to this and willingly give up a morning in exchange for free car rental, tours, or other perks. If your time is tight, however, steer clear.

CITY LAYOUT The main street, **Avenida Juárez,** leads to the town square from Hwy. 307. On the way, it crosses several numbered avenues running parallel to the beach, all of which are multiples of 5. The east-west streets parallel to Juárez are in multiples of two. A wonderful bike path along Avenida 10 provides fairly safe passage for *tricilcos* (bike taxis) and cyclists.

Avenida Quinta (Fifth Avenue), often simply "La Quinta," runs 1 to 2 blocks inland from the beach and is the most popular street in the Riviera Maya. It's closed to traffic from Avenida Juárez to Calle 12 (and some blocks beyond, in the evening). However, taxis and drivers are allowed to access hotels on side streets. Hotels, restaurants, shops, clubs, and chains like Starbucks and Dairy Queen line Fifth Avenue and its side streets. **Avenida Constituyentes** delineates the newest part of rapidly growing Playa. Several hip restaurants and pricey condo developments are located here.

Playacar, a golf-course development with private residences and several resort hotels, is located just south of Avenida Juárez.

Playa del Carmen's ferry terminal.

[Fast FACTS] PLAYA DEL CARMEN

Area Code The telephone area code is **984.**

ATMs & Banks Playa has several banks and ATMs.

Currency Exchange Many *casas de cambio* or currency-exchange houses are close to the pier or along Avenida Quinta at Calle 8.

Doctor For serious medical attention, go to **Hospiten** (✆ **984/803-1002**), on Hwy. 307 at the second Playacar exit, just south of Sam's Club. **Dr. G. Ambriz** speaks English and was trained in the U.S. and Europe. His office is at the corner of Avenida 30 and Calle 14 (✆ **984/109-1245**)

Drugstore The **Farmacía del Carmen,** Avenida Juárez between avenidas 5 and 10 (✆ **984/873-2330**), is open 24 hours.

Internet Access Internet cafes are all over town; most have fast connections. Most hotels have Wi-Fi, at least in public areas.

Parking Parking on the street in Playa is tough, as spots are hard to come by and police are quick to ticket violators. The **Estacionamiento México,** at avenidas Juárez and 10 (where the entrance is located) is open daily 24 hours and charges 20 pesos per hour, 120 pesos per day. There's also a **24-hour lot** a few blocks from the pier on Avenida 10 and Calle 3 Sur. Very few hotels have on-site parking, but some can get you reduced rates at nearby lots.

Post Office The *correo,* on Avenida Juárez, 3 blocks from the plaza, is on the right past the Hotel Playa del Carmen and the launderette.

Seasons The main high season is from mid-December to Easter. A mini high season is in August and around Thanksgiving. Low season is all other months, though many hotels further divide these into several micro seasons.

Exploring Playa del Carmen

Playa del Carmen is best enjoyed from a lounge chair on the sand or over an evening strolling **Avenida Quinta ★★**, paralleling the beach for 20 blocks from the ferry pier to the north. The area around the ferry terminal, predictably, is rife with trinket emporiums, hawkers, and chain eateries, but the avenue mellows into bistros, cool bars, sweet clothing shops, and sophisticated restaurants as you go north.

Playa's most active pursuits revolve around simply enjoying the good life. The best **sandy beaches** for swimming and sunning are north of Avenida Constituyentes; for the most part, central Playa's beach is pocked with sharp limestone and is best for dining, partying, and watersports. The best stretch of sand in this area, offering a breather from encroaching hotels, is Playa El Faro, between calles 8 and 10. A decent patch also lies between the dock and Las Ruinas Beach Club at Calle 2. The most beautiful beach, though—and unfortunately the most crowded—extends from Constituyentes north for 5 blocks to Las Mamitas and Kool beach clubs, between calles 28 and 30. Its gradually deepening waters and breaking waves farther out provide ample fodder for water play. The sublime sands farther north are increasingly being squeezed by condo developments.

Playa's offshore reef offers decent **diving,** though it doesn't compare to Cozumel (p. 155) or Puerto Morelos (p. 181). Its primary virtue, which has earned it scores of dive shops, is access to Cozumel and a chain of inland cenotes. Reef

Countless watersports outfitters line the beach.

dives generally cost $45 to $50 for one tank and $70 to $75 for two; two-tank cenote trips are around $110 to $120. Prices for Cozumel trips vary more and are noted below. (Cozumel dives almost always require you to take the ferry on your own and board the dive boat on the island.) Dedicated divers should look for the discounted multi-dive deals and dive/hotel packages offered by many shops. **Buceo Cyan Ha** (✆ **984/803-2517;** www.cyanha.com), the first shop in Playa and still one of the most respected, recently opened a second site at the Petite Lafitte Hotel (p. 186). **Tank-Ha Dive Center** (✆ **984/873-0302;** www.tankha.com) is the only operator that takes divers to Cozumel directly from Playa. **Yucatek Divers** (✆ **984/803-2836;** www.yucatek-divers.com) specializes in cenote diving and in dives for people with disabilities. The **Abyss Dive Center** (✆ **984/873-2164;** www.abyssdiveshop.com) has its own hotel. You won't go wrong with any of these.

The best **snorkeling** spots are not along Playa's shore but at Moché reef to the north and Inna reef to the south. Most dive shops offer guided snorkeling tours for $35 to $45, or $55 to $65 for cenote snorkeling. Before you book, ask whether gear is included, the size of your group, how long the trip will last, and how many reefs or cenotes you'll visit. Small boats docked up and down the beach also offer snorkeling tours for a little less than dive-shop prices, and they'll launch as soon as you show up.

Countless **watersports** outfitters line the beach and La Quinta, offering excursions inland to cenotes, ruins, and adventure parks. Banana boating, tubing, and jet-skiing are just a few of the (pricey) watersports you can enjoy in Playa's calm waters.

Playa makes a great base for excursions up and down the Riviera Maya. It's easy to shoot out to Cozumel on the ferry, drive south to the nature parks and the ruins at Tulum and Cobá, or drive north to Cancún. Directly south of town

Stock up on souvenirs at any number of stores on Avenida Quinta.

is the Playacar development, which has a golf course, several large all-inclusive resorts, and a residential development. My favorite outfitter for unusual trips is **Alltournative** (✆ **800/507-1092** in the U.S., or 984/803-9999; www.alltour native.com; p. 79), on La Quinta between calles 12 and 14.

Shopping

Playa is the Caribbean coast's retail heart, and meandering Avenida Quinta and its side streets to ferret out the latest boutiques and shops makes a fine late-afternoon diversion. Once you get past the ferry terminal area, low-key, locally owned shops vie for your vacation dollar with high-end clothing, Cuban cigars, specialty tequila, handcrafts, jewelry, and beach wear. Credit cards are widely accepted. The best folk art and boutiques are concentrated between calles 4 and 10; Calle Corazón, a leafy pedestrian area between calles 12 and 14, has art galleries, restaurants, a spa, and still more boutiques.

Some favorite shops along La Quinta, south to north: **Colors Collection Boutique,** Calle 2, west of Avenida Quinta (✆ **984/879-3272**), an unsung little side-street shop selling locally designed *manta* (Mexican cotton) clothes for women, and some for men (also available in the larger but less tranquil De Beatriz Boutique at the beach); **Caracol,** between calles 6 and 8 (✆ **984/803-1504**), with tasteful and unique textiles, crafts, and clothing from throughout Mexico; **La Calaca,** between calles 12 and 14 (✆ **984/873-0174**), for its wondrous variety of wooden masks, quirky carvings of angels, devils, and skeletons, and *alebrijes* (the famous Oaxacan carved, whimsically painted animals); **Casa Tequila,** at Calle 16 (✆ **984/873-0195**), for its impressive selection of fine silver jewelry as well as 100 types of specialty tequila (you sample before you buy); and **Ah Cacao,** at Constituyentes (✆ **984/803-5748;** www.ahcacao.com), for its intense and rare criollo chocolate, the Maya's "food of the gods," in bars, cocoa, or roasted beans—the cafe's fudgy mochas, frappes, and chocolate shots will ruin you for Starbucks.

Paseo del Carmen, at the south end of Avenida Quinta, has distinguished itself from Playa's plethora of generic shopping malls by acquiring a collection of interesting shops, galleries, and restaurants. **InArt** (**© 984/803-3968;** inart mexico.com), a jewelry gallery that also sells gorgeous, unique silver pieces embedded with Mexican semiprecious gems and stones, is worth the trip in itself.

Where to Stay

Playa has a lot of affordable small hotels that give you a better feel for the town than staying in one of the resorts in Playacar. Don't hesitate to book a place that's not on the beach. Town life here is much of the fun, and staying on the beach in Playa has its disadvantages—in particular, the noise from a couple of beach bars. Beaches are public property in Mexico, and you can lay out your towel anywhere you like. There are some beach clubs in north Playa where, for a small sum or the price of a meal, you have use of lounge chairs, towels, and food and drink.

When tourism is slow you can score some great walk-in offers. Promotional rates and packages pop up online as well. Reservations are essential around holidays, however. Rates listed below include the 12% hotel tax. I don't include rates for Christmas to New Year's, which are even higher than standard high-season rates.

EXPENSIVE

Deseo Hotel + Lounge ★★ The lounge serves as lobby, restaurant, bar, and pool area all at once. It's a raised open-air platform with bar, pool, self-serve kitchen, and daybeds for sunning or sipping an evening drink when the action is in full swing. It's filled with a hip Mexico City clientele during national holidays and is popular with the 20 to 50 set. Guest rooms are comfortable, original, and striking, but they don't tempt one to stay indoors—no TV, no cushy armchair. Their simplicity gives them an almost Asian feel, heightened by nice touches like sliding wood-and-frosted-glass doors. The bottom of each bed has a little drawer that slides out with a night kit containing incense, earplugs, and condoms.

The owners also operate the cleverly styled **Hotel Básico** (**© 984/879-4448;** www.hotelbasico.com). It's a fun mix of industrial and '50s styles, built with concrete, plywood, and plastics. As with Deseo, the common areas are not wasted space.

Av. 5 (at Calle 12), 77710 Playa del Carmen, Q. Roo. **© 984/879-3620.** Fax 984/879-3621. www.hoteldeseo.com. 15 units. $199–$233 lounge view; $222–$255 balcony; $278–$311 suite. Rates include continental breakfast. AE, MC, V. No parking. No children 17 and under. **Amenities:** Bar; Jacuzzi; small rooftop pool; room service. *In room:* A/C, hair dryer (on request), minibar.

MODERATE

Hotel Lunata ★★ In the middle of Playa, there isn't a more comfortable or more attractive place to stay than this small hotel on Avenida Quinta. Rooms offer character and polished good looks. The few standard rooms are midsize and come with a queen-size or a double bed. Large deluxe rooms come with a king-size bed and small fridge; junior suites come with two doubles. The well-designed bathrooms have good showers. I stayed in a room facing the street, with double-glazed glass doors opening to a balcony. I enjoyed looking out over La Quinta, and, with the doors shut, the noise was not bothersome. Still, light sleepers should ask for a room facing the garden.

Av. 5 (btw. calles 6 and 8), 77710 Playa del Carmen, Q. Roo. ✆ **984/873-0884.** Fax 984/873-1240. www.lunata.com. 10 units. High season $129 double, $159–$179 deluxe and junior suite; low season $110 double, $125–$145 deluxe and junior suite. Rates include continental breakfast. AE, MC, V. Secure parking $5. No children 12 and under. **Amenities:** Bikes; smoke-free rooms; watersports. *In room:* A/C, fan, TV, fridge (in some), hair dryer (on request), Wi-Fi (in some).

La Tortuga ★★★ You'll have a hard time staying anywhere else when you can get amiable service, a variety of rooms, and all the amenities you need at these digs. The word's out, and travelers fill the rooms—though there's usually a good choice for returning guests. Some rooms edge the sinuous pool; others have tiny balconies overlooking rooftops. Suites have whirlpool tubs, balconies, and extras like irons and robes. All rooms have plenty of shelves and tables for stowing your belongings, coffee machines, and alarm clocks (blessings for business travelers). The cozy living room space by the pool has a bar, a book exchange, and comfy couches, and the restaurant is always improving. Guests have a private entrance to the Zen Eco Spa next door.

Avenida 10 (btw. calles 12 and 14), 77710 Playa del Carmen, Q. Roo. ✆ **984/873-1484.** www.hotellatortuga.com. 51 units. $180–$269 double, $200–$300 suite. Rates include reduced-rate parking at an indoor lot, breakfast, and beach passes. MC, V. **Amenities:** Restaurant; bar; outdoor pool; Wi-Fi. *In room:* AC, fan, TV, Jacuzzi (in suite), minibar, MP3 dock (in suite).

Playa Maya ★ There are plenty of reasons to choose this over other beach hotels in downtown Playa—good location, good price, comfortable rooms, and friendly, helpful management, to name a few. But what really sets it apart is that you enter the hotel from the beach. This seemingly inconsequential detail sets the mood and creates a little separation from the busy street. What's more, the design blocks out noise from nearby bars and neighboring hotels. Rooms are large, with midsize bathrooms. A couple have private garden terraces with Jacuzzis; others have balconies facing the beach. High-season rates here extend from Christmas through August, and minimum stays are required.

Zona FMT (btw. calles 6 and 8 Norte), 77710 Playa del Carmen, Q. Roo. ✆ **984/803-2022.** www.playa-maya.com. 20 units. High season $145–$195 double; low season $112–$180 double. Rates include continental breakfast. MC, V. Limited street parking. **Amenities:** Restaurant; bar; Jacuzzi; outdoor pool; room service. *In room:* A/C, TV, fridge, hair dryer, Wi-Fi.

INEXPENSIVE

Hotel Lab Nah Good rooms in a central location for a good price are the main attraction at this economy hotel in the heart of Playa. The cheapest rooms have windows facing Avenida Quinta, allowing in some noise—mostly late-night bar hoppers. It didn't bother me much, but I think it's worth the money to get one of the partial-oceanview standards with balcony on the third floor, which are quieter and larger. Garden-view rooms directly below the oceanviews are just as large and quiet, but not quite as fixed up. And the difference in price is little. The largest unit, a rooftop *palapa,* is good for three or four people.

Calle 6 (and Av. 5), 77710 Playa del Carmen, Q. Roo. ✆ **984/873-2099.** www.labnah.com. 33 units. High season 550–750 pesos double, 1,050 pesos rooftop *palapa;* low season 490–650 pesos double, 860 pesos rooftop *palapa.* Rates include continental breakfast. MC, V. Limited street parking. **Amenities:** Small outdoor pool. *In room:* A/C, hair dryers (in some), no phone.

Jardín de Marieta Besides the reasonable rates, I like this pleasant, quirky place for its central, yet half-hidden location in a small, quiet interior property without any street frontage on La Quinta. Rooms vary a good bit, but most are large, bright, and cheerful. Four rooms have kitchenettes, adequate for simple meals. Most rooms encircle a tree-shaded patio with a few shops and a restaurant.

Av. 5 Norte 173 (btw. calles 6 and 8), 77710 Playa del Carmen, Q. Roo. ✆ **984/873-0224.** www.jardindemarieta.com. 10 units. High season $60–$100 double; low season $50–$90 double. No credit cards. Limited street parking. **Amenities:** Restaurant. *In room:* A/C, TV, fridge, kitchenette (in some), no phone, Wi-Fi.

Where to Dine

For a delicious Veracruz-style breakfast in pleasant, breezy surroundings, try the upstairs terrace restaurant of the **Hotel Básico,** at Avenida Quinta and Calle 10 Norte. For fish tacos and inexpensive seafood, try **El Oasis,** on Calle 12, between avenidas 5 and 10 (no phone). For *arrachera* (fajita) tacos, the place to go is **Super Carnes H C de Monterrey** (✆ **984/803-0488**), on Calle 1 Sur between avenidas 20 and 25.

EXPENSIVE

La Casa del Agua ★★ EUROPEAN/MEXICAN Excellent food in inviting surroundings. Instead of obtrusive background music, you hear the sound of falling water. The German owners present what they like best about the old and new worlds. They do a good job with seafood—try the grilled seafood for two. For a mild dish, try chicken in a scented sauce of fine herbs accompanied by fettuccine; for something heartier, there's a tortilla soup listed as "Mexican soup." A number of cool and light dishes are appetizing for lunch or an afternoon meal, such as avocado stuffed with shrimp and flavored with a subtle horseradish sauce on a bed of alfalfa sprouts and julienne carrots—a good mix of tastes and textures. For dessert, try the chocolate mousse. This is an upstairs restaurant under a large and airy *palapa* roof.

Av. 5 (at Calle 2). ✆ **984/803-0232.** Reservations recommended in high season. Main courses 165–280 pesos. MC, V. Daily 10am–midnight.

Yaxché ★★★ YUCATECAN The menu here employs many native foods and spices to present a more elaborate regional cooking than the usual offerings at Yucatecan restaurants. Excellent examples are a cream of *chaya* (a native leafy vegetable) and an *xcatic* chili stuffed with *cochinita pibil.* I also like the classic Mexican-style fruit salad with lime juice and dried powdered chili. Seafood dishes are fresh and well prepared.

Calle 8 (btw. avenidas 5 and 10). ✆ **984/873-2502.** Reservations recommended in high season. Main courses 119–230 pesos. AE, MC, V. Daily noon–midnight.

MODERATE

Casa Mediterránea ★ ITALIAN Tucked away on a quiet little patio off Avenida Quinta, this small, homey restaurant serves excellent Italian cuisine. Maurizio Gabrielli and Mary Michelon make it a habit to greet customers and make recommendations. Maurizio came to Mexico to enjoy the simple life, and it shows in the restaurant's welcoming, unhurried atmosphere. The menu is mostly northern Italian, with several dishes from other parts of Italy. The lobster is prepared beautifully. There are daily specials, too. Pastas (except penne and spaghetti) are made in-house, and none is precooked. Try fish and shrimp ravioli or penne alla Veneta. There are several wines, mostly Italian, to choose from.

Av. 5 (btw. calles 6 and 8; look for the Hotel Marieta sign). ✆ **984/876-3926.** Reservations recommended in high season. Main courses 120–220 pesos. No credit cards. Wed–Mon 2–11pm.

La Cueva del Chango ★★ MEXICAN/HEALTH FOOD Good food in original surroundings with a relaxed attitude makes this quirky place enduringly popular (expect a wait on weekend mornings). True to its name (The Monkey's Cave), the place is cave-like and has little waterways meandering through it, with wicker and fabric monkeys hanging about. You'll enjoy great juices, blended fruit drinks, salads, soups, Mexican specialties with a natural twist, and handmade tortillas. The fish is fresh and delicious, and the warm panella cheese with tortillas is divine. Mosquitoes can sometimes be a problem at night, but the management has bug spray for the guests.

Calle 38 (btw. Av. 5 and the beach). ✆ **984/116-3179.** Main courses 80–140 pesos. No credit cards. Mon–Sat 8am–11pm; Sun 8am–2pm.

La Vagabunda ITALIAN/MEXICAN This place has the charm of old-style Playa. A large *palapa* shelters several simple wood tables sitting on a gravel floor. It's low key and quiet—a good place for breakfast, with many options, including delicious blended fruit drinks, waffles, and omelets. The specials are a good value. In the afternoon and evening, they serve light fare such as panini, pastas, and ceviche.

Av. 5 (btw. calles 24 and 26). ✆ **984/873-3753.** Reservations not accepted. Breakfast 40–60 pesos; main courses 70–120 pesos. MC, V. High season daily 7am–11:30pm; low season daily 7am–3:30pm.

Media Luna ★★ FUSION The inventive menu here favors grilled seafood, sautés, and pasta dishes. Everything is fresh and prepared beautifully. Try the tasty pan-fried fish cakes with mango and honeyed hoisin sauce, or the black pepper–crusted fish. And keep an eye on the daily specials. For lunch, you can get sandwiches and salads, as well as black-bean quesadillas and crepes.

Av. 5 (btw. calles 12 and 14). ✆ **984/873-0526.** Breakfast 40–60 pesos; sandwich with salad 50–70 pesos; main courses 80–150 pesos. No credit cards. Daily 8am–11:30pm.

INEXPENSIVE

Las Mañanitas MEXICAN The set price breakfast is a steal here—around $5 for eggs scrambled with tomatoes, chilies, and onions, with toast, coffee, and OJ. Tables fill with hotel and shop workers in early morning. Travelers wander in around 9am and continue claiming tables under the piñatas through lunch. In the evening, diners observe the action from sidewalk tables as they feast on fresh fish, a bountiful chilled seafood platter, pasta, and meats. The vibe is low key and the waiters friendly.

Av. 5 between calles 4 and 6. ✆ **984/873-0114.** Main courses 50–120 pesos. MC, V. Daily 7am–10pm.

La Tarraya Restaurant/Bar SEAFOOD/YUCATECAN THE RESTAURANT THAT WAS BORN WITH THE TOWN, proclaims the sign. It's right on the beach, and the owners are fishermen. The catch of the day is so fresh it's still practically wiggling. The wood hut doesn't look like much, but they also have tables right on the beach. You can have your fish prepared in several ways. If you haven't tried the Yucatecan specialty *tik-in-xic*—fish with *achiote* and bitter-orange sauce, cooked in a banana leaf—this is a good place to start. I also recommend the ceviche and the beer.

Calle 2 Norte. ✆ **984/873-2040.** Reservations not accepted. Main courses 50–100 pesos; whole fish 100 pesos per kilo (2.2 lb.). No credit cards. Daily noon–9pm.

Los Carboncitos ★ MEXICAN The menu is simple, but there's hardly anything to steer clear of. One of the top choices is the tacos, which are mainly grilled meat, such as fajitas *(arrachera)* or *al pastor.* These are served with a great collection of salsas. I also recommend the soups, especially the Mexican-style chicken soup *(caldo xochitl)* and the traditional *pozole.* For the seafood, try the shrimp al chipotle or the shrimp kabobs. The great lineup of sides includes fried crispy cheese *(chicharrón de queso)* and guacamole.

Calle 4 (btw. avenidas 5 and 10). ✆ **984/873-1382.** Reservations not accepted. Main courses 60–110 pesos; order of tacos 40–60 pesos. No credit cards. Daily 9am–1am.

Playa Del Carmen After Dark

It seems as if everyone in town is out strolling La Quinta until midnight; there's pleasant browsing, dining, and drinking available at any number of establishments. Here's a quick rundown of the bars that you won't find on Avenida Quinta. The beach bar that is an institution in Playa is the **Blue Parrot** (✆ **984/873-0083**). It gets live acts, mostly rock, and attracts a mixed crowd. It's between calles 12 and 14. Just to the south is **Om** (no phone), which gets a younger crowd with louder musical acts.

Alux (✆ **984/110-5050**) is a one-of-a-kind club occupying a large cave with two dramatically lit chambers and several nooks and sitting areas. The local conservancy group approved all the work. The club books music acts and usually charges no cover. The bar is cash only and is open Tuesday to Sunday from 7pm to 2am. Take Avenida Juárez across to the other side of the highway—2 blocks down on your left.

Avenida Quinta is constantly bustling at night.

CHOOSING AN all-inclusive IN THE RIVIERA MAYA

All-inclusive resort rooms far outnumber those in regular hotels in the Riviera Maya. And the trend continues to dominate new construction, along with vacation-ownership developments. Most folks are familiar with the AI (short for all-inclusive) concept—large hotels that work with economies of scale to offer lodging, food, and drink all for a single rate. Some AIs offer convenience and economy, especially for families with many mouths to feed. Because they are enclosed areas, they make it easy for parents to watch their children. The system makes it easy to hold multiple-generation family reunions and group meetings, and seasonal deals offer amazingly cheap getaways.

All-inclusive resorts aren't for everyone; think of it as a cruise vacation on land. A certain sameness pervades these hotels. Colored bracelets designate various AI plans, which usually include all buffet meals, drinks of varying quality, specialty restaurants (some with an additional charge), elaborate pool areas with activities, evening entertainment, and so on. Some charge extra for use of golf courses, spas, and fitness centers.

If you decide all-inclusive is the way to go, choose a resort whose amenities suit your desires. This type of all-inclusive is best booked through a vacation packager or travel agent. Their air and AI packages usually beat anything you can get by booking your own flight and room, even if you have frequent-flier miles to burn.

I came to understand and appreciate this type of vacation while staying at the **Iberostar** (www.iberostar.com) complex on Paraíso Beach north of Playa del Carmen. The enormous compound includes five hotels in all price ranges, a golf course, shopping center, nightclubs, spacious beach, and terrific spa. A tram travels between the resorts. (Guests at the higher-end hotels can use the amenities at all hotels.) Despite the size, I never felt overwhelmed and enjoyed watching families play together and apart.

With several resorts of varying quality and style, **Palace Resorts** (www.palaceresorts.com) also merits attention, though their vacation ownership salespeople can be very pushy. Wyndham hotels has taken over management of some Palace properties, which could mean some changes are in store.

A new all-inclusive concept swings totally in the other direction, with beyond-luxurious resorts offering fabulous suites, spas, pools, and beaches along with exceptional gourmet dining. Daily rates can soar beyond $1,000 per person per day. But more and more resort companies are moving in this direction, and big spenders have outstanding options. The **Grand Velas Riviera Maya** (p. 185) excels in this category. The pricey **Royal Hideaway Playacar** (www.royalhideaway.com) is acclaimed as an idyllic wedding and honeymoon setting. The exclusive resorts sometimes have some odd rules. For example, my husband and I weren't able to enjoy the specialty restaurants at one resort because men were required to wear closed-toe dress shoes—even dressy leather sandals were verboten. Be sure you know such things before you go.

Though they technically close around sunset, several beach clubs north of Avenida Constituyentes book live acts occasionally. Look for action at the foot of calles 30 to 36.

SOUTH OF PLAYA DEL CARMEN

A succession of small communities, resorts, and nature parks flank a 56km (35-mile) stretch of highway leading south from Playa del Carmen. This section covers them from north to south.

Renting a car is the best way to move around down here. The best buses might do is get you close to your destination; from the highway, it can be a hot walk to the coast. Another option is to hire a car and driver.

Beyond Paamul, you'll see signs for this or that cenote or cave. The Yucatán has thousands of cenotes, and each is slightly different (p. 202). These turnoffs are less visited than the major attractions and can make for a pleasant visit.

Punta Venado: Horseback Riding

A few places along the highway offer horseback rides. The best of these, **Rancho Punta Venado,** is just south of Playa, past the Calica Pier. This ranch is the least touristy, and the owner takes good care of his horses. It has a nice stretch of coast with a sheltered bay and offers kayaking and snorkeling outings. Make arrangements in advance so that they can schedule you on a day when they have fewer customers. E-mail (ptavenado@yahoo.com) is the best way to reach them; sometimes they don't answer their office number, ✆ **984/803-5224.** Another option is to call the ranch's cellphone from Mexico (✆ **984/116-3213**); there is a charge for the call. Talk to Gabriela or Francisco; both speak English. Or try dropping by. The turnoff for the ranch is 2km (1¼ miles) south of the Calica overpass near Km 279.

Río Secreto: Wondrous Cavern

More spiritual than commercial, this community-based eco-park teaches visitors about Maya beliefs regarding the "underworld" as they explore a 600-m (less than a ½ mile) long cavern hidden from view for centuries. As the story goes, a local *campesino* was chasing a meaty lizard into the brush and under a rock pile. The *campesino* followed, digging through rocks, until he heard a splash. The lizard, it seemed, had discovered a hiding place. Digging a bit farther, the man found the entrance to a cave filled with stalactites and stalagmites. Local naturalists heard about the find and discovered a dazzling series of chambers with rock formations dating back 2.5 million years. The area was declared a nature reserve and opened to the public in April 2008.

Visitors must be accompanied by guides and wear short wetsuits and helmets as they walk and swim through the cavern. At times, it is so dark you feel like you're totally blind (if you turn off your handy flashlight). Other times, sunshine streams through holes in the roof, illuminating the green trees above ground and the blue and pink striations caused by mineral-rich water dripping over earth-toned stone. An occasional swim through an emerald green pool adds to the fun, as does the guide's banter and knowledge. From donning your wetsuit to downing a filling lunch after the 90-minute underground tour, it will take about 3 hours. Hot showers and lockers are available. The basic tour without transportation costs $49. Call ahead for reservations. Río Secreto is located off

Marvel at the stalactites and stalagmites of Río Secreto.

Hwy. 307, 5 minutes south of Playa del Carmen (between Xcaret and the Calica Port). For more info, call ✆ **800/985-2664** in the U.S. or 984/877-2377, or go to www.riosecretotours.com.

Xcaret: Tribute to the Yucatan

A billboard in distant Guadalajara's airport reads in Spanish, "And when visiting Xcaret, don't forget to enjoy the pleasures of the Riviera Maya, too." An exaggeration, yes, but a point well taken: Xcaret ("eesh-ca-*ret*") is the biggest attraction in these parts and even has its own resort. Thousands visit every week; stay away if you like solitude. Xcaret samples everything the Yucatán—and the rest of Mexico—has to offer, and action junkies take full advantage of the pricey admission fee.

The myriad activities include scuba and snorkeling; cavern diving; hiking through tropical forest; horseback riding; an underwater river ride; swinging in a hammock under palms; and meeting native Maya people. Exhibits include the best folk art museum outside Mexico City; a bat cave; a butterfly pavilion; mushroom and orchid nurseries; and a petting aquarium. Native jaguars, manatees, sea turtles, monkeys, macaws, and flamingos are also on display. The evening show celebrates Mexico in music and dance, and the costumes and choreography are unequaled anywhere in Mexico. I'm not Xcaret's biggest fan, preferring my adventures in the wild, but this show is a genuinely mesmerizing spectacle. It presents so many aspects of the Mexican nation that you feel like you've toured the whole country by the time the performers take their last bow.

A costumed dancer performs at Xcaret.

Xcaret is 10km (6¼ miles) south of Playa del Carmen; you'll know when you get to the turnoff.

UNDERGROUND adventures

The Yucatán Peninsula's land surface is a thin limestone shelf jutting out like a footprint between the Gulf of Mexico and the Caribbean Sea. Rainwater seeps through the surface into cenotes, freshwater sinkholes that dot the underground world. Some cenotes are like small wells. Others are like giant green ponds with high rock walls—tempting sights to would-be Tarzans. Cenotes often provide access to magical caves where sunlight from holes in the land's surface glimmers on icicle-like stalactites and stalagmites. The Riviera Maya is filled with these formations, and it seems every farmer and landowner has posted a sign offering access to their pools and caverns for a few pesos. More elaborate parks include underground rivers and cenotes among their many attractions. Several, including Xcaret, Hidden Worlds, Río Secreto, and Aktun Chen are described in this chapter. Dozens of smaller cenotes and caves deserve your attention as well, and entry costs much less than at the big parks. Adventuresome types, should seek out newly opened sites marked with rustic wooden signs. Below are a few *cenotes* accessible from Hwy 307. Most have bathrooms, are open daily from about 8 or 9am until 5 or 6pm, and charge about 30 to 50 pesos.

Cenote Azul (approximately 2km/1 mile south of Puerto Aventuras, just south of Ecopark Kantun Chi): Situated close to the highway with several large pools, Cenote Azul has a fun jump-off point on a section of overhanging rock, and a wooden lounging deck jutting over the water. Walkways along the edge make it easier to get in and swim with the abundant catfish.

Gran Cenote (about 3 km/1½ miles west of Tulum on the road to Cobá): Divers are especially fond of this aptly named bottomless, crystal-clear cenote leading to caverns that seem to have no end. Snorkelers can follow the dive lights into caves close to the surface and see fantastic rock formations. Since it's off the main highway, this fabulous cenote is less popular with groups and feels like it's buried in jungle.

Jardín del Edén (1.6km/1 mile north of Xpu-Há, just south of Cenote Azul): "El Edén" is one of my favorite cenotes because it's run by an accommodating family and has lots of rocky outcroppings where you can lounge in the warm sun after the freezing water leaves you covered in goose bumps. There's plenty of room along the edges of the cenote, which looks like a huge swimming pool. Shrieks fill the air as daredevils attempt swan dives from a high jump-off point. Snorkelers and divers find plenty of tropical fish and eels.

It's open daily from 8:30am to 9pm. Basic admission prices are $69 for adults, $34 for children 5 to 12; many activities and facilities cost extra. The Xcaret at Night rate is a good deal at $49 for adults and $30 for children. You enter the park after 3pm and have plenty of time to play and explore before the night show. For more info, call ✆ **998/883-0470** or visit www.xcaret.net.

The people who created Xcaret recently opened **Xplor** (✆ **998/849-5275;** www.xplor.travel) next door. The adventure park has a zip line, four-wheel-drive track, and an underground river ride. Admission is $109 for adults, $55 for children (8 or over); you get a 10% discount for booking online 3 days in advance.

Manatí (Tankhah, east of the highway 10km/6 miles north of Tulum): The large, open lagoon near Casa Cenote restaurant is part of a long underwater cave system that ends at the sea. Fresh water bubbling up into ocean waters creates significant but not dangerous currents that attract a great variety of saltwater and freshwater fish. The cenote was named for the manatees that used to show up occasionally; the shy creatures have disappeared as the region has gained popularity.

Xunaan ha (outside of Chemuyil, 12km/7.5 miles south of Akumal): Gaining popularity because of its sense of authenticity, this one is reached by winding through a Maya village and growing town that is home to locals who work in and around Akumal. Signs point to the small cenote nearly hidden in the jungle, where you can swim, float, or snorkel with schools of fish and the occasional freshwater turtle. Be prepared: no bathrooms here.

Most dive shops along the Riviera Maya offer cenote diving as well as reef dives. Recommended outfitters that specialize in cenote dives include **Yukatek Divers** (✆ **984/803-2836;** www.yucatek-divers.com) and **Go Cenotes** (✆ **984/803-3924;** www.gocenotes.com), both in Playa del Carmen, and **Cenote Dive Center** (✆ **984/871-2232;** www.cenotedive.com) and **Xibalba Dive Center** (✆ **984/871-2953;** www.xibalbadivecenter.com) in Tulum. All charge $120 for two-tank cavern dives, which take place in open cenotes where you are always within reach of air and natural light; cave diving requires advanced technical training and specialized gear, and is more expensive.

Four kilometers (2½ miles) south of the entrance to Xcaret is the turnoff for **Puerto Calica,** the cruise-ship pier. Passengers disembark here for tours of Playa, Xcaret, the ruins, and other attractions on the coast.

Paamul: Seaside Getaway ★

About 15km (9¼ miles) beyond Xcaret and 25km (16 miles) from Playa del Carmen is Paamul (also written Pamul) 🎁, which in Mayan means "a destroyed ruin." The exit is clearly marked. You can enjoy the Caribbean in relative quiet here. The water at the out-of-the-way beach is wonderful, but the shoreline is

RV campers park at Paamul.

rocky. There are four rooms for rent, a restaurant, and many trailer and RV spaces with hookups, available by the day or month.

Scuba-Mex (✆ **984/875-1066;** fax 984/874-1729; www.scubamex.com) is a fully equipped PADI- and SSI-certified dive shop next to the cabañas. Using two boats, the staff takes guests on dives 8km (5 miles) in either direction. If it's too choppy, the reefs in front of the hotel are also good. The cost for a one-tank dive with rental gear is $39. They also have multi-dive packages and certification instruction.

Cabañas Paamul ★ Paamul works mostly with the trailer crowd, but there are also 12 modern "junior suites" on or near the water's edge. They are spacious and comfortable, and come with a kitchenette and two queen beds. Slightly cheaper, but more limited in size and amenities, are the "eco-cabañas." Trailer guests have access to 12 showers and separate bathrooms for men and women. Laundry service is available nearby. The large, breezy *palapa* restaurant is open to the public, and customers are welcome to use the beach, which is rocky along this stretch of the coast. Prices vary according to season.

Carretera Cancún–Tulum Km 85. ✆ **984/875-1051.** www.paamul.com. 22 units; 190 trailer spaces (all with full hookups). $100–$150 junior suite; $80–$120 cabaña. RV space with hookups $30 per day, $600 per month. No credit cards. Ask about discounts for stays longer than 1 week. Free parking. **Amenities:** Restaurant; bar; outdoor pool; dive shop. *In room:* A/C, TV, kitchenette.

Puerto Aventuras: Dolphins & Shipwrecks

Five kilometers (3 miles) south of Paamul and 104km (64 miles) from Cancún, Puerto Aventuras is a glitzy condo/marina development with a 9-hole golf course on Chakalal Bay. At its center is a collection of restaurants, bordering a dolphin pool,that offer Mexican and Italian food, steaks, and pub grub. The major attraction is swimming with the dolphins in a highly interactive program; make reservations well in advance with

Avoiding the Cruise-Ship Crowds

Fewer ships arrive on weekends than on weekdays, which makes the weekend a good time for visiting the coast's major attractions.

Dolphin Discovery (✆ **998/849-4757;** www.dolphindiscovery.com). The surest way is through the website.

Puerto Aventuras has the region's only maritime museum, **Museo Sub-Acuatico CEDAM** ★ (✆ **984/873-5000;** www.puertoaventuras.com/services.html). This is a compelling display of coins, weapons, gold dentures, clay dishes, and other items from colonial-era shipwrecks. All were recovered by members of the "Explorations and Water Sports Club of Mexico" (CEDAM), a group of former World War II frogmen. Most of the artifacts came from a Cuban ship that foundered near Akumal in 1741. Other displays include Maya offerings dredged from the peninsula's cenotes, finds from local archaeological sites, vintage diving equipment, and early photos of cenote explorations. The museum is on the second floor of a pink building near the entrance.

Puerto Aventuras is also popular for boating and deep-sea fishing. **Capt. Rick's Sportfishing Center** (✆ **888/449-3562** in the U.S., or 984/873-5195; www.fishyucatan.com) will combine a fishing trip with some snorkeling, which makes for a leisurely day. The best fishing on this coast is from March to August.

Despite the reasons to visit Puerto Aventuras, I've never been tempted to stay there. It has a few hotels, but most residential development is upscale condos and vacation homes. The most prominent hotel, the **Omni Puerto Aventuras** (✆ **800/843-6664** in the U.S., or 984/873-5101), is nice, but even with recession-induced specials knocking the starting price back to $200, this color-coordinated, self-contained enclave isn't interesting enough to compel me to spend that much to stay there.

Xpu-Ha: Sublime Beach

Three kilometers (1¾ miles) beyond Puerto Aventuras is **Xpu-Ha** (*eesh-poo-hah*) ★★★, a wide bay lined by a broad, beautiful sandy beach. Much of the shore is filled with private houses and condos, along with a few all-inclusive resorts. The beach is one of the best on the coast and is long enough to

A display at the Museo Sub-Acuatico CEDAM.

accommodate hotel guests, residents, and day-trippers without feeling crowded.

Besides the hotels reviewed below, a few others offer basic lodging—a couple of beds, cement floors, and a small private bathroom. They rent on a first-come, first-served basis for 500 to 800 pesos a night, depending on how busy they are. Nearby Akumal has better choices; if you're renting a car, you can come to the beach for a day.

In Case of Emergency

The Riviera Maya, south of Puerto Aventuras, is susceptible to power failures that can last for hours. Gas pumps and cash machines shut down when this happens, and once the power returns, they attract long lines. It's a good idea to keep a reserve of gas and cash.

Al Cielo ★ This is a good choice if you want a small hotel on the beach where you can go native. The four rooms (two upstairs, two down) occupy a large thatched building right on the beach. The restaurant is popular, but the rooms are rustic and simple, which sometimes draws guests into the beach experience as an escape from the modern world. If you're looking for more amenities, this won't be for you.

Carretera Cancún-Tulum Km. 118, 77710 Xpu-Ha, Q. Roo. ✆ **984/840-9012**. www.alcielohotel.com. 4 units. $212–$258 double. MC, V. No children. Rates include full breakfast. Free secure parking. **Amenities:** Restaurant; bar; Hobie cat; room service. *In room:* Fan, hair dryer, no phone, Wi-Fi.

Esencia ★★★ No other property on this coast epitomizes leisure and escape more than Esencia. Originally built as a private villa for an Italian duchess, the hotel now includes a few rooms in the original villa and guesthouse. I'd be thrilled to spend a few romantic nights in the villa's beach-view rooms—one of those lottery dreams. Families spread out in the two-story cottages surrounded by lush plants and gardens. Every room throughout the property has lots of space, lots of beauty, lots of privacy, and an air of serenity (decorations are tastefully minimalist, like three oranges on a driftwood tray). Of course, the magnificent beach includes private day beds under A-framed thatch shades. Service is personal and understated (a service fee is added to the room rate) and the food is outstanding. If the spa were any more relaxing, it would be an out-of-body experience. The hotel offers 2 hours of complimentary babysitting per day for guests using the spa or restaurant.

Predio Rústico Xpu-Ha, Fracc. 16 y 18, L. 18, 19 (exit Xpu-Ha-2), 77710 Xpu-Ha, Q. Roo. ✆ **877/528-3490** in the U.S. or Canada, or 984/873-4830. www.hotelesencia.com. 29 units. High season $569 and up double or suite; low season $479 and up double or suite. Rates include full breakfast. Internet specials sometimes available. AE, MC, V. Free valet parking. **Amenities:** Restaurant; 2 bars; babysitting; concierge; Jacuzzi; 2 outdoor pools; room service; smoke-free rooms; spa. *In room:* A/C, TV/DVD, hair dryer, Internet, minibar.

Akumal: Beautiful Bays & Cavern Diving

Continuing south on Hwy. 307 for 2km (1¼ miles), the turnoff for Akumal ("Place of the Turtles") is marked by a traffic light. The ecologically oriented tourism community is spread among four bays, with two entrances off the frontage road that runs parallel to the highway. The main entrance, labeled Akumal, leads to hotels, rental condos, and vacation homes. Take the Akumal Aventuras entrance to the Grand Oasis all-inclusive hotel and more condos and homes. No waterside road connects the two, so you'll need to know which exit to take. A

Scuba-diving in Akumal.

Akumal is home to sea turtles from May through July.

white arch delineates the main entrance to the tourism community (years ago, the original residents were moved across the highway to a separate, fast-growing town where many workers and business owners reside). Just before the arch are a couple of grocery stores and a laundry service. Just inside the arch, to the right, is the Hotel Akumal Caribe. If you follow the road to the left and keep to the left, you'll reach Half Moon Bay, lined with two- and three-story condos, and eventually Yal-ku Lagoon, a snorkeling park. To rent a condo, contact **Akumal Vacations** (✆ **800/448-7137** in the U.S.; www.akumalvacations.com) or **Loco Gringo** (www.locogringo.com).

Both bays have sandy beaches with rocky or silt bottoms. This is a popular diving area and home to Mexico's original diving club. Three dive shops are in town and at least 30 dive sites are offshore. The **Akumal Dive Shop** (✆ **984/875-9032;** www.akumal.com), one of the oldest and best dive shops on the coast, offers cavern-diving trips and courses in technical diving. The friendly owner and dive masters know all the secret spots in the area and can offer all sorts of insider tips. It and **Akumal Dive Adventures** (✆ **888/425-8625** in the U.S., or 984/875-9157), at the Vista del Mar hotel on Half Moon Bay, offer resort courses as well as full open-water certification.

Yal-ku Lagoon ☺ snorkeling park is like a miniature Xel-Ha without all the pricey amusements. Modern sculptures punctuate gardens beside the clear lagoon, which is about 700m (2,296 ft.) long and 200m (656 ft.) at its widest. You can paddle around comfortably in sheltered water and see fish and a few other creatures. It's a perfect place to learn how to snorkel and let kids swim about safely. Of course, there are many spots along the bays where you can snorkel for free, but this little park is an easy, relaxing outing. It's open daily from 8am to 5:30pm. Admission is 80 pesos for adults, 45 pesos for children 3 to 14.

The gentle crescent of **Akumal Bay,** washing a wide, soft beach shaded by coconut palms, is one of the few places where you'll often be surprised by a sea turtle swimming along with you. During nesting season (May through July), visit **Centro Ecológico Akumal ★★★** (✆ **984/875-9005;** www.ceakumal.org) in the morning to sign up for that evening's 9pm turtle walk (Monday through Friday). You'll help staff search for new nests, protect exhausted mothers making their way back to sea, and remove eggs to hatcheries where they can incubate safely.

WHERE TO STAY

Rates below are for two people and include taxes. During the holidays, most hotels and condo rentals charge higher rates than those listed.

Hotel Akumal Caribe ★★ ☺ The first accommodations on Akumal Bay were simple thatch-roofed cabañas beside a gorgeous beach. When I stayed here in the 1980s I felt like I had discovered the best hideaway on the coast. Since then, the property has morphed into a large resort with 40 tile-roofed bungalows spread about dense gardens. Simply and comfortably furnished, with kitchenettes, spacious showers, and jugs of purified water, the bungalows are still a great place to stay for a night or a week (as many families do). The 21 rooms in the three-story beachside hotel have one king- or two queen-size beds, kitchenettes, and fancier furnishings than in the bungalows. The hotel also has a freshwater pool (open to all guests), but I still prefer the homey bungalows. The hotel also books condos and attractive villas on Half Moon Bay. The four villas, which share a pool, have two or three bedrooms and large living, dining, and kitchen areas, as well as lovely furnished patios just steps from the beach. The property's best asset is its placement at the edge of beautiful Akumal Bay. Visiting its restaurants and shops will get you past the guards who turn non-guests away.

Carretera Cancún–Tulum (Hwy. 307) Km 104. ✆ **984/206-3500.** www.hotelakumalcaribe.com. (Reservations: P.O. Box 13326, El Paso, TX 79913; ✆ **800/351-1622** in the U.S., 800/343-1440 in Canada, or 915/584-3552.) 70 units. High season $110–$119 bungalow, $139–$149 double, $255–$375 villa or condo; low season $89 bungalow, $109 double, $137–$190 villa or condo. Reservations with prepayment by check only. AE, MC, V. Free parking. Low-season packages available. **Amenities:** 2 restaurants; bar; babysitting; seasonal children's activities; dive shop; large outdoor pool. *In room:* A/C, Internet (in some), kitchenette (in some), no phone (in some).

Vista del Mar Hotel and Condos ★ This beachside property rents hotel rooms at good prices and large, fully equipped condos that you can rent by the day or week. The lovely, well-tended beach in front of the hotel has chairs and umbrellas. The on-site dive shop eliminates the hassle of organizing dive trips. Hotel rooms are small and contain either a queen-size or a double and a twin bed. They consist of a well-equipped kitchen, a living area, two or three bedrooms, and up to three bathrooms. All have balconies or terraces facing the sea and are furnished with hammocks. Several rooms come with whirlpool tubs.

Half Moon Bay, 77760 Akumal, Q. Roo. ✆ **877/425-8625** in the U.S. Fax 505/988-3882. www.akumalinfo.com. 27 units. High season $102 double, $207–$325 condo; low season $84 double, $124–$196 condo. MC, V. Limited free parking. **Amenities:** Restaurant; bar; dive shop; small outdoor pool; watersports. *In room:* A/C, TV, CD player, fridge, kitchenette, no phone.

WHERE TO DINE

Akumal has about 10 places to eat, and there's a convenient grocery store, **Super Chomak** (with an ATM), by the arch. Just inside the arch a collection of businesses includes a bakery and coffeehouse. At the Hotel Akumal Caribe, **Lol-Ha** serves good breakfasts and dinners and has free Wi-Fi, and the **Palapa Snack** bar dishes out everything from ice cream cones to burgers with poblano chilies and avocado. Tell the guards at the hotel's entrance that you're there for a meal and they'll direct you to special parking areas—and they don't notice if you take some time to wander along the hotel's beautiful beach.

La Buena Vida SEAFOOD/REGIONAL This beach restaurant is just plain fun. Where else can you scale a *mirador* (crow's nest) to dine while under the influence of the coast's best view of Half Moon Bay? The menu is varied and the fare excellent, especially the Maya chicken, *tik-in-xic* fish (grilled after marinating in *achiote* and sour orange), and other regional specialties. Afterward, belly up to swings at the sand-floored bar, which blends its own unique cocktails in addition to serving a barrage of special tequilas.

Half Moon Bay beach (btw. Akumal and Yal-ku Lagoon). ✆ **984/875-9061.** www.akumalinfo.com/restaurant.htm. Main courses 80–285 pesos. AE, MC, V. Daily 11am–1am.

Turtle Bay Cafe & Bakery ★ AMERICAN Yummy pancakes with pecan maple syrup, fried eggs with hash browns, and eggs benedict with Canadian bacon satisfy the expats dining beneath the palms. More adventuresome eaters go for *huevos rancheros* or a breakfast burrito with eggs, corn, and mushrooms. Lunches are equally tempting—you can even get a lentil burger—and cool smoothies and pastries are served throughout the day. Dinner might start with coconut shrimp and move on to crab cakes over mashed potatoes or a bodacious steak sandwich with caramelized onions. There's free Wi-Fi and plenty of friendly folks conversing with travelers.

Plaza Ukana. ✆ **984/875-9138.** Main courses 88–180 pesos. V, MC. Daily 7am–3pm, Tues–Fri 6–9pm.

Xel-Ha: Snorkeling & Swimming ★★

Two miles south of Akumal you'll see the turnoff for **Aktun Chen** ★★ (✆ **984/109-2061;** www.aktunchen.com). This is one of the Yucatán's best caverns, with lots of geological features, good lighting, several underground pools, and large chambers, all carefully preserved. And it has thrived under management by the local community rather than outside tour companies. The cavern tour takes about 90 minutes and requires a lot of walking, but the footing is good. It costs $25 for adults and $13 for children. You can also snorkel in a cenote ($20 adults and children), or soar above the jungle on zip lines ($36 adults and children). There is also a zoo with spider monkeys and other local fauna; some critters are allowed to run about freely. Aktun Chen is open from 9am to 4pm daily (closed Christmas and New Year's days). The turnoff is to the right, and the cave is about 4km (2½ miles) from the road.

Snorkel in Xel-Ha lagoon.

Thirteen kilometers (8 miles) south of Akumal is **Xel-Ha** ☺ (✆ **998/884-9422** in Cancún, 984/873-3588 in Playa, or 984/875-6000 at the park; www.xelha.com.mx). The centerpiece is a large, beautiful lagoon where freshwater and saltwater meet. You can swim, float, and snorkel in beautifully clear water surrounded by jungle. A small train takes you to a drop-off point upriver, and you float back down on water moving calmly toward the sea. With no waves or currents to pull you around, snorkeling here is more comfortable than in the open sea, and the water has several species of fish, including rays.

Inside the park, you can rent snorkeling equipment and an underwater camera. Platforms allow nonsnorkelers to view the fish. Even better, use the park's Snuba gear—a contraption that allows you to breathe through 6m (20-ft.) tubes connected to scuba tanks floating on the surface. It rents for about $45 for an hour. Like Snuba but more involved is sea-trek, an elaborate plastic helmet with air hoses that allows you to walk around on the bottom, breathing normally, and perhaps help to feed the stingrays.

The dolphin area offers several interactive programs. A 1-hour swim costs $134 plus park admission; a shorter program costs $100. Make reservations at least 24 hours in advance by calling ✆ **998/883-0524**.

Other attractions include a plant nursery; an apiary for the local stingerless bees; and a lovely path through the tropical forest bordering the lagoon. Admission includes use of inner tubes, life vest, shuttle train to the river, and changing rooms and showers. (Though not listed on the website, the park often discounts admission on weekends.) Xel-Ha is open daily from 8:30am to 6pm. Parking is free. Admission is $40

FROM TOP: **Rent snuba gear in Xel-Ha; A cenote in Hidden Worlds.**

adults and $30 children ages 5 to 11; children younger than 5 enter free. An all-inclusive option includes all rentals plus food and beverages: $79 adults, $39 children. (These prices are not discounted.) The park has five restaurants, two ice-cream shops, a store, and an ATM. Bring biodegradable sunblock.

Signs clearly mark the turnoff to Xel-Ha, close to the ruins of Tulum. A popular day tour from Cancún or Playa combines the two. If you're traveling on your own, the best time to enjoy Xel-Ha without the crowds is during the weekend from 9am to 2pm.

About 2km (1¼ miles) south of Xel-Ha is **Hidden Worlds Cenotes ★★★** (✆ **984/877-8535;** www.hiddenworlds.com.mx), which offers an excellent opportunity to snorkel or dive in a couple of nearby caverns. The caverns are part of a vast network that makes up a single underground river system. The water is crystalline (and cold), and the rock formations impressive. These caverns were filmed for the IMAX production *Journey into Amazing Caves.* The snorkel tour costs $30 and takes you to two different caverns (a half-tour costs $20). The main form of transportation is "jungle mobile," with a guide tossing out information and lore about the jungle plant life you see. You'll be walking some, so take shoes or sandals. I've toured several caverns, but floating through one gave me an entirely different perspective. For divers, a one-tank dive is $60, two tanks $100. The owners have also installed a 180m (590-ft.) zip line on the property.

Tankah Bay: Bubbling Cenote

Tankah Bay (about 3km/2 miles from Hidden World Cenotes) has a handful of private villas and some rental houses and condos. The most interesting hotel is **Casa Cenote** (✆ **998/874-5170;** www.casacenote.com). Its underground river surfaces at a cenote in the back of the property, then goes underground and bubbles up into the sea just a few feet offshore. Casa Cenote has seven beach bungalows. The double rate runs from $125 to $175, depending on the season (excluding holidays) and includes breakfast. The American owner provides kayaks and snorkeling gear and can arrange dives, fishing trips, and sailing charters.

TULUM ★★★

Tulum (130km/80 miles from Can-cún) is best known for its archaeological site, a walled Maya city of the post-Classic age perched dramatically on a rocky cliff overlooking the Caribbean. The coastline south of the site is packed with *palapa* hotels and upscale retreats for a well-heeled crowd seeking a "rustic" hideaway.

This stretch of incredible white beaches has become the unofficial center of the Tulum Hotel Zone—a collection of about 30 *palapa* hotels stretching from the Tulum ruins south to the entrance to the Sian Ka'an Biosphere Reserve. Hotels here rely on freshwater deliveries and rain tanks, and must generate their own electricity to provide power for a few hours after sundown (though someone with the right connections managed to build a larger property and connect it to the town's electrical grid). Plugs in the main office are usually open for guests' chargers, and Wi-Fi is sometimes available in public areas. The slow arrival of technology hasn't deterred entrepreneurs; new hotels are crammed in among the coast's old-timers, and traffic can be frustrating. Meanwhile, various federal agencies are randomly closing hotels that may not have all the proper papers.

The official town of Tulum is bisected by Hwy. 307, where it intersects the road to Cobá. The commercial center sprawls along both sides of Hwy. 307 for about 20 blocks jam-packed with gas stations, auto repair shops, *farmacias,* banks, markets, tour offices, and eateries. Two *glorietas* (traffic circles) slow the traffic through town; frontage roads allow access to parking spaces and driveways. Restaurants and hotels pop up along side streets around the municipal building and concrete plaza. Anyone who thinks of Tulum as a charming pueblo hasn't been here for a few years. The growth is astounding and shows no sign of slowing.

Getting to the Beach

If you're staying elsewhere but want some beach time in Tulum, the easiest way is to drive to El Paraíso Beach Club, about 1km (a half-mile) south of the ruins (take a left at the T junction). This is a great place—there's a long, broad beach that is pure sand, and access is free. The owners make money by selling food and drink, so they ask you not to bring your own. If you want isolation, drive down the dirt road toward Punta Allen. After you pass the last of the beach hotels, there are a couple of places where the beach comes into view. You can pull over and spread out your beach towel.

ORIENTATION To visit the Tulum area, get a rental car; it will make everything much easier. From the north, you pass the entrance to the ruins before you enter town. When you come to an intersection with a traffic light, the highway to the right leads to the ruins of Cobá (p. 219); to the left is Tulum's beach Hotel Zone, beginning about 2km (1¼ miles) away. The road sign reads BOCA PAILA. When you come to a T junction, there will be hotels in both directions. If you turn left (north), you'll be heading toward the back entrance to the ruins. If you take a right, you'll pass a long line of more *palapa* hotels until you reach the entrance to Sian Ka'an.

The Tulum ruins overlook a white-sand beach and the Caribbean Sea.

A Tulum beach.

In the town of Tulum, Hwy. 307 widens and is called Avenida Tulum. One place that I find handy is a travel agency/communications/package center called **Savana** (✆ **984/871-2081**), on the east side of Avenida Tulum between calles Orion and Beta. Most of the staff speaks English and can answer questions about tours and calling home.

Exploring the Tulum Ruins

Thirteen kilometers (8 miles) south of Xel-Ha are the ruins of Tulum, a Maya fortress-city on a cliff above the sea. They are open daily from 7am to 5pm in winter, 8am to 6pm in summer. It's best to go early, before the crowds start showing up (around 9:30am). At the entrance, you'll find artisans' stands, a bookstore, a museum, a restaurant, several large bathrooms, and a ticket booth. It's about a 5-minute walk from the entrance to the archaeological site. Admission is 51 pesos. If you want to ride the shuttle from the visitor center to the ruins, it's another 15 pesos. Parking is 30 pesos. A video camera permit costs 45 pesos. Licensed guides at the stand next to the path to the ruins charge 200 pesos for a 45-minute tour in English, French, or Spanish for up to four people. In some ways, they are performers who will tailor their presentation to the responses they get from you. Some will try to draw connections between the Maya and Western theology, and they will point out architectural details that you might otherwise miss.

By A.D. 900, the end of the Classic period, Maya civilization had begun its decline, and the large cities to the south were abandoned. Tulum is one of the small city-states that rose to fill the void. It came to prominence in the 13th century as a seaport, controlling maritime commerce along this section of the coast, and remained inhabited well after the arrival of the Spanish. The primary god here was the diving god, depicted on several buildings as an upside-down figure above doorways. Seen at the Palace at Sayil and Cobá, this curious, almost comical figure is also known as the bee god.

The most imposing building in Tulum is a large stone structure above the cliff called the **Castillo** (castle). A temple as well as a fortress, it was once

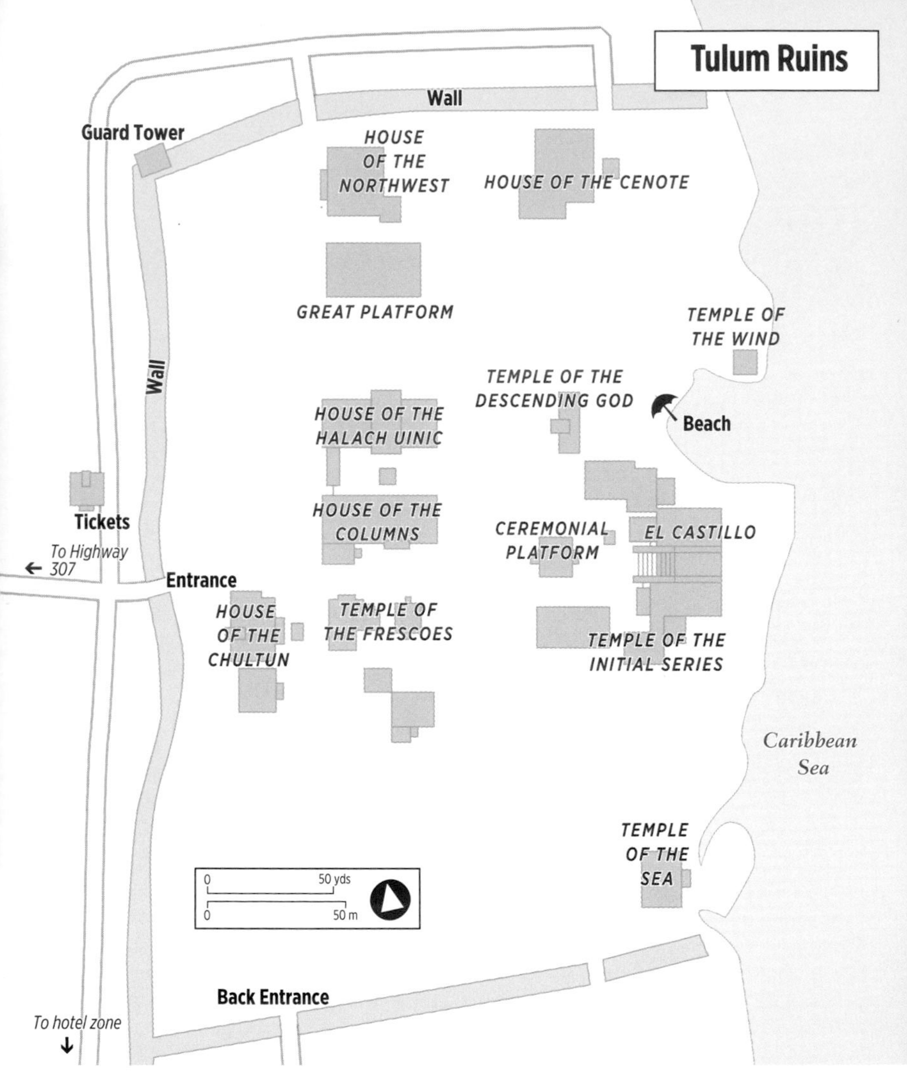

covered with stucco and paint. In front of the Castillo are several unrestored palace-like buildings partially covered with stucco. Tourists swim and sunbathe on the **beach** below, where the Maya once came ashore.

The **Temple of the Frescoes,** directly in front of the Castillo, contains interesting 13th-century wall paintings, though entrance is no longer permitted. Distinctly Maya, they represent Chaac, the rain god, and Ixchel, goddess of weaving, women, the moon, and medicine. The cornice of this temple has a relief of Chaac's head; from a slight distance, you can make out the eyes, nose, mouth, and chin. Notice the remains of the red-painted stucco—at one time all of Tulum's buildings were painted bright red.

Much of what we know of Tulum at the time of the Spanish Conquest comes from the writings of Diego de Landa, third bishop of the Yucatán. He wrote that Tulum was a small city inhabited by about 600 people who lived in platform dwellings along a street and supervised the trade traffic from Honduras to the Yucatán. Though it was a walled city, most inhabitants probably lived outside the walls, leaving the interior for the ceremonial structures and residences of governors and priests. Tulum survived for about 70 years after the conquest before finally being abandoned. Because of the great number of visitors this site receives, it is no longer possible to climb all of the ruins. In some cases, visitors are asked to remain behind roped-off areas.

Where to Stay

If you can afford to stay at one of the small beach hotels in Tulum, it's an enjoyable and relaxing experience. But the beach's popularity among moneyed yet eco-conscious travelers has pushed beachside prices inexorably into the stratosphere. The last bastion for budget travelers, a collection of unabashedly basic concrete bungalows beloved for their prime location on the same gorgeous beach that commands $300 a night at Ana y Jose next door, has changed owners and joined the upscale ranks. We can still recommend **Cabañas Tulum,** Carretera Punta Allen Km 7 (✆ **984/115-9912;** www.hotelstulum.com), but if you return after staying there last year for $60 to $70 a night, be prepared now to pay upwards of $157 to $218, depending on location and season, for 16 colorfully redecorated rooms (half of the original rooms have been closed), new beds, and a new restaurant and beach club.

Even at such prices, beach hotels offer few amenities. Most don't accept credit cards (though there's now an ATM on the beach road), and air-conditioning is still a rarity. Demand is high, supply is limited, and the hotels must generate their own electricity (bring a flashlight). With the under-$100-a-night room on the beach approaching extinction, budget travelers are better off staying in town and making day trips to the beach. The good news is that the town's supply of comfortable and increasingly sophisticated hotels has been steadily growing.

Dozing in a hammock on a peaceful Tulum beach.

Relaxing at a beach in Tulum.

ON THE BEACH

Very Expensive

Ana y José ★★ This *palapa* hotel has gone "boutique," with a spa, suites, and serious remodeling of rooms. It's a far cry from what it used to be—a simple collection of cabins and a restaurant on the beach. Now there are marble countertops, marble tile floors, and wood terraces with a table and chairs. Rooms range from garden- and pool- view doubles with soaring *palapa* ceilings to pricey oceanfront suites with private pools. All have hammocks swinging near the door. Accoutrements include a spa and wedding planners (ceremonies on the excellent white-sand beach are very popular). Ana y José is 6.5km (4 miles) south of the Tulum ruins.

Carretera Punta Allen Km 7 (Apdo. Postal 15), 77780 Tulum, Q. Roo. ✆ **998/880-5629.** Fax 998/880-6021. www.anayjose.com. 23 units. $303–$447 double. AE, MC, V. Free parking. **Amenities:** Restaurant; outdoor pool; spa. *In room:* A/C, fan.

Moderate

Posada Dos Ceibas ★ Of all the places along this coast, this is closest to the way hotels in Tulum used to be: simple, quiet, and ecological without being pretentious. This is a good choice for a no-fuss beach vacation. Bright yellow, blue, and pink one- and two-story cottages are spread out through dense vegetation. Simply furnished rooms come with ceiling fans, and most have private patios or porches with hammocks. Prices vary with room size, and are high for what you get. The grounds are well tended. The solar-generated electricity kicks in at 6pm. The hotel is near the entrance to Sian Ka'an and is more private than those bunched together to the north.

Carretera Tulum-Boca Paila Km 10, 77780 Tulum, Q. Roo. ✆ **984/877-6024.** www.dosceibas.com. 8 units. High season $75–$170 double; low season $60–$110 double. MC, V. **Amenities:** Restaurant; Wi-Fi (in restaurant); yoga. *In room:* No phone.

Zamas ★★ A couple from San Francisco has made this rustic getaway most enjoyable by concentrating on the essentials: comfort, privacy, and good food. The cabañas are simple, attractive, and well situated for catching the breeze. Rooms right on the beach were once simple huts, but storms and high tides kept knocking them down. They're solid concrete now, with *palapa* roofs and hammocks swinging over sand. Most rooms are in individual structures; the suites and oversize rooms are in two-story buildings. Some are by the beach, while others are nestled in dense jungle across the street. For the money, I like the garden *palapas*, which are attractive, spacious, and comfortable, with a queen-size bed and a twin or a king- and queen-size bed. The most expensive rooms are the upstairs oceanview units, which enjoy a large terrace and lots of sea breezes. They come with a king- and a queen-size bed or two queen-size beds. The restaurant serves the freshest seafood, often right off the boat. A white-sand beach curves in a scenic cove between rocky areas.

Carretera Punta Allen Km 5, 77780 Tulum, Q. Roo. ✆ **415/387-9806** in the U.S. www.zamas.com. 20 units. High season $165 beachfront double, $135–$165 garden double, $200 oceanview double; low season $125–$150 beachfront double, $100–$125 garden double, $155 oceanview double. No credit cards. Limited parking. **Amenities:** Restaurant. *In room:* Fan; no phone.

Inexpensive

Don Diego de la Playa ★ An offshoot of the hugely popular Don Diego de la Selva in town, this simple little eco-hotel is buried in palms beside a quiet swath

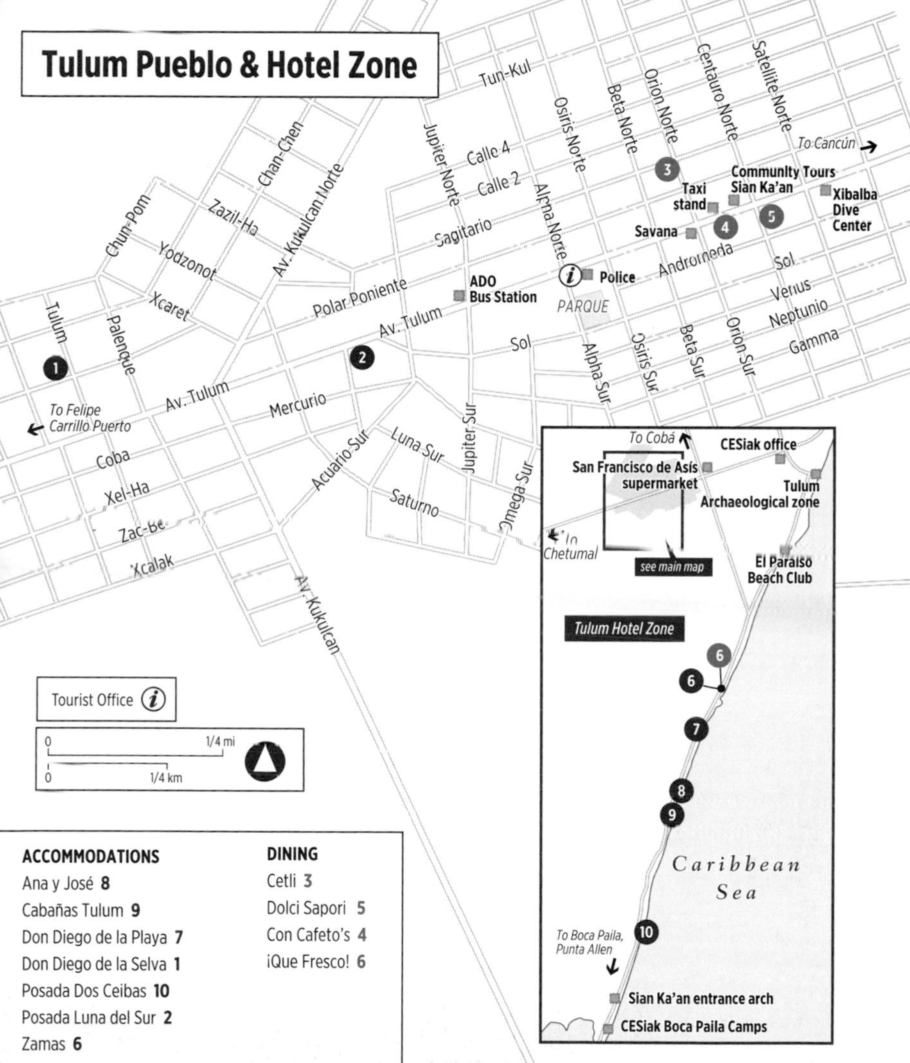

of sand. The least expensive accommodations are in Bedouin tents with wooden floors. Their small net windows catch some breeze, but not enough to keep you cool on sweltering summer nights. Two cement cabañas with thatch roofs are more comfortable. All rooms share common bathrooms with hot water showers. Carretera Punta Allen Km 4.5, 77780 Tulum, Q. Roo. ✆ **984/114-9744** in town. www.dtulum.com. High season $75–$95 tent, $95–$125 cabaña; low season $60–$75 tent, $76–$95 cabaña. No credit cards. Limited parking. **Amenities:** Restaurant. *In room:* Fan; no phone.

IN TOWN

Don Diego de la Selva ★★ The combination of a wild garden setting and easy town and beach accessibility keeps guests coming back to this stylish hotel and restaurant. It feels like you're in the jungle with all the benefits of civilization—24/7 electricity; immaculate rooms; a large, clear swimming pool; and a huge *palapa* restaurant that attracts diners from town and the beach. The gregarious French owners serve drinks and mingle with guests each night, and the concierge dotes on you like a loving nanny. Eight spacious, air-conditioned rooms open to garden patios with chairs and hammocks. Rooms have one king-size or two double beds with orthopedic mattresses, hot showers with skylights, thick towels, and simple, elegant furnishings. Two large bungalows come with queen-size beds and are cooled by ceiling fans. Room rates include a filling breakfast with fresh fruit and a different cake baked every morning.

Av. Tulum, Mza. 24 Lote 3 (1km/half mile so. of ADO bus station), 77780 Tulum, Q. Roo. ✆ **984/114-9744.** www.dtulum.com. 10 rooms. High season $95–$145 with A/C, $75–$120 with fan; low season $76–$195 with A/€, $60–$75 with fan. Rates include breakfast. MC, V. Parking lot. **Amenities:** Restaurant; bar; common fridge; outdoor pool. *In room:* A/C (in some), fan, Wi-Fi.

Posada Luna del Sur ★★ Guests have been known to linger days beyond their planned departure date at this convenient, comfortable inn. Jugs of purified water, coffee pots, utensils, and refrigerators make each room feel like home. Guests pick up eats and treats at produce stands and grocery stores along Avenida Tulum and prepare inexpensive meals in their rooms or share goodies on the rooftop terrace. Rooms open to gardens, bougainvillea bushes, and banana trees; those on the second story have balconies. The owners are gradually remodeling the perfectly adequate rooms, combining modern sinks and furnishings with Mexican tiles and folk art. Dozens of restaurants are within walking distance, and the beach is a 10-minute drive away.

Calle Luna Sur 5, 77780 Tulum, Q. Roo. ✆ **984/871-2984.** www.posadalunadelsur.com. High season $80 double; low season $70 double. Rates include continental breakfast. No credit cards. Covered parking. No children under 16. **Amenities:** Wi-Fi. *In room:* A/C, fan, TV, kitchenette.

Where to Dine

Tulum's dining scene is surprisingly sophisticated, given its laid-back beach vibe. The variety is best in town, where classy restaurants, rowdy bars, and barebones taco stands crowd together along Avenida Tulum and side streets. Many beach hotels have great food as well, though the prices are sometimes appallingly high. Several markets and grocery stores provide do-it-yourself supplies.

Cetli ★★★ MEXICAN You'd think Chef Claudia Pérez Rívas would be a culinary star in Mexico City or New York, but she's applying her considerable talents to create *alta cocina mexicana* (gourmet Mexican cuisine) in a gorgeous old home in downtown Tulum. She grinds spices and herbs in stone *metates* for authentic *moles* (sauces with multitudinous ingredients), places grilled shrimp atop a bed of *huitlacoche* (a savory corn mushroom), and stuffs chicken breasts with *chaya* (similar to spinach). Linen-covered tables are spaced far enough apart for quiet conversation, though diners tend to share opinions and recommend favorites. Dining here is both a pleasure and a culinary adventure.

Calle Polar Poniente at Calle Orion Norte, downtown Tulum. ✆ **984/108-0681.** Main courses 170–210 pesos. No credit cards. Thurs–Tues 5–10pm.

Dolci Sapori ★★ ITALIAN Lasagna doesn't get much better than the 3-inch-high servings at this tiny cafe with a half-dozen outdoor tables and, indoors, an open kitchen with glass cases displaying irresistible tiramisu and pastries. Homemade pastas, tender calamari, and crunchy focaccia go well with the imported Chiantis, and owner Roberto Deligios is happy to help diners choose between the linguini with pesto and shrimp or the awesome lasagna. Fresh croissants, orange juice, and espresso hit the spot in the morning—all meals are a treat here.

Calle Centauro Sur btw. Av. Tulum and Andromeda Oriente, downtown Tulum. ✆ **984/111-3147.** Main courses 75–130 pesos. No credit cards. Daily 8am–11pm.

Don Cafeto's ★ MEXICAN The first place I head for homestyle *huevos rancheros* or *camarones mojo de ajo* (grilled shrimp with oil and garlic) is this sometimes noisy, always interesting cafe. The coffee's strong, the margaritas are perfectly mixed, and the salsas range from mild to *muy picante*. Background music varies from marimbas to mariachis to romantic guitars, and the waiters are always friendly and patient with non-Spanish speakers. It's like a dependable diner, but with far more interesting cuisine.

Av. Tulum btw. calles Centauro and Orion, downtown Tulum. ✆ **984/871-2207.** Main courses $8–$15. MC, V. Daily 7am–11pm.

¡Que Fresco! ★★ AMERICAN/MEXICAN Start the day with fragrant coffee from Chiapas, homemade bread and marmalade, and yogurt with papaya, all served at a bright yellow table on the sand beside a gorgeous beach. Snack on crisp chips and salsas with midday margaritas, and dine on grilled shrimp or filet mignon after dark. Why leave? Well-deserved rave reviews cover the walls at the Zamas hotel's barefoot cafe, and I've yet to see an unhappy diner even when the place is packed.

Carretera Punta Allen Km 5 on the beach. ✆ **415/387-9806** in the U.S. Main courses $7–$15. No credit cards. Daily 7am–10pm.

COBÁ RUINS ★★★

168km (104 miles) SW of Cancún

Older than most of Chichén Itzá and much larger than Tulum, Cobá was the eastern Yucatán's dominant city before A.D. 1000. The site is widely spread out, with thick forest growing between the temple groups. Rising high above the forest canopy are tall, steep pyramids of the Classic Maya style. Of the major sites, this one is the least reconstructed, with mounds that are sure to be additional structures still covered in vines and roots. Since they have been left in the condition in which they were found, most of the stone sculptures are worn down and impossible to make out. But the structures themselves, the surrounding jungle, and the twin lakes are impressive and

Bikers ride along tree-shaded trails in Cobá.

enjoyable. The forest canopy is higher than in the northern part of the peninsula, and the town of Cobá is much like those in Yucatán's interior.

Cobá is my favorite easy escape from the action on the coast. Spending a night here gives you a chance to roam through the archaeological site in early morning when birds chatter, butterflies hover over flowers, and trees shade solitary trails. In the evening, you can easily spot turtles and crocodiles in the lake and graceful white egrets fishing for their dinners. Locals walk along the lakeside and gather outside their simple homes, chatting and watching children run about. I often wish I could spend several nights in this peaceful enclave.

Essentials

GETTING THERE & DEPARTING **By Car** The road to Cobá begins in Tulum and continues for 65km (40 miles). Watch out for *topes* (speed bumps) and potholes. The road has been widened and repaved and should be in good condition. Close to the village of Cobá, you will come to a triangle; be sure to follow the road to Cobá and not Nuevo Xcan or Valladolid. The entrance to the ruins is a short distance down the road past some small restaurants and the large lake.

By Bus Several buses a day leave Tulum and Playa del Carmen for Cobá. Several companies offer bus tours.

Exploring the Cobá Ruins

The Maya built many intriguing cities in the Yucatán, but few as grand as Cobá ("water stirred by wind"). Much of the 67-sq.-km (26-sq.-mile) site remains unexcavated. Scholars believe Cobá was an important trade link between the Caribbean coast and inland cities. A 100km (62-mile) *sacbé* (raised road) through the jungle linked it to Yaxuná, once an important Maya center 50km (31 miles) south of Chichén Itzá. This is the Maya's longest-known *sacbé,* and at least 50

Visitors climb the Cobá ruins.

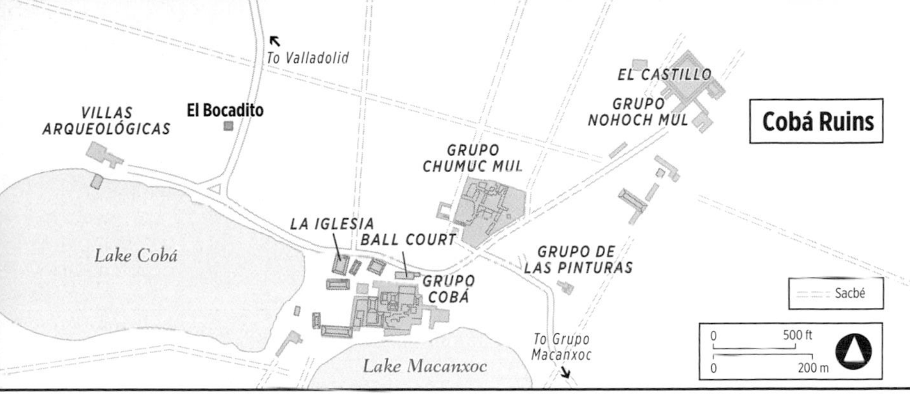

shorter ones lead from here. An important city-state, Cobá flourished from A.D. 632 (the oldest carved date found here) until after the rise of Chichén Itzá, around 800. Then Cobá faded in importance and population until it was finally abandoned.

Once at the site, keep your bearings—you can get turned around in the maze of dirt roads in the jungle. Branching off from every labeled path, you'll see unofficial narrow paths into the jungle, used as shortcuts by locals. These are good for birding, but be careful to remember the way back.

The **Grupo Cobá** holds an impressive pyramid, **La Iglesia (the Church).** Take the path bearing right after the entrance. Resist the urge to climb the temple; the view is better from El Castillo in the Nohoch Mul group farther back.

Return to the main path and turn right, passing a sign pointing to the restored ***juego de pelota*** **(ball court).** Continuing for 5 to 10 minutes, you'll come to a fork in the road, where you'll notice jungle-covered, unexcavated pyramids to the left and right. At one point, a raised portion of the *sacbé* to Yaxuná is visible as it crosses the pathway. Throughout the area, carved stelae stand by pathways or lie forlornly in the underbrush. Although protected by crude thatched roofs, most are weatherworn enough to be indiscernible.

The left fork leads to the **Nohoch Mul Group,** which contains **El Castillo.** Except for Structure 2 in Calakmul, this is the tallest pyramid in the Yucatán, outreaching El Castillo at Chichén Itzá and the Pyramid of the Magician at Uxmal. From the top, you can see unexcavated, jungle-cloaked pyramids poking through the forest canopy all around. Climbing the Castillo was forbidden for a short time as archaeologists determined that all the traffic wasn't disturbing the pyramid's inner temples. Climbing had resumed in late 2009.

The right fork (more or less straight on) goes to the **Conjunto Las Pinturas**, whose main attraction is the **Pyramid of the Painted Lintel,** a small structure with traces of its original bright colors above the door. You can climb up for a close look.

Admission is 51 pesos, free for children younger than 12. Parking is 50 pesos, and video camera permits 35 pesos. The site is open daily from 8am to 5pm, sometimes longer. ***Note:*** Visit Cobá in the morning or after the heat of the day has passed. Mosquito repellent, drinking water, and comfortable shoes are imperative. Bicycles are available for rent for $3 per hour at a stand just past the entrance. You can also hire a *triciclo* with driver to carry you around the site; rates start at $10. Clever *triciclo* drivers also park at Nohuch Mul to carry hot, tired passengers back to the entrance.

Where to Stay & Dine

Cobá offers a few hotels, restaurants, and markets, and food choices abound at stands near the entrance when the archaeological site is open. Prices are refreshingly realistic, and the locals enjoy chatting with travelers. A few truly rustic hostelries offer hard mattresses and cold-water showers for budget travelers, and a couple of hotels are on the road to Tulum. Making reservations is difficult, as phone and Internet service is spotty, but it's a good idea to give it a shot during high season.

Serene Cobá lake.

El Bocadito Cobá's longtime family-run hotel is always changing as the owners add air-conditioning and TVs to some rooms while keeping others bare-bones basic. The adjacent large restaurant (popular with groups at lunch) sits on the main road through town, right where buses to Playa del Carmen depart. Bathrooms in the cheapest rooms are so small that the seatless toilet is practically in the cold-water shower, and the single beds take up nearly all the space. Size and comfort levels gradually increase with the rates, up to the four rooms with TVs and one with air-conditioning. Guests gather at picnic tables beneath banana and orange trees in a narrow courtyard or in the Internet cafe with several communal computers. It's hard to make reservations, since phone and Internet service is unreliable.

A Day in the Life of a Maya Village

In the tropical forest near Cobá, a village of 27 families exists much as their long-ago ancestors did, living in round thatch huts with no electricity, indoor plumbing or paved roads, gathering plants in the jungle for medicinal and other uses on their way to dip into a hidden *cenote*, appealing to the gods for successful crops. And every day, the people of Pac Chen open their homes to as many as 80 tourists who want to know what Maya village life is in the 21st century.

The only way to visit Pac Chen is on trips with **Alltournative** (✆ **800/507-1092** in the U.S., or 984/803-9999; www.alltournative.com), an eco-tour company that works with villagers to help them become self-sustaining. Farming continues, but tourism income allows them to survive without burning their land to squeeze out the last remaining nutrients.

The arrangement is a boon to tourists, too. On your own, it would be pretty well impossible to walk into a Maya village and be ushered through the jungle and lowered into a cenote or to glide through the forest canopy on a zip line, kayak a lagoon full of howler monkeys, eat lunch cooked by village women and receive a copal-incense blessing from a village elder for a safe trip home.

The Maya Encounter tour costs $119 for adults and $95 for children.

Anatomy of a Biosphere Reserve

Unlike its national parks, which focus on historical and aesthetic features, Mexico's biosphere reserves were created purely to protect its last natural ecosystems. Recognition by UNESCO (United Nations Educational, Scientific and Cultural Organization), requires that the biosphere contain at least 10,000 hectares (about 39 sq. miles), at least one pristine area of biological diversity, and threatened or endangered endemic species.

Mexico pioneered the zoning system that allows some carefully managed tourism. The core area—the heart of the reserve—is limited to scientific research and is surrounded by a buffer zone that allows only conservation-related activity. On the periphery, a transition zone permits sustainable use of natural resources to benefit local communities, as CESiaK's tours do. Biosphere reserves allow original residents to remain; local people, in fact, are recruited to research, monitor, and manage the ecosystem while developing sustainable activities such as ecotourism.

On main road through Cobá town. ✆ **985/852-0052** or 984/876-3738. www.cancunsouth.com/bocadito; bocadito@hotmail.com. 9 units. 100–350 pesos double. MC, V (10% charge). **Amenities:** Restaurant. *In room:* A/C (in one), fan (in some), Internet (for a fee).

Villas Arqueológicas Cobá ★★ Lovingly maintained for several decades, this peaceful compound facing the lake is removed from town on a private road. Its cool blue pool, good restaurant, attentive service from faithful local workers and a superb library make it the best choice in the area. The rooms have a double and a single bed in semiprivate niches, a small bathroom with hot-water shower, a sink outside the bathroom door, and dreadful lighting. Bougainvillea, palms, and ferns flourish in the central courtyard, shading the pool and dining terraces. The restaurant's Mexican/Continental food is very good, if a bit overpriced (bring water or pay 10 pesos for each tiny bottle). An excellent library contains tomes on the Maya, archaeology, and Mexican art—and a pool table for guests bored by the lack of activities after dark.

West of the ruins beside the lake. ✆ **984/206-7001.** www.villasarqueologicas.com.mx. 43 units. $65–$125 double. MC, V. Parking lot. **Amenities:** Restaurant; bar; outdoor pool; room service; tennis court; Wi-Fi (in pubic areas). *In room:* A/C, hair dryer.

SIAN KA'AN & THE PUNTA ALLEN PENINSULA ★★★

Just past Tulum's last cabaña hotel is the entrance arch to the vast (526-hectare/1.3 million-acre) **Sian Ka'an Biosphere Reserve.** This inexpressibly beautiful tract of wild land is the domain of howler monkeys, ocelots, crocodiles, jaguars, tapirs, sea turtles, and thousands of species of plants. The Mexican government created this reserve in 1986; the following year, the United Nations declared it a World Heritage Site. Sian Ka'an protects 10% of Quintana Roo's land mass, including almost one-third of the Caribbean coastline, from development.

The entrance to the Punta Allen Peninsula, a small portion of the reserve, is one of two main entrances to the reserve; the other entrance is from the community of Muyil off Hwy. 307 south of Tulum (you take a boat down canals, built by the Maya, that connect to the Boca Paila lagoon).

A mangrove in Sian Ka'an Biosphere Reserve.

Legends still swirl about the 4 hours it takes to drive the 50km (31 miles) over potholes, ruts, and rivulets to the town of Punta Allen at road's end. In fact, the road has been much improved, though it is still dirt, still pockmarked to varying degrees, and subject to weather-related conditions. Guards at the entrance gate are fond of declaring it's now a 1-hour trip, and no doubt that's true for the locals who sailed past me in my rented compact sedan. Driving cautiously after a stretch of rainy weather, it took me a little less than two hours. Those driving 4-wheelers or other robust vehicles should plan to spend about 1½ hours on the road.

If you don't fancy yourself a road warrior, you can drive through the entrance arch in Tulum (entry 25 pesos per person) and take a path at the guard station to the clear, cool Ben-Ha cenote for a swim—or continue south a short way to one of several places where the beach comes into view, pull over and spread out your beach towel.

The Punta Allen Peninsula

As you drive the skinny peninsula, which separates the Boca Paila Lagoon from the sea, you'll find no trails leading into the jungle, but you can swim or snorkel off the beaches that come into view. Guided tours are the only way to see most of the reserve. Otherwise, there is no practical way to visit Sian Ka'an except by car.

THE SIAN KA'AN BIOSPHERE RESERVE ★★★

Maya life in ancient times remains essentially a mystery, but there's no wondering why they named this land Sian Ka'an (see-*an* caan), Mayan for "where the sky is born." Sunrise here truly is like witnessing the birth of a day.

The reserve encompasses most of the ecosystems that exist on the entire Yucatán Peninsula: medium- and low-growth jungles, beaches, savannas, marshes, freshwater and brackish lagoons, cenotes, underground rivers, and untouched coral reef. Numerous archaeological sites have also been found within its borders.

More than 2,000 people, most of them Maya, live in Sian Ka'an. All are original residents of the area, or their descendants. Tours to the reserve are often led by locals, who grew up nearby in homes occupied for countless generations. They'll almost never consult a field guide; their knowledge about the birds, the plants, the water, and the ruins are simply a part of their lives.

To access the reserve beyond the road, arrange for a tour in Tulum. Two organizations in particular keep their groups small and work only through the local people.

The **Centro Ecológico Sian Ka'an,** or CESiaK, Hwy. 307 just south of Tulum ruins turnoff (✆ **984/871-2499;** www.cesiak.org), which runs the Sian Ka'an Visitor Center, is a nonprofit group supporting the reserve with education and community development programs. Its popular all-day canal tour ($77 per person, including lunch and tax), includes a guided walk through coastal dunes and jungle, continuing with a boat trip across two brackish lagoons where fresh water cenotes well up from under the ground. Boats follow a narrow channel through mangroves and grass savanna to a small temple where Maya traders stopped to make offerings and ask for successful negotiations. You'll don life jackets and float part of the way in the currents of a freshwater lagoon and snorkel in a cenote before the day is over. Other tours include a sunset bird-watching trip and single- and multi-day fly fishing packages.

Community Tours Sian Ka'an, Av. Tulum btw. calles Centauro and Orión (✆ **984/114-0750;** www.siankaantours.org) is a local guides' cooperative that runs snorkeling, birding, and adventure tours into the biosphere. Their

Visitors float down a canal in Sian Ka'an.

SLEEPING where the sky is born

To see the sun rise in Sian Ka'an as the Maya did, you can stay in CESiaK's **Boca Paila Camps ★★**, 4km/2.5 miles past the entrance arch. The eco-lodge's tent cabins are tucked into the edge of the jungle on a clean, white beach, raised on platforms to avoid interfering with the sand's natural processes. The fine linens and solid wood furniture make it feel less like camping, but when night falls and you're stumbling around by candlelight, it feels plenty rustic. Guests share scrupulously clean bathrooms equipped with composting toilets, housed in buildings whose rooftop lookouts grant views of the sea and lagoon that give "panoramic" new meaning—you'll actually see the curvature of the earth. Cabins with one double and one single bed rent for $65, while deluxe cabins with one queen and ocean or lagoon views are $80. Meals are extra. The camp has no electricity—guests get battery-powered lamps—but wind and solar power provide hot water. Things do not always run perfectly smoothly: The restaurant, which is reasonably priced and turns out better meals than it has any right to in this remote location, sometimes runs out of ingredients for a popular menu item, and one time I was assigned to a tent that was already occupied (and quickly reassigned). But this place makes Tulum's vaunted sands look like Panama City Beach in springtime—and its staff knows the reserve's plants, animals, and local culture backward and forward.

"Forest and Float" canal tours ($99 per adult, $70 child) begin with a visit to the Muyil archaeological site and enter the reserve from that side.

THE ROAD TO PUNTA ALLEN

About 11km (6.8 miles) past the arch, you'll come to the **Boca Paila Fishing Lodge** (www.bocapaila.com). Not for the general traveler, it specializes in weeklong, all-inclusive packages for fly-fishers. The peninsula is so narrow here that you see the Boca Paila lagoon on one side and the sea on the other. In another 3km (1.9 miles), you will be flooded by false hope when you reach a smooth, concrete roadway—this is the foot of the Boca Paila Bridge, which spans the inlet between the ocean and the lagoon, and the pavement disappears as quickly as it appeared. You'll often see people fishing off the sides. This is a good place to stop and stretch your legs while taking in ethereal water views from either side.

After the bridge, it's mostly deserted coastline until you get to Punta Allen. About 8km (5 miles) before you do, you'll come to **Rancho Sol Caribe** (www.solcaribe-mexico.com), with four comfortable cabañas and a stunning beach it has all to itself.

Punta Allen

Punta Allen, the peninsula's only town, is a lobster fishing village on a palm-studded beach perched between Ascension Bay and the Caribbean Sea. About 100 families survive by lobster fishing and, increasingly, tourism; many of the young men now are expert fly-fishing guides.

Isolated and rustic, this is very much the end of the road. The town has a lobster cooperative, a few sand streets with modest homes, and a lighthouse. The generator, when it's working, comes on for a few hours in the morning and a few more at night. Your cellphone won't work here, and no one takes credit cards. Without the help of a friendly local, it's a challenge to figure out when any of the businesses are open.

This is slowly beginning to change. The few lodges that bravely set up shop here 10 or 15 years ago have acquired some upstart young neighbors, and 80 more guest rooms have been approved (no telling how long it will take for those to materialize). For now, unless you're a fishing enthusiast, there's not a lot to do in Punta Allen except kick back, snorkel a little, and eat your fill of fresh seafood.

Casa de Ascención ★ Of the newer places in town, this home run by a Swiss/Argentine couple is the most impressive in town. Positioned between the beach in one direction and the bay in the other—100m (less than a mile) either way—it offers three cool, tidy rooms whose furniture and decor take cues from Mexican design. They surround a shared living room with a book exchange, Internet computer, and satellite TV. Solar power cranks out electricity 24 hours a day. The helpful owners live upstairs behind the restaurant, which turns out an impressive array of international dishes, pizza, and fresh fish specials. All-inclusive fly-fishing packages are available, too.

One block west of entrance to town. ✆ **984/801-0034.** www.casadeascension.com. 3 units. High season $65–$85 double; low season $60–$80 double. No credit cards. *In room:* No phone.

Cuzan Guesthouse One of the town's original fishing lodges, this collection of basic, *palapa*-roofed wood cabañas on a sandy beach also has one of the town's best restaurants and a full bar. Despite the increasing competition, it has a loyal following. Cuzan's bread and butter is its all-inclusive fishing packages, but it will rent a *cabaña* to anyone interested in passing some time in Punta Allen. The guesthouse also offers a variety of birding, snorkeling, and other boat tours.

Apartado 24, Felipe Carrillo Puerto, 77200 Q. Roo. ✆ **983/834-0358.** www.flyfishmx.com. 12 units. $50– $110 cabañas. No credit cards. *In room:* No phone.

Fishing boats in Punta Allen.

Serenidad Shardon This retreat on the coastal road just south of town—we're talking about the equivalent of 3 or 4 blocks—can put you in a three-bedroom beach house or one of two sweet, private cabañas, all with private bathrooms, contemporary decoration, and views of the Caribbean from decks or windows. In high season, owner Niki Allen puts up four sturdy tent cabins, equipped with lights and fans, to accommodate more guests. She'll also set you up with tours if you want them, and think of a dozen other ways to make sure you are happy.

Beach road south of town square. ✆ **616/827-0204** in the U.S., or 984/876-1827. www.shardon.com. 3 units (7 in high season). $150–$200 cabañas, $350 beach house ($250 lower floor only), 200 pesos per person tent cabins. No credit cards. *In room:* No phone.

The ruins of Muyil.

En Route to the Lower Caribbean Coast

About 25km (16 miles) south of Tulum on Hwy. 307, a sign points to the small but interesting ruins of **Muyil** (take bug spray), on the western edge of Sian Ka'an. The principal ruins are a small group of buildings and a plaza dominated by the Castillo. It's one of the Caribbean coast's taller structures but is more interesting for the unique, solid round masonry turret at the top. From here, a canal dug by the Maya enters the biosphere reserve and empties into a lake, with other canals going from there to the saltwater estuary of Boca Paila. The local community offers a boat ride through these canals and lakes. The 3½-hour tour includes viewing some otherwise inaccessible ruins, snorkeling the canal, and floating in its current.

Felipe Carrillo Puerto (pop. 60,000) is the first large town on the road to Ciudad Chetumal. The town was a rebel stronghold during the War of the Castes and home to the millenarian cult of the "Talking Cross." A sizable community of cult believers still practices its own brand of religion and is respected by the entire town. Of primary interest to travelers, however, are Carrillo Puerto's two gas stations, a market, a bus terminal, and a bank next to the gas station in the center of town, which has an ATM. From Carrillo Puerto, Hwy. 184 goes into the peninsula's interior and eventually to Mérida, making it a turning point on the "short circuit" of the Yucatán Peninsula.

MAHAHUAL, XCALAK & THE CHINCHORRO REEF

Tourism has been late to arrive on the quiet southern half of the Caribbean coast. The recently dubbed Costa Maya is tucked under the Sian Ka'an Biosphere Reserve on a wide peninsula jutting out from the mainland. It remained largely unnoticed—except by fly-fishers—while resorts gobbled up the beaches of Cancún and the Riviera Maya over the past few decades.

Lying 354km (220 miles) from Cancún's airport and more than 48km (30 miles) from the highway, the Costa Maya's beaches might never see Riviera Maya-scale development, but changes have already come since Carnival Cruise Line and government tourism officials brought a huge cruise port to the tiny fishing village of Mahahual (sometimes spelled Majahual) in 2001. New roads built to smooth the way for cruise passenger bus tours have cut the trip to the

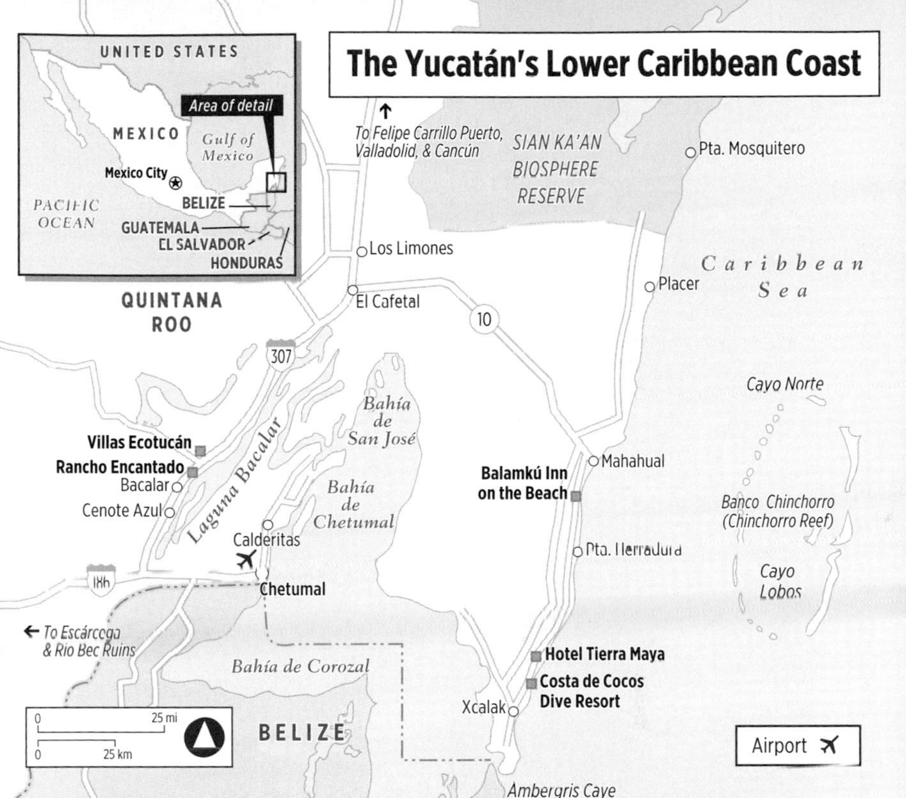

even smaller and more remote village of Xcalak (eesh-kah-*lahk*)—the Mexican Caribbean's southernmost settlement—from four hours to less than one. Luxury developments are rumored to be on the drawing boards, but tourism officials vow to abandon the Cancún/Riviera Maya model, integrating the local population into restrained development of small, eco-friendly hotels and nature tours.

So far, the Costa Maya remains a landscape of mangrove marshes, low jungle, and long stretches of palm-fringed, white-sand beaches. Affordable bungalows and small restaurants serving fresh-caught fish await visitors drawn to the region's cenotes, ancient villages, Maya ruins, and incomparable snorkeling and diving.

ORIENTATION About 45 minutes south of Felipe Carrillo Puerto, a few kilometers past the town of Limones at a place called El Cafetal (there's a gas station before the turnoff), you reach the clearly marked turnoff for Mahahual and Xcalak. It's 50km (31 miles) on a good paved road to the coast at Mahahual. The turnoff for the new road to Xcalak comes 2km (1¼ miles) before you reach Mahahual, at a military checkpoint. Xcalak is 55km (34 miles) to the south, less than an hour's drive.

Mahahual

The cruise ship pier (north of the road entering town) has given Mahahual a split personality. The port has expanded into a small tourist zone with a beach club, shopping mall, and tour companies offering dozens of excursions, and a

DIVING the chinchorro reef

The **Chinchorro Reef Underwater National Park,** about 30km (20 miles) off this coastline, is by most accounts the largest coral atoll in the Northern Hemisphere, at 38km (24 miles) long and 13km (8 miles) wide. Its coral formations, massive sponges and abundant sea life are certainly among the most spectacular. Locals claim this is the last virgin reef system in the Caribbean. The oval reef is as shallow as 1m (3¼ ft.) at its interior and as deep as 900m (2,952 ft.) at its exterior. It's invisible from the ocean side and has doomed scores of ships. Contrary to popular misconception, the 30 or so **shipwrecks** that decorate the underwater landscape cannot be dived—they are protected by the Banco Chinchorro Biosphere. However, the reef offers at least a dozen stellar dive sites. And most wrecks, including the famous **40 Cannons** on the northwest side, are quite shallow and can be explored by snorkeling. The west side of the reef is a wonderland of walls and coral gardens.

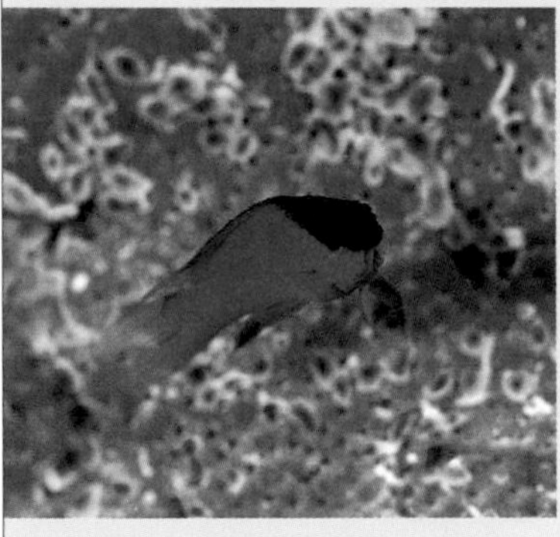

The number of divers who have tried to dive Chinchorro Reef and never got there is kind of a running joke along the Costa Maya. It can be a challenge to get to the reef, partly because of fickle sea conditions and partly because of the strict limit on permits. **XTC Dive Center** (✆ **983/839-8865;** www.xtcdivecenter.com) in Xcalak specializes in trips to Chinchorro—the company's name stands for "Xcalak to Chinchorro." XTC also offers a lineup of dives to local reefs and cenotes.

mini-city with its own suburb of homes and apartments has sprouted nearby. On port days, the town's packed-sand main street brims with tipsy, sunburned passengers who elect beach time over bus tours, only to empty at night and return to somnolence.

Your best bet is to keep your distance from the pier and stay in the lower Mahahual area (or repair to Xcalak). Even when devoid of cruise passengers, I don't find Mahahual a particularly appealing town, though its new *malecón* (seafront promenade) makes for a pleasant walk along a fine white beach. Beach areas north and south of town, though, are the stuff of dreams. Most of its hotels and services are on the sand road running through town and south along the coast.

Balamkú Inn on the Beach ★★★ This comfortable, friendly place on the coast road south of town rents rooms in stylish, one- and two-story thatched bungalows distributed across 110m (361 ft.) of dazzling white beach. They are large and breezy, with comfortable mattresses, large attractive bathrooms, and louvered windows to let you control the amount of breeze. All have terraces facing the beach. The friendly Canadian owners are environmentally minded to the extreme. All the inn's energy comes from wind and sun—enough to provide 24-hour power without using a diesel generator. Even more impressive, they rely on a large rainwater collection system and route shower and sink wastewater to nourish the wetlands, and use a composting waste system instead of polluting septic tanks—they not only allow but urge guests to flush paper down the toilet. For travelers with any ecological leanings at all, it adds yet another layer of relaxation to the supremely comfortable and beautiful surroundings.

Carretera Costera Km 5.7, Mahahual, Q. Roo. ✆ **983/839-5332.** www.balamku.com. 10 units. High season $90 double, mid-season $85 double; low season $80 double. Rates include full breakfast. AE, MC, V for deposits; no credit cards at hotel. Free guarded parking. **Amenities:** Restaurant (breakfast & lunch); bar (afternoons); airport transfer; smoke-free rooms; watersports. *In room:* No phone, Wi-Fi.

Xcalak

Quintana Roo's last stand before the channel marking Mexico's border with Belize, **Xcalak** (eesh-kah-*lahk*) is a depopulated, weather-beaten fishing village with a few comfortable places to stay and a couple of restaurants. A former military outpost, it once had a population as large as 1,200 before the 1958 hurricane washed most of the town away; now it has about 600 permanent residents. Fly-fishers started coming in the 1980s and are still pulling prizes out of the water. The town has a certain shabby charm, but the real lure is the inns just beyond town that offer a little patch of paradise safe from anything resembling a crowd.

Costa de Cocos Dive & Fly-Fishing Resort ★★ Freestanding cabañas sit around a large, attractive sandy beach graced with coconut palms. Co-owner Ilana Randal epitomizes a "life is too short" philosophy that makes you feel all is right with the world. The comfortable cabañas come with one king- or queen-size bed or two doubles; one cabaña is a two-bedroom unit with two bathrooms. They have been recently remodeled and have plenty of cross-ventilation, ceiling fans, hot water, and comfortable mattresses. Wind and solar power provides 24-hour electricity. Activities include kayaking, snorkeling, scuba diving, and fly-fishing. The resort has experienced English-speaking fishing guides and a dive instructor. The casual restaurant/bar, which offers good home-style cooking, is open late.

Carretera Mahahual-Xcalak Km 52, Q. Roo. ✆ **983/839-8537.** www.costadecocos.com. 16 cabañas. High season $90 double; low season $85 double. Dive and fly-fishing packages available by e-mail request. Rates include breakfast buffet. AE, MC, V. Free parking. **Amenities:** Restaurant; bar; dive shop; watersports. *In room:* Wi-Fi, no phone.

Hotel Tierra Maya ★ This is a comfortable, modern-style hotel on the beach. Rooms in the two-story building are spacious and designed for good cross-ventilation. They come with ceiling fans. Each has a private balcony or terrace that looks out to the sea, hammocks, and bottled purified water. Solar generators provide 24-hour electricity. Bathrooms are large, and beds are either twins or queen-size. The owners arrange diving, fishing, and snorkeling trips for guests. Guests have use of kayaks and bikes.

Carretera Mahahual-Xcalak Km 54, Q. Roo. ✆ **800/216-1902** in the U.S. Fax 941/627-0089. www.tierramaya.net. 7 units. High season $85–$150 double; low season $75–$135 double. Rates include continental breakfast. MC, V for advance payments; cash only at hotel. Limited free parking. **Amenities:** Restaurant; bar; bikes; kayaks. *In room:* Wi-Fi, no phone.

Laguna Bacalar.

LAGUNA BACALAR ★★★

104km (64 miles) SW of Felipe Carrillo Puerto; 37km (23 miles) NW of Chetumal

On a sunny day, you will see why Laguna Bacalar is nicknamed *Lago de los Siete Colores* (Lake of the Seven Colors): The white-sandy bottom makes the crystalline water pale turquoise in shallow areas, morphing to vivid turquoise and through a spectrum to deep indigo in the deeper center. The colors shift with the passing of the day, making a mesmerizing backdrop for a day or two of exploring.

Considered Mexico's second-largest lake, Bacalar is actually a lagoon, with a series of waterways leading eventually to the ocean. Fed not by surface runoff but by underground cenotes, it is almost 50km (31 miles) long. You'll glimpse the jewel-toned water long before you reach the town of Bacalar, about two-thirds of the way down, where you must go for swimming or kayaking.

The town of Bacalar is quiet and traditional, though it seems every year brings a new cadre of expats looking for a different kind of life. There's not a lot of action in town, but you shouldn't miss the **Fuerte San Felipe Bacalar,** built in 1733 to protect the Spanish from the pirates and Maya rebels who regularly raided the area. Admission is 52 pesos. Overlooking the lake on the eastern edge of the central plaza, the fort houses an excellent museum devoted to regional history, with a focus on the pirates who repeatedly descended upon these shores.

As if to prove the water gods smile upon Bacalar, Mexico's biggest and deepest cenote is about a mile south of town, at Km 15. Measuring 185m (607 ft.) across, **Cenote Azul** is surrounded by lush flowers and trees, and filled with water so clear that you can see 60m (200 ft.) down into its nearly 91-m (300-ft.) depth.

Some lovely inns dot the lagoon's western shore, which makes Bacalar an appealing alternative base to Chetumal for exploring the Maya ruins in the nearby Río Bec area.

ORIENTATION Driving south on Hwy. 307, the town of Bacalar is 1½ hours beyond Felipe Carrillo Puerto, clearly marked by signs. If you're driving north from Chetumal, it takes about a half-hour. Buses going south from

Cancún and Playa del Carmen stop here, and there are frequent buses from Chetumal. There are now a couple of gas stations on the highway in town.

Where to Stay

You can stay quite comfortably in Bacalar for very little money. My favorite inn is **Amigos B&B Laguna Bacalar ★★** (✆ **987/872-3868;** www.bacalar.net), with five rooms of various sizes and configurations overlooking the water on Avenida Costera, about a mile south of the plaza. Doubles run 600 to 700 pesos including breakfast, 500 to 600 pesos without. A little closer to the center of town on the same road, I also quite like the quirky and endearing **Casita Carolina** (✆ **983/834-2334;** www.casitacarolina.com), with three units in a converted family home that share a common living room and kitchen, and three separate *casitas* scattered through a large, grassy garden sloping to the lake's shore. The owner, who lives on-site, hosts an artist's retreat every February. Prices range from 300 to 600 pesos, making this a great value. If you want to really get away from it all, **Villas Ecotucán** (✆ **983/834-2516;** www.villasecotucan.info) commands about 40 hectares (99 acres) of largely undeveloped land and focuses on the outdoors; its five spacious *palapa*-roofed cabañas (made out of native materials from the property) and two suites have separate sitting rooms and rent for 550 pesos; for 850 pesos you can have your own houseboat on the lake. They also offer more jungle walks, swimming, and kayaking tours than you could go through in a week. Ecotucán is 5km (3 miles) north of town and 1km (less than a mile) off Hwy. 307; look for the tall, rainbow-colored tree, flags, and welcome sign.

Climbing the price scale just a bit gets you all-out luxury. The all-suites **Villas Bakalar ★** (✆ **983/835-1400;** www.villasbakalar.com) on Avenida 3, a couple of blocks north of the plaza, has 15 new and modern one- and two-bedroom suites for 1,130 pesos and 1,780 pesos, respectively, set in a veritable botanical garden of native flora—a passionate interest of the owner. It's a block from the shore but has sweeping lake views. And the well-known **Rancho Encantado ★** (✆/fax **983/101-3358;** www.encantado.com) near Hwy. 307 north of town, rents 13 large white stucco cottages scattered over a shady lawn beside the lake, surrounded by native trees, orchids, and bromeliads. It charges $130 to $150 in high season, $65 to $85 in low season.

Cenote Azul in Bacalar.

Fuerte San Felipe Bacalar.

Where to Dine

I've had good, simple meals at **Laguna de Bacalar** on the town square, and great dinners at the more upscale **Los Aluxes** on Avenida Costera, south of Amigos B&B. And **Restaurante Cenote Azul** (✆ **983/834-2460;** www.cenoteazul.com.mx), with its vantage point overlooking the cenote, wouldn't even have to serve decent food to attract a following, but it does all the same. While you're there, you can take a dip in the cenote, as long as you aren't wearing lotions or deodorant.

CHETUMAL

251km (156 miles) S of Tulum; 37km (23 miles) S of Lago Bacalar

Quintana Roo's capital and second-largest city (after Cancún), Chetumal (pop. 210,000), is a tourist destination only in the sense that it's the gateway to Belize, Tikal (Guatemala), and the Río Bec ruins (p. 236). It has little to offer a tourist, with the one huge exception of its museum devoted to Maya culture, perhaps the best outside of Mexico City. The old part of town down by the Río Hondo has an intriguing Caribbean atmosphere, but otherwise there's not much to hold you here.

Essentials

GETTING THERE & DEPARTING

BY PLANE Mexicana's regional carrier, **Click** (✆ **01-800/112-5425** or 983/832-6675; www.mexicana.com), flies between Chetumal (Airport code CTM) and Mexico City. The airport is west of town, just north of the entrance from the highway.

BY CAR Chetumal is just over 3 hours from Tulum. If you're heading to Belize, be aware that rental companies don't allow you to take their cars across the border. To get to the ruins of Tikal in Guatemala, you must go through Belize to the border crossing at Ciudad Melchor de Mencos.

BY BUS The main bus station (✆ **983/832-5110**) is 20 blocks from the town center on Insurgentes at Avenida Héroes. Buses go to Cancún, Tulum, Playa del Carmen, Puerto Morelos, Mérida, Campeche, Villahermosa, and Tikal, Guatemala.

To Belize: Buses depart from the Lázaro Cárdenas market, most often called Mercado Nuevo (Héroes and Circuito). Ask for **Autobuses Novelo,** which has local service every 45 minutes (140 pesos) and four express buses per day (185 pesos).

VISITOR INFORMATION

The **State Tourism Office** (✆ **983/835-0860,** ext. 1811) is at Calzada del Centenario 622, between Comonfort and Ciricote. It's open Monday to Friday from 9am to 6pm.

ORIENTATION

The telephone **area code** is **983.**

Traffic enters the city from the west on Hwy. 186 and feeds onto Avenida Obregón into town. Stay on Obregón and don't take the exit veering left for Avenida Insurgentes. You'll cross Avenida Héroes, the main north–south street.

A Museum Not to Miss

Museo de la Cultura Maya ★★★ This sophisticated museum unlocks the complex world of the Maya through interactive exhibits and genuine artifacts. Push a button, and an illustrated description appears, explaining medicinal and domestic uses of plants with their Mayan and scientific names; another exhibit describes the social classes of the Maya by their manners of dress. One of the most fascinating exhibits describes the Maya's ideal of personal beauty, which prompted them to deform craniums, scar the face and body, and induce cross-eyed vision.

An enormous screen flashes aerial images of more than a dozen Maya sites from Mexico to Honduras. Another large television shows the architectural variety of Maya pyramids and how they were probably built. Then a walk on a glass floor takes you over representative ruins in the Maya world. In the center of the museum is the three-story, stylized, sacred Ceiba tree, which the Maya believed connected Xibalba (the underworld), Earth, and the heavens. Try to see the museum before you tour the Río Bec ruins. The museum now closes at 2pm because of budget cutbacks.

Av. Héroes s/n (btw. Colón and Gandhi, 8 blocks from Av. Obregón, just past the Holiday Inn). ✆ **983/832-6838.** Admission 52 pesos. Tues–Sun 9am–2pm.

Where to Stay

I prefer Bacalar (see above), only about 30 minutes away, as a base for exploring this region. If you do need to stay over in the capital, a couple of hotels stand above the rest.

Hotel Holiday Inn Chetumal Puerta Maya This modern hotel is a reliable if not inspiring option. It has the best air-conditioning in town and is only a block from the Museo de la Cultura Maya. Most rooms are midsize and come with one king-size or two double beds. Bathrooms are roomy and well lit.

Av. Héroes 171, 77000 Chetumal, Q. Roo. ✆ **800/465-4329** in the U.S., or 983/835-0400. Fax 983/832-1676. 85 units. 865 pesos double. AE, MC, V. Free secure parking. From Av. Obregón, turn left on Av. Héroes, go 6 blocks, and look for the hotel on the right. **Amenities:** Restaurant; bar; fitness room; midsize outdoor pool; room service. *In room:* A/C, TV, Wi-Fi.

Hotel Los Cocos Renovated rooms are positively sleek, bathrooms are scrupulously clean, and the small but inviting pool is in the middle of a lush garden. Ask for a room facing the courtyard—the view is better. The open-air restaurant, popular with museum visitors, does a good job with Mexican favorites. This three-story hotel is 2 blocks south of the museum.

A display in the Museo de la Cultura Maya.

Av. Héroes 134 (corner of Chapultepec), 77000 Chetumal, Q. Roo. ✆ **983/832-3232.** 176 units. 900 pesos double. AE, MC, V. Off-street parking. **Amenities:** Restaurant; bar; Internet terminal; 2 outdoor pools; room service. ***In room:*** A/C, TV, fridge.

Where to Dine

For an economical meal with some local atmosphere, try **Restaurante Pantoja,** on the corner of calles Ghandi and 16 de Septiembre (✆ **983/832-3957**), 2 blocks east of the Museum of Maya Culture. It offers a cheap daily special, good green enchiladas, and Yucatecan specialties. It's open Monday to Saturday from 7am to 7pm. To sample excellent *antojitos,* the local supper food, try **El Buen Gusto,** on Calzada Veracruz across from the market (no phone). A Chetumal institution, it serves excellent *salbutes* and *panuchos*, tacos, and sandwiches. It's open from the morning until 2pm and again from about 7pm to midnight. Another alternative is next door at **La Ideal,** which many locals hold to be the better of the two supper joints. It has delicious *tacos de pierna* (soft tacos with thinly sliced pork shoulder) and *agua de horchata* (water flavored with rice, vanilla, and toasted pumpkin seed).

Onward from Chetumal

The Maya ruins of Lamanai, in Belize, are an easy day trip if you have transportation (not a rental car). You can explore the Río Bec route (see below) directly west of the city by taking Hwy. 186.

SIDE TRIPS TO MAYA RUINS FROM CHETUMAL

A few miles west of Bacalar and Chetumal begins an area of Maya settlement known to archaeologists as the Río Bec region. A number of ruins stretch from close to Bacalar well into the state of Campeche. They are intriguing for their heavily stylized, lavishly decorated architecture. Excavation has brought restoration, but these cities have not been rebuilt to the same degree as those at Uxmal and Chichén Itzá. Often, buildings were in such great shape that reconstruction was unnecessary.

Nor have these sites been cleared of jungle growth like the marquee ruins mentioned above. Trees and vines grow in profusion around the buildings, giving the sites the feel of lost cities. In visiting them, you can imagine what John Lloyd Stephens and Frederick Catherwood must have felt when they traipsed through the Yucatán in the 19th century. And watch for wildlife; fauna along the entire route is especially rich. You might see a toucan, a grand curassow, or a macaw hanging about, and orioles, egrets, and several birds of prey are extremely common. Gray fox, wild turkey, *tesquintle* (a bushy-tailed, plant-eating rodent), the coatimundi (raccoon kin with long tapered snout and tail), and armadillos inhabit the area in abundance. Several bands of spider and howler monkeys circulate Calakmul and the surrounding jungle.

THE ROUTE Halfway between Bacalar and Chetumal is the well-marked turnoff for Hwy. 186 to Escárcega (about 20km/12 miles from either town). This same road leads to Campeche, Palenque, and Villahermosa. A couple of gas stations are en route, including one in the town of Xpujil. Keep plenty of cash with you, as credit cards are rarely accepted in the area.

> **Opening Hours**
>
> **The archaeological sites along the Río Bec (except for Calakmul, which has its own opening days and hours) are open daily, 8am to 5pm.**

The Río Bec sites are at varying distances off this highway. You pass through a guard station at the border with Campeche State. The guards might ask you to present your travel papers, or they might just ask you where you've been and where you are going, then wave you on. You can divide your sightseeing into several day trips from Bacalar or Chetumal, or you can spend the night in this area and see more the next day. If you get an early start, you can easily visit a few of the sites mentioned here in a day.

Evidence, especially from Becán, shows that these ruins were part of the **trade route** linking the Caribbean coast at Cobá to Edzná and the Gulf Coast, and to Lamanai in Belize and beyond. At one time, a great number of cities thrived here; much of the land was dedicated to cultivation of maize. Today everything lies hidden under a dense jungle, which blankets the land from horizon to horizon.

The following sites are listed in east-to-west order, the way you would see them driving from the Caribbean coast. If you decide to tour these ruins, take the time to visit the Museo de la Cultura Maya (p. 235) in Chetumal first. It will lend context to what you see. If you want a guide to show you the area, you can't do better than **Luis Téllez** (✆ **983/832-3496;** www.mayaruinsandbirds.com) in Chetumal. He's knowledgeable, speaks English, and drives safely and well. Most important, he's acquainted with most of the archaeologists excavating these ruins and stays current with their discoveries. He also knows the local wildlife and guides many tours for birders.

Entry to each site is 31 to 49 pesos. Informational signs at each building are in Mayan, Spanish, and English. Few if any refreshments are available at the ruins, so bring your own water and food. All the principal sites have toilets.

FOOD & LODGING The only town in the Río Bec region offering basic tourist services is Xpujil, which doesn't have much else going for it. Of the basic affordable hotels in town, the best food and lodging is at **Restaurant y Hotel Calakmul** (✆ **983/871-6029**), which rents air-conditioned doubles with TV for 550 to 600 pesos. They have tile floors, private bathrooms with hot water, and good beds. The restaurant is reliable and is open daily from 6am to midnight. Main courses cost 45 to 120 pesos.

If you have a rental car, I'd suggest staying outside of town. Just beyond Xpujil, across from the ruins of the same name, is **Chicanná Eco Village** at Carretera Escárcega Km 296 (✆ **981/811-9191** in Campeche for reservations; www.hoteldelmar.com.mx). Its 42 comfortable, nicely furnished rooms are distributed among several two-story thatched bungalows. They offer doubles or a king-size bed, ceiling fans, a large bathroom, and screened windows. The manicured lawns and flower beds are lovely, with pathways linking the bungalows to one another and to the restaurant and swimming pool. Double rooms go for 1,200 pesos

Río Bec Dreams ★★ (✆ **983/871-6057;** www.riobecdreams.com), 11km (7 miles) west of Xpujil right after you pass through Becán, rents "jungalows"—small, wooden cabins on stilts—scattered through a

Overgrown trees dominate the ruins of Kinichna.

tropical forest. The cabins have good screens and such niceties as curtains, tile counters, hand-painted sinks, porches, and very comfortable beds with mosquito netting (which I didn't need), for 500 pesos a night. Each cabin has a wash basin, but guests share spotless bathrooms (the one unit with its own bathroom, the larger Orchida, costs 575 pesos). Nicer still are the cabañas, which have screened-in porches and private bathrooms; these cabañas rent for 878 pesos to 990 pesos, with a 2-night minimum stay. In the coming year, more of the jungalows will be enlarged and equipped with their own toilets. For all its rusticity, the hotel provides wireless Internet. The Canadian owners have lived in the area a long time and are devoted students of Río Bec architecture who guide tours of the ruins; tours run from short excursions to smaller ruins for 250 pesos to all-day treks through Calakmul for 1,500 pesos. The owners are a wonderful resource for their guests, and good companions around the open-air bar. The restaurant is the best in this region.

Dzibanche & Kinichna

The turnoff, 37km (23 miles) from the highway intersection, is well marked; another 23km (14 miles) brings you to the ruins. Ask about the condition of the road before setting out. These unpaved roads can go from good to bad pretty quickly, but this is an important enough site that road repair is generally kept up. Dzibanché (or Tzibanché) means "place where they write on wood"—obviously not the original name, which remains unknown. It dates from the Classic period (A.D. 300–900) and was occupied for around 700 years. Exploration began here in 1993, and the site opened to the public in late 1994. Scattered over 42 sq. km (16 sq. miles) are several groupings of buildings and plazas; only a small portion is excavated.

Recommended Reading

For a bit of background reading to help you make the most of your visit, try *A Forest of Kings: The Untold Story of the Ancient Maya,* by Linda Schele and David Freidel; *The Blood of Kings: Dynasty and Ritual in Maya Art,* by Linda Schele and Mary Ellen Miller; and *The Maya Cosmos,* by David Freidel and Linda Schele. The best companion book to have is Joyce Kelly's *An Archaeological Guide to Mexico's Yucatán Peninsula,* even though it lacks historical and cultural information, and many sites have expanded since it was written.

TEMPLES & PLAZAS Two large adjoining plazas have been cleared. The most important structure yet excavated is the **Temple of the Owl** in the main plaza, Plaza Xibalba. Archaeologists found a stairway descending from the top of the structure and deep into the pyramid to a burial chamber (not open to visitors), where they uncovered some beautiful polychromatic lidded vessels, one of which has an owl painted on the top handle with its wings spreading onto the lid. White owls were messengers of the underworld gods of the Maya religion. Also found here were the remains of a sacrificial victim and what appear to be the remains of a Maya queen, which is unique in Maya archaeology.

Opposite the Temple of the Owl is the **Temple of the Cormorant,** named after the bird depicted on a polychromed drinking vessel found here. Archaeologists also found evidence here of an interior tomb similar to the one in the Temple of the Owl, but excavations have not yet begun. Other magnificently preserved pottery pieces found during excavations include an incense burner with an almost three-dimensional figure of the diving god attached to the outside, and another incense burner with an elaborately dressed representation of the god Itzamná attached.

Situated all by itself is **Structure VI,** a miniature rendition of Teotihuacán's style of *tablero* and *talud* architecture. Each step of the pyramid is made of a *talud* (sloping surface) crowned by a *tablero* (vertical stone facing). Teotihuacán was near present-day Mexico City, but its influence stretched as far as Guatemala. At the top of the pyramid, a doorway with a wooden lintel is still intact after centuries of weathering. This detail gave the site its name. Date glyphs for the year A.D. 733 are carved into the wood.

Another nearby city, **Kinichná** (Kee-neech-*nah*) is about 2.5km (1½ miles) north. The road leading there becomes questionable during the rainy season, but an Olmec-style jade figure was found there. It has a large acropolis with five buildings on three levels, which have been restored and are in good condition. Fragments of the original stucco are visible.

Kohunlich ★

Kohunlich (Koh-*hoon*-leech), 42km (26 miles) from the turnoff for Hwy. 186, dates from around A.D. 100 to 900. Turn left off the road, and the entrance is 9km (5½ miles) farther. Enter the grand, parklike site, cross a large, shady ceremonial area flanked by four large, conserved pyramids, continue walking straight ahead.

Just beyond this grouping you'll come to Kohunlich's famous **Pyramid of the Masks** under a thatched covering. These enormous plaster faces on the facade date from around A.D. 500. Each elongated face wears a headdress with a mask on its crest and a mask on the chin piece—essentially masks within masks.

An enormous plaster face from Kohunlich's famous Pyramid of the Masks.

The carving on the pupils suggests a solar connection, possibly with the night sun that illuminated the underworld. This may mean that the person had shamanic vision. It's speculated that masks covered much of the facade of this building, which was built in the Río Bec style with rounded corners, a false stairway, and a false temple on the top. At least one theory holds that the masks are a composite of several rulers at Kohunlich.

In the buildings immediately to the left after you enter the site, recent excavations uncovered two intact pre-Hispanic skeletons and five decapitated heads that were probably used in a ceremonial ritual. To the right, follow the shady path through the jungle to another recently excavated plaza. The fine architecture of the rooms and the high quality of pottery found there suggests this complex housed priests or rulers. Scholars believe overpopulation led to the decline of Kohunlich.

Xpujil

Xpujil (Eesh-poo-*heel;* also spelled Xpuhil), meaning either "cattail" or "forest of kapok trees," flourished between A.D. 400 and 900. This small, well-preserved site is easy to get to; look for a blue sign on the highway pointing to the right. The entrance is just off the highway. After buying a ticket, you have to walk 180m (590 ft.) to the main structure. Along the path are some *chechén* trees, recognizable by their blotchy bark. Don't touch; they are poisonous and a stick from one will provoke blisters. On the right, you'll see a platform supporting a restored two-story building with a central staircase on the eastern side. Remnants of a decorative molding and two galleries are connected by a doorway. About 90m (295 ft.) farther you come to **Structure I,** the site's main structure—a rectangular ceremonial platform 2m (6½ ft.) high and 50m (164 ft.) long supporting the palace, decorated with three tall towers shaped like miniature versions of the pyramids in Tikal, Guatemala. These towers are purely decorative, with false stairways and temples that are too small to serve as such. The effect is beautiful. The main body of the building holds 12 rooms, which are now in ruins.

Becán ★★★

Becán (Beh-*kahn*) is about 7km (4½ miles) beyond Xpujil, visible on the right side of the highway. Becán means "moat filled by water," and, in fact, it was protected by a moat spanned by seven bridges. The extensive site dates from the early Classic to the late post-Classic (600 B.C.–A.D. 1200) period. Although it was abandoned by A.D. 850, ceramic remains indicate that there may have been a population resurgence between 900 and 1000, and it was still used as a ceremonial site as late as 1200. Becán was an administrative and ceremonial center with political sway over at least seven other cities in the area, including Chicanná, Hormiguero, and Payán.

The first plaza group you see after you enter was the center for grand ceremonies. From the highway, you can see the back of **Structure I,** a pyramid with two temples on top. Beyond and in between the two temples you can see the Temple atop **Structure IV,** which is opposite Structure I. When the high priest appeared exiting the mouth of the earth monster in the center of this temple (which he reached by way of a hidden side stairway that's now partially exposed), he would have been visible from well beyond the immediate plaza. It's thought that commoners had to watch ceremonies from outside the plaza—thus the site's position was for good viewing purposes. The back of Structure IV is believed to have been a civic plaza where rulers sat on stone benches. The second plaza group dates from around A.D. 850 and has perfect twin towers on top. Under the platform supporting the towers are 10 rooms that are thought to be related to Xibalba (Shee-*bahl*-bah), the underworld. Hurricane Isidore damaged them, and they are still closed. Earth-monster faces probably covered this building (and appeared on other buildings as well). Remains of at least one ball court have been

The ruins of Xpujil.

unearthed. Next to the ball court is a well-preserved figure in an elaborate headdress behind glass. He was excavated not far from where he is now displayed. The markings are well defined, displaying a host of details.

Chicanná

Slightly over 1.5km (1 mile) beyond Becán, on the left side of the highway, is Chicanná, which means "house of the mouth of snakes." Trees loaded with bromeliads shade the central square surrounded by five buildings. **Structure II,** the site's outstanding building, features a monster-mouth doorway and an ornate stone facade with more superimposed masks. As you enter the mouth of the earth monster, note that you are walking on a platform configured as the open jaw of the monster with stone teeth on both sides. Again you find a lovely example of an elongated building with ornamental miniature pyramids on each end.

Calakmul ★★★

This area is both a massive Maya archaeological zone, with at least 60 sites, and a 70,000-hectare (172,900-acre) rainforest designated in 1989 as the Calakmul Biosphere Reserve, including territory in both Mexico and Guatemala. The best way to see Calakmul is to spend the night at Xpujil or Chicanná and leave early in the morning for Calakmul. If you're the first to drive down the narrow access road to the ruins (1½ hr. from the highway), you'll probably see plenty of wildlife. On my last trip to the ruins, I saw two groups of spider monkeys swinging through the trees on the outskirts of the city and a group of howler monkeys sleeping in the trees in front of Structure II. I also saw a couple of animals that I couldn't identify, and heard the growl of a jungle cat that I wasn't able to see.

The site is open Tuesday to Sunday from 7am to 5pm, but it gets so wet during the rainy season from June to October that it's best not to go during that time.

The ruins of Becán.

Note the monster-mouth doorway of Structure II from the ruins of Chicanná.

THE ARCHAEOLOGICAL ZONE Since 1982, archaeologists have been excavating the ruins of Calakmul, which date from 100 B.C. to A.D. 900. It's the largest of the area's 60 known sites. Nearly 7,000 buildings have been discovered and mapped. At its zenith, at least 60,000 people may have lived around the site, but by the time of the Spanish Conquest in 1519, there were fewer than 1,000 inhabitants. Visitors arrive at a large plaza filled with a forest of trees. You immediately see several stelae; Calakmul contains more of these than any other site, but they are much more weathered and indistinguishable than the stelae of Palenque or Copán in Honduras. On one of them you can see the work of looters who carefully used some sort of stone-cutting saw to slice off the face of the monument. By Structure XIII is a stele of a woman, thought to have been a ruler, that dates from A.D. 652.

Some structures here are built in the Petén style and others in the Río Bec style. **Structure III** must have been the residence of a noble family. Its design is unique and quite lovely; it managed to retain its original form and was never remodeled. Offerings of shells, beads, and polychromed tripod pottery were found inside. **Structure II** is the tallest pyramid in the Yucatán, at 54m (177 ft.). From the top, you can see the outline of the ruins of El Mirador, 50km (31 miles) across the forest in Guatemala. Notice the two stairways that ascend along the sides of the principal face of the pyramid in the upper levels, and how the masks break up the space of the front face.

Temple IV charts the line of the sun from June 21, when it falls on the left (north) corner; to September 21 and March 21, when it lines up in the east behind the middle temple on the top of the building; to December 21, when it falls

A Driving Caution

Numerous curves in the road obscure oncoming traffic (what little there is).

A yellow orchid from the Calakmul Biosphere Reserve.

on the right (south) corner. Numerous jade pieces, including spectacular masks, were uncovered here, most of which are on display in the Museum of Mayan Culture in Campeche (p. 297). **Structure VII** is largely unexcavated except for the top, where, in 1984, the most outstanding jade mask yet to be found at Calakmul was uncovered. In their book *A Forest of Kings,* Linda Schele and David Freidel tell of wars among the Calakmul, Tikal, and Naranjo (the latter two in Guatemala), and how Ah-Cacaw, king of Tikal (120km/74 miles south of Calakmul), captured King Jaguar-Paw in A.D. 695 and later Lord Ox-Ha-Te Ixil Ahau, both of Calakmul.

CALAKMUL BIOSPHERE RESERVE Set aside in 1989, this is the peninsula's only high forest, a rainforest that annually records as much as 5m (16 ft.) of rain. The canopy of the trees is higher here than in the forest of Quintana Roo. It lies very close to the border with Guatemala, but, of course, there is no way to get there. Among the plants are cactus, epiphytes, and orchids. Endangered animals include the white-lipped peccary, jaguar, and puma. So far, more than 250 species of birds have been recorded. At present, no overnight stay or camping is permitted. If you want a tour of a small part of the forest and you speak Spanish, you can inquire for a guide at one of the two nearby *ejidos* (cooperatives). Some old local *chicleros* (the men who tap sapodilla trees for their gum) have expert knowledge of flora and fauna and can take you on a couple of trails.

The turnoff on the left for Calakmul is located 53km (33 miles) from Xpujil, just before the village of Conhuas. There's a guard station there where you pay 40 pesos per car. From the turnoff, it's an hour's drive on a paved one-lane-road. Admission to the site is 41 pesos.

It's advisable to take with you some food and drink and, of course, bug spray.

Balamkú ★★

Balamkú (Bah-lahm-*koo*) is easy to reach and worth the visit. A couple of buildings in the complex were so well preserved that they required almost no reconstruction. Inside are three impressive figures of men sitting in the gaping maws of crocodiles and toads as they descend into the underworld. The concept behind this building, with its molded stucco facade, is life and death. On the head of each stucco figure are the eyes, nose, and mouth of a jaguar figure, followed by the full face of the human figure, then a neck formed by the eyes and nose of another jaguar, and an Olmec-like face on the stomach, with its neck ringed by a necklace. These figures were saved from looters who managed to get away with a fourth one. Now they're under the protection of a caretaker, who keeps the room under lock and key. If you speak Spanish, you can get the caretaker to explain something of the figures and their complex symbolism. A beautiful courtyard and another set of buildings are adjacent to the main group.

Elaborate carvings from Balamkú.

8

MÉRIDA, THE MAYA INTERIOR & CHICHÉN ITZÁ

by Christine Delsol

Long before Cancún was a glimmer in some computer programmer's eye, all roads led to **Mérida.** The great "White City"—still the region's cultural heart and soul—presided over a peninsula rich with legacies of colliding civilizations. The trove of ancient cities left behind by that cataclysm has enticed visitors ever since New York writer John Lloyd Stephens and illustrator Frederick Catherwood ventured south to investigate rumors of lost cities in the jungle.

The splendors of the ancient Maya world are still the Yucatán's biggest draw beyond the Caribbean coast. **Chichén Itzá,** every bit as wondrous as its coronation as a "new" Wonder of the World suggests, has many worthy companions. **Uxmal, Edzná, Cobá, Calakmul** and several smaller ancient cities are all infused with an ancient spirit that only tenuously survives Chichén Itzá's celebrity status.

The thoughtful visitor, though, will soon learn the Maya heartland is far more than a living museum revealing an extraordinary culture— it is the evolution of that civilization. Whether you stay in a restored hacienda and indulge in a massage from the granddaughter of a Maya shaman, attend Mérida's weekly *Vaquería* with traditional Yucatecan cowboy music and dancing, or visit a village whose people live in thatch-roof huts and still speak the Yucatec Mayan language, you'll find past and present converging as they do nowhere else.

The best way to see the Yucatán is by car. The terrain is flat, highways are well-maintained and hypnotically straight, and traffic beyond the cities is light. Secondary roads are narrow and sometimes rough, though a flurry of road projects has improved a good percentage of them in the past couple of years. Add about 30 percent to the time you think any particular trip should take—not only will you miss a lot by speeding through, you will also run afoul of innumerable *topes* (*toh*-pehs), or speed bumps. These might be a rope across the road, a concrete island, or they might be a row of metal half spheres that will eat your undercarriage for breakfast (if they don't flip your car over). Most have warning signs, but sometimes they appear out of nowhere—or the signs might appear but the *topes* do not. You *will* slow down, either to ease over the *topes* or to ask around for a repair shop.

Renting a car (p. 67) isn't cheap, but some promotional deals are available, especially in low season. And some of your most memorable experiences will be in places not easily reached by bus. Plenty of buses serve major towns and ruins, but service to smaller towns and ruins, and the haciendas, is sparse. Autobuses del Oriente (ADO) controls most of the first-class bus service and does a good job with the major destinations. Second-class buses go to some out-of-the-way places, but they make countless stops and often aren't air-conditioned; they are best for short distances. If you don't want to rent a car, a few tour operators transport small groups to more remote ruins, cenotes, and villages. Alternatively, hiring a taxi for a half or full day can be less expensive than renting a car.

FACING PAGE: **The main square in Valladolid.**

The Yucatán is ***tierra caliente*** (the hot lands); always travel with a hat, sun block, mosquito repellent, and water. November to February are the coolest months, April to June the hottest. Thunderstorms moderate temperatures from July to October. More tourists visit the interior in winter, but the high season/low season distinction is far less pronounced than on the Caribbean coast.

Between tramping through ruins, swimming in the cool, clear waters of a cenote (natural underground pools), staking out your own private beach, or spotting flamingos in an estuary, you won't lack for diversions. But the greatest pleasure of all is slowing down, lazing in the town square, eating regional food prepared with centuries-old techniques, and making conversation with the proud, gentle people whose ancestors created the ancient empires we admire today.

MÉRIDA: GATEWAY TO THE MAYA HEARTLAND ★★★

1,440km (893 miles) E of Mexico City; 320km (198 miles) W of Cancún

Mérida, capital of the state of Yucatán, has been the peninsula's lodestar since the Spanish Conquest, yet many visitors treat it merely as a base camp for forays to the surrounding ruins. Though "The White City" (named after its limestone buildings) endures the traffic and noise common to many of Mexico's colonial cities, its vibrancy, its eye-popping architecture, and its kind, dignified people are what you remember. The heady brew of ancient and modern is at its most piquant in the bustling, genial historic center, and the Meridanos' celebratory proclivities are infectious. This is also the best place to shop for regional specialties, such as hammocks, Panama hats, *guayabera* shirts, and embroidered *huipiles,* the colorful native blouses. Expatriates have been flocking to the city in recent years,

the best websites FOR THE YUCATÁN

- **Yucatán Today: www.yucatantoday.com** One of the least commercial privately run sites, with cultural notes; detailed maps; transportation advice; history; and lists of hotels, restaurants, and events in Yucatán state and beyond, by the editors of an enormously helpful monthly tourist magazine.
- **Yucatán Living: www.yucatanliving.com** Destination and cultural articles, and in-depth reviews of restaurants and attractions, are written by and for expatriates but also give visitors an inside view on life in the Yucatán, with an emphasis on Mérida.
- **TravelYucatan.com** Loaded with practical tips and detailed articles by travelers and residents, quarterly news roundups, with such useful graphics as authorized taxi cabs and dive-site maps rather than just glamour shots. You might not notice that it's also a booking site until you go to the "accommodations" link.
- **Yucatán Travel Guide: www.mayayucatan.com** Yucatán's Ministry of Tourism site, which has an update section and good general information on the state's destinations.

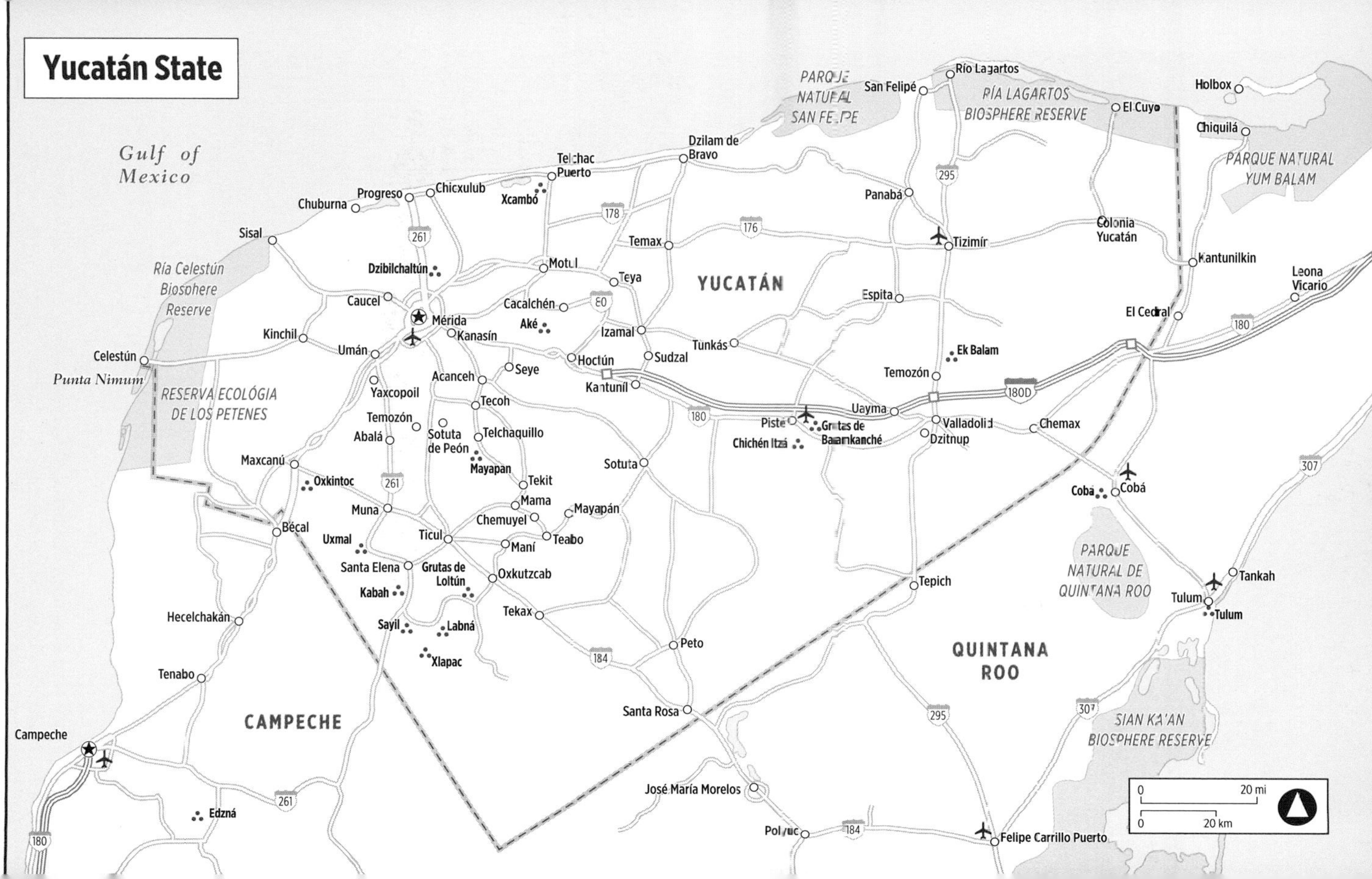
Yucatán State
Gulf of Mexico
Ría Celestún Biosphere Reserve
Reserva Ecológia de los Petenes
Punta Nimum
Celestún
Sisal
Chuburna
Progreso
Chicxulub
Telchac Puerto
Xcambó
Dzilam de Bravo
Parque Natural San Felipe
San Felipé
Río Lagartos
Ría Lagartos Biosphere Reserve
El Cuyo
Holbox
Chiquilá
Parque Natural Yum Balam
Dzibilchaltún
Mérida
Caucel
Kinchil
Umán
Kanasín
Motul
Teya
Cacalchén
Aké
Izamal
Temax
Panabá
Tizimír
Colonia Yucatán
Kantunilkin
YUCATÁN
Espita
Tunkás
Sudzal
Hoctún
Kantunil
Seye
Acanceh
Tecoh
Yaxcopoil
Temozón
Abalá
Sotuta de Peón
Telchaquillo
Mayapan
Maxcanú
Oxkintoc
Muna
Tekit
Mama
Chemuyel
Mayapán
Teabo
Ticul
Maní
Bécal
Uxmal
Santa Elena
Grutas de Loltún
Oxkutzcab
Kabah
Tekax
Sayil
Labná
Xlapac
Hecelchakán
Tenabo
CAMPECHE
Campeche
Edzná
Sotuta
Peto
Santa Rosa
José María Morelos
Polyuc
Piste
Chichén Itzá
Grutas de Balankanché
Uayma
Temozón
Ek Balam
Valladolid
Dzitnup
Chemax
El Cedral
Leona Vicario
Tepich
Cobá
Parque Natural de Quintana Roo
QUINTANA ROO
Tulum
Tankah
Sian Ka'an Biosphere Reserve
Felipe Carrillo Puerto
0 20 mi
0 20 km
180
180D
176
178
261
295
307
184
80

Mérida's busy Plaza Grande.

not only retirees but young couples with boundless energy to explore and show off their adopted home. It all adds up to a cultural explosion; you never have to look far to find a festival, concert, theater production or art exhibition. It also has produced a remarkable bounty of bed-and-breakfasts and beautifully restored colonial homes, many of which are rented out for part of the year.

Essentials

GETTING THERE & DEPARTING

BY PLANE **Aeroméxico** (✆ **800/237-6639** in the U.S. or 01-800/021-400 in Mexico; www.aeromexico.com) flies nonstop to and from Miami and Mexico City. **Mexicana** (✆ **01-800/801-2010** in Mexico, or 877/801-2010; www.mexicana.com.mx) flies nonstop to and from Mexico City. **Continental** (✆ **999/946-1888,** -1900; www.continental.com) flies nonstop to and from Houston. (American, Delta, and Alaska also serve Mérida through code shares, usually at significantly higher fares.) **Click** (✆ **01-800/112-5425;** www.mexicana.com), Mexicana's budget airline, provides nonstop service to and from Mexico City and Veracruz. AeroMéxico's regional carrier, **Aerolitoral** (✆ **800/237-6639** in the U.S. or 01-800/021-400 in Mexico; www.aerolitoral.com), flies to and from Mexico City and Villahermosa. **Volaris** (✆ **01-800/122-8000** in Mexico; www.volaris.com.mx) is a discount domestic air carrier that flies to and from Toluca. In 2009, the airline added connecting flights from San Francisco and Los Angeles. Another Mexican budget line, **VivaAerobus** (✆ **01-81/8215-0150;** www.vivaaerobus.com), flies between Monterrey and Mérida and offers connecting flights from Austin and Las Vegas.

BY CAR **Hwy. 180** is the old *carretera federal* (federal highway) between Mérida and Cancún. The trip takes about 6 hours on a good road that passes through many Maya villages. A four-lane divided *cuota,* or *autopista* (toll road) parallels Hwy. 180 and begins at the town of Kantunil, 56km (35 miles) east of Mérida. For a toll of 338 pesos each way, you avoid the tiny villages and their not-so-tiny speed bumps. Coming from the direction of Cancún, Hwy. 180 feeds into Mérida's Calle 65, which passes 1 block south of the main square.

Coming from the south (Campeche or Uxmal), you enter the city on Avenida Itzáes. To get to the town center, turn right on Calle 59 (the first street after the zoo).

A *periférico* (loop road) circles Mérida, making it possible to skirt the city. Directional signs into the city are generally good, but lapping the city on the loop requires vigilance.

BY BUS Mérida is the Yucatán's transportation hub. Of its five bus stations, two offer first-class buses and the other three provide local service to nearby destinations. The larger first-class station, **CAME,** is on Calle 70, between calles 69 and 71 (see "City Layout," below). The ADO bus line and its affiliates operate the station, which is also used by Clase Elite and other long-distance lines. In the row of ticket windows that greets you, all but the last couple to the right sell first-class tickets. The last two sell tickets for ADO's deluxe services. ADO-GL is a small step up from first class, while UNO has superwide seats with lots of leg room. Unless it's a long trip, I go for the bus with the most convenient departure time. Tickets can be purchased in advance; ask the agent for ticket options and departure times for the route you need.

To and from Cancún: You can pick up a bus almost every hour at the CAME for the 3- to 4-hour trip. Some lines also collect passengers at the Fiesta Americana Hotel on Calle 60 at Av. Colón, across from the Hyatt; you can buy a ticket in the hotel's shopping arcade at the **Ticket Bus** agency (which also takes reservations at www.ticketbus.com.mx) or at the Elite ticket agency. Cancún is 4 hours away; a few buses stop in **Valladolid.** If you're downtown, you can purchase tickets from the agency in Pasaje Picheta, a mall next to the Palacio de Gobierno on the main square.

To and from Chichén Itzá: Three buses per day (2½-hr. trip) depart from the CAME. Tour operators in Mérida hotels also offer day trips.

To and from Playa del Carmen, Tulum, and Chetumal: From the CAME, there are at least 10 departures per day for Playa del Carmen (5 hours away), six for Tulum (6 hours), and eight for Chetumal (7 hours).

To and from Campeche: The CAME station has about 40 departures per day. It's a 2½-hour trip.

To and from Palenque and San Cristóbal de las Casas: There are three departures a day from the CAME to San Cristóbal and four to Palenque. Minor thefts have been reported on buses to Palenque, so don't take second-class buses; check your luggage so that it's stowed in the cargo bay; and put your carry-on in the overhead rack, not on the floor.

The main **second-class terminal** is around the corner from the CAME on Calle 69, between calles 68 and 70.

To and from Uxmal: There are four buses per day. (You can also pick up a tour through most hotels or any travel agent or tour operator in town.) ATS offers one daily round-trip Ruta Puuc bus, combining Uxmal with the other sites to the south (Kabah, Sayil, Labná, and Xlapak). It takes all day, stopping for 2 hours at Uxmal and 30 minutes at each of the other sites.

To and from Progreso and Dzibilchaltún: Transportes Auto-Progreso offers service to and from its downtown station at Calle 62 no. 524, between calles 65 and 67. The trip to Progreso takes an hour by second-class bus.

To and from Celestún: Buses depart 10 times a day from the Noreste second-class station on Calle 50 between calles 65 and 67. The trip takes 1½ to 2 hours, depending on how many stops the bus makes. Other destinations include **Izamal** (20 buses a day), Río Lagartos, and Chiquilá (ferry terminal for Isla Holbox).

ORIENTATION

ARRIVING BY PLANE Mérida's airport is 13km (8 miles) from the city center on the southwestern outskirts of town, near the entrance to Hwy. 180. The airport has desks for rental cars, hotel reservations, and tourist information. Taxi tickets to town (150 pesos) are sold outside the airport doors, under the covered walkway.

VISITOR INFORMATION The city tourism offices and state tourism offices have different resources; if you can't get the information you're looking for at one, go to the other. I have better luck with the city's **visitor information office** (✆ **999/942-0000,** ext. 80119), which is on the ground floor of the Ayuntamiento building, facing the main square on Calle 62. Look for a glass door under the arcade. Hours are Monday to Saturday from 8am to 8pm, and Sunday from 8am to 2pm. The staff offers a free walking tour of the area around the main square at 9:30am, Monday through Saturday. The state operates two downtown tourism offices: One in the **Teatro Peón Contreras,** facing Parque de la Madre (✆ **999/924-9290**), and the other on the main plaza, in the **Palacio de Gobierno** (✆ **999/930-3101,** ext. 10001), immediately to the left as you enter. These offices are open daily from 8am

Mérida's grand boulevard, Paseo de Montejo.

to 9pm. It also has information booths at the airport and the CAME bus station.

Keep your eye out for the free monthly magazine *Yucatán Today;* it's packed with information about Mérida and the rest of the region.

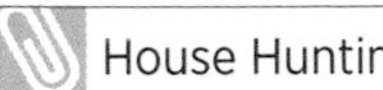

House Hunting

Address numbers bear little relation to a building's physical location, so addresses almost always include cross-streets. In "Calle 60 no. 549 x 71 y 73," for example, the "x" is shorthand for the word *por* (meaning "by"), and *y* means "and." So this address is on Calle 60 between calles 71 and 73. This tidy system disappears outside of downtown, where street numbering gets erratic (to say the least). It's important to know the name of the *colonia* (neighborhood) where you're going. This is the first thing taxi drivers will ask you.

CITY LAYOUT Downtown Mérida's grid layout is typical of the Yucatán: Even-numbered streets run north and south; odd-numbered streets run east and west. The numbering begins on the north and the east sides of town, so if you're walking on an odd-numbered street and the even numbers of the cross-streets are increasing, you are heading west; likewise, if you are on an even-numbered street and the odd-numbered cross-streets are increasing, you are going south. Most downtown streets are one-way.

Mérida's main square is the busy **Plaza Grande,** bordered by calles 60, 61, 62, and 63. Calle 60, the *centro's* (downtown's) central artery, runs in front of the cathedral and it connects the main square with several smaller plazas, some theaters and churches, and the University of Yucatán, just to the north. Handicraft shops, restaurants, and hotels are concentrated here. Around Plaza Mayor are the cathedral, the Palacio de Gobierno (state government building), the Ayuntamiento (town hall), and the Palacio Montejo. The plaza always has a crowd, and it overflows on Sundays, when the surrounding streets are closed for an enormous street fair. (See "Festivals & Events in Mérida," below.) Within a few blocks are several smaller plazas and the bustling market district.

Mérida's most fashionable district is the wide, tree-lined boulevard **Paseo de Montejo** and its surrounding neighborhood. The Paseo de Montejo parallels Calle 60 and begins 7 blocks north and a little east of the main square. Though it has trendy restaurants, modern hotels, bank and airline offices, and a few clubs, the boulevard is mostly known for its stately mansions built during the boom times of the *henequén* industry. Near the Paseo's intersection with Avenida Colón, you'll find the Hyatt and the Fiesta Americana hotels.

GETTING AROUND **By Car** In general, reserve your car in advance from home to get the best weekly rates during high season (Nov–Feb); in low season, renting a car after you reach Mérida usually yields better deals. Local rental companies are competitive and have promotional deals that you can get only if you are there. Make sure you compare apples to apples; ask if the price quote includes the IVA tax and insurance coverage. Practically everybody offers free mileage. For tips on saving money on car rentals, see "Getting There & Getting Around," in chapter 3. Rental cars are generally a little more expensive (unless you find a promotional rate) than similar rentals in the U.S., though less than in Cancún. If your visit will be primarily in

Mérida except for a couple of day trips you'll do better to rent for just a day or two, which also spares you the high cost of Mérida's parking lots. These *estacionamentos* often charge one price for the night and double that if you leave your car for the following day. Many hotels offer free parking, but make sure that includes daytime hours.

By Taxi Taxis are easy to come by and much cheaper than in Cancún, usually 30 to 60 pesos around town.

By Bus City buses are a little tricky to figure out but aren't needed often because almost everything of interest is within walking distance of the main plaza. The most useful buses run between downtown and Paseo de Montejo, which is a bit of a hike from the plaza. Catch an "Itzimná" bus on Calle 59, between calles 56 and 58, to visit points along the boulevard. You can also take a minibus, or *colectivo* that is heading north on Calle 60. Most take you within a couple of blocks of Paseo de Montejo. The *colectivos* or *combis* (usually painted white) line up along the side streets next to the plaza and fan out in several directions from the main plaza along simple routes.

[FastFACTS] MÉRIDA

Area Code The telephone area code is **999.**

Business Hours Generally, businesses are open Monday to Saturday from 10am to 2pm and 4 to 8pm.

Consulates The **American Consulate** is at Calle 60 no. 338-K between calles 29 and 31 (✆ **999/942-5700**), 1 block north of the Hyatt hotel (Col. Alcalá Martín). Office hours are Monday to Friday from 9am to 1pm.

Currency Exchange I prefer *casas de cambio* (currency exchange offices) over banks. Mérida has plenty; one called **Cambios Portales,** Calle 61 no. 500 (✆ **999/923-8709**), is on the north side of the main plaza in the middle of the block. It's open daily from 8:30am to 8:30pm. There are also many ATMs; one is on the south side of the same plaza.

Drugstore Farmacía Yza, Calle 63 no. 502-A, between calles 60 and 62 (✆ **999/924-9510**), on the south side of the plaza, is open 24 hours.

Hospitals The best hospital is **Centro Médico de las Américas,** Calle 54 no. 365 between 33-A and Avenida Pérez Ponce. The main phone number is ✆ **999/926-2611;** for emergencies, call ✆ **999/927-3199.** You can also call the **Cruz Roja (Red Cross)** at ✆ **999/924-9813.**

Internet Access You hardly have to walk more than a couple of blocks to find an Internet access provider; rates hover around 15 pesos per hour. Most hotels provide free Wi-Fi, and since 2007, the city has been installing free Wi-Fi in city parks. The Plaza Grande, Parque San Juan, Parque de las Américas and Parque Zoológico del Centenario are among the parks currently connected.

Police Mérida has a special body of English-speaking police to assist tourists. They patrol the downtown area and Paseo de Montejo, wearing white shirts with a POLICIA TURISTICA patch on the sleeve. Their phone number is ✆ **999/942-0060.**

Post Office The *correo* is near the market at the corner of calles 65 and 56, with its own entrance separate from the new city museum. It's open Monday to Friday from 8am to 7pm, Saturday from 9am to 1pm.

Seasons Mérida has two high seasons, but they aren't as pronounced as on the Caribbean coast. One is in July and August, when Mexicans take their vacations, and the other is between November 15 and Easter Sunday, when Canadians and Americans flock to the Yucatán to escape winter weather.

Weather From November to February, the weather can be pleasantly cool and windy. In other months, it's just hot, especially during the day. Rain can occur any time of year, especially during the rainy season (July–Oct), and usually comes in the form of afternoon tropical showers.

festivals & events IN MÉRIDA

Many Mexican cities offer weekend concerts in parks and plazas, but Mérida surpasses them all by offering performances every day of the week. Unless otherwise indicated, admission is free.

Sunday From 9am to 9pm, the *centro* stages a fair called *Mérida en Domingo* (Mérida on Sunday). The plaza and a section of Calle 60 extending to Parque Santa Lucía close to traffic. Parents stroll with their children, taking in the food and drink booths, the lively little flea market and used-book fair, children's art classes, and educational booths. At 11am, musicians play everything from jazz to classical and folk music in front of the Palacio del Gobierno, while the police orchestra performs Yucatecan tunes in Santa Lucía park. At 11:30am, you'll find bawdy comedy acts at Parque Hidalgo, on Calle 60 at Calle 59. After a midafternoon lull, the plaza fills up again as people walk around and visit with friends. Around 7pm in front of the Ayuntamiento, a large band starts playing mambos, rumbas, and cha-chas with great enthusiasm; you may see 1,000 people dancing in the street. Afterward, folk ballet dancers reenact a typical Yucatecan wedding inside.

Monday At 9pm in front of the *Palacio Municipal,* performers dance and play *Vaquería regional* (traditional cowboy music) to celebrate the Vaquerías feast, which was associated originally with the branding of cattle on the haciendas. Performers include dancers with trays of bottles or filled glasses balanced on their heads—a sight to see.

Tuesday At 9pm in Parque Santiago, Calle 59 at Calle 72, the Municipal Orchestra plays Latin and American big-band music from the 1940s.

Wednesday At 9pm in the Teatro Peón Contreras, Calle 60 at Calle 57, the University of Yucatán Ballet Folklórico presents *Yucatán and Its Roots.* Admission is 50 pesos. Auditorio Olimpio, on the Calle 62 side of the plaza, hosts guitar *trovas* (boleros or ballads) and other live music and theater performances, free of charge.

Thursday At 9pm in Parque Santa Lucía, the Serenata Yucateca presents regional music, dance, and spoken-word performances.

Friday At 9pm in the courtyard of the University of Yucatán, Calle 60 at Calle 57, the University of Yucatán Ballet Folklórico performs typical regional dances from the Yucatán.

Saturday At 8pm in the park at Paseo de Montejo and Calle 47, Noche Mexicana features traditional Mexican music and dance performances with crafts booths and food stands selling great *antojitos* (finger foods), drinks, and ice cream. At 9pm, Calle 60 closes between Plaza Grande and Calle 53 for En El Corazón de Mérida, a festival featuring several live bands joined by stilt walkers, mariachis, and crafts and food stands.

Where to Stay

Mérida soothes the budget, especially if you've come from the Caribbean resorts. Though winter is the most popular time, the stream of visitors is steadier than on the coast, so many hotels don't have high- and low-season rates. That said, promotional rates are more plentiful during low season. Large trade shows can fill the hotels, so reservations are a good idea. Rates quoted here include the 17% tax (always ask if the price includes tax). Most hotels in Mérida offer at least a few air-conditioned rooms, and some also have pools. But many inexpensive places haven't figured out how to provide a comfortable bed; either the mattresses are hard or the bottom sheet is too small to stay tucked in. One last note: Without exception, every hotel in Mérida that doesn't have its own parking has an arrangement with a nearby garage, letting you park for a fee. If you can find a parking space on the street, cars are generally safe from vandalism. Some hotels offer free parking, but sometimes it's free only at night, with a charge incurred during the day.

VERY EXPENSIVE

Hacienda Xcanatún ★★★ This magnificent example of the Yucatán's converted haciendas was built in the mid-18th century at the edge of present-day Mérida and later became one of the region's most important *henequén* (sisal) plantations. Restoration with handcrafted local hardwood, wrought iron, marble, and stone has resuscitated its original luster and then some: The *hacendados* likely did not have capacious bathrooms with double-sized, carved-stone waterfall tubs, and they certainly didn't have Casa de Piedra, one of Mexico's top-rated restaurants, in the machinery house. Fountains and a bridged stream grace the extensive, jungle-like gardens, and the spa's ancient Maya healing techniques use local plants and flowers. The hacienda recently began a program of private guided cultural tours.

Km. 12 Carretera Mérida-Progreso, Mérida, Yuc. ✆ **888/883-3633** in the U.S. and Canada, or 999/930-2140. Fax 999/941-0319. www.xcanatun.com. 18 units. $317–$340 double; $346–$382 deluxe suites; $382–$417 master suites. Rates include breakfast. Ask about Best Available Rate promotion. AE, MC, V. Free parking. No children under 12 without prior arrangement. **Amenities:** Restaurant; 2 bars; concierge; garden; golf privileges at nearby Jack Nicklaus course; 2 outdoor pools; private day-trip program; spa; Wi-Fi on patios, in restaurant, and lobby. *In room:* A/C, hair dryer, minibar, outdoor whirlpool tubs (in suites).

Hotel Indigo Mérida Hacienda Misné ★★ 🎁 The latest addition to the region's corps of hacienda hotels is a rarity: A country estate located in Mérida itself, operated by the family who bought it for a summer home years before it became a hotel in 2007. It's a beauty, with long red-tiled colonnades stretching along vast gardens peppered with ponds and fountains. The family has worked hard to preserve the hacienda's original character while creating luxurious modern rooms behind the traditional exteriors. Some even have private sitting pools. It's about a 15-minute drive from downtown, just off Calle 65 (the road to and from Cancún) about a half kilometer (less than half a mile) from the *periférico*. The neighborhood's confounding street numbering system makes it tricky to find the first time, but it's easy enough after that—especially since Calle 6B has a tree in the middle of the road at Calle 65.

Calle 19 no. 172 (at Calle 6B), Fracc. Misné 1, 97173 Mérida, Yuc. ✆ **877/846-3446** in the U.S. and Canada, or 999/940-7150. Fax 999/940-7160. www.haciendamisne.com.mx. 50 units. $240 double, $273 executive, $316 junior suite, $343 deluxe. See website for promotional rates. AE, DC, DISC, MC, V. Free parking. **Amenities:** Restaurant; bar; concierge; library; 2 outdoor pools; room service; spa. *In room:* A/C, TV, CD and MP3 players, hair dryer, Wi-Fi.

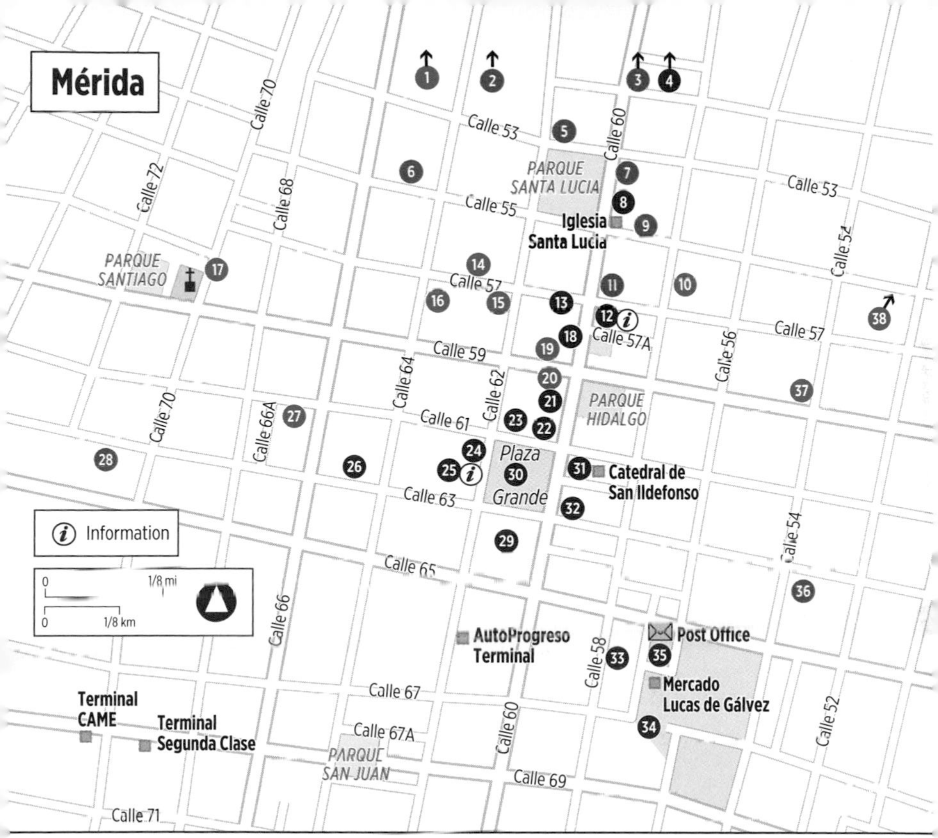

Mérida
Calle 53
Calle 55
Calle 57
Calle 57A
Calle 59
Calle 61
Calle 63
Calle 65
Calle 67
Calle 67A
Calle 69
Calle 71
Calle 52
Calle 54
Calle 56
Calle 58
Calle 60
Calle 62
Calle 64
Calle 66
Calle 66A
Calle 68
Calle 70
Calle 72
PARQUE SANTA LUCIA
Iglesia Santa Lucia
PARQUE SANTIAGO
PARQUE HIDALGO
Plaza Grande
Catedral de San Ildefonso
Information
0 1/8 mi
0 1/8 km
AutoProgreso Terminal
Post Office
Mercado Lucas de Gálvez
Terminal CAME
Terminal Segunda Clase
PARQUE SAN JUAN

Gulf of Mexico
Mérida
Cancún
YUCATÁN
YUCATÁN PENINSULA
CAMPECHE
QUINTANA ROO
Caribbean Sea

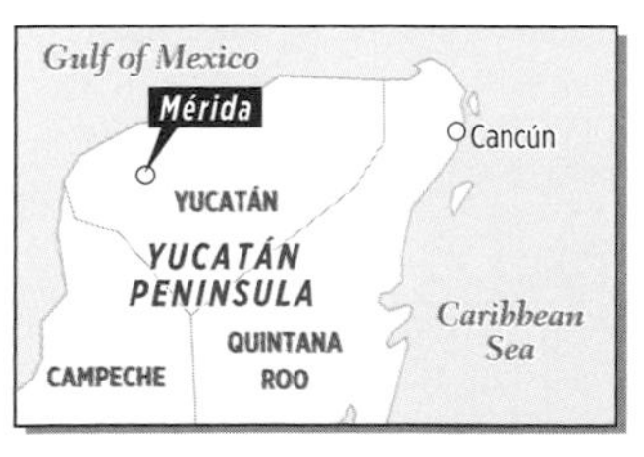

ATTRACTIONS

Bazaar de Artesanías **34**
Casa del Alguacil **23**
Casa de las Artesanías **26**
Cathedral **31**
Centro Cultural Olimpo **24**
Iglesia de Jesús **18**
Iglesia de Santa Lucía **8**
Museo de Arte Contemporáneo **32**
Museo de la Ciudad **35**
Palacio Cantón/Museo Regional de Antropología **4**
Palacio de Gobierno **22**
Palacio Montejo **29**
Palacio Municipal **25**
Plaza Mayor Grande **30**
Portal de Granos **33**
Teatro Ayala **21**
Teatro Peón Contreras **12**
Universidad de Yucatán **13**

ACCOMMODATIONS

Casa Álvarez **5**
Casa del Balam **11**
Casa Santiago **28**
Fiesta Americana Mérida **3**
Hotel Dolores Alba **36**
Hotel Maison Lafitte **7**
Hotel Marionetas **2**
Hotel MedioMundo **6**
Luz en Yucatán **9**

Dining

Alberto's Continental **16**
Amaro **19**
Café Alameda **10**
Casa de Frida **27**
Eladio's **37**
El Portico del Peregrino **14**
La Chaya Maya **15**
La Flor de Santiago **17**
Restaurante Kantún **1**
Restaurante Los Almendros **38**
Vito Corleone **20**

EXPENSIVE

Casa del Balam ★★★ I could happily spend all my nights in Mérida at this onetime colonial mansion, converted in 1968. Even with a king-size bed and massive wooden furniture, suites in the original owners' bedrooms have space enough to do cartwheels. My favorite overlooks Calle 60, with heavy cedar doors opening onto the street and windows onto the lush courtyard dining room, where piano strains waft up at times. These rooms still feel more like a colonial mansion than a hotel, but with the added comforts of air-conditioning and double-paned windows. Standard rooms in the newer annex are more modest but supremely comfortable, with tile floors and wrought-iron headboards honoring the colonial atmosphere. The plaza is just 2 blocks away, and staff members treat you like their favorite niece or nephew.

Calle 60 no. 488 at Calle 57, 97000 Mérida, Yuc. ✆ **800/624-8451** U.S. & Canada, or 999/924-8844. www.casadelbalam.com. 51 units. $85–$117 double, $95–$146 honeymoon, $110–$187 master suites. AE, DISC, MC, V. Free parking. **Amenities:** Restaurant; bar; babysitting; concierge; golf club access; outdoor pool; room service; spa services; Wi-Fi. *In room:* A/C, TV, hair dryer, minibar.

Fiesta Americana Mérida This six-story hotel on Paseo de Montejo, built in the fin-de-siècle style of the old mansions along the boulevard, is the grand dame of Mérida's luxury chain hotels. Guest rooms around the soaring lobby face outward and have views of one of the avenues. Rooms are comfortable and large, with innocuous modern furnishings and decorations in light, tropical colors. The floors are tile and the bathrooms large and well equipped. Except for the pool area's noisy air-conditioners, common areas are stunning, from the stained-glass ceiling in the lobby to the luxurious spa and the tony ground-floor shopping center. The hotel was built with local materials and at least a nod to Mexican design. I prefer it to the cookie-cutter Hyatt across the street—the service is more attentive, too.

Av. Colón 451, corner of Paseo Montejo, 92127 Mérida, Yuc. ✆ **800/343-7821** in the U.S. and Canada, or 999/942-1111. Fax 999/942-1112. www.fiestaamericana.com.mx. 350 units. $120–$135 double; $163 executive level; $227 junior suite. AE, DC, MC, V. Free secure parking. **Amenities:** 2 restaurants; bar; babysitting; children's programs; concierge; executive-level rooms; health club w/saunas, men's steam room; unisex whirlpool; midsize outdoor pool; room service; tennis court. *In room:* A/C, TV w/pay movies, hair dryer, Internet, minibar.

Hotel Marionetas ★ This quiet, attractive B&B, 6 blocks north of the main square, has a comforting feel. Sofi (Macedonian) and Daniel (Argentinean) are engaging, interesting people and attentive innkeepers who have created a lovely space with common areas in front, rooms in back, and a lush garden/pool area in between. Each room is different, but all have handmade tile floors, liberal use of bold but not overbearing color, and large, colonial-style windows and doors.

Calle 49 no. 516 (btw. calles 62 and 64), 97000 Mérida, Yuc. ✆ **999/928-3377.** www.hotelmarionetas.com. 8 units. $100–$120 double, $130–$170 suite. Rates include full breakfast. 2-night minimum stay. MC, V. Free secure parking for compact cars. No children under 10. **Amenities:** Small outdoor pool; smoke-free rooms. *In room:* A/C, TV, fridge, hair dryer, Wi-Fi.

MODERATE

Casa Santiago ★★★ This B&B, whose four recently remodeled guest rooms open off the wide central corridor of a lovely colonial home, is an absolute pleasure. With the gregarious manager, Vince, living on-site, it offers an ideal blend of comfort and privacy, traditional detail, and modern style. Casa Santiago is part of a compound that includes Casa Feliz, whose two large, newly restored rooms are available individually when the entire house isn't rented, and Casa Navidad, with one more room. Each room has its own distinct theme, and guests in one house may use either pool or garden. All have the original pasta tile floors (made in Mérida for centuries with a technology brought over from Spain), handmade furniture, and some of the most comfortable mattresses in Mexico or anywhere else. Its Parque Santiago neighborhood is 5 easy blocks from the main plaza. Guests have use of the house's immaculate, modern kitchen.

Calle 63 no. 562 (btw. calles 70 and 72), 97000 Mérida, Yuc. ✆ **314/266-1888** U.S. & Canada, or **999/162-9528**. www.casasantiago.net. 7 units. $59–$125 double. Rates include full breakfast. No credit cards (Paypal for deposits). Limited free parking. No children under 14. **Amenities:** 2 outdoor pools; common kitchen; phone for local calls. *In room:* A/C, Wi-Fi.

Hotel Maison Lafitte ★ This newish three-story hotel has modern, attractive rooms with good air-conditioning, and tropical touches such as wooden window louvers and light furniture with caned backs and seats. Rooms are medium to large, with midsize bathrooms that have great showers and good lighting. Most come with either two doubles or a king-size bed. Rooms are quiet and overlook a pretty little garden with a fountain, though a few don't have windows. The location is excellent.

Calle 60 no. 472 (btw. calles 53 and 55), 97000 Mérida, Yuc. ✆ **800/538-6802** in the U.S. and Canada, or 999/928-1243. Fax 999/923-9159. www.maisonlafitte.com.mx. 30 units. 896 pesos, double. Rates include full breakfast. AE, MC, V. Free limited secure parking for compact cars. **Amenities:** Restaurant; bar; small outdoor pool; room service. *In room:* A/C, TV, hair dryer, minibar, Wi-Fi.

Hotel MedioMundo ★ Bright colors and lush gardens distinguish this quiet courtyard hotel, well located 3 blocks north of the main plaza. The simple, beautiful rooms have their original tile floors. The English-speaking owners, Nicole and Nelson, have invested their money in the right places, going for pillow-top mattresses, good lighting, quiet air-conditioning, lots of space, and good bathrooms with strong showers. What they didn't invest in were TVs, which adds to the serenity. The eight rooms with air-conditioning cost $10 more, but all units have windows with good screens and get ample ventilation. A generous breakfast is served in one of the two attractive courtyards.

Calle 55 no. 533 (btw. calles 64 and 66), 97000 Mérida, Yuc. ✆/fax **999/924-5472.** www.hotelmediomundo.com. 12 units. $75–$90 double. MC, V. Limited street parking. No children under 8. **Amenities:** Small outdoor pool; smoke-free rooms; Wi-Fi in public areas. *In room:* A/C (in some), no phone.

Luz en Yucatán ★★★ Behind a deceptively plain wall next to Santa Lucia Church, this inn offers a dizzying variety of rooms, suites, studios, and apartments in the main building (rumored to have been Santa Lucia's convent) and tucked into the garden around the pool. Every unit is different, thoughtfully decorated with Mexican arts and crafts, and the place is full of nooks and crannies for visiting or lounging. A large kitchen and dining room that seats 12 at a beautiful wooden table is available for guests in rooms without kitchens. The beds are among the best in Yucatán. The amiable and knowledgeable manager, who lives on site, delights in taking guests under his wing. Oh, and did we mention the free bar cart?

haciendas & **HOTELS**

During the colonial period, **haciendas** in the Yucatán were isolated, self-sufficient fiefdoms. Mostly they produced foodstuffs—enough for the needs of the owners and peasants, plus a little extra that the owners could sell for a small sum in the city. The owners, though sometimes politically powerful, were never rich.

This changed in the 19th century, when the expanding world market created high demand for *henequén*—more commonly known in the U.S. as sisal—an agave cactus fiber that was used to bale hay. Haciendas shifted to *henequén* production *en masse,* and the owners became wealthy as prices and profits kept climbing through the end of the century and into the 20th. Then came the bust. Throughout the 1920s, prices and demand fell, and no other commodity could replace sisal. The haciendas entered a long decline, but by then, *henequén* cultivation and processing had become part of local culture.

Visiting a hacienda is a way to see and understand what the golden age was like. **Sotuta de Peón** (p. 273) has been refurbished and operates much as in the old days—a living museum involving an entire community. At another, **Yaxcopoil** (p. 279), you can wander about the shell of a once-bustling estate and take in the faded splendor.

Today another boom of sorts has brought haciendas back, this time as hotels, retreats, and country residences. The hotels convey an air of the past—elegant gateways, thick walls, open arches, and high ceilings—and extravagant suites and personal service genuinely make a guest feel like lord and master. What I find most striking when visiting haciendas is the contrast between their domains and the world outside. They are little islands of order and tranquillity in a sea of chaos.

Six of the region's hacienda hotels are pure luxury. The most opulent is La **Hacienda Xcanatún ★★★** (p. 256) on the outskirts of Mérida, off the highway to Progreso.

Calle 55 no. 499 (btw. calles 60 and 58), 97000 Mérida, Yuc. ✆/fax **999/924-0035.** www.luzenyucatan.com. 15 units. $50–$75 double, $60–$70 studio with kitchen, $70–$90 apartment; weekly and monthly discounts. No credit cards. Discounted parking in secure lot $5 a day. **Amenities:** Outdoor pool; communal kitchen and dining room; Wi,-Fi. *In room:* A/C, TV, fridge.

INEXPENSIVE

Casa Alvarez Guest House ★ Many guests come to this inn, 4blocks from the plaza, for extended stays with the kind and hospitable Enrique and Miriam Álvarez. Each spacious room is different, all featuring light but vivid colors and a variety of wooden, iron, and painted headboards. Larger rooms have air-conditioning and command the higher prices. The large eat-in kitchen where guests may prepare their own meals is stocked with coffee, tea, spices, and sometimes breakfast food and invariably becomes a social center. The owners go out of their way to keep children happy.

Calle 62 no. 448 at Calle 53, 97000 Mérida, Yuc. ✆ **999/924-3060.** www.casaalvarezguesthouse.com. 8 units. 400–550 pesos. No credit cards. Free parking. **Amenities:** Kitchen for guests' use; Wi-Fi in public areas and some rooms.

Hotel Dolores Alba Cheerful, comfortable rooms offer respite from a busy and not particularly pleasant street 3½ blocks from the main square. It's a good

Four more luxury hotels are owned by Roberto Hernández, one of Mexico's richest men, and are affiliated with Starwood Hotels (✆ **800/325-3589** in the U.S. and Canada; www.luxury collection.com). The owner has taken great pains to restore all four haciendas to their original condition, and they are quite beautiful. **Temozón** (p. 261), off the highway to Uxmal, is the most magnificent. **Uayamón ★★★**, located between the colonial city of Campeche and the ruins of Edzná, is perhaps the most romantic, with its exterior preserved in a state of arrested decay. **Hacienda San José Cholul ★** is east of Mérida toward Izamal, and picturesque **Santa Rosa** lies southwest of Mérida, near the town of Maxcanú. Packages are available for staying at more than one of these haciendas. All offer personal service, activities, and spas.

The newest luxury hotel, **Hacienda Misné ★★** (p. 256), is within Mérida city limits and is run by the family who once used it as a summer home.

Several haciendas offer more affordable lodging. Between Mérida and Campeche, just off the highway, **Hacienda Blanca Flor** (✆ **999/925-8042;** www.blancaflor.com.mx), is the only converted hotel that still operates as a hacienda, producing most of the food served there. On the western outskirts of Mérida on the highway to Cancún is **Hacienda San Pedro Nohpat** (✆ **999/988-0542;** www.hacienda holidays.com). It retains only the land immediately surrounding the residence, but its large, comfortable rooms, attractive garden, and pool area are a bargain.

Two more haciendas can be leased by small groups for retreats and vacations: **Hacienda Petac** (✆ **800/225-4255** in the U.S.; www.haciendapetac.com) and **Hacienda San Antonio** (✆ **999/910-6144;** www.haciendasan antonio.com.mx). Both have beautiful rooms, common areas, and grounds.

deal for an inviting swimming pool, good air-conditioning, and free parking. The newer three-story section (with elevator) surrounding the courtyard offers spacious, more stylish rooms with good-size bathrooms. Beds (two doubles or one double and one twin) have supportive mattresses, usually in a combination of one medium-firm and one medium-soft. All rooms have windows or balconies looking over the pool. An old mango tree shades the front courtyard. The older rooms in this section are decorated with local crafts and have small bathrooms. The family that owns the Hotel Dolores Alba outside Chichén Itzá manages this hotel; you can make reservations at one hotel for the other.

Calle 63 no. 464 (btw. calles 52 and 54), 97000 Mérida, Yuc. ✆ **999/928-5650.** Fax 999/928-3163. www.doloresalba.com. 100 units. 475 pesos double. Internet specials available. MC, V (with 8% surcharge). Free guarded parking. **Amenities:** Restaurant; bar; outdoor pool; room service. *In room:* A/C, TV.

Where to Stay Outside of Mérida

Hacienda Temozón ★★★ This magnificent 17-century estancia presides over 37 hectares (91 acres) of subtropical gardens and cenotes, 39km (24 miles) from Mérida. Built in 1655 by Don Diego de Mendoza, Temozón was the region's most productive livestock estancia in the early 18th century, then the top sisal producer in the late 1800s. Meticulously restored in 1997, it's now a Starwood property employing local workers and using organic produce from nearby farms in the restaurant. Spacious Spanish colonial–style rooms have 5.5m (18-ft.) ceilings with exposed rafters, fans, and thick whitewashed walls; Spanish-tile floors and baths; hammocks positioned to catch natural breezes; dark, tropical hardwood furniture; and large, plush beds with white linens adorned daily with fresh flowers. Suites have tubs, private terraces, and plunge pools. The Casa del Patrón suite has accommodated many global heads of state.

KM 182 Carretera Merida-Uxmal, 97825 Temozon Sur, Yuc. ✆ **888-625-5144** or 999/923-8089. www.haciendasmexico.com/temozon. Fax 999/923-7963. 28 units. $325 double; $405 junior suite; $480 deluxe suite. AE, MC, V. **Amenities:** Restaurant; free airport transfers; bikes; horseback riding; concierge; health club; outdoor pool; room service; smoke-free rooms; spa; outdoor tennis court. *In room:* AC; fan; CD and MP3, Internet.

Where to Dine

The people of Mérida have strong ideas and traditions about food. Certain dishes are always associated with a particular day of the week. In households across the city, Sunday would feel incomplete without *puchero* (a kind of stew). On Monday, at any restaurant that caters to locals, you are sure to find *frijol con puerco* (pork and beans). Likewise, you'll find *potaje* (potage) on Thursday; fish, of course, on Friday; and *chocolomo* (a beef dish) on Saturday. These dishes are heavy and slow to digest; they are for the midday meal and not suitable for supper. What's more, Meridanos don't believe seafood is a healthy supper food. Seafood restaurants in Mérida close by 6pm unless they cater to tourists. The preferred supper food is turkey, and it's best served in the traditional *antojitos—salbutes* (small, thin rounds of *masa* fried and topped with meat, onions, tomatoes, and lettuce) and *panuchos* (*salbutes* with the addition of bean paste)—and turkey soup.

Mérida also has a remarkable number of Middle Eastern restaurants. A large influx of Lebanese immigrants around 1900 has strongly influenced local society; Meridanos think of kibbe almost the way Americans think of pizza. Speaking of pizza, if you want to get some to take back to your hotel room, try **Vito Corleone,** on Calle 59 between calles 60 and 62. Its pizzas have a thin crust with a slightly smoky taste from the wood-burning oven.

Downtown Mérida is well-endowed with good midrange and budget restaurants, but the best upscale restaurants are in outlying districts. For something special, I recommend dining at **Hacienda Xcanatún** (p. 256), whose French-trained chef excels at a fusion of French, Caribbean, and Yucatecan dishes.

***Cochinita pibil* (pit-baked pork), a Yucatecan specialty.**

EXPENSIVE

Alberto's Continental ★ LEBANESE/YUCATECAN There's nothing quite like dining here at night in a softly lit room or on the wonderful old patio framed in Moorish arches. Elegant *mudejar*-patterned tile floors, simple furniture, and a gurgling fountain create a romantic mood, though prices are on the expensive side. For supper, you can choose a sampler plate of four Lebanese favorites, or traditional Yucatecan specialties, such as *pollo pibil* or fish Celestún (bass stuffed with shrimp), and finish with Turkish coffee.

Calle 64 no. 482 (at Calle 57). ✆ **999/928-5367.** Reservations recommended. Main courses 80–220 pesos. AE, MC, V. Daily 1–11pm.

Casa de Frida ★★ MEXICAN If you're longing for classic Mexican food from the central highlands, try this place. It serves fresh, healthful versions of some of Mexico's best-known dishes, such as *mole poblano* and *chiles en nogada*. The *mole* was good when I was last there, as was an interesting *flan de berenjena* (a kind of eggplant timbale). This is a comfortable, no-nonsense sort of place with fuchsia pink walls and peacock blue trim, a la Frida. The menu's breadth will satisfy any appetite.

Calle 61 no. 526 (at Calle 66). ✆ **999/928-2311.** Reservations recommended. Main courses 100–130 pesos. No credit cards. Mon–Fri 6–10pm; Sat noon–5pm & 6–10pm; Sun noon–5pm.

El Pórtico del Peregrino INTERNATIONAL When I first ate here 10 years ago, I swooned over the *berenjenas al horno*, layers of eggplant, chicken, and cheese baked in tomato sauce—kind of a hybrid of lasagna and moussaka that seems to personify Mérida's Italian and Lebanese influences. I stand by my recommendation for this unassuming entrée, and the small, vine-covered patio is one of the sweetest dining areas in Mérida. The higher-priced meat and fish dishes, though—even the traditional specialties—no longer seem to have the zip that I've come to expect in the Yucatán.

Calle 57 no. 501 (btw. calles 60 and 62). ✆ **999/928-6163.** Main courses 70–175 pesos. AE, MC, V. Daily noon to midnight.

MODERATE

Amaro VEGETARIAN/YUCATECAN This peaceful courtyard restaurant, with its walls providing gallery space for local art, lists some interesting vegetarian dishes, such as *crema de calabacitas* (cream of squash soup), apple salad, and avocado pizza. It also offers a few fish and chicken dishes; you might want to try the Yucatecan chicken. The *agua de chaya* (chaya is a spinach-like vegetable prominent in the Maya diet) is refreshing on a hot afternoon. All desserts are made in-house.

Calle 59 no. 507 Interior 6 (btw. calles 60 and 62). ✆ **999/928-2451.** Main courses 50–90 pesos. MC, V. Daily 11am–2am.

El Príncipe Tutul Xiú ★★ YUCATECAN Authentic Yucatecan specialties from a limited menu are served here in a Yucatecan village atmosphere by staff in traditional Maya dress. The owner of the original restaurant in the town of Maní opened this location in response to persistent pressure from Meridanos. This is a great place to try the famous *sopa de lima* and one of the six typical main courses, such as *pavo escabeche,* served with great handmade tortillas. Meat is cooked over a charcoal grill. The flavored waters, such as *horchata* or *tamarindo*, are especially good here. It's a short taxi ride from downtown, and to return you can pick up a local bus that passes by the restaurant.

Calle 123 no. 216 (btw. calles 46 and 46b), Colonia Serapio Rendón. ✆ **999/929-7721.** Reservations not accepted. Main courses 58 pesos. MC, V. Daily 11am–7pm.

La Chaya Maya ★★ YUCATECAN Ladies in traditional Maya garb slap tortillas onto the grill in an open space in the dining room of this spotless, comfortable restaurant devoted to Yucatecan cooking made with ultra-fresh ingredients. I can't imagine skipping the cream of *chaya* (a spinach-like vegetable that has sustained the Maya through the centuries). This is the place to find traditional dishes that rarely grace restaurant menus, such as *mucbil pollo* (chicken tamale casserole), traditionally served for Day of the Dead, and *sikil p'aak,* an earthy paste of ground squash seeds, tomatoes and chiles served with the complimentary chips. The friendly, professional staff does a better job than most with large groups, too.

Calle 57 no. 481 (at Calle 62). ✆ **999/928-4780.** Main courses 60–90 pesos. Cash only. Daily 7am–11pm.

Restaurante Kantún ★★ SEAFOOD This modest restaurant serves up the freshest seafood for incredibly low prices. The owner-chef is always on the premises taking care of details. The menu includes excellent ceviche and seafood cocktails, and fish cooked to order with delicate seasonings and sauces, including such specials as the *especial Kantún,* lightly battered and stuffed with lobster, crab, and shrimp. The dining room is air-conditioned, the furniture comfortable, and the service attentive.

Calle 45 no. 525-G (btw. calles 64 and 66). ✆ **999/923-4493.** Reservations recommended. Main courses 60–120 pesos. MC, V. Daily noon–8pm (occasionally closed on Mon).

Restaurante Los Almendros YUCATECAN As the first place to offer tourists such Yucatecan specialties as *salbutes, panuchos* and *papadzules, cochinita pibil,* and *poc chuc*, this place is an institution. That doesn't mean it produces the best of these dishes, but the food is good and reliable—and photographs on the menu make it a good place to try Yucatecan food for the first time. It's 5 blocks east of Calle 60, facing the Parque de la Mejorada. A new branch in the Fiesta Americana offers a less traditional but more inspiring setting, and the service is better.

Calle 50A no. 493. ✆ **999/928-5459.** Reservations recommended on Sunday. Main courses 60–100 pesos. AE, MC, V. Daily 10am–11pm.

INEXPENSIVE

Café Alameda MIDDLE EASTERN/VEGETARIAN The trappings here are simple and informal (metal tables, plastic chairs), and it's a good place for catching a light meal. The trick is figuring out the Spanish names for popular Middle Eastern dishes. Kibbe is *quebbe bola* (not *quebbe cruda*), hummus is *garbanza,* and shish kabob is *alambre*. I leave it to you to figure out what a spinach pie is called (and it's excellent). Café Alameda is a treat for vegetarians, and the umbrella-shaded tables on the patio are perfect for morning coffee and *mamules* (walnut-filled pastries).

Calle 58 no. 474 (btw. calles 55 and 57). ✆ **999/928-3635.** Main courses 22–58 pesos. No credit cards. Daily 8am–5pm.

Eladio's ★ YUCATECAN Locals have come to this open-air restaurant since 1952 to relax, drink very cold beer, and snack on Yucatecan specialties. Five of these restaurants are now scattered about the city; this one is the closest to the historic center. You can order a beer and enjoy *una botana* (a small portion that accompanies a drink—in this case, usually a Yucatecan dish), or order from the menu. *Cochinita, poc chuc,* and *relleno negro* (turkey flavored with burnt chiles) are all good. You'll often be treated to live music. The restaurant is 3 blocks east of Parque de la Mejorada.

Calle 59 (at Calle 44). ✆ **999/923-1087.** Main courses 40–85 pesos. AE, MC, V. Daily noon–9pm.

La Flor de Santiago YUCATECAN This is an atmospheric place with a loyal clientele. The dining area is classic—fans spinning under a high ceiling, dark wood furniture, one wall lined by bakery cases for fresh treats from a wood fired stove. The service, though friendly, can be classically slow, too. It's especially popular for breakfast, but I like to stop in for one of its Yucatecan specialties on the way to the weekly big-band dancing in Parque Santiago across the street.

Calle 70 no. 478 (btw. calles 57 and 59). ✆ **999/928-5591.** Comida corrida 40 pesos; main courses 40–75 pesos. No credit cards. Daily 7am–11pm.

Exploring Mérida

Most of Mérida's attractions are within walking distance from downtown. One easy way to see more of the city is on the popular, open-air **Carnavalito City Tour Bus.** It leaves Santa Lucia Park (calles 60 and 55) at 10am and 1, 4, and 7pm (no 7pm tour on Sundays). The guided tour costs 75 pesos per person and lasts 2 hours. A national company, **Turibus** (www.turibus.com.mx), operates modern, bright-red, double-decker buses that provide earphones with a recorded narrative in English and five other languages. You can ride the entire circuit in less than 2 hours, or hop off at any stop to explore at will and grab the next bus to continue. Pick them up in front of the cathedral, or at any scheduled stop, every half-hour. The tour costs 100 pesos. Another sightseeing option is a ***calesa*** (horse-drawn carriage), best at night or on Sunday morning when traffic is light. A 45-minute ride around central Mérida costs 250 pesos. You can usually find *calesas* beside the cathedral on Calle 61.

PLAZA GRANDE ★★★ Downtown Mérida has a casual, relaxed feel. Buildings lack the severe baroque and neoclassical features that characterize central Mexico; most are finished in stucco and painted light colors. Mérida's many gardens add to the languid tropical atmosphere. Rather than trying to control nature, gardeners strive for natural exuberance, allowing plants to grow in wild profusion. The city's plazas are a slightly different version of this aesthetic: Unlike the highland plazas with their carefully sculpted trees, Mérida's squares are typically built around large trees that are left to grow as tall as possible.

The natural starting point to explore Mérida, the plaza is a comfortable and informal place to gather with friends. Even when no orchestrated event is in progress, the park is full of people strolling or sitting on benches and talking. Big as Mérida is, the plaza bestows a personal feel and sense of community. Mérida's oldest buildings, beautiful in their scale and composition, surround the square.

The most prominent, the fortress-like **cathedral**—which was in fact designed as a fortress as much as a place of worship—is the oldest on the continent, built between 1561 and 1598. Much of the stone in its walls came from the ruined buildings of the Maya city of T'hó (sometimes Tiho). The original finish was stucco, and you can see some remnants still clinging

Mérida's fortress-like cathedral.

to the bare rock. The two top levels of the bell towers are built off-center from their bases, revealing them as later additions. Inside, decoration is sparse, all smooth white stone, with a conspicuous absence of gold adornments seen in many of Mexico's cathedrals. The most notable item is a picture of Ah Kukum Tutul Xiú, chief of the Xiú people, visiting the Montejo camp to make peace; it hangs over the side door on the right.

To the left of the main altar is a small shrine with a curious figure of Christ that replicates one recovered from a burned-out church in the town of Ichmul. In the 1500s a local artist carved the original figure from a miraculous tree that was hit by lightning and burst into flames—but did not char. The statue later became blistered in the church fire at Ichmul, but it survived. In 1645, it was moved to Mérida, where the locals attached great powers to the figure, naming it *Cristo de las Ampollas* (Christ of the Blisters). It did not, however, survive the sacking of the cathedral in 1915 by revolutionary forces, so a new figure was modeled after the original. Take a look in the side chapel (daily 8–11am and 4:30–7pm), which contains a life-size diorama of the Last Supper. The Mexican Jesus is covered with prayer crosses brought by supplicants asking for intercession.

Next door to the cathedral is the old bishop's palace, now converted into the city's contemporary art museum, **Museo de Arte Contemporáneo Ateneo de Yucatán ★** (**✆ 999/928-3258;** www.macay.org), or MACAY. The palace was confiscated and rebuilt during the Mexican Revolution in 1915. The museum entrance faces the cathedral from the reconstructed walkway between the two buildings called the Pasaje de la Revolución. The 17 exhibition rooms display work by contemporary artists, mostly from the Yucatán. (The best known are Fernando García Ponce and Fernando Castro Pacheco, whose works also hang in the government palace described below.) Nine rooms hold the museum's permanent collection; the rest are for temporary exhibits. It's open Wednesday to Monday from 10am to 6pm, until 8pm Friday and Saturday. Admission is free.

As you move clockwise around the plaza, **Palacio Montejo** is on the south side. The heavy, elaborate decoration around the doorway and windows is carved in the Spanish plateresque architectural style, but the content is very much a New World creation. Conquering the Yucatán was the Montejo family business, begun by the original Francisco Montejo and continued by his son and nephew, both also named Francisco Montejo. Francisco Montejo El Mozo ("The Younger") started construction of the house in 1542. Bordering the entrance, figures of conquistadors stand on the heads of vanquished Indians—borrowed, perhaps, from the pre-Hispanic custom of portraying victorious Maya kings treading on their defeated foes. The conquistadors' quixotic posture and somewhat cartoonish expressions make them less imposing than the Montejos might have intended. A bank now occupies the building, but you can enter the courtyard, view the garden, and imagine what home must have been like for the Montejos and their descendants, who lived here as recently as the 1970s. (Mérida society keeps track of Montejo's descendants, as well as those of the last Maya king, Tutul Xiú.)

In stark contrast to the severity of the cathedral and Casa Montejo is the light, unimposing **Ayuntamiento** or **Palacio Municipal (city hall).** The exterior dates from the mid–19th century, an era when a tropical aesthetic tinged with romanticism began asserting itself across coastal Latin America. On the second floor, you can see the city council's meeting hall and enjoy a view of the plaza from the balcony. Next door to the Ayuntamiento is the recently completed **Centro Cultural de Mérida Olimpo.** It follows the lines of the historic building it replaced, but inside it is a large, modern space that hosts art exhibits, films, and lectures. It houses the **Arcadio Poveda Ricalde Planetarium** on the lower level and also holds concert and gallery space, a bookstore, and a lovely courtyard. A comfortable cafe is under the arches.

A mural by Fernando Castro Pacheco, located in the Palacio de Gobierno.

Cater-corner from the Olimpo is the old **Casa del Alguacil (Magistrate's House).** Under its arcades is something of an institution in Mérida: the **Dulcería y Sorbetería Colón,** an ice cream and sweet shop that will appeal to those who prefer less-rich ice creams. A spectacular side doorway on Calle 62 bears viewing, and across the street is the **Cine Mérida,** with two movie screens showing art films and one stage for live performances. Returning to the main plaza, down from the ice cream store, is a **shopping center** of boutiques and convenience food vendors called **Pasaje Picheta.**

At the end of the arcade is the **Palacio de Gobierno (state government building) ★**, dating from 1892. Large murals by Yucatecan artist Fernando Castro Pacheco, completed between 1971 and 1973, decorate the courtyard walls with scenes from

Maya and Mexican history. The painting over the stairway depicts the Maya spirit with ears of sacred corn, the "sunbeams of the gods." Nearby is a painting of mustachioed President Lázaro Cárdenas, who, in 1938, expropriated 17 foreign oil companies and was hailed as a Mexican liberator. The long, wide upstairs gallery holds more of Pacheco's paintings, which have an almost photographic double-exposure effect. The palace is open Monday to Saturday from 8am to 8pm, Sunday from 9am to 5pm (and often later). A small tourism office is to the left of the entrance.

A few blocks from Plaza Mayor, on Calle 56 between 65 and 65A, the **Museo de la Ciudad (City Museum)** ★ has moved into the grand old post office building. An exhibit outlining Mérida's history includes explanatory text in English. Hours are Tuesday to Friday from 8am to 8pm, Saturday and Sunday from 8am to 2pm. Admission is free.

CALLE 60 Heading north from Plaza Mayor up Calle 60, you'll see many of Mérida's old churches and squares, as well as stores selling gold-filigree jewelry, pottery, clothing, and folk art. A stroll along this street leads to the Parque Santa Ana and continues to the fashionable boulevard Paseo de Montejo and its **Museo Regional de Antropología (Anthropology Museum).**

The **Teatro Daniel Ayala Pérez,** on the left between calles 61 and 59, is of interest because it sometimes schedules interesting performances. On the right side, is the small Parque Cepeda Peraza, more often called **Parque Hidalgo,** named for 19th-century Gen. Manuel Cepeda Peraza and was part of Montejo's original city plan. Small outdoor restaurants front hotels on the park, making it a popular stopping place at any time of day—for locals, tourists, and hammock vendors alike. Across Calle 59 is the **Iglesia de Jesús,** or El Tercer Orden (the Third Order). Built by the Jesuits in 1618, it has the richest interior of any church in Mérida, making it a favorite spot for weddings. If you look at the church's west wall carefully, you'll find stones that still bear Mayan inscriptions from their previous life. The entire block on which the church stands belonged to the Jesuits, who are known for being great educators. The school they left behind after their expulsion became the Universidad de Yucatán.

On the other side of the church is the **Parque de la Madre,** with a copy of Renoir's statue of the *Madonna and Child.* Beyond the park is the **Teatro Peón Contreras,** an opulent theater designed by Italian architect Enrico Deserti a century ago. The theater is noted for its Carrara marble staircase and frescoed dome. National and international performers appear here often; duck inside and check the schedule for performances taking place during your stay. In the southwest corner of the theater, facing the Parque de la Madre, is a **tourist information office.** Across Calle 60 is the main building of the **Universidad de Yucatán.** The *ballet folklórico* performs in its flagstone courtyard on Friday nights.

A block farther north, across from **Iglesia de Santa Lucía** (1575), is **Parque Santa Lucía.** Bordered by an arcade on the north and west sides, this square was where early visitors first alighted from the stagecoach. The park holds a used-book market on Sundays and hosts popular entertainment several evenings a week, including a performance of Yucatecan songs and poems on Thursday nights.

Four blocks farther up Calle 60 is **Parque Santa Ana;** turn right to get to the beginning of Paseo de Montejo in 2 blocks.

PASEO DE MONTEJO The Paseo de Montejo, a broad, tree-lined boulevard modeled after Paris' Champs Elyesées, runs north–south starting at Calle 47, 7 blocks north and 2 blocks east of the main square. In the late 19th century, Mérida's upper crust (mostly plantation owners) decided the city needed something grander than its traditional narrow streets lined by wall-to-wall town houses. They built this monumentally proportioned boulevard and lined it with mansions. It came to a halt when the *henequén* industry went bust, but numerous mansions survive—some in private hands, others as offices, restaurants, or consulates. Today this is the fashionable part of town, home to restaurants, trendy dance clubs, and expensive hotels.

Of the surviving mansions, the most notable is the Palacio Cantón, a Beaux Arts confection that houses the **Museo Regional de Antropología ★★** (Anthropology Museum; ✆ **999/923-0557**), Mérida's most impressive museum. Enrico Deserti, the architect of the Teatro Peón Contreras, designed and built this between 1909 and 1911, during the last years of the Porfiriato. It was the home of Gen. Francisco Cantón Rosado, who enjoyed his palace for only 6 years before his death. For a time, the mansion served as the governor's official residence.

A visit to the museum offers the irony of one of Mérida's most extravagant examples of European architecture housing a tribute to the ancient civilization the Europeans did their best to extinguish. The exhibition of pre-Columbian cultures covers the Yucatán's cosmology, history, and culture, with a special focus on the inhabitants' daily life. Displays illustrate such strange Maya customs as tying boards to babies' heads to create the oblong shape that they considered beautiful, and filing or perforating teeth to inset jewels. Drawings and enlarged photos of several archaeological sites illustrate various styles of Maya dwellings. Captions for the permanent displays are mostly in Spanish, but it's a worthwhile stop even if you barely know the language for the background it provides for explorations of Maya sites. The museum is open Tuesday to Saturday from 8am to 8pm, Sunday from 8am to 2pm. Admission is 41 pesos.

Ecotours & Adventure Trips

The Yucatán Peninsula has been enjoying a recent explosion of companies that organize nature and adventure tours. One well-established outfit with a great track record is **Ecoturismo Yucatán,** Calle 3 no. 235, Col. Pensiones (✆ **999/920-2772;** fax 999/925-9047; www.ecoyuc.com). Alfonso and Roberta Escobedo create itineraries to meet your special or general interest in the Yucatán or southern Mexico. Alfonso has been creating adventure and nature tours for more than a dozen years. Specialties include archaeology, birding, natural history, and kayaking. The company also offers day trips that explore contemporary Maya culture and life in villages in the Yucatán. Package and customized tours are available.

Mayan Ecotours, Calle 80 no. 561 x 13-1, Col. Pensiones 6a Etapa (✆ **999/987-3710;** www.mayanecotours.com) also comes highly recommended. The young company specializes in low-impact visits to unspoiled natural areas and pueblos absent from tourist maps. A new Mayan Life tour combines swimming in a cenote, weaving jipijapa (palm leaves that Panama hats are made of) the traditional way—in a cave—and a home cooking lesson in a Maya village. Custom tours are also available.

Shopping

A vendor selling balloons in Mérida.

Mérida is known for hammocks, *guayaberas* (lightweight men's shirts worn untucked), and Panama hats. Local baskets and pottery are sold in the central market. Mérida is also the place to pick up prepared *adobo,* a pastelike mixture of ground *achiote* seeds (annatto), oregano, garlic, and other spices used as a marinade for such dishes as *cochinita pibil* (pit-baked pork).

Hordes of people come to Mérida's bustling **market district,** a few blocks southeast of the Plaza Grande, to shop and work. It is by far the most crowded part of town. Behind the former post office (at calles 65 and 56, now the city museum) the oldest part of the market is the **Portal de Granos (Grains Arcade),** a row of maroon arches where grain merchants once sold their goods. Just east, between calles 56 and 54, is the market building, **Mercado Lucas de Gálvez.** The city built a new municipal market on the south side of this building, but has had difficulty persuading the market vendors to move. When they do, the city plans to tear down the Lucas de Gálvez and replace it with a plaza. If you can abide the chaos, you can find anything inside from fresh fish to flowers to leather and other locally made goods. A secondary market is on Calle 56, labeled **Bazaar de Artesanías (crafts market)** in big letters. Still another crafts market, **Bazaar García Rejón,** lies a block west of the main market on Calle 65 between calles 58 and 60.

The English-language bookstore **Amate Books** (✆ **999/924-2222**) is at Calle 60 453-A, by Calle 51. It stocks a large selection of books and is open Tuesday through Sunday from 10:30am to 8:30pm. **The Librería Dante,** Calle 59 between calles 60 and 62 (✆ **999/928-3674**), has a small selection of English-language cultural-history books on Mexico.

CRAFTS

Casa de las Artesanías ★ This state-run store, occupying the front of a restored monastery, sells a wide selection of crafts, 90% of which come from the Yucatán. The quality of work is higher than elsewhere, but so are the prices. The monastery's back courtyard is used as a gallery, with rotating exhibits on folk and fine arts. It's open Monday to Saturday from 10am to 8pm, Sunday from 10am to 2pm. Calle 63 no. 513 (btw. calles 64 and 66). ✆ **999/928-6676**.

Miniaturas This fun little store is packed to the rafters with miniatures, a traditional Mexican folk art form that has been evolving into social and political satire, pop art, and bawdy humor. The owner collects these hand-crafted items from around Mexico and offers plenty of variety, from traditional miniatures such as dollhouse furniture and *arboles de vida* (trees of life), to popular cartoon characters and old movie posters. Hours are Monday to Saturday from 10am to 8pm. Calle 59 no. 507A-4 (btw. calles 60 and 62). ✆ **999/928-6503**.

¿Habla Español?

Maya scholars, Spanish teachers, and archaeologists from the United States are among the students at the Centro de Idiomas del Sureste, Calle 52 no. 455 (btw. calles 49 and 51; ✆ 999/923-0954; www.cisyucatan.com.mx). The school has two other locations: the Norte campus in Colonia México and the Poniente campus in Colonia García Ginerés. Students live with local families or in hotels; sessions running 2 weeks or longer are available for all levels of proficiency and areas of interest.

The older Benjamin Franklin Institute (✆ 999/928-6005; www.benjaminfranklin.com.mx), which claims Mérida's longest-running Spanish program for English speakers, also has many satisfied customers with its somewhat more formal and structured program. The choice depends on what kind of a student you are.

GUAYABERAS

Instead of sweltering in business suits in Mérida, businessmen, bankers, and bus drivers alike wear the *guayabera*, a loose-fitting shirt decorated with narrow tucks, pockets, and sometimes embroidery, worn over the pants rather than tucked in. Mérida is famous as the best place to buy *guayaberas*, which can go for less than 150 pesos at the market or for more than 650 pesos custom made; a linen *guayabera* can cost about 800 pesos. Most are made of cotton, although other materials are available. The traditional color is white.

Most shops display ready-to-wear shirts in several price ranges. *Guayabera* makers strive to outdo one another with their own updated versions of the shirt. When shopping, here are a few things to keep in mind: When Yucatecans say *seda*, they mean polyester; *lino* is linen or a linen/polyester combination. Look closely at the stitching and such details as the way the tucks line up over the pockets; with *guayaberas*, details are everything.

Guayaberas Jack The craftsmanship here is good, the place has a reputation to maintain, and some of the salespeople speak English. Prices are as marked. This will give you a good basis of comparison if you want to hunt for a bargain elsewhere. If the staff does not have the style and color of shirt you want, they will make it for you in about 3 hours. This shop also sells regular shirts and women's blouses. Hours are Monday to Saturday from 10am to 8pm, Sunday from 10am to 2pm. Calle 59 no. 507A (btw. calles 60 and 62). ✆ **999/928-6002**.

HAMMOCKS

Natives across tropical America used hammocks long before Europeans reached the New World, and they are still in use throughout Latin America. They come in many forms, but none is so comfortable as the Yucatecan hammock, which is woven with cotton string in a fine mesh. While we might think of a hammock as garden furniture to laze in for an hour or two, they are beds for the majority of Yucatecans, who generally eschew mattresses. Hotels that cater to Yucatecans always provide hammock hooks in the walls because many guests travel with their own hammock.

A good shop will gladly hang a hammock for you to test-drive. Look to see that there are no untied strings. The woven part should be cotton, it should be made with fine string, and the strings should be so numerous that when you get in it and stretch out diagonally (the way you're meant to sleep in them), the gaps between the strings remain small. Don't pay attention to descriptions of a hammock's size; they have become practically meaningless. Good hammocks don't cost a lot of money (250–350 pesos). Superior hammocks are made with fine crochet thread—*hilo de crochet*—and be prepared to pay as much as 1,200 pesos.

You can also see what street vendors are offering, but you have to know what to look for, or they are likely to take advantage of you.

Hamacas El Aguacate El Aguacate sells hammocks wholesale and retail. It has the greatest variety and is the place to go for a really fancy or extra-large hammock. A good hammock is the no. 6 in cotton; it runs around 340 pesos. The store is open Monday to Friday from 8:30am to 7:30pm, Saturday from 8am to 5pm. It's 6 blocks south of the main square. Calle 58 no. 604 (at Calle 73). ✆ **999/923-0152**.

Tejidos y Cordeles Nacionales This place near the municipal market sells only cotton hammocks, priced by weight—a pretty good practice because hammock lengths are fairly standardized. The prices are better than at El Aguacate, but quality control isn't as good. My idea of a good hammock is one that weighs about 1½kg (3½ lb.) and runs about 270 pesos. Calle 56 no. 516-B (btw. calles 63 and 65). ✆ **999/928-5561**.

PANAMA HATS

Another useful and popular item is this soft, pliable hat made from the fibers of the jipijapa palm in several towns south of Mérida along Hwy. 180, especially Becal, in the neighboring state of Campeche. Hat makers in these towns work inside caves so that the moist air keeps the palm fibers pliant.

Jipi hats come in various grades determined by the pliability, softness, and fineness of the fibers and closeness of the weave. A fine weave gives the hat more body and helps it to retain its shape. You'll find Panama hats for sale in several places, but often without much selection. One of the market buildings has a hat store: Walk south down Calle 56 past the post office; just before the street ends in the marketplace, turn left into a passage with hardware stores at the entrance. The fourth or fifth shop is **Casa de los Jipis.**

Mérida After Dark

For nighttime entertainment, see the box, "Festivals & Events in Mérida," p. 255, or check out the theaters noted here.

Teatro Peón Contreras, Calle 60 at Calle 57, and **Teatro Ayala,** Calle 60 at Calle 61, feature a wide range of performing artists from Mexico and around the world. **Centro Cultural de Mérida Olimpo,** on the main square, schedules frequent concerts; and **Cine Mérida,** a half-block north of the Olimpo, has two screens for showing classic and art films, and one live stage.

Mérida's club scene offers everything from ubiquitous rock/dance music to some one-of-a-kind spots. Most of the dance clubs are in the big hotels or on trendy Paseo de Montejo, such as the ever-so-cool **El Cielo Lounge** at Prolongación Montejo and Calle 25. For dancing, a small cluster of clubs on Calle 60, around the corner from Santa Lucía, offer live rock and Latin music. For salsa, go to **Mambo Café** in the Plaza las Américas shopping center.

SIDE TRIPS FROM MÉRIDA

Hacienda Sotuta de Peón ★

What started out as one man's hobby has grown into one of the best living museums you'll ever see. If you've passed one of the Yucatán's elegantly decaying haciendas and wondered what it was like during its heyday, here's your chance to find out. The owner didn't just restore the buildings, he put the entire hacienda into working order and is now turning out 10 to 15 tons of *henequén* per month.

You can arrange transportation from any of Mérida's hotels by calling **Hacienda Sotuta de Peón** at ✆ **999/941-8639** or going to **www.haciendatour.com**. Be sure to get precise directions if you plan to take your own car. After a welcome drink and a tour of the beautiful main house, you'll visit the *henequén* fields via mule-drawn "trucks," or carts. You get to see harvesting and, later, processing at the *casa de máquinas,* and learn how to spin the fiber into twine. You'll also learn about the culture surrounding *henequén* production, visiting one of the workers in his traditional Maya home. Bring your bathing suit because you'll have time for a swim in a cenote on the property. You can also sample fine regional cooking in a restaurant on the premises. Admission is 300 pesos per adult, 150 pesos per child; transportation is 200 pesos extra. Packages are available that combine entrance fee, transportation from Mérida, and a meal. The hacienda is open from Monday to Saturday, with tours at 10am and 1pm.

Izamal ★★

Izamal, about 80km (50 miles) east of Mérida, presents one of Mexico's most vivid juxtapositions of three cultures: Ancient pyramids surround one of the largest monasteries the Spanish ever built in Mexico, while contemporary Maya artisans do a brisk trade in their traditional crafts.

The entire city center glows with ochre-yellow paint—the market, all the colonial buildings, and the massive Franciscan convent of **San Antonio de Padua ★★** for which Izamal is best known. Walking along the colonnades high over the plaza, you know why priests believed they were close to God. The porticoed atrium, reputedly second in size only to the Vatican's, presents a sound-and-light show on Tuesday, and Thursday to Saturday at 8:30pm. Admission is 48 pesos; headphones with English narration cost another 30. Bishop Fray Diego de Landa, who was to became infamous for his brutal *auto-da-fé* at Maní, leveled a Maya pyramid here to build the monastery and

Sisal production at Hacienda Sotuta de Peón.

Izamal's ochre-colored convent of San Antonio de Padua.

church. Inside is a beautifully restored altarpiece and, among many statues, the Nuestra Señora de Izamal, brought from Guatemala in 1652 and still drawing pilgrims every August who climb the staircase on their knees to plead for miracles.

The new **Centro Cultural y Artesanal ★** (20 pesos) across the square from the convent provides an excellent introduction to Izamal's proliferation of handicrafts. The shop sells fine-quality hammocks, clothing, and other work of local artists. Follow up with a self-guided tour, available at the center, of folk art workshops in town. A good way to reach them is by *victoria,* the horse-drawn buggies that serve as taxis here.

Of the four pyramids overlooking the town center, **Kinich Kakmó** on Calle 28 at Calle 25 (daily 8am–8pm; free admission), is the Yucatan's largest pre-Hispanic building. Impressing with sheer size rather than fine architecture, it looks like a strangely symmetrical hill, but you can climb the restored stairways on its south face for grand views and a fresh breeze.

The easiest way to get to Izamal from Mérida is to take Hwy. 180 toward Cancún. At Km 68, follow the signs for the *cuota* (toll road) until just past the Kantunil turnoff. Before you reach the toll plaza, the exit for Izamal will be on the left. You'll head north, passing through the villages of Xanaba and Sudzal, for 7.7 km (4¾ miles) to Izamal.

Izamal, which had meager lodging options only a few years ago, is enjoying a bit of a boom. Long-standing favorite **Macan ché Bed and Breakfast,** in the middle of town at Calle 22 no. 305 between calles 33 and 35 (✆ **988/954-0287;** www.macanche.com), recently opened a second house suited for families and long-term stays as well as a new building with four quirky, highly designed rooms. Rates range from $40 to $55 for rooms, $90 to $135 for a house. Just east of the city center, on Calle 18 between calles 33 and 35, an Austrian entrepreneur has turned a ranch into **Hotel Rancho Santo Domingo** (✆ **988/967-6136;** www.izamalhotel.com). Bungalows in a tropical garden house bright, modern rooms for $65 to $75, including tax, breakfast, and some refreshments. I visited just before the first two bungalows opened, and it looks like a great value. At press time, the hotel was aiming to expand to 10 units by the end of 2010.

Celestún National Wildlife Refuge: Flamingos & Other Waterfowl

On the Gulf Coast west of Mérida, Celestún is the gateway to a wildlife reserve harboring one of North America's only two flamingo breeding colonies (the other is Ría Lagartos, p. 318). The long, shallow estuary, where salty Gulf waters mix with fresh water from about 80 cenotes, is sheltered from the open sea by a skinny strip of land, creating ideal habitat for flamingos and other waterfowl. This *ría* (estuary) is shallow (.3–1m/1–3¼ ft. deep) and thick with mangroves. You can ride a launch through an open channel just .5km (a quarter-mile) wide and 50km (31 miles) long to see flamingos dredging the shallows for a species of small crustacean and a favorite insect that form the bulk of their diet. You may also see frigate birds, pelicans, spoonbills, egrets, sandpipers, and other waterfowl. At least 15 duck species have been counted. Nonbreeding flamingos remain year-round; breeding birds take off around April to nest in Ría Lagartos, returning to Celestún in October.

The old days of approaching a fisherman under the bridge to negotiate a trip to the flamingos are over; immediately to the left after you cross the bridge into town is a modern visitor center with a small museum, snack bar, clean bathrooms, and a ticket window. Tour prices are fixed at about 750 pesos for a 75-minute tour for up to six people. You can join others or hire a boat by yourself. In addition to flamingos, you'll see mangroves close up, and you might stop for a swim in a cenote. It's a pleasant ride through calm waters on wide, flat-bottom skiffs with canopies for shade. *Don't ask boatmen to get closer to the flamingos than they are allowed to.* If pestered too much, the birds will abandon the area for another, less-fitting habitat.

Celestún is an easy 90-minute drive from Mérida. (For bus info, see "Getting There & Departing: By Bus," p. 252.) Leave downtown on Calle 57, which ends

Flamingos flock to Celestún National Wildlife Refuge.

just past Santiago Church and doglegs onto Calle 59-A. After crossing Avenida Itzáes, it becomes Jacinto Canek; continue until you see signs for Celestún Hwy. 178. After Hunucmá, the road joins Hwy. 281. Continue to the bridge, and you are in Celestún.

WHERE TO STAY

Casa de Celeste Vida ★★ This newish guest house, 1.5 km north of town on a quiet, unspoiled beach that stretches for miles, hits the perfect balance between comfort and economy, seclusion and convenience. Two studios and a one-bedroom apartment have ocean views, kitchens stocked with utensils and food staples, and use of bikes, kayaks, and outdoor grills. The amiable Canadian owners, who live on-site, gladly arrange tours and sometimes even accompany guests on errands in town. They are highly tuned in to local culture and provide enormous insights into the lives of local fishermen and their families.

49-E Calle 12, Celestún, Yuc. ✆ **988/916-2536.** www.hotelcelestevida.com. 3 units. $75 studios, $100 apartment. Weekly/monthly rates available. AE, DISC, MC, V. Free parking. **Amenities:** Kitchen; bikes; kayaks; Wi-Fi.

Hotel Eco Paraíso Xixim This resort has drawn accolades for its ecological practices. Composting, reusing treated wastewater, and developing barely more than 1% of its 25 hectares (62 acres) is certainly laudable, and the 5km (3 miles) of pristine beach are sublime. The *palapa*-roof bungalows are exquisitely private and generally comfortable. For its five-star rating and its rates, though, I expect more consistent cleaning standards and restaurant service. And if you don't relish bouncing over 11km (7 miles) of potholes whenever you want to explore, you are captive to the resort's services. This hotel is best for well-off travelers looking to cosset themselves away for a week.

Antigua Carretera a Sisal Km 10, 97367 Celestún, Yuc. ✆ **988/916-2100.** Fax 988/916-2111. www.ecoparaiso.com. 15 units. High season $270 double; low season $250 double. Rates include breakfast. AE, MC, V. Free parking. **Amenities:** Restaurant; bar; midsize outdoor pool. *In room:* Hair dryer.

Dzibilchaltún: Maya Ruins & Museum

This small archaeological site can be a quick day trip or part of a longer trip to the Yucatán's Gulf coast. It stands 14km (8¾ miles) north of Mérida along the Progreso road, 4km (2½ miles) east of the highway. Take Calle 60 out of town and follow signs for Progreso and Hwy. 261. Turn right at the sign for Dzibilchaltún, which also reads UNIVERSIDAD DEL MAYAB; the entrance is a few miles farther. If you don't want to drive, take one of the *colectivos* lined up at Parque San Juan.

The ruins of Dzibilchaltún.

Dzibilchaltún was founded about 500 B.C., flourished around A.D. 750, and began its decline long before the conquistadors arrived. Since their discovery in 1941, more than 8,000 buildings have been mapped, but only about a half-dozen have been excavated. The site covers almost 15 sq. km (5¾ sq. miles); of greatest interest are the buildings surrounding two plazas next to the cenote and a third connected by a *sacbé* (causeway). At least 25 stelae have been found in Dzibilchaltún, which means "place of the stone writing."

Start with the **Museo del Pueblo Maya,** which exhibits artifacts from sites around the Yucatán and provides fairly thorough bilingual explanations. Displays include a beautiful plumed serpent from Chichén Itzá and a finely designed incense vessel from Palenque. The museum moves on to artifacts specifically at Dzibilchaltún, including the curious dolls that gave the site's main attraction its name. Another exhibit covers Maya culture through history, including a collection of *huipiles,* the woven blouses worn by Indian women. From here, a door leads out to the site.

You first encounter the *sacbé.* To the left is the **Temple of the Seven Dolls,** whose doorways and the *sacbé* line up with the rising sun at the spring and autumnal equinoxes. To the right are the buildings grouped around the Cenote Xlacah, the sacred well, and a complex of buildings around **Structure 38,** the **Central Group** of temples. Yucatán's State Department of Ecology has added nature trails and published a booklet (in Spanish) of birds and plants seen along the mapped trail.

The site is open daily from 8am to 5pm (museum closes at 4pm). Admission is 79 pesos, including the museum; children under 13 free.

Progreso, Uaymitun & Xcambo: Gulf Coast City, Flamingo Lookout & More Maya Ruins

Puerto Progreso is Mérida's refuge when the weight of summer heat descends on the city. And though it doesn't occur to most U.S. travelers, it is also a gateway to the trove of undiscovered white sands and mangrove-lined estuaries. Except for the vacation homes within easy reach of Mérida, most of the Yucatán's 378 seafront kilometers (235 miles)—stretching from near Isla Holbox to Celestún—belongs to some scattered fishing villages, a lot of flamingos, and an increasing number of American and Canadian expats and snowbirds.

Progreso has been the Yucatán's main port of entry since the 1870s, when *henequén* shipped all over the world. Today, it's a major stop for cruise ships. The cruise business has allowed the city to spruce up the Malecón, its 16-block seaside promenade that skims past well-groomed, white-sand beaches. Though the water is green and murky compared with the Caribbean, it's clean, and good for swimming. Fancy restaurants have been added (many sell good seafood), and vendors now ply their wares on the beach, but it's still pretty quiet most of the time. The 7km (4½-mile) pier, which seems to disappear in the distance, became the world's longest when a new section was added to accommodate cruise ships, which dock twice a week. The sea is so shallow here that large ships cannot get any closer to shore.

From Mérida, buses to Progreso leave from the AutoProgreso terminal (p. 252) every 15 minutes or so, taking almost an hour and costing 35 pesos. If you drive, take Paseo Montejo or Calle 60 north; either funnels you onto Hwy. 261 leading to Progreso.

If you have time, a drive east on the coastal road toward Telchac Puerto will reveal the other side of the Yucatán's coast. The shoreline along Hwy. 27 from

Chuburna to the village of Dzilam de Bravo is dubbed La Costa Esmeralda (the Emerald Coast), after the clear, green Gulf waters. First up: the sleepy beach town of **Chicxulub,** about 8km (5 miles) east of Progreso. To winter-phobic northerners, it's a bit of paradise. To scientists, it's the site of a buried impact crater, about 161km (100 miles) in diameter, left by a meteor that smashed into the earth 65 million years ago; it is blamed for extinguishing the dinosaurs and probably created the Yucatán's cenotes. Less than 10km (6 miles) farther, in **Uaymitun,** a large wooden tower looming on the right is an observation post for viewing a new colony of flamingos that migrated from Celestún in recent years. Binoculars are provided free of charge. You might also spot some of the rosy birds about 20 minutes down near the turnoff for the road to Dzemul.

The road to Dzemul also leads to the small but intriguing Maya site of **Xcambó**, which was (and still is) a salt production center. Archaeologists have reconstructed the small ceremonial center, including several platforms and temples. A rough-hewn Catholic church, complete with altar, flowers, and statues, rises from some of the ruins. Admission is free.

You can continue on the same road through the small town of Dzemul to Baca, where you can pick up Hwy. 176 back to Mérida or Progreso, or you can return to the coast road and continue east until it ends in **Dzilam de Bravo,** final resting place of "gentleman pirate" Jean Lafitte. On the way, you'll pass through **Telchac Puerto,** which holds little interest unless you're hungry for some decent seafood, and the appealing village of **San Crisanto,** where a group of fishermen will paddle you through shallow canals in the mangroves to an array of newly accessible cenotes.

A church in the village of Telchac Puerto.

The Catholic church in Xcambó.

WHERE TO STAY

Hotel Yakunah ★★ ☺ This beautiful former colonial home is owned by a generous, outgoing Dutch family who have turned it into an expat gathering place as well as an exemplary B&B. The quiet location is a 10-minute walk from the Progreso city center but right across the street from the beach. Spacious rooms have a romantic air, with large beds, pasta tile, and armoires. Gleaming tiled bathrooms have large showers. A two-bedroom garden apartment with fully equipped kitchen and private terrace is also available. Co-owner Gerben Hartskeerl is a talented chef who turns out breakfasts and dinners (extra charge) that will spare you the tribulations of finding a restaurant.

Calle 23 no. 64 (btw. calles 48 and 50), Col. Ismael García, Progreso, Yuc. ✆ **969/935-5600.** www.hotelyakunah.com.mx. 7 units. 750 pesos double, 1,400 pesos 2-bedroom casita. Rates include light breakfast; extra charge for full breakfast. Minimum stay 2 nights. MC, V. **Amenities:** Restaurant; bar; library; outdoor pool; non-smoking rooms. *In room:* A/C, TV, Wi-Fi.

En Route to Uxmal

Two routes go to Uxmal, about 80km (50 miles) south of Mérida. The most direct is Hwy. 261, via Umán and Muna. Hwy. 18 is a longer, more scenic road sometimes called the Convent Route. You might also make the trip to Uxmal into a loop by going one way and coming back the other, with an overnight stay at Uxmal. Arriving at Uxmal in late afternoon, you could attend the evening sound-and-light show, and see the ruins the next morning while it is cool and uncrowded.

Both of these roads will lead you to the central square in one small village after another, and many lack signs to point you in the right direction. Get used to poking your head out the window and saying, *"Buenos días. ¿Dónde está el camino para . . . ?"* ("Good day. Where is the road to . . . ?") I've usually had the best luck asking a policeman, if I can find one. Sometimes you have to ask more than one person before you get back on track. Streets in these villages are full of children, bicycles, and animals, so drive carefully, and learn to recognize unmarked *topes* from a distance.

Churches on these routes are open daily from 10am to 1pm and 4 to 6pm; ruins are open daily from 8am to 5pm.

HWY. 261: YAXCOPOIL & MUNA From downtown Mérida, take Calle 65 or 69 west and then turn left on Avenida Itzáes, which feeds onto the highway. To save some time by looping around the busy market town of Umán, take the exit for Hwy. 180 to Cancún and Campeche, and follow signs toward Campeche. Keep going south on Hwy. 180 until it intersects with Hwy. 261 and take the Uxmal exit.

You'll soon come to the town and **Hacienda Yaxcopoil** (yash-koh-po-*eel;* ✆ **999/900-1193;** www.yaxcopoil.com), 32km/20 miles south of Mérida. The ruined hacienda, immediately identifiable by its double Moorish arches, has been preserved but not restored, making for an eerie but particularly vivid trip back in time. Tours take in the *casa principa,* with its large lounges and drawing rooms, the extensive gardens, a small Maya museum, and the *henequén* factory. It's open Monday to Saturday from 8am to 6pm, and Sunday 9am to 5pm. Admission is 50 pesos.

The hacienda is no secret, but few travelers seem to know you can stay overnight in the ***Casa de Visitas*** **★★★**, a guest house behind the manor house that is not open to the public. It is roomy, with a sitting and dining

An artisan crafts a ceramic vase in Muna.

room, and charming, with a patterned tile floor and colonial-style furniture. After 6 p.m., it's just you, the entire empty hacienda, the deep starry sky, and the utter silence. It's a unique experience that I look forward to repeating, but it's not for travelers whose comfort level requires a front desk ready to snap to attention at any hour of the day or night. The guest house rents for $60 a night; another $20 per person gets you a homemade tamale dinner and a hearty breakfast, delivered and served by a local woman in town.

South of Yaxcopoil, the little market town of **Muna** (65km/40 miles from Mérida) sells excellent reproductions of Maya ceramics, created by artisan Rodrigo Martín Morales, who has worked 25 years to replicate the ancient Maya's style and methods. As you enter Muna, watch for two large Ceiba trees on the right side of the road, with handcraft and food stalls in a small plaza under the branches. Turn right, and in about 45m (148 ft.) the Taller de Artesanía Los Ceibos (&997/971-0036) will be on your left. The family works in the back, and only Spanish is spoken. The store is open from 9am to 6pm daily. Uxmal is 15km (9¼ miles) beyond Muna.

HWY. 18: THE CONVENT ROUTE From downtown Mérida, take Calle 63 east to Circuito Colonias and turn right, then look for a traffic circle with a small fountain and turn left. This feeds onto Hwy. 18 to Kanasín (kah-nah-*seen*) and then Acanceh (ah-kahn-*keh*). In **Kanasín,** the highway divides into two; go to the right, and the road curves to flow into the next parallel street. Pass the market, church, and main square on your left, and then stay to the right when you get to a fork.

Shortly after Kanasín, the upgraded road now bypasses a lot of villages. Follow the sign pointing left to **Acanceh.** Across the street from and overlooking Acanceh's church is a restored pyramid. On top, under a makeshift roof, are some stucco figures of Maya deities. The caretaker will guide you up to see them and give you a little explanation (in Spanish). Admission is 25 pesos. A few blocks away, at some other ruins called **El Palace de los Stuccoes,** a stucco mural was found in mint condition there in 1908.

The ruins of Mayapán.

Exposure deteriorated it somewhat, but it is sheltered now. You can still distinguish the painted figures in their original colors. To leave Acanceh, head back to the highway on the street that passes between the church and the plaza.

The next turnoff will be for **Tecoh,** on the right side. Its ornate and crumbling parish church and convent sit on the base of a massive pre-Columbian ceremonial complex that was sacrificed to build the church. The three carved *retablos* (altarpieces) inside are covered in gold leaf and unmistakably Indian in style. About 9km (6 miles) farther on, you come to the ruins of Mayapán, the last of the great city-states.

MAYAPÁN ★

Founded, according to Maya lore, by the man-god Kukulkán (Quetzalcóatl in central Mexico) in about A.D. 1007, Mayapán quickly established itself as northern Yucatán's most important city. For almost 2 centuries, it was the capital of a Maya confederation of city-states that included Chichén Itzá and Uxmal. Sometime before 1200, Mayapán attacked and subjugated the other two cities, leading to a revolt that eventually toppled Mayapán. It was abandoned during the mid-1400s.

The city extended out at least 4 sq. km (1½ sq. miles), but the ceremonial center is quite compact. Several buildings bordering the principal plaza have been reconstructed, including one that is similar to Chichén Itzá's El Castillo. Excavation has uncovered murals and stucco figures that provide more grist for the mill of conjecture: atlantes (supporting columns in the form of a human figure), skeletal soldiers, macaws, entwined snakes, and a stucco jaguar. This place is definitely worth a stop.

The site is open daily from 8am to 5pm. Admission is 35 pesos. Use of a personal video camera is 45 pesos.

FROM MAYAPÁN TO TICUL About 20km (12 miles) after Mayapán, take the highway for **Mama** on your right, and the narrow road quickly enters town. Some parts of this village are quite pretty. The main attraction is the church and former convent, with several fascinating *retablos* sculpted in a native form of baroque. Colonial-age murals and designs were uncovered and restored during the restoration of these buildings. You can peek at them in the sacristy. From Mama, continue on about 20km (12 miles) to Ticul, a large (for this area) market town with a couple of simple hotels.

TICUL

Best known for the cottage industry of *huipil* (native blouse) embroidery and the manufacture of women's dress shoes, Ticul is an especially exciting stop and a convenient place to wash up and spend the night. It's also a center for large-scale pottery production—most of the widely sold sienna-colored pottery painted with Maya designs is made here. If it's a cloudy, humid day, potters may not be working (part of the process requires sun drying). They still welcome visitors to purchase finished pieces.

Ticul is only 20km (12 miles) northeast of Uxmal, making a good alternative to the expensive hotels at the ruins, especially if you want to do the Puuc Route one day and the Convent Route the next. On the main square is the **Hotel Plaza,** Calle 23 no. 202, near Calle 26 (✆ **997/972-0484**). It's a modest but comfortable hotel. A double room with air-conditioning costs 340 pesos. A 5% charge applies to payments made by credit card (MC and V accepted). Get an interior room to avoid noise from Ticul's lively plaza. From Ticul, you can head straight for Uxmal via Santa Elena, or loop around the Puuc Route (p. 283) the long way to Santa Elena.

FROM TICUL TO UXMAL Follow the main street (Calle 23) west through town. Turn left on Calle 34 and drive 15km (9¼ miles) to Santa Elena; it will be another 15km (9¼ miles) to Uxmal. In Santa Elena, by the side of Hwy. 261, is a clean restaurant with good food, **El Chaac Mool,** and on the opposite side of the road the **Flycatcher Inn B&B** (see listing, below).

Ticul is known for its pottery.

THE RUINS OF UXMAL ★★★

80km (50 miles) SW of Mérida; 19km (12 miles) W of Ticul; 19km (12 miles) S of Muna

The ceremonial complex of Uxmal ("oosh-*mahl*") is one of the masterworks of Maya civilization. It is strikingly different from all other Maya cities for its expansive and intricate facades of carved stone. Unlike other sites in northern Yucatán, such as Chichén Itzá and Mayapán, Uxmal isn't built on a flat plane, but incorporates the varied elevations of the hilly landscape. And then there is the strange and beautiful oval-shaped Pyramid of the Magician, unique among the Maya. The great building period took place between A.D. 700 and 1000, when the population probably reached 25,000. After 1000, Uxmal fell under the sway of the Xiú princes (who may have come from central Mexico). In the 1440s, the Xiú conquered Mayapán, and not long afterward, the age of the Maya ended with the arrival of the Spanish conquistadors.

Close to Uxmal, four smaller sites—**Sayil, Kabah, Xlapak,** and **Labná**—can be visited in quick succession. With Uxmal, these ruins (p. 284) are collectively known as the **Puuc route.**

Essentials

GETTING THERE & DEPARTING **By Car** The two main routes to Uxmal from Mérida are described in "En Route to Uxmal," above. *Note:* There's no gasoline at Uxmal.

By Bus See "Getting There & Departing" (p. 251) for information about bus service between Mérida and Uxmal. To return, wait for the bus on the highway at the entrance to the ruins. To see the sound-and-light show, sign up with a tour operator from Mérida.

ORIENTATION Entrance to the ruins is through the visitor center where you buy tickets (two per person; hold on to both). It has a restaurant; toilets; a first-aid station; shops selling soft drinks, ice cream, film, batteries, and books; a state-run Casa de Artesanía (crafts house); and a small museum, which isn't very informative. The site is open daily from 8am to 5pm. Admission to the archaeological site is 51 pesos, and you'll pay 40 pesos more for the evening sound-and-light show. Bringing in a video camera costs 45 pesos and parking is 10 pesos. If you're staying the night in Uxmal, it is possible (and I think preferable) to get to the site late in the day and buy a ticket that combines the sound-and-light show that evening with entry to the ruins the next morning to explore them before it gets hot. Make sure the ticket vendor knows what you intend to do, and keep the ticket.

Guides at the entrance of Uxmal give tours in several languages, charging $40 for a single person or a group. The guides frown on it, but you can ask other English speakers if they'd like to join you in a tour and split the cost. As at other sites, the guides vary in quality but will point out areas and architectural details you might otherwise miss. Think of these guided tours as performances—the guides try to be as entertaining and adjust their presentations according to the group's interests.

Included in the price of admission is a 45-minute **sound-and-light show** each evening at 7pm. It's in Spanish, but you can rent headsets for 25 pesos that narrate the program in several languages. It's part Hollywood, part high school, but the lighting of the buildings is worth making the effort to see it. After the show, the chant *"Chaaac, Chaaac"* will echo in your mind for weeks.

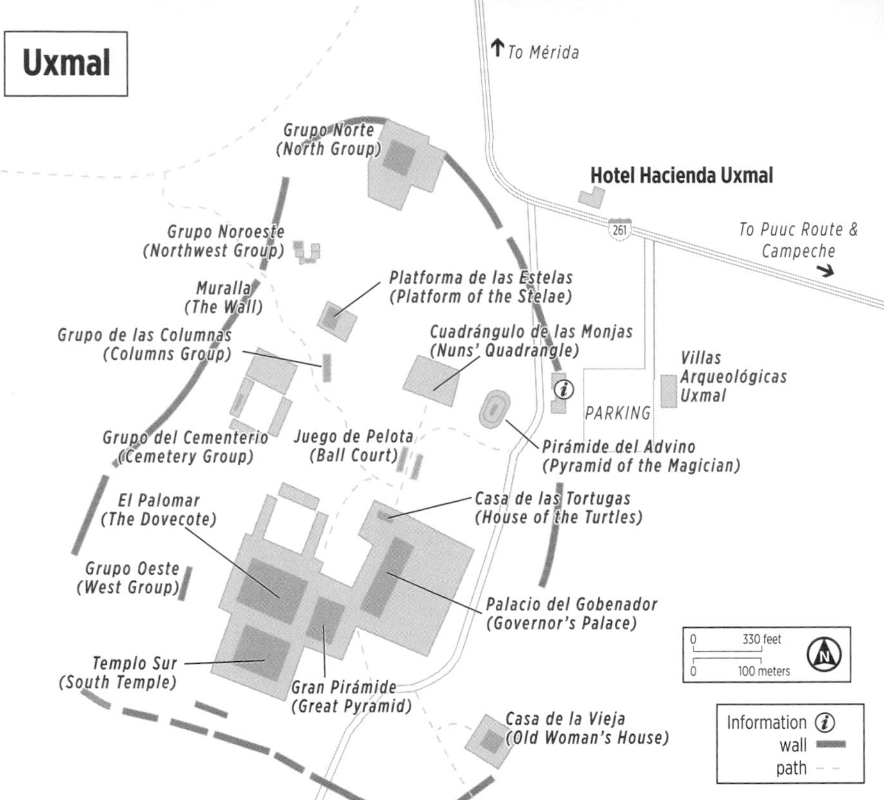

A Tour of the Ruins

THE PYRAMID OF THE MAGICIAN ★★ As you enter the ruins, note a *chultún,* or cistern, where Uxmal stored its water. Unlike most of the major Maya sites, Uxmal stands about 30m (100 ft.) above sea level, so it has no cenotes to supply fresh water from the subterranean rivers. The city's inhabitants depended on rainwater, and consequently venerated the rain god Chaac with unusual devotion.

Rising in front of you is the Pirámide del Adivino, the city's tallest structure at 38m (125 ft.). The name comes from a myth about a magician-dwarf who reached adulthood in a single day after being hatched from an egg and built this pyramid in 1 night. It is built over five earlier structures. The pyramid has an oval base and rounded sides. You are looking at the east side. Walk around the left, or south, side to see the main face on the west side. The pyramid was designed so that the east side rises less steeply than the west side, which shifts the crowning temples to the west of the central axis of the building, causing them to loom above the plaza below. The temple doorway is heavily ornamented, characteristic of the Chenes style, with 12 stylized masks representing Chaac.

THE NUNNERY QUADRANGLE To get from the plaza to the large Nunnery Quadrangle, walk out the way you walked into the plaza, turn right, and follow the wall of this long stone building until you get to the building's main door—a corbelled arch that leads into the quadrangle. You'll be in another plaza, bordered on each side by stone buildings with elaborate facades. The 16th-century Spanish historian Fray Diego López de Cogullado gave the quadrangle its name when he decided its layout resembled a Spanish convent.

The quadrangle does have a lot of small rooms, about the size of a nun's cell. Poke your head into one to see the shape and size, but don't bother trying to explore them all. These rooms were long ago abandoned to the swallows that fly above the city. No interior murals or stucco work have been found here, at least not yet. The richness of Uxmal lies in the stonework on its exterior walls.

The Nunnery is a great example. The first building that catches your eye when you enter the plaza is the north building in front of you. It is the tallest, and the view from the top includes all the city's major buildings, making it useful for the sound-and-light show. The central stairway is bordered by doorways supported by rounded columns, a common element in Puuc architecture. Remnants of the facade on the second level show elements used in the other three buildings and elsewhere in the city; a crosshatch pattern and a pattern of square curlicues, called a step-and-fret design, and the vertical repetitions of the long-nosed god masks—found so often on the corners of Uxmal's buildings that they have acquired the nickname "Chaac stacks." Though the facades of these buildings share these and other common elements, their composition varies. On the west building, long, feathered serpents are intertwined at head and tail. A human head stares out from a serpent's open mouth. There are many interpretations of this motif, repeated elsewhere in Maya art, and that's the trouble with symbols: They are usually the condensed expression of multiple meanings, so any one interpretation could be true, but only partially true.

THE BALL COURT Leaving the Nunnery the same way you entered, you will see a ball court straight ahead. What Maya city would be without a ball court?

Uxmal's Pyramid of the Magician.

The Governor's Palace in Uxmal.

This one is a particularly good representative of the hundreds found elsewhere in the Maya world. It even has a replica of one of the stone rings the players aimed at, using their knees, hips, and maybe their arms to strike a solid rubber ball (the Maya knew about natural rubber and extracted latex from a couple of species of rubber trees). Spectators are thought to have observed the game from atop the two structures.

THE GOVERNOR'S PALACE Continuing south, you come to the large raised plaza supporting the Governor's Palace, which runs north and south. The surface area of the raised plaza measures 140m x 170m (459 ft. x 558 ft.), and it is raised about 10m (33 ft.) above the ground—quite a bit of earth moving. Most of this surface is used as a ceremonial space facing the front (east side) of the palace. In the center is a double-headed jaguar throne, which is seen elsewhere in the Maya world. From here, you get the best view of the building's remarkable facade. Like the other palaces here, the first level is smooth and the second is ornate. A series of Chaac masks moves diagonally across a crosshatch pattern. Crowning the building is an elegant cornice projecting slightly outward from above a double border, which could be an architectural reference to the original crested thatched roofs of the Maya. Human figures adorned the main doors, though only the headdress of the central figure survives.

THE GREAT PYRAMID Behind the palace, the platform descends in terraces to another plaza with a large temple, known as the Great (or Grand) Pyramid, on its south side. On top is the Temple of the Macaws, for the repeated image of macaws on the face of the temple, and the ruins of three other temples. The view from the top is extraordinary.

THE DOVECOTE This building is remarkable, in that roof combs weren't a common feature of temples in the Puuc hills, although Sayil's El Mirador has one of a very different style.

Where to Stay

Flycatcher Inn B&B ★★ This pleasant bed-and-breakfast is 15 minutes southeast of Uxmal in the village of Santa Elena, just off Hwy. 261. Spacious rooms are attractive and quiet, and they come with pillow-top orthopedic mattresses and decorative ironwork made by one of the owners, Santiago Domínguez. The other owner, his wife, is Kristine Ellingson, an American from the Northwest who has lived in Santa Elena for years and has voluminous information on travel and local culture to share with guests. The large, attractive grounds include a recently discovered little Maya ruin along the nature trail that runs through the property. The inn's new Owl's Cottage, a secluded house with a small kitchen and large living/dining room, is designed for longer stays.

Carretera Uxmal–Kabah, 97840 Santa Elena, Yuc. ✆ **997/102 0865.** www.flycatcherinn.com. 8 units. $55–$75 double, $75 suite, $50–$85 cottage (3-night minimum). Rates include full breakfast. No credit cards. Free secure parking. Not set up to accommodate young children. *In room:* A/C.

Hacienda Uxmal ★★ The Hacienda is the oldest hotel in Uxmal. Located just up the road from the ruins, it was built for the archaeology staff. Large, airy rooms exude a feel of days gone by, with patterned tile floors, heavy furniture, and louvered windows. Room nos. 202 through 214 and 302 through 305 are the nicest of the superiors. Larger corner rooms are labeled A through F and come with Jacuzzi tubs. A handsome garden courtyard with towering royal palms, a bar, and a pool adds to the air of tranquility. A guitar trio usually plays on the open patio in the evenings.

Carretera Mérida–Uxmal Km 80, 97844 Uxmal, Yuc. ✆ **800/235-4079** in the U.S., or 997/976-2012; fax 987/976-2011. www.mayaland.com. 82 units. High season $164–$185 double, $238–$249 superior; low season $110–$140 double, $144–$196 superior. AE, MC, V. Free guarded parking. **Amenities:** Restaurant; bar; 2 outdoor pools; smoke-free rooms. *In room:* A/C, TV, hair dryer (upon request), minibar.

Villas Arqueológicas Uxmal ★★ Still the best value among the hotels clustered around the ruins' entrance, the Villas and its sister properties have new owners that have added some polish, though the food seems blander than before. A basic two-story quadrangle around a garden patio and pool is admirably prettied up by lush vegetation, Maya statues, and a paint job with a semblance of traditional style. At guests' disposal are a tennis court, a library, and an audiovisual show on the ruins in English, French, and Spanish. Each of the modern, medium-size rooms has a double and a twin bed fit into spaces that are walled on three sides (very tall people should look elsewhere). Ask about rates for half- (breakfast plus lunch or dinner) or full (3 meals) board.

Ruinas Uxmal, 97844 Uxmal, Yuc. ✆ **987/872-9300,** ext. 8101. www.islandercollection.com. 48 units. 989 pesos double Sun–Thurs, 1,106 pesos Fri & Sat. AE, MC, V. Free guarded parking. **Amenities:** Restaurant; bar; outdoor pool; tennis court; Wi-Fi in public areas. *In room:* A/C, hair dryer.

Where to Dine

You can eat well at the hotel restaurant of the **Lodge at Uxmal** if you order the Yucatecan specialties, which are fresh and well prepared. In Santa Elena, the **Pickled Onion** offers a menu of mostly Mexican dishes with a few international twists; the food is good, and the owner's hospitality is legendary. The *palapa* restaurants by the highway as you approach the ruins from Mérida are a mixed bag. They do a lot of business with bus tours, so the best time to try them is early afternoon.

THE PUUC MAYA ROUTE

South and east of Uxmal are several other ancient Maya cities, small and largely unexcavated but worth visiting for their unique architecture.

Kabah is 28km (17 miles) southeast of Uxmal via Hwy. 261 through Santa Elena, and only a couple kilometers farther to Sayil. Xlapak is almost walking distance (through the jungle) from Sayil, and Labná is just a bit farther east. A short drive beyond Labná brings you to the caves of Loltún. Oxkutzcab is at the road's intersection with Hwy. 184, which you can follow west to Ticul or east all the way to Felipe Carrillo Puerto. If you aren't driving, a daily bus from Mérida (p. 251) goes to all these sites, with the exception of Loltún.

Puuc Maya Sites

KABAH ★ From Uxmal, head southwest on Hwy. 261 to Santa Elena (1km/½ mile), then south to Kabah (13km/8 miles). The ancient city lies along both sides of the highway. Turn right into the parking lot.

The outstanding building at Kabah, to the right as you enter, is the **Palace of Masks,** or Codz Poop ("rolled-up mat"), named for its decorative motif. Its Chenes-style facade is completely covered in a repeated pattern of 250 masks of Chaac, each with curling remnants of the god's elephant trunk–like nose. It is unique in all of Maya architecture. For years, parts of this building lay lined up in the weeds like pieces of a puzzle awaiting assembly. Sculptures from this building are in the anthropology museums of Mérida and Mexico City.

Just behind and to the left of the Codz Poop is the **Palace Group** (also called the East Group), with a fine Puuc-style colonnaded facade. Originally, it had 32 rooms. On the front are seven doors, two divided by columns—a common feature of Puuc architecture. Across the highway is what was once the **Great Temple,** and beyond that is a **great arch.** It was

The Palace of Masks in Kabah.

The ruins of Sayil.

much wider at one time and may have been a monumental gate into the city. A *sacbé* linked this arch to Uxmal. Compare this corbelled arch to the one at Labná (below), which is in much better shape.

SAYIL About 4km (2½ miles) south of Kabah is the turnoff (left, or east) to Sayil, Xlapak, Labná, Loltún, and Oxkutzcab. The ruins of **Sayil** ("place of the ants") are 4km (2½ miles) along this road.

Sayil is famous for **El Palacio ★★**. With more than 90 rooms, the palace is impressive for its size alone. Climbing is not permitted, but the facade that makes this a masterpiece of Maya architecture is best appreciated from the ground. It stretches across three terraced levels, and its rows of columns give it a Minoan appearance. The upside-down stone figure known to archaeologists as the Diving God, or Descending God, over the doorway on the second level is the same motif used at Tulum a couple of centuries later. The large circular basin on the ground below the palace is an artificial catch basin for a *chultún* (cistern); this region has no natural cenotes (wells) for irrigation.

In the jungle beyond El Palacio is **El Mirador,** a small temple with an oddly slotted roof comb. Beyond El Mirador, a crude stele (tall, carved stone) is carved with a fertility god burdened with a phallus of monstrous proportions. Another building group, the Southern Group, is a short distance down a trail that branches off from the one heading to El Mirador.

Seeing the Puuc Maya Sites

These sites are undergoing excavation and reconstruction, and some buildings may be roped off when you visit. The sites are open daily from 8am to 5pm. Admission is 37 pesos for each city and 50 pesos for Loltún. Loltún has tours at 9:30 and 11am, and 12:30, 2, 3, and 4pm. Even if you're the only person there when a tour is scheduled, the guide must give you a tour, and he can't charge you as if you were contracting his services for an individual tour (though sometimes they try). Use of a video camera at any time costs 45 pesos; if you visit Uxmal the same day, you pay only once for video permission and present your receipt as proof at each ruin.

Labná's El Palacio.

XLAPAK Xlapak (*shla*-pahk) is a small site with one building; it's 5.5 km (3½ miles) down the road from Sayil. The Palace at Xlapak bears the masks of the rain god Chaac. If you're running out of steam, this is the one to skip.

LABNÁ Labná, dating from between A.D. 600 and 900, is 30km (19 miles) from Uxmal and only 3km (1¾ miles) past Xlapak. The entrance has a snack stand and toilets. Descriptive placards fronting the main buildings are in Spanish, English, and German.

As soon as you enter you'll see **El Palacio,** a magnificent Puuc-style building on your left that is much like the one at Sayil, but in poorer condition. Over one doorway is a large, well-conserved mask of Chaac with eyes, a huge snout nose, and jagged teeth around a small mouth that seems on the verge of speaking. Jutting out on one corner is a highly stylized serpent's mouth from which pops a human head with an unexpectedly serene expression. From the front, you can gaze out to the enormous grassy interior grounds flanked by vestiges of unrestored buildings and jungle.

From El Palacio, you can walk on a reconstructed *sacbé* leading to Labná's **corbelled arch.** At one time, there were probably several such arches through the region. This one has been extensively restored, although only remnants of the roof comb are visible. It was once part of a more elaborate structure now lost to history. Chaac's face occupies the corners of one facade, and stylized Maya huts are fashioned in stone above the two small doorways. You can pass through the arch to reach **El Mirador** or El Castillo. Towering above a large pile of rubble, the remains of a pyramid, is a singular room crowned with a roof comb piercing the sky.

LOLTÚN The caverns of Loltún are 31km (19 miles) past Labná on the way to Oxkutzcab, on the left side of the road. One of the Yucatán's largest and most fascinating cave systems, they were home to the ancient Maya and were used as a refuge during the War of the Castes (1847–1901). Inside are statues, wall carvings, and paintings, *chultunes* (cisterns), and other signs of

The caverns of Loltún.

Maya habitation. Guides will explain much of what you see, though their English isn't always easy to understand.

The admission price includes a 90-minute tour. These begin daily at 9:30 and 11am, and 12:30, 2, 3, and 4pm. The floor of the cavern can be slippery in places; take a flashlight if you have one.

To return to Mérida from Loltún, drive the 7km (4¼ miles) to Oxkutzcab. From there, you can take the slow route through Maní and Teabo, which will allow you to see some convents and return by Hwy. 18, known as the "Convent Route" (p. 279). The other option is to head toward Muna to hook up with Hwy. 261 (p. 279).

Oxkutzcab

Oxkutzcab (ohsh-kootz-*kahb*), 11km (6¾ miles) from Loltún, is the center of the Yucatán's fruit-growing region. Oranges abound. The tidy village of 21,000 centers on a beautiful 16th-century church and the market. **Su Cabaña Suiza** (no phone) is a dependable restaurant in town. The last week of October and first week of November is the **Orange Festival,** when the village turns exuberant, with a carnival and orange displays in and around the central plaza.

En Route to Campeche

From Oxkutzcab, head back 43km (27 miles) to Sayil, and then drive south on Hwy. 261 to Campeche (126km/78 miles). After crossing the state line, you'll pass through the towns of Bolonchén and Hopelchén, both of which have gas stations. The drive is pleasant, and there's little traffic. Watch carefully for directional traffic signs in these towns to stay on the highway. From Hopelchén, Hwy. 261 heads west. After 42km (26 miles), you'll find yourself at Cayal and the well-marked turnoff for the ruins of the city of Edzná (p. 301), 18km (11 miles) farther south. If you're taking this route to Campeche, this could be the time to see this tranquil, underappreciated ancient city.

CAMPECHE ★★

251km (156 miles) SW of Mérida; 376km (233 miles) NE of Villahermosa

Campeche, the capital of the state of the same name, is a splendidly restored colonial city that is woefully overlooked by travelers. All the historic center's facades have been repaired and painted, electrical and telephone cables moved underground, and the streets paved to resemble cobblestone. Several period films have been shot here, including *Che,* Steven Soderbergh's epic two-part biography of Che Guevara.

Those who do come to Campeche often are on their way to the ruins at Palenque (chapter 9) or the Río Bec region (chapter 7), or they are accidental wanderers by nature. It must be said that Campeche is not geared to foreign tourism the way Mérida is—though it is catching up—so expect less English translation at museums, ruins, and services. Also, expect less in the way of nightlife, except on weekend nights when the main square becomes one huge street party.

Campeche's history is laden with drama. The conquistadors arrived in 1517, when Francisco de Córdoba landed here while exploring the coast and stayed just long enough to celebrate Mass. Native resistance thwarted attempts to settle here until Montejo the Younger managed to secure a settlement in 1540.

In the 17th and 18th centuries, pirates repeatedly sacked the city. The list of attackers reads like a who's who of pirating. On one occasion, several outfits banded together under the famous Dutch pirate Peg Leg (the likely inspiration for many a fictional one-legged sailor) and managed to capture the city. The Campechanos grew tired of hosting pirate parties and erected walls around the city, with *baluartes* (bastions) at critical points. For added security, they built two forts, complete with moats and drawbridges, on the hills flanking Campeche. There were four gates through the wall, two of which still stand: the Puerta de Mar (Sea Gate) and the Puerta de Tierra (Land Gate). The pirates never cared to return, but in Mexico's stormy political history, the city did withstand a couple of sieges by different armies. Eventually, in the early 1900s, the wall was razed, but the bastions and main gates remain, along with the two hilltop fortresses. Most of the bastions and both forts now house museums.

Essentials

GETTING THERE & DEPARTING **By Plane** **Aeroméxico** (✆ **800/237-6399** in the U.S., 01-800/021-4000 in Mexico or 981/816-6656; www.aeromexico.com.mx) flies once daily to and from Mexico City. Campeche's **airport** is several kilometers northeast of the town center, and you'll have to take a taxi into town (about 100 pesos).

By Car Hwy. 180 goes south from Mérida, passing near the basket-making village of Halacho and near Becal, known for its Panama-hat weavers. The trip takes 2½ hours. The longer way from Mérida is along Hwy. 261 past Uxmal.

When driving from Campeche to Mérida via Hwy. 180, go north on Avenida Ruiz Cortines, bearing left to follow the water (this becomes Av. Pedro Sainz de Baranda, but there's no sign). Follow the road as it turns inland to Hwy. 180, where you turn left (there's a gas station at the intersection).

ATTRACTIONS
Baluarte San Juan **19**
Botanical Garden **3**
Casa 6 Centro Cultural **7**
Casa de Artesanías Tukulná **11**
Mansion Carvajal **4**
Museo de la Ciudad **16**
Museo de la Cultura Maya **8**
Puerta de Tierra **13**

ACCOMMODATIONS
Hacienda Puerta Campeche **12**
Hotel Castelmar **14**
Hotel Del Mar **9**
Hotel Francis Drake **17**
Hotel López **15**

DINING
Cactus **18**
Casa Vieja **6**
Cenaduria los Portales **1**
La Parroquia **5**
La Pigua **2**
Marganzo **10**

To go from Campeche to Edzná and Uxmal, drive north on either Ruiz Cortines or Gobernadores and turn right on Madero, which feeds onto Hwy. 281. To go south to Villahermosa, take Ruiz Cortines south.

By Bus **ADO** (✆ **981/816-2802**) offers a first-class *de paso* (passing through) bus to Palenque (6 hrs.; 254 pesos) four times a day and buses to Mérida (2½ hr.; 144 pesos) every hour from 5:30am to midnight. The ADO **bus station** is on Avenida Patricio Trueba at Avenida Casa de Justicia, almost 2km (1.2 miles) from the Puerta de Tierra. The second-class bus station, with service to nearby cities and to Mérida, is at Avenida Gobernadores and Calle 45 (also called Calle Chile on the east side of Gobernadores).

INFORMATION The **State of Campeche Office of Tourism** (✆ **981/811-9229;** fax 981/816-6767; http://campeche.travel) is in Plaza Moch-Couoh, Avenida Ruiz Cortines s/n (btw. calles 63 and 65). Hours are daily 8am to 4pm and 6 to 9pm. This is one of the state buildings between the historic center and the shore. Tourist information offices are also in the bastions of Baluarte San Pedro (daily 9am–1pm and 5–9pm) and in Casa 6 (daily 9am–9pm). The city's **Tourism and Culture Office** (✆ **981/811-3989**) is on Calle 55 between calles 10 and 8; open daily 9am to 9pm.

CITY LAYOUT By far the most interesting feature of the city is the restored old part, most of which once lay within the walls. Originally, the seaward wall was at the water's edge, but land has been gained from the sea between the old walls and the coastline. This is where you'll find most of the state government buildings, which were built in a glaringly modernist style around **Plaza Moch-Couoh:** buildings such as the office tower **Edificio de los Poderes (Judicial Building)** or **Palacio de Gobierno (headquarters for the state of Campeche),** and the futuristic **Cámara de Diputados (Chamber of Deputies),** which looks like a cubist clam.

Campeche's street numbering system is typical of the Yucatán, except that numbers of the north–south streets increase as you go east instead of the reverse.

GETTING AROUND Most recommended sights, restaurants, and hotels are within walking distance of the old city, except for the two fort-museums. Campeche isn't easy to negotiate by bus, so take taxis for sights beyond walking distance—they are inexpensive.

[FastFACTS] CAMPECHE

Area Code The telephone area code is **981.**

ATMs More than 10 cash machines are around the downtown area.

Internet Access Plenty of places to check e-mail are in town—just look for signs with the words INTERNET or CYBERCAFE.

Post Office The *correo* is in the Edificio Federal, at Avenida 16 de Septiembre and Calle 53 (✆ **981/816-2134**), near the Baluarte de Santiago; it's open Monday to Saturday from 7:30am to 8pm.

Campeche's Parque Principal by night.

Exploring Campeche

With beautiful surroundings, friendly people, and an easy pace of life, Campeche is made for walking. Its more than 1,000 refurbished facades and renovations, grand mansions, monumental buildings, and ornate churches can be sampled in half a day or savored, along with a few day trips, over a week.

INSIDE THE CITY WALLS

The natural starting point is the modest but exceedingly pretty *zócalo,* or **Parque Principal ★**, bounded by calles 55 and 57 running east and west, and calles 8 and 10 running north and south. On Saturday nights and Sundays, the streets are closed and bands set up in the gazebo. People set up tables in the streets, and an exuberant street party ensues. Construction of the **cathedral** on the north side, whose crown-shaped bell towers dominate the square, began in 1650 and was finally completed 150 years later. A pleasant way to see the city is to take the *tranvía* (trolley) tour leaving the plaza approximately every hour between 9am and 1pm and 5 to 9pm. The cost is 70 pesos for a 45-minute tour.

Baluarte San Juan The city's smallest bastion holds an exhibition on the history of the baluartes and an old underground dungeon. The only remaining chunk of the old city wall connects San Juan with the Puerta de Tierra. The short walk between the two offers incomparable views of the new as well as the old city.

Calle 18, btw. calles 8 and 10. No phone. Free admission. Tues–Sun 8am–7:30pm.

Botanical Garden The Jardín Botánico Xmuch'haltun is a riot of some 250 species of exotic and common plants, including an enormous *ceiba* tree, in a tiny courtyard surrounded by the stone walls of the last bastion Campeche built (Baluarte de Santiago).

Av. 16 de Septiembre and Calle 49. No phone. Free admission. Mon–Fri 9am–8pm; Sat–Sun 9am–1pm.

Casa 6 Centro Cultural ★★ Some rooms in this remodeled colonial house are decorated with period furniture and accessories. The traditional stucco and terra cotta kitchen is arranged just as many Campechanos use them today. The patio of mixtilinear arches supported by simple Doric columns is striking. The front of the house is now a cultural center with a patio restaurant and a bookstore focusing on Campeche's history. One bedroom has been turned over to exhibition space.

Calle 57 no. 6. No phone. Free admission. Daily 9am–9pm.

Mansion Carvajal ★ Another remarkable colonial mansion, built by one of the Yucatán's wealthiest *hacendados* in the early 19th century, has been put to more prosaic contemporary use for state offices but is open to the public on weekdays. It is most famous for its massive Carrara marble stairway, curving to the open, light-filled second story as if ascending to the heavens. Surrounded by pale mint-green walls punctuated by white columns and sinuous Moorish arches, you feel like you're standing on a colossal tiered wedding cake. Art Nouveau curlicues in the iron railings and black-and-white checkerboard floors are, well, the icing on the cake.

Calle 10 btw. calles 51 and 53. No phone. Free admission. Mon–Fri 8am–2:45pm.

Museo de la Ciudad The Museo de la Ciudad, or city museum, with the Baluarte de San Carlos, deals primarily with the design and construction of the fortifications. A model of the city shows how it looked in its glory days and provides a good overview for touring within the city walls. There are several excellent ship models as well. All text is in Spanish.

Circuito Baluartes and Av. Justo Sierra. No phone. Admission 25 pesos. Tues–Sat 9am–8pm; Sun 9am–1pm.

Museo de la Cultura Maya The Baluarte de la Soledad, next to the sea gate, houses the Museo de la Cultura Maya. Four rooms of Maya artifacts recovered from throughout the state, including columns from Edzná, provide an excellent overview of Maya writing, sculpture, and architecture. Many of the stelae are badly worn, but line drawings beside the stones allow you to appreciate their former design.

Calle 57 and Calle 8, opposite Plaza Principal. No phone. Admission 25 pesos. Tues–Sat 9am–8pm; Sun 9am–1pm.

Puerta de Tierra ☺ The Land Gate, unlike the reconstructed Sea Gate at the opposite end of calle 59, is the original, and is connected to the last remaining patch of the old city wall. A small museum displays portraits of pirates and the city founders. The 1732 French 5-ton cannon in the entryway was discovered in 1990. On

A colorful cobblestone street in Campeche.

Fuerte-Museo San José el Alto.

Tuesday, Friday, and Saturday at 8pm, it holds a light-and-sound show, as long as enough people buy tickets. A variation on the popular shows at the archaeological sites, this re-enacts pirate tales with blazing cannons and flashing lights. A little over the top, but fun, and kids are enthralled.

Calle 59 at Circuito Baluartes/Av. Gobernadores. No phone. Free admission to museum; show 52 pesos adults, 15 pesos children younger than 11. Daily 9am–9pm.

OUTSIDE THE WALLS: SCENIC VISTAS

Fuerte-Museo San José el Alto This fort is higher and has a more sweeping city and coastline views than Fuerte San Miguel—its sloping lawns are a popular picnic spot—but it houses only a small exhibit of 16th- and 17th-century weapons and scale miniatures of sailing vessels. The rogue's gallery of pirates is irresistible. Take a cab; you will pass an impressive statue of Juárez on the way.

Av. Morazán s/n. No phone. Admission 27 pesos. Tues–Sun 9:30am–5:30pm.

Fuerte-Museo San Miguel ★★ For a good view of the city and a great little museum, take a cab up to Fuerte–Museo San Miguel, a small fort with a moat and a drawbridge. Built in 1771, it was the most important of the city's defenses. General Santa Anna captured it when he attacked Campeche in 1842. The **Museum of Mayan Culture** was renovated in 2000 and is worth seeing. Artifacts are organized around central issues in Maya culture. The room devoted to Maya concepts of the afterlife displays a captivating *in situ* burial scene with jade masks and jewelry from Maya tombs at Calakmul. Another room explains Maya cosmology, one depicts war, and another explains the gods. The history of the fort has its own exhibits.

Ruta Escénica s/n. No phone. Admission 34 pesos. Tues–Sat 9am–8pm; Sun 8am–noon.

Campeche's Malecón.

Malecón ★★ Not everything Campeche has to offer is lodged in the past. The flurry of renovation also lined about 3km (2 miles) of the waterfront with this broad, palm-lined sea walk, encompassing fountains, cannons, exercise stations, gardens, and monuments. The jogging and bike path bustles with energetic locals in the cool of early morning and late-night hours. Join them as the day's heat breaks for a sunset you won't soon forget.

Shopping

Casa de Artesanías Tukulná This store, run by a government family-assistance agency, occupies a restored mansion and sells top-quality examples of everything that is produced in the state, from textiles to clothing to furniture. An elaborate display of regional arts and crafts in the back includes a hammock in the making and a replica of a mud-walled Maya house. Calle 10 no. 333 (btw. calles 59 and 61). ✆ **981/816-9088**. Mon–Sat 10am–8pm.

Where to Stay

Rates quoted include the 17% tax.

VERY EXPENSIVE

Hacienda Puerta Campeche ★★★ This beautiful and original hotel was created from several adjoining colonial homes, just inside the Puerta de Tierra in Campeche's colonial center. There is a tropical garden in the center and a pool that runs through the ruined walls of one house. Rooms are colonial with flair—large with old tile floors, distinctive colors, and beamed ceilings. "Hacienda" is in the name to make it apparent that this is connected to the hacienda properties managed by Starwood hotels (p. 261).

Calle 59 no. 71 (btw. Calles 16 and 18), 24000 Campeche, Camp. ✆ **800/325-3589** in the U.S. or Canada, or 981/816-7508. Fax 999/923-7963. www.luxurycollection.com. 15 units. High season $325–$445 superior; $405 and up suite; low season $245–$360 superior; $325 and up suite. AE, MC, V. Free guarded parking. **Amenities:** Restaurant; 2 bars; airport transfer; babysitting; concierge; outdoor pool; room service; spa. *In room:* A/C, TV, fridge, hair dryer, Internet, minibar.

EXPENSIVE

Hotel Del Mar ★ It's your typical concrete rectangle, but rooms in this modern four-story hotel are large, bright, and comfortably furnished. All have balconies facing the Gulf of Mexico. The beds (two doubles or one king-size) are comfortable. The Del Mar is on the main oceanfront boulevard, between the coast and the city walls. You can make a reservation here to stay in the Río Bec area, or you can buy a package that includes guide and transportation.

Av. Ruiz Cortines 51 (at calle 59), 24000 Campeche, Camp. ✆ **981/811-9192,** -9193. Fax 981/811-1618. www.delmarhotel.com.mx. 145 units. $90 double. AE, MC, V. Free parking. **Amenities:** 2 restaurants; bar; babysitting; gym w/sauna; large outdoor pool; room service; smoke-free rooms. *In room:* A/C, TV, hair dryer.

MODERATE

Hotel Castelmar ★★ ☺ This remarkable transformation of a one-time flophouse was restored in 2006. Pillars, archways, and tall wooden doors are reminiscent of Puerta de Campeche. The original floor plans and tiles (different patterns in each room) remain, and rooms are all shapes and sizes. But the bathrooms, swimming pool, and sun deck are new. I like the rooms with double doors opening onto a tiny balcony overlooking the street, though some people find them too noisy. It's a great *centro histórico* (historical district) location, two blocks from the *zócalo*.

Calle 61 no. 2, btw. calles 8 and 10, 24000 Campeche, Camp. ✆ **981/811-1204.** Fax 702/297-6826. www.castelmarhotel.com. 22 units. 850 pesos double, 950 pesos superior, 1,150 pesos junior suite. AE, MC, V. Free parking. **Amenities:** Concierge; outdoor pool; sundeck. *In room:* A/C, TV, hair dryer (on request), Wi-Fi.

Hotel Francis Drake ★ This three-story hotel in a quiet *centro histórico* location has comfortable, midsize rooms with upscale touches not often seen at the rates they charge. The rooms are attractive, with tile floors and one king-size bed, two doubles, or two twins. The modern marble bathrooms have large showers. Suites are larger and better furnished than the standard rooms. Service is attentive, if not particularly warm by Campeche standards. The small restaurant, with a whimsical sky scene painted in the ceiling coves, serves fine examples of local dishes at very reasonable prices.

Calle 12 no. 207 (btw. calles 63 and 65), 24000 Campeche, Camp. ✆ **981/811-5626,** -5627. www.hotelfrancisdrake.com. 24 units. 795 pesos double, 905 pesos junior suite, 1,030 pesos suite. AE, MC, V. Limited free parking. **Amenities:** Restaurant; concierge; room service. *In room:* A/C, TV, hair dryer, minibar.

INEXPENSIVE

Hotel López Unique among the historic center's hotels, the López is all Art Deco verve, with curlicued ironwork swooping around layers of curved walkways above an oval-shaped, open-air courtyard. The 1950 building was rehabilitated several years ago, now with gleaming tile bathrooms, a new waterfall pool, and a small cafe. Guest rooms are small and not nearly as stylish as the public areas, but they are comfortable enough and clean. It's the best hotel in its price range.

Calle Calle 12 no. 189 (btw. calles 61 and 63), 24000 Campeche, Camp. ✆ **981/816-3344.** www.hotelllopezcampeche.com. MC, V. 48 units. 500 pesos. **Amenities:** Outdoor pool. *In room:* A/C, TV.

Where to Dine

Campeche is a fishing town, known for its fresh seafood, but restaurants also offer classic Yucatecan pork, chicken, turkey, and beef dishes. Campeche also has its own regional cuisine, fusing Spanish dishes, recipes brought by pirates from all over the world, and the region's own exotic fruits and vegetables. Make a point to try the No. 1 specialty, *pan de cazón* (baby shark casserole)—a stack of tortillas layered with baby shark and refried beans, then smothered with tomato sauce. For an inexpensive introduction to Campechano cuisine, sample the home-cooked food served in stalls around the *zócalo* on weekend evenings.

MODERATE

Cactus STEAKS/MEXICAN If seafood isn't to your taste, or you've just had enough, this steakhouse is a favorite with the locals. The rib-eyes are good, as is everything but the *arrachera,* which is the same tough cut of meat used for fajitas.

Av. Malecón Justo Sierra. ✆ **981/811-1453.** Main courses 120–250 pesos. No credit cards. Daily 7am–2am.

Casa Vieja INTERNATIONAL/MEXICAN Casa Vieja has gotten a little, well, old. While the blend of Yucatecan and Cuban food still holds interest, there's been a drop in effort. But this is still the city's prettiest dining space, in an upstairs arcade overlooking the main square. Stick with simple regional dishes, and if you're lucky, they'll be on the upswing in that mysterious cycle of quality through which so many restaurants operate.

Calle 10 no. 319. ✆ **981/811-1311.** Reservations not accepted. Main courses 60–160 pesos. No credit cards. Tues–Sun 9am–2am; Mon 5:30pm–2am.

La Pigua ★★★ SEAFOOD The dining area is an air-conditioned version of a traditional Yucatecan cabin, but with walls of glass looking out on green vegetation. Sure to be on the menu is fish stuffed with shellfish, which I recommend. If you're lucky, you'll also find pompano in a green sauce seasoned with a peppery herb known as *hierba santa.* Other standouts are coconut-battered shrimp with applesauce and *chiles rellenos* with shark. Service is excellent, and the accommodating owner can have your favorite seafood prepared in any style you want.

Av. Miguel Alemán no. 179A. ✆ **981/811-3365.** Reservations recommended. Main courses 120–260 pesos. AE, MC, V. Daily noon–8pm. From Plaza Principal, walk north on Calle 8 for 3 blocks; cross Av. Circuito by the botanical garden where Calle 8 becomes Miguel Alemán; the restaurant is 1½ blocks farther, on the right.

Marganzo ★ SEAFOOD The menu veers toward the expensive side if you indulge in the seafood—its specialty—but if you stick to the Yucatecan dishes such as *poc chuc* and *pollo pibíl,* you'll eat quite well for 75 pesos or so. If you spring for seafood, white fish filled with seafood is a local favorite. Either way, you'll leave satisfied; the kitchen knows what it's doing. Though it isn't the bargain it used to be, breakfast is still the most popular meal here.

Calle 8 no. 267 (in front of the Sea Gate). ✆ **981/816-3899.** www.marganzo.com. Main courses 82–228 pesos. MC, V. Daily 7am–11pm.

INEXPENSIVE

Cenaduría los Portales ★ ANTOJITOS This is a traditional Campechano supper place, a small restaurant under the stone arches facing the Plaza San

Francisco in the *barrio* (neighborhood) of San Francisco. This is the oldest part of town, but it lies just outside the walls to the north. Start with the *horchata* (a sweet, milky-white drink made, in this case, with coconut). Try the delicious turkey soup and the *sincronizadas* (tostadas) and *panuchos*.

Calle 10 no. 86, Portales San Francisco. ✆ **981/811-1491.** *Antojitos* 4–15 pesos. No credit cards. Daily 6pm–midnight.

La Parroquia MEXICAN This local hangout offers good, inexpensive fare. It's best for breakfasts and the afternoon *comida corrida,* which might offer pot roast, meatballs, pork, or fish, with rice or squash, beans, tortillas, and fresh fruit–flavored water.

Calle 55 no. 9. ✆ **981/816-8086.** Breakfast 50 pesos; main courses 50–130 pesos; *comida corrida* (served noon–3pm) 45–55 pesos. MC, V. Daily 24 hr.

Side Trips from Campeche

EDZNÁ ★★

Don't skip **Edzná** just because you've seen Chichén Itzá, Uxmal, or other famous ruins. There are several reasons to see this city. The area was populated as early as 600 B.C., with urban formation by 300 B.C. Edzná grew impressively, displaying considerable urban-planning skills. It has an ambitious and elaborate canal system that must have taken decades to complete, but would have allowed for a great expansion in agricultural production and therefore, concentration of population.

Another construction boom began around A.D. 500, during the Classic period—the city's most prominent feature, the **Great Acropolis,** was started

Edzná's Pyramid of Five Stories.

then—and rose to its height as a grand regional capital between A.D. 600 and 900. This was a crossroads between cities in present-day Chiapas, Yucatán, and Guatemala, and influences from all those areas appear in the city's elegant architecture.

Sitting atop the Great Acropolis are five main pyramids, the largest being the much-photographed **Pyramid of Five Stories.** It combines the features of temple platform and palace. Maya architecture typically consists of palace buildings with many vaulted chambers or solid pyramidal platforms with a couple of interior temples or burial passages. The two types of construction are mutually exclusive—except here. Such a mix is found only in the Puuc and Río Bec areas, and in only a few examples there. None are similar to this, which makes this pyramid a bold architectural statement.

Each of the Acropolis' four lesser pyramids is each constructed in a different style, and each is a pure example of that style. It's as if the city's rulers were flaunting their cosmopolitanism, showing that they could build in any style they chose but preferred creating their own, superior architecture.

West of the Acropolis, across a large open plaza, is a long, raised building whose purpose isn't quite clear. But its size, as well as that of the plaza, makes you wonder just how many people this city actually held to necessitate such a large public space. Other major structures to explore include the **Platform of the Knives,** where flint knives were recovered, and the **Temple of the Big Masks,** flanked by twin sun-god faces with protruding crossed eyes (a sign of elite status).

To reach Edzná, take Hwy. 261 east from Campeche to Cayal, then Hwy. 188 south for 18km (11 miles). Buses from Campeche leave from a small station behind Parque Alameda, which is next to the market. Plan to spend an hour or two. The site is open daily from 8am to 5pm. Admission is 111 pesos, including the evening light-and-sound show, plus 45 pesos if you use a video camera.

CALAKMUL & RÍO BEC

If you're interested in seeing the ruins along the Río Bec route, see "Side Trips to Maya Ruins from Chetumal," in chapter 7. **Calakmul ★★★** (p. 242) is an important site, with the tallest pyramid in the Yucatán peninsula; Balamkú and other Río Bec sites are well worth seeing while you're in the area. You can get information and book a tour in Campeche, or rent a car. Calakmul is too far away for a day trip.

From the Calakmul area, it's easy to cross over the peninsula to Yucatán's southern Caribbean coast. Then you can head up the coast and complete a loop of the peninsula.

THE RUINS OF CHICHÉN ITZÁ ★★★

179km (111 miles) W of Cancún; 120km (74 miles) E of Mérida; 138km (86 miles) NW of Tulum

The fabled ruins of Chichén Itzá (chee-*chen* eet-*zah*) are by far the Yucatán's best-known ancient monuments. Sadly, its coronation as a "New World Wonder" has made the great city harder to appreciate. Still, walking among these stone temples, pyramids, and ball courts gives you a feel for this civilization that books

The fabled ruins of Chichén Itzá.

cannot approach, and there's no other way to comprehend the city's sheer scale. The ceremonial center's plazas would have been filled with thousands of people during one of the mass rituals that occurred here a millennium ago—and that is the saving grace for hordes of tourists that now flow through every day.

Much of what is said about the Maya (especially by tour guides) is merely educated guessing. We do know the area was settled by farmers as far back as the 4th century A.D. The first signs of an urban society appear in the 7th century in construction of stone temples and palaces in the Puuc Maya style, found in the "Old Chichén" section of the city. In the 10th century (the post-Classic Era), Chichén Itzá came under the rule of the Itzáes, who arrived from central Mexico by way of the Gulf Coast. They may have been a mix of highland Toltec Indians, who built the city of Tula in central Mexico, and lowland Putún Maya, a thriving population of traders. Following centuries brought Chichén Itzá's greatest growth. The style of the grand architecture built during this age clearly reveals Toltec influence.

The new rulers might have been refugees from Tula. A pre-Columbian myth from central Mexico tells of a fight between the gods Quetzalcóatl and Tezcatlipoca that forced Quetzalcóatl to leave his homeland and venture east. In another mythic tale, the losers of a war between Tula's religious factions fled to the Yucatán, where they were welcomed by the local Maya. Over time, the Itzáes adopted more and more the ways of the Maya. Sometime at the end of the 12th century, the city was captured by its rival, Mayapán.

Though it's possible to make a day trip from Cancún or Mérida, staying overnight here or in nearby Valladolid makes for a more relaxing trip. You can see the light show in the evening and return to see the ruins early the next morning when it is cool and before the tour buses start arriving.

Essentials

GETTING THERE & DEPARTING **By Car** Chichén Itzá is on old Hwy. 180 between Mérida and Cancún. The fastest way to get there from either city is to take the *autopista* (or *cuota*). The toll is 71 pesos from Mérida (1½hours), 267 pesos from Cancún (2½ hours). From Tulum, take the highway leading to Cobá and Chemax, which connects to Hwy. 180 a bit east of Valladolid. Exiting the *autopista*, turn onto the road to Pisté. In the village, you'll reach a T junction at Hwy. 180 and turn left to the ruins; the entrance is well marked. On the same highway a few kilometers beyond, you'll come to the Hotel Zone exit at Km 121 (first, you'll pass the eastern entrance to the ruins, which is usually closed).

By Bus First-class buses run from Mérida's CAME station nearly every hour, and some first-class buses to Cancún and Playa also stop here. Cancún and Valladolid also have first-class service. Day trips to Chichén Itzá are also widely available from Mérida, Cancún, and Playa del Carmen (and almost any destination in the Yucatán).

AREA LAYOUT The village of **Pisté,** where most of the budget hotels and restaurants are located, is about 2.5km (1½ miles) west of the ruins. Public buses can drop you off here. Another budget hotel, the Dolores Alba (p. 310) is on the old highway 2.5km (1½ miles) east of the ruins. Three luxury hotels are situated right at Chichén Itzá's entrance.

Exploring the Ruins

The site occupies 6.5 sq. km (2½ sq. miles), requiring most of a day to see it all. The ruins are open daily from 8am to 5pm, service areas from 8am to 10pm. Admission is 51 pesos, free for children 11 and younger. A video camera permit costs 45 pesos. Parking is extra. *You can use your ticket to re-enter on the same day.* The **sound-and-light show** (worth seeing as you're being charged for it anyway), is held at 7pm or 8pm depending on the season, and is in Spanish, but headsets are available for rent in several languages. The narrative is okay, but the real reason for seeing the show is the lights, which show off the beautiful geometry of the city.

The large, modern visitor center at the main entrance consists of a museum, an auditorium, a restaurant, a bookstore, and bathrooms. Licensed guides who speak English or Spanish usually wait at the entrance and charge around 450 pesos for one to six people (there's nothing wrong with approaching a group of people who speak the same language and offering to share a guide). You can also see the site on your own, but the guides can point out architectural details you might miss on your own.

Chichén Itzá has two parts: the central (new) zone, which shows distinct Toltec influence, and the southern (old) zone, with mostly Puuc architecture. The most important structures are in New Chichén, but the older ones are also worth seeing.

EL CASTILLO As you enter from the tourist center, the icon of Yucatán tourism, the magnificent 25m (82-ft.) El Castillo (also called the Pyramid of Kukulkán) is straight ahead across a large, open grassy area. It was built with the Maya calendar in mind. The four stairways leading up to the central platform each have 91 steps, which, added to the platform, totals the

The sound-and-light show illuminates the pyramids of Chichén Itzá.

365 days of the solar year. The 18 terraces flanking the stairways on each face of the pyramid add up to the number of months in the Maya religious calendar. The terraces contain a total of 52 panels, representing the 52-year cycle when the solar and religious calendars reconverge. The pyramid, now closed to climbers, is aligned so that the **spring** or **fall equinox** (Mar 21 or Sept 21), triggers an optical illusion: The setting sun casts the terraces' shadow onto the northern stairway, forming a diamond pattern suggestive of a snake's geometric designs. As it meets the giant serpent's head at the bottom, the shadow appears to slither down the pyramid as the sun sets, a phenomenon that brings hordes of visitors every year. (The effect is more conceptual than visual, and frankly, the ruins are much more enjoyable on other days when they are less crowded.)

Like most Maya pyramids, El Castillo was built over an earlier structure. A narrow stairway at the western edge of the north staircase leads inside to a sacrificial altar-throne—a red jaguar encrusted with jade. The stairway is open from 11am to 3pm and is cramped, usually crowded, humid, and uncomfortable. A visit early in the day is best. Photos of the jaguar figure are not allowed.

JUDGE DE PELOTA (MAIN BALL COURT) Northwest of El Castillo is Chichén's main ball court, the largest and best preserved anywhere, and only one of nine ball courts built in this city. Carved on both walls are scenes showing Maya figures dressed as ball players and decked out in heavy protective padding. A headless player kneels with blood shooting from his neck; another player holding the head looks on.

Players on two teams tried to knock a hard rubber ball through one of the two stone rings placed high on either wall, using only their elbows, knees, and hips. According to legend, losers paid for defeat with their lives. However, some experts say the victors were the only appropriate sacrifices for the gods. Either way, the game, called pok-ta-pok, must have been riveting, heightened by the ball court's wonderful acoustics.

Players tried to knock a hard rubber ball through this stone ring placed high on the wall, using only their elbows, knees, and hips.

THE NORTH TEMPLE Temples stand at both ends of the ball court. The North Temple has sculptured pillars and more sculptures inside, as well as badly ruined murals. The acoustics of the ball court are so good that from the North Temple, a person speaking can be heard clearly at the opposite end, about 135m (443 ft.) away.

TEMPLE OF JAGUARS Near the southeastern corner of the main ball court is a small temple with serpent columns and carved panels showing warriors and jaguars. Up the steps and inside the temple, a mural chronicles a battle in a Maya village.

TZOMPANTLI (TEMPLE OF THE SKULLS) To the right of the ball court, the Temple of the Skulls, obviously borrows from the post-Classic cities of central Mexico. Notice the rows of skulls

The Temple of the Skulls.

carved into the stone platform; when a sacrificial victim's head was cut off, it was impaled on a pole and displayed with others in a tidy row. Also carved into the stone are pictures of eagles tearing hearts from human victims. The word *Tzompantli* is not Mayan, but comes from central Mexico.

PLATFORM OF THE EAGLES Next to the Tzompantli, this small platform has reliefs showing eagles and jaguars clutching human hearts in their talons and claws, as well as a human head emerging from the mouth of a serpent.

PLATFORM OF VENUS East of the Tzompantli and north of El Castillo, near the road to the Sacred Cenote, is the Platform of Venus. In Maya and Toltec lore, a feathered monster or a feathered serpent with a human head in its mouth represented Venus. This is also called the tomb of Chaac-Mool, for the figure that was discovered "buried" within the structure.

SACRED CENOTE Follow the dirt road (actually an ancient *sacbé,* or causeway) leading north from the Platform of Venus for 5 minutes to get to the great natural well that may have given Chichén Itzá (the Well of the Itzáes) its name. This well was used for ceremonial purposes, and the bones of both children and adult sacrificial victims were found at the bottom.

Edward Thompson, who was the American consul in Mérida and a Harvard professor, purchased the ruins of Chichén early in the 20th century and explored the cenote with dredges and divers. He uncovered a fortune in gold and jade, most of which ended up in Harvard's Peabody Museum of Archaeology and Ethnology—a matter that disconcerts Mexican classicists to this day. Excavations in the 1960s yielded more treasure, and studies of the recovered objects show that the offerings came from throughout the Yucatán and even farther away.

TEMPLO DE LOS GUERREROS (TEMPLE OF THE WARRIORS) The Toltec influence is especially evident on the eastern edge of the plaza. Due east of El Castillo is one of Chichén Itzá's most impressive structures, the Temple of the Warriors, named for the carvings of warriors marching along its walls. The temple and the rows of almost Greco-Roman columns flanking it are also called the Group of the Thousand Columns, and it recalls the great Toltec site of Tula. A figure of Chaac-Mool sits at the top of the temple (visible only from a distance now that the temple is closed to climbers), surrounded by impressive columns carved in relief to look like enormous feathered serpents. South of the temple was a square building that archaeologists call **El Mercado (The Market);** a colonnade surrounds its central court.

The main Mérida–Cancún highway once ran straight through the ruins of Chichén, and though it has been diverted, you can still see the great swath it cut. South and west of the old highway's path are more impressive ruined buildings.

TUMBA DEL GRAN SACERDOTE (TOMB OF THE HIGH PRIEST) Past the refreshment stand to the right of the path, the Tomb of the High Priest shows both Toltec and Puuc influence. The 9-m (30-ft.) pyramid, with stairways on each side depicting feathered serpents, bears a distinct resemblance to El Castillo. Beneath its foundation is an ossuary (a communal graveyard) in a natural limestone cave, where skeletons and offerings have been found.

CASA DE LOS METATES (TEMPLE OF THE GRINDING STONES) This building, the next one on your right, is named after the Maya's concave corn-grinding stones.

TEMPLO DEL VENADO (TEMPLE OF THE DEER) Past Casa de los Metates is this fairly tall, though ruined, building. The relief of a stag that gave the temple its name is long gone.

CHICHANCHOB (LITTLE HOLES) This temple has a roof comb with little holes, three masks of the rain god Chaac, three rooms, and a good view of surrounding structures. It's one of Chichén's oldest buildings, built in the Puuc style during the late Classic period.

Chichén Itzá's El Caracol is shaped like a snail.

EL CARACOL (THE OBSERVATORY) One of Chichén Itzá's most intriguing structures is in the old part of the city. From a distance, the rounded tower of El Caracol ("The Snail," for its shape), sometimes called The Observatory, looks like any modern observatory. Construction of this complex building with its circular tower was carried out over centuries, acquiring additions and modifications as the Maya's careful celestial observations required increasingly exact measurements. Quite unlike other Maya buildings, the entrances, staircases, and angles are not aligned with one another. Four doors lead into the tower and a circular chamber, where a spiral staircase leads to the upper level. The slits in the roof are aligned with the sun's equinoxes. Astronomers observed the cardinal directions and the approach of the all-important spring and autumn equinoxes, as well as the summer solstice.

On the east side of El Caracol, a path leads north into the bush to the **Cenote Xtoloc,** a natural limestone well that provided the city's daily water supply. If you see lizards sunning there, they may well be *xtoloc,* the species for which this cenote is named.

TEMPLO DE LOS TABLEROS (TEMPLE OF THE PANELS) Just south of El Caracol are the ruins of a *temazcalli* (a steam bath) and the Temple of Panels, named for the carved panels on top. A few traces remain of the much larger structure that once covered the temple.

EDIFICIO DE LAS MONJAS (EDIFICE OF THE NUNS) This enormous nunnery is reminiscent of the palaces at sites along the Puuc route. The new edifice was built in the late Classic period over an older one. To prove this, an early 20th-century archaeologist put dynamite between the two and blew away part of the exterior, revealing the older structures within. Indelicate, perhaps, but effective.

On the east side of the Edifice of the Nuns is **Anexo Este (annex),** constructed in highly ornate Chenes style with Chaac masks and serpents.

LA IGLESIA (THE CHURCH) Next to the annex is another of Chichén's oldest buildings, the Church. Masks of Chaac decorate two upper stories; a close look reveals armadillo, crab, snail, and tortoise symbols among the crowd of Chaacs. These represent the Maya gods, called *bacah,* whose job it was to hold up the sky.

AKAB DZIB (TEMPLE OF OBSCURE WRITING) Beloved of travel writers, this temple lies east of the Edifice of the Nuns. Above a door in one of the rooms are some Mayan glyphs, which gave the temple its name because the writings are hard to make out. In other rooms, traces of red handprints are still visible. Reconstructed and expanded over the centuries, Akab Dzib might be the oldest building on the site.

CHICHÉN VIEJO (OLD CHICHÉN) For a look at more of Chichén's oldest buildings, constructed well before the time of Toltec influence, follow signs from the Edifice of the Nuns southwest into the bush to Old Chichén, about 1km (a half-mile) away. Be prepared for this trek with long trousers, insect repellent, and a local guide. Attractions here include the **Templo de los Inscripciones Iniciales (Temple of the First Inscriptions),** with the oldest inscriptions discovered at Chichén, and the restored **Templo de los Dinteles (Temple of the Lintels),** a fine Puuc building. Some of these buildings are being restored.

Where to Stay

The expensive hotels in Chichén all occupy beautiful grounds, are close to the ruins, serve decent food, and have toll-free reservations numbers. They do a brisk business with tour operators—they can be empty one day and full the next. From these hotels, you can easily walk to the back entrance of the ruins, next to the Hotel Mayaland. Several inexpensive hotels are just to the west of the ruins in the village of Pisté, which has little else to recommend it. Another option is to stay in the colonial town of Valladolid (p. 311), 40 minutes away.

EXPENSIVE

Hacienda Chichén Resort ★★ The smallest and most private of the hotels at the ruins' entrance is also the quietest. A one-time hacienda that served as headquarters for the Carnegie Institute's excavations in 1923, the bungalows built for institute staff residences now house one or two units with a dehumidifier, a ceiling fan, and good air-conditioning. The floors are ceramic tile, ceilings are stucco with wood beams, and walls are adorned with carved stone. Trees and tropical plants fill manicured gardens that you can enjoy from your private porch or from the terrace restaurant, which occupies part of the original main house. Standard rooms come with a queen-size, two twin, or two double beds; suites have king-size beds.

Zona Arqueológica, 97751 Chichén Itzá, Yuc. ✆/fax **985/851-0045.** www.haciendachichen.com. (Reservations office in Mérida: 877/631-4005 in the U.S., or 999/920-8407.) 28 units. High season $165–$180 double, $200–$280 suite; low season $120 double, $135–$180 suite. Promotional rates available. AE, MC, V. Free guarded parking. **Amenities:** Restaurant; 2 bars; large outdoor pool; smoke-free rooms; spa. *In room:* A/C, hair dryer, minibar, no phone.

MODERATE

Villas Arqueológicas Chichén Itzá ★ ☺ Similar to its sister property at Uxmal, this hotel is built around a courtyard and pool and is a happy compromise between low-budget lodging and the more lavish hotels nearby. It's by far the best deal if you want to stay near the entrance to the ruins (a 5- to 10-minute walk on a peaceful road). The grounds are lush with two massive royal Poinciana trees and bougainvillea-draped walls. Rooms are modern, clean, and quite comfortable, unless you're 1.9m (6 ft., 2 in.) or taller—each bed is in a niche, with walls at the head and foot. Most rooms have one double bed and a twin bed, and Islander has added a few suites. You can also book a half- or full-board plan.

Zona Arqueológica, Km 120 Carratera Mérida Valladolid, 97751 Chichén Itzá, Yuc. ✆ **985/856-6000.** Fax 985/856-6008. www.islandercollection.com. 45 units. $58–$83 double, $121–$173 suite. Rates include continental breakfast. Half-board (breakfast plus lunch or dinner) $20 per person; full board (3 meals) $35 per person. AE, MC, V. Free parking. **Amenities:** Restaurant; bar; large outdoor pool; tennis court; Wi-Fi in public areas. *In room:* A/C, hair dryer.

INEXPENSIVE

Hotel Dolores Alba This longtime budget favorite is of the motel variety, and it is a bargain for what you get: two pools (one fed by a natural spring); hammocks hanging under *palapas*; and large, comfortable rooms with some colorful hacienda-style accents that come with two double beds. The restaurant serves good meals at moderate prices. The hotel provides free transportation to the ruins and the Caves of Balankanché during visiting hours, though you will have to take a taxi back. It is located on the highway 2.5km (1½ miles) east of the ruins (toward Valladolid).

Carretera Mérida-Valladolid Km 122, Yuc. ✆ **985/858-1555.** www.doloresalba.com. (Reservations: Hotel Dolores Alba, Calle 63 no. 464, 97000 Mérida, Yuc.; ✆ **999/928-5650**; fax 999/928-3163.) 40 units. 550 pesos double. MC, V (8% service charge). Free parking. **Amenities:** Restaurant; bar; 2 outdoor pools; room service. *In room:* A/C, TV, no phone.

Where to Dine

This area has no great food, but it has plenty of decent food; simple choices are the best. The restaurant at the ruins' visitor center serves decent snack food. The hotel restaurants mostly do a fair job, though they are more expensive than they should be. In the village of Pisté, you can try one of the restaurants along the highway that cater to the bus tours, such as **Fiesta** (✆ **985/851-0111**). The best time to go is during early lunch or regular supper hours, when the buses are gone.

Other Attractions in the Area

Ik-Kil is a large, deep cenote on the highway across from the Hotel Dolores Alba, 2.5km (1½ miles) east of the main entrance to the ruins. Getting down to the water's edge requires navigating many steps, but they are easier to manage than those at Dzitnup. The view from both the top and the bottom is dramatic, with lots of tropical vegetation and curtains of hanging tree roots stretching all the way to the water's surface. The best swimming is before 11:30am, when bus tours begin to arrive. These tours are the main business of Ik-Kil, which also has a restaurant and souvenir shops. The cenote is open from 8am to 5pm daily. Admission is 60 pesos per adult, 30 pesos per child 7 to 12 years old.

The **Cave of Balankanché** is 5.5km (3⅓ miles) from Chichén Itzá on the road to Valladolid and Cancún. Taxis will make the trip and wait. The entire excursion takes about a half-hour, but the walk inside is hot and humid. This is the tamest of the Yucatán's cave tours, with good footing and the least amount of walking and climbing. It includes a cheesy and uninformative recorded tour. The highlight is a round chamber with a central column that resembles a large tree. The cave became a hideout during the War of the Castes, and you can still see traces of carving and incense burning, as well as an underground stream that supplied water to the refugees. Outside, meander through the botanical gardens, where nearly everything is labeled with common and botanical names.

Admission is 48 pesos, free for children 6 to 12 (younger than 6 not admitted). Use of a video camera costs 45 pesos (free if you bought a video permit in Chichén earlier in the day). Tours in English are at 11am and 1 and 3pm, and, in Spanish, at 9am, noon, and 2 and 4pm. Double-check these hours at the main entrance to the Chichén ruins.

VALLADOLID

40km (25 miles) E of Chichén Itzá; 160km (99 miles) SW of Cancún; 98km (61 miles) NW of Tulum

Valladolid (pronounced "bah-yah-doh-*leed*")is a small colonial city halfway between Mérida and Cancún. One of the first Spanish strongholds and crucible of the War of the Castes (p. 31), the city still has handsome colonial buildings and 19th-century structures that make it a pleasant place to bask in the real Yucatán. People are friendly and informal, and the only real challenge is the heat. The city's economy is based on commerce and small-scale manufacturing. It's close to a

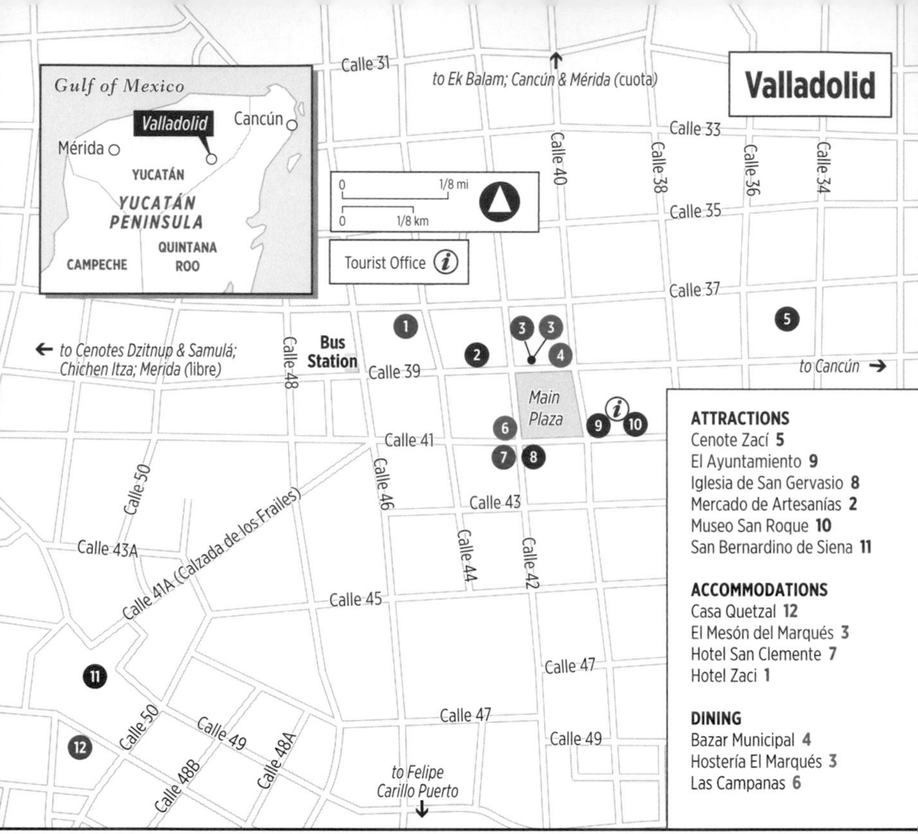

couple of famous cenotes, the intriguing ruins of Ek Balam, Ría Lagartos' nesting flamingos, and the sandy beaches of Isla Holbox (p. 319). It's closer to Chichén Itzá than Mérida is, making it a good alternative base for exploring.

Essentials

GETTING THERE & DEPARTING **By Car** From Mérida or Cancún, you can take either the Hwy. 180 *cuota* (toll road) or Hwy. 180 *libre* (free). The toll is 214 pesos from Cancún and 124 pesos from Mérida. The ***cuota*** passes 2km (1¼ miles) north of the city; the exit is at the crossing of Hwy. 295 to Tizimín. **Hwy. 180 *libre*,** passing through a number of villages (with their requisite *topes*) takes significantly longer. Both 180 and 295 lead straight to downtown. Leaving is just as easy: From the main square, Calle 41 turns into 180 East to Cancún; Calle 39 heads to 180 West to Chichén Itzá and Mérida. To take the *cuota* to Mérida or Cancún, take Calle 40 (see "City Layout," below).

By Bus Buses leave throughout the day for Mérida (134 pesos) and Cancún (82 pesos). You can also get several buses a day to Playa del Carmen (96 pesos) and Tulum (64 pesos). To get to Chichén Itzá, take a second-class bus, which leaves at least every hour. The recently remodeled bus station is at the corner of calles 39 and 46.

VISITOR INFORMATION The small **tourism office** is in the Palacio Municipal, open Monday to Friday from 8am to 9pm, Saturday and Sunday 9am to 9pm.

CITY LAYOUT Valladolid's layout is the standard for towns in the Yucatán: Streets running north–south are even numbers; those running east–west are odd numbers. The main plaza is bordered by Calle 39 on the north, 41 on the south, 40 on the east, and 42 on the west. The plaza is named Parque Francisco Cantón Rosado, but everyone calls it **El Centro.** Taxis are easy to come by.

Exploring Valladolid

Before it became Valladolid, the city was a Maya settlement called Zací (zah-*kee*), which means "white hawk." The old name lives on in the cenote in a small park at the intersection of calles 39 and 36. The long but easily navigable stepped trail at **Cenote Zací ★** leads past caves, stalactites, and hanging vines that give the place a prehistoric feel, but the cenote's partially open roof lightens the atmosphere. It's a fine place to cool off, whether you jump in for a swim, dangle your feet in the water and let the fish nibble your toes, or just walk down to escape city heat and noise. After several trips to both, I find Zací more peaceful and just as pretty as the famous cenotes outside of town (p. 317). The park, which has a large *palapa* restaurant overlooking the cenote, is free; entry to the cenote is 15 pesos.

Ten blocks southwest of the main square is the Franciscan monastery of **San Bernardino de Siena ★★**, dating from 1552. The monastery complex was sacked during the War of the Castes but a fine baroque altarpiece and some striking 17th- century paintings remain. Most of the compound was built in the early 1600s; a large underground river is believed to pass under the convent and surrounding neighborhood, which is called Barrio Sisal. ("Sisal," in this case, is

Cenote Zací.

San Bernardino de Siena monastery.

a corruption of the Mayan phrase *sis-ha,* meaning "cold water.") The *barrio* has been extensively restored and is a delight. For a real treat, walk there along the **Calzada de los Frailes (Walkway of the Friars) ★**. From the corner of calles 41 and 46, follow Calle 41A, the cobblestone street running diagonally to the southwest, about 1km (1/2 mile) to the monastery. The road is lined by huge clay planters and passes elegantly painted colonial homes.

Valladolid's **main plaza** is the town's social center and a thriving market for Yucatecan dresses. The square was renovated in the winter of 2009–2010, and all of the lush old shade trees were preserved. The Old World benches and *confidenciales* (S-shaped chairs inviting friends or lovers to chat or nuzzle face-to-face), were either replaced or repainted. Although the buildings flanking the square were repainted, new lighting was added, and walking paths were repaved, the square still retains its old colonial feel.

On the plaza's south side is the imposing cathedral, **Iglesia de San Gervasio** (sometimes called Parroquia de San Servacio). Its thick stone walls weren't enough to stop the Maya rebels who sacked it in 1847, touching off the War of the Castes. Vallesoletanos, as the locals are known, believe most all cathedrals in Mexico point east, and they cherish a local legend to explain why theirs points north—but don't believe a word of it. On the east side, the municipal building, **El Ayuntamiento,** is the repository for dramatic paintings outlining the peninsula's history, including a wonderful depiction of a horrified Maya priest foreseeing the arrival of Spanish galleons. On Sunday nights, beneath the stone arches of the Ayuntamiento, the municipal band plays *jaranas* and other traditional music of the region.

For an overview of arts and crafts from surrounding Maya villages, find the pink, fortresslike building that houses **Museo San Roque** on Calle 41 between calles 38 and 40. Signs are in Spanish, but the displays mostly speak for themselves. Ancient stone masks, pottery, and bones unearthed at nearby Ek Balam (p. 317) are also on exhibit. The museum is open Monday through Saturday, 9am to 9 pm. Entry is free.

Iglesia de San Gervasio

Shopping

The **Mercado de Artesanías de Valladolid (crafts market),** at the corner of calles 39 and 44, gives you an overview of the local merchandise. Perhaps the town's primary handicraft is embroidered Maya dresses, which you can buy here or from women around the main square. **Yalat,** on Calle 39 at Calle 40, looks like a gallery but sells unique folk art from throughout Mexico, specializing in the Yucatán.

Valladolid is in cattle country, making it a good place to buy inexpensive, locally made leather goods such as *huaraches* (sandals) and bags. On the main plaza is a small shop above the municipal bazaar. A good sandal maker has a shop called **Elios,** Calle 37 no. 202, between calles 42 and 44 (no phone). An Indian named **Juan Mac** makes *alpargatas,* the traditional Maya sandal, in his shop on Calle 39, 1 block from the main plaza near Calle 38 (across from the Bar La Joya). There's no sign, but the door jamb is painted yellow. Juan Mac is working there most mornings. Most of his output is for locals, but he's happy to knock out a pair for visitors.

Where to Stay

Aside from lodging listed below, Valladolid's best budget hotels are **Hotel San Clemente,** on Calle 42 between calles 41 and 43 (✆ **985/856-3161;** www.hotelsanclemente.com.mx, 448 pesos per night; MC, V) and **Hotel Zací,** Calle 44 between calles 37 and 39 (✆ **985/856-2167;** www.hotelzaci.com; 468 pesos; no credit cards).

For something a bit different, you can stay in a small ecohotel in the nearby village of Ek Balam, close to the ruins, at **Genesis Retreat Ek Balam** (✆ **985/858-9375;** www.genesisretreat.com). The Canadian owner, Lee Christie, takes guests on village tours that unveil daily life for the contemporary Maya. She rents simple cabañas (with shared or private bathrooms) surrounding a lovely pool and a restaurant.

Casa Quetzal ★ The landlady, Judith Fernández, is a gracious Mexican woman who moved to Valladolid to slow down. She has created airy, attractive lodging in the refurbished Barrio Sisal, within easy walking distance of the main square. Emphasis is on comfort and service—good linens and mattresses, quiet air-conditioning, and a large and inviting central courtyard. English is spoken, and Sra. Fernández has lined up a good guide you can contract to take you to outlying areas.

Calle 51 no. 218, Barrio Sisal, 97780 Valladolid, Yuc. ✆/fax **985/856-4796.** www.casa-quetzal.com. 8 units. $60–$75 double, $80 junior suite, $90 casita. Rates include full breakfast. No credit cards. Free secure parking. **Amenities:** Babysitting; small outdoor pool; room service; spa. *In room:* A/C, TV, no phone, Wi-Fi.

El Mesón del Marqués ★★ Originally an early 17th-century house, the doyen of Valladolid's plaza has grown by adding new construction in back. All the rooms (most with two double beds) are quite comfortable, though the new buildings don't have the wow factor of the original porticoed courtyard, which drips with bougainvillea and hanging plants and is mostly occupied by the restaurant (see "Where to Dine," below). The pretty, fairly large pool is another modern addition. The hotel is on the north side of the plaza, opposite the church.

Calle 39 no. 203 (btw. calles 40 and 42), 97780 Valladolid, Yuc. ✆ **985/856-2073.** Fax 985/856-2280. www.mesondelmarques.com. 90 units. 700–770 pesos double; 865–950 pesos superior; 1,330–1,460 pesos junior suite. AE, MC, V. Free secure parking. **Amenities:** Restaurant; bar; outdoor pool; room service. *In room:* A/C, TV, Wi-Fi.

Where to Dine

Valladolid is not a hotbed of haute cuisine, but the regional specialties are reliably good. **Hostería El Marqués** ★★ at the Hotel El Mesón del Marqués, turns out the best food in town—Yucatecan classics and international dishes—in

Women embroider fabric in Valladolid.

an achingly romantic setting. Also on the main square, friendly, informal **Las Campanas** serves tasty food for reasonable prices. Locals like to visit over a meal at the stalls in the **Bazar Municipal,** next door to the Mesón del Marqués; I like them for a quick, cheap breakfast or a huge tumbler of fresh-squeezed orange juice when the heat gets to me (you can also take it to go in a plastic bag with a straw).

Side Trips from Valladolid

CENOTES DZITNUP & SAMMULÁ

The **Cenote Dzitnup** ✋ (also known as Cenote Xkekén) is 4km (2½ miles) west of Valladolid off Hwy. 180 toward Chichén Itzá. It's said to be the most photographed cenote in the Yucatán, and it's easy to see why. The deep, glassy, blue water, beneath a thicket of stalactites and ropey tree roots straining for a drink, is a spectacle to behold. The beautiful pictures, however, don't reveal the treacherous stone steps, the unrelenting humidity even on an otherwise comfortable day (wear contacts instead of glasses, which will be constantly fogged), and the somewhat claustrophobic feeling if you're there with a crowd (which is most of the time). It's an awesome sight, to be sure, and you should see it at least once. Bring a suit and take a swim; it will revive you for the climb back out.

The cenote is open daily from 7am to 7pm; admission is 25 pesos. If it's crowded, you can go for a swim about 90m (295 ft.) down the road on the opposite side in a smaller, less developed but also beautiful cenote, **Sammulá.**

EK BALAM: DARK JAGUAR ★★★

About 18km (11 miles) north of Valladolid, off the highway to Río Lagartos, are the spectacular ruins of **Ek Balam,** which, owing to a certain ambiguity in Mayan, may mean "black jaguar," "dark jaguar," or "star jaguar." Though tourists have yet to catch on, these ruins could prove to be a more important discovery than Chichén Itzá. Archaeologists began work only in 1997, and their findings have Maya scholars all aquiver. Built between 100 B.C. and A.D. 1200, the smaller buildings are architecturally unique—especially the large, perfectly restored **Oval Palace** (also sometimes called La Redonda or Caracol).

The imposing central pyramid, known as **El Torre** ★★ or the Acropolis, is about 160m (525 ft.) long and 60m (197 ft.) wide. At more than 30m (98 ft.) high, it easily surpasses El Castillo in Chichén Itzá. To the left of the main stairway, archaeologists have uncovered a large ceremonial doorway of perfectly preserved stucco work. Designed in the Chenes style associated with Campeche, it forms an astonishingly elaborate representation

The ruins of Ek Balam.

Cenote Etiquette

If you swim in a cenote, be sure you don't have creams or other chemicals on your skin—including deodorant. They damage the habitat of the small fish and other organisms living in the water. No alcohol, food, or smoking is allowed.

of the gaping mouth of the underworld god. Around it are several beautifully detailed human figures, including what appear to be winged warriors. Known as Mayan Angels, they are unique in Maya architecture. Excavation inside the pyramid revealed a long chamber (so far closed to the public) filled with hieroglyphic writing that suggests the scribes probably came from Guatemala. The script revealed the name of one of the city's principal kings—Ukit Kan Le'k Tok', whose tomb was uncovered about two-thirds of the way up the pyramid. Climb to the top and you see untouched ruins masquerading as overgrown hills to the north, and the tallest structures of **Cobá,** 50km (31 miles) to the southeast.

Also visible are the Maya's ***sacbeob,*** or raised causeways, appearing as raised lines in the forest. More than any of the better-known sites, Ek Balam inspires a sense of mystery and awe at the scale of Maya civilization and the utter ruin to which it fell.

A new road runs from the highway to the ruins. Take Calle 40 north out of Valladolid to Hwy. 295 and go 20km (12 miles) to a large marked turnoff. Ek Balam is 13km (8 miles) from the highway; admission is 31 pesos, 45 pesos per video camera. The site is open daily from 8am to 5pm.

RÍA LAGARTOS NATURE RESERVE ★

About 80km (50 miles) north of Valladolid (40km/25 miles north of Tizimín) on Hwy. 295, Ría Lagartos is a 50,000-hectare (123,500-acre) refuge established in 1979 to protect the largest nesting flamingo population in North America. The nesting area is off-limits, but you can see plenty of flamingos, as well as many other species of waterfowl, on an enjoyable boat ride around the estuary.

Río Lagartos, at west end of the estuary, is the place to get boats to the flamingos. Misnamed by Spaniards who mistook the long, narrow *ría* (estuary) for a *río* (river), it's a small fishing village of about 3,000 people who make their living from the sea and from the occasional tourist who shows up to see the flamingos. Colorful houses face the *malecón* (oceanfront street), and brightly painted boats dock here and there.

When you drive into town, keep going straight until you get to the shore. Where Calle 10 intersects with the *malecón,* near a modern church, is a little kiosk where the guides can be found (no phone). You can book a 2-hour tour, which costs about 750 pesos for two to three people. The guides also like to show you the evaporation pools used by the local salt producer at Las Coloradas (a good source of employment for the locals until it was mechanized) and a freshwater spring bubbling out from below the saltwater estuary.

The best time to see flamingos is in the early morning, so you might want to stay overnight in town. Río Lagartos has a few simple hotels charging about 250 pesos a night, including **Posada Leyli** (✆ **986/862-0106**) and **Posada Lucy** (no phone). Another option is **Hotel San Felipe** (✆ **986/862-2067**) in the pleasant fishing village of San Felipe, 9km (5½ miles) to the west. Still another is **Hotel 49** (✆ **986/863-2136**) near the main square in Tizimín, which you pass through on the way from Valladolid.

Flamingos in Ría Lagartos.

ISLA HOLBOX ★

A sandy strip of an island off the northeastern corner of the Yucatán Peninsula, Isla Holbox (pronounced "hohl-*bosh*") is in Quintana Roo, and is actually closer to Cancún than Valladolid. But, unless Cancún tourists take a boat tour, they have to drive almost to the Yucatán border to get to the road north. Given the challenges of driving in Cancún, it makes sense to visit Holbox from the Yucatán side.

Holbox was a half-deserted fishing village in a remote corner of the world before tourists started showing up for the beach. Now it's a semiprosperous little community that makes its livelihood from tourist services, employment at the beach hotels, and tours. It's most popular with visitors from May to September, when more than a hundred **whale sharks ★★★** congregate in nearby waters to feed on the plankton and krill churned up by the collision of Gulf and Caribbean waters. Whale sharks are much larger than other sharks, reaching as much as 18m (59 ft.), and they filter their food much as baleen whales do. These peaceable giants swim slowly along the surface of the water and don't seem to mind the boat tours and snorkelers that come for the thrill of swimming alongside them. That said they can do some mischief if you annoy them.

Besides swimming with whale sharks, most tourists come to Holbox to laze on the broad beach of fine-textured sand. The water, though, is not the amazing blue of the Caribbean but a murkier green. Diving, snorkeling, sportfishing and nature tours of **Laguna Yalahu,** the shallow lagoon separating Holbox from the mainland, are the primary other diversions. It's not a place for Type-A types.

Posada Mawimbi (✆ **984/875-2003;** www.mawimbi.net), starting at $75 to $90 a night depending on season, hits the best balance between price and comfort

A Matter of Timing

You'll see some flamingos any time of year (and probably ducks, hawks, cranes, cormorants, and osprey as well). But to see great rosy masses of them, go between April and October. After the birds complete their courtship rituals in Celestún, they fly to Ría Lagartos to nest, lay their eggs, and prepare their young for the return journey in October.

Visiting the Whale Sharks of Isla Holbox

In 2002, Mexico's whale sharks were designated an endangered species. The government, along with environmental groups, closely monitors their activity and the tours that visit them off Isla Holbox. Several restrictions apply to how tours are run, and all tour operators must abide by them. See details of the restrictions, and learn more about the whale sharks, at www.domino.conanp.gob.mx/rules.htm.

Whale shark tours are kept small; just two people at a time are allowed to snorkel with the sharks. Tours typically cost around $80 to $100 per person and last 4 to 6 hours. Many hotels or outfitters on the island can arrange a tour.

among the beach hotels in town. **Casa Sandra** (✆ **984/875-2171;** www.casasandra.com) charges $220 and (way) up in low season, $290 and up in high season, but travelers who want only the best will find it here, along with air-conditioning, a rarity in Holbox. Just beyond town, **Villas Delfines,** which has an office in Cancún (✆ **998/884-8606;** www.villasdelfines.com), is an ecohotel charging $90 to $150 in low season, $120 to $180 high season, for thatched-roof beach bungalows.

From Valladolid, take Hwy. 180 east for about 90km (56 miles) toward Cancún; turn north after Nuevo Xcan at the tiny crossroads of El Ideal. Drive nearly 100km (62 miles) north on a state highway to the tiny port of Chiquilá, where you can park your car in a secure parking lot; walk 180m (590 ft.) to the pier, and catch the ferry to the island. It runs 10 times per day and costs 70 pesos per person. When you arrive in the village, you can contract with one of the golf-cart taxis for a ride to your hotel.

Whale sharks congregate in Isla Holbox from May to September.

TABASCO & CHIAPAS

by David Baird

9

The states of Tabasco and Chiapas, in southernmost Mexico, are largely covered in jungle and rainforest. In Preclassic times (before A.D. 300) a large part of this area was homeland to Mexico's "mother culture," the Olmec, who in many ways gave form to the cultural development of the civilizations that would come afterward. And in both pre-classic and classic times (A.D. 300 to 900) this was the homeland of the Maya, whose descendants still populate the region. The ruins that these people left behind, as well as the villages of the present-day Maya, attract many visitors to this region: The giant stone heads of the Olmec, the ancient ceremonial centers of the Maya, such as Palenque and Toniná, and the living Maya cultures of both highland and lowland Chiapas.

There is also great natural beauty. The lowland jungle with its high canopy offers a tremendous variety of flora and fauna. Placid lakes dot the land and provide the only open vistas in this densely packed landscape. The mountainous central highlands of Chiapas are also thickly forested and often shrouded in mist. Rivers, including Mexico's two largest, the Grijalva and the Usumacinta, cut their way down to the lowlands, through rugged canyons and tumbling waterfalls. And the cool mountain air feels refreshing after you've experienced the heat and humidity of the Yucatán lowlands.

Tabasco is a small, oil-rich state along the Gulf Coast. The capital, **Villahermosa,** is the main port of entry into this region. It has a boomtown feel and an intriguing history. But the large state of **Chiapas** holds the greatest attractions. In its eastern lowland jungle is the ancient ceremonial center of **Palenque.** Near the border with Guatemala are the smaller but dramatic sites of **Yaxchilán** and **Bonampak.** Between these lowlands and the central highlands are many waterfalls and rapids as well as the ruins of **Toniná.** Located high in the mountains and surrounded by Indian communities is the colonial city of **San Cristóbal de las Casas,** with its beautiful old town and market center.

VILLAHERMOSA

142km (88 miles) NW of Palenque; 469km (291 miles) SW of Campeche; 160km (99 miles) N of San Cristóbal de las Casas

Villahermosa (pop. 600,000) is the capital of the state of Tabasco and its largest city. It lies in a shallow depression about an hour's drive from the Gulf Coast, at the confluence of two rivers: the Grijalva and the Carrizal. This location makes the city susceptible to flooding. The land is marshy, with shallow lakes scattered here and there. For most of the year it's hot and humid.

PREVIOUS PAGE: **Maya women.**

Oil has brought money to this town and raised prices. Villahermosa is one of the most expensive cities in the country and contrasts sharply with inexpensive Chiapas. Though there's a lot of money, it's all being pulled to the modern western sections surrounding a development called Tabasco 2000. This area, especially the neighborhoods around the **Parque–Museo La Venta,** is the most attractive part of town, dotted by small lakes. The historic center has been left to decay. It's gritty, crowded, and unpleasant. The main reason to be downtown is for the cheap hotels.

Two names that you will likely see and hear are Carlos Pellicer Cámara and Tomás Garrido Canabal; both were interesting people. The first was a mid-20th-century Tabascan poet and intellectual. The best known of Mexico's *modernista* poets, he was a fiercely independent thinker. Garrido Canabal, socialist governor of Tabasco in the 1920s and 1930s, was even more fiercely independent. He wanted to turn the conservative, backwater state of Tabasco into a model of socialism and fought for many socialist causes. But his enmity for Mexico's Catholic Church is what he is most remembered for today. He went so far as to name his son Lucifer and his farm animals Jesus and the Virgin Mary.

Essentials

GETTING THERE & DEPARTING

BY PLANE Villahermosa's airport (airport code: VSA) is the main port of entry into this region. **Continental ExpressJet** (✆ **800/525-0280** in the U.S., or 01-800/900-5000 in Mexico; www.continental.com) has direct service to/from Houston on a regional jet. **Mexicana** (✆ **800/531-7921** in the U.S., or 01-800/800-2010 in Mexico; www.mexicana.com) and **Aeroméxico** (✆ **800/237-6639** in the U.S., or 01-800/021-4000 in Mexico; www.aeromexico.com) and their subsidiaries have direct flights to and from Mexico City, Monterrey, Mérida, and Veracruz. Mexican discount carrier, **VivaAerobus** (✆ **01-81/8215-0150** in Mexico; www.vivaaerobus.com) has a direct flight to/from Monterrey.

BY CAR Highway 180 connects Villahermosa to Campeche (6 hr.). Highway 186, which passes by the airport, joins Highway 199 to Palenque and San Cristóbal de las Casas. The road to Palenque is a good one, and the drive takes 2 hours. Between Palenque and San Cristóbal, the road enters the mountains and takes 4 to 5 hours. On any of the mountain roads, conditions are apt to get worse during the rainy season from May to October.

BY BUS The **bus station** is at Mina and Merino (✆ **993/312-8900;** www.ticketbus.com.mx), three blocks off Highway 180. There are eight nonstop buses per day to/from Palenque (2½ hr.). There are seven nonstop buses per day to Mexico City (10 hr.), six deluxe services on **ADO-GL,** and two superdeluxe on **UNO.** To Campeche, there are seven buses nonstop per day (7 hr.); some of these go on to Mérida.

ORIENTATION

ARRIVING Villahermosa's **airport** is 16km (8 miles) east of town. The trip takes between 20 and 30 minutes. Once you cross the bridge over the Río Grijalva, turn left to reach downtown. Taxis to the downtown area cost 150 pesos.

Parking downtown can be difficult; it's best to find a parking lot. Use one that's guarded round-the-clock.

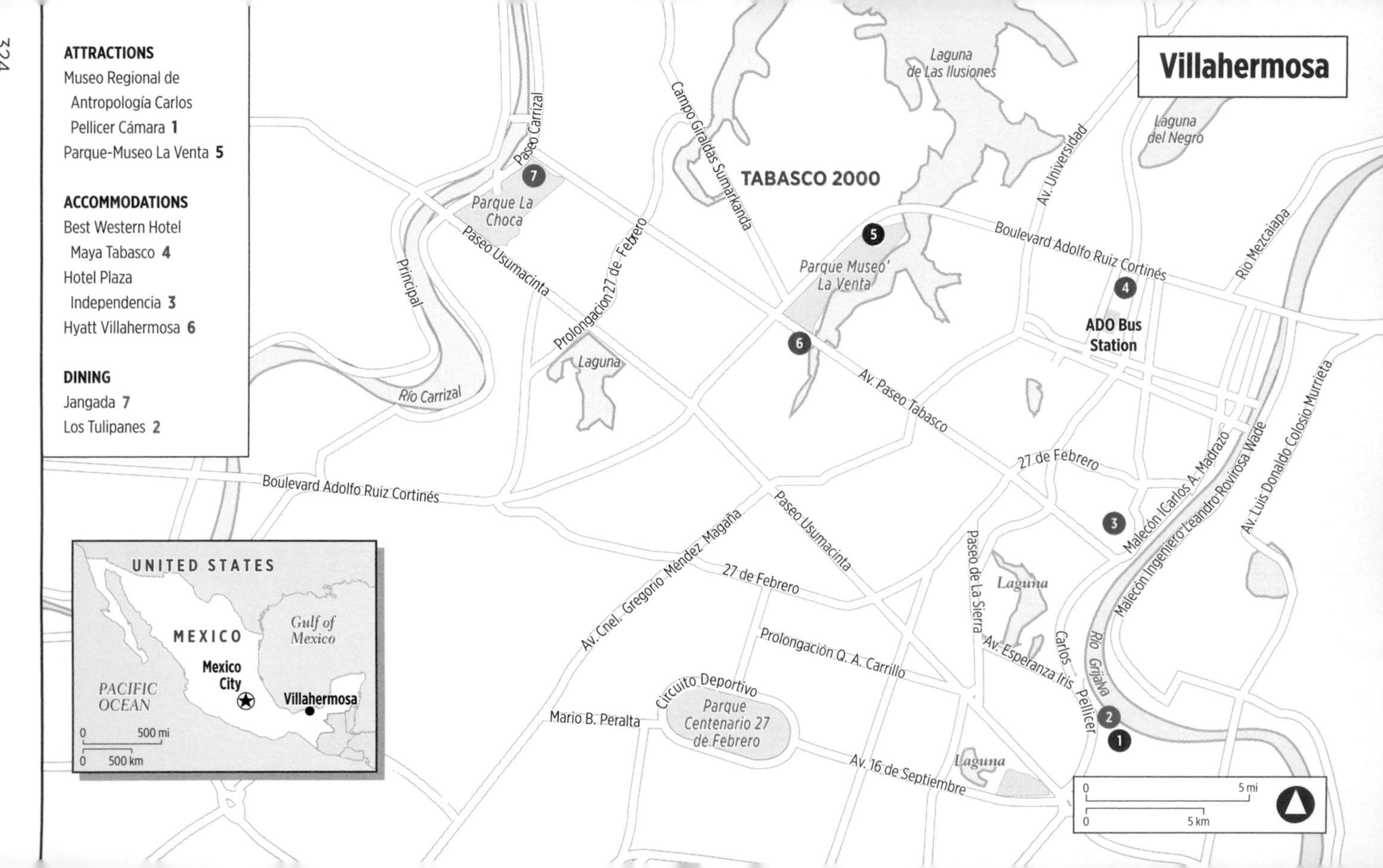
Villahermosa
ATTRACTIONS
Museo Regional de Antropología Carlos Pellicer Cámara 1
Parque-Museo La Venta 5
ACCOMMODATIONS
Best Western Hotel Maya Tabasco 4
Hotel Plaza Independencia 3
Hyatt Villahermosa 6
DINING
Jangada 7
Los Tulipanes 2
TABASCO 2000
Laguna de Las Ilusiones
Laguna del Negro
Parque Museo La Venta
Parque La Choca
ADO Bus Station
Parque Centenario 27 de Febrero
Laguna
Laguna
Laguna
Río Carrizal
Río Grijalva
Río Mezcalapa
Paseo Carrizal
Principal
Paseo Usumacinta
Prolongacion 27 de Febrero
Campo Giraldas Sumarkanda
Av. Universidad
Boulevard Adolfo Ruiz Cortinés
Av. Paseo Tabasco
27 de Febrero
Malecón (Carlos A. Madrazo
Malecón Ingeniero Leandro Rovirosa Wade
Av. Luis Donaldo Colosio Murrieta
Paseo de La Sierra
Av. Esperanza Iris
Carlos Pellicer
Av. Cnel. Gregorio Méndez Magaña
Prolongación Q. A. Carrillo
Circuito Deportivo
Mario B. Peralta
Av. 16 de Septiembre
0 5 mi
0 5 km
UNITED STATES
MEXICO
Gulf of Mexico
PACIFIC OCEAN
Mexico City
Villahermosa
0 500 mi
0 500 km

VISITOR INFORMATION The **State Tourism Office** (✆ **993/316-5122,** ext. 229) has two information booths: The one at the **airport** is staffed daily from 10am to 5pm; the one at **Parque–Museo La Venta** (next to the ticket counter for the park) is staffed Monday to Friday from 9am to 1pm.

CITY LAYOUT The downtown area, including the pedestrian-only **Zona Luz,** is on the west bank of the Grijalva River. About 1.5km (1 mile) upstream (south) is **CICOM,** an academic organization with the large archaeology museum named for the poet Carlos Pellicer Cámara. The **airport** is on the east side of the river. Highway 180 passes the airport and crosses the river just north of downtown, becoming **Bulevar Ruiz Cortines.** To get to the downtown area, turn left onto **Madero** or **Pino Suárez.** By staying on Ruiz Cortines you can reach the city's biggest attraction, the Parque–Museo la Venta. It's well marked. Just beyond that is the intersection with **Paseo Tabasco,** the heart of the modern hotel and shopping district.

GETTING AROUND **Taxis** are your best way to get around town. Villahermosa is rare for being a Mexican city without a capable public transportation system.

FAST FACTS The telephone **area code** is **993.** There aren't a lot of *casas de cambio,* but you can exchange money at the airport, the hotels, and downtown banks on calles Juárez and Madero. ATMs are plentiful.

Exploring Villahermosa

Villahermosa is not a pleasant city; the downtown area is poor and gritty, the modern western part of the city is largely without character. You'll probably want to get in and out as fast as you can. The two major attractions, the **Parque–Museo La Venta** and the **Museo Regional de Antropología Carlos Pellicer Cámara** (when it opens in summer of 2010) can be seen in a day.

If you're bound and determined to get to know the city, take a stroll about the pedestrian-only Zona Luz in the old city center, and you'll see signs that investment might be returning to the downtown area. Outside the Zona Luz, things get more unpleasant, with lots of traffic and crowds of pedestrians. You can walk south along the banks of the Grijalva until you come to a pedestrian bridge with an observation tower. That's the highlight. You won't miss much by keeping away.

Museo Regional de Antropología Carlos Pellicer Cámara This museum on the west bank of the river about 1.5km (1 mile) south of the town center was damaged in the flood of 2007. It has remained closed ever since, while it awaits the completion of its new home. The new museum is on the same site and will be larger. It should open in the second half of 2010. The permanent collection of pre-Colombian sculpture and pottery is well worth a visit. It focuses on the cultures of the region—Olmec and Zapotec—but also includes pieces from other parts of Mexico and Central America.

CICOM Center, Av. Carlos Pellicer Cámara 511. ✆ **993/312-6344.** Admission 45 pesos. Tues–Sun 9am–5pm.

Parque–Museo La Venta ★★ The Olmec created the first civilization in Mexico and developed several cultural traits that later would be adopted by all subsequent civilizations throughout Mesoamerica. In addition to their monumental works, they carved small exquisite figurines in jade and serpentine, which can be seen in the Museo Regional de Antropología (see above). This *parque-*

museo occupies a portion of a larger park named after Tomás Garrido Canabal, which includes a serene lake, a zoo, a natural history museum, and a lot of green space with several walkways frequented by joggers. Once inside the *parque-museo,* a trail leads you from one sculpture to the next. Most of the pieces are massive heads or altars. These can be as tall as 2m (6½ ft.) and weigh as much as 40 tons. The faces seem to be half adult, half infant. Most have highly stylized mouths with thick fleshy lips that turn down (known as the "jaguar mouth," this is one of the identifying characteristics of Olmec art). At least 17 heads have been found: 4 at La Venta, 10 at San Lorenzo, and 3 at Tres Zapotes—all Olmec cities on Mexico's east coast. The pieces in this park were taken from La Venta, a major city during the pre-Classic period (2000 B.C.–A.D. 300). Most were sculpted around 1000 B.C. without the use of metal chisels. The basalt rock used for these heads and altars was transported to La Venta from more than 113km (70 miles) away. It is thought that the rock was transported most of the distance by raft. Most of these pieces were first discovered in 1938. Now all that remains at La Venta are some grass-covered mounds that were once earthen pyramids. An exhibition area at the entrance to the park does a good job of illustrating how La Venta was laid out and what archaeologists think the Olmec were like.

As you stroll along, you will see labels identifying many species of local trees, including a grand ceiba tree of special significance to the Olmec and, later, the Maya. A few varieties of local critters scurry about, seemingly unconcerned with the presence of humans or with escaping from the park. Allow at least 2 hours for wandering through the jungly sanctuary and examining the 3,000-year-old sculpture. ***Note:*** Don't forget the mosquito repellent.

Bulevar Ruiz Cortines s/n. ✆ **993/314-1652.** Admission 40 pesos. Tues–Sun 8am–4pm.

A giant Olmec head in Parque-Museo La Venta.

Where to Stay

Hotel rooms in Villahermosa are a little pricier than in other Mexican cities. Rates listed below include the 18% tax. Rates can go up during conventions, but there is no high-season/low-season split. Most hotels have live music on weekends. This makes it difficult to sleep in several of the inexpensive downtown hotels. The only inexpensive hotel I could find that didn't have this problem is listed below.

VERY EXPENSIVE

Hyatt Villahermosa ★★ I like this property more than the Camino Real (which is the other top hotel in the city), for its better location and service. A short walk away is the Parque–Museo La Venta. The entire hotel was completely remodeled in 2009. The rooms have a sleek, modern design with sharp-looking furnishings, fixtures, and accents. This is true of the bathrooms as well, which are large and made to feel larger by the use of sliding doors and minimal clutter.

Av. Juárez 106, 86000 Villahermosa, Tab. ✆ **800/233-1234** in the U.S., or 993/310-1234. Fax 993/315-1963. www.villahermosa.regency.hyatt.com. 206 units. $227–$289 double; $265–$335 Regency Club room; $330–$375 junior suite. Weekend rates often discounted. AE, DC, MC, V. Free guarded parking. **Amenities:** Restaurants; 2 bars (1 w/live music, 1 sports bar); concierge; well-equipped exercise room; outdoor pool, wading pool; room service; concierge-level rooms; smoke-free rooms. *In room:* A/C, TV, hair dryer, minibar, Wi-Fi (for a fee).

EXPENSIVE

Best Western Hotel Maya Tabasco This hotel is centrally located between the downtown area and the modern western section. It's close to the Parque–Museo La Venta, the bus station, and the city's principal restaurant district. Rooms are larger than the norm. Most have ceramic tile floors and are simply furnished. Midsize bathrooms are attractive and have good counter space. A lush pool area separates the hotel from the hotel's bar, which gets fairly good live talent.

Bulevar Ruiz Cortines 907, 86000 Villahermosa, Tab. ✆ **800/528-1234** in the U.S. and Canada, or 993/358-1111, ext. 822. Fax 993/358-1118. www.hotelmaya.com.mx. 151 units. 1,270 pesos double; 1,975 pesos junior suite. AE, MC, V. Free guarded parking. **Amenities:** Restaurant; bar; free airport transfer; large outdoor pool; room service; smoke-free rooms. *In room:* A/C, TV, hair dryer, Wi-Fi.

INEXPENSIVE

Hotel Plaza Independencia 🏷 The Plaza Independencia is the only hotel in this price range with a pool and enclosed parking. It's located downtown, by the pedestrian bridge, and not far from the Anthropology Museum. Rooms are a little small but are better lit than the norm. End rooms, whose numbers end in 01, 02, 14, and 15, have balconies and are generally preferable.

Independencia 123, 86000 Villahermosa, Tab. ✆ **993/312-1299,** -7541. Fax 993/314-4724. www.hotelesplaza.com.mx. 90 units. 720 pesos double. AE, MC, V. Free secure parking. **Amenities:** Restaurant; bar; small outdoor pool; room service. *In room:* A/C, TV, hair dryer, minibar, Wi-Fi.

Where to Dine

Like other Mexican cities, Villahermosa has seen the arrival of U.S. franchise restaurants, but as these things go, I prefer the Mexican variety: **Sanborn's,** Av. Ruiz Cortines 1310, near Parque–Museo La Venta (✆ **993/316-8722**), and **VIPS,** Av. Fco. I. Madero 402, downtown (✆ **993/312-3237**). Both usually do an okay job with traditional dishes such as enchiladas or *antojitos.*

Jangada ★★ SEAFOOD My favorite restaurant in the city is an all-you-can-eat seafood buffet. Start with a small glass of delicious seafood broth and an appetizing empanada of *pejelagarto,* a freshwater fish for which Tabasco is famous. Next to the salad and cold seafood bar, which offers a seafood salad made with freshwater lobster, different kinds of ceviche, and seafood cocktails made to order. There's a variety of soups—especially good is the shrimp-and-*yuca* chowder. And then, of course, there are the main dishes, including charcoal-grilled *pejelagarto* (mild taste—light and almost nutty), and fish kabobs. Jangada is in the fancy western part of town in La Choca neighborhood. It closes early, but next door is a good Brazilian-style steakhouse (Rodizio) that stays open until 9pm.

Paseo de la Choca 126, Fracc. La Choca. ✆ **993/317-6050.** Reservations not accepted. 340 pesos per person, excluding drinks and dessert. AE, DC, MC, V. Daily 12:30–7pm.

Los Tulipanes SEAFOOD/STEAKS/REGIONAL Los Tulipanes is an old-school Mexican restaurant downtown, next to the Pellicer Museum of Anthropology. The food is good so long as you stick to the Mexican dishes and steer clear of the international. Before you order, *tostones de plátano macho*—mashed and fried plantain crisps are brought to your table as an appetizer. Included on the menu are such Mexican specialties as *chiles rellenos,* tacos, and enchiladas. Dishes that are out of the ordinary include *tortilla de maíz nuevo* (oversize tortilla made with fresh corn and stuffed with shrimp or other seafood). For breakfast, the *tamales de chipilín* (an herb) are quite good.

CICOM Center, Periférico Carlos Pellicer Cámara 511. ✆ **993/312-9209,** -9217. Main courses 90–210 pesos; Sun buffet 205 pesos. MC, V. Mon–Sat 8am–7pm; Sun 12:30– 7pm.

PALENQUE ★★

142km (88 miles) SE of Villahermosa; 229km (142 miles) NE of San Cristóbal de las Casas

The ruins of Palenque look out over the jungle from a tall ridge that juts out from the base of steep, thickly forested mountains. It is a dramatic sight colored by the mysterious feel of the ruins themselves. The temples here are in the Classic style, with high-pitched roofs crowned with elaborate combs. Inside many are representations in stone and plaster of the rulers and their gods, which give evidence of a cosmology that is—and perhaps will remain—impenetrable to our understanding. This is one of the grand archaeological sites of Mexico.

Eight kilometers (5 miles) from the ruins is the town of Palenque. There you can find lodging and food, as well as make travel arrangements. Transportation between the town and ruins is cheap and convenient.

Essentials

GETTING THERE & DEPARTING

BY CAR Hwy. 186 from Villahermosa should take about 2 hours. You may encounter military roadblocks that involve a cursory inspection of your travel credentials and perhaps your vehicle. The 230km (143-mile) trip from San Cristóbal to Palenque takes 5 hours and passes through lush jungle and mountain scenery. Take it easy, though, and watch out for potholes and other hindrances.

BY BUS **ADO/Cristóbal Colón** (✆ **916/345-1344**) has regular service to and from Villahermosa and San Cristóbal, as wells as Campeche (six per day, 5 hr.), Villahermosa (nine per day, 2 hr.), Mérida (two per day, 9 hr.), and Playa del Carmen (once per day, 12 hr.). The station is located on Avenida Juárez between the town center and La Cañada.

ORIENTATION

VISITOR INFORMATION The downtown tourism office is a block from the main square at the corner of Avenida Juárez and Abasolo. It's open Monday to Saturday from 9am to 9pm, Sunday from 9am to 1pm. There's no phone at the downtown office. To get info over the phone, call the tourism office's business office (✆ **916/345-0356).**

CITY LAYOUT **Avenida Juárez** is Palenque's main street. At one end is the **plaza;** at the other a traffic circle adorned with a monument imitating the iconic figure of a Maya head, which was discovered at the ruins. To the right of the statue is the entrance to La Cañada; to the left is the road to the ruins, and straight ahead past the statue is the highway to Villahermosa. The distance between the town's main square and the monument is about 1.5km (1 mile).

La Cañada is a restaurant and Hotel Zone tucked away in the forest. Aside from the main plaza area, this is the best location for travelers without cars, because the town is within a few blocks, and the buses that run to the ruins pass right by.

GETTING AROUND The cheapest way to get back and forth from the ruins is on the white vans *(colectivos)* that run down Juárez every 10 minutes from 6am to 6pm. The buses pass La Cañada and hotels along the road to the ruins, and can be flagged down at any point, but they may not stop if they're full. The cost is 10 pesos per person.

FAST FACTS The telephone **area code** is **916.** As for the **climate,** Palenque's high humidity is downright oppressive in the summer, especially after rain showers. During the winter, the damp air can occasionally be chilly in the evening. Rain gear is handy at any time of year. **Internet service** and **ATMs** are easily available.

Exploring Palenque

The reason to come here is the ruins; although you can tour them in a morning, many people savor Palenque for days. There are no must-see sights in town.

PARQUE NACIONAL PALENQUE ★★★

A **museum and visitor center** sits not far from the entrance to the ruins. Though it's not large, the museum is worth the time it takes to see; it's open Tuesday to Sunday from 10am to 5pm and is included in the price of admission to the ruins. It contains well-chosen and artistically displayed exhibits, including jade from recently excavated tombs. Text in Spanish and English explains the life and times of this magnificent city. New pieces are sometimes added as they are uncovered in ongoing excavations.

The **main entrance,** about 1km (½ mile) beyond the museum, is at the end of the paved highway. There you'll find a large parking lot, a refreshment stand, a ticket booth, and several shops. Among the vendors selling souvenirs are often some Lacandón Indians wearing white tunics and hawking bows and arrows.

The Temple of the Inscriptions in Palenque.

Admission to the ruins is 73 pesos. The fee for using a video camera is 50 pesos. Parking at the main entrance and at the visitor center is free. The site and visitor center shops are open daily from 8am to 4:45pm.

TOURING THE RUINS Pottery shards found during the excavations show that people lived in this area as early as 300 B.C. By the Classic period (A.D. 300–900), Palenque was an important ceremonial center. It peaked around A.D. 600 to 700.

Ornate stone carvings from the ruins of Palenque.

When John Stephens visited the site in the 1840s, the ruins that you see today were buried under centuries of accumulated earth and a thick canopy of jungle. The dense jungle surrounding the cleared portion still covers unexcavated temples, which are easily discernible in the forest even to the untrained eye. But be careful not to drift too far from the main path—there have been a few incidents where tourists venturing alone into the rainforest were assaulted.

Of all Mexico's ruins, this is the most haunting, because of its majesty; its history, recovered by epigraphers; and its mysterious setting. Scholars have identified the rulers and constructed their family histories, putting visitors on a first-name basis with

Palenque Ruins

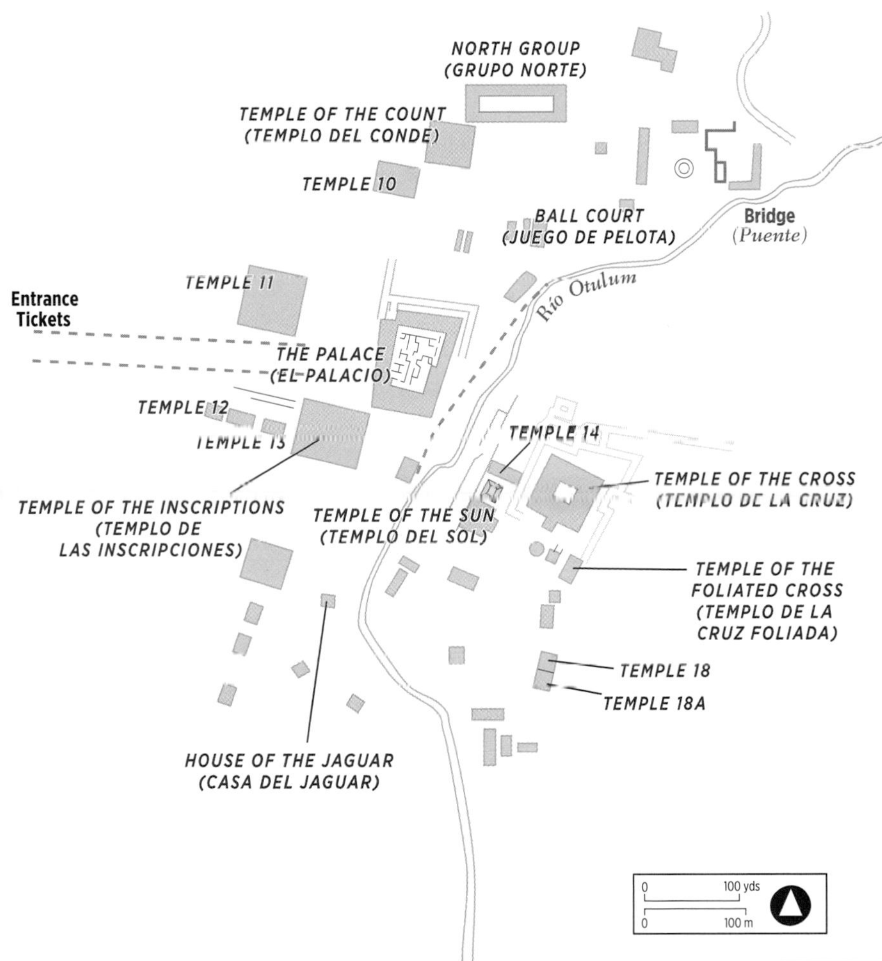

these ancient people etched in stone. You can read about it in *A Forest of Kings,* by Linda Schele and David Freidel.

As you enter the ruins, the building on your right is the **Temple of the Inscriptions,** named for the great stone hieroglyphic panels found inside. (Most of the panels, which portray the family tree of King Pacal, are in the National Anthropological Museum in Mexico City.) This temple is famous for the crypt of King Pacal deep inside the pyramid, but the crypt is closed to the public. The archaeologist Alberto Ruz Lhuillier discovered the tomb in the depths of the temple in 1952—an accomplishment many scholars consider one of the great discoveries of the Maya world. In exploratory excavations, Ruz Lhuillier found a stairway

The Palace in the ruins of Palenque.

leading from the temple floor deep into the base of the pyramid. The original builders had carefully concealed the entrance by filling the stairway with stone. After several months of excavation, Ruz Lhuillier finally reached King Pacal's crypt, which contained several fascinating objects, including a magnificent carved stone sarcophagus. Ruz Lhuillier's own gravesite is opposite the Temple of the Inscriptions, on the left as you enter the park.

Just to your right as you face the Temple of the Inscriptions is **Temple 13,** which is receiving considerable attention from archaeologists. They recently discovered the burial of another richly adorned personage, accompanied in death by an adult female and an adolescent. Some of the artifacts found there are on display in the museum.

Back on the main pathway, the building directly in front of you is the **Palace,** with its unique tower. The explorer John Stephens camped in the Palace when it was completely covered in vegetation, spending sleepless nights fighting off mosquitoes. A pathway between the Palace and the Temple of the Inscriptions leads to the **Temple of the Sun,** the **Temple of the Foliated Cross,** the **Temple of the Cross,** and **Temple 14.** This group of temples, now cleared and in various stages of reconstruction, was built by Pacal's son, Chan-Bahlum, who is usually shown on inscriptions with six toes. Chan-Bahlum's plaster mask was found in Temple 14 next to the Temple of the Sun. Archaeologists have begun probing the Temple of the Sun for Chan-Bahlum's tomb. Little remains of this temple's exterior carving. Inside, however, behind a fence, a carving of Chan-Bahlum shows him ascending the throne in A.D. 690. The panels depict Chan-Bahlum's version of his historic link to the throne.

To the left of the Palace is the North Group, also undergoing restoration. Included in this area are the **Ball Court** and the **Temple of the Count.** At least three tombs, complete with offerings for the underworld journey, have been found here, and the lineage of at least 12 kings has been deciphered from inscriptions left at this site.

Just past the North Group is a small building (once a museum) now used for storing the artifacts found during restorations. It is closed to the public. To the right of the building, a stone bridge crosses the river, leading to a pathway down the hillside to the new museum. The rock-lined path descends along a cascading stream, on the banks of which grow giant ceiba trees. Benches are placed along the way as rest areas, and some small temples have been reconstructed near the base of the trail. In the early morning and evening, you may hear monkeys crashing through the thick foliage by the path; if you keep noise to a minimum, you may spot wild parrots as well. Walking downhill (by far the best way to go), it will take you about 20 minutes to reach the main highway. The path ends at the paved road across from the museum. The *colectivos* (minibuses) going back to the village will stop here if you wave them down.

Where to Stay

English is spoken in all the more expensive hotels and about half of the inexpensive ones. The quoted rates include the 18% tax. High season in Palenque is limited to Easter week, July to August, and December. Palenque gets most of its visitors through bus tours, which originate in Cancún; if you want to avoid running into large groups, pick a small hotel.

EXPENSIVE

Chan-Kah Resort Village ★ This is a pretty property located between the town and the ruins. It's a grouping of comfortable bungalows, called casitas, surrounded by tropical forest. Staying here offers a measure of privacy and quiet in the tropical surroundings. The grounds are well tended, and an inviting freshwater pool fed by a stream runs through the property. The bungalows are made of stone and plaster. They are spacious, and each comes with its own terrace and two rocking chairs. The master suites are two-bedroom bungalows. Christmas prices will be higher than those quoted here, and you may be quoted a higher price if you reserve a room in advance from outside the country. Room service is pricey.

Carretera Las Ruinas Km 3, 29960 Palenque, Chi. © **916/345-1100.** Fax 916/345-0820. www.chan-kah.com.mx. 73 units. 1,580 pesos casita; 3,861 pesos master suite. Promotional rates Sept–Nov. MC, V. Free guarded parking. **Amenities:** Restaurant; bar; 3 outdoor pools (1 large w/natural spring); room service; smoke-free rooms; Wi-Fi (in common areas). *In room:* A/C, TV, hair dryer.

MODERATE

Hotel Ciudad Real Though not fancy, this hotel does the important things right—the rooms are ample, quiet, well lit, and are comfortably furnished. Most units hold two double beds; a few have king-size beds. All rooms have a small balcony, which, in the best case, overlooks tropical vegetation. When making a reservation, specify the hotel in Palenque (there's also a Ciudad Real in San Cristóbal). It's at the edge of town in the direction of the airport. Though it works with bus tours, as other large hotels do, this hotel works well for individual travelers who have their own car.

Carretera a Pakal-Na Km 1.5, 29960 Palenque, Chi. © **916/345-1343** (reservations: © 967/678-4400). www.ciudadreal.com.mx. 72 units. High season 1,330 pesos double, 1,695 pesos junior suite; low season 900 pesos double, 1,150 pesos junior suite. AE, MC, V. Free secured parking. Internet discounts sometimes available. **Amenities:** Restaurant; bar; outdoor pool; baby pool; room service; smoke-free rooms; Wi-Fi (in lobby and restaurant). *In room:* A/C, TV, hair dryer.

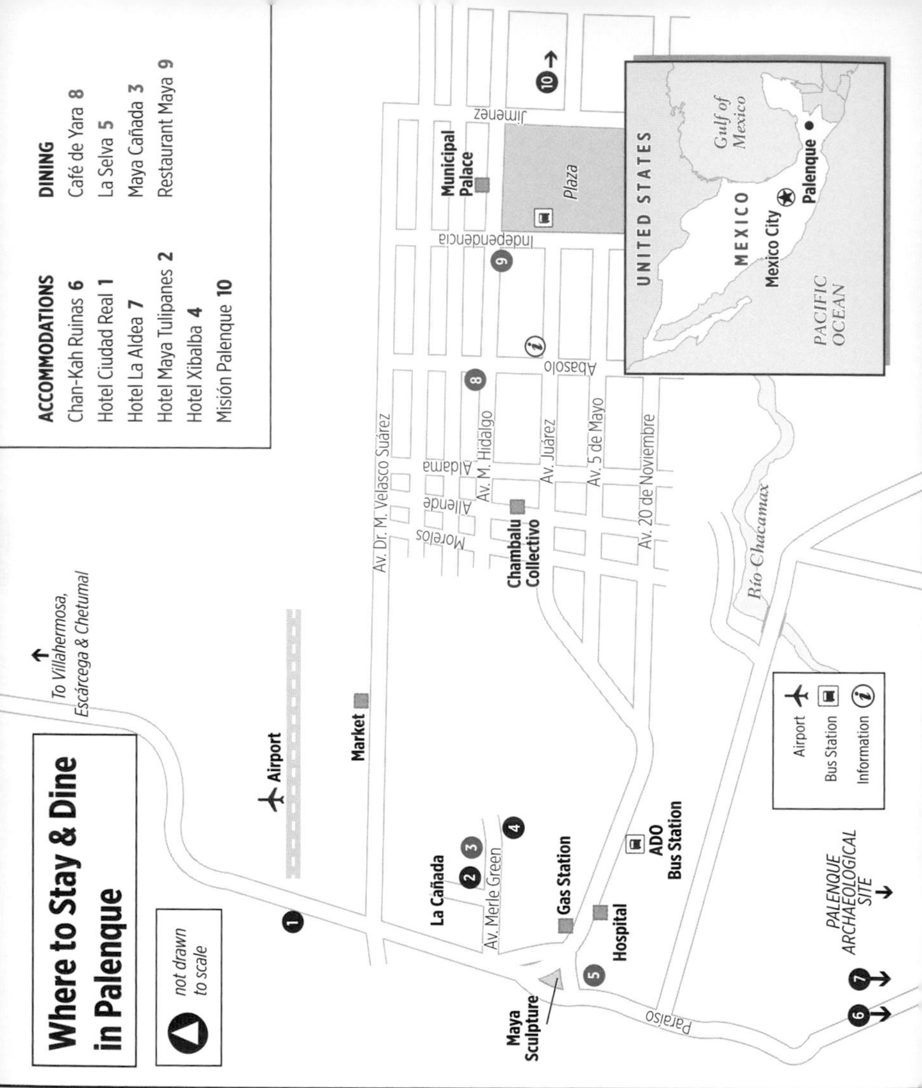

Hotel La Aldea This hotel on the way to the ruins enjoys the same lush surroundings as the more expensive Chan-Kah Resort Village, but it's smaller and most often quieter. It is a family-owned hotel, designed and managed by an architect. The rooms show a good deal of thought went into making them attractive and functional. They are in a collection of free standing bungalows set on rising ground (mostly two rooms per bungalow). A few of the rooms (number 10 in particular) have views of the forest. All rooms are large, with good space for luggage. Each has an outdoor sitting area. In terms of layout and decor, I like them better than those in the neighboring Chan-Kah Village.

Carretera Las Ruinas Km 2.8, 29960 Palenque, Chi. ✆/fax **916/345-1693.** www.hotellaaldea.net. 28 units. 1,100 pesos double. Low season discounts of 20%–30% MC, V. Free secured parking. **Amenities:** Restaurant; bar; outdoor pool; smoke-free rooms; Wi-Fi (in common areas). *In room:* A/C, no phone.

Hotel Maya Tulipanes This is an attractive hotel tucked away in the Cañada. I like it for its location and management. Service and upkeep are both good. Rooms are medium to large and come with a queen-size, a king-size, or two double beds. Tropical vegetation adorns the grounds, along with some reproductions of famous Maya architecture. The Maya Tulipanes has an arrangement with a sister hotel at the ruins of Tikal, in Guatemala. The travel agency operates daily tours to Bonampak and other attractions.

Calle Cañada 6, 29960 Palenque, Chi. ✆ **916/345-0201,** -0258. Fax 916/345-1004. www.mayatulipanes.com.mx. 74 units. High season 1,190 pesos double; low season 795–1,000 pesos double. Internet packages available. AE, MC, V. Free secured parking. **Amenities:** Restaurant; bar; ground transportation to/from Villahermosa airport; outdoor pool; room service; smoke-free rooms. *In room:* A/C, TV, hair dryer, Wi-Fi.

Misión Palenque ★ This hotel has returned to being among the most comfortable in the city after a total remodeling that includes new air-conditioning and other amenities. Rooms are medium-size and attractively furnished with light, modern furniture. Bathrooms are spacious, with ample counters. The hotel has extensive grounds and is very quiet. In one corner of the property, a natural spring flows through an attractive bit of jungle, where the hotel has installed the spa. Part of the spa is a *temazcal,* or sweat lodge. There's also a mud bath along with the more common elements. The hotel is a few blocks east of the town's main square.

Periférico Oriente s/n, 29960 Palenque, Chi. ✆ **916/345-0241,** or 01/800-900-3800 in Mexico. Fax 916/345-0300. www.hotelesmision.com.mx. 156 units. 1,100 pesos double; 2,925 pesos junior suite. AE, MC, V. Free guarded parking. **Amenities:** Restaurant; babysitting; exercise room; Jacuzzi; outdoor pool; wading pool; room service; spa; 2 tennis courts. *In room:* A/C, TV, hair dryer (on request), Wi-Fi.

INEXPENSIVE

Hotel Xibalba This budget hotel recently expanded to handle larger groups, but the price is still right. You can ask for a room in back if a group is being noisy. The medium-to-small rooms are basic but clean, with functioning air-conditioning, which is not always the case at the budget level. The upstairs units are a little smaller than the downstairs units. Most of the beds have firm mattresses. Check out the full-size replica of Pacal's sarcophagus lid on the premises.

Calle Merle Green 9, Col. La Cañada, 29960 Palenque, Chi. ✆ **916/345-0392.** Fax 916/345-0411. www.hotelxibalba.com. 35 units. 500–700 pesos double. MC, V. Free parking. **Amenities:** Restaurant; bar; Wi-Fi. *In room:* A/C, TV, no phone.

Where to Dine

Palenque and, for that matter, the rest of backwater Chiapas, is not for gourmets. Who'd a thunk? I had an easy time eliminating a number of restaurants that didn't even seem to be keeping up the appearance of serving food. But the situation has been improving, and you can at least get some decent Mexican food.

MODERATE

La Selva INTERNATIONAL/MEXICAN At La Selva (the jungle), you dine under a large, attractive thatched roof beside well-tended gardens. The menu includes seafood, freshwater fish, steaks, and Mexican specialties. The most expensive thing on the menu is *pigua,* freshwater lobster caught in the large rivers of southeast Mexico. These can grow quite large—the size of small saltwater lobsters. This and the finer cuts of meat have been frozen, but you wouldn't want otherwise in Palenque. I liked the fish stuffed with shrimp, and the *mole* enchiladas. La Selva is on the highway to the ruins, near the statue of the Maya head.

Carretera Palenque Ruinas Km 0.5. ✆ **916/345-0363.** Main courses 145–220 pesos. MC, V. Daily 11:30am–11:30pm.

INEXPENSIVE

Café de Yara MEXICAN A small, modern cafe and restaurant with a comforting, not overly ambitious menu. The cafe's strong suit is healthful salads (with disinfected greens) and home-style Mexican entrees, such as the beef or chicken *milanesa* or chicken cooked in a *chile pasilla* sauce. It also offers decent tamales. In the evenings it occasionally offers live music.

Av. Hidalgo 66 (at Abasolo). ✆ **916/345-0269.** Main courses 60–105 pesos. MC, V. Daily 7am–11pm.

Restaurant Maya and Maya Cañada ★ MEXICAN These two are the most consistently good restaurants in Palenque. One faces the main plaza from the corner of Independencia and Hidalgo, the other is in La Cañada (✆ **916/345-0216**). Menus differ a bit, but much is the same. Both do a good job with the basics—good strong, locally grown coffee and soft, pliant tortillas. The menu offers a combination of Mexican standards and regional specialties. If you're in an exploratory mood, try one of the regional specialties such as the *mole chiapaneco* (dark red, like *mole poblano,* but less sweet) or any of the dishes based on *chaya* or *chipilin* (mild-flavored local greens), such as the soup with *chipilin* and *bolitas de masa* (corn dumplings). If you want something more comforting, go for the chicken, rice, and vegetable soup, or the *sopa azteca.* The plantains stuffed with cheese and fried Mexican style are wonderful. Waiters sometimes offer specials not on the menu, and these are often the thing to get. You can also try *tascalate,* a pre-Hispanic drink made of water, *masa,* chocolate, and *achiote,* and served room temperature or cold.

Av. Independencia s/n (at Hidalgo). ✆ **916/345-0042.** Breakfast 50–80 pesos; main courses 50–160 pesos. MC, V. Daily 7am–11pm.

Road Trips from Palenque

BONAMPAK & YAXCHILÁN: MURALS IN THE JUNGLE

Intrepid travelers may want to consider the day trip to the Maya ruins of Bonampak and Yaxchilán. The **ruins of Bonampak ★**, southeast of Palenque on the Guatemalan border, were discovered in 1946. The site is important for the vivid and well-preserved **murals** of the Maya on the interior walls of one temple. Particularly striking is an impressive battle scene, perhaps the most important painting of pre-Hispanic Mexico.

Several tour companies offer a day trip. The drive to Bonampak is 3 hours. From there you continue by boat to the **ruins of Yaxchilán ★**, famous for its

Vivid Maya murals from Bonampak.

highly ornamented buildings. Bring rain gear, boots, a flashlight, and bug repellent. All tours include meals and cost about 900 pesos. No matter what agency you sign up with, the hours of departure and return are the same. You leave at 6am and return at 7pm.

Try **Viajes Na Chan Kan** (✆ **916/345-2154;** www.nachankan.com), at Hidalgo 5, across from the main square offers all the usual side trips as well as ecological and cultural tours to outlying Indian communities.

WATERFALLS AT MISOL HA & AGUA AZUL

Misol Ha is 20km (12 miles) from Palenque, in the direction of Ocosingo. It takes about 30 minutes to get there, depending on the traffic. The turn-off is clearly marked; you'll turn right and drive another 1.5 km (1 mile). The place is absolutely beautiful. Water pours from a rocky cliff into a broad pool of green water bordered by thick tropical vegetation. There's a small restaurant and some rustic cabins for rent for around 500 pesos per night, depending on the size of the cabin. The place is run by the *ejido* cooperative that owns the site, and it does a good job of maintaining the place. To inquire about the cabins, call ✆ **916/345-1506.** Admission for the day is 25 pesos.

A Lacandón Indian near Bonampak.

Approximately 44km (27 miles) beyond Misol Ha are the **Agua Azul**

A waterfall in Misol Ha.

waterfalls—270m (886 ft.) of tumbling falls with lots of water. There are cabins for rent here, too, but I would rather stay at Misol Ha. You can swim either above or below the falls, but make sure you don't get pulled by the current. You can see both places in the same day or stop to see them on your way to Ocosingo and San Cristóbal. Agua Azul is prettiest after 3 or 4 consecutive dry days; heavy rains can make the water murky. Check with guides or other travelers about the water quality before you decide to go. The cost to enter is 25 pesos per person. Trips to both of these places can be arranged through just about any hotel.

OCOSINGO & THE RUINS OF TONINÁ

By the time you get to Agua Azul, you're halfway to Ocosingo, which lies halfway between Palenque and San Cristóbal. So instead of returning for the night to Palenque, you can go on to Ocosingo. It's higher up and more comfortable than Palenque. It's a nice little town, not touristy, not a lot to do other than see the ruins of Toniná. But it is a nice place to spend the night so that you can see the ruins early before moving on to San Cristóbal. There are about a half-dozen small hotels in town; the largest is not the most desirable. I would stay at the **Hospedaje Esmeralda** (✆ **919/673-0014**) or the **Hotel Central** (✆ **919/673-0024**), on the main square. Both of these are small and simple, but welcoming. The restaurant in front of Hotel Central has good cooking.

RUINS OF TONINÁ ★★ The ruins of Toniná (the name translates as "house of rocks") are 14km (8¾ miles) east of Ocosingo. You can take a cab there and catch a *colectivo* to return. The city dates from the Classic period and covered a large area, but the excavated and restored part is all on one steep hillside that faces a broad valley. This site is not set up to handle lots of tourists (and doesn't really receive many). There is a good bit of climbing involved, and some of it is a little precarious. This is not a good place to take kids. Admission is 41 pesos.

This complex of courtyards, rooms, and stairways is built on multiple levels that are irregular and asymmetrical. The overall effect is that of a ceremonial area with multiple foci instead of a clearly discernable center. It affords beautiful and intriguing perspectives from just about any spot.

As early as A.D. 350, Toniná emerged as a dynastic center. In the 7th and 8th centuries, it was locked in a struggle with rival Palenque and, to a lesser degree, with faraway Calakmul. This has led some scholars to see Toniná as more militaristic than its neighbors—a sort of Sparta of the classic Maya. Toniná's greatest victory came in 711, when, under the rule of Kan B'alam, it attacked Palenque and captured its king, K'an Joy Chitam, depicted on a stone frieze twisted, his arms bound with rope.

But the single most important artifact yet found at Toniná, is up around the fifth level of the acropolis—a large stucco frieze divided into panels by a feathered framework adorned with the heads of sacrificial victims (displayed upside down) and some rather horrid creatures. The largest figure is a skeletal image holding a decapitated head—very vivid and very puzzling. There is actually a stylistic parallel with some murals of the Teotihuacán culture of central Mexico. The other special thing about Toniná is that it holds the distinction of having the last ever date recorded in the long count (A.D. 909), which marks the end of the Classic period.

SAN CRISTÓBAL DE LAS CASAS ★★★

229km (142 miles) SW of Palenque; 80km (50 miles) E of Tuxtla Gutiérrez; 74km (46 miles) NW of Comitán; 166km (103 miles) NW of Cuauhtémoc; 451km (280 miles) E of Oaxaca

San Cristóbal is a colonial town of white stucco walls and red-tile roofs, of cobblestone streets and narrow sidewalks, of graceful arcades and open plazas. It lies in a green valley 2,120m (6,954 ft.) high. The city owes part of its name to the 16th-century cleric Fray Bartolomé de las Casas, who was the town's first bishop and spent the rest of his life waging a political campaign to protect the indigenous peoples of the Americas.

San Cristóbal de las Casas.

Surrounding the city are many villages of Mayan-speaking Indians who display great variety in their language, dress, and customs, making this area one of the most ethnically diverse in Mexico. San Cristóbal is the principal market town for these Indians, and their point of contact with the outside world. Most of them trek down from the surrounding mountains to sell goods and run errands

Several Indian villages lie within reach of San Cristóbal by road: **Chamula,** with its weavers and unorthodox church; **Zinacantán,** whose residents practice their own syncretic religion; **Tenejapa, San Andrés,** and **Magdalena,** known for brocaded textiles; **Amatenango del Valle,** a town of potters; and **Aguacatenango,** known for embroidery. Most of these "villages" consist of little more than a church and the municipal government building, with homes scattered for miles around and a general gathering only for church and market days (usually Sun).

Many Indians now live on the outskirts of town because they've been expelled from their villages over religious differences. They are known as *los expulsados.* No longer involved in farming, they make their living in commerce and handicrafts. Most still wear traditional dress, but they've adopted Protestant religious beliefs that prevent them from partaking in many of their community's civic and religious celebrations.

The influx of outsiders hasn't created in most Indians a desire to adopt mainstream customs and dress. It's interesting to note that the communities closest to San Cristóbal are the most resistant to change. The greatest threat to the cultures in this area comes not from tourism, but from the action of large market forces, population pressures, environmental damage, and poverty. The Indians aren't interested in acting or looking like the foreigners they see. They may steal glances or even stare at tourists, but mainly they pay little attention to outsiders, except as potential buyers for handicrafts.

You may see or hear the word *Jovel,* San Cristóbal's Indian name, incorporated often in the names of businesses. You'll hear the word *coleto,* used in reference to someone or something from San Cristóbal. You'll see signs for *tamales coletos, pan coleto,* and *desayuno coleto* (Cristóbal breakfast).

Essentials

GETTING THERE & DEPARTING

BY PLANE The local airport is little used, and the closest airport with regular service is in Tuxtla Gutiérrez (p. 357).

BY CAR From Palenque (5 hr.), the beautiful road provides jungle scenery, but portions of it may be heavily potholed or obstructed during rainy season. Check with the local state tourism office before driving. From Tuxtla Gutiérrez, the 1½-hour trip winds through beautiful mountain country.

BY TAXI Taxis from Tuxtla Gutiérrez to San Cristóbal cost around 600 pesos.

BY BUS The **ADO** station (which also handles the affiliates Altos, Cristóbal Colón, and Maya de Oro) is at the corner of Insurgentes and Bulevar Juan Sabines, 8 blocks south of the main square. This company offers service to and from Tuxtla (12 buses per day), Palenque (almost every hour), and several other destinations: Mérida (two buses per day), Villahermosa (two buses per day), Oaxaca (two buses per day), and Puerto Escondido (two buses per day). To buy a bus ticket without going down to the station, go to the **Ticket Bus** agency, Real de Guadalupe 24 (© **967/678-8503**). Hours are Monday to Saturday from 7am to 10pm.

The best cheap way to get to and from nearby Tuxtla Gutiérrez is by "*microbus,*" 16-seat buses that depart every 5 to 15 minutes from the small bus station across the street from the ADO bus station. The company is called **Omnibuses de Chiapas** (no phone). Look for white buses that say *omni* or *expreso* on the front. The fare is 35 pesos and the trip takes an hour. There are also vans making the run every 15 to 30 minutes. They can be found just off Juan Sabines by the bus station. You'll have to ask someone to point them out to you because there isn't a sign. The problem with these is that they pack too many passengers in them for comfort.

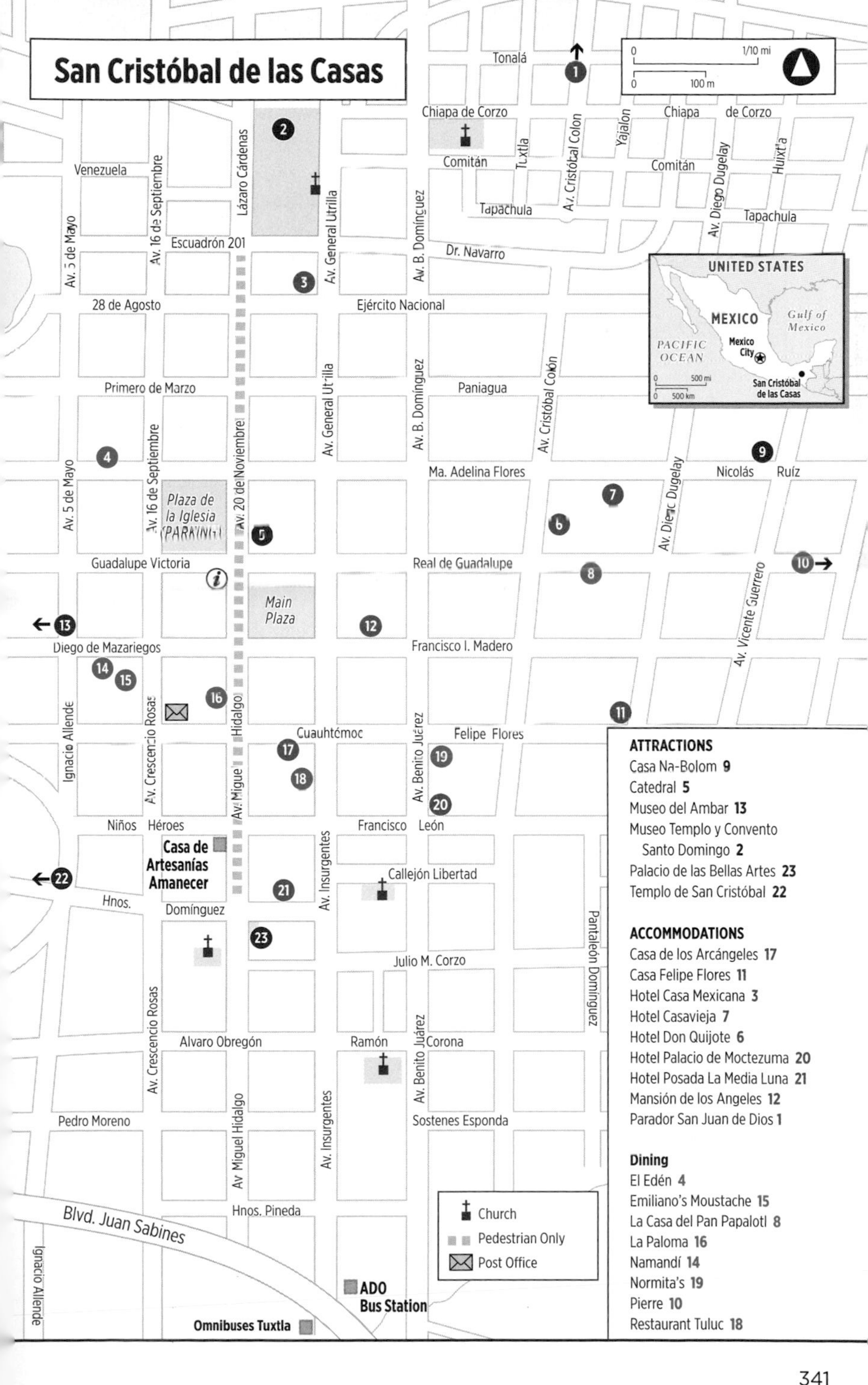
San Cristóbal de las Casas
0 1/10 mi
0 100 m
UNITED STATES
MEXICO
Gulf of Mexico
PACIFIC OCEAN
Mexico City
San Cristóbal de las Casas
0 500 mi
0 500 km
Tonalá
Chiapa de Corzo
Comitán
Tapachula
Venezuela
Escuadrón 201
Dr. Navarro
28 de Agosto
Ejército Nacional
Primero de Marzo
Paniagua
Ma. Adelina Flores
Nicolás Ruíz
Guadalupe Victoria
Real de Guadalupe
Diego de Mazariegos
Francisco I. Madero
Cuauhtémoc
Felipe Flores
Niños Héroes
Francisco León
Callejón Libertad
Hnos. Domínguez
Julio M. Corzo
Alvaro Obregón
Ramón Corona
Pedro Moreno
Sostenes Esponda
Hnos. Pineda
Blvd. Juan Sabines
Av. 5 de Mayo
Av. 16 de Septiembre
Lázaro Cárdenas
Av. General Utrilla
Av. B. Domínguez
Tuxtla
Av. Cristóbal Colón
Yajalon
Av. Diego Dugelay
Huixtla
Av. 20 de Noviembre
Av. Vicente Guerrero
Ignacio Allende
Av. Crescencio Rosas
Av. Miguel Hidalgo
Av. Insurgentes
Av. Benito Juárez
Pantaleón Domínguez
Plaza de la Iglesia (PARKING)
Main Plaza
Casa de Artesanías Amanecer
ADO Bus Station
Omnibuses Tuxtla
Church
Pedestrian Only
Post Office
ATTRACTIONS
Casa Na-Bolom 9
Catedral 5
Museo del Ambar 13
Museo Templo y Convento Santo Domingo 2
Palacio de las Bellas Artes 23
Templo de San Cristóbal 22
ACCOMMODATIONS
Casa de los Arcángeles 17
Casa Felipe Flores 11
Hotel Casa Mexicana 3
Hotel Casavieja 7
Hotel Don Quijote 6
Hotel Palacio de Moctezuma 20
Hotel Posada La Media Luna 21
Mansión de los Angeles 12
Parador San Juan de Dios 1
Dining
El Edén 4
Emiliano's Moustache 15
La Casa del Pan Papalotl 8
La Paloma 16
Namandí 14
Normita's 19
Pierre 10
Restaurant Tuluc 18

THE zapatista movement & CHIAPAS

In January 1994, Indians from this area rebelled against the Mexican government over health care, education, land distribution, and representative government. Their organization, the **Zapatista Liberation Army,** known as EZLN (Ejército Zapatista de Liberación Nacional), and its leader, Subcomandante Marcos, became symbols of the struggle for social justice. Times have changed. The situation has long since quieted, and there is no longer any talk of armed revolt. Subcomandante Marcos has become a social critic and commentator, and the EZLN has become an independent political organization not tied to any particular party. Even the town's graffiti reflects the new mood, with political exhortations disappearing in favor of the more artsy, more obscure scribblings, resembling the graffiti in the U.S.

ORIENTATION

ARRIVING To get to the town square from the highway, turn on to **Avenida Insurgentes** (at the traffic light). From the bus station, the main plaza is 8 blocks north up Avenida Insurgentes (a 10-min. walk, slightly uphill). Cabs are cheap and plentiful.

VISITOR INFORMATION The **Municipal Tourism Office** (✆/fax **967/678-0665**) is in the town hall, west of the main square. It's open daily from 9am to 9pm. Check the bulletin board here for apartments, shared rides, cultural events, and local tours.

CITY LAYOUT San Cristóbal is laid out on a grid; the main north–south axis is **Insurgentes/Utrilla,** and the east–west axis is **Mazariegos/Madero.** All streets change names when they cross either of these streets. The *zócalo* (main plaza) lies where they intersect. An important street to know is **Real de Guadalupe,** which runs from the plaza eastward to the church of Guadalupe; located on it are many hotels and restaurants. The market is 7 blocks north of the *zócalo* along Utrilla.

Take note that this town has at least three streets named Domínguez and two streets named Flores. There are Hermanos Domínguez, Belisario Domínguez, and Pantaleón Domínguez; and María Adelina Flores and Dr. Felipe Flores.

GETTING AROUND Most of the sights and shopping in San Cristóbal are within walking distance of the plaza.

***Urbano* buses** (minibuses) take passengers between town and the residential neighborhoods. All buses pass by the market and central plaza on their way through town. Utrilla and Avenida 16 de Septiembre are the two main arteries; all buses use the market area as the last stop. Any bus on Utrilla will take you to the market.

Colectivos to outlying villages depart from the public market at Avenida Utrilla. Buses late in the day are usually very crowded. Always check to see when the last or next-to-last bus returns from wherever you're

San Cristóbal's Av. 20 de Noviembre.

going, and then take the one before that—those last buses sometimes don't materialize, and you might be stranded. I speak from experience!

Recommended Books

The People of the Bat: Mayan Tales and Dreams from Zinacantán, **by Robert M. Laughlin, is a priceless collection of beliefs from that village near San Cristóbal. Another good book with a completely different view of today's Maya is** ***The Heart of the Sky,*** **by Peter Canby, who traveled among the Maya to chronicle their struggles (and wrote his book before the Zapatista uprising).**

Rental cars come in handy for trips to the outlying villages and may be worth the expense when shared by a group, but keep in mind that insurance is invalid on unpaved roads. Try **Optima Car Rental,** Av. Mazariegos 39 (✆ **967/674-5409**). Office hours are daily from 9am to 1pm and 5 to 8pm. You'll save money by arranging the rental from your home country; otherwise, a day's rental with insurance will cost around 700 pesos for a VW Beetle with manual transmission, the cheapest car available.

Scooters can be rented from **Croozy Scooters** (✆ **967/631-4329**), at Belisario Domínguez 7-A. Passport and 500 pesos deposit required.

Bikes are another option for getting around the city; a day's rental is about 120 pesos. **Los Pingüinos,** Av. Ecuador 4-B (✆ **967/678-0202;** pinguinosmex@yahoo.com), offers bike tours to a few out-of-town locations. Tours in the valley around San Cristóbal last 4 to 6 hours and cost 300 to 400 pesos. It's open daily from 10am to 2:30pm and 4 to 7pm.

[FastFACTS] SAN CRISTÓBAL DE LAS CASAS

Area Code The telephone area code is **967.**

ATMs San Cristóbal has a number of ATMs.

Currency Exchange There are at least five *casas de cambio* on Real de Guadalupe, near the main square, and a couple under the colonnade facing the square. Most are open until 8pm, and some are open Sunday.

Doctor Try **Dr. Roberto Lobato,** Av. Belisario Domínguez 17, at Calle Flavio A. Paniagua (✆ **967/678-7777**). Don't be unsettled by the fact that his office is next door to Funerales Canober.

Internet Access Internet cafes are everywhere.

Parking Use the underground public lot in front of the cathedral, just off the main square on 16 de Septiembre. Entry is from Calle 5 de Febrero.

Post Office The *correo* is at Crescencio Rosas and Cuauhtémoc, a block south and west of the main square. It's open Monday to Friday from 8am to 7pm, Saturday from 9am to 1pm.

Spanish Classes The **Centro Bilingüe,** at the Centro Cultural El Puente, Real de Guadalupe 55, 29250 San Cristóbal de las Casas, Chi. (✆ **800/303-4983** in the U.S., or ✆/fax 967/678-3723), offers classes in Spanish and can arrange home stays for their students.

Weather San Cristóbal can be chilly when the sun isn't out, especially during the winter. It's 2,120m (6,954 ft.) above sea level. Most hotels are not heated, although some have fireplaces. There is always a possibility of rain, but I would avoid going to San Cristóbal from late August to late October, during the height of the rainy season.

Exploring San Cristóbal

San Cristóbal is a lovely town in a lovely region. A lot of people come for the beauty, but the main thing that draws most visitors here is the highland Maya. They can be seen anywhere in San Cristóbal, but most travelers take at least one trip to the outlying villages to get a close-up of Maya life.

Casa Na-Bolom ★ This is the old headquarters of anthropologists Frans and Trudy Blom, who made this little corner of the world their home and their passion. It became a gathering place for those studying in the region. Frans Blom (1893–1963) led many early archaeological studies in Mexico, and Trudy (1901–1993) was noted for her photographs of the Lacandón Indians and her efforts to save them and their forest homeland. A room at Na-Bolom contains a selection of her Lacandón photographs, and postcards of the photographs are on sale in the gift shop (daily 9am–2pm and 4–7pm). The house is now a museum. A tour covers the displays of pre-Hispanic artifacts collected by Frans Blom; the cozy library, with its numerous volumes about the region and the Maya (weekdays 10am–2pm); and the gardens Trudy Blom started for the ongoing reforestation of the Lacandón jungle. The tour ends with a showing of *La Reina de la Selva,* an excellent 50-minute film on the Bloms, the Lacandón, and Na-Bolom.

The 17 guest rooms, named for surrounding villages, are decorated with local objects and textiles. All rooms have fireplaces and private bathrooms. Prices

A display from the Museo del Ambar.

A display from Casa Na-Bolom.

(including admission to the museum) are 970 to 1,110 pesos for a double; 1,250 to 1,520 pesos for a suite.

Even if you're not a guest here, you can come for a meal, usually an assortment of vegetarian and other dishes. Just be sure to make a reservation at least ½ hours in advance, and be on time. The colorful dining room has one large table, and the eclectic mix of travelers sometimes makes for interesting conversation. Breakfast costs 60 pesos; lunch and dinner cost 150 pesos each. Dinner is served at 7pm. Following breakfast (8–10am), a guide not affiliated with the house offers tours to San Juan Chamula and Zinacantán (see "The Nearby Maya Villages & Countryside," below) on everyday but Monday.

Av. Vicente Guerrero 33, 29200 San Cristóbal de las Casas, Chi. ✆ **967/678-1418.** Fax 967/678-5586. www.nabolom.org. Group tour and film 45 pesos. Tours daily 11:30am (Spanish only) and 4:30pm.

Catedral San Cristóbal's main cathedral was built in the 1500s. Make note of the interesting beamed ceiling and a carved wooden pulpit.

Calle 20 de Noviembre at Guadalupe Victoria. No phone. Free admission. Daily 7am–6pm.

El Mercado Once you've visited Santo Domingo (see listing below), meander through the San Cristóbal town market and the surrounding area. Every time I do, I see something different to elicit my curiosity.

By Santo Domingo church. No phone. Mon–Sat 8am–7pm.

Museo del Ambar If you've been in this town any time at all, you know what a big deal amber is here. Chiapas is the third-largest producer of amber in the world, and many experts prefer its amber for its colors and clarity. A couple of stores tried calling themselves museums, but they didn't fool anybody. Now a real museum moves methodically through all the issues surrounding amber—mining, shaping, and identifying it, as well as the different varieties found in other parts of the world. It's interesting, it's cheap, and you get to see the restored area of the old convent it occupies. There are a couple of beautiful pieces of worked amber that are on permanent loan—make sure you see them. In mid-August, the museum holds a contest for local artisans who work amber; they do remarkable work.

Exconvento de la Merced, Diego de Mazariegos s/n. ✆ **967/678-9716.** Admission 25 pesos. Tues–Sun 10am–2pm and 4–7pm.

San Cristóbal's main cathedral.

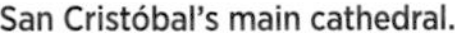

A gilded altar from Museo Templo y Convento Santo Domingo.

Museo Templo y Convento Santo Domingo Inside the front door of the carved-stone facade is a beautiful gilded wooden altarpiece built in 1560, walls with saints, and gilt-framed paintings. Attached to the church is the former Convent of Santo Domingo, now a small museum about San Cristóbal and Chiapas. It has changing exhibits and often shows cultural films. It's 5 blocks north of the *zócalo*, in the market area.

Av. 20 de Noviembre. ✆ **967/678-1609.** Free admission to church; museum 41 pesos. Museum Tues–Sun 9am–6pm; church daily 10am–2pm and 5–8pm.

Palacio de las Bellas Artes Bellas Artes periodically hosts dance events, art shows, and other performances. The schedule of events is usually posted on the door if the Bellas Artes is not open. A public library is next door. Around the corner, the Centro Cultural holds concerts and other performances; check the posters on the door to see what's scheduled.

Av. Hidalgo, 4 blocks south of the plaza. No phone.

Templo de San Cristóbal For the best view of San Cristóbal, climb the seemingly endless steps to this church and *mirador* (lookout point). A visit here requires stamina. There are 22 more churches in town, some of which also demand strenuous climbs.

At the very end of Calle Hermanos Domínguez.

HORSEBACK RIDING

The **Casa de Huéspedes Margarita,** Real de Guadalupe 34, can arrange horseback rides for around 150 to 180 pesos, including a guide. The excursions are around 4½ hours long. Reserve your steed at least a day in advance. Possible places to visit might include San Juan Chamula, some nearby caves, or some of the outlying hills, depending upon interest.

THE NEARBY MAYA VILLAGES & COUNTRYSIDE

The Indian communities around San Cristóbal are fascinating worlds unto themselves. If you are unfamiliar with these indigenous cultures, you will understand and appreciate more of what you see by visiting them with a guide, at least for your first foray out into the villages. Guides are acquainted with members of the communities and are viewed with less suspicion than newcomers. These communities have their own laws and customs—and visitors' ignorance is no excuse. Entering these communities is tantamount to leaving Mexico, and if something happens, the state and federal authorities will not intervene except in case of a serious crime.

The best guided trips are the locally grown ones. Three operators go to the neighboring villages in small groups. They all charge the same price (175 pesos per person), use minivans for transportation, and speak English. They do, however, have their own interpretations and focus.

Pepe and Ramiro leave from **Casa Na-Bolom** (see above) for daily trips to San Juan Chamula and Zinacantán at 10am, returning to San Cristóbal between 2 and 3pm. They look at cultural continuities, community relationships, and religion.

Alex and Raúl can be found in front of the cathedral between 9:15 and 9:30am. They are quite personable and get along well with the Indians in the communities. They focus on cultural values and their expression in social behavior, which provides a glimpse of the details and the texture of life in these communities (and, of course, they talk about religion). Their tour is very good. They can be reached at ✆ **967/678-3741** or chamul@hotmail.com.

For excursions farther afield, see "Road Trips from San Cristóbal," later in this chapter. Also, Alex and Raúl can be contracted for trips to other communities besides Chamula and Zinacantán; talk to them.

CHAMULA & ZINACANTÁN A side trip to the village of San Juan Chamula will get you into the spirit of life around San Cristóbal. Sunday, when the market is in full swing, is the best day to go for shopping; other days, when you'll be less impeded by eager children selling their crafts, are better for seeing the village and church.

The village, 8km (5 miles) northeast of San Cristóbal, has a large church, a plaza, and a municipal building. Each year, a new group of citizens is chosen to live in the municipal center as caretakers of the saints, settlers of disputes, and enforcers of village rules. As in other nearby villages, on Sunday local leaders wear their leadership costumes, including beautifully woven straw hats loaded with colorful ribbons befitting their high position. They solemnly sit together in a long line somewhere around the central square. Chamula is typical of other villages, in that men are often away working in the "hot lands," harvesting coffee or cacao, while women stay home to tend the sheep, the children, the cornfields, and the fires.

Don't leave Chamula without seeing the **church interior.** As you step from bright sunlight into the candlelit interior, you feel as if you've been transported to another country. Pine needles scattered amid a sea of lighted candles cover the tile floor. Saints line the walls, and before them people are often kneeling and praying aloud while passing around bottles of Pepsi-

A Zinacantán villager.

Cola. Shamans are often on hand, passing eggs over sick people or using live or dead chickens in a curing ritual. The statues of saints are similar to those you might see in any Mexican Catholic church, but beyond sharing the same name, they mean something completely different to the Chamulas. Visitors can walk carefully through the church to see the saints or stand quietly in the background.

Just to the south, in Zinacantán, a wealthier village than Chamula, you must sign a strict form promising *not to take any photographs* before you see the two side-by-side **sanctuaries.** Once permission is granted and you have paid a small fee, an escort will usually show you the church, or you may be allowed to see it on your own. Floors may be covered in pine needles here, too, and the rooms are brightly sunlit. The experience is an altogether different one from that of Chamula. You may be approached by children who will offer to show you to their home where their female relatives will most likely be weaving or working at some other craft.

AMATENANGO DEL VALLE About an hour's ride south of San Cristóbal is Amatenango, a town known mostly for its **women potters.** You'll see their work in San Cristóbal—small animals, jars, and large water jugs—but in the village, you can visit the potters in their homes. Just walk down the dirt streets.

A woman potter in Amatenango.

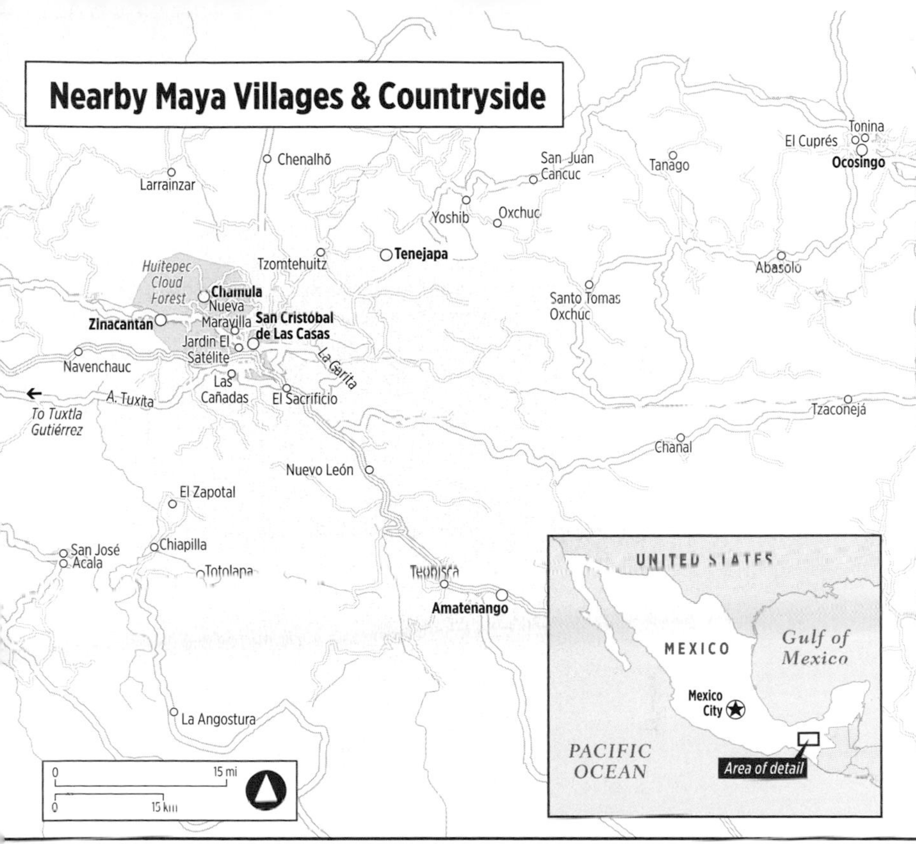

Villagers will lean over the walls of family compounds and invite you in to select from their inventory. You may even see them firing the pieces under piles of wood in the open courtyard or painting them with color derived from rusty iron water. The women wear beautiful red-and-yellow *huipiles,* but if you want to take a photograph, you'll have to pay. To get here, take a *colectivo* from the market in San Cristóbal. Before it lets you off, be sure to ask about the return-trip schedule.

AGUACATENANGO This village, 16km (10 miles) south of Amatenango, is known for its **embroidery.** If you've visited San Cristóbal's shops, you'll recognize the white-on-white and black-on-black floral patterns on dresses and blouses for sale. The locals' own regional blouses, however, are quite different.

TENEJAPA The **weavers** of Tenejapa, 28km (17 miles) northeast from San Cristóbal, make some of the most beautiful and expensive work you'll see in the region. The best time to visit is on market day (Sun and Thurs, though Sun is better). The weavers of Tenejapa taught the weavers of San Andrés and Magdalena—which accounts for the similarity in their designs and colors. To get to Tenejapa, try to find a *colectivo* in the very last row by the market, or hire a taxi. On Tenejapa's main street, several stores sell locally woven regional clothing, and you can bargain for the price.

THE HUITEPEC CLOUD FOREST Pronatura, Av. Benito Juárez 11-B (✆ **967/678-5000**), a private, nonprofit, ecological organization, offers environmentally sensitive tours of the cloud forest. The forest is a haven for **migratory birds,** and more than 100 bird species and 600 plant species have been discovered here. Guided tours run from 9am to noon Tuesday to Sunday. They cost 250 pesos per group of up to eight people. Make reservations a day in advance. To reach the reserve on your own, take the Chamula road north; the turnoff is at Km 3.5. The reserve is open Tuesday to Sunday from 9am to 4pm.

Shopping

Many Indian villages near San Cristóbal are noted for **weaving, embroidery, brocade work, leather,** and **pottery,** making the area one of the best in the country for shopping. You'll see beautiful woolen shawls, indigo-dyed skirts, colorful native shirts, and magnificently woven *huipiles,* all of which often come in vivid geometric patterns. A good place to find textiles as well as other handicrafts, besides what's mentioned below, is in and around Santo Domingo and the market. The stalls and small shops in that neighborhood make for interesting shopping. Working in leather, the craftspeople are artisans of the highest caliber. Tie-dyed *jaspe* from Guatemala comes in bolts and is made into clothing. The town is also known for **amber,** sold in several shops; two of the best are mentioned below.

For the best selection of new and used books and reading material in English, go to **La Pared,** Andador Eclesiásticos 13 (✆ **967/678-6367**). The owners keep a large collection of books on the Maya, and Mexico in general, both fiction and nonfiction. Hours are Monday through Saturday 10am to 7:30pm.

CRAFTS

El Encuentro The owner has been in business for more than 50 years and has quite a list of local artisans who sell her merchandise. She specializes in textiles, but also sells other forms of handicrafts, such as work made with agave fibers, forged iron, carved wood, or shaped tin. The store is open Monday to Saturday from 9am to 8pm. Calle Real de Guadalupe 63-A (btw. Dugelay and Colón). ✆ **967/678-3698**.

La Galería This art gallery beneath a cafe shows the work of national and international painters. Also for sale are paintings and greeting cards by Kiki, the owner, a German artist who has found her niche in San Cristóbal. There are some Oaxacan rugs and pottery, plus unusual silver jewelry. It's open daily from 10am to 9pm. Hidalgo 3. ✆ **967/674-7273**.

Lágrimas de la Selva "Tears of the Jungle" deals in amber and jewelry, and few shops have the variety, quality, or artistic flair of this one. It's not a bargain hunter's turf, but a great place for the curious to go. Often you can watch the jewelers in action. Open Monday through Saturday from 10am to 8pm; Sunday from noon to 8pm. Hidalgo 1-C (half-block south of the main square). ✆ **967/674-6348**.

Piedra Escondida This is another excellent choice for out-of-the-ordinary amber and jewelry. Open daily from 8:30am to 8pm. 20 de Noviembre 22. No phone.

Tienda Chiapas This showroom has examples of every craft practiced in the state. It is run by the government in support of Indian crafts. You should take a look, if only to survey what crafts the region practices. It's open Monday to Friday from 9am to 9pm, Saturday 10am to 8pm, and Sunday 10am to 2pm. Niños Héroes at Hidalgo. ✆ **967/678-1180**.

A weaver in Tenejapa.

TEXTILES

El Telar "The Loom" sells textiles all handmade in San Cristóbal, and most are from the store's workshop, which you can visit in the northwest part of town, next to the hotel Rincón del Arco. It specializes in textiles made on large floor looms. Open Monday to Saturday from 9am to 2 pm and 4 to 8pm. Calle 28 de Agosto 3 (next door to Hotel Casa Mexicana). © **967/678-4422.** www.eltelar.com.mx.

Plaza de Santo Domingo The plazas around this church and the nearby Templo de Caridad fill with women in native garb selling their wares. Here you'll find women from Chamula weaving belts or embroidering, surrounded by piles of loomed woolen textiles from their village. Their inventory includes Guatemalan shawls, belts, and bags. There are also some excellent buys on Chiapanecan-made wool vests, jackets, rugs, and shawls, similar to those at Sna Jolobil (described below), if you take the time to look and bargain. Vendors arrive between 9 and 10am and begin to leave around 3pm. Av. Utrilla. No phone.

Sna Jolobil Meaning "weaver's house" in Mayan, this place is in the former convent (monastery) of Santo Domingo, next to the church of Santo Domingo. Groups of Tzotzil and Tzeltal craftspeople operate the cooperative store, which has about 3,000 members who contribute products, help run the store, and share in the moderate profits. You'll find some elegant huipiles and other weavings; prices are high, as is the quality. It's open Monday to Saturday from 9am to 2pm and 4 to 6pm; credit cards are accepted. Calzada Lázaro Cárdenas 42 (Plaza Santo Domingo, btw. Navarro and Nicaragua). © **967/678-2646.**

Unión Regional de Artesanías de los Altos Also known as J'pas Joloviletic, this cooperative of weavers is smaller than Sna Jolobil (described above) and not as sophisticated in its approach to potential shoppers. It sells blouses, textiles, pillow covers, vests, sashes, napkins, baskets, and purses. It's near the market and worth looking around. Open Monday to Saturday from 9am to 2pm and 4 to 7pm, Sunday from 9am to 1pm. Av. Utrilla 43. © **967/678-2848.**

Where to Stay

Among the most interesting places to stay in town is the seminary-turned-hotel-and-museum **Casa Na-Bolom** (p. 344).

Hotels in San Cristóbal are inexpensive. You can do tolerably well for $50 to $70 per night per double. Rates listed here include taxes. High season is Easter week, July, August, and December.

EXPENSIVE

Parador San Juan de Dios ★★ This is the handsomest property in San Cristóbal. It's located in the north end of town in some old buildings that belonged to a 17th-century farm. The rooms are large, plush, and distinctive, with something of the air of the old adobe and stone buildings. Most have fireplaces and period pieces mixed with a few modern comforts. Bathrooms are large and beautifully finished. In the suites they include Jacuzzi tubs. Most rooms also come with their own stone terraces (and in some cases two terraces), which afford views of the extensive grounds. The hotel is a long walk or short taxi ride from the main square.

Calzada Roberta 16, Col. 31 de Marzo, 29229 San Cristóbal de las Casas, Chi. ✆/fax **967/678-1167,** -4290**.** www.sanjuandios.com. 12 units. High season 1,800 pesos double, 3,300–4650 pesos suite; low season 1,600 pesos double, 2,200–4100 pesos suite. AE, MC, V. Free secure parking. **Amenities:** Restaurant; bar; room service; smoke-free rooms. *In room:* TV, hair dryer, Wi-Fi.

MODERATE

Casa Felipe Flores ★ This beautifully restored colonial house is the perfect setting for getting a feel for San Cristóbal. The patios and common rooms are relaxing and comfortable, and their architectural details are so very *coleto*. The guest rooms are nicely furnished and full of character and are heated in winter. The owners, Nancy and David Orr, enjoy sharing their appreciation and knowledge of Chiapas and the Maya.

Calle Dr. Felipe Flores 36, 29230 San Cristóbal de las Casas, Chi. ✆/fax **967/678-3996.** www.felipeflores.com. 5 units. $95–$125 double. Rates include full breakfast. 10% service charge. No credit cards. Limited street parking. **Amenities:** Library. *In room:* No phone.

Hotel Casa Mexicana ★ This colonial hotel with well-manicured courtyards offers attractive, comfortable lodging. The management is attentive and keeps the property looking sharp. Service is great. The standard rooms are carpeted and come with two double beds or one king-size. They have good lighting, electric heaters, and spacious bathrooms. Across the street in another colonial house are several suites that are much larger, have distinctive clay tile floors and larger bathrooms. The hotel handles many tour groups; it can be quiet and peaceful one day, full and bustling the next.

28 de Agosto 1 (at General Utrilla), 29200 San Cristóbal de las Casas, Chi. ✆ **967/678-1348,** -0698. Fax 967/678-2627. www.hotelcasamexicana.com. 55 units. High season $105 double, $160 junior suite, $180 suite; low season $85 double, $140 junior suite, $170 suite. AE, MC, V. Free secure parking 1½ blocks away. **Amenities:** Restaurant; bar; babysitting; room service; sauna, smoke-free rooms. *In room:* TV, hair dryer, Wi-Fi.

Hotel Casavieja Unlike Casa Mexicana, this old colonial house has retained some of the original creakiness, at least in the original section. Most of the rooms, however, are in the new section, where construction has been faithful to the original design in essentials such as wood-beam ceilings. Half the rooms have carpeted floors, and half have tile or laminate flooring. Rooms are medium size and not brightly lit. Some have smallish bathrooms.

María Adelina Flores 27 (btw. Cristóbal Colón and Diego Dugelay), 29200 San Cristóbal de las Casas, Chi. ✆/fax **967/678-6868,** -0385. www.casavieja.com.mx. 40 units. 780–1,100 pesos double; 1,100–1,350 junior suite. Internet specials often available. AE, MC, V. Free parking. **Amenities:** Restaurant; bar. *In room:* TV, Wi-Fi.

Casa de los Arcángeles The owner of a large courtyard restaurant decided to convert the rooms surrounding the courtyard into hotel rooms. This kind of afterthought is often a recipe for disaster, but it works in this case. The rooms, each with a queen-size bed, are large, comfortable, attractive, and well priced. The restaurant closes early so noise isn't a factor, and the location just south of the main square is excellent.

Cuauhtémoc 4, 29200 San Cristóbal de las Casas, Chi. ✆ **967/678-1531,** -1936. casadelosarcangeles@hotmail.com. 7 units. 950–1,100 pesos double. Rates include full breakfast. MC, V. Free parking. **Amenities:** Restaurant; bar; smoke-free rooms. *In room:* TV, hair dryer, Wi-Fi.

Mansión de los Angeles This colonial hotel is clean and attractive. Guest rooms are medium-size and come with either a single and a double bed or two double beds. They are more attractive, warmer, and better lit than most hotels in this town. They are also quiet. Some of the bathrooms are small. Most rooms have windows that open onto a pretty courtyard with a fountain. The rooftop sun deck is a great siesta spot.

Calle Francisco Madero 17, 29200 San Cristóbal de las Casas, Chi. ✆ **967/678-1173,** -4371. www.hotelmansiondelosangeles.com. 20 units. 600–800 pesos double. MC, V. Limited street parking. *In room:* TV.

INEXPENSIVE

Hotel Don Quijote Rooms in this three-story hotel (no elevator) are small but quiet, carpeted, and well lit, but a little worn. All have two double beds with reading lamps over them, tiled bathrooms, and plenty of hot water. There's complimentary coffee in the mornings.

Cristóbal Colón 7 (near Real de Guadalupe), 29200 San Cristóbal de las Casas, Chi. ✆ **967/678-0920.** Fax 967/678-0346. 25 units. 250–350 pesos double. MC, V. Free parking 1 block away. *In room:* TV.

Hotel Palacio de Moctezuma The rooms in this three-story hotel have windows facing one of the two courtyards. They are quiet, minimally furnished, carpeted, and poorly lit. Most are medium size and come with two double beds, but a few are large. On the third floor is a solarium with comfortable tables and chairs and a view of the city.

Juárez 16 (at León), 29200 San Cristóbal de las Casas, Chi. ✆ **967/678-0352,** -1142. Fax 967/678-1536. 48 units. 300–500 pesos double. MC, V. Free limited parking. **Amenities:** Restaurant; smoke-free rooms. *In room:* TV, hair dryer, Wi-Fi.

Hotel Posada La Media Luna A modern two-story hotel in the downtown area with medium-size, attractive rooms for a good price. The bathrooms are larger than the norm, and the staff is helpful and friendly, and some speak English.

Hermanos Domínguez 5, 29200 San Cristóbal de las Casas, Chi. ✆ **967/631-5590.** www.hotellamedialuna.com. 11 units. 350 pesos double. MC, V. **Amenities:** Restaurant. *In room:* TV, no phone, Wi-Fi.

Where to Dine

San Cristóbal is not known for its cuisine, but you can still eat well. For baked goods, try the **Panadería La Hojaldra,** Insurgentes 14 (✆ **967/678-4286**). It's a traditional Mexican bakery that's open daily from 8am to 9:30pm. (It will move one block south sometime in late 2010/early 2011.) In addition to the restaurants listed below, consider making reservations for dinner at **Casa Na-Bolom** (p. 344).

MODERATE

El Edén ★ INTERNATIONAL This is a small, quiet restaurant inside the Hotel El Paraíso where the food and service are consistently good, better than in most restaurants in San Cristóbal. The steaks are tender, and the margaritas are especially dangerous (one is all it takes). Specialties include Swiss cheese fondue for two, Edén salad, and brochettes.

In the Hotel El Paraíso, Av. 5 de Febrero 19. ✆ **967/678-5382.** Breakfast 35–55 pesos; main courses 60–150 pesos. AE, MC, V. Daily 8am–10:30pm.

La Paloma ★ INTERNATIONAL/MEXICAN La Paloma I particularly like in the evening because the lighting is so well done. For starters, I enjoyed the quesadillas Mexico City style (small fried packets of *masa* stuffed with a variety of fillings). Don't make my mistake of trying to share them with your dinner companion—it will only lead to trouble. Mexican classics include *albóndigas en chipotle* (meatballs in a thick chipotle sauce), Oaxacan black *mole,* and a variety of *chiles rellenos.* Avoid the *profiteroles.* Live music nightly 9 to 10:30pm.

Hidalgo 3. ✆ **967/678-1547.** Main courses 100–140 pesos. MC, V. Daily 9am–midnight.

Pierre FRENCH Who would have thought that you could get good French food in San Cristóbal? And yet Frenchman Pierre Niviere offers an appealing selection of traditional French dishes, simplified and tweaked for the tropical surroundings. I showed up on a Sunday, enjoyed the fixed menu, and left well satisfied.

Real de Guadalupe 73. ✆ **967/678-7211.** Main courses 150–200 pesos; Sun fixed menu 130 pesos. No credit cards. Fri–Wed 1:30–10pm.

INEXPENSIVE

Emiliano's Moustache 🎁 MEXICAN/TACOS Like any right-thinking traveler, I initially avoided this place on account of its unpromising name and some cartoonlike figures by the door. But a conversation with some local folk overcame my prejudice and tickled my sense of irony. Sure enough, the place was crowded with *coletos* enjoying the restaurant's popular *comida corrida.* You can choose from a menu of taco plates (a mixture of fillings cooked together and served with tortillas and a variety of hot sauces). Live music Thursday through Saturday.

Crescencio Rosas 7. ✆ **967/678-7246.** Main courses 70–90 pesos; taco plates 40–50 pesos; *comida corrida* 48 pesos. No credit cards. Daily 8am–midnight.

La Casa del Pan Papalotl VEGETARIAN This place is best known for its vegetarian lunch buffet with salad bar. The vegetables and most of the grains are organic. Kippy, the owner, has a home garden and a field near town where she grows vegetables. She buys locally grown, organic red wheat for her breads. These are all sourdough breads, which she likes because she feels they are easily digested and have good texture and taste. The pizzas are a popular item. The restaurant shares space with other activities in the cultural center El Puente, which has gallery space, a language school, and cinema.

Real de Guadalupe 55 (btw. Diego Dugelay and Cristóbal Colón). ✆ **967/678-7215.** Main courses 50–70 pesos; pizzas 50–140 pesos; lunch buffet 60–70 pesos. No credit cards. Mon–Sat 9am–10pm, lunch buffet 2–5pm.

Namandí INTERNATIONAL/REGIONAL If you're looking for a light meal or snack this place would be the perfect choice. Excellent quality fair-trade coffee and delicious Mexican items such as enchiladas or tostadas. The crepes are excellent, but on my last visit I really enjoyed the local tamales, which were delicious and different. The restaurant space is modern, light, and airy.

Mazarriegos 16. ✆ **967/678-8054.** Crepes, salads, and sandwiches 40–75 pesos; breakfasts 35–50 pesos. MC, V. Mon–Sat 8am–11:30pm; Sun 8:30am–11pm.

Normita's MEXICAN Normita's is famous for its *pozole,* a chicken and hominy soup to which you add extra ingredients at the table. It also offers cheap, short-order Mexican mainstays. This is a "people's" restaurant; the open kitchen takes up one corner of the room, the rest of which is filled with simple tables and chairs.

Av. Juárez 6 (at Dr. José Flores). No phone. Breakfast 30–40 pesos; *pozole* 35 pesos; tacos 30 pesos. No credit cards. Daily 7am–11pm.

Restaurant Tuluc MEXICAN/INTERNATIONAL The owner hails from Puebla, but learned the restaurant business in Germany and Belgium. On my visits I often see him attending to his customers. The house specialty is *filete Tuluc,* a beef filet wrapped around spinach and cheese served with fried potatoes and green beans; while not the best cut of meat, it's certainly priced right. The *tampiqueña* steak, served with a plethora of sides is certainly good and filling. The Chiapaneco breakfast is a filling quartet of juice, toast, two Chiapanecan tamales, and coffee. Lighter favorites include the sandwiches and enchiladas.

Av. Insurgentes 5 (btw. Cuauhtémoc and Francisco León). ✆ **967/678-2090.** Breakfast 35–50 pesos; main courses 68–85 pesos; *comida corrida* (served 2–5pm) 65 pesos. No credit cards. Daily 7am–10pm.

COFFEEHOUSES

Because Chiapas-grown coffee is highly regarded, it's not surprising that coffeehouses proliferate here. Most are concealed in the nooks and crannies of San Cristóbal's side streets. Try **Café La Selva,** Crescencio Rosas 9 (✆ **967/678-7244**), for coffee served in all its varieties and brewed from organic beans; it is open daily from 9am to 11pm. A more traditional-style cafe, where locals meet to talk over the day's news, is **Café San Cristóbal,** Cuauhtémoc 1 (✆ **967/678-3861**), between Hidalgo and Insurgentes. It's open daily 7:30am to 10pm, Sunday from 9am to 9pm.

San Cristóbal After Dark

San Cristóbal is blessed with a variety of nightlife, both resident and migratory. There is a lot of live music, surprisingly good and varied. The bars and restaurants are cheap. And they are easy to get to: You can hit all the places mentioned here without setting foot in a cab. Weekends are best, but on any night you'll find something going on.

Almost all the clubs in San Cristóbal host Latin music of one genre or another. **El Cocodrilo** (✆ **967/678-1140**), on the main plaza in the Hotel Santa Clara, has acoustic performers playing Latin folk music *(trova, andina)* from 9 to 11pm daily. Relax at a table in what usually is a not-too-crowded environment. After that, your choices vary. One of the two most popular bars is **Café Bar Revolución** (© **967/678-6664**), on the pedestrian-only 20 de Noviembre at 1 de Marzo. It has two live acts every night—usually blues, reggae, latin, or rock, and always rock on Saturday nights. Usually it winds down around midnight. For Latin dance music, there's a club on the corner of Madero and Juárez, called **Latino's** (© **967/678-9972**)—good bands playing a mix of salsa, merengue, and cumbia. On weekends it gets crowded, but it has a good-size dance floor. There's a small cover on weekends. The place is dark and has a bit of an urban edge to it. For a relaxing place to have a drink, try the bar at the **Hotel Posada Real de Chiapas.** It's across the street from Latino's. There's a piano player on Saturdays, and soft recorded music the rest of the week.

Road Trips from San Cristóbal

For excursions to nearby villages, see "The Nearby Maya Villages & Countryside," earlier in this chapter; for destinations farther away, there are several local travel agencies. But first you should try **Alex and Raúl** (p. 347). You can also try **ATC Travel and Tours,** Calle 5 de Febrero 15, at the corner of 16 de Septiembre (© **967/678-2550;** fax 967/678-3145), across from El Fogón restaurant. The agency has bilingual guides and reliable vehicles. ATC regional tours focus on birds and orchids, textiles, hiking, and camping.

Strangely, the cost of the trips includes a driver but not necessarily a bilingual guide or guided information of any kind. You pay extra for those services, so when checking prices, be sure to flesh out the details.

PALENQUE, BONAMPAK & YAXCHILÁN

For information on these destinations, see the section on Palenque, earlier in this chapter.

CHINCULTIC RUINS, COMITÁN & MONTEBELLO NATIONAL PARK

Almost 160km (99 miles) southeast of San Cristóbal, near the border with Guatemala, is the **Chincultic** archaeological site and **Montebello National Park,** with 16 multicolored lakes and exuberant pine-forest vegetation. Seventy-

The view from the acropolis of the Chincultic ruins.

The Montebello lakes.

four kilometers (46 miles) from San Cristóbal is **Comitán,** a pretty hillside town of 40,000 inhabitants known for its flower cultivation and a sugar cane–based liquor called *comiteco.* It's also the last big town along the Pan-American Highway before the Guatemalan border.

The Chincultic ruins, a late Classic site, have barely been excavated, but the main **acropolis,** high up against a cliff, is magnificent to see from below and is worth the walk up for the view. After passing through the gate, you'll see the trail ahead; it passes ruins on both sides. More unexcavated tree-covered ruins flank steep stairs leading up the mountain to the acropolis. From there, you can gaze upon distant Montebello lakes and miles of cornfields and forest. The paved road to the lakes passes six lakes, all different colors and sizes, ringed by cool pine forests; most have parking lots and lookouts. The paved road ends at a small restaurant. The lakes are best seen on a sunny day, when their famous brilliant colors are optimal.

Most travel agencies in San Cristóbal offer a daylong trip that includes the lakes, the ruins, lunch in Comitán, and a stop in the pottery-making village of Amatenango del Valle. If you're driving, follow Hwy. 190 south from San Cristóbal through the pretty village of Teopisca and then through Comitán; turn left at La Trinitaria, where there's a sign to the lakes. After the Trinitaria turnoff and before you reach the lakes, there's a sign pointing left down a narrow dirt road to the Chincultic ruins.

TUXTLA GUTIÉRREZ

82km (51 miles) W of San Cristóbal; 277km (172 miles) S of Villahermosa; 242km (150 miles) NW of Ciudad Cuauhtémoc on the Guatemalan border

Tuxtla Gutiérrez (altitude 557m/1,827 ft.) is the commercial center of Chiapas. Coffee is the basis of the region's economy, along with recent oil discoveries. Tuxtla (pop. 350,000) is a business town, and not a particularly attractive one. Most travelers simply pass through Tuxtla on their way to San Cristóbal, the Sumidero Canyon, or Oaxaca.

Essentials

GETTING THERE & DEPARTING

BY PLANE Tuxtla's airport (airport code: TGZ) is 45 minutes south of the city. There is taxi service at the airport. With the demise of **Aviacsa,** air traffic has declined. **Mexicana** (✆ **01-800/801-2030** in Mexico; www.mexicana.com) and its subsidiary, **Click** (✆ **01-800/122-5425** in Mexico; www.mexicana.com), have nonstop flights to and from Mexico City, Oaxaca, and

Mérida. **Continental Airlines** (www.continental.com) recently announced that it will start nonstop service between Tuxtla and Houston, Texas, Tuxtla twice a week, starting in June 2010.

BY CAR From Oaxaca, you'll enter Tuxtla by Hwy. 190. From Villahermosa, or Palenque and San Cristóbal, you'll enter at the opposite end of town on the same highway from the east. In both cases, you'll arrive at the large main square at the center of town, La Plaza Cívica (see "City Layout," below).

From Tuxtla to Villahermosa, take Hwy. 190 east past the town of Chiapa de Corzo; soon you'll see a sign for Hwy. 195 north to Villahermosa. To San Cristóbal and Palenque, take Hwy. 190 east. The road is beautiful but tortuous. It's in good repair to San Cristóbal, but there may be bad spots between San Cristóbal and Palenque. The trip from Tuxtla to Villahermosa takes 8 hours by car; the scenery is beautiful.

BY BUS The **ADO bus station** (✆ **961/612-2624**) is a mile northwest of the city center on Avenida 5 Norte Poniente, at the Plaza del Sol. There are eight buses a day to Villahermosa, three or four buses a day to Oaxaca, and five to Palenque. There's usually no need to buy a ticket ahead of time, except during holidays. Small buses (microbuses) to San Cristóbal leave every 5 to 15 minutes from the station at the intersection of Av. 4 Sur and Calle 15 Oriente.

ORIENTATION

ARRIVING There is taxi service from the airport to town (220 pesos) and taxi service at the bus station.

VISITOR INFORMATION Information desks are on the main square and on Avenida Central across from Parque de la Marimba. They are open daily from 9am to 2pm and from 4 to 8pm. Some staff speak English and can provide good maps.

CITY LAYOUT Tuxtla is laid out on a grid. The main street, **Avenida Central,** is the east–west axis and is the artery through town for Hwy. 190. West of the central district, it's called **Bulevar Belisario Domínguez,** and in the east, it's **Bulevar Angel Albino Corzo. Calle Central** is the north–south axis. The rest of the streets have names that include one number and two directions. This tells you how to get to the street. For example, to find the street 5 Norte Poniente (5 North West), you walk 5 blocks north from the center of town and turn west. To find 3 Oriente Sur, you walk 3 blocks east from the main square and turn south. When people indicate intersections, they can shorten the names because it's redundant.

GETTING AROUND Taking taxis is the easiest way to get around in this city. They are plentiful and easy to come by. **Buses** to all parts of the city converge upon the Plaza Cívica along Calle Central.

FAST FACTS The telephone **area code** is **961.** If you need medical help, the best **clinic** in town is Sanatorio Rojas, Calle 2 Sur Poniente 1847 (✆ **961/611-2079** or 612-5414).

Exploring Tuxtla

Miguel Alvarez del Toro Zoo (ZOOMAT) Located in the forest called El Zapotal, ZOOMAT is one of the best zoos in Mexico. The collection of animals and birds indigenous to this area gives the visitor a tangible sense of what the wilds of Chiapas are like. The zoo keeps jaguars, howler monkeys, owls, and many more

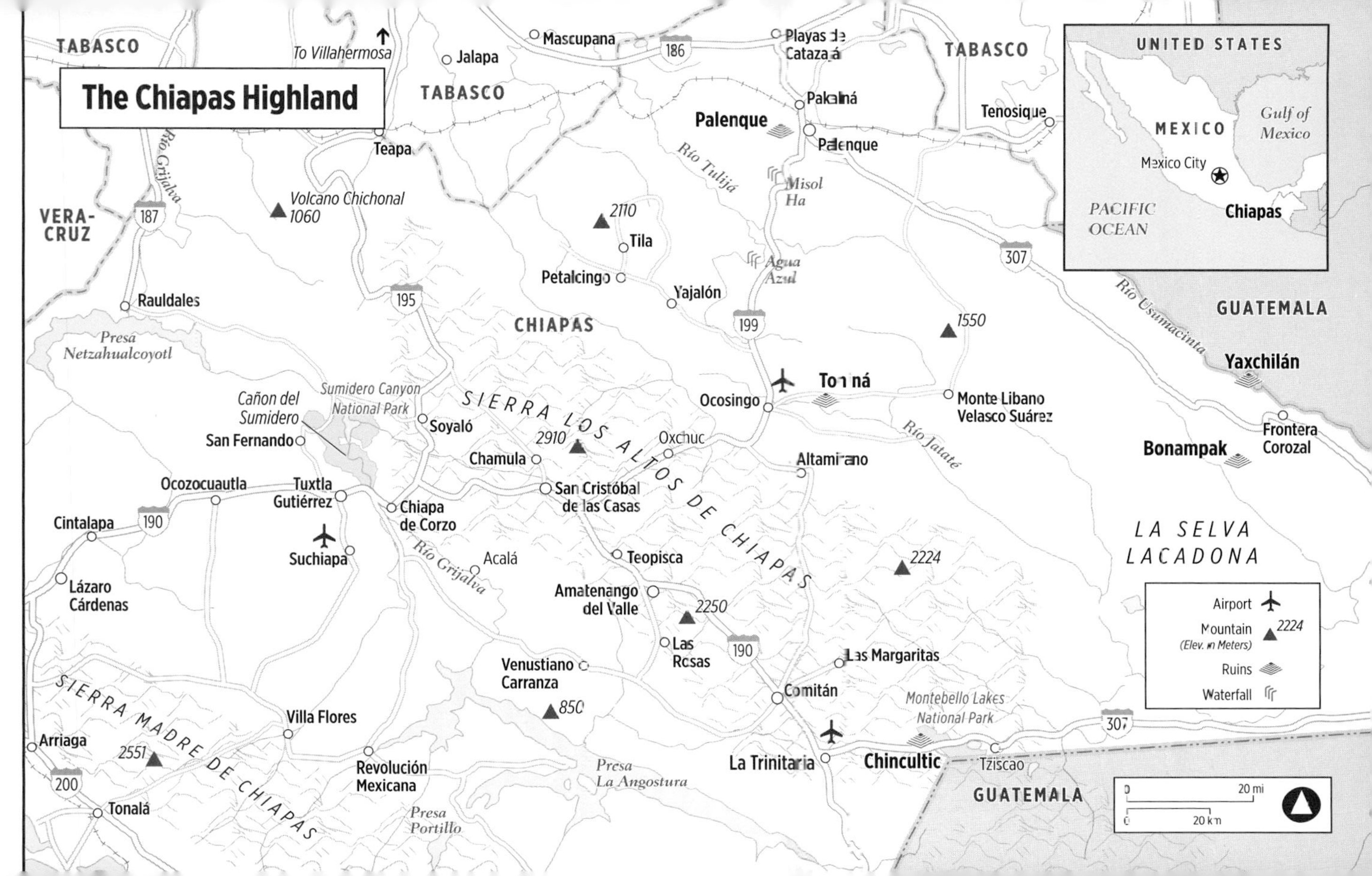

The Chiapas Highland
To Villahermosa
TABASCO
VERA-CRUZ
CHIAPAS
GUATEMALA
UNITED STATES
MEXICO
Mexico City
Chiapas
Gulf of Mexico
PACIFIC OCEAN
LA SELVA LACADONA
SIERRA LOS ALTOS DE CHIAPAS
SIERRA MADRE DE CHIAPAS
Airport
Mountain (Elev. in Meters)
Ruins
Waterfall
2224
20 mi
20 km
0
Río Grijalva
Río Usumacinta
Río Tulijá
Río Jatatė
Presa Netzahualcoyotl
Presa La Angostura
Presa Portillo
Sumidero Canyon National Park
Cañon del Sumidero
Montebello Lakes National Park
Volcano Chichonal 1060
Misol Ha
Agua Azul
Palenque
Yaxchilán
Bonampak
Toniná
Chincultic
Teapa
Jalapa
Mascupana
Playas de Catazajá
Pakalná
Tenosique
Frontera Corozal
Monte Libano Velasco Suárez
Tila
Petalcingo
Yajalón
Ocosingo
Oxchuc
Altamirano
Las Margaritas
Comitán
La Trinitaria
Tziscao
Soyaló
Chamula
San Cristóbal de las Casas
Teopisca
Amatenango del Valle
Las Rosas
Acalá
Chiapa de Corzo
Tuxtla Gutiérrez
Suchiapa
San Fernando
Ocozocuautla
Cintalapa
Lázaro Cárdenas
Rauldales
Venustiano Carranza
Revolución Mexicana
Villa Flores
Arriaga
Tonalá
186
187
190
195
199
200
307
1550
2110
2910
2250
850
2551

exotic animals in roomy cages that replicate their home terrain; the whole zoo is so deeply buried in vegetation that you can almost pretend you're in a natural habitat. Unlike at other zoos I've visited, the animals are almost always on view.

Bulevar Samuel León Brinois, southeast of downtown. No phone. 20 pesos general admission. Tues–Sun 9am–5:30pm. The zoo is about 8km (5 miles) southeast of downtown; catch a bus along Av. Central and at the Calzada.

Shopping

The government-operated **Instituto Marca Chiapas,** Bl. Domínguez 2035 (✆ **961/602-9800**), endeavors to support artisans and promote the crafts from all parts of the state. The store is subsidized, making the prices here quite reasonable. The two stories of rooms feature an extensive collection of crafts grouped by region and type from throughout the state of Chiapas. It's open Monday to Saturday from 9am to 8pm and Sunday from 10am to 2pm.

Where to Stay

As Tuxtla booms, the center of the hotel industry has moved out of town, west to Hwy. 190. You'll notice the new motel-style hotels, such as the **Hotel Flamboyán, Palace Inn, Hotel Laganja,** and **La Hacienda.**

Camino Real Tuxtla Gutiérrez ★★ Bold modern architecture is the hallmark of the Camino Real chain, and this one is no exception, with stark lines and bright colors. This one makes subtle references to the Maya culture and the local region. The center of the hotel is open air and filled with a spot of jungle, a small cascade, and tropical birds flying freely about. This is a relaxing hotel; walking to and from your room, you hear bird song and the falling of water. Guest rooms have two doubles or a king, are carpeted and comfortably furnished. Bathrooms are large.

Bulevar Domínguez 1159, 29060 Tuxtla Gutiérrez, Chi. ✆ **800/7CAMINO** in the U.S. or Canada, or 961/617-7777. Fax 961/617-7779. 210 units. 2,200 pesos double; 2,600 pesos and up suite. Internet promotions often available. AE, MC, V. Free secured parking. **Amenities:** 2 restaurants; bar; babysitting; concierge; executive floor; health club and spa; pool; room service, smoke-free rooms. *In room:* A/C, TV hair dryer, minibar, Wi-Fi.

Hotel María Eugenia This is a centrally located, well-managed property with plain, medium-size rooms. The white walls and white ceramic tile make them seem even plainer, but clean and uncluttered. Beds have comfortable mattresses and come either as two doubles or one king. There is good space for luggage.

Av. Central Oriente 507, 29000 Tuxtla Gutiérrez, Chi. ✆ **961/613-3767** or 01-800/716-0149 in Mexico. 83 units. 800 pesos double. AE, MC, V. Free guarded parking. **Amenities:** Restaurant; bar; pool; room service; smoke-free rooms. *In room:* A/C, TV, Wi-Fi.

Hotel Regional San Marcos For a discount hotel, this was the best I could find in central Tuxtla. It's in the downtown zone and close to the *colectivos* that go to Chiapa de Corzo. Rooms are distributed on four floors (no elevator). They are medium in size but not too depressing. The air-conditioning window units can be a bit noisy.

1 Sur Oriente 176 (at Av. 4 Oriente), 29000 Tuxtla Gutiérrez, Chi. ✆ **961/613-1940,** -1887. hotelsanmarcos@prodigy.net.mx. 40 units. 409 pesos double. MC, V. *In room:* A/C, TV, Wi-Fi.

Where to Dine

For a full sit-down meal, you can try local Chiapan food at **Las Pichanchas,** Av. Central Oriente 837 (✆ **961/612-5351**). It's festively decorated and pretty to look at. The emphasis is on meat, with several heavy dishes on the menu. I would recommend the *filete simojovel* (a thin steak in a not-spicy chile sauce) or the *comida grande,* which is beef in a pumpkin-seed sauce. Eating here is a cultural experience, but I usually prefer to head over to the **Flamingo,** 1 Poniente Sur 168, just off Avenida Central (✆ **961/612-0922**), which serves standard Mexican dishes: enchiladas, *mole,* roast chicken. The restaurant is owned by a Spaniard, who also owns an elegant steakhouse called El Asador Castellano, which is on the west side of town. Take a taxi.

If all you want is tacos, there are several good places around the **El Parque de la Marimba.** This plaza has free *marimba* music nightly and is enjoyable. There you'll find a couple of local taco restaurants bordering the plaza, such as **Parrilla Suiza** and **El Fogón Norteño.** Both have good grilled tacos. The Parque de la Marimba is on Avenida Central Poniente, 8 blocks west of the main square.

Chiapa de Corzo & the Sumidero Canyon

The real reason to stay in Tuxtla is to take a boat trip through the **Canyon of El Sumidero** ★★. The canyon is spectacular, and the boat ride is fun. Boats leave from the docks in **Chiapa de Corzo,** a colonial town of about 50,000 inhabitants that bumps up to Tuxtla. To get there, take a taxi or hop on the bus operated by Transportes Chiapa-Tuxtla (Av. 1 Sur btw. calles 5 and 6 Oriente). Buses leave every couple of minutes and cost 9 pesos. The ride takes a half-hour. Ask to get off at the main square (*parada del parque*). The two main boat cooperatives have ticket booths under the archways bordering the square. But you don't have to look for these; just go straight to the boats at the pier (*embarcadero*) 1½ blocks below the square.

Marimba musicians perform nightly in El Parque de la Marimba.

As you pass the church of Santo Domingo, you'll see a large **ceiba** tree shading the churchyard. In better circumstances these trees get even larger than this, but this one has taken up an interesting position in front of the church. The Maya felt that these trees embodied the connection between the heavens, the world of men, and the underworld because they extend into all three realms.

The Canyon of El Sumidero.

The **two cooperatives** (the reds and the greens identified by the color of their boats) offer the same service. They work together sharing passengers and such. Boats leave as soon as a minimum of 12 people show up. The interval can be up to an hour or as short as 10 minutes, depending on the season. The cost is 150 pesos. The ride takes 2 hours. This river is the Grijalva, which flows to the Gulf of Mexico from Guatemala and is one of Mexico's largest. Besides the canyon vistas, you're likely to see some crocodiles and other things of interest. The boat's pilot will explain a few things in Spanish, but much of what he says adds little to the tour. At the deepest point in the canyon, our pilot said the walls stretch up vertically 1,000m (3,280 ft.) above the water, which, in turn, is about 100m (328 ft.) deep at that point. I wasn't about to double-check this statement—all I know is that the view was really something. There are some interesting things happening on the walls; water seeps out in places, creating little micro-environments of moss, grass, and mineral deposits. One of these places is called the Christmas Tree, for its form. Our boat glided slowly by as a fine mist fell on us from the plants.

The boats operate from 8am to 4pm. They are fast, and the water is smooth. The best times to see the canyon are early or late in the day, when the sun is at an angle and shines on one or the other of the canyon walls. The boats are necessarily open, so you should take an adjustable cap or a hat with a draw string or some sunscreen. A pair of earplugs would come in handy, too.

If you'd rather stay in Chiapa de Corzo than Tuxtla, check out the simple but nice hotel off the main square: **Hotel Los Angeles,** at Av. Julián Grajales 2 (**✆ 916/616-0048**). It offers rooms with or without air-conditioning for 400 to 500 pesos per night.

FAST FACTS

[FastFACTS] YUCATÁN, TABASCO & CHIAPAS

10

Business Hours Most businesses in larger cities are open between 9am and 7pm; in smaller towns many close between 2 and 4pm. Most close on Sunday. In resort areas stores commonly open in the mornings on Sunday, and shops stay open late, until 8 or even 10pm. Bank hours are Monday through Friday from 9 or 9:30am to anywhere between 3 and 7pm. Banks open on Saturday for at least a half-day.

Drinking Laws The legal drinking age in Mexico is 18; however, asking for ID or denying purchase is extremely rare. Grocery stores sell everything from beer and wine to national and imported liquors. You can buy liquor 24 hours a day, but during major elections, dry laws often are enacted by as much as 72 hours in advance of the election—and they apply to tourists as well as local residents. Mexico does not have laws that apply to transporting liquor in cars, but authorities are beginning to target drunk drivers more aggressively. It's a good idea to drive defensively.

It's illegal to drink in the street; but many tourists do. If you are getting drunk, you shouldn't drink in the street, because you are more likely to get stopped by the police.

Electricity The electrical system in Mexico is 110 volts AC (60 cycles), as in the United States and Canada. In reality, however, it may cycle more slowly and overheat your appliances. To compensate, select a medium or low speed on hair dryers. Many older hotels still have electrical outlets for flat two-prong plugs; you'll need an adapter for any plug with an enlarged end on one prong or with three prongs. Adapters are available in most Mexican electronics stores. Many better hotels have three-hole outlets (*trifásicos* in Spanish). Those that don't may loan adapters, but to be sure, it's always better to carry your own.

Embassies & Consulates They provide valuable lists of doctors and lawyers, as well as regulations concerning marriages in Mexico. Contrary to popular belief, your embassy cannot get you out of jail, provide postal or banking services, or fly you home when you run out of money. Consular officers can provide advice on most matters and problems, however. Most countries have an embassy in Mexico City, and many have consular offices or representatives in the provinces.

The Embassy of **Australia** in Mexico City is at Rubén Darío 55, Col. Polanco (✆ **55/1101-2200;** www.mexico.embassy.gov.au). It's open Monday through Thursday from 9:30am to noon.

The Embassy of **Canada** in Mexico City is at Schiller 529, in Polanco (✆ **55/5724-7900** or for emergencies 01-800/706-2900); it's open Monday through Friday from 9am to 1pm and 2 to 5pm. Visit www.dfait-maeci.gc.ca or www.canada.org.mx for addresses of consular agencies in Mexico. Canadian consulates are in Acapulco (✆ 744/484-1305), Cancún (✆ 998/883-3360), Guadalajara (✆ 333/671-4740), Mazatlán (✆ 669/913-7320), Monterrey (✆ 818/344-2753, -3200), Oaxaca (✆ 951/513-3777), Playa del Carmen (✆ 984/803-2411), Puerto Vallarta (✆ 322/293-0098), San José del Cabo (✆ 624/142-4333), and Tijuana (✆ 664/ 684-0461).

The Embassy of **Ireland** in Mexico City is at Cda. Bl. Manuel Avila Camacho 76, 3rd floor, Col. Lomas de Chapultepec (✆ **55/5520-5803**). See http://www.irishembassy.com.mx. It's open Monday through Thursday from 8:30am to 5pm, and Friday from 8:30am to 1:30pm.

The Embassy of **New Zealand** in Mexico City is at Jaime Balmes 8, 4th Floor, Col. Los Morales, Polanco (✆ **55/5283-9460;** www.nzembassy.com/home.cfm?c=50). It's open Monday through Thursday from 8:30am to 2pm and 3 to 5:30pm, and Friday from 8:30am to 2pm.

The Embassy of the **United Kingdom** in Mexico City is at Río Lerma 71, Col. Cuauhtémoc (✆ **55/5207-2089** or 5242-8500; http://ukinmexico.fco.gov.uk/en). It's open Monday through Thursday from 8am to 4pm and Friday from 8am to 1:30pm.

The Embassy of the **United States** in Mexico City is at Paseo de la Reforma 305, next to the Hotel María Isabel Sheraton at the corner of Río Danubio (✆ **55/5080-2000**); hours are Monday through Friday from 8:30am to 5:30pm. Visit **http://www.usembassy-mexico.gov** for information related to U.S. Embassy services. U.S. consulates are at Paseo de la Victoria #3650, Ciudad Juárez (✆ 656/227-3000); Progreso 175, Col. Americana, Guadalajara (✆ 333/268-2100); Av. Constitución 411 Poniente, Monterrey (✆ 818/345-2120); Av. Tapachula 96, Col. Hipodromo, Tijuana (✆ 664/622-7400); Calle Monterrey 141 Poiniente, Col. Esqueda, Hermosillo (✆ 662/289-3500); Av. Primera 200 y Azaleas, Matamoros (✆ 868/812-4402); Calle 60 No. 338 K x 29 y 31, Col. Acala Martin, Mérida (✆ 999/942-5700); Calle San Jose, Fraccionamiento "Los Alamos" Nogales (✆ 631/311-8150); and Allende 3330, Col. Jardin, Nuevo Laredo (✆ 867/714-0512). In addition, there are consular agencies in Acapulco (✆ 744/469-0556 or 484-0300), Cabo San Lucas (✆ 624/143-3566), Cancún (✆ 998/883-0272), Cozumel (✆ 987/872-4574), Ixtapa/Zihuatanejo (✆ 755/553-2100), Mazatlán (✆ 669/916-5889), Oaxaca (✆ 951/516-2853 or 514-3054), Playa del Carmen (✆ 984/873-0303), Puerto Vallarta (✆ 322/222-0069), Reynosa ✆ 882/823-9331), San Luis Potosí (✆ 444/811-7802, -7803), and San Miguel de Allende (✆ 415/152-2357).

Emergencies In case of emergency, dial ✆ **060** from any phone within Mexico. Dial ✆ **065** for the Red Cross. For police emergency numbers, turn to the "Fast Facts" sections in each of the individual chapters. The 24-hour **Tourist Help Line** in Mexico City is ✆ **01-800/987-8224** in Mexico or 55/5089-7500, or you can now simply dial ✆ **078.** The operators don't always speak English, but they are always willing to help.

Insurance For information on traveler's insurance, trip cancelation insurance, and medical insurance while traveling visit www.frommers.com/planning.

Language Spanish is the official language in Mexico. English is spoken and understood to some degree in most tourist areas. Mexicans are very accommodating with foreigners who try to speak Spanish, even in broken sentences. See chapter 11 for a glossary of simple phrases for expressing basic needs.

Mail Postage for a postcard or letter varies depending on its destination; it may take a few weeks to arrive. The price for registered letters and packages depends on the weight. The recommended way to send a package or important mail is through FedEx, DHL, UPS, or another reputable international mail service.

Passports See www.frommers.com/planning for information on how to obtain a passport.

Police Several cities, including Cancún, have a special corps of English-speaking Tourist Police to assist with directions, guidance, and more. In case of emergency, dial ✆ **060** from any phone within Mexico. For police emergency numbers, turn to "Fast Facts" in the individual chapters.

Smoking See p. 73 in chapter 3.

Taxes The 15% IVA (value-added) tax applies on goods and services in most of Mexico, and it's supposed to be included in the posted price. This tax is 10% in Cancún, Cozumel, and Los Cabos. There is a 5% tax on food and drinks consumed in restaurants that sell alcoholic beverages with an alcohol content of more than 10%; this tax applies whether you drink alcohol or not. Tequila is subject to a 25% tax. Mexico imposes an exit tax on every foreigner leaving the country by plane.

Telephones See p. 83 in chapter 3.

Time Central Time prevails throughout the Yucatán, Tabasco, and Chiapas. All of Mexico observes **daylight saving time.**

Tipping Most service employees in Mexico count on tips for the majority of their income, and this is especially true for bellboys and waiters. Bellboys should receive the equivalent of 5 to 15 pesos per bag; waiters generally receive 10% to 15%, depending on the level of service. It is not customary to tip taxi drivers, unless they are hired by the hour or provide touring or other special services.

Toilets Public toilets are not common in Mexico, but an increasing number are available, especially at fast-food restaurants and Pemex gas stations. These facilities and restaurant and club restrooms commonly have attendants, who expect a small tip (about 5 pesos).

Visas See p. 61 in chapter 3.

Visitor Information The **Mexico Tourism Board** (✆ **866/640-0597** in the U.S.; or 01-800/006-8839 or ✆ **078** from within Mexico; www.visitmexico.com) is an excellent source for general information; you can request brochures and get answers to the most common questions from the exceptionally well-trained, knowledgeable staff.

The **Mexican Government Tourist Board's** main office is in Mexico City (✆ **55/5278-4200**). Satellite offices are in the U.S., Canada, and the UK. In **Canada:** Toronto (✆ **416/925-0704**). In the **United Kingdom:** London (✆ **020/7488-9392**). In the **United States:** Chicago (✆ **312/228-0517**), Houston (✆ **713/772-2581**), Los Angeles (✆ **213/739-6336**), Miami (✆ **786/621-2909**), and New York (✆ **212/308-2110**).

The **Chiapas Tourism Board** is at Blvd. Belisario Dominguez 950, CP29060 Tuxtla Gutiérrez, Chiapas (✆ **961/613-9396**). The **Quintana Roo Tourist Board** is at Carr. a. Calderitas 622, CP77010 Chetumal, Quintana Roo, (✆ **983/835-0860**). The **Tabasco Tourism Board** is at Av. Los Rios s/n, Tabasco 2000, CP86035 Villahermosa, Tabasco (✆ **993/316-5134**). The **Yucatán Tourism Board** is at Calle 59 No. 514, Centro, CP97000 Mérida, Yucatán (✆ **999/924-9389**).

The **Mexican Embassy** in **Canada** is at 055 Rue Peel, Ste. 1000, Montreal, QUE, H3A 1V4 (✆ **514/288-2502**); Commerce Court West, 199 Bay St., Suite 4440, Toronto, ON, M5L 1E9 (✆ **416/684-3522**); 411-117 W. Hastings Street, 4th Floor, Vancouver, BC, V6E2K3 (✆ **604/684-1859**); and 1500-45 O'Connor St., Ottawa, ON, K1P 1A4 (✆ **613/233-8988;** fax 613/235-9123).

The Mexican Embassy (Consular Section) in the **United Kingdom** is at 16 Georges Dr., London, W1S1FD (✆ **020/7235-6393**).

The **Mexican Embassy** in the **United States** is at 1911 Pennsylvania Ave. NW, Washington, DC 20006 (✆ **202/728-1600**).

Water Tap water in Mexico is generally not potable and it is safest to drink purified bottled water. Some hotels and restaurants purify their water, but you should ask rather than assume this is the case. Ice may also come from tap water and should be used with caution.

AIRLINE WEBSITES

MAJOR AIRLINES

Aeroméxico
www.aeromexico.com

Alaska Airlines/Horizon Air
www.alaskaair.com

American Airlines
www.aa.com

British Airways
www.british-airways.com

Continental Airlines
www.continental.com

Delta Air Lines
www.delta.com

Iberia Airlines
www.iberia.com

North American Airlines
www.flynaa.com

United Airlines
www.united.com

US Airways
www.usairways.com

Virgin America
www.virginamerica.com

Virgin Atlantic Airways
www.virgin-atlantic.com

BUDGET AIRLINES

Click Mexicana
www.mexicana.com

Frontier Airlines
www.frontierairlines.com

Interjet
www.interjet.com.mx

JetBlue Airways
www.jetblue.com

Volaris
www.volaris.com.mx

SURVIVAL SPANISH

Most Mexicans are very patient with foreigners who try to speak their language; it helps a lot to know a few basic phrases. Included here are simple phrases for expressing basic needs, followed by some common menu items.

ENGLISH-SPANISH PHRASES

English	Spanish	Pronunciation
Good day	Buen día	**Bwehn *dee*-ah**
Good morning	Buenos días	***Bweh*-nohs *dee*-ahs**
How are you?	¿Cómo está?	***Koh*-moh eh-*stah***
Very well	Muy bien	**Mwee byehn**
Thank you	Gracias	***Grah*-syahs**
You're welcome	De nada	**Deh *nah*-dah**
Goodbye	Adiós	**Ah-*dyohs***
Please	Por favor	**Pohr fah-*bohr***
Yes	Sí	**See**
No	No	**Noh**
Excuse me	Perdóneme	**Pehr-*doh*-neh-meh**
Give me	Déme	***Deh*-meh**

English	Spanish	Pronunciation
Where is . . . ?	¿Dónde está . . . ?	***Dohn*-deh eh-*stah***
the station	la estación	**lah eh-stah-*syohn***
a hotel	un hotel	**oon oh-*tehl***
a gas station	una gasolinera	***oo*-nah gah-soh-lee-*neh*-rah**
a restaurant	un restaurante	**oon res-tow-*rahn*-teh**
the toilet	el baño	**el *bah*-nyoh**
a good doctor	un buen médico	**oon bwehn *meh*-dee-coh**
the road to . . .	el camino a/hacia	**el cah-*mee*-noh ah/*ah*-syah**
To the right	A la derecha	**Ah lah deh-*reh*-chah**
To the left	A la izquierda	**Ah lah ees-*kyehr*-dah**
Straight ahead	Derecho	**Deh-*reh*-choh**
I would like	Quisiera	**Key-*syeh*-rah**
I want	Quiero	***Kyeh*-roh**
to eat	comer	**koh-*mehr***
a room	una habitación	***oo*-nah ah-bee-tah-*syohn***
Do you have . . . ?	¿Tiene usted . . . ?	**Tyeh-neh oo-*sted***
a book	un libro	**oon *lee*-broh**
a dictionary	un diccionario	**oon deek-syoh-*nah*-ryoh**
How much is it?	¿Cuánto cuesta?	***Kwahn*-toh *kweh*-stah**
When?	¿Cuándo?	***Kwahn*-doh**
What?	¿Qué?	**Keh**
There is (Is there . . . ?)	(¿)Hay (. . . ?)	**Eye**
What is there?	¿Qué hay?	**Keh eye**
Yesterday	Ayer	**Ah-*yer***
Today	Hoy	**Oy**
Tomorrow	Mañana	**Mah-*nyah*-nah**
Good	Bueno	***Bweh*-noh**
Bad	Malo	***Mah*-loh**
Better (best)	(Lo) Mejor	**(Loh) Meh-*hohr***
More	Más	**Mahs**
Less	Menos	***Meh*-nohs**
No smoking	Se prohibe fumar	**Seh proh-*ee*-beh foo-*mahr***
Postcard	Tarjeta postal	**Tar-*heh*-tah poh-*stahl***
Insect repellent	Repelente contra insectos	**Reh-peh-*lehn*-teh *cohn*-trah een-*sehk*-tohs**

MORE USEFUL PHRASES

English	Spanish	Pronunciation
Do you speak English?	¿Habla usted inglés?	***Ah*-blah oo-*sted* een-*glehs***
Is there anyone here who speaks English?	¿Hay alguien aquí que hable inglés?	**Eye *ahl*-gyehn ah-*kee* keh *ah*-bleh een-*glehs***
I speak a little Spanish.	Hablo un poco de español.	***Ah*-bloh oon *poh*-koh deh eh-spah-*nyohl***
I don't understand Spanish very well.	No (lo) entiendo muy bien el español.	**Noh (loh) ehn-*tyehn*-doh mwee byehn el eh-spah-*nyohl***
The meal is good.	Me gusta la comida.	**Meh *goo*-stah lah koh-*mee*-dah**
What time is it?	¿Qué hora es?	**Keh *oh*-rah ehs**
May I see your menu?	¿Puedo ver el menú (la carta)?	***Pweh*-doh vehr el meh-*noo* (lah *car*-tah)**
The check, please.	La cuenta, por favor.	**Lah *kwehn*-tah pohr fa-*borh***
What do I owe you?	¿Cuánto le debo?	***Kwahn*-toh leh *deh*-boh**
What did you say?	¿Mande? (formal)	***Mahn*-deh**
	¿Cómo? (informal)	***Koh*-moh**
I want (to see) . . .	Quiero (ver) . . .	***kyeh*-roh (vehr)**
a room	un cuarto or una habitación	**oon *kwar*-toh, *oo*-nah ah-bee-tah-*syohn***
for two persons	para dos personas	***pah*-rah dohs pehr-*soh*-nahs**
with (without) bathroom	con (sin) baño	**kohn (seen) *bah*-nyoh**
We are staying here only . . .	Nos quedamos aquí solamente. . .	**Nohs keh-*dah*-mohs ah-*kee* soh-lah-*mehn*-teh**
one night.	una noche.	***oo*-nah *noh*-cheh**
one week.	una semana.	***oo*-nah seh-*mah*-nah**
We are leaving . . .	Partimos (Salimos) . . .	**Pahr-*tee*-mohs (Sah-*lee*-mohs)**
tomorrow.	mañana.	**mah-*nya*-nah**
Do you accept . . . ?	¿Acepta usted . . . ?	**Ah-*sehp*-tah oo-*sted***
traveler's checks?	cheques de viajero?	***cheh*-kehs deh byah-*heh*-roh**
Is there a laundromat . . . ?	¿Hay una lavandería . . . ?	**Eye *oo*-nah lah-*bahn*-deh-*ree*-ah**
near here?	cerca de aquí?	***sehr*-kah deh ah-*kee***
Please send these clothes to the laundry.	Hágame el favor de mandar esta ropa a la lavandería.	***Ah*-gah-meh el fah-*bohr* deh mahn-*dahr eh*-stah *roh*-pah a lah lah-*bahn*-deh-*ree*-ah**

NUMBERS

English	Spanish	Pronunciation
one	uno	***ooh*-noh**
two	dos	**dohs**
three	tres	**trehs**
four	cuatro	***kwah*-troh**
five	cinco	***seen*-koh**
six	seis	**sayes**
seven	siete	***syeh*-teh**
eight	ocho	***oh*-choh**
nine	nueve	***nweh*-beh**
ten	diez	**dyehs**
eleven	once	***ohn*-seh**
twelve	doce	***doh*-seh**
thirteen	trece	***treh*-seh**
fourteen	catorce	**kah-*tohr*-seh**
fifteen	quince	***keen*-seh**
sixteen	dieciséis	**dyeh-see-*sayes***
seventeen	diecisiete	**dyeh-see-*syeh*-teh**
eighteen	dieciocho	**dyeh-see-*oh*-choh**
nineteen	diecinueve	**dyeh-see-*nweh*-beh**
twenty	veinte	***bayn*-teh**
thirty	treinta	***trayn*-tah**
forty	cuarenta	**kwah-*ren*-tah**
fifty	cincuenta	**seen-*kwen*-tah**
sixty	sesenta	**seh-*sehn*-tah**
seventy	setenta	**seh-*tehn*-tah**
eighty	ochenta	**oh-*chehn*-tah**
ninety	noventa	**noh-*behn*-tah**
one hundred	cien	**syehn**
two hundred	doscientos	**do-*syehn*-tohs**
five hundred	quinientos	**kee-*nyehn*-tohs**
one thousand	mil	**meel**

TRANSPORTATION TERMS

English	Spanish	Pronunciation
Airport	Aeropuerto	**Ah-eh-roh-*pwehr*-toh**
Flight	Vuelo	***Bweh*-loh**
Rental car	Arrendadora de autos	**Ah-*rehn*-da-doh-rah deh *ow*-tohs**
Bus	Autobús	**Ow-toh-*boos***
Bus or Truck	Camión	**Ka-*myohn***
Lane	Carril	**Kah-*reel***
Nonstop (bus)	Directo	**Dee-*rehk*-toh**
Baggage (claim area)	Equipajes	**Eh-kee-*pah*-hehss**
Intercity	Foraneo	**Foh-rah-*neh*-oh**
Luggage storage area	Guarda equipaje	***Gwar*-dah eh-kee-*pah*-heh**
Arrival gates	Llegadas	**Yeh-*gah*-dahss**
Originates at this station	Local	**Loh-*kahl***
Originates elsewhere	De paso	**Deh *pah*-soh**
Are seats available?	Hay lugares disponibles?	**Eye loo-*gah*-rehs dis-pohn-*ee*-blehss**
First class	Primera	**Pree-*meh*-rah**
Second class	Segunda	**Seh-*goon*-dah**
Nonstop (flight)	Sin escala	**Seen ess-*kah*-lah**
Baggage claim area	Recibo de equipajes	**Reh-*see*-boh deh eh-kee-*pah*-hehss**
Waiting room	Sala de espera	***Sah*-lah deh ehss-*peh*-rah**
Toilets	Sanitarios	**Sah-nee-*tah*-ryohss**
Ticket window	Taquilla	**Tah-*kee*-yah**

DINING TERMINOLOGY

Meals

desayuno Breakfast.

comida Main meal of the day, taken in the afternoon.

cena Supper.

Courses

botana A small serving of food that accompanies a beer or drink, usually served free of charge.

entrada Appetizer.

sopa Soup course. (Not necessarily a soup—it can be a dish of rice or noodles, called *sopa seca* [dry soup].)

ensalada Salad.

plato fuerte Main course.

postre Dessert.

comida corrida Inexpensive daily special usually consisting of three courses.

menú del día Same as *comida corrida.*

Degree of Doneness

término un cuarto Rare, literally means one-fourth.

término medio Medium rare, one-half.

término tres cuartos Medium, three-fourths.

bien cocido Well-done.

Note: Keep in mind, when ordering a steak, that *medio* does not mean "medium."

Miscellaneous Restaurant Terminology

cucharra Spoon.

cuchillo Knife.

la cuenta The bill.

plato Plate.

plato hondo Bowl.

propina Tip.

servilleta Napkin.

tenedor Fork.

vaso Glass.

IVA Value-added tax.

fonda Strictly speaking, a food stall in the market or street, but now used in a loose or nostalgic sense to designate an informal restaurant.

Popular Mexican & Yucatecan Dishes

a la tampiqueña (Usually *bistec a la t.* or *arrachera a la t.*) A steak served with several sides, including but not limited to an enchilada, guacamole, rice, and beans.

achiote Small red seed of the *annatto* tree, with mild flavor, used for both taste and color.

adobo Marinade made with chiles and tomatoes, often seen in adjectival form *adobado/adobada.*

agua fresca Any sweetened fruit-flavored water, including *limonada* (limeade), *horchata* (see below), *tamarindo* (see below), *sandía* (watermelon), and *melón* (cantaloupe).

alambre Brochette.

albóndigas Meatballs, usually cooked in a *chile chipotle* sauce.

antojito Literally means "small temptation." It's a general term for tacos, *tostadas, quesadillas,* and the like, which are usually eaten for supper or as a snack.

arrachera Skirt steak, fajitas.

arroz Rice.

atole A thick, hot drink made with finely ground corn and flavored with fruit usually, but also can be flavored with chile, chocolate, or spices.

bistec Steak.

bolillo Small bread with a crust much like a baguette.

buñuelos Fried pastry dusted with sugar. Can also mean a large, thin, crisp pancake that is dipped in boiling cane syrup.

café con leche Hot coffee with milk. In cheap restaurants, often made with powdered instant coffee.

cajeta Thick caramel sauce made from goat's milk.

calabaza Zucchini squash.

caldo tlalpeño Chicken and vegetable soup, with rice, *chile chipotle,* avocado, and garbanzos. Its name comes from a suburban community of Mexico City, Tlalpan.

caldo xochitl Mild chicken and rice soup served with a small plate of chopped onion, chile serrano, avocado, and limes, to be added according to individual taste.

camarones Shrimp. For common cooking methods, see ***pescado.***

carne Meat.

carnitas Slow-cooked pork dish from Michoacán and parts of central Mexico, served with tortillas, guacamole, and salsa or pickled jalapeños.

cebolla Onion.

cecina Thinly sliced pork or beef, dried or marinated, depending on the region.

ceviche Fresh raw seafood marinated in fresh lime juice and garnished with chopped tomatoes, onions, chiles, and sometimes cilantro.

chalupas poblanas Simple dish from Puebla consisting of handmade tortillas lightly fried but left soft, and topped with different chile sauces.

chayote A type of spiny squash boiled and served as an accompaniment to meat dishes.

chilaquiles Fried tortilla quarters softened in either a red or a green sauce and served with Mexican sour cream, onion, and sometimes chicken *(con pollo).*

chile Any of the many hot peppers used in Mexican cooking, in fresh, dried, or smoked forms.

chile ancho A dried *chile poblano,* which serves as the base for many varieties of sauces and *moles.*

chile chilpotle (or **chipotle**) A smoked jalapeño sold dried or canned in an *adobo* sauce.

chile en nogada *Chile poblano* stuffed with a complex filling of shredded meat, nuts, and dried, candied, and fresh fruit, topped with walnut cream sauce and a sprinkling of pomegranate seeds.

chile poblano Fresh pepper that is usually dark green in color, large, and not usually spicy. Often stuffed with a variety of fillings *(chile relleno).*

chile relleno Stuffed pepper.

chimichurri Argentine sauce made with olive oil, oregano, parsley, and garlic, served with grilled meats.

chivo Kid or goat.

churro Fried pastry dusted with sugar and served plain or filled. The Spanish equivalent of a donut.

cochinita pibil Yucatecan dish of pork, pit-baked in a *pibil* sauce of *achiote,* sour orange, and spices.

col Cabbage. Also called *repollo.*

consomé Clear broth, usually with rice.

cortes Another way of saying steaks; in full, it is *cortes finas de carne* (fine cuts of meat).

cuitlacoche Variant of *huitlacoche.*

elote Fresh corn.

empanada For most of Mexico, a turnover with a savory or sweet filling. In Oaxaca and southern Mexico, it is corn masa or a tortilla folded around a savory filling and roasted or fried.

empanizado Breaded.

enchilada A lightly fried tortilla, dipped in sauce and folded or rolled around a filling. It has many variations, such as *enchiladas suizas* (made with a cream sauce), *enchiladas del portal* or *enchiladas placeras* (made with a predominantly *chile ancho* sauce), and *enchiladas verdes* (in a green sauce of tomatillos, cilantro, and chiles).

enfrijoladas Like an enchilada, but made with a bean sauce flavored with toasted avocado leaves.

enmoladas Enchiladas made with a *mole* sauce.

ensalada Salad.

entomatadas Enchiladas made with a tomato sauce.

escabeche Vegetables pickled in a vinegary liquid.

fideo Angel hair pasta.

flan Custard.

flautas Tortillas that are rolled up around a filling (usually chicken or shredded beef) and deep-fried; often listed on a menu as *taquitos* or *tacos fritos.*

frijoles refritos Beans mashed and cooked with lard.

gorditas Thick, fried corn tortillas, slit open and stuffed with meat or cheese filling.

horchata Drink made of ground rice, melon seeds, ground almonds, or coconut and cinnamon.

huazontle A vegetable vaguely comparable to broccoli, but milder in taste.

huevos mexicanos Scrambled eggs with chopped onions, *chiles serranos,* and tomatoes.

huevos rancheros Fried eggs, usually placed on tortillas and bathed in a light tomato sauce.

huitlacoche Salty and mild-tasting corn fungus that is considered a delicacy in Mexico.

jitomate Tomato.

lechuga Lettuce.

limón A small lime. Mexicans squeeze these limes on everything from soups to tacos.

lomo adobado Pork loin cooked in an ***adobo.***

masa Soft dough made of corn that is the basis for making tortillas and tamales.

menudo Soup made with beef tripe and hominy.

milanesa Beef cutlet breaded and fried.

molcajete A three-legged mortar made of volcanic stone and used for grinding. Often used now as a cooking dish that is brought to the table steaming hot and filled with meat, chiles, onions, and cheese.

mole Any variety of thick sauce made with dried chiles, nuts, fruits or vegetables, and spices. Variations include *m. poblano* (Puebla style, with chocolate and sesame), *m. negro* (black *mole* from Oaxaca, also with chocolate), and *m. verde* (made with herbs and/or pumpkin seeds, depending on the region).

pan Bread. A few of the varieties include *p. dulce* (general term for a variety of sweet breads), *p. de muerto* (bread made for the Day of the Dead holidays), and *p. Bimbo* (packaged sliced white bread).

panuchos A Yucatecan dish of *masa* cakes stuffed with refried black beans and topped with shredded turkey or chicken, lettuce, and onion.

papadzules A Yucatecan dish of tortillas stuffed with hard-boiled eggs and topped with a sauce made of pumpkin seeds.

papas Potatoes.

parrillada A sampler platter of grilled meats or seafood.

pescado Fish. Common ways of cooking fish include *al mojo de ajo* (pan seared with oil and garlic), *a la veracruzana* (with tomatoes, olives, and capers), and *al ajillo* (seared with garlic and fine strips or rings of *chile guajillo*).

pibil See ***cochinita pibil.*** When made with chicken, it is called *pollo pibil.*

picadillo Any of several recipes using shredded beef, pork, or chicken and onions, chiles, and spices. Can also contain fruits and nuts.

pipián A thick sauce made with ground pumpkin seeds, nuts, herbs, and chiles. Can be red or green.

poc chuc Pork with onion marinated in sour orange and then grilled; a Yucatecan dish.

pollo Chicken.

pozole Soup with chicken or pork, hominy, lettuce, and radishes, served with a small plate of other ingredients to be added according to taste (onion, pepper, lime juice, oregano). In Jalisco it's red *(p. rojo),* in Michoacán it's clear *(p. blanco),* and in Guerrero it's green *(p. verde).* In the rest of Mexico, it can be any one of these.

puerco Pork.

pulque A drink made of fermented juice of the maguey plant; most common in the states of Hidalgo, Tlaxcala, Puebla, and Mexico.

quesadilla Corn or flour tortillas stuffed with white cheese and cooked on a hot griddle. In Mexico City, it is made with raw masa folded around any of a variety of fillings (often containing no cheese) and deep-fried.

queso Cheese.

res Beef.

rompope Mexican liqueur, made with eggs, vanilla, sugar, and alcohol.

salbute A Yucatecan dish much like a *panucho,* but without bean paste in the middle.

solomillo Filet mignon.

sopa azteca Tortilla soup.

sopa tarasca A blended soup from Michoacán made with beans and tomatoes.

sope Small fried masa cake topped with savory meats and greens.

tacos al pastor Small tacos made with thinly sliced pork marinated in an *adobo* and served with pineapple, onion, and cilantro.

tallarines Noodles.

tamal (Not "tamale.") *Masa* mixed with lard and beaten until light and folded around a savory or sweet filling, and encased in a cornhusk or a plant leaf (usually corn or banana) and then steamed. *Tamales* is the plural form.

taquitos See ***flautas.***

tinga Shredded meat stewed in a *chile chipotle* sauce.

torta A sandwich made with a bolillo.

INDEX

See also Accommodations and Restaurant indexes, below.

General Index

D

I

J

K

L

M

N

O

P

Q

R

S

T

U

Accommodations

Restaurants

PHOTO CREDITS

p. i: © Eric Blanc; p. iii, iv, v: © Jose Granados; p. 1: © Jose Granados; p. 2: © George Oze / Alamy; p. 3: © Jose Granados; p. 7, left: © Martha Roque; p. 7, right: © Martha Roque; p. 8: © Jon Davison / Lonely Planet Images; p. 9, top: © Chris A. Crumley / Alamy; p. 9, bottom: © Eric Blanc; p. 10: © Jose Granados; p. 11, top: © Martha Roque; p. 11, bottom: © Martha Roque; p. 12: © Axiom / Photolibrary; p. 14, top: © Martha Roque; p. 14, bottom: © Courtesy JW Marriott Cancún; p. 17: © Richard Broadwell / Alamy; p. 18: © Jose Granados; p. 19: © Vojtech Vlk / allphoto / AGE Fotostock; p. 21: © Martha Roque; p. 22: © Martha Roque; p. 26: © Ivan Luckie; p. 27, box: © Jose Granados; p. 28: © Jose Granados; p. 30: © Giraudon / The Bridgeman Art Library International; p. 31: © Martha Roque; p. 32, box: © Charles Sleicher / Danita Delimont Stock Photography; p. 35: © Jose Granados; p. 36: © Jose Granados; p. 37, left: © mm-iamges / Blickwinkel / AGE Fotostock; p. 37, right: © Eric Blanc; p. 39: © Jose Granados; p. 41: © Martha Roque; p. 42: © Ivan Luckie; p. 43: © WILDLIFE GmbH / Alamy; p. 44: © Miguel Nuñez; p. 47, left: © Miguel Nuñez; p. 47, right: © Martha Roque; p. 48: © Martha Roque; p. 50 © Fernando Mundo; p. 53: © Fernando Mundo; p. 54, top: © Martha Roque; p. 54, bottom: © Martha Roque; p. 55: © Miguel Nuñez; p. 86: © Eric Blanc; p. 88: © Eric Blanc; p. 89: © Mark Callanan / Photolibrary; p. 89: © Pixtal Images / Photolibrary; p. 90: © Miguel Nuñez; p. 91: © Eric Blanc; p. 94, left: © Strigl Egmont / Prisma / AGE Fotostock; p. 94, right: © Eric Blanc; p. 95: © Jose Granados; p. 96: © Eric Blanc; p. 98: © Eric Blanc; p. 100, left: © Egmont Strigl / AGE Fotostock; p. 100, right: © Leonardo Díaz Romero / AGE Fotostock; p. 101: © Avatra Images / Alamy; p. 103: © Eric Blanc; p. 104: © Eric Blanc; p. 107: © Martha Roque; p. 110: © Eric Blanc; p. 113: © John Mitchell / Alamy; p. 127, top: © Martha Roque; p. 127, bottom: © Eric Blanc; p. 128: © PAPHOTO / Alamy; p. 129: © Eric Blanc; p. 132: © Courtesy Hilton Cancun Golf And Spa Resort; p. 134: © Martha Roque; p. 136: © Martha Roque; p. 138: © Miguel Nuñez; p. 142: © Martin Moxter / Imagebroker / Alamy; p. 143: © Martha Roque; p. 144: © Martha Roque; p. 147: © Andrew Woodley / Alamy; p. 148: © Orchidpoet / Alamy; p. 149: © McPHOTO / Blickwinkel / AGE Fotostock; p. 150, left: © Martha Roque; p. 150, right: © Martha Roque; p. 154: © Martha Roque; p. 158: © Miguel Nuñez; p. 162: © Miguel Nuñez; p. 163: © Miguel Nuñez; p. 165, top: © Miguel Nuñez; p. 165, bottom: © Miguel Nuñez; p. 167, top: © M. Timothy O'Keefe / Alamy; p. 168: © Miguel Nuñez; p. 173: © Miguel Nuñez; p. 175: © Miguel Nuñez; p. 176: © Martha Roque; p. 180: © Martha Roque; p. 182: © Martha Roque; p. 183: © Martha Roque; p. 186: © Courtesy Mayakoba El Camaleón Golf; p. 187: © Eric Blanc; p. 190: © Miguel Nuñez; p. 192: © Wagner Gerd / Alamy; p. 193: © Miguel Nuñez; p. 198: © Miguel Nuñez; p. 201, top: © Eric Blanc; p. 201, bottom: © Martha Roque; p. 203, box: © Eric Blanc; p. 204: © Jose Granados; p. 205: © Martha Roque; p. 207, left: © Woody Welch / Aurora Photos; p. 207, right: © Photo by Hamid Rad, courtesy Centro Ecológico Akumal.; p. 209: © Eric Blanc; p. 210, top: © Courtesy Xel-Há; p. 210, bottom: © Courtesy Hidden Worlds Cenote Park; p. 212: © Eric Blanc; p. 213: © Jose Granados; p. 215, left: © Sola / parasola.net / Alamy; p. 215, right: © Juan Carlos Longos / Alamy; p. 219: © Eric Blanc; p. 220: © Eric Blanc; p. 222: © Eric Blanc; p. 224: © Andoni Canela / AGE Fotostock; p. 225: © Eric Blanc; p. 227: © PCL / Alamy; p. 228: © Juergen Ritterbach / Vario Images / Alamy; p. 230: © B. Jones & M. Shimlock / NHPA / AGE Fotostock; p. 232: © Eric Blanc; p. 233, left: © Andrea Matone / Alamy; p. 233, right: © Alexander Pöschel / Imagebroker / Alamy; p. 235: © travelstock.ca / Alamy; p. 238: © Jose Granados; p. 240: © Jose Granados; p. 241: © Jose Granados; p. 242: © Jose Granados; p. 243: © Jose Granados; p. 244: © Juergen Ritterbach / Vario Images / Alamy; p. 245: © Doug McKinlay / Lonely Planet Images; p. 246: © Martha Roque; p. 250: © Martha Roque; p. 252: © Martha Roque; p. 262: © Jose Granados; p. 266: © Martha Roque; p. 267: © Martha Roque; p. 270: © Dan Leeth / Alamy; p. 273: © Dennis Johnson / Lonely Planet Images; p. 274: © Eric Blanc; p. 275: © Robert Harding Picture Library Ltd / Alamy; p. 276: © Witold Skrypczak / Alamy; p. 278, left: © Julie Eggers / Danita Delimont Stock Photography / Alamy; p. 278, right: © Jose Granados; p. 280: © Jose Granados; p. 281: © Jose Granados; p. 282: © Jose Granados; p. 285: © Jose Granados; p. 286: © Eric Blanc; p. 288: © Jose Granados; p. 289: © Jose Granados; p. 290: © Jose Granados; p. 291: © Bruno Perousse / AGE Fotostock; p. 295: © Martin Norris / Alamy; p. 296: © Gordon Sinclair / Alamy; p. 297: © Mauricio Ramos / TMC Images / AGE Fotostock; p. 298: © Alessandro Gandolfi / Index Stock Imagery / Photolibrary; p. 301: © Florian Schulz / Alamy; p. 303: © Jose Granados; p. 305: © Jose Granados; p. 306: © Jose Granados; p. 307: © Egmont Strigl / Imagebroker / AGE Fotostock; p. 308: © Jose Granados; p. 313: © J. Moreno / Arco Images

/ AGE Fotostock; p. 314: © Martha Roque; p. 315: © Martha Roque; p. 316: © Cris Haigh / Alamy; p. 317: © Jose Granados; p. 319: © Frans Lemmens / Alamy; p. 320: © Paul Nicklen / National Geographic / Getty Images; p. 321: © Adalberto Ríos Szalay / AGE Fotostock; p. 326: © Ivan Luckie; p. 330, top: © Eric Blanc; p. 330, bottom: © Eric Blanc; p. 332: © Eric Blanc; p. 337, top: © Eric Blanc; p. 337, bottom: © Robert Cundy / Robert Harding Picture Library / Alamy; p. 338: © Stefano Paterna / AGE Fotostock; p. 339: © Fernando Mundo; p. 343: © Fernando Mundo; p. 345, left: © Fernando Mundo; p. 345, right: © Fernando Mundo; p. 346, left: © Fernando Mundo; p. 346, right: © Diana Bier / Alamy; p. 348, top: © Mel Longhurst / AGEfotostock; p. 348, bottom: © Miriam Reik / Impact / AGE Fotostock; p. 351: © S. Rocker / Blickwinkel / AGE Fotostock; p. 356: © Ignacio Guevara / AGE Fotostock; p. 357: © Charles Crust / Danita Delimont Stock Photography / Alamy; p. 361: © Fernando Mundo; p. 362: © Fernando Mundo.

NOTES